MERGERS, CORPORATE CONCENTRATION AND POWER IN CANADA

MERGERS, CORPORATE CONCENTRATION AND POWER IN CANADA

Edited by
R.S. Khemani
D.M. Shapiro
W.T. Stanbury

The Institute for Research on Public Policy/
L'Institut de recherches politiques

Printed in Canada

Legal Deposit Third Quarter
Bibliothèque nationale du Québec

Canadian Cataloguing in Publication Data

Main entry under title:

Mergers, corporate concentration and power in
Canada

Prefatory material in English and French.
Proceedings of a conference held in
Montreal, March 23-24, 1987.
ISBN 0-88645-067-5

1. Consolidation and merger of corporations
— Canada — Congresses. I. Khemani, R.S.
II. Shapiro, Daniel M., 1947-. III. Stanbury,
W.T., 1943-. IV. Institute for Research on
Public Policy.

HD2810.M47 1988   338.8'3'0971   C88-098641-7

The camera-ready copy for this publication was created
on a Xerox 6085 Desktop Publishing System.

The Institute for Research on Public Policy/
L'Institut de recherches politiques
P.O. Box 3670 South
Halifax, Nova Scotia   B3J 3K6

Contents

Foreword

In a wide variety of discussions on topics ranging from corporate concentration to sustainable development, it is generally accepted that the energy and dynamism of the free enterprise system must be channelled within some stable framework of public policy. At a national conference on Mergers, Corporate Concentration and Corporate Power organized in Montreal last year by this Institute, in association with Concordia University's School of Community and Public Affairs, this same consensus recognized that one major challenge for public policy is to find a framework which permits a degree of corporate concentration sufficient to sustain a dynamic domestic economy and a strong competitive position internationally while avoiding undue market power or concentration of political power within the Canadian community. A subsidiary task is to find the appropriate balance between measures to anticipate potential abuses in this area and the tolerance to await evidence of actual damage.

The conference proceedings contained in the present volume explore several key questions along these lines, ranging from specific concerns with concentrated ownership and cross-ownership, the extent to which biases in market allocation decisions are driven by tax policy, by other public policies, or induced by other distortions in market structures, to more general questions of corporate governance and the efficiency of "markets for corporate control," or even the possibility of distinguishing speculative churning ("paper entrepreneurship") from productive investment in the "real" economy. A great deal of new analysis and empirical evidence is contained in the papers prepared for the conference and subsequently edited extensively for this proceedings volume.

A more fundamental question underlying much of the discussion was a concern with the evident asymmetry of resources available to the various — honest and legitimate — influences in the public policy process, and the related problem of the links from economic concentration to the distribution of political power in a pluralist society. Whether the potential contestability of markets offers sufficient protection of the public interest in the face of all the actual distortions (either tax-driven or arising from existing patterns of cross-ownership) in market decisions and market behaviour is a question left unanswered at the Montreal meeting.

Over the decade since the Royal Commission on Corporate Concentration (the Bryce Commission) completed its work, this Institute has explored the topic of competition policy and corporate concentration in a number of publications arising out of a work program organized by Professor Bill Stanbury of UBC. (One can see earlier Institute books, including *Competition Policy in Canada: Stage II, Bill C-13* (Rowley and Stanbury, 1978); *Perspectives on the Royal Commission on Corporate Concentration* (Gorecki and Stanbury, 1979); *Canada's Competition Policy Revisited: Some New Thoughts on an Old Story* (Brecher, 1982); and *The Objectives of Canadian Competition Policy, 1888-1983* (Gorecki and Stanbury, 1984)). There remains, however, much more work to be done on the linkages between mergers, corporate concentration, corporate power, and political power. And there remains the puzzle of potential irreversibilities in addressing the problem of corporate concentration if we should, at some time in the future, judge that the process has gone too far.

The Institute is proud to make this important document available for wider study and debate, and I should like personally to express thanks to the editors and all the participants who have contributed to a lively and provocative exchange of views on a subject of fundamental importance in Canadian public policy. As we approach the centenary of competition policy in Canada, the questions addressed in this volume continue to demand the most intense scrutiny.

Rod Dobell
President
September 1988

Avant-propos

Au cours des discussions de toutes sortes qui portent sur un vaste ensemble de problèmes, allant de la concentration des entreprises au développement durable, il est généralement reconnu que l'énergie et le dynamisme propres au système de la libre entreprise doivent être tempérés par des mesures de politique générale appropriées et stables. Lors d'un congrès national sur les fusions et les concentrations de corporations et sur leurs pouvoirs, organisé l'an dernier à Montréal par l'Institut, avec la collaboration de l'École des affaires commerciales et publiques de l'Université Concordia, la même unanimité se reformait pour convenir qu'une des difficultés majeures en politique était de pouvoir trouver une solution satisfaisante qui permette un degré de concentration des corporations suffisant pour assurer le dynamisme de l'économie domestique et une position concurrentielle avantageuse sur le plan international, sans pour autant donner à celles-ci une emprise non désirable sur le marché et un pouvoir politique excessif à l'intérieur de la communauté canadienne. Cela entraîne l'intervention d'un système d'équilibre adéquat entre les mesures de prévention d'abus possibles et la modération, qui s'avère nécessaire pour éviter d'agir sans avoir l'évidence de dommages véritables.

Les actes du congrès repris dans le présent volume examinent plusieurs questions clés dans cet esprit. Cela va des préoccupations suscitées par la concentration des droits de propriétés et les participations croisées, au problème de savoir dans quelle mesure le favoritisme en matière d'attribution des marchés provient de la politique fiscale, d'autres mesures politiques ou bien d'autres distorsions structurelles du marché, en passant par les questions plus générales des politiques propres aux corporations et de l'efficacité des "marchés pour le contrôle des corporations", ou encore par le problème de savoir s'il est possible de distinguer les activités purement spéculatives, par simple artifice d'écritures, des investissements productifs effectués dans une économie "réelle". Les communications présentées au congrès ont offert un grand nombre d'analyses nouvelles et d'exemples concrets. Ce sont ces données, soigneusement révisées, qui figurent dans ce volume.

Une question plus fondamentale, qui se trouvait à l'arrière-plan de la plus grande partie des débats, provenait de la préoccupation causée par l'asymétrie évidente qui existe entre les ressources dont disposent les diverses influences légitimes et honnêtes intervenant dans le processus politique et le problème connexe des liens entre la concentration économique et la distribution du pouvoir politique dans une société pluraliste. Le problème de savoir si la situation de concurrence potentielle des marchés offre une protection suffisante pour le public vis-à-vis des distorsions existantes (soit d'ordre fiscal, soit du fait de l'existence des participations croisées) dans le contexte économique (décisions et comportement du marché) n'a pas pu trouver de réponse au cours de la rencontre de Montréal.

Depuis les travaux de la Commission royale pour l'étude de la concentration des entreprises, l'Institut a examiné, au cours de la décennie, la question de la politique concurrentielle par rapport à la concentration des entreprises. Il en est résulté un certain nombre de publications issues du programme de travail dirigé par le professeur Bill Stanbury, de l'Université de Colombie-Britannique, et publiées par l'Institut (notamment: *Competition Policy in Canada: Stage II, Bill C-13* (Rowley et Stanbury, 1978); *Perspectives on the Royal Commission on Corporate Concentration* (Gorecki et Stanbury, 1979); *Canada's Competition Policy Revisited: Some New Thoughts on an Old Story* (Brecher, 1982); et *The Objectives of Canadian Competition Policy, 1888-1983* (Gorecki et Stanbury, 1984)). Il reste encore beaucoup de travail à faire pour l'étude des rapports qui existent entre les fusions et la concentration des corporations, la puissance de celles-ci et le pouvoir politique. En outre, subsiste la question compliquée des irréversibilités potentielles qui se présente quand on veut régler le problème de la concentration des entreprises, si l'on devait juger dans l'avenir que le processus de concentration est allé trop loin.

L'Institut est fier d'être en mesure de publier ce document important et de le soumettre à l'examen d'un plus large public. Je voudrais personnellement profiter de cette occasion pour présenter mes remerciements aux éditeurs et à tous ceux qui ont contribué à ces débats animés et stimulants sur un sujet d'une importance fondamentale pour la politique générale canadienne. Comme nous approchons du centenaire du système de la politique de concurrence au Canada, les questions traitées dans ce volume continuent d'exiger la plus grande attention.

Rod Dobell
Président

Septembre 1988

Mergers, Corporate Concentration and Power in Canada: Introduction and Executive Summary

R. S. Khemani
D. M. Shapiro
W. T. Stanbury

1.0 ORIGINS AND BACKGROUND

The papers in this volume grew out of a conference held in March 1987, sponsored by both the Institute for Research on Public Policy and the School of Community and Public Affairs, Concordia University. At the time the conference was conceived, Canada, like other countries, was in the midst of an unprecedented merger boom.[1] There were various indications that the Canadian economy was becoming increasingly dominated by a small number of large firms which were in turn owned by a small number of individuals and families.[2] At the same time, the federal government and several provinces were embarking on a process of financial deregulation which raised serious issues regarding concentration of firms and ownership in the financial sector.[3] Another recent policy initiative was the enactment of the new *Competition Act* which came into force in June 1986, with provisions that could affect both the financial and non-financial sectors.[4] These events largely defined both the theme of the conference and the papers in this volume, most of which were presented at the conference.[5]

2.0 THE ROYAL COMMISSION REVISITED

At the time of writing, it is 10 years since the publication of the *Report* of the Royal Commission on Corporate Concentration.[6] The event that led to the creation of the Commission was the attempted takeover of Argus Corporation by Power Corporation in 1975, an event which seems benign by the takeover standards of 1985-1987.[7] It would be fair to say that the Commission made no significant policy recommendations with respect to corporate concentration. Indeed, the thrust of the *Report* was that the nature of the Canadian economy was such that high levels of concentration were inevitable. Furthermore, the deleterious consequences of high concentration could be minimized by a combination of more stringent competition legislation[8] and market forces. Thus, the Commission supported reform of the competition laws to more effectively counter restrictive practices.[9]

With respect to mergers, the Commission's analysis and recommendations were more controversial.[10] The Commission (1978, p. 156) concluded that "no long-run general relationship between merger activity and concentration can be identified in Canada during the period since 1945." It also stated that "there is insufficient evidence to conclude that most of the mergers taking place in Canada [an average rate of 358 p.a. between 1970 and 1977] add very much to real efficiency in production and distribution" (RCCC 1978, p. 155). The Commission (1978, p. 160) concluded that competition policy "should deal in a prohibitory way with proven anti-competitive conduct ...[and] corporate mergers should not be subject to a review process or require official approval or consent before they are completed." In other words, mergers were only to be addressed *ex post* if they resulted in an abuse of dominant position, a price-fixing conspiracy, or other restraint of trade.

While admitting that "conglomerate diversification has probably decreased the efficiency of resource allocation in the Canadian economy,"[11] the Commission was content to rely on the forces of competition to overcome the problem.[12] With respect to large conglomerate mergers, in effect, the Commission handed the problem back to the federal Cabinet suggesting that it review those that appeared not to be in the public interest. It was to do so without any new legislation or even a list of criteria to assess such large mergers.[13]

Given the events described above, a re-examination of the issues raised by the Royal Commission is in order. In particular, we seek to provide new empirical evidence on trends in corporate concentration; to survey recent theoretical and empirical evidence relating to mergers; to examine recent changes in the financial sector; and to critically assess recent policy initiatives, particularly the *Competition Act* and financial deregulation.

3.0 CONCENTRATION AND ITS CONSEQUENCES

Any assessment of the costs and benefits associated with corporate concentration requires a clear definition of terms. Khemani (Chapter 1) distinguishes among aggregate concentration (the relative position of large firms in the economy as a whole or in broadly defined sectors such as financial and non-financial); ownership concentration (the extent to which share ownership of the largest firms is restricted to a relatively small number of individuals and families); conglomerate concentration (the relative position of large, diversified firms in the economy) and market concentration (the relative position of large firms in specific industries). It is the first three concepts that were of concern at the conference and in this volume.

Although there is considerable disagreement over the causes and consequences of *market* concentration, economists and policy makers at least have a clearly defined framework for debate. The relevant parameters at issue (economies of scale, barriers to entry, innovative activity, collusion) have all been widely studied within the context of traditional economic analysis.

The same cannot be said for aggregate concentration, ownership concentration and conglomerate concentration. In these cases policy analysis is made difficult by the absence of an agreed upon framework for the analysis. Each of these topics has been investigated by economists, political scientists, sociologists, journalists, and business theorists and each brings a different, and sometimes conflicting, approach.[14] It is evident that there is no consensus about which issues are most salient and how they should be analyzed.

3.1 Aggregate Concentration

As an example, consider the issue of aggregate concentration in the non-financial sector. The evidence produced by Khemani (Chapter 1) and Marfels (Chapter 3) shows unambiguously that aggregate concentration in Canada is high by international standards. Moreover, it is rising. Khemani's data indicate that the 25 largest non-financial enterprises in Canada held 29.5 per cent of total sector assets in 1977 and this rose continuously to 35.3 per cent in 1984. Marfels (Chapter 3) shows that while aggregate concentration in Canada is increasing, it has been declining in the U.S., Japan, and West Germany. As a consequence, aggregate concentration in Canada is very high by international standards. As of 1984, the leading 100 Canadian non-financial enterprises held 52 per cent of total corporate non-financial assets. This contrasts with 24.8 per cent for West Germany, 24.8 per cent for Japan and 28.2 per cent (1982) in the United States. Moreover, contrary to the prediction of the Royal Commission on Corporate Concentration (1978), new data presented by Niosi (Chapter 2) indicates that the growth of a few large conglomerates is a major source of increasing aggregate concentration. The evidence is clear, but its interpretation is not.

3.2 Power and Efficiency

Political scientists and sociologists, among others, are concerned with the problems of political and social power and how such power influences policy making. In the domestic context, figures such as those reported above would be viewed with alarm since they indicate a considerable concentration of potential power within a nation. The analysis tends to focus on the potential for undue influence over the political process, the formation of public policy, and the articulation of national goals (in part through the media). It also emphasizes the importance of a social system which is just and fair and seen to be so. In fact, these are among the issues raised by André (Chapter 20), Blenkarn (Chapter 23), Martin (Chapter 18), Kerton (Chapter 19), and Stanbury (Chapter 17).

Economists, on the other hand, tend to be primarily concerned with two types of efficiency: productive and allocative.[15] The former is related to economies of scale and scope and is achieved when firms choose the appropriate size and product mix which minimizes costs. The latter is related to pricing, and is achieved when prices are maintained at competitive levels through the forces of competition. Economists have long been aware that these two goals may be conflicting: the benefits of scale and scope economies may be achieved only through the existence of a small number of relatively large firms (particularly in a small market), which implies a lessening of competition.[16]

Economists tend to look beyond national boundaries in assessing both scale and scope economies and the degree of competition. Thus, many economists would not view the high degree of aggregate concentration in Canada with alarm. Indeed, they would point out that while the largest Canadian firms are large relative to the Canadian economy, they are small relative to the largest firms in the world. This suggests that Canadian firms have not fully achieved the necessary size to become globally competitive and some economists would argue that yet larger firms are therefore necessary, even if concentration increases. Such views are clearly articulated by Brander (Chapter 5) and Parizeau (Chapter 16) in the context of both industrial and financial industries. Although they are aware that domestic concentration would increase, their global orientation minimizes this concern. Essentially they argue that in an open economy, domestic concentration is irrelevant since competition is assured at the international level.[17] Indeed, these same considerations lead most Canadian orthodox economists to favour free trade and to oppose policies which overly restrict the emergence of large firms.

Organizational and managerial theorists are also concerned with efficiency. However, recent work in this area, most notably that of Oliver Williamson (1975, 1985), has been highly critical of the orthodox (neo-classical) economists' approach. Essentially they argue that in treating the firm as a "black-box," economists have ignored the potential for increasing efficiency through the appropriate organizational design. In contrast, the new organizational economists pay particular attention to the internal functioning of firms and tend to emphasize incentives, bureaucracy, flexibility, innovation and entrepreneurship. David Teece's paper (Chapter 4) is illustrative of this approach and indicates how it can lead to conclusions quite different from those of orthodox economists.

Teece implies that economies of scale and scope are over-emphasized as determinants of efficiency and international competitiveness because they do not include factors such as corporate governance, managerial practices, and the potential for innovation. Moreover, Teece suggests that we may be entering an era of the "post-modern corporation," a firm which is typically small to medium sized, less bureaucratic and more entrepreneurial and open to employee participation in management and ownership. In terms of policy, the outcome of Teece's analysis leaves room for interventionist industrial strategies, the relaxing of restrictions on cooperation among firms, and restrictions on size-increasing mergers, particularly conglomerate mergers. Thus, two approaches to the theory of the firm, one emphasizing economies of scale and scope and the second emphasizing corporate governance lead to completely different policy conclusions.

The basic point to be made is that if one is addressing the question "does aggregate concentration matter?" the answer will depend critically on the framework for analysis. Moreover, the articulation of public policy in this regard is rendered difficult by the fact that the various approaches do not intersect to any great degree. It is therefore evident that in making public policy, weights must be attached to the various arguments and there seems to be no *a priori* way of doing so.

4.0 MERGER ACTIVITY

There seems to be little debate over the contention that much of the increase in aggregate concentration can be explained by a dramatic increase in mergers and takeovers. Khemani (Chapter 1), Mason (Chapter 6) and Appendix 1 describe the extent to which the phenomenon accelerated in the 1980s. In the 1970s the average number of mergers per year in Canada was 380, while in 1986 there were 938 and in 1987 there were 1,082.[18] Moreover, it appears that the number of *large* transactions has also increased. For example, in 1984 there were four takeovers in which the value of the transaction exceeded $100 million ($778 million in total) whereas in 1986 there were 42 and in 1987 there were 47 such deals with a total value of $16.2 billion and $26.1 billion respectively — see Appendix 1.

As Brander (Chapter 5), Walter (Chapter 11), Eckbo (Chapter 7), and Mason (Chapter 6) suggest, there are a variety of potential motivations for a merger or takeover, one of which is the desire to achieve synergistic effects. Synergy implies that the whole is greater than the sum of its parts and that a consolidation of business activities is more efficient than operating them independently.[19] Economies of scale and scope, when they exist, create synergistic effects which may motivate a merger or takeover and should result in efficiency gains as a consequence. However, synergy is not the only potential cause of increased post-merger efficiency. It is argued, particularly by Eckbo in Chapter 7, that takeovers may best be understood in terms of a market for corporate control. In this market inefficient managers see their firms acquired by investors who will appoint more efficient managers. Corporate efficiency is thus enhanced, not only by takeovers, but also by the threat of being taken over. (As Samuel Johnson noted, the thought of being hanged shortly wonderfully concentrates a man's mind.) If one could verify that takeover activity does result in efficiency gains, either through synergy or through the market for corporate control, then that would certainly alleviate some of the concerns over aggregate concentration.

There has been a considerable amount of academic research undertaken with respect to this question. Unfortunately, no consensus has emerged in part because the frameworks for analysis have differed. Essentially, two analytical frameworks have been employed, the first relying on evidence derived from stock market reactions to mergers, or the announcement of proposed mergers (event studies), and the second relying on the analysis of accounting data (primarily measures of profitability). The two sides of the debate are forcefully presented by Professors Eckbo (Chapter 7) and Scherer (Chapter 8). The intricacies of the methodologies and results are such that they cannot be readily summarized here. In any event, they are described by the respective authors in this volume and elsewhere.

Scherer reports that an analysis of 6,000 mergers in the U.S. between 1950 and 1977 reveals that, on average, acquired companies had superior profit records *prior* to the merger. Nor can the average decline of post-merger profitability to one-half of pre-merger profitability be considered minor. Scherer concludes in Chapter 8 that, on average, most mergers were unlikely to have resulted in efficiency gains and cites the post-merger "divorce rate" of one-third as corroborating evidence.

Walter (Chapter 11) points out the difficulties in managing merged institutions, thus supporting Scherer's position. Similar points are made by Adams in Chapter 10. In addition, Walter (Chapter 11) presents survey evidence suggesting that there are a variety of motivations for merging (of which economies of scale/scope are but one), and that the importance of each depends on the nature of the merger.

Eckbo, on the other hand, in Chapter 7 surveys the results of a large number of studies which show that merger or takeover announcements coincide with increases in the target firms' shares prices of between 29 per cent and 50 per cent. This is interpreted to indicate that stock markets evaluate the merger favourably because of anticipated efficiency gains. Moreover, the evidence surveyed by Eckbo discounts merger motivations other than those related to efficiency.[20] It should be noted that Scherer's evidence is influenced to a great degree by the merger boom of the late 1960s, while the studies surveyed by Eckbo usually include more recent mergers. This may account for some of the differences. However, as matters stand, there is simply no agreement over the costs and benefits of mergers and takeovers.

The market for corporate control, as a means of disciplining inefficient managers, has assumed some importance in recent years in that it provides a market solution to problems associated with the separation of ownership from control. As noted by Khemani (Chapter 1), the vast majority of large U.S. firms are characterized by the fact that their shares are widely-held. Widely dispersed shareholdings, it is argued, reduces the power of shareholders to monitor their appointed agents (managers). Put another way, it increases "agency costs." Managers, therefore have effective control over corporate policy and are free from the discipline of owners — thus allowing for the possibility that inefficient managers may *not* be fired. An effective market for corporate control can alleviate this concern by providing the necessary discipline: inefficient managers' firms will be taken over and incumbent management will be displaced. Some empirical evidence consistent with the premise that increased shareholder concentration may reduce the so-called "agency costs" and lead to improved managerial firm performance is offered by Jog and Riding (Chapter 9). In their analysis of both stock market and financial returns data, the authors find that firm performance improves after a change in ownership control take place by means of a partial acquisition.

With respect to ownership concentration, Canada is very different from the U.S. Khemani indicates in Chapter 1 that the vast majority of large Canadian firms are closely-held, that is, a controlling interest is held by an individual or identifiable group. Indeed, whereas in the U.S. some 80 per cent of the largest 500 industrials are widely-held, the opposite is the case in Canada. There appears to be some agreement that ownership concentration is a source of concern. Jog and Riding (Chapter 9) and McFetridge (Chapter 14) emphasize the possible adverse effects on the market for corporate control and minority shareholder rights. It must be noted, however, that it is not clear whether the disciplinary effects of an active takeover market are necessary when owners have the power and incentive to monitor corporate managers.

5.0   FROM ECONOMIC TO POLITICAL POWER

In terms of political and social power, Stanbury (Chapter 17) discusses the means by which economic power (emanating from the combination of high ownership and corporate concentration) may be translated into political power and influence over public policy. He also indicates the limitations on corporate political power and the dynamics of countervailing power by other interest groups. In this regard, the paper by Kerton (Chapter 19) is illuminating, illustrating both how passively the majority of Canadians regard the phenomenon of corporate power as well the unequal participation of interest groups in Canada's "political markets." Equally interesting are Adams' comments in Chapter 10 on the same issues in the United States. Adams suggests that large U.S. corporations have used their influence to extract various concessions from the U.S. government, including protectionist measures. The fact that the major business groups (including U.S.-owned firms) in Canada have supported free trade underscores the complexities of analyzing interest group behaviour, even for what many believe to be a relatively homogeneous interest.[21]

6.0   THE FINANCIAL SECTOR

The issues addressed by the papers on the financial sector closely parallel those discussed above, albeit primarily in the context of proposals for financial reform and deregulation. Concentration in the financial sector, diversification within the financial sector, conglomeration between financial and non-financial firms, and concentration of ownership regulations have all generated considerable interest and debate.

Ryba (Chapter 13) discusses the general trend towards increased integration and conglomeration in financial sectors as well as the globalization of financial markets in the context of issues currently confronting Canadian financial institutions. He notes that, although concentration in various financial market segments is high, there exists healthy and increasing competition in the provision of financial services in Canada. Ryba therefore supports the recommendations of the White Paper presented by the Hon. Tom Hockin in December 1986. In Chapter 22 Hockin outlines the major elements of the White Paper which, among other things, supports ownership integration and product networking among financial services. He explains the Conservative government's reasons for rejecting the continued separation of the "four pillars" (commercial banking, trust companies, insurance companies and investment dealers), the hallmark of financial regulation in Canada. Parizeau (Chapter 16) supports the emergence of larger and more diversified financial entities because of the demands of global competition. Jackman (Chapter 15) is critical of these proposals which he regards as being designed to sustain the power of the (already) large banks and to discourage competition. Almost all observers expect concentration in the financial sector to increase, but they differ on its effects.

Ryba also raises the issue of the co-mingling of financial and non-financial activities in Chapter 13. He opposes them because of the potential for self-dealing and conflicts of interest, both of which may undermine confidence in the stability and solvency of the financial system. Similar points are made by Hockin. McFetridge (Chapter 14) and Courchene (Chapter 24) review the general issues and proposals regarding ownership regulations. McFetridge acknowledges that dispersion of ownership removes some of the incentives for self-dealing but, it may also impact adversely on efficiency. Mandatory dispersed ownership requirements will tend to insulate firm management from the discipline of the market for corporate control. He advocates caution since the magnitude of the efficiency gains forgone is not known. Courchene, who provides a comprehensive commentary on the different ownership regulation proposals for financial institutions put forward during the past few years also advocates caution. The ownership issue has become the subject of heated debate as Blenkarn indicates in Chapter 23. Courchene argues in Chapter 24 that while there may well be a case for wide ownership, convincing arguments have not yet been put forward.

7.0 POLICY RESPONSES

The final group papers represent the views and interpretations of those directly involved in the policy process. As noted above, Hockin (Chapter 22) presents and defends the proposals of his White Paper. Goldman (Chapter 21) describes the major provisions of the new *Competition Act* as they relate to the issue of corporate concentration. These provisions include the abuse of dominant market position, mergers, refusal to deal and tied selling and apply to financial as well as industrial companies. Thus rigorous application of the new *Act* may alleviate some concerns regarding concentration, particularly in the area of financial services and mergers. However, Goldman notes that the *Act* primarily relates to market concentration and not to the broader issues of aggregate and ownership concentration.

Blenkarn (Chapter 23) also notes the possible deterrent effect the new *Competition Act* may have on future merger activity as a source for increased corporate concentration. He is skeptical of the efficiencies that arise from takeovers and points to the adverse impact they tend to have on employment. One area of potential reform which he identifies is tax policy. In order to make the takeover game less profitable, he suggests rethinking the deductibility of interest on debt to finance takeovers. The particular merger and interest deductibility provisions of the corporate tax system are described briefly by Wolfson (Chapter 12). His data suggest an "inverted U-shaped" relationship between corporate size and effective tax rates; that is, both large and small sized corporations pay less tax. While the tax system may encourage the growth of small business, questions no doubt arise as to whether it should facilitate the growth of large corporations which may in turn enhance corporate concentration. Wolfson's data clearly point to the need to reassess the tax system in terms of its effects on concentration.

8.0 CONCLUSIONS

What broad conclusions can be drawn from this extensive re-examination of the issues surrounding the degree of corporate concentration in Canada? What do we know now that we did not know a decade ago? One conclusion is obvious: the trend towards increased aggregate corporate concentration has not been arrested since the *Report* of the Royal Commission on Corporate Concentration in 1978. Any concerns which existed then are amplified now. Yet it is still not clear how important these concerns are. The number of mergers, notably large mergers, has increased greatly and conglomerate diversification has also increased. There is, however, no agreement over their causes and effects, although the literature has expanded greatly. Large firms have grown relatively larger but there is considerable disagreement over the efficient size and scope of the modern corporation.

For some observers, the passage of the *Competition Act*, combined with enhanced international competition, alleviates any concern regarding concentration in both the financial and non-financial sectors. Indeed, they would argue that increasing concentration is a necessary response to the demands of global, particularly American, competition. Fundamentally, this position is the same as that enunciated by the Royal Commission 10 years ago. It is somewhat paradoxical that some of the strongest challenge to this viewpoint comes from the American authors. Their various contributions suggest that U.S. industrial firms have become too large (in part through merging) and too inflexible. The (North) American comparative advantage may well reside in smaller, more specialized, more technology-intensive firms. Thus, while some vocal Canadians worry that our firms are too small to compete with the Americans, at least some Americans argue that their firms have become too large to compete successfully in increasingly "globalized" markets.

The question of corporate political power and influence remains a complex and elusive issue. In this regard, no specific policy proposals seem to elicit wide support. However, it does appear to be the case that the Canadian political system is now more dominated by organized interest groups than it was 10 years ago, and that the character of Canadian democracy is changing. The data in Figure 1 suggest a majority of Canadians view the situation with some apprehension.

Perhaps the only thing that can be stated with certainty is that these same issues will be debated for many years to come. If this book contributes to this process it will have been a success.

Figure 1
Poll on Corporate Concentration

Question	Results
What would you say has happened to corporate concentration in Canada over the past few years?	**53%** Increased **33%** Not Really Changed **10%** Decreased **4%** No Opinion
In general, how concerned are you about corporate concentration of ownership?	**42%** Somewhat Concerned **22%** Not Very Concerned **19%** Not Concerned At All **17%** Very Concerned
Which one of the following three things concern you the most about corporate concentration of ownership? Is it that the people who own these companies have too much power over prices and limit competition, that they take too much wealth out of the economy for their own use, or that they have too much political power and influence?	**40%** Too Much Power Over Prices/Competition **39%** Too Much Political Power/Influence **19%** Too Much Wealth **2%** No Opinion

Source: Quarterly Report of Decima Research conducted in 1987, based on a random sample of 1500 Canadians 18 years and older; published in The *Financial Times*, March 28, 1988, p. 3.

NOTES

1. Data on mergers in Canada can be found in Marfels (Chapter 3), Brander (Chapter 6) and in Appendix 1.

2. See the data in Khemani (Chapter 1), Niosi (Chapter 2), Marfels (Chapter 3), André (Chapter 20), and Francis (1986).

3. See Hockin (Chapter 22) and Courchene (Chapter 24).

4. See Goldman (Chapter 21) and Stanbury (1986b).

5. As editors, we provided each author with guidelines regarding the purpose, scope and length of their papers. Since the contributors were both academics and non-academics, they responded in different ways. Other than adding references and putting sub-headings into the same format, we chose not to impose stylistic homogeneity. Some of the papers therefore appear largely as they were presented – as speeches; others are written in traditional academic form. Papers which exceeded the length limitations were not arbitrarily shortened. For the most part these were surveys of literature and ideas whose coherence would have been adversely affected. However, we did not solicit longer papers from some authors and length is therefore not related to the importance we attach to any paper.

6. A number of critiques of the *Report* can be found in Gorecki and Stanbury eds. (1979).

7. See Appendix 1 of this volume.

8. The state of Canada's competition legislation in 1978 is described in Rowley & Stanbury eds. (1978) and Prichard, Stanbury and Wilson eds. (1979).

9. The Bureau of Competition Policy (1979) notes that the Commission was not supportive of proposed new legislation (Bill C-13 introduced in November 1977) in respect to mergers and joint monopolization.

10. See, for example, Stanbury & Waverman (1979).

11. Royal Commission on Corporate Concentration (1978, p. 132).

12. For a critique, see Gorecki (1979).

13. It should be noted that in none of the official proposals for reform (e.g., Bill C-13 in 1977 or Bill C-29 in 1984) or in the new *Competition Act* is there any provision dealing with pure conglomerate mergers, no matter how large. See Stanbury (1986b).

14. See the papers by Stanbury (Chapter 17), Martin (Chapter 18), and Kerton (Chapter 19) and the book by Francis (1986).

15. In general, there is much less emphasis on what might be called "dynamic efficiency." It is the ability of a firm to be efficient over time

by means of innovation and technological change. The greatest gains in real wealth are created by new products and by new methods of production and distribution, e.g., television, nylon, the jet engine, transistors, micro-circuits, etc.

16. This point is specifically addressed in the new merger provisions of the *Competition Act* which came into effect June 19, 1986. It provides for an efficiency gains "defence." See Goldman (Chapter 21) and Stanbury (1986b).

17. It should be noted that not all goods and services are traded, nor will they be under the draft free trade agreement between Canada and the U.S. signed in January 1988. The proposition that global competition can be relied upon to obviate any problems of domestic concentration, market or aggregate, is often exaggerated.

18. Data provided by the Bureau of Competition Policy.

19. It should be noted that in the U.S., in particular, in the period 1986-1987 a significant fraction of all takeovers consisted of "spinoffs" of divisions of large conglomerate enterprises. In other words, through management buyouts and purchases by smaller, more specialized firms, "de-conglomeratization" was also occurring. This suggests that for some firms at least the synergy was negative.

20. He notes, for example, that while the market value of the acquiring firm may increase little or even decline, the net result is an increase in the combined value of the two firms.

21. More generally, see Stanbury (1986a) and Pross (1986).

REFERENCES

Bureau of Competition Policy (1979) "The Royal Commission on Corporate Concentration – Recommendations and Comments Directly Relevant to Bill C-13" in P.K. Gorecki & W.T. Stanbury (eds.) *Perspectives on the Royal Commission on Corporate Concentration* (Montreal: The Institute for Research on Public Policy), Ch. 12.

Francis, Diane (1986) *Controlling Interest* (Toronto: Macmillan).

Gorecki, P.K. (1979) "The Conglomerate Enterprise in Canada: Evidence and Policy" in P.K. Gorecki & W.T. Stanbury (eds.) *Perspectives on the Royal Commission on Corporate Concentration* (Montreal: The Institute for Research on Public Policy), Ch. 11.

Gorecki, P.K. and W.T. Stanbury (1979) *Perspectives on the Royal Commission on Corporate Concentration* (Montreal: The Institute for Research on Public Policy).

Prichard, J.R.S., W.T. Stanbury and T.A. Wilson eds. (1979) *Canadian Competition Policy: Essays in Law and Economics* (Toronto: Butterworths).

Pross, A. Paul (1986) *Group Politics and Public Policy* (Toronto: Oxford University Press).

Rowley, J.W. and W.T. Stanbury eds. (1978) *Competition Policy in Canada: Stage II, Bill C-13* (Montreal: The Institute for Research on Public Policy).

Royal Commission on Corporate Concentration (1978) *Report* (Ottawa: Minister of Supply and Services Canada).

Stanbury, W.T. (1986a) *Business-Government Relations in Canada* (Toronto: Methuen).

_____ (1986b) "The New Competition Act and Competition Tribunal Act: 'Not With a Bang, But a Whimper'," *Canadian Business Law Journal*, Vol. 12(1), October, pp. 2-42.

Stanbury W.T. & Leonard Waverman (1979) "Merger Policy of the Royal Commission on Corporate Concentration: Conclusions without Evidence" in P.K. Gorecki & W.T. Stanbury (eds.) *Perspectives on the Royal Commission on Corporate Concentration* (Montreal: The Institute for Research on Public Policy), Ch. 10.

Williamson, O.E. (1975) *Markets and Hierarchies* (New York: The Free Press).

_____ (1985) *Economic Institutions of Capitalism* (New York: The Free Press).

Dimensions of Corporate Concentration

Chapter 1

The Dimensions of Corporate Concentration in Canada

R.S. Khemani*
Senior Policy Advisor
Bureau of Competition Policy
Department of Consumer & Corporate Affairs
Ottawa-Hull

1.0 INTRODUCTION

Concerns regarding corporate concentration have been a recurrent theme in Canadian public policy since the turn of the century. The discussions over time, however, have tended to be fragmented by focusing on only one or two dimensions of the phenomenon of corporate concentration. The term corporate concentration embodies at least three distinct concepts: *aggregate concentration*, which measures the relative position of large enterprises in the economy; *industry or market concentration*, which measures the relative position of large enterprises in the provision of specific goods or services such as automobiles or mortgage loans; and *ownership concentration*, which measures the extent to which shares of stock exchange listed companies are widely or narrowly (closely) held. This last concept is often extended to describe the wealth or control of corporate assets among individual families or business entities. In addition, discussions regarding corporate concentration frequently include matters such as conglomerates, i.e., the extent to which large enterprises have operations across a number of industries or sectors and, inter-locking directorates, i.e., multiple ties between the boards of directors of large corporations.[1]

*   The views expressed in this paper are held solely by the author and do not necessarily reflect those of the Bureau of the Department of Consumer and Corporate Affairs Canada. The author wishes to particularly thank W.T. Stanbury for providing unpublished data and volumes of other material used in the preparation of this paper including an extensive unpublished manuscript on corporate concentration in Canada. The research assistance of David Bloom is gratefully acknowledged.

The central theme of this chapter is that these different dimensions of corporate concentration are inter-related and that the ramifications of high levels in one type of concentration cannot be fully gauged without reference to prevailing levels of other types of concentration. Because of the interconnections, public policies formulated to address concerns in respect to any one type of concentration will tend to affect other areas which may not be intended or desirable. The realization of this point is particularly acute in Canada where empirical information suggests there exists a possibly unique configuration of high levels of all three types of concentration namely, aggregate, industry and ownership concentration.

The remaining sections of this paper are organized as follows: Section 2 briefly describes the rationale for measuring, and the concerns associated with, different types of corporate concentration. Section 3 provides a brief historical overview of earlier Canadian studies on corporate concentration. Section 4 presents the most up-to-date statistical information available on different dimensions of corporate concentration. Section 5 discusses some implications of the particular configuration of corporate concentration in Canada. Section 6 offers some concluding comments.

2.0 RATIONALE FOR MEASURING CORPORATE CONCENTRATION

There exist various rationales for computing different measures of corporate concentration. Briefly, *aggregate concentration* has interested economists, sociologists and political scientists mainly in the context of theories relating to actual and potential economic-political power of big business in modern capitalistic economies. A typical theory or hypothesis is that in highly concentrated economies, the freedom of action of democratically elected government to enact public policies which are not supported by the interests of a few large corporations or families becomes severely constrained.[2] As aggregate concentration increases, large enterprises may control the most important means of production and be in a position such that their decisions necessarily have wide economic and social consequences. Beck (1985, p. 182) has observed:

It is well recognized that the largest corporations such as Bell Canada, MacMillan Bloedel, CPR and CP Enterprises, Power Corporation and Imperial Oil, to name a few, exercise power that extends far beyond their obvious function as efficient producers of goods and providers of services. In spite of the rise of manifold regulations and the alleged play of pluralist, countervailing forces, the large corporation wields power that commands, directs and influences large segments of society. Indeed, the international division of labour, the technological and communications revolutions, and the internationalization of capital aided by the electronic transfer of funds have given the corporation a freedom to move and a power to act that is greater today than it has ever been.

Since those who control mega corporations exercise power in pursuit of the interests of the corporation, there is no reason to believe that the exercise of such power will necessarily coincide with the public interest (Galbraith 1973, p. 6).

Other concerns that have been expressed with respect to aggregate concentration is that large enterprises tend to be large diversified conglomerates and are more likely to meet their counterparts in many markets, sometimes as competitors, sometimes as buyers and sellers. The resulting multiple interdependence will foster competition-lessening policies such as mutual forbearance, reciprocity and cross-subsidization. On the positive side, it has been argued that large conglomerate enterprises are able to more efficiently transfer financial resources from less to higher valued uses than does the external capital market, better withstand business cycles, and diversify risk.

The rationale underlying the measurement of *industry or market concentration* is the industrial organization economics theory which suggests that other things being equal, high levels of market concentration are more conducive to firms engaging in monopolistic practices which leads to the misallocation of resources and poor economic performance.

In highly concentrated industries, it is argued, firms have greater latitude and discretionary power in making decisions regarding price, output and other related matters. They have this power because the presence of only a few rivals enables them to act interdependently and to effectively coordinate their respective business policies. In contrast, when industry concentration is low, the existence of many rival firms forces each to behave independently, and firms will have less discretionary power over prices, output and related factors. In this latter case, market forces rather than individual firms determine the levels of prices and output.

This particular theory has been buttressed by empirical research which suggests a positive relationship exists between concentration levels and profits, that is, due to monopoly pricing industries with high concentration levels will tend to have higher than average profits. The interpretation of the empirical results, as well as the theory itself, has been subject to significant criticism. The alternative viewpoint suggests that high concentration and high profits may not reflect so much the exercise of market power as much as the efficiency and superior competitive performance of large firms. In addition, it has been argued that the presence of a large number of firms is not a necessary condition for competition to prevail in an industry. Effective competition in the form of inter-firm rivalry may exist when there are few firms of relative equal size. Moreover, competitive price and output levels may be observed in industries with only one or few firms if there are no barriers to the entry of new firms. The threat of potential entry will force incumbent firms to price and output at competitive levels.[3]

While the controversy over the meaning and effects of industry or market concentration remain unresolved, there does exist some consensus that the concept itself is not irrelevant to analyzing competition in an industry when it is accompanied with an examination of other structural and behavioural factors.

Ownership concentration is measured in order to gauge the extent to which there is separation between the ownership and control of stock exchange-listed companies. Analysis of the ownership structure of corporations is motivated by various hypotheses relating to the extent to which corporate control is exercised by large shareholders or by professional managers, the incentives and rights of majority vs. minority shareholders, and other such matters as the composition, role and power of the board of directors.

Modern corporations are typically owned by stockholders who delegate decision-making authority regarding day-to-day business to hired professional managers. Stockholders are in essence investors who provide capital whereas managers provide the knowledge and skills necessary for the operation of large, complex organizations. However, this difference in roles and specialization between stockholders and managers is not without risk. If ownership of a corporation is widely distributed across numerous shareholders, no one shareholder may have the ability nor the incentive to ensure management interests in operating the corporation coincide with those of the shareholders. Management may thus control and run corporations in their best interests instead of maximizing shareholder value. As a consequence, corporate assets may not be put to their highest valued uses and a misallocation of resources may take place.

The risks of such occurrences can, to some extent, be held in check if share ownership is concentrated among fewer investors so that there will exist greater incentives to monitor the performance of corporate management. Poor corporate management performance may also be deterred by what has been referred to as the *market for corporate control*, that is, the process of takeovers.[4] According to this hypothesis, poor management performance will tend to be reflected in lower share prices than the market would otherwise establish. Consequently, bidders foreseeing an opportunity to make profits will directly approach stockholders and offer a premium to purchase shares so as to take over control and replace incumbent management. The successful strategy to avoid being taken over is to maintain high levels of corporate performance and to ensure the stock price is also high relative to an outsider's estimate of its potential value.[5]

These mechanisms may, however, have an adverse impact in other areas. Ownership concentration, while mitigating the possibility of abuses by corporate management, may give rise to problems of shareholders' democracy if majority shareholders adopt policies which discriminate against minority shareholders. The process of takeovers may increase the level of industry or market concentration and give rise to concerns regarding competition or accentuate concerns that stem from high levels of aggregate concentration.

The interconnections between different dimensions of corporate concentration become clearer when considered in the context of how the different measures of concentration are computed. This is illustrated by Figure 1.

Figure 1

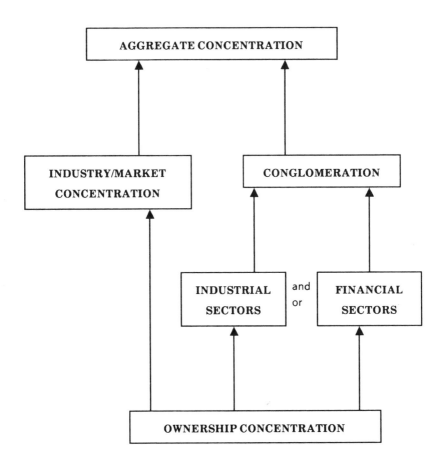

For purposes of computing aggregate and/or industry concentration measures, the first step is to examine the ownership structure and inter-corporate links among individual corporations or firms. These "firms" are then grouped together, according to "common control," into "enterprises." Common control is established on the basis of individuals or corporate entities holding directly or indirectly, 50 per cent or more of the common voting shares of a firm. The enterprises are then ranked within individual industries or in the economy as a whole in order to arrive at industry or aggregate concentration measures, respectively. The groupings of large enterprises used to compute aggregate concentration measures may therefore comprise of large single firm enterprises that operate in a single industry and/or of large multi-firm enterprises with conglomerate operations across wide range of industries. Thus, absolute corporate size as well as market concentration may underlie prevailing levels of aggregate concentration.

3.0   HISTORICAL REVIEW

In some measure, concerns expressed about corporate concentration formed the basis for enactment of the first competition legislation in 1889.[6] While debates in Parliament at that time (and during subsequent amendments to the law) dealt primarily with issues of unfair market practices and high prices, questions relating to large aggregations of capital and economic power were also raised.[7]

It was, however, not until the early part of this century that the first empirical measures of corporate concentration were put forward. According to Myers (1914, pp. i-iii), less than 50 men controlled one-third of Canada's material wealth as expressed in railways, banks, factories, mines, land and other properties and resources. The rapid concentration of wealth was viewed as "no mere fancy" and the process of centralization was described as steadily going on for 35 years. The role played by mergers was recognized and expected to increase as "economic forces are more powerful than statute laws." Myers (1914) also alluded to political influence and failure of government to exercise any control over the process: "the machinery of Government is administered at all times either directly by the beneficiaries or by the representatives of those ruling forces, no matter by what political name they may be pleased to call themselves."

The Royal Commission on Price Spreads (1935) put forward the first, and fairly comprehensive, set of official data on aggregate, industry and ownership concentration and concluded that corporate concentration levels were high in Canada and had increased over time. It was estimated that in 1923, the 100 largest companies accounted for 25.5 per cent of total assets which by 1932 had grown to 35 per cent. However, these computations excluded the assets of the two railways (CNR, CPR), which loomed large in the economy at that time. When included, the corresponding concentration statistics for the two years were 65 and 70 per cent respectively.

The commission also stated that corporate concentration "manifested itself in numerous cases of economic exploitation and was one of the main sources of our economic problems" (Report, p. 27). The economic problem particularly mentioned was resistance towards readjustment in many parts of the Canadian economy.

In its analysis of ownership and control of the 145 largest non-financial companies, 34 per cent (23 per cent of assets) were deemed to be closely held, i.e., at least 50 per cent of the voting stock was in the hands of one or a small group of individuals. For one-half of these large corporations, there was separation between ownership and control.

The commission put forward a wide set of proposals which were insightful, and in many respects ahead of the times. The recommendations included strengthening competition legislation, government supervision of financial reports, prohibitions on insider trading, buttressing internal governance of firms, and greater information disclosure.

In the post-war period,[8] the subject of corporate concentration was revisited by the Royal (Gordon) Commission on Canada's Economic Prospects (1957); the Economic Council of Canada (1969); most extensively by the Royal (Bryce) Commission on Corporate Concentration (1978) and most recently by the Royal (Macdonald) Commission on the Economic Union and Development Prospects for Canada (1986). While the views expressed in these reports vary, it was commonly acknowledged that large corporate size in and of itself is not inherently against the public interest. The need for strengthening competition legislation was identified, particularly with respect to mergers that were likely to increase market concentration resulting in adverse economic effects. No radical changes in laws governing conglomerate mergers and/or forms of corporate activity that would specifically affect aggregate corporate concentration were deemed to be necessary.

4.0   EMPIRICAL INFORMATION ON CORPORATE CONCENTRATION

Data on various measures of corporate concentration in Canada is presented below. In interpreting this information, the drawbacks and methodological problems which generally affect concentration measures must be borne in mind. First, the consolidation of corporations into enterprises, as described earlier, is based on examining inter-corporate ownership links and defining effective control as ownership of 50 per cent or more of common voting shares. Actual control can, however, be exercised at lower voting share ownership thresholds and through the use of devices such as voting trusts. To the extent this occurs, the prevailing degree of aggregate and industry concentration will be understated. Second, the identity and rank of enterprises that form the basis of concentration measures may change over time. In other words, not all of the leading 25 or 100 enterprises will remain the same over time. Turnover among enterprises may take place.[9] Third, while various economic units such as assets, sales, employment, tend to be highly correlated, divergence in the rank size of enterprises may occur at any given point in time and/or over time depending on the measure chosen. Sales and employment measures are, for example, more sensitive to business conditions than assets. Also, enterprises that rank large in terms of sales such as retail chains, may not rank similarly in terms of assets.

4.1   Total Corporate Sector

Traditionally, in the computation of aggregate concentration measures, the holdings of enterprises which span both the financial and non-financial sector are consolidated separately within each of the respective sectors. This understates the relative significance of these enterprises in the economy as a whole. In order to correct for this, Table 1 presents data on the relative size of the 25, 50 and 100 largest enterprises, regardless of the sector in which they operate. The table indicates that as a per cent of total corporate assets, aggregate concentration has increased between 1977 and 1983, the latest year for which these statistics are available. There, however, is some variation in the composition of the increase in concentration. Examining the leading 25 enterprises, the data shows that their share of non-financial sector assets decreased from 37.6 per cent to 32.7 per cent whereas, in the financial sector their share increased from 48.9 per cent to 59.7 per cent between 1977 and 1983. The same does not hold for the leading 50 and 100 enterprises indicating that the move towards inter-sectoral conglomeration that has occurred is primarily among the largest enterprises.

4.2   Economy Wide Conglomerates

The confidentiality provisions of the *Statistics Act* preclude identification of individual enterprise names and sizes but, the list of the 50 largest (in 1977) would certainly include the following 'economy-wide conglomerates', that is, corporate entities whose activity spans three or more major standard industrial classification categories including but not necessarily financial services.

- Belzberg/First City
- Black/Revelston
- Canadian Pacific
- Edper/Brascan
- Hiram Walker
- Nova/Husky
- Southern/Atco
- Weston/Loblaws

- Bell Canada Enterprises
- Cemp/Seagrams
- Desmarais/Power
- Genstar
- Imasco
- Reichman/Olympia York
- Thomson/Hudson's Bay

Each of these conglomerates have book value of assets in excess of $1 billion. These conglomerates and their subsidiaries generally tend to be wholly or closely owned. The total *Canadian* asset holdings of these conglomerates and their size relative to the corporate sector as a whole are presented in Table 2. Enterprises such as Alcan, Canada Packers, Chrysler Corporation, which are among these leading enterprises, are not viewed as "conglomerates" given their activity is primarily within one major industrial sector.

Table 1

Leading 25, 50 & 100 Enterprises in the Canadian Economy
(Non-financial and Financial Sectors)

	Year	Total Enterprise Assets ($ millions)	% of Total Corporate Sector Assets	% of Non-financial Sector Assets	% of Financial Sector Assets
25 Leading Enterprises	1977	$230,480	42.5	37.6	48.9
	1983	$512,633	45.3	32.7	59.7
50 Leading Enterprises	1977	$295,081	54.5	45.7	65.7
	1983	$645,467	57.0	49.9	65.1
100 Leading Enterprises	1977	$351,173	64.8	59.8	71.3
	1983	$756,931	66.9	63.4	70.9

Source: Statistics Canada Special Tabulation (1986)

Table 2
Asset Share of Selected Economy-wide Conglomerates, 1977-1985[1]

	1977	1980	1983	1985[2]
Total Conglomerate Assets ($Billions)	37	74	135	211[2]
Conglomerate Assets as a Percentage of Total Corporate Sector Assets	6.8%	8.8%	11.9%	16.0%[2]
Total Corporate Sector Assets (Including Financial Sector) ($Billions)	542	842	1,132	1,318

Notes:

1. A group of 15 conglomerates in existence in 1977 was reduced to 12 in 1985 due to mergers and acquisitions.

2. Estimated

Sources: Statistics Canada Special Tabulation - (Corporate Sector Assets 1977 to 1983) Statistics Canada "Calura Pt.I," Cat. No. 61-210, Annual Reports of Individual Corporations, Financial Post Cards

Table 2 indicates there has been a consistent upward trend in the relative size of the 15 conglomerates. In 1977 they accounted for approximately 7 per cent of total corporate sector assets which grew to 12 per cent by 1983 and 16 per cent by 1985. In absolute terms, over the same period, these 15 conglomerates experienced a near six-fold increase in size, while the growth in total corporate assets in the Canadian economy increased by approximately two and one-half times. Increase in congloerate relative size has particularly accentuated since 1980. This growth in relative size is in part, if not importantly the result of "mega merger activity" which the conglomerates have been involved in. By 1985, the number of 15 economy-wide conglomerates was reduced to 12 because of such activity within the group itself.[10] Moreover, given the fact that these statistics do not reflect the most recent acquisitions, further increase in conglomeration and aggregate concentration has likely occurred since 1985. (See also Niosi, Chapter 2 in this volume.)

4.3 The Non-financial Sector
The extent to which the non-financial sector is dominated by a small number of large enterprises is indicated in Table 3. In 1984, the 25 largest enterprises, which include those operated by federal and provincial governments, accounted for 35.3 per cent of sector assets whereas in 1975 the corresponding figure is 29.2 per cent. The most dramatic increases in the relative size of these enterprises occurred during the periods of 1968-1975 and 1980-1982. It may be noted there was significant merger activity in the Canadian economy in selected years during those time periods as well. Similar trends are evident when the relative size of the 50 and 100 largest enterprises are examined.

Once again, because of the *Statistics Act*, information on the identity and rank of individual enterprises is not available. However, analyses of the 100 largest corporations listed in the *Financial Post 500* is indicative of the turnover among large firms. Of the 100 largest corporations in 1984, 94 were in the group in 1983, 76 in 1980 and 48 in 1975.[11] Only 41 corporations remained ranked among the 100 largest throughout the 1975-1984 period. There were also changes in the ranks of the 10 largest corporations but, their composition generally tends to be more stable over time. Eight corporations have remained ranked among the top 10 throughout the past decade or so.

The leading enterprises consist of government, foreign and Canadian private sector owned or controlled enterprises. As Figure 2 suggests, the share of assets accounted for by the foreign enterprises have remained fairly stable. In contrast, the share of assets of both the Canadian private and government sector enterprises have tended to increase, though not consistently in all years. Government enterprises, as much as private sector enterprises, have contributed significantly towards higher levels of aggregate concentration. A similar pattern may be observed in terms of the composition of the 50 and 100 largest enterprises. Overall, since 1965, there has been a consistent upward trend in aggregate concentration in the non-financial sector of the Canadian economy.

4.4 Financial Sector
The Economic Council of Canada (1987) has published data on concentration of assets among major groups of financial institutions such as chartered banks, trust and loan companies and life insurance companies.[12] This information suggests that the four largest institutions accounted for 46 per cent of sector assets in 1967, 55 per cent in 1979 and 52 per cent in 1984.[13] In terms of different financial activities accounted for by the four largest companies, concentration had declined between 1979 and 1984 in domestic deposits (from 54 to 48 per cent) and in domestic and personal loans (from 70 to 63 per cent) but not in mortgages (30 to 33 per cent).[14] The Council states that the concentration figures tend to underestimate the nature of competition as they do not take into account substitution between different financial instruments. (See also Ryba, Chapter 13 of this volume.)

Table 3
Ownership Composition and Shares of Assets of the 25, 50, and 100 Largest Non-Financial Enterprises in Canada (Ranked in terms of Sales) 1965-1984

	Leading 25 Enterprises — Percentage Share of Assets and Type of Ownership *				Leading 50 Enterprises — Percentage Share of Assets and Type of Ownership *				Leading 100 Enterprises — Percentage Share of Assets and Type of Ownership *				Total Non-Financial Sector Assets For Classified Enterprises only *** ($ millions)			Grand Total - includes non-classified enterprises ***
	Foreign	Canadian Pvt.	Gov't	Total	Foreign	Canadian Pvt.	Gov't	Total	Foreign	Canadian Pvt.	Gov't	Total	Foreign	Canadian Pvt.	Canadian Gov't**	
1965-%				23.8				30.6				38.6				$77,296
1968-%				22.5				29.4				37.3				$99,711
1973-%				25.2				32.4				40.1				$183,713
1975-%	5.4	10.0	13.8	29.2	8.6	14.2	13.8	36.6	14.5	16.6	15.4	46.5	$79,367	$112,411	$43,152	$245,459
-#	9	12	4		23	23	4	50	56	37	7	100	3,608	56,663	318	208,528
1976-%	5.4	9.6	14.7	29.6	9.8	13.7	14.7	38.2	14.0	16.5	16.5	46.9	$83,369	$125,848	$51,622	$273,440
-#	9	12	4	25	21	25	4	50	53	40	7	100	3,643	65,181	321	231,273
1977-%	5.5	8.7	15.3	29.4	8.8	13.4	15.3	37.5	14.5	15.8	17.3	47.6	$92,719	$139,489	$60,569	$305,107
-#	9	12	4	25	21	25	4	50	53	40	7	100	3,590	71,614	339	249,272
1978-%	5.3	9.7	15.4	30.4	8.4	13.4	15.4	37.3	13.6	16.1	18.1	47.8	$99,817	$164,001	$69,855	$347,055
-#	9	12	4	25	21	25	4	50	52	40	8	100	3,625	81,134	325	276,955
1979-%	5.8	11.6	13.3	30.7	9.1	15.7	13.3	38.1	14.0	19.8	14.7	48.5	$116,592	$208,031	$64,317	$403,129
-#	9	13	3	25	22	25	3	50	51	44	5	100	3,227	95,741	15	307,030
1980-%	5.8	10.0	14.3	30.2	8.5	15.7	14.7	38.8	13.5	19.6	16.3	49.4	$126,715	$241,552	$79,851	$463,698
-#	9	12	3	25	20	25	5	50	47	45	8	100	3,515	108,826	23	343,563
1981-%	5.6	13.3	13.2	32.1	8.0	17.8	15.6	41.5	12.6	20.3	17.1	50.0	$138,160	$291,007	$97,565	$543,355
-#	9	13	3	25	18	27	5	50	46	46	8	100	3,348	122,493	34	373,678
1982-%	5.5	13.0	15.6	34.1	8.3	17.6	16.5	42.4	12.1	21.3	18.4	51.9	$141,906	$326,762	$109,373	$578,041
-#	9	12	4	25	19	26	5	50	43	48	9	100	3,608	385,058	41	388,707
1983-%	5.7	12.6	16.0	34.3	8.7	17.3	17.0	43.1	12.3	21.1	18.7	52.1	$147,388	$341,321	$117,019	$605,728
-#	9	12	4	25	20	26	5	50	45	47	8	100	3,351	351,588	19	354,958
1984-%	6.6	12.2	16.4	35.3	8.3	17.5	17.4	43.2	12.1	20.8	19.2	52.1	$160,354	$373,642	$129,765	$663,762
-#	10	11	4	25	17	28	5	50	42	49	8	99	3,136	386,884	22	390,042

Sources: 1975 onward: Statistics Canada, Corporations and Labour Unions Returns Act, Part I (Cat. 61-210) Annual, Table 1.
Prior to 1975: Royal Commission on Corporate Concentration, Study 31 (1977), "Concentration Levels and Trends in the Canadian Economy, 1965-1973," C. Marfels, Supply and Services Canada, Ottawa.

* Percentages expressed are proportion of total non-financial sector assets.
** Excludes regionally and municipally controlled enterprises from 1979 onward.
*** Non-Classified Enterprises have assets less than $500,000 and sales less than $250,000, and, as such, do not report under CALUPA.

Figure 2
25 Largest Non-financial Enterprises

Ownership Composition and Trends

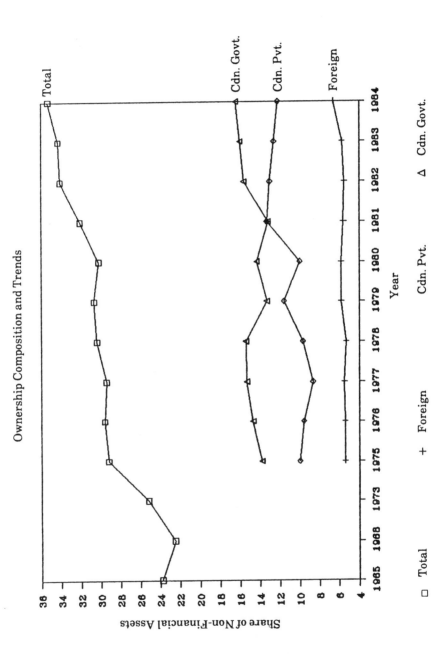

4.5 Industry Concentration

In Khemani (1986), information on concentration levels and trends in major industrial sectors and particularly in Canadian manufacturing is presented. An examination of individual industries indicates four-firm concentration levels of greater than 75 per cent in tobacco, coal and coke, department stores, variety stores, air transportation, railways, pipelines, electric power, telephones, gas distribution, banks, consumer loan companies and other financial agencies. Over the period 1975-1980, concentration levels in the majority of these industries tended to increase. In the manufacturing sector, 95 per cent or 3,943 of 4,131 five-digit industry products such as four-door passenger cars and canned soups, were produced by four or less firms accounting for 50 per cent or more of the total domestic output. The study also documents that while in the post-war period, there had been until 1972 a consistent tendency towards higher concentration levels, in recent years this trend has been moderate if not declined. Concentration levels in Canadian manufacturing, however, remain higher than those prevailing in other Western industrialized countries.

4.6 Ownership Concentration

The Securities Industry Committee on Take-Over Bids (1983) indicates that of the 283 companies having shares included in the TSE (Toronto Stock Exchange) 300 Composite Index, 137 or 48.4 per cent were under legal control that is, where 50 per cent or more of voting stock was held by one or a small group of shareholders; another 85 or 30 per cent of the companies were under effective control (20 - 49.9 per cent of voting stock) and only 61 or 21.6 per cent of the companies could be viewed as being widely held.[15] The corresponding statistics for the U.S. Standard and Poor's (S & P) 500 Index are six companies or 1.2 per cent, 68 companies or 13.6 per cent and 426 companies or 85.2 per cent respectively.[16] In other words, while the majority or nearly 80 per cent of the TSE 300 companies are closely held, 85 per cent of the S & P 500 companies are widely held.

5.0 SINGLE, DOUBLE OR TRIPLE JEOPARDY?

The preceding section indicates that the particular configuration of corporate concentration in Canada is such that there simultaneously exists high levels of aggregate, industry and ownership concentration. There also exists significant conglomerate activity across various industrial sectors, including in recent years, across financial and non-financial sectors. There is some indication that these dimensions of corporate concentration have been increasing over time or, at least, been relatively stable.

While a multitude of economic, institutional and other factors underlie the phenomenon of corporate concentration, the focus of attention in recent years has been on corporate takeover activity. The Speech from the Throne in October 1986 stated that the

> . . . government is concerned about the increasing concentration of corporations, particularly where takeovers serve to increase

corporate size without creating new jobs or stimulating economic growth in Canada. Some aspects of this essentially non-productive activity will be examined and considered. . . .

The Bureau of Competition Policy Merger Register indicates the number of mergers and acquisitions reported in the financial press have been consistently increasing since 1980. In that year there were 414 acquisitions whereas in 1986 the number stood at 938.[17] During the first 10 months of 1987 there were 895 completed or proposed takeovers reported. While these statistics do not represent the total number of mergers and acquisitions in Canada, they are likely indicative of the trends in this activity. Moreover, in recent years the number of large merger transactions have probably increased. Data collected by W.T. Stanbury (see Appendix 1) lists 13 acquisitions in 1980 with transaction values in excess of $100 million; 42 in 1986 and 47 in 1987.

Decima (1987), the public opinion polling firm has indicated that in recent years, 6 in 10 Canadians noted an increase in mergers and takeovers and 7 in 10 expressed concerns about such activity. A subsequent poll suggests that public perceptions and levels of concern about corporate concentration had actually increased. Specially notable is the high level of concern expressed by well educated professionals in urbanized provinces such as British Columbia and Ontario. The concerns expressed focus primarily on the power over prices, competition and policies that concentrated ownership gives to individuals (Decima 1987, p. 27).

The different sets of concerns which takeover activity and corporate concentration give rise to are summarized in Figure 3. The chart is self-evident and indicates the major issues posed as well as the public policy instruments that are available to address them. Note, however, needs to be made of the inter-connections between the various issues and policies. While takeover activity may raise particular questions regarding corporate governance or economic growth, policies enacted in one area may impact in other areas. For example, ownership restrictions may alleviate some concerns regarding corporate governance but insulate firms from the market for corporate control and adversely affect competition and efficiency. Caution therefore needs to be exercised in formulating policies which otherwise appear to have a narrow focal point.

An overall question that is worth exploring is: What explains the configuration of high levels of aggregate, industry and ownership concentration, which casual evidence suggests, is unique to Canada?

Takeover activity no doubt forms part of the answer to this question. However, a more fundamental explanation that may be ventured is that it is importantly linked to the past state of competition in various industrial and financial sectors of the Canadian economy.

The Canadian economy has historically been characterized as being composed of industrial and financial sectors which have been insulated from competition due to tariff and non-tariff barriers, government regulation and ineffective competition laws. It is likely this lack of competition provided the

Figure 3
Corporate Concentration
Analytical Framework

The Environment of Corporate Concentration in the Mid-1980s

- Failure of 2 banks and 14 trust companies
- Increasing concentration of ownership
- Increase in very large takeovers
- Conflict of interest allegations against public officials
- Fear of reduced competition
- New takeover tactics, especially in financing
- Conglomeration
- New awareness of paper entrepreneurship
- Non-financial takeovers of financial institutions
- Growth of financial services industry
- Hostile takeovers
- Perceived failure of regulatory supervision
- Non-arms length deals/ risk of increased conflict of interest

	Firm Performance/ Economic Growth	Competition	Financial Institutions/ Financial Risk	Corporate Governance	Distribution of Wealth	Management of the Government/Business Relationship
Main Concept	Firm Performance/ Economic Growth	Competition	Financial Institutions/ Financial Risk	Corporate Governance	Distribution of Wealth	Management of the Government/Business Relationship
Main question	Do takeovers contribute to economic growth?	Does concentration reduce competition?	Does blending of financial and non-financial institutions increase financial risk?	Are shareholder rights protected?	Do takeovers further entrench the corporate elite?	Does concentration increase corporate political influence?
Issues	• Effects of takeovers on firm performance; • Growth: efficiency; employment; investment and inflation • Effects of concentration on aggregate economic performance	• Anticompetitive behaviours in markets • Conglomerates and competition	• solvency and depositor's protection • system stability • competition • conflict of interest	• Closely held/widely held • Separate Ownership and Control: • Shareholders/ Directors/Managers • Acquisitors/Targets	The Corporate Elite: • smaller • closely held ownership • mobility • distribution of wealth	• Public Confidence • Business as lobby • Business as community leader • Commonality of interests • Conflict of interest
Instruments	• regulatory framework • securities law • corporations law • tax law • sectoral policy • bankruptcy law • monetary policy • Crown divestiture policy	• competition law • sectoral policy • trade policy • investment policy	• financial institution regulation • Competition Act • corporations law	• corporations law • securities law • tax law	• tax law • investment incentives • ownership limits	• consultation • lobbying policy • adequacy of regulatory framework • government as entrepreneur/financier • sectoral policy • conflict of interest guidelines

Source: Consumer and Corporate Affairs Canada. Presentation to House of Commons Standing Committee on Consumer and Corporate Affairs, May 21, 1987.

initial impetus for concentration to take place in these sectors. Other things being equal, high levels of industry concentration also tend to provide opportunities for charging higher prices and earning excess profits. However, in an industrial environment which is insulated from competitive pressures, it is not easy to ascertain whether the level of profits earned represent the efforts of corporate management to minimize costs. The lack of competition may lead to organizational slack and X-inefficiency.

In addition, if the firms are widely held, shareholders may not be able to exercise control and corporate management will become entrenched and likely to pursue their own private goals instead of maximizing corporate and shareholder value. The extent to which this arises provides incentives for ownership concentration to increase and for an active market for corporate control. While both of these mechanisms will enable better monitoring of corporate management performance, the pursuit of profit maximization will not reduce the high prices and excess profits earned by the firms in the market for their goods and services. Income transfers from consumers to owner-producers will continue as long as there is a lack of competition in the markets the firms serve. These transfers will accentuate income and eventually wealth inequality in society. Further, an active market for corporate control will accentuate industry and aggregate concentration as well as ownership concentration. Moreover, the tendency towards ownership concentration will not cease at levels necessary to effectively monitor corporate management performance. The lack of competition in the industrial and financial sectors will generate higher than normal risk adjusted profits. Through increased ownership, a greater proportion of these profits can be retained as against being distributed in the form of dividends. With the leverage provided by high profits, new financing when required will likely be funded through increased debt and/or the issuance of non-voting stock, without diluting ownership control.

Thus, the adverse effects of a non-competitive economic environment can be widespread and generate self-sustaining tendencies towards all three types of corporate concentration. In contrast, if vigorous competition exists, firms will tend to earn normal, risk-adjusted profits. Any attempts by corporate management to depart from maximizing profits and shareholder wealth will be effectively held in check by both the market for corporate control and the degree of competition prevailing in markets. The extent to which ownership concentration does arise will likely be due to perceived problems of otherwise monitoring corporate performance. If ownership concentration is sought for exercise of power at the sacrifice of profits, the corporation will tend to decline over time as competitive pressures are exercised by more aggressive and innovative firms.

6.0 CONCLUDING COMMENTS
The issue of corporate concentration, in one form or another, has been raised in Canada since the late nineteenth century if not earlier. Questions regarding the phenomenon traditionally tend to arise during periods of peak merger activity, when amendments to competition legislation are before

Parliament and/or when regulatory problems and institutional failures occur.

Unlike the United States, in Canada there exists no consistent populist underpinnings for measures aimed at preventing excessive accumulation of corporate economic power. In the United States, antitrust and related policies include in the conceptual framework, the objectives of "diffusion of economic power," "diversity in decision making units," "preservation of free enterprise" and "fairness." Indeed, there appears to be a rough consensus in American society which attaches equal if not higher value to these objectives than to economic efficiency.

The lack of similar consensus in Canada, coupled with the complex nature of the issues, has generally led to a schizoid reaction to the concentration phenomenon. On the one hand, recognizing the relative small size of the Canadian economy, high levels of concentration are often viewed as being necessary to enable firms to exploit various economies of scale and scope and to compete internationally. On the other hand, with higher levels of aggregate concentration and increased conglomeration among firms, concerns are expressed about the emergence of an economic oligarchy which will wield undue economic, social and political influence.

The issues that corporate concentration poses are unlikely to be resolved without objective in-depth research. However, even in the face of such research, one may anticipate differences in views to persist. The issues are not merely those relating to economic statistics and methodologies, but of ideological beliefs and fundamental values as well. If future discussions are to be intelligent and productive, the responsibility lies not just with government and/or academic institutions studying the matter but also with the executives and management of large corporations. Greater information is required on corporate objectives and activity in Canada. The current set of information disclosure requirements are fragmented across different jurisdictions and agencies and generally inadequate. In addition, corporate executives tend to display reticence in discussing issues of broad public concern.[18] The first step that needs to be taken towards resolving many of the questions regarding corporate concentration is enhanced and more timely disclosure of information.

NOTES

1. The issue of inter-locking directorates is not examined in this paper. Extensive analysis in this area in the Canadian context has been conducted by Carroll (1986).

2. More generally, see Stanbury, Chapter 17 in this volume.

3. See, for example, Baumol *et al.* (1982).

4. See Manne (1965). An excellent synthesis of this hypothesis and empirical evidence is contained in U.S. Council of Economic Advisors (1985, Ch. 6).

5. More generally, see Eckbo, Chapter 7 in this volume, and Job and Riding, Chapter 9 in this volume.

6. See, for example, the discussion in Gorecki and Stanbury (1984).

7. The development of corporate capitalism in Canada, including the power exercised by an industrial-political-financial 'elite' is described by Clement (1975, Ch. 2) and citations therein.

8. See also McCollum (1947).

9. See the analysis of Carroll (1986) which covered the period 1946-1976 for the top 100.

10. See also the data collected by W.T. Stanbury reported in Appendix 1.

11. See also the work of Carroll (1986) which examined the period 1946-1976.

12. See also Ryba, Chapter 13 in this volume.

13. Economic Council (1987, Table 3-1, p. 28).

14. Economic Council (1987, Table 3-4, p. 30).

15. Securities Industry Committee (1983, p. 69).

16. Securities Industry Committee (1983, p. 75).

17. More generally, see Brander, Chapter 5 in this volume.

18. Statements reported in the financial pages citing Conrad Black, Marshall Cohen, Trevor Eyton and Bernard Ghert are among the notable exceptions.

REFERENCES

Baumol, W., Panzar, J.C., and Willig, R.D. (1982), *Contestable Markets and the Theory of Industry Structure* (New York: Harcourt & Brace Jovanovich).

Beck, S.M. (1985), "Corporate Power and Public Policy" in I. Bernier & A. Lajoie (eds.) *Consumer Protection and Environmental Law and Corporate Power*, (Toronto: University of Toronto Press) pp. 181-219.

Berle, A.A. and Means, G.C. (1933), *The Modern Corporation and Private Property* (New York: MacMillan).

Black, C. (1986), "The Survival of the Fattest," *Globe and Mail Report on Business* (Toronto), February, pp. 97-98.

Brozen, Y. (1982), *Concentration, Mergers and Public Policy*, (New York: MacMillan).

Carroll, W.K. (1986), *Corporate Power and Canadian Capitalism* (Vancouver: University of British Columbia Press).

Clement, W. (1975), *The Canadian Corporate Elite: An Analysis of Economic Power* (Toronto: McClelland and Stewart Ltd.).

Cohen, M. (1986a), *A Corporate Strategy for Success in an Unpredictable Sector of the Economy*, Remarks to The Financial Post Executive Day (Toronto), September 3, pp. 1-8.

Cohen, M. (1986b), *Shaping Canada's Economic Destiny in the Global Village*, Remarks to The Canadian Club (Toronto), October 27, pp. 1-8.

Decima (1987), *The Decima Quarterly Report: Public Affairs Trends* (Toronto: Decima), Vol. VIII, No. 2.

Demsetz, H. and Lehn, K. (1985), "The Structure of Corporate Ownership: Causes and Consequences", *Journal of Political Economy*, Vol. 93(6), pp. 1155-1177.

Economic Council of Canada (1969), *Interim Report on Competition Policy*, (Ottawa: Queen's Printer).

Economic Council of Canada, (1987), *Framework for Financial Regulation* (Ottawa: Supply and Services Canada).

Fama, E.F., and Jensen, M.C. (1983), "Separation of Ownership and Control," *Journal of Law and Economics*, Vol. 26, pp. 301-325.

Galbraith, J.K. (1973), "On the Economic Image of Corporate Enterprise" in R. Nader & M.J. Green (eds.) *Corporate Power in America*, (New York: Grossman Publishers), pp. 3-9.

Ghert, B.I. (1985), "Brief on the Green Paper: Regulation of Canadian Financial Institutions" (Toronto: Cadillac Fairview Corporation Ltd.)

Gorecki, P.K. & W.T. Stanbury (1984) *The Objectives of Canadian Competition Policy, 1888-1983* (Montreal: The Institute for Research on Public Policy).

Hunter, L.A.W. (1985), "Notes for an Address to the Conference on the Changing Regulatory Environment for Canadian Financial Institutions" (Ottawa: Bureau of Competition Policy).

Khemani, R.S. (1986), "The Extent and Evolution of Competition in the Canadian Economy" in D.G. McFetridge (ed.), *Canadian Industry in Transition* (Toronto: University of Toronto Press), pp. 135-176.

Marfels, C. (1978), *Concentration Levels and Trends in the Canadian Economy*, 1965-73 Study 31 prepared for the Royal Commission on Corporate Concentration (Ottawa: Supply and Services Canada).

McCollum, W.H. (1947), *Who Owns Canada?*, (Ottawa: Wordsworth House Publishers).

McGee, J.S. (1983), "Professor Weiss on Concentration," *Journal of Law and Economics*, Vol. 26(2), pp. 457-465.

McKinley, D.F. (1985), "Concentration, Conglomerates and Contestability," *Canadian Competition. Policy Record*, June, Vol. 6(2), pp. 1-11.

Myers, G. (1914), *A History of Canadian Wealth* (Chicago: Charles H. Kerr) Two vols.

Royal Commission on Price Spreads (1935) *Report*, (Ottawa: King's Printers).

Royal Commission on Corporate Concentration (1978) *Report*, (Ottawa: Supply and Services Canada).

Royal Commission on the Economic Union and Development Prospects for Canada (1986) *Report*, Vol. II, (Ottawa: Supply and Services Canada).

Securities Industry Committee on Take-over Bids (1983) *The Regulation of Take-over Bids in Canada: Premium Private Agreement Transactions*, (Toronto), November.

Stanbury, W.T. (1986), *Business-Government Relations in Canada: Grappling with Leviathan* (Toronto: Methuen).

U.S. Council of Economic Advisors (1985), *The Economic Report of the President*, (Washington, D.C. Government Printing Office), pp. 187-216.

Weiss, L.W. (1983), "The Extent and Effects of Aggregate Concentration", *Journal of Law and Economics*, Vol. 26(2), pp. 429-453.

Young, R.A. (1987), "Conglomerates: The Need to Know," *Policy Options*, May, pp. 35-37.

Chapter 2

The Rise of the Conglomerate Economy

Jorge Niosi*
Statistics Canada, and
University of Quebec at Montreal

1.0 INTRODUCTION

Many studies (Rosenbluth 1957; Berkovitz *et al* 1976; Khemani 1980; Caves *et al.* 1980) estimated Canadian industrial concentration both at the technical (establishment) and economic (corporation) levels. Several statistical surveys regularly publish data on this issue (Statistics Canada, Cat. 31-402 and 61-210). These studies, and data for the last 25 years, show a slow but steady growth of sellers' concentration for the Canadian economy and for particular industries.

Parallel to this rise of economic and technical concentration, but a less studied phenomenon, is a trend towards higher concentration at the enterprise level. Enterprises are groups of corporations under common control. Two different types of enterprises will be distinguished in this paper: the specialized and the conglomerates.

The specialized enterprise is a group of corporations operating in the same line of business. A group of pulp and paper companies, or a group of insurance and reinsurance corporations would, for example, be considered a specialized enterprise (see Section 2 on definitions). The conglomerate

---

* I am grateful to the persons who read and commented on the preliminary version of this paper: R.S. Khemani, Bill Krause, Danny Shapiro and Michael Wolfson. Susan Leroux put her computer talents at work to build the data on which this paper is based. This work was supported by the Social and Economics Studies Division, Statistics Canada. The views expressed in this paper are those of the author, and in no way necessarily reflect those of Statistics Canada, nor the colleagues who commented on earlier drafts of it.

enterprise is a group of corporations operating in different, unrelated industries. It is my contention that for the last 25 years the growth of financial concentration in the Canadian economy has been very rapid, and that it has superseded the trend towards higher technical and economic concentration. The growth of conglomerates has been particularly swift. New conglomerates have been created in Canada since the 1960s and, as the conglomerate wave swept the American economy at the same time, foreign conglomerates migrated to Canada as well, forging local replicas of their parent counterparts. Most conglomerates enjoyed a high rate of growth during the period, and they represent an increasing proportion of the sales, profits or assets of the Canadian economy. These trends have seldom been recognized, and still less studied, other than in a journalistic way. The goal of this report is to shed light on the main dimensions of the rise of the conglomerates, with quantitative, although preliminary, estimates for the largest of them.

2.0   BASIC DATA AND DEFINITIONS

Inter-corporate Ownership surveys (collected under the *Corporations and Labour Unions Returns Act*) provide the main empirical basis for the study. Starting in 1962, with the most recent data available for 1984, they cover a fairly long time span (22 years) and thus permit estimates of changes in the composition both of specialized and of conglomerate enterprises. This source was complemented with corporate financial information available from data bases created with *Corporations and Labour Unions Returns Act* Administration (CALURA) and other Statistics Canada surveys. Owing to the large number of corporations involved in this study (more than 1,500 every year) and to limits on the resources and time available, we decided to start the study in 1969 instead of 1965, the first year for which machine readable financial data for all corporations exist. I have also examined large enterprises for 1984 (latest available year) and for 1978, an intermediate point for which financial data, and the Inter-corporate Ownership publication (an occasional survey) were also available.

   Statistics Canada data was complemented with information for corporations available from other sources: annual company reports, Financial Post Surveys, Moody's Manuals, financial periodicals, Ontario and Quebec Securities Commissions Bulletins.

   My definition of an enterprise is not the same as that from CALURA used in their Statistics Canada data bases. In CALURA's basic definition a corporation controls another if it owns at least 50 per cent of its voting shares. CALURA also recognizes cases of apparent minority control by taking into account the number of directors of the holding company that are also members of the subsidiary's board, and the distribution of the remaining shares. In fact, control is often held with less than 50 per cent; empirical studies (Berle and Means 1932; Larner 1970; Chevalier 1970; Morin 1975; Niosi 1978) use a threshold as low as 5 per cent for minority control, while the U.S. government statistics and the Quebec, Ontario and Alberta

Securities Commissions use a 20 per cent lower limit for minority control. Thus, some of our enterprises are larger than those Statistics Canada data would suggest, because we have added a few minority-controlled subsidiaries not identified by CALURA.

A conglomerate is a diversified enterprise. For an enterprise to be considered diversified, more than 30 per cent of its sale must be in a different line of business from its main activity. Conversely, where 70 per cent and more of the sales are in the same line of business, the enterprise is classified as specialized.

Conglomerates thus are groups of corporations under common control operating in different, unrelated industries. "Different" means that they operate in at least two industries, classified at a three-digit level, and that these industries are not in the same line of business. Integrated enterprises, thus, are not conglomerates. The concept of "related industries," developed by Wrigley (1970), and applied by Rumelt (1974), Caves *et al.* (1977 and 1980), Lecraw and Thompson (1978), has been used here.

As to control, it can be held either by a management company (a financial corporation classified with a 756 SIC number), by a corporation operating in manufacturing, commerce, transportation, real estate or other industry, or even by a charitable foundation. I find the same kind of situation in specialized enterprises, in which, however, operating holding companies are the rule.

Conglomerates can be under either public or private control. Some public enterprises are as diversified as privately held conglomerates. Some of them are under federal control, while others are controlled by provincial governments. Government-controlled conglomerates are, however, presented separately from privately-held ones.

In this analysis, conglomerates were ranked by sales. This decision gives a more balanced weight to the overall picture, because, if ranked by assets, financial institutions (with huge assets but small sales) would have taken the major part of the list. This methodological decision is also in line with previous Canadian studies. In this study, however, insurance companies and cooperative credit unions are excluded.

A final remark has to be made on the geographical restriction of the data. Statistics Canada data bases are for Canada only. Foreign operations are excluded. Therefore, if a multinational enterprise under Canadian control is specialized in Canada, but conglomerate on a worldwide basis, it will be classified as "specialized" in this study. There is at least one case falling in this category.

3.0 FINDINGS

With these definitions in mind, lists of the largest 35 conglomerates in 1969, 1978 and 1984 were prepared. I now present the preliminary findings from the analysis.

3.1 Turnover

I produced three lists of the largest conglomerates in Canada for 1969, 1978 and 1984, involving information on 57 conglomerates; 16 of them appear in the three lists. This means that a fair proportion (28 per cent) of Canada's largest conglomerates already existed in 1969.

Fourteen conglomerates in the 1969 list disappeared from the subsequent lists: they were either displaced to lower positions, (two cases), absorbed by larger conglomerates (six cases), dismembered (three cases), or became specialized (three cases).

Nine conglomerates from the 1978 list disappeared in 1984, for the same reasons as before. Four enterprises became specialized, three others merged within larger conglomerates, while two others became too small to remain in the top 35.

Survivors are falling within the ranks of the conglomerate ladder: most of them occupy in 1984 a lower position than the one they had in 1969 (Table 1). And only five enterprises remain in 1984 in the same quintile they were in 1969.

Table 1
Turnover Among 22 Conglomerates Ranked Both in 1969 and 1984

		Rank in 1984				
		1-7	8-14	15-21	22-28	29-35
	1-7	4	2	1		
	8-14		1	3	1	
Rank in 1969	15-21			-	2	1
	22-28				-	1
	29-35					-

Finally, five survivors are foreign (31 per cent) roughly the same proportion as in the total samples. Canadian and foreign-controlled groups seem to have the same ability to survive.

3.2 Age

While conglomerates have drawn attention from economists only in the late 1960s and early 1970s (Blair 1972, Ch. 12), some of them have their origins well before 1960. In Canada at least three of the largest existed before the Second World War, while several others have been founded or began their diversification in the 1940s and 1950s. Five of the 35 conglomerates in the 1984 list have their origins before the merger period of the 1960s and 1970s.

The majority (62 per cent) of the conglomerates in the 1984 list were created in the 1960-1979 period. In many cases this process involved the incorporation of new holding companies. In other cases a specialized enterprise diversified into totally unrelated industries. This was the case for two of the largest tobacco manufacturers and one of the largest breweries in the 1960s. Finally, foreign conglomerates either invested in Canada through subsidiaries operating in different industries or acquired control, in Canada, or corporations in new lines of businesses. Only eight of the conglomerates in the 1984 list (23 per cent) were created in the 1980s. This sublist includes the largest in Canada, which diversified only in 1983 and two others, among the largest conglomerates in 1984, diversified in 1980 into totally unrelated industries.

3.3 Originating Industries
From what industries do conglomerates emerge? Analysis of the 1984 list shows a varied sectoral distribution, as shown in Table 2.

Table 2
Industrial Origins of the 1984 Canadian Conglomerates

Services	5
Finance	6
Commerce	1
Resources	4
Manufacturing	19

These figures, of course, do not take into account the four conglomerates under government control that we present separately and that existed in 1984: Canadian National Railways (CNR) and the Canada Development Corporation (CDC) groups (federal) and the Société generale de financement du Quebec (SGF) and the Crown Investment Corporation (CIC) of Saskatchewan (provincial). Two of these governmental enterprises were created in the 1960s and 1970s (the SGF and the CDC), one between the Wars (CNR) and one in the 1980s (the CIC of Saskatchewan).

Among private conglomerates manufacturing is by far the most important originating industry (54 per cent of the 35): most cases are those of slow growth, high profits industries like alcoholic beverages, tobacco manufacturing and food. In services also, enterprises diversify into unrelated industries to escape from sluggish (like residential telephone services) or highly cyclical activities (like real estate and engineering).

3.4 Country of Control
In 1984, large conglomerates in Canada were mostly (66 per cent) Canadian-owned and controlled, not including the four state-owned groups. Canadian-owned and controlled conglomerates include the nine largest in Canada in 1984.

Table 3 shows the picture for 1984 and compares it with that of 1969.

The small rise of foreign conglomerates as a proportion of the largest ones in Canada seems to be the consequence of two different trends. The first is the amalgamation of foreign subsidiaries in Canada produced by the conglomeration of their parent companies abroad. Thus, previously specialized subsidiary enterprises have been absorbed into larger conglomerates. The second is the regrouping of some Canadian conglomerates into larger units, and the phasing out (either by absorption or by dismembering) of several regionally-based ones.

Table 3
Country of Control of Conglomerates, 1969 and 1984

	1969	1984
Canada	27 (77%)	23 (66%)
U.S.A.	6 (17%)	8 (23%)
Other foreign	2 (6%)	4 (12%)
Total foreign	8 (23%)	12 (35%)
Total	35 (100%)	35 (100%)

3.5 Concentration

As conglomerates operate over widely diverse industries, the issue of concentration only makes sense here with reference to the overall economy. It is possible to calculate "absolute" concentration, i.e., the proportion of sales, assets, profits or any other corporate characteristic in the total sales, assets, profits, etc., in the Canadian economy.

I calculated three of the five "major" financial variables in the corporate data bases of Statistics Canada: sales, total assets and profits for all corporations and for the largest 35 conglomerates. We are aware that each measure has its difficulties. Sales and profits are volatile and can vary enormously from one year to the other; all three are plagued with double counting, especially in large enterprises.

I also decided to compare large conglomerate enterprises with large but specialized firms. Table 4 present the results for 1984. This table shows how highly skewed the distribution of enterprises is by size. Even though the analysis considers the 35 largest enterprises, the largest 20 or 30 account for most of their economic activity. Correspondingly, extending the analysis to the 50 largest enterprises, say, would not change the picture appreciably.

By any measure, conglomerates are large, but smaller than specialized enterprises. The difference between conglomerates and non-diversified enterprises is wider in terms of assets, because the specialized list includes several banks and oil corporations with huge assets, compared to sales and profits. But the difference seems smaller in terms of profits; in other terms, conglomerates seem more profitable than specialized enterprises of comparative size. This hypothesis will be tested later in this paper.

As to trends in the 1969-1984 period, Table 5 shows that the conglomerate part of the Canadian economy diminished during the 1969-1978 period, then grew at a rapid pace, whatever the variable employed to measure it.

It is not easy to explain this non-linear trend from only three observations in time. The explanation lies probably not in the conglomerate enterprises themselves but in the specialized ones. Several specialized enterprises grew very rapidly during the 1969-1978 period: oil and gas producers,

Table 4
Conglomerate Concentration in Canada, 1984

	Conglomerates			Specialized Firms		
	Sales	Assets	Profits	Sales	Assets	Profits
Top 4	5%	7%	9%	6%	7%	7%
Top 8	7%	10%	13%	9%	13%	14%
Top 12	7%	10%	14%	12%	21%	16%
Top 20	9%	13%	17%	16%	26%	20%
Top 30	10%	13%	18%	18%	28%	22%
Top 35	10%	14%	18%	19%	28%	23%

Table 5
Trends of Conglomerate Concentration, 1969-1984

	Sales			Assets			Profits		
	1969	1978	1984	1969	1978	1984	1969	1978	1984
Top 4	4%	4%	5%	5%	3%	7%	6%	6%	9%
Top 8	5%	4%	7%	6%	4%	10%	8%	7%	13%
Top 12	6%	5%	7%	8%	5%	10%	10%	9%	14%
Top 20	6%	6%	9%	9%	6%	13%	10%	10%	17%
Top 30	6%	6%	10%	9%	6%	13%	11%	9%	18%
Top 35	7%	6%	10%	11%	7%	14%	11%	9%	18%

hydro-electric public utilities, car manufacturers and banks. The growth of conglomerates was probably less swift in that period, and they lost some share of the Canadian economy.

The opposite trend prevailed after 1981-82. Energy prices fell, and energy enterprises stagnated or even sold some of their assets; car manufacturers stumbled under foreign competition, and banks stopped growing because of bad loans to oil companies and to Third World countries.

With the resumption of growth in 1983, conglomeration became possible again: the stock markets reached new heights, interest rates fell and the long term trend worked its way out anew.

3.6 Profitability

The most surprising finding is that conglomerates appear (subject to data limitations such as double counting) more profitable than specialized enterprises. I used two measures of profitability: profits on sales, and profits on total assets. In both cases, conglomerates are strikingly more profitable. And the difference remains constant through time (see Table 6). this pattern is not sensitive to one or two of the largest conglomerates being reclassified as specialized enterprises.

The opposite, however, is true with government-owned conglomerates, that are less profitable than specialized public enterprises of comparative size, and have also lower profits than private conglomerates of the same volume of sales.

It would be difficult to explain this difference in terms of the particular composition of the lists. In both there are commercial corporations which have comparatively low profits to sales. In both private conglomerate and specialized enterprises lists there are Canadian firms and foreign subsidiaries.

This result runs against most literature on conglomerate enterprises (Blair 1972; Meeks 1977; Narver 1967) and certainly merits a more thorough analysis. Other measures of profitability (and particularly profits on capital invested) should be used to confirm (or qualify) this finding. As well, all variables used, both in conglomerate and specialized enterprises should be adjusted to remove double counting (a complex but feasible task which is under way).

3.7 Diversification

Diversification grows with size, but the relationship between the two variables is not very strong. Table 7 shows diversification for the conglomerates in the 1969 and 1984 lists, ranked by sales and divided into five classes of seven enterprises each.

A diversification index has been calculated for each conglomerate with the formula

$$1 - \frac{Pr}{Total\ sales}$$

where Pr is the value of sales of the principal activity. Firms are re-ranked each year.

Table 6
Profitability of Large Canadian Enterprises

Private

	Specialized			Conglomerates		
	1969	1978	1984	1969	1978	1984
Profits on sales	9.6%	7.4%	8.7%	12.5%	11.2%	13.3%
Profits on assets	3.0%	2.7%	3.4%	5.3%	6.6%	5.7%

Governmental

	Specialized			Conglomerates		
	1969	1978	1984	1969	1978	1984
Profits on sales	7.1%	10.9%	11.3%	-1.0%	6.1%	6.1%
Profits on assets	0.8%	1.6%	2.4%	-0.3%	2.8%	3.0%

Table 7
Diversification in Canadian Conglomerates, 1969 and 1984*
(by sales quintiles)

	1969	1984
First	0.66	0.51
Second	0.50	0.45
Third	0.47	0.46
Fourth	0.63	0.53
Fifth	0.57	0.49
Total	0.57	0.49

*   Arithmetic averages for each group of seven enterprises.

The first group includes in 1984 the most diversified conglomerate in the country; it also includes (and is headed by) one of the least diversified conglomerates.

During the 15-year period, diversification within conglomerates has decreased, as shown in Table 7. Some very large conglomerates started a process of reorganization and rationalization and became less diversified; several small, regional, and very diversified groups disappeared both from the lists and from the economic landscape. It also appears that a number of conglomerates have pulled back from half a dozen or more markets to concentrate in two or three major areas.

4.0   CONCLUSIONS

During the last 25 years there is a general sense that a new type of economic centralization has been growing in Canada, namely conglomerate concentration. Mergers and acquisitions have reduced the number of independent corporations and increased the ranks and sizes of large diversified enterprises operating in different, unrelated markets. The preliminary results reported in this analysis tend to support this view.

Three independent lists of the 35 largest conglomerates in Canada spanning a 15-year period with data for 1969, 1978 and 1984 have produced 57 names; we also produced a list of the 35 largest specialized enterprises for each year. Among the conglomerates, 16 appear in all three lists, yielding a high turnover rate of 72 per cent. Survivors are more often large Canadian enterprises and foreign firms of any size. Disappearing conglomerates are more often regionally-based Canadian enterprises of small size.

Most conglomerates (62 per cent) have been created in the 1960s and 1970s either through the incorporation of management holding companies or through the acquisition, by previously specialized enterprises, of independent operating corporations.

Diversified enterprises originate mostly in manufacturing, finance and services. But each industry shows a different tendency to conglomeration, the highest being railways, telephone services, food and beverages.

Conglomerates in Canada are both locally and foreign-controlled; while the largest of them are domestically owned and controlled (not including four under governmental control) 40 per cent of them are the Canadian counterparts of conglomerate parents abroad.

Conglomerate concentration is significant and appears to have increased over the last 15 years in the Canadian economy. However, the trend does not appear uniform; absolute concentration of conglomerate enterprises fell from 1969 to 1978 and then increased at a more rapid pace from 1978 to 1984. This pattern is probably explained mostly by the changing fortunes of large specialized enterprises (which abound in energy, banking and vehicle manufacturing): these enterprises achieved their best performance in the late 1970s and then stagnated in the 1980s. Conglomerates then experienced their more rapid growth.

Contrary to most literature, conglomerates in Canada seem to show a better record than specialized enterprises in terms of profitability. Preliminary data on returns to assets and profit margins on sales are higher for private sector conglomerates over the entire period. This conclusion is however not true for government-owned conglomerates, which are less profitable than their private sector counterparts, as well as specialized governmental enterprises.

Diversification in Canadian conglomerates has been decreasing through time. Recent rationalization of large enterprises and the disappearance of small very diversified groups explains this pattern. Diversification also tends to increase slightly with the size of the enterprise.

The rise of conglomerate concentration, if it proceeds at the same swift pace of the latest period, will produce a new type of economy and society. Far from the mythical model of pure and perfect competition, and rather different also from the more realistic imperfect or oligopolistic schemes, new types of enterprises and markets are emerging that challenge our present understanding of Canadian society.

REFERENCES

Berkovitz, S.D. *et al.* (1976) *Enterprise Structure and Corporate Concentration,* Technical Report prepared for the Royal Commission on Corporate Concentration (Ottawa: Minister of Supply and Services).

Berle, A.A. and G. Means (1932) *The Modern Corporation and Private Property* (New York: Harcourt, Brace & World (rev. ed. 1968)).

Blair, J. (1972) *Economic Concentration* (New York: Harcourt, Brace & Jovanovich).

Caves, R. *et al.* (1977) *Studies in Canadian Industrial Organization,* Study No. 26, Royal Commission on Corporate Concentration (Ottawa: Minister of Supply and Services).

Chevalier, H.M. (1970) *La structure financiere de l'Industrie Americaine* (Paris: Cujas).

Gort, M. (1962) *Diversification and Integration in American Industry* (Princeton: Princeton University Press).

Khemani, R.S. (1980) *Concentration in Canadian Manufacturing Industries* (Ottawa: Consumers and Corporations Canada).

Larner, R. (1970) *Management Control and the Large Corporation* (New York: Dunellen).

Lecraw, D.J. and D.N. Thompson (1978) *Conglomerate Mergers in Canada,* Study No. 32, Royal Commission on Corporate Concentration (Ottawa: Minister of Supply and Services).

Meeks, G. (1977) *Disappointing Marriage: A Study of Gains from Merger* (Cambridge: Cambridge University Press).

Morin, F. (1975) *La structure financiere du capitalisme francais* (Paris: Calmann-Levy).

Narver, J.C. (1967) *Conglomerate Merger and Market Competition* (Los Angeles: University of California Press).

Niosi, J. (1978) *Le controle financier du capitalisme Canadien* (Montreal: les Presses de l'Université du Québec). (English Translation: *The Economy of Canada: A Study of Ownership and Control,* Montreal, Black Rose).

Penrose, E. (1959) *The Theory of the Growth of the Firm* (Oxford: Basil Blackwell).

Rosenbluth, G. (1957) *Concentration in Canadian Manufacturing Industries* (Princeton: Princeton University Press).

Rumelt, R.P. (1974) *Strategy, Structure and Economic Performance* (Boston: Harvard University).

Wrigley, L. (1970) "Divisional Autonomy and diversification" (Unpublished Doctoral Dissertation, Harvard Business School).

Periodicals and other sources:

Maclean Hunter Ltd: *Financial Post Survey of Industrials*, Toronto, Annual.

Maclean Hunter Ltd: *Financial Post Survey of Mines and Energy Resources*, Toronto, Annual.

Moody's Investor Service Inc: *Moody's Industrial Manual*, New York, Annual.

Moody's Investor Service Inc: *Moody's Bank & Finance*, New York, Annual.

Ontario Securities Commission: *Insiders Trading Bulletin*, Toronto, monthly.

Commission des valeurs mobilières du Québec: *Bulletin mensuel*, Montreal.

Chapter 3

Aggregate Concentration in International Perspective: Canada, Federal Republic of Germany, Japan and the United States[1]

Christian Marfels
Department of Economics
Dalhousie University

1.0 INTRODUCTION

Ever since Berle and Means pioneered the study of aggregate concentration in 1932 the issue of control of the entire economy or large parts thereof by the largest firms has been the subject of continuous debate. Critics have often questioned the meaning of concentration measurement going beyond specific markets since it was felt that anti-competitive conduct and lessening of competition can only happen in cases where the shares of the participant firms add up (see Duke 1982, pp. 1-2). However, in the wake of multi-billion-dollar mergers between firms in unrelated industries and markets a restriction of concentration measurement to 4-digit industries is unrealistic, particularly in view of the power exerted by mega-corporations beyond the economic domain (see Stanbury, Ch. 17 in this volume). Nowhere does this gain more momentum than in the Canadian economy which, according to an earlier study (Marfels 1976), was found to show high levels of industry concentration in international perspective.

The present study is an attempt to relate levels and trends of aggregate concentration in Canada to those of its major trading partners. Availability of data restricted the inclusion of countries to the Federal Republic of Germany, Japan, and the United States which account for about 82 per cent of Canada's foreign trade, the United States alone for 75 per cent. The period of analysis refers to the past two decades since a systematic compilation of data on aggregate concentration is of fairly recent origin, with the exception of the U.S. First, the meaning of aggregate concentration and the limitations of its measurement will be discussed. Next, data on aggregate concentration in the four countries will be presented. Finally, trends of aggregate concentration will be compared among the four countries.

1.1   What is Aggregate Concentration?

Aggregate concentration refers to the measurement of concentration in (i) divisions of the economy (Manufacturing, Trade, etc.), and (ii) the entire economy. Thus, it seems advisable to designate the latter as "overall concentration." The broader approach of overall concentration has the definite advantage of presenting the corporation or other unit of measurement in its entirety without running the risk of a distortion of the concentration ratio. By contrast, the measurement of, e.g., aggregate concentration in the manufacturing sector requires the exclusion of non-manufacturing activities of the top corporations or else concentration is overstated.

The measurement of overall concentration has traditionally been limited to the non-financial industries of the economy in order to avoid a kind of double-counting inasmuch as the assets of the financial sector are the liabilities of the non-financial sector. This approach makes sense whenever assets are employed as a measure of corporate size and, usually, this is the case. But when value-added data are available there is no need to exclude the financial sector and, thus, have "true" overall concentration.

1.2   What Can be Measured?

The only meaningful measure for both overall and aggregate concentration is the humble but simplistic method of concentration ratios in their capacity as a discrete measure of concentration. The discreteness, i.e., the truncation at a specific number of top firms, is necessary because the magnitude of firms involved makes the employment of a summary measure of concentration inoperational. The reference to a fixed number of firms in a concentration ratio means that, over time, the largest firms in each year rather than identical firms are considered. Consequently, the homogeneity of the group of top firms will become the lesser the longer the period of observation. For instance, of the top 25 identical corporations of the Fortune 500 in 1975, 19 were still in that group in 1985; however, of the top 25 of 1955, only 13 were left in that group in 1985.

Corporate size can be measured in terms of assets, sales, value added or employment. Depending on the measure, higher or lower levels of concentration will be obtained. According to concentration data published by Statistics Canada for the non-financial sector, asset concentration exceeds sales concentration by a wide margin (Statistics Canada, Cat. No. 61-210). Similarly, data on aggregate concentration in the manufacturing sector have shown sales concentration to be higher than value-added concentration and this, in turn, to be higher than employment concentration (Statistics Canada, Cat. No. 31-402). Assets are widely used as the reference measure for corporate size because they tend to exhibit greater stability than sales or employment (Duke 1982, p. 25). But there can be no doubt that value added is the more sophisticated measure since it refers to the net addition to product value and, thus, avoids distortions among stage of production.

However, value added concentration data are rarely available beyond the manufacturing sector — see below.

2.0 CANADA

Levels of overall and aggregate concentration in Canada are high and rising, see Table 1. As of 1983, the 25 largest non-financial enterprises held more than one-third of total non-financial assets, the 100 largest held more than one-half, and the 500 largest more than two-thirds. All these shares were significantly up from 1975 and 1965 levels, respectively. By economic division, the top 100 controlled more than 80 per cent of the assets in Transportation/Communications/Utilities, more than 50 per cent in Mining and in Manufacturing, about 30 per cent in Trade, 18 per cent in Finance, 12 per cent in Services, and negligible amounts in Agriculture/Forestry/Fishing and Construction. See Table 2. Again, these levels of control had increased in all divisions since 1975. These data are published annually by the *Corporations and Labour Unions Returns Act* Administration (CALURA) of Statistics Canada (Statistics Canada, Cat. No. 61-210). The unit of measurement in the CALURA statistics is the enterprise which comprises all majority-controlled corporations. Enterprises are ranked by sales, and concentration data are presented in terms of sales, assets, equity, and profits.

In order to secure comparability with the concentration data for Japan and the U.S., asset concentration rather than sales concentration was selected. This means a very slight downward bias, if any, because of the ranking by sales rather than by assets. Furthermore, CALURA data include privately held corporations and exclude foreign assets. The only sources of distortion of "true" concentration levels are (i) the omission of non-corporate businesses, and (ii) the neglect of minority control. Since the impact of the two items works in opposite directions — the former causes an overstatement of concentration levels and the latter an understatement — the net effect on concentration is unclear. Turning to aggregate concentration in divisions of the Canadian economy, 1983 asset concentration in terms of the top 4 enterprises was highest in Transportation/Communications/Utilities and Finance, see Table 3. Concentration levels are *over*stated to the extent of inclusion of non-divisional activities of enterprises and to the extent that these multi-divisional activities are more pronounced with the top enterprises. Finally, the series on value-added-concentration levels in manufacturing comes closest to "true" concentration levels except for the omission of minority control, see Table 4. The share of the top 100 increased by 3.5 points from 1965 levels to reach 47.1 per cent in 1982, which was 14 points above the respective level in the U.S., (see below).

3.0 FEDERAL REPUBLIC OF GERMANY

Data on overall and aggregate concentration in the F.R. of Germany are available in unusual detail and accuracy. First, all firms regardless of type of organization are included rather than corporations only. This is a meaningful procedure since the corporate sector accounts for less than one-half of all business activity compared to more than 70 per cent in Japan, almost 80 per cent in Canada, and close to 90 per cent in the U.S. (see part 4 of Table 5). In fact, in 1984, 10 non-corporate firms (including seven partnerships) were even prominently represented among the top 100 firms and, thus, made it into the numerator of the aggregate concentration ratio. Second, and most importantly, in a pioneering approach the Monopolies Commission employs total value added as the reference measure of firm size in its biennial directory of the top 100 since 1978. Concentration is measured in terms of the domestic operations of consolidated enterprises, i.e., including subsidiaries. The employment of value added makes a meaningful combination of the non-financial and the financial sectors possible and, thus, portrays true overall concentration. The inclusion of the financial sector is of great significance for concentration in the West German economy since banks and insurance companies have a long tradition of extending their influence into non-financial industries (see below).

After a slight increase between 1978 and 1980 concentration levels of the top 100 have declined by 0.6 points to 18.7 per cent in 1984. See part 1 of Table 2. This decline can be attributed to the overproportionate growth of the service economy (non-financial and financial services): when the service economy is excluded concentration levels based on the non-service firms among the top 100 have increased between 1978 and 1984; e.g., in 1982 the 13 service firms contributed only 8.6 per cent to the numerator of the top 100 ratio but the total service economy contributed a hefty 31 per cent to its denominator (Monopolkommission 1984-85, p. 121). Not surprisingly, Manufacturing held the lion's share of the top 100 in 1984 with 63 firms and 72.7 per cent of the top 100's total value added: next were Finance (11: 8 per cent), Transportation/Utilities (9: 7.1 per cent), Trade (8: 4.6 per cent), Mining (3: 5 per cent), Services (3: 1.5 per cent), and Construction (3.1.1 per cent).

In 1984, the three leading banks ("Big Three") – Deutsche Bank, Dresdner Bank, and Commerzbank – held ranks 12, 21, and 34, respectively, among the top 100, which certainly is not representative of their enormous power. Furthermore, Deutsche Bank was only one-third of Siemens, the largest firm in terms of 1984 value added. However, it must be noted that the "Big Three" had moved up since 1978 when they had held ranks 19, 27, and 36. The top non-identical firms among the top 100 have been traced back to 1970. Their share rose from 6.6 per cent in 1970 to a peak of 7.5 per cent in 1980 from where it tapered off to 7.3 per cent in both 1982 and 1984 (see part 1 of Table 2). A glance at trends of aggregate concentration of the top 10 firms in various divisions and subdivisions in part 4 of Table 2 reveals a similar slight decline during 1978-1984, with the exception of the industrial sector where concentration had increased by an overall 1.2 points; however, even here did concentration decline between 1982 and 1984 by 0.2 points.

Beyond concentration levels and trends, the Monopolies Commission provides an analysis of the top 100 with regard to ownership, joint ventures, interlocking directorates, and merger activity, all of which have a significant impact on overall concentration.

Ownership links among the top 100 are important: in 1984, 33 firms from the top 100 held ownership stakes in 29 firms from this exclusive group for a total of 88 cases of stockholdings (Monopolkommission 1984-85, p. 138); the latter number was up from 73 cases in 1978 (Monopolkommission 1980-81, p. 116). Most prominent among the owners are the "Big Three" and the leading insurance company, Allianz-Versicherung. Their holdings increased from 27 cases in 1978 to 35 in 1984. In fact, Deutsche Bank held minority control of two of the top 100 firms, among them the second largest firm, Daimler-Benz. But there is more. The combined holdings of the four financial giants ("Big Four") add up to minority control in five firms, and even to majority control in another two firms. This means that a total of nine firms of the top 100 were controlled by the "Big Four". Yet, this is only the tip of the iceberg: according to the latest edition of an authoritative guide to capital links in the F.R. of Germany, the "Big Four" held direct ownership stakes in 189 firms (Deutsche Bank: 62; Dresdner Bank: 50; Commerzbank: 44; Allianz-Versicherung: 33); individual control was held in 77 firms, and joint control in another 16 firms (Commerzbank 1985). Some major holdings of the "Big Three" are portrayed in Figure 1. Using a 25 per cent stake as a benchmark – the lower threshold of merger control in Sec. 23 GWB – the Monopolies Commission found some 282 cases of inter-firm links via joint majority control in 194 firms among 67 of the top 100 firms in 1984, up from 275 cases, 193 firms and 68 firms, respectively, in 1980 (Monopolkommission 1982-83, pp. 120-127; *id.*, 1984-85, pp. 146/154). Of the 194 controlled firms, five belonged to the top 100 (1980:6).

The intricate network of control is further reinforced by a system of interlocking directorates when members of the management boards of the top 100 serve on the supervisory boards of at least two other firms in this group (see Figures 2 and 3). In 1984, a total of 1,200 interlocking directorates existed among the top 100, up from 1,054 in 1978 (Monopol-kommission 1980/81, p. 136; and 1984-85, p. 161). Again, the "Big Four" took a leading role in the creation of these interlocking directorates: Deutsche Bank sent members of its management to the supervisory boards of 39 of the top 100 firms, Dresdner Bank to 22 firms, Allianz to 17 firms, and Commerzbank to 15 firms. Altogether, the "Big Four" accounted for 40 per cent of the 233 initial personal links between the top 100; Deutsche Bank alone accounted for 17 per cent. These links led to interlocking directorates between 20 of the top 100 firms through managers of the Deutsche Bank; the respective numbers for Dresdner Bank were 25, for Allianz 36, and for Commerzbank 15 (see Figure 2). Interlocking directorates have an immediate impact on concentration as a potential breeding ground for collusive activities whenever the same or similar product/service lines are concerned. The Monopolies Commission identified 17 such cases in 1984, 4 of which were *not* based upon capital links (Monopolkommission, 1984-85, p. 161).

Finally, the Monopolies Commission reports merger activity of the top 100. During 1980-81, a total of 1,254 mergers and acquisitions (mergers) were reported to the Federal Cartel Bureau according to Sec. 23 GWB;[2] in 1982-83, the number was 1,109, and in 1984-85 1,284. In these years, the top

100 participated in 528 (42.1 per cent), 381 (34.4 per cent), and 402 mergers (31.3 per cent), respectively. Despite this declining trend, the "Big Four" expanded their merger activity from 18 mergers in 1980-81 (3 per cent of all 604 merger cases)[3] to 36 in 1982-83 (8 per cent of 460 cases) to 53 in 1984-85 (11 per cent of 402 cases).

The indicated awesome power of the West German banks comes from a rather liberal regulatory framework of the banking system which permits banks to be a bank, trust company, stockbroker, and investment dealer all in one. Beyond that, banks may exercise proxy vote for shareholders not attending annual meetings of corporations. Since this absenteeism is the rule rather than the exception banks can easily achieve a kind of "make or break" position. In fact, there appears to be no end to the continuous expansion of the realm of influence of the "Big Four" and of other members of the financial community. Indications are that the only way for new activity of the financial giants is to penetrate the hitherto respected territories within the financial sector: the stage for potential confrontation was set in the Fall of 1986 when the no. 5 insurance firm, Aachener und Muenchener Beteiligungs-AG (AMB), acquired the no. 11 bank, Bank fuer Gemeinwirtschaft (BfG). To be sure, there have been earlier moves from insurance into banking, and *vice versa*, but only on a very modest scale: insurance companies have offered life-insured savings plans, and banks have offered basically the same vehicle; the only difference, albeit an important one, is that the former are tax-free after 12 years' duration and the latter are not (*Der Spiegel*, No. 48, 1986, pp. 52-58). At this time, the initiative appears to be with the insurance companies: after AMB's move, Allianz, the undisputed no. 1 insurance company, is contemplating its options following a corporate reorganization with a new holding company at the helm which is not subject to the control of the Superintendent of Insurance (*Der Spiegel*, No. 48, 1986, p. 56). Meanwhile, the banks try to keep a low profile amidst new claims that a bank should not be permitted to own more than 5% of the voting shares of a corporation. This goes back to a recommendation of the Monopolies Commission issued in its First Report in 1976 and reiterated in its Sixth Report (Monopolkommission 1973-75, p. 296; *id.*, 198-/85, p. 176). Judging from the benign neglect of the Commission's earlier recommendation it is unlikely that the 5 per cent threshold will become subject to legislative moves.

4.0   JAPAN

Concentration in Japan has been declining steadily since the late 1960s. This trend is reflected in all four series in Table 3. In terms of assets of non-financial corporations the share of the top 100 eased by a hefty five points from one-quarter in 1967 to one-fifth in 1984 (see part 1 of Table 3). This decline can be attributed to underproportionate growth of the top 100: during 1967-1980, total assets of the top 100 increased by 380 per cent; this compares to 473 per cent for all non-financial corporations the number of which increased from 0.73 million to 1.57 million during that period.[4] A classification of the top 100 by their principal division in part 4 of Table 3 indicates, again, declining levels of concentration in all sectors except for services where seven corporations – all in the leasing business – had entered the top 100 since 1967. In the manufacturing sector, the share of assets held by the top 100 manufacturing corporations declined by 4.2 points during 1967-1984 (see part 3 of Table 3).

Japanese concentration data have to be treated with some caution since they refer to unconsolidated statements only and, thus, exclude subsidiaries. Consequently, the relatively low concentration levels are somewhat deceptive. In a special investigation, the Fair Trade Commission (FTC) included majority-controlled subsidiaries of the top 100 non-financial corporations from 1978 to 1984. The same trend of decline prevailed as with the unconsolidated data but concentration levels rose by about four points vis-à-vis the unconsolidated data (see part 1 of Table 3). To put this in proper perspective, it must be noted that 1 per cent of total corporate assets in non-financial industries stood at about 5 trillion Yen in 1980 ($26 billion) or the equivalent of the total assets of the largest Japanese non-financial corporation, by assets, *viz.* Tokyo Electric Power Co. (see part 5 of Table 5).

The omission of inter-corporate ownership links is the more deplorable since there is an intricate reciprocal network of ownership links among Japanese corporations which extends from the non-financial sector into the financial sector and back. In 1970, there were 270 "large" shareholders who owned more than 1 per cent each of the shares issued by any of the top 100 non-financial corporations: 21.1 per cent of the large shareholders were members of the top 100, another 25.6 per cent were other non-financial corporations, and 26.6 per cent were financial institutions (White Papers of Japan, 1972-73, p. 140). Going beyond their own turf and including all other non-financial corporations the top 100 held more than 10 per cent each of the stock of 7,612 corporations, more than 25 per cent each of 5.881 corporations, and more than 50 per cent each of 2,818 corporations (White Papers of Japan, 1972-73, p. 139).

Most prominent among corporate stockholders are the large Japanese trading houses (Sogo Shosha). Their principal business is wholesale trade and they act as intermediaries to sell products of other firms worldwide on a commission basis. But there is more. The trading houses form the nucleus of large enterprise groups which wield enormous power. In a special investigation, the Fair Trade Commission found that the six largest trading houses (Mitsubishi, Mitsui, Marubeni, C. Itoh, Sumitomo, and Nissho-Iwal) along with majority-controlled subsidiaries held 25.1 per cent of the total assets of all Japanese corporations in 1974; this share rose to 30.9 per cent when holdings of more than 10 per cent were included (OECD, Annual Reports on Competition Policy, 1976/No. 1, p. 84). Furthermore, the six trading houses handled 19.6 per cent of Japan's wholesale business in 1972-73, 40 per cent of the exports, and 50 per cent of the imports (OECD, Annual Reports on Competition Policy, 1975/No. 1, p. 32).

A case in point is the Mitsubishi-Group which rotates around its nucleus, Mitsubishi Corp., Japan's largest trading house with 1984-85 sales of 16.4 trillion Yen ($94.6 billion) and assets of 6.3 trillion Yen ($36.3 billion). Excluding the nucleus and using a cumulative stockholding of 10%

or more as a benchmark, the Group included some 15 large non-financial corporations (with assets of more than 100 billion Yen each) with total assets of 12 trillion Yen ($70 billion) in 1984-85, and four financial firms (excl. Meiji Mutual Life Insurance Co.) with assets of 38 trillion Yen ($218 billion). Among them are the leading Japanese firms in chemicals (Mitsubishi Chemicals), industrial equipment (Mitsubishi Heavy Industries), glass (Asahi Glass), beverages (Kirin Brewery), marine transportation (Nippon Yusen), trust banking (Mitsubishi Trust Co.), the number four bank (Mitsubishi Bank), and the number five electronical and electronics firm (Mitsubishi Electric). It is worth noting that reciprocal stockholdings of members of the Group are usually less than 10 per cent, but they cumulate to minority or majority control with an average stockholding of 21.8 per cent (as of 1985) for the 20 firms, e.g., the Group jointly holds 25.2 per cent of the Mitsubishi Corp. itself.[5] This reciprocal network of stockholdings is a reflection of the prohibition of holding companies under the Antimonopoly Act (Caves/Uekusa 1976, p. 142) and tends to reinforce the closedness of the Group. *Cum grano salis*, the same scenarios apply for the other enterprise groups.

5.0 UNITED STATES

Recent studies of overall and aggregate concentration in the United States suggest that concentration has not increased in recent years (White 1980; Duke 1982; Weiss 1983). To begin with, the Federal Trade Commission's (FTC) overall concentration series for non-financial corporations shows a slight increase from 1958 to 1967 and, thereafter, a gradual decline to 1982 (see part 1 of Table 4); beyond that, a further slight decline to 1984 has been estimated by the Economic Analysis Group of the Antitrust Division (EAG-Memorandum 1986). Similarly, in its capacity as the most authoritative series of aggregate concentration data in the U.S., the Census Bureau's value-added-concentration series for manufacturing companies depicts a rather marked increase between 1947 and 1963 from where concentration literally leveled off: the share of the top 50 declined by 1 point to reach 24 per cent in 1982, and the top 100 remained virtually unchanged at 33 per cent; only the top 200 increased their share beyond 1967 to reach a peak of 44 per cent in 1977 from where it declined to 43 per cent in 1982 (see part 2 of Table 4). By contrast, the FTC series on asset concentration of manufacturing *corporations* in Table 4, part 3, portrays a scenario of increasing concentration from 1974 to 1985. However, some qualifications have to be made. First, there is the issue of foreign operations of U.S. mega-corporations. Like their Canadian, German, and Japanese counterparts, U.S. multinationals increasingly maintain production facilities abroad. These activities should not be included in an aggregate concentration ratio since it refers to conditions in the domestic market. This gains momentum if one looks at the annual Forbes Directory of the 100 Largest U.S. Multinationals (ranked by foreign revenue): in 1985, foreign assets accounted for an average 28 per cent of the top 100's total assets; for three members of the top 100 this share exceeded 50 per cent, and for another 55 it exceeded the 25 per cent mark. Consequently, an inclusion of foreign assets leads to an *over*statement of aggregate concentration levels since large corporations maintain an overproportionate extent of foreign operations. A reinforcement of this bias occurs whenever foreign assets are represented unequally in the numerator and in the denominator. This happens to be the case with the FTC series on non-financial corporations where the denominator (based on IRS Statistics of Income) includes assets of foreign branches of U.S. corporations but omits assets of their foreign subsidiaries; by contrast, the numerator (based on Moody's and Standard and Poor's COMPUSTAT) includes all foreign assets (Duke 1982). In fact, this means that the decline of the share of the top 100 non-financial corporations was stronger than the numbers suggest.

The Census Bureau's series for the manufacturing sector is based on the domestic assets only, and the FTC series on manufacturing corporations (based on the Quarterly Financial Report data of the Commerce Department) includes the net equity position of foreign holdings on a cost basis. Other sources of bias of aggregate concentration are (i) the exclusion of non-corporate businesses, (ii) the exclusion of privately held corporations, and (iii) the extent of inclusion of non-manufacturing activities when manufacturing corporations are considered. All of the FTC series refer to the corporate economy only. Since the non-corporate businesses would affect the denominator of an aggregate concentration ratio but not its numerator, the level of "true" concentration is *over*stated. However, according to estimates by Scherer, this overstatement is on a decreasing scale with the decline of the non-corporate sector in terms of business receipts in all industries from 25.8 per cent in 1958 to 13 per cent in 1978 (Scherer, 1986). Presumably, this would translate into even lower shares in terms of assets (see Statistics Canada, Cat. No. 61-521, 1986). In fact, corporate concentration in the manufacturing sector comes very close to "true" concentration levels since non-corporate firms accounted for a scant 1.2 per cent of business receipts in 1978, down from 4.2 per cent in 1958 (Scherer 1986). Next, the vast majority of U.S. corporations is privately held and, thus, not required to disclose financial data. Unlike non-corporate businesses some of the multi-billion dollar privately held corporations like Cargill, Continental Grain, and Bechtel would likely make it into the numerator of the FTC series on non-financial corporations where they are omitted. Since privately held corporations are included in the denominator their partial omission causes an *under*statement of concentration levels, albeit a negligible one. Finally, another *up*ward bias occurs in the FTC series on manufacturing corporations to the extent that non-manufacturing activities are included and that multi-sectoral activities are more pronounced among the top corporations. The net effect of these distortions would most likely mean a stronger than indicated decline in the FTC series on non-financial corporations in the post-1967 era and a less than indicated increase in the FTC series on manufacturing corporations during 1974-1984. The Census Bureau's series is unaffected by all of these qualifications and, thus, comes closest to reflect "true" concentration levels. Both Census and FTC series are based on consolidated statements, i.e., they take account of majority control. Yet this implies an *under*statement of concentration levels to the extent of omission of minority control.

Why did overall and aggregate concentration not show any significant increase during the 1960s, 1970s, and early 1980s? On a grander scale, Weiss has attributed the decline of overall concentration in the U.S. during 1958-1977 relative to 1929, the reference year in the seminal Berle/Means study, to changes in the regulated industries (Weiss 1983). These changes refer primarily to (i) the decline of railroads vis-à-vis smaller transportation carriers (trucks, airplanes), and (ii) the reorganization of public utility holding companies. In an interesting albeit speculative analysis, Weiss retraces concentration levels from 1929 to 1977 in a scenario that assumes these changes had not happened: instead of declining from 49.2 per cent in 1929 to 38.3 per cent in 1977, the share of the top 200 non-financial corporations would have climbed to 55.2 per cent (Weiss 1983).

Weiss also notes the only very modest influence of the merger wave of 1965-1969 on levels of overall concentration referred to by him as an "uptick" (Weiss 1983, p. 431). A glance at part 1 of Table 4 confirms this observation for the years 1963 and 1967. Again, some qualifications must be made. To begin with, the "numerical obstacles to increased concentration" as Davidson put it are enormous (Davidson 1985, p. 284): for example, in order to just maintain the 1977 share of the top 100 non-financial corporations of 29.7 per cent in 1982 would have required an asset growth of US $523 billion, and an increase of one point to reach 30.7 per cent would have required an additional US $43 billion for a total of US $566 billion. Yet, the top 100 had a "growth deficit" of US $70 billion and US $113 billion, respectively, to reach the aforementioned levels and, thus, their share declined to 28.2 per cent in 1982.

Since mega-corporations are very active acquirers, the merger component of growth will most certainly have prevented a more pronounced decline of the share of the top 100. Consequently, the modest increase of overall concentration in the mid-1960s and its decline in the late 1970s and early 1980s somewhat becloud the "true" contribution of mergers in compensating the lagging internal growth of the top 100 relative to the economy. An integral part of the numerical obstacles to increased concentration is the lopsided size distribution of assets among the top corporations: for instance, in 1975 the top 50 non-financial corporations held almost as many assets as the next 350 (Davidson 1985, p. 284). The respective proportion for the Fortune 500 in 1985 read 30 to 470. Consequently, only mega-mergers of the Chevron-Gulf and Texaco-Getty calibre will have a noticeable impact on aggregate concentration, and even this impact is fading rapidly beyond the top 100 ratio. Most recently, a further downward impact on overall concentration was the approximate US $100 billion AT&T divestiture in 1984, estimated to have caused about 0.7 point reduction of the top 100 ratio (EAG-Memorandum 1986).

6.0 INTERNATIONAL COMPARISONS

An international comparison of overall and aggregate concentration has to be treated with some caution because of the divergent statistical bases of concentration data. The group of the top 100 has been singled out for comparison since it is available for all of the four countries, and it has become somewhat of a reference in the measurement of overall and aggregate concentration.

Beginning with overall concentration, Figure 4 depicts asset concentration for Canada, Japan, and the U.S., and sales/value added concentration for the F.R. of Germany. What is surprising is not so much the lofty height of the Canadian series but its sharp increase of 13.6 points during 1965-1983. This has to be evaluated against the decline of (i) the Japanese series by 4.9 points during 1967-1984, (ii) the U.S. series by 3.4 points during 1958-1982, and (iii) the West German value-added series by 0.7 points during 1978-1984; the West German sales series shows a steady decline from 1974 to 1978 and estimates have shown a further decline to 1984. This means that overall concentration in Canada increased substantially at the time when it declined in the economies of its leading trading partners. The high levels of concentration in Canada vis-à-vis the three pillars of the world economy can be explained mainly by the relative smallness of Canada's domestic market.

In terms of its 1985 population Canada was 42 per cent the size of the F.R. of Germany, 21 per cent of Japan, and 11 per cent of the U.S. And in terms of Canada's 1984 GDP (at 1980 prices and exchange rates) the respective relations were 31 per cent, 21 per cent, and 9 per cent. Some further indicators of the corporate economy in international perspective are presented in Table 5. First, the number of non-financial corporations in relation to the total population ("corporate density") is highest in Canada and the increase during 1975-1984 was second to that of the F.R. of Germany (see part 1 of Table 5). More importantly, the relative size of Canadian mega-corporations appears to outpace its counterparts abroad. The average sales of the top 10 industrial corporations in Canada in relation to GDP were ahead of the respective ratios in both Japan and the U.S. on a widening scale and only slightly behind West Germany (see part 3 of Table 5). Extending the spectrum to the average assets of the top 10 non-financial corporations as a per cent of GDP and excluding government enterprises, Canada assumed a clear lead in 1985 with 2.3 per cent vs. 1.9 per cent for the F.R. of Germany, 1.7 per cent for Japan, and 1.2 per cent for the U.S. Finally, the relatively high level of concentration in Canada is perhaps best reflected by the fact that as many as 14 non-financial corporations held more than 1 per cent each of total assets in non-financial industries compared to 3 in the U.S., 2 in the F.R. of Germany, and only 1 in Japan (see part 5 of Table 5).

Turning to aggregate concentration in the manufacturing sector in Figure 5 the series for Canada is situated way above the other series: an increase of 3.5 points during 1965-1982 compares to a decline of 4.2 points in Japan during 1967-1984, unchanged concentration levels in the U.S. during 1963-1982, and an increase of 2.9 points in the F.R. of Germany during 1978-

1984. However, looking just at the most recent development since 1980, Canada is, again, the only country showing increasing concentration.

In view of the contribution of mergers to overall and aggregate concentration, available merger statistics have been presented in Tables 6-9. It must be noted that a comparison between countries is somewhat restricted due to varying methods of compilation and different measures for large mergers. Nevertheless, it is remarkable to observe the increase of merger activity in the 1980s as depicted in Figure 6: the average number of mergers during the entire period from 1970 to 1986 was 485 in Canada, 495 in the F.R. of Germany, 1,572 in Japan, and 1,820 in the U.S. Yet, during 1980-1986 the respective average numbers rose to 631, 635, 1,807, and 2,683. A similar upward trend with large mergers can be seen in Figure 7.

7.0 CONCLUSION

In his discussion of the factors influencing concentration John Blair (1972, p. 255) once referred to the interaction of the centrifugal forces which tend to reduce concentration and the centripetal forces which operate in the opposite direction. Reviewing the recent evidence on overall and aggregate concentration it would appear that, on balance, in the F.R. of Germany, Japan and the U.S. the centrifugal forces have come to overcompensate the centripetal forces whereas in Canada the reverse holds true.

NOTES

1.   Financial support from the Research Develoment Fund at Dalhousie University is gratefully acknowledged.

2.   Given certain size criteria of the merger partners (combined sales of at least DM 500 million or a combined workforce of at least 10,000 employees) a merger has to be reported to the FCB whenever (i) at least 25 per cent of the voting shares (ii) 50 per cent of the voting shares of a firm are to be acquired.

3.   The number does not coincide with the number of mergers because of multiple acquirers in a merger.

4.   Unless otherwise noted, data come from two documents of the Fair Trade Commission.

5.   Tokyo M. and F. Insurance 6.4 per cent; Meiji Mutual Life Insurance 5.5 per cent, Mitsubishi Bank 5.4 per cent; Mitsubishi Trust 4.1 per cent; Mitsubishi Heavy Industries 3.8 per cent (Japan Company Handbook, 1st Half 1986).

Table 1
Overall and Aggregate Concentration in Canada: Four Series

Part 1. Per cent of Total Corporate Assets Held by the 25, 100, and 500
Largest Non-Financial Enterprises, 1975-1983[a]

	1965	1975	1980	1983
Top 25	23.8	29.2	30.2	34.0
Top 100	38.6	46.5	49.4	52.2
Top 500	n.a.	65.0	65.3	68.2

Note:
a. An enterprise consists of a group of corporations under common control;
enterprises ranked by sales.

Sources: Statistics Canada, *Corporations and Labour Unions Returns Act*,
Cat. No. 61-210 Annual, Ottawa; Khemani, R.S., "The Extent and
Evolution of Competition in the Canadian Economy," *Canadian
Industry in Transition*, D.G. McFetridge (Research Coordinator),
Toronto, 1986, p. 144.

Part 2. Per cent of Total Divisional Corporate Assets Held by the 100
Largest Non-Financial Enterprises, 1975 and 1983[a]

Division	Top 100	
	1975	1983
Agriculture/Forestry/Fishing	n.a.	4.7
Mining	51.2	59.7
Manufacturing	47.0	50.9
Construction	3.4	2.5[b]
Transportation/Communications/Utilities	75.6	82.2
Trade	26.5	30.6[c]
Finance	17.3	18.3
Services	9.6	12.1

Notes:
a. Enterprises ranked by sales.
b. Excl. government enterprises.
c. 1982.

Source: Communication from the Corporations and Labour Unions Returns
Act Administration, Statistics Canada, Ottawa.

Table 1 cont'd

Part 3. Per cent of Total Divisional Corporate Assets Held by the 4 Largest Enterprises in Each Division, 1975-1983[a]

Division	Top 4		
	1975	1980	1983
Agriculture/Forestry/Fishing	4.1	3.6	2.6
Mining	18.2[b]	17.1	18.4
Manufacturing	7.9[b]	8.3	11.1
Construction	6.0	3.0	4.7
Transportation/Communications/Utilities	26.4[b]	34.2	47.7
Trade	7.2[b]	10.5	15.7
Finance	32.8	37.6	33.2
Services	5.9	13.5	6.0

Notes:
a. Enterprises ranked by sales.
b. 1976.

Source: see part 2 of this table

Part 4. Per cent of Manufacturing Value Added Held by the 4 and 100 Largest Manufacturing Firms, 1965-1982

	1965	1974	1982
Top 4	7.7	7.2	9.3
Top 100	43.6	46.2	47.1

Source: Communication from the Manufacturing and Primary Industries Division, Statistics Canada, Ottawa.

Table 2
Overall and Aggregate Concentration in the F.R. of Germany:
Four Series

Part 1. Per cent of Total Value Added Held by the 10, 50, and 100 Largest Firms, 1970-1984

	1970	1978	1980	1982	1984
Top 10	6.6	7.0	7.5	7.3	7.3
Top 50	n.a.	15.5	15.6	15.5	15.1
Top 100	n.a.	19.3	19.5	19.1	18.7
Top 100a	n.a.	24.4	24.9	25.3	24.8

Note:
a. Percent held by the non-service firms among the top 100 firms.

Source: Monopolkommission, *Gesamtwirtschaftliche Chancen und Risiken wachsender Unternehmensgroessen*, Hauptgutachten 1984-1985, Baden-Baden, 1986, pp. 121-123; communication from the Monopolies Commission.

Part 2. Per cent of Total Sales Held by the 100 Largest Non-Financial Firms, 1972-1978

	1972	1974	1976	1978
Top 100	21.7	24.6	24.4	24.2

Source: Monopolkommission, *Fusionskontrolle bleibt vorrangig*, Hauptgutachten 1978/1979, Baden-Baden, 1980, p. 68.

Part 3. Per cent of Total Sales Held by the 50 and 100 Largest Firms in Manufacturing, Mining, Construction, Electric Power & Gas, 1954-1973

	1954	1962	1965	1971	1973
Top 50	25.4	31.8	35.5	43.4	42.8
Top 100	33.6	37.2	42.0	51.8	50.1

Source: Mueller, J. and R. Hochreiter, *Stand und Entwicklungs-tendenzen der Konzentration in der Bundesrepublik Deutschland*, Goettingen, 1975, p. 117.

Table 2 cont'd

Part 4. Per cent of Total Activity Accounted for by the Largest Firms, by Economic Division or Subdivision, 1978-1984

	1978	1980	1982	1984
	Manufacturing, Mining, Construction, Electric Power & Gas[a]			
Top 10	13.5	14.0	14.9	14.7
Top 100	36.6	37.0	39.5	39.5
	Trade[a]			
Top 10	7.6	7.2	7.7	7.3
Top 20	11.1	10.7	11.3	10.9
	Banks[b]			
Top 10	37.3	36.9	35.8	36.6
	Insurance Companies[c]			
Top 10	37.5	38.5	37.1	37.1
	Transportation, Services[a]			
Top 10	7.8	7.9	7.9	7.7

Notes:
a. By sales.
b. By assets.
c. By premium revenue.

Sources: Monopolkommission, *Gesamtwirtschaftliche* .... pp. 97-109; Marfels, C., "Economic Criteria for the Application of Antitrust," *The Antitrust Bulletin*, Vol. 31, No. 4, Winter 1986, p. 1081.

Table 3
Overall and Aggregate Concentration in Japan: Four Series

Part 1. Per cent of Total Corporate Assets Held by the 100 Largest Non-Financial Corporations, 1967-1984[a]

	1967	1975	1978	1980	1984
Top 100[b]	25.6	23.9	21.8	21.4	20.7
Top 100[c]	n.a.	n.a.	25.7	25.2	24.8

Notes:
a. Fiscal Years.
b. Excl. subsidiaries.
c. Incl. majority-controlled domestic subsidiaries.

Source: Fair Trade Commission, Tokyo.

Part 2. Per cent of Total Share Capital Held by the 100 Largest Non-Financial Corporations Listed on the Stock Exchanges, 1953-1980[a]

	1953	1958	1963	1965	1970	1975	1980
Top 100	32.1	35.3	39.4	37.5	32.8	28.7	25.2

Note:
a. Fiscal years.

Source: Fair Trade Commission, Tokyo.

Part 3. Per cent of Total Corporate Assets Held by the 100 Largest Manufacturing Corporations, 1967-1984[a]

	1967	1976	1978	1980	1982	1984
Top 100	37.2	35.9	34.3	33.8	34.5	33.0

Note:
a. Fiscal years.

Source: Fair Trade Commission, Tokyo.

Table 3 cont'd

Part 4.   Per cent of Total Corporate Assets Held by the 100 Largest Non-Financial Corporations, by Economic Division, 1967 and 1984

Division	1967[a] No.	%	1984[a] No.	%
Agriculture/Forestry	1	19.5	0	0
Mining	1	5.8	0	0
Construction	5	15.2	8	12.1
Manufacturing	57	30.6	50	25.1
Trade	15	18.1	14	15.4
Real Estate	1	4.4	2	3.1
Transportation/ Communications	9	21.2	7	14.0
Electric Power	9	94.8	12	93.6
Gas & Water	2	73.3		
Services	0	0	7	11.1

Note:
a. Fiscal year.

Source: Fair Trade Commission, Tokyo.

Table 4
Overall and Aggregate Concentration in the United States:
Four Series

Part 1. Per cent of Total Non-Financial Corporate Assets Held by the 50, 100, and 200 Largest Non-Financial Corporations, 1958-1982

	1958	1963	1967	1972	1977	1982
Top 50	23.9	24.2	24.5	23.2	22.7	21.8
Top 100	31.6	31.3	31.9	30.5	29.7	28.2
Top 200	40.0	39.9	41.0	39.7	38.3	36.1

Source: Memorandum of the Bureau of Economics, Federal Trade Commission, Washington, D.C., 1986 (Mimeograph); by kind permission.

Part 2. Per cent of Value Added by Manufacture Held by the 50, 100, and 200 Largest Manufacturing Companies, 1947-1982

	1947	1963	1967	1972	1977	1982
Top 50	17	25	25	25	24	24
Top 100	23	33	33	33	33	33
Top 200	30	41	42	43	44	43

Source: U.S. Bureau of the Census, *1982 Census of Manufactures, Subject Series: Concentration Ratios in Manufacturing*, Cat. No. MC82-S-7, Washington, D.C., 1986, p. 3.

Part 3. Per cent of Total Corporate Assets in Manufacturing Held by the 100 and 200 Largest Manufacturing Corporations, 1974-1984

	1974	1976	1978	1980	1982	1985
Top 100	44.4	45.5	45.5	46.8	47.7	49.1
Top 200	56.7	58.0	58.3	59.9	60.9	61.0

Source: Memorandum of the Bureau of Economics, Federal Trade Commission, Washington, D.C., 1986 (Mimeograph); by kind permission.

Table 4 cont'd

Part 4. Per cent of Total Corporate Assets Held by the 50, 200, and 500 Largest Corporations in Various Sectors, 1968-1974

	1968	1970	1972	1974
		All Industries		
Top 50	20.8	21.4	21.4	23.1
Top 200	34.3	35.5	35.3	36.9
Top 500	45.9	47.3	47.1	48.6
		All Non-Financial Industries		
Top 50	25.1	25.9	25.3	25.7
Top 200	42.2	43.6	42.9	42.9
Top 500	53.9	55.8	55.2	55.6
		Manufacturing		
Top 50	36.6	37.7	37.5	38.0
Top 200	57.2	59.8	59.7	60.5
Top 500	68.6	71.6	71.9	73.2
		Transportation, Communications, and Public Utilities		
Top 50	57.9	59.9	60.4	60.5
Top 200	84.7	86.5	86.7	86.8
Top 500	91.8	92.9	93.4	93.4
		Trade		
Top 50	20.0	21.1	20.6	21.7
Top 200	28.2	30.0	29.4	30.9
Top 500	33.6	35.6	35.2	37.1
		Finance		
Top 50	28.4	29.7	29.5	32.2
Top 200	43.8	45.0	45.1	47.8
Top 500	55.0	56.0	56.5	59.2
		Services		
Top 50	21.3	20.1	20.6	20.2
Top 200	31.8	31.0	32.0	33.5
Top 500	n.a.	38.4	39.8	41.2

Source: Shenefield, J.H., "Statement," *Mergers and Economic Concentration Hearings*, Pt. 1, U.S. Senate Subcommittee on Antitrust, Monopoly, and Business Rights, Washington, D.C., 1979, pp. 86-92.

Table 5
Number and Size of Non-Financial Corporations in
International Perspective: Five Series

Part 1. "Corporate Density": Number of Persons per Non-Financial
Corporation, 1975 and 1984

	1975	1984	Change (%)
Canada	105	63	-40
F.R. of Germany	464	190	-59
Japan	92	66	-28
United States	107	94a	-12

Note:
a. 1982.

Sources: Institut der deutschen Wirtschaft, *International Economic Indicators 1987*, Koeln, 1987, p. 1; *Statistisches Jahrbuch der Bundesrepublik Deutschland; Statistical Abstract of the United States*; Fair Trade Commission, Tokyo; Communication from the Industrial Organization and Finance Division, Statistics Canada, Ottawa.

Part 2. Number of Industrial Corporations with Sales over US$1 Billion, 1975 and 1985

	1975	1985	Change (%)
Canada	14	31	121
F.R. of Germany	34	50	47
Japan	45	134	198
United States	203	307	51

Source: Institut der deutschen Wirtschaft, *International* ...., p. 40.

Part 3. Average Sales of the 10 Largest Industrial Corporations as Per cent of GDP, 1975 and 1985

	1975	1985	Change
Canada	1.6	1.9	0.3
F.R. of Germany	1.7	2.1	0.4
Japan	1.1	1.2	0.1
United States	1.4	1.4	0

Sources: *Fortune Directories*; Institut der deutschen Wirtschaft, *International* ...., p. 11.

Table 5 cont'd

Part 4.   Corporations as Per cent of All Types of Businesses in Non-Financial Industries

	Number of Businesses	Total	Activity
Canada (1983)	33.4	78.4	(Taxable Income)
F.R. of Germany (1984)	10.0	46.7	(Sales)
Japan (1981)	32.6[a]	71.9	(Employment)
United States (1982)	19.9[b]	89.6	(Business Receipts)

Notes:
a.   Establishments
b.   Excl. sole proprietorships in farming.

Sources: Statistics Canada, *Corporation Taxation Statistics, 1983*, Cat. No. 61-208 Annual, Ottawa, 1986, p. XI; *Statistisches Jahrbuch fuer die Bundesrepublik Deutschland*; *Japan Statistical Yearbook*; *Statistical Abstract of the United States*.

Part 5.   The Monetary Equivalent of 1 per cent of the Denominator of an Aggregate Concentration Ratio

	Units (Bill.)		C$ (Bill.)	Dominant Corporation & Rank[c]
Canada (1983)[a]	$	6.1	6.1	Noranda Mines (14)
F.R. of Germany (1984)[b]	DM	12.0	5.5	Daimler-Benz (2)
Japan (1980)[a]	Y	4,994.1	25.7	Tokyo Electric Power (1)
United States (1982)[a]	US$	42.9	52.9	General Motors (3)

Notes:
a.   Corporate assets in non-financial industries.
b.   Total value added in all industries.
c.   Domestic non-financial corporation closest to 1% mark; rank in terms of all non-financial corporations.

Sources: Statistics Canada; *The Financial Post 500*; Monopolkommission; Fair Trade Commission; *The Forbes Foreign 100 Directory*; Statistical Abstract of the United States; *The Forbes Assets 500*.

Table 6
Mergers and Acquisitions in Canada, 1970-1986

Year	Number	of which:		
		Horizontal[a]	Others[a]	Large[b]
1970	427	224	203	n.a.
1971	388	215	173	n.a.
1972	429	238	191	n.a.
1973	352	227	125	n.a.
1974	296	158	138	n.a.
1975	264	179	85	3
1976	313	214	99	3
1977	395	261	134	1
1978	449	231	218	9
1979	511	290	221	9
1980	414	220	194	13
1981	491	302	189	23
1982	576	284	292	2
1983	628	352	276	3
1984	641	345	296	4
1985	714	370	344	16
1986	953	383	570	42

Notes:
a. Based on two-digit industries for manufacturing and one-digit divisions for other sectors.
b. Value of transaction over $100 million.

Sources: Consumer and Corporate Affairs Canada, Bureau of Competition Policy Merger List, Annual, Ottawa; data compiled by the author and W.T. Stanbury.

Table 7
Mergers and Acquisitions in the Federal Republic of Germany, 1970-1986

Year	Numbera	of which:		
		Horizontalb	Others	Largec
1970	305	n.a.	n.a.	n.a.
1971	220	n.a.	n.a.	n.a.
1972	269	n.a.	n.a.	n.a.
1973	242	n.a.	n.a.	n.a.
1974	318	235	103	n.a.
1975	448	336	109	n.a.
1976	453	283	170	n.a.
1977	554	367	187	n.a.
1978	558	396	162	n.a.
1979	602	386	216	n.a.
1980	635	401	234	n.a.
1981	618	387	231	41
1982	603	376	227	48
1983	506	335	171	29
1984	575	377	198	29
1985	709	449	260	52
1986	802	571	231	65

Notes:
a.   Notifications to the Federal Cartel Bureau according to Para. 23 GWB.
b.   Incl. market-extension mergers.
c.   Acquired firm's sales over DM 500 million.

Source: Federal Cartel Bureau, Berlin.

Table 8
Mergers and Acquisitions in Japan, 1970-1986a

Year[b]	No. of Mergers[c]	of which Horizontal[d,e]	of which Others[e]	of which Large[f]	No. of Acquisitions[g]
1970	1,147	677	626	47	413
1971	1,178	627	736	39	449
1972	1,184	518	789	45	452
1973	1,028	399	737	37	443
1974	995	372	803	35	420
1975	957	390	728	36	429
1976	941	365	699	32	511
1977	1,011	408	739	37	646
1978	898	415	603	32	595
1979	871	373	668	38	611
1980	961	576	650	33	680
1981	1,044	557	639	462	771
1982	1,040	468	761	178	815
1983	1,020	526	699	436	702
1984	1,096	478	771	470	790
1985	1,113	581	695	538	807

Notes:
a. Notifications to the Fair Trade Commission; excl. acquisitions of stock and acquisitions by foreign firms.
b. Fiscal year.
c. Consolidation of two or more firms (Sec. 15(2) of the Antimonopoly Act).
d. Incl. market-extension mergers.
e. Refers to number of firms involved in mergers.
f. Capital of the merger partners over 1 billion yen.
g. Transfers of business (Sec. 16 of the Antimonopoly Act).

Source: Japan Fair Trade Commission, Tokyo.

Table 9
Mergers and Acquisitions in the United States, 1970-1986[a]

Year	Number	of which: Large[b]	Total Value Paid[c] $ Bill.
1970	1,318	n.a.	n.a.
1971	1,269	n.a.	n.a.
1972	1,263	n.a.	n.a.
1973	1,064	n.a.	n.a.
1974	926	n.a.	n.a.
1975	981	6	n.a.
1976	1,145	16	n.a.
1977	1,209	37	n.a.
1978	1,452	36	n.a.
1979	1,526	61	34.2
1980	1,565	59	33.1
1981	2,326	119	67.0
1982	2,295	107	60.4
1983	2,345	108	52.3
1984	3,064	189	125.2
1985	3,165	243	139.1
1986	4,022	352	190.0

Notes:
a. Completed transactions at end of year; value of transaction of $1 million or more; transfers of at least 5 per cent of a firm's assets or equity.
b. Over $100 million paid for acquired firm.
c. Transactions for which valuation data are publicly recorded.

Source: *Mergers & Acquisitions*, Philadelphia: MLR Enterprises; communication from MLR Ent.

Figure 1
The Great Entrepreneurs

Selected Cases of Ownership of West German Firms by the "Big Three"

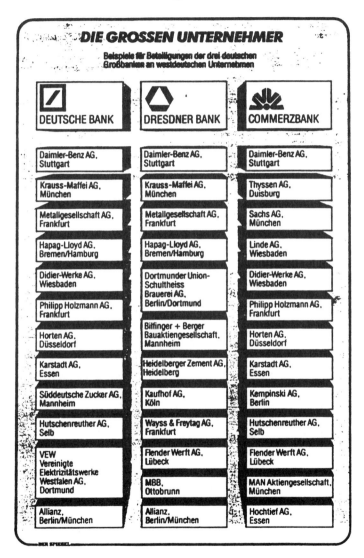

Source: "Koennen nur die Mammuts ueberleben?," *Der Spiegel*, No. 49, 1986, p. 91; by kind permission.

Figure 2
A Cozy Group

Number of Top 100 Firms Linked via Interlocking Directorates with the Indicated Firm, 1984

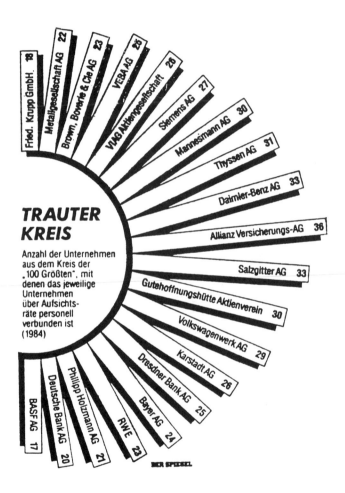

TRAUTER KREIS

Anzahl der Unternehmen aus dem Kreis der „100 Größten", mit denen das jeweilige Unternehmen über Aufsichts-räte personell verbunden ist (1984)

Fried. Krupp GmbH. 18
Metallgesellschaft AG 22
Brown, Boveri & Cie AG 23
VEBA AG 23
VIAG Aktiengesellschaft 23
Siemens AG 27
Mannesmann AG 30
Thyssen AG 31
Daimler-Benz AG 33
Allianz Versicherungs-AG 36
Salzgitter AG 33
Gutehoffnungshütte Aktienverein 30
Volkswagenwerk AG 29
Karstadt AG 26
Dresdner Bank AG 25
Bayer AG 24
RWE 23
Philipp Holzmann AG 21
Deutsche Bank AG 20
BASF AG 17

DER SPIEGEL

Source: "Koennen nur die Mammuts ueberleben?," *Der Spiegel*, No. 49, 1986, p. 97; by kind permission.

Figure 3
A Powerful Man

Rudolf v. Bennigsen-Foerder
President, VEBA AG

Select Cases of the more than 600 Firms under the Potential Sphere of Influence of VEBA (White Blocks: VEBA subsidiaries; Shaded Blocks: Non-aligned firms where Mr. v. Bennigsen-Foerder is a member of the supervisory board; Names in bold face: Firms with equity capital of DM 100 million or more)

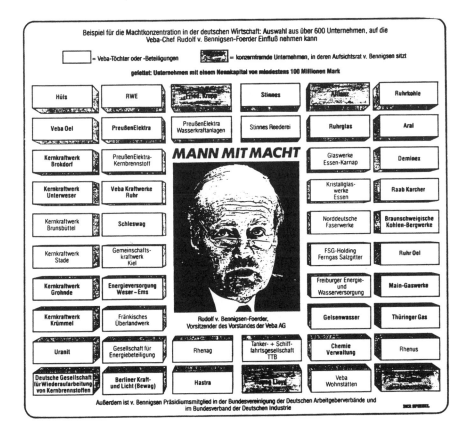

Source: "Koennen nur die Mammuts ueberleben?," *Der Spiegel*, No. 49, 1986, p. 83; by kind permission.

Figure 4
Share of Total Non-Financial Activity Held by the
100 Largest Non-Financial Corporations

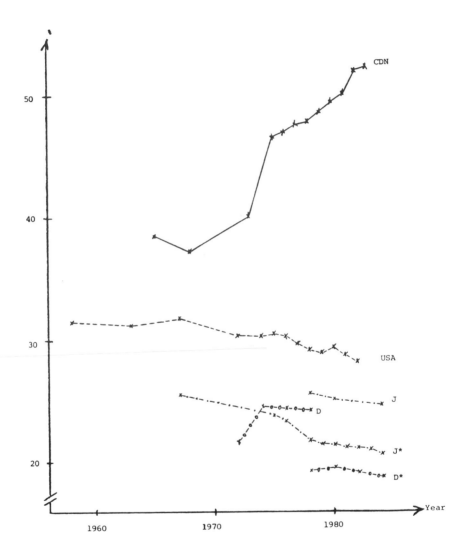

Legend: CDN: Canada (Assets);   USA: United States (Assets);   J: Japan
(Assets, incl. domestic subsidiaries); D: F.R. of Germany (Sales, all
firms); J*: Japan (Assets, excl. subsidiaries); D*: F.R. of Germany
(Value added, all firms)

Source: *vid.* Tables 1-4.

Figure 5
Share of Total Manufacturing Activity Held by the
100 Largest Manufacturing Firms

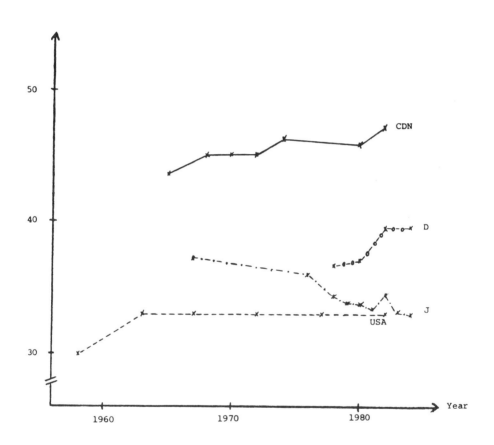

Legend: CDN: Canada (Value added); D: F.R. of Germany (Sales, incl. Mining, Construction, Electric Power & Gas); J: Japan (Assets, corporations only); USA: United States (Value added)

Source: *vid.* Tables 1-4.

Figure 6
Number of Mergers and Acquisitions

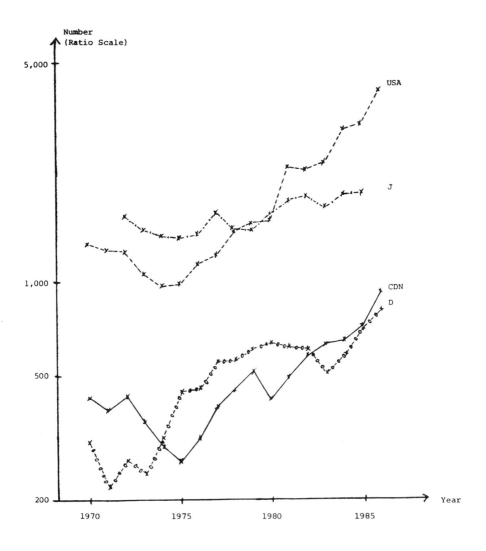

Legend: USA: United States; J: Japan; CDN: Canada; D: F.R. of Germany

Source: *vid.* Tables 5-8.

Figure 7
Number of Large Mergers and Acquisitions

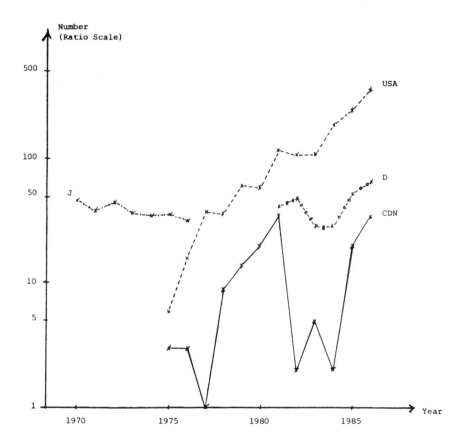

Legend: USA: United States; J: Japan (Mergers only); D: F.R. of Germany;
CDN: Canada

Source: *vid.* Tables 5-8.

REFERENCES

Berle, A.A. and G.C. Means, (1932) *The Modern Corporation and Private Property*, New York.

Blair, J.M., (1972) *Economic Concentration*, (New York: Harcourt, Brace & Jovanovich).

Canada, Statistics Canada, *Industrial organization and concentration in the manufacturing, mining and logging industries*, Cat. 31-402 Biennial, Ottawa.

_____, *Corporation Taxation Statistics*, Cat. 61-208 Annual, Ottawa.

_____, *Corporations and Labour Unions Returns Act*, Pt. I-Corporations, Cat. 61-210 Annual, Ottawa.

_____, *Small Business in Canada: A Statistical Profile 1981-1983*, Cat. 61-521, Ottawa, Oct. 1986.

Caves, R.E. and M. Uekusa, (1976) *Industrial Organization in Japan* (Washington, D.C., Brookings Institution).

Commerzbank, (1985) *wer gehoert zu wem*, 15 e., Frankfurt A.M.

Davidson, K.M., (1985) *Megamergers*, (Cambridge, Mass.: Ballinger).

"Die Zeit der Erbhoefe ist vorbei," (1986) *Der Spiegel*, No. 48, pp. 52-58.

Der Spiegel, "Koennen nur die Mammuts ueberleben?," No. 49, 1986, pp. 77-100.

Duke, D., (1982) *Trends in Aggregate Concentration*, (Washington, D.C.: Federal Trade Commission, Bureau of Economics, Working Paper No. 61, June).

Federal Republic of Germany, Monopolkommission, (1976) *Mehr Wettbewerb ist moeglich*, Hauptgutachten I, 1973-1975, Baden-Baden.

_____, (1982) *Fortschritte bei der Konzentrationserfassung*, Hauptgutachten IV, 1981-1982, Baden-Baden.

_____, (1984) *Oekonomische Kriterien fuer die Rechtsanwendung*, Hauptgutachten V, 1982-1983, Baden-Baden.

_____, (1986) *Gesamtwirtschafliche Chancen und Risiken wachsender Unternehmensgroessen*, Hauptgutachten VI, 1984-1985, Baden-Baden.

Japan, Fair Trade Commission, (1982) *The Recent Trend of Production Concentration and Overall Concentration*, Tokyo, (Mimeograph).

_____, (1986) *Combination of Firms*, Tokyo, (Mimeograph).

Japan, Japan Institute for International Affairs, (1974) *White Papers of Japan, 1972-73*, Tokyo.

Khemani, R.S., (1986) "The Extent and Evolution of Competition in the Canadian Economy," In D.G. McFetridge (ed.) *Canadian Industry in Transition*, (Toronto: University of Toronto Press), pp. 135-176.

_____, (1988) "The Dimensions of Corporate Concentration in Canada" (Chapter 1 in this volume).

Marfels, C., (1977) *Concentration Levels and Trends in the Canadian Economy*, Royal Commission on Corporate Concentration Study No. 31 (Ottawa: Minister of Supply & Services Canada).

_____, (1986) "Economic Criteria for the Application of Antitrust," *The Antitrust Bulletin*, Vol. 31, No. 4, Winter, pp. 1067-1087.

Mueller, J. and R. Hochreiter, (1975) *Stand und enwicklungstendenzen der Konzentration in der Bundesrepublik Deutschland*, Goettingen.

OECD, *Annual Reports on Competition Policy* (Paris: OECD).

Scherer, F.M., (1986) *The Ownership of U.S. Corporations*, (Swarthmore College, Mimeograph).

Schenefield, J.H., (1979) "Statement," *Mergers and Economic Concentration Hearings*, Pt. 1, U.S. Senate Subcommittee on Antitrust, Monopoly and Business Rights (Washington, D.C.), pp. 61-95.

Stanbury, W.T. (1988) "Corporate Power and Political Influence: Concerns, Sources, Manifestations and Limitations," (Chapter 17 in this volume).

United States, Bureau of the Census, (1986) *1982 Census of Manufactures, Subject Series: Concentration Ratios in Manufacturing*, Cat. No. MC82-S-7 (Washington, D.C.).

United States, Department of Justice, Economic Analysis Group (1986) *Memorandum re. Aggregate Concentration* (Washington, D.C., Mimeograph).

United States, Federal Trade Commission, Bureau of Economics, (1986) *Memorandum re. Concentration and Mergers* (Washington, D.C., Mimeograph).

Weiss, L.W., (1983) "The Extent and Effects of Aggregate Concentration," *Journal of Law and Economics*, Vol. 31, June, pp. 429-455.

White, L.R., (1980) "What Has Been Happening to Aggregate Concentration in the United States?," *Journal of Industrial Economics*, Vol. 29(3), pp. 223-230.

Rethinking the Modern Corporation

Chapter 4

Reconceptualizing the Corporation and Competition: Preliminary Remarks

David J. Teece
School of Business Administration
University of California, Berkeley

1.0 INTRODUCTION

Two somewhat independent shifts are causing academics, businessmen and policy makers to rethink fundamental ideas about the corporation and competition. The first is the increased level of international competition, particularly from the Japanese and developing countries which have relentlessly been challenging American and European corporations in the global marketplace. These competitive pressures are leading, at least in some circles, to a re-evaluation of American institutions and policies. The second and more subtle shift is occurring within the discipline of economics and is driven by a dissatisfaction with orthodox theory. Textbook views of the corporation as a black box, or production function, are giving way to views of the corporation as an institution for economizing on transactions costs, for housing organizational learning, and as a vehicle for capturing value from technological innovation. In addition, some fundamental rethinking is occurring with respect to how corporations ought to cooperate and compete. This latter issue has not gone very far to date, but it will probably become an increasingly important consideration in the years ahead. In this paper, I briefly survey and interpret these recent developments and indicate the directions in which the new thinking might productively gravitate.

2.0 THE CORPORATION
2.1 Traditional Views
Economists and managers both have had their own stylized view of the corporation in the post-war period. Each perspective is quite distinct and will be examined separately.

(a) **Neoclassical Perspectives**. Academic economists, relying on the classical economists and in particular Ricardo and Marshall, have always tended to view the firm as a mechanism for converting inputs into outputs, using known technologies, in accord with the dictates of marginal analysis. This view has proved to be useful as the underpinnings of a theory of production and enables much of traditional industry analysis as well as price theory to proceed.

The theory of the firm as developed by the classical economists has had a remarkable stability, with very little new insights provided until quite recently. But to view the firm as an input conversion mechanism is extraordinarily limited and often downright misleading. It has tended to focus attention on cost conditions and, in particular, economies of scale and more recently of scope. But in today's world, if not in earlier periods, the key economic functions of the corporation relate to learning and innovation, to organizational control and coordination, and to economizing on the transactions costs which would be incurred if the economic activity (which is internalized) had to proceed between stand-alone firms in the market.

A key limiting aspect of the production function view is that it avoids governance and agency issues. How is the firm to be organized and managed, and how are the top managers going to be policed? These complex and real issues are not part of the basic conceptualization contained in the production function view, and to the extent they were dealt with at all, it was in special theories which were not successfully grafted onto the underlying theory of production.

Equally remiss has been the treatment of know-how and knowledge generation and retention with the business enterprise. The most common theoretical approach, evidence for which can be found in practically all of the textbooks on microeconomics or price theory, is to take technology as given, ignoring completely the fact that managers almost always have the option to invest in R&D in order to bring about improvement in products and processes. On the occasions when this pattern is broken by explicit attention to technological change, the treatment of states of knowledge and changes therein is usually simplistic and misleading. It is common to assume in models of competition that technology is available to all at zero cost (or at least under the same cost conditions). If proprietary, it is considered to reside in a "book of blueprints" that can be traded just like a bushel of wheat or a ton of coal. In reality, "know-how" cannot, except in some circumstances, be transferred at zero cost from organization to organization. The book of blueprints metaphor implies that know-how is codified, when more often than not it is tacit. The book of blueprints metaphor caricatures the development and transfer of know-how.

Evidence of the inadequacy of the received orthodoxy can be found in by the complete inability of the theory to explain the organization and structure of the modern corporation. There is nothing in orthodoxy theory, except chance, to explain why firms diversify, and nothing to explain why the observed diversification is not completely random. Clearly, most firms do not diversify in a completely random fashion, and some firms, like IBM, are remarkably specialized. Nor is there anything, other than appeals to monopoly incentives, to explain vertical integration. Even explaining the size of the firm and limits thereto is beyond the means of orthodox theory.

Hence, without too much exaggeration, one can say that the orthodoxy found in practically all the textbooks tells us virtually nothing about the modern multi-product, multi-divisional, vertically integrated corporation. It might constitute an acceptable model of the nineteenth century English farm, but nineteenth century agriculture is quite some organization and technological distance from the modern post-war American or Japanese corporation.

As mentioned above, orthodox theory even has trouble explaining the limits to firm size. Oliver Williamson (1985) has referred to this as a "chronic puzzle" in the theory of the firm. Primitive formulations of the theory of the firm appeal to exhaustion of scale economies; but while limits to production level economics may explain why plants reach a certain size, they do not explain why *firms* cannot expand indefinitely. Knight's (1965, pp. 286-878) answer was that a man could not "adequately manage a business enterprise of indefinite size and complexity" because of "effective uncertainty." Coase (1937) posed the question of "why is not all production carried on in one big firm?" but seemed unable to answer his own question.

(b) **Institutional-Managerial Perspectives.** It is much more complex to characterize institutional-managerial views of the corporation. Institutionalists' and historians' concepts of the corporation have been shaped less by theory than by actual facts and circumstances.

Different methods for organizing work have shaped the corporation, both here and abroad. Early organizational forms included the "putting out" system. The capitalist firm, personified by the putter-outer and his agents, supplied rural workers in the early nineteenth century with raw materials that would be processed in the home to produce woolen and cotton goods. The finished goods would then be collected and paid for at a previously agreed upon piece rate.

The putting out system reduced the capitalists' fixed costs, but it did not provide control, and the ability to quickly introduce productivity enhancing investments. Also, division of labour was limited as the workers could only communicate with each other via the putter-outer and his agent. The *factory* afforded a potential solution to throughput and productivity problems. In capital-intensive activities like spinning, the mechanized factory system came in during the 1770s, and half a century later in weaving.

In the nineteenth century British factories, operatives took on functions now commonly thought of as management functions (Pollard 1968, Ch. 5). They recruited and trained workers, and often acted as inside subcontractors. Such shop floor control was later parlayed into powerful and enduring unions. Senior adult workers utilized the management and apprenticeship system to play the major role in the development of the labor force. The early British firms were thus akin to vertically specialized factories. The reliance on skilled labour for managerial functions lessened the need to develop managerial hierarchies. Regional concentration permitted external economics to be realized so that British industry was viable, even if scale was limited (Lazonick 1987).

The 1920s witnessed a second industrial revolution, dominated by U.S. manufacturing companies. The second industrial revolution was based on additional mechanization and on organizational innovation. In the nineteenth century, a distinctive "American system of manufacturers" had emerged in wood working and metal working, and particularly in armaments where long-term government procurement contracts, justified investments in special purpose machinery (Smith 1977; Hounshell 1984; Lazonick 1987). These investments economized on skilled labor and lowered costs by achieving parts interchangeability. The "Lowell system" of cotton textile manufacture similarly encouraged skills in cotton textile manufacture. The trend towards mass production and vertical integration reached its full expression in Henry Ford's giant River Rouge facility for manufacturing the Model T.

Henry Ford, with his introduction of the moving assembly line and his perfection of the interchangeability of parts, was first and foremost an organizational innovator. Ford and his contemporary, Frederick Taylor, made significant contributions to managerial thinking by stressing the need to share productivity gains with workers, and the importance of scheduling and coordination. However, both Ford and Taylor erred in treating human effort as purely an expandable marketable commodity. As the specialized capital required for efficient production expanded, so did the need for commitment from the work place. In subsequent decades, as their market power increased, American firms came to offer *de facto* extended employment through internal job ladders (Lazonick 1983).

American managers were the first to learn how to structure large corporations to overcome the problems associated with the loss of control and to facilitate long-term planning. The multi-divisional structure was developed in the 1920s and diffused rapidly thereafter. The separation of operational from strategic decision making which the M-form accommodated created a new concept of the business enterprise.

The passing of economic leadership from Britain to the U.S. in the inter war years changed the institutional nature of global capitalism. The British model of the family firm was displaced by the American model of the large multidimensional enterprise with ownership separate from control. British business institutions ossified; the American ones continued to change. Craft control of the shop floor and the family firm structure in Britain impeded innovation and exchange. The superiority of American management over the British was apparent to all by 1950. The British system, based on aristocratic values, the family firm, and the inability of the education system to offer the pre-employment foundations for management development, could no longer compete in global products against a better system. The relative levels of living of the British had to decline, along with Britain's economic and political power.

However, the American epoch of economic prowess was to be short lived. The American concept of the corporation and strategy took on some distinctive properties – some would say debilitating qualities – during the post-war years. Diversification expanded and took on a conglomerate dimension during the 1960s. It was widely believed, and for a while the stock market seemed to bear it out, that the way to profitability was through growth and the fastest way to grow was to diversify, through mergers and acquisitions if necessary. This belief was fueled by an explosion in strategic management tools and, in particular, the product portfolio concept of the Boston Consulting Group (BCG).

BCG held that, because of experience curve effects, the acquisition of market share was the key to profitability. Moreover, a firm had to have a balanced portfolio of businesses with different cash flow profiles. The cash generated by "cash cow" businesses ought to be used to finance new businesses, as if there was no venture capital market (there was not much of one in the 1960s), and as if mature markets could never be revitalized through reinvestment and innovation. The investment banking community facilitated and encouraged growth via merger and acquisition.

By the 1970s, however, it had become apparent that the American system was being challenged by smarter capitalists from across the Pacific – the Japanese. Prominent institutional features of the Japanese industrial system include enterprise groups, consensus decision making, and permanent employment for a substantial fraction of the labor force of large firms. The Japanese manager's concept of the corporation is very different from his American counterpart. If the U.S. has a "control model" to accomplish hierarchical integration, then the Japanese have a commitment model. The transition from the first to the second requires transformation in both the traditional division of labor between managers and workers as well as in skills and attitudes of workers and managers.

Important and possibly critical differences in the relationship of finance to industry characterize the U.S. and Japan. The Japanese economy has grown largely independently of an active reliance on stock markets – either as a major source of corporate capital or of discipline on corporation management (Gerlach 1987). True, institutions have in Japan, as in the U.S., replaced individuals as the primary controller of shareholdings. About 43 per cent of shares of U.S. firms were held by institutional investors in the early 1980s, while the figure in Japan was 62 per cent (Aoki 1984, pp. 10-11). But the nature of this relationship is markedly different in the two countries. In the U.S., nearly two-thirds of institutional investors are pension funds and personal trust funds. In Japan, equity is held instead by business partners. These equity links signify inter-firm relationships which tend to be markedly stable over time.

2.2   New Perspectives

(a)   **The Organizational Economics Perspective**. Most applied economists have now abandoned the traditional production function view of the firm. A new perspective has emerged which views the corporation as simultaneously a mechanism for internalizing certain transactions which would proceed much less efficiently, if at all, were they forced into a market context and as a mechanism to facilitate path dependent learning.

The transactions cost perspective has its origins with Ronald Coase's (1937) seminal article on the nature of the firm. The perspective has been further developed by Williamson (1975, 1985), who has turned transactions costs reasoning into a theory of the firm by specifying the circumstances under which contractual linkages among unaffiliated parties are likely to break down, and when superior hierarchical alternatives exist. This theory points to the importance of the technological requirements of efficient production in determining desirable organizational arrangements. When efficient production requires special purpose equipment which is idiosyncratic to a particular set of buyer-seller relationships, or investment in firm or customer specific know-how, then firms will probably need to internalize these assets if they wish production to proceed efficiently. Specialized assets turn out to be the key discriminating factor in the transactions cost theory of the firm, and they help explain complex forms of business organization and especially vertical integration.

But transactions costs approaches leave much about the corporation unexplained. Diversification is a case in point. Neoclassical concepts such as economies of scope cannot explain diversification either. Orthodox theory would imply that since economies of scope arise from the sharing of a common input, a specialist firm ought to be able to own the common input and rent its services to other specialist firms who would pursue their own particular product line strategy. Multi-product firms would exist in the world of orthodox micro theory and frictionless markets, but only as flukes. Transactions cost reasoning, which emphasizes the shortcomings of contractual investments for leasing the services of specialized assets, can explain why firms might become multi-product (Teece 1982). However, additional factors must be introduced to explain observed reality, and particularly the fact that firms often start specialized and become diversified. There is nothing in orthodox theory, or in transactions cost theory, to explain why it is rarely observed that firms begin large and diversified and subsequently become specialized.[1] Generally, of course, firms begin as specialized enterprises and later diversify.

To explain such phenomenon, one must reconceptualize the corporation. Firms need to be understood and their boundaries explained in terms of their *economizing* and *learning* capabilities, in terms of their *path-dependent growth*, and not their resource conversion capabilities as orthodox theory would have it. Important aspects of each are now briefly examined.

Important aspects of *economizing* are the following. Internalizing economic activity is more efficient than the market alternative when efficient production requires highly (transaction) specialized investments in plant and equipment, in location, and in learning. Otherwise, there is a great risk that these investments will be stranded as a result of recontracting by unaffiliated parties whose prior contractual commitments are important to the profitability of the investment in question.

Important characteristics of learning inside the corporation are that it is cumulative, it involves the development of organization rather than individual skill, and that the knowledge generated by learning is best conceptualized as residing in organizational securities and not in some mythical book of blueprints. The rate of learning is powerfully influenced by changes in the science and technology which underpin the industry.

It is also important to recognize that the growth of business firms is path-dependent, being constrained by significant irreversibilities as well as forward constraints. There are several reasons for this. First, firms typically arise as governance structures to protect specialized idiosyncratic physical and human capital. These assets are not generic and generally cannot be deployed outside the line of business for which they were developed in the first place. Secondly, and notwithstanding notable exceptions, there are cognitive limits on the capacities of managers which permit them from knowing all technologies and markets equally well.

Once reconceptualized along these lines, a rather interesting and empirically satisfying set of propositions emerge about the firm, its capabilities and its boundaries. A firm is likely to have one or more "core businesses" defined by the technological and market paths it has historically traversed. The degree of coherence displayed among the firm's businesses will be a function of the interaction of learning, path dependencies, and the strength of the competitive environment in which the firm has operated. With rapid learning, as in many high technology industries, and tight path dependencies, one should expect to see single product (specialist) firms growing rapidly. With slow learning and path dependencies, one can expect to see specialist firms displaying some degree of lateral integration. With high learning and low path dependency, fast-moving "network" firms and "hollow" corporations should be viable. Conglomerates may exist where there is low path dependency, slow learning, and weak competitive pressures. Learning, path dependencies, and the selection environment the firm occupies will thus explain the coherence of the corporation.

(b) **Institutional and Managerial Perspectives**. Since the 1970s, a rather different view, or at least an alternative view, of the corporation has begun to emerge in America. Alfred Chandler (1977), basing his observations on the period before the Second World War, defined the modern corporation as follows:

> Modern business enterprise . . . has two specific characteristics: it contains many distinct operating units and it is managed by a hierarchy of executives. Each unit . . . has its own administrative office . . . In contrast, the traditional American business firm was a single-unit business enterprise . . .

But the modern American corporation in the 1980s is not necessarily of the type Chandler describes. A whole new class of specialized, rapidly-growing firms has emerged, usually in high technology industries. These firms represent possibly an alternative paradigm for organizing business. These firms also have a different ownership structure, displaying considerable employee ownership, and different corporate cultures. They sometimes have close links with established firms. For instance, the new biotechnology firms often have close links with established pharmaceutical companies. They are typically funded by venture capital firms, with the venture capitalists playing important advisory and sometimes managerial roles.

These firms do not take their boundaries as given. Two key dynamics are whether technology should be developed internally or sourced from the outside, and whether manufacturing and other key vertical stages should be performed in-house or serviced externally. Technology strategy in these new companies is thus just not a question of how much to spend on R&D and on what, but also should one license in and license out, and should one commercialize innovation using in-house marketing and manufacturing, or should one collaborate and/or joint venture with firms better positioned in these complementary assets. These concerns are now a critical decision variable for big firms as well as small firms, but it is the newer firms which have been the most willing, possibly because of necessity, to consider their boundaries as a decision variable.

Larger traditional firms have in some instances attempted to adopt the small company model internally, creating new venture groups with considerable autonomy. Not many have been successful. What is evident, however, is a clear tension between the virtues of bigness and of smallness, of centralization and decentralization, of integration and contract. The challenge of management is to balance these properties and attempt to capture benefits from simultaneously maintaining some of each structure. This is what American management has experimented with in the 1970s and 1980s, so far with mixed success. Perhaps the internal logic of each form is so strong that mixed structural forms are not viable.

3.0   COMPETITION
3.1   Traditional Views
The basic tenet of received orthodoxy is that competition drives resource allocation towards efficient outcomes, while market power distorts and detracts. The image of competition which informs this view is that of the activities in neoclassical perfectly competitive industries. This model employs a long list of assumptions, including atomistic competitors with fixed technology and perfect information. In this model, the effect of monopoly is to reduce output, raise price, and create excess profits. If there is any redeeming virtue of monopoly, it is the case of "natural" monopoly, where the economies of scale gained through monopolization yield cost savings of great value.

In the orthodox formulation, price is considered to be the sharpest competitive weapon. Non-price competition, through product and process innovation, "can have real effects but it is less direct and hard hitting" (Shepherd 1979, p. 301). Cooperation is generally analyzed *only* in terms of its negative impacts on economic welfare. Indeed, coordination of prices is often the only form of cooperation recognized in the textbooks. For instance, Shepherd (1979, Ch. 15) has an entire chapter devoted to the topic of "cooperation among firms" which is entirely a discussion of cartels, as if it were the only kind of interfirm cooperation. One must look in vain for analysis of interfirm collaborative research in the Western literature on research and development published before 1970 (Samuels 1987). And in the economic literature, there is practically no mention of cooperative R&D, let alone analysis of it, until about the 1980s.

Embedded in the orthodox literature is a hostility towards cooperation, even when it involves R&D. Cooperation is feared because it would preclude multiple paths to invention and dull the incentives to be creative. Furthermore, collaborative habits might migrate from the laboratory to product development and marketing, with attendant antisocial consequences.

This conceptualization of competition informs antitrust or competition policy in North America. It leads to a hostility towards many forms of business conduct, particularly if agreements with competitors are at issue. It also informs industrial policy in many Western nations. Economies are often sought and protected in the formulation of public policy. However, because economies of scale are practically the only economies recognized in orthodox theory, the avenues in which government can assist industrial development, and the matters upon which the government should restrict business behaviour, tend to be construed narrowly. For instance, notions of "critical" or "strategic" industries cannot find a foundation in received orthodoxy — nor can the strategic use of trade barriers or the use of export promotion mechanisms. The result is a world in which government, particularly in North America, restrict complex forms of business behaviour, such as the exchange of competitor information and collaboration with respect to new product commercialization, while finding nothing objectionable about conglomerate mergers, even if they are efficiency destroying.[2]

3.2   Challenges to Orthodoxy

A reconceptualization of competition, and in particular horizontal collaboration, would appear to be warranted. In many circles, not much is new with respect to the fashion in which competition and cooperation is assessed. Nevertheless, elements of a new approach can be identified.

The underpinnings of a new approach can reside in the observation that an essential aspect of economic organization is the need to coordinate economic activity and, in particular, investments. It is the essence of the private enterprise economy that although its individual members are independent, their activities are nevertheless interrelated. Any single investment will, in general, only be profitable provided first, that the volume of competitive investment does not exceed a limit set by demand, and second, that the volume of complementary investment reaches the correct level (Richardson 1960, p. 31).

However, orthodox theorists often fail to recognize that there is no special machinery in a private enterprise, market economy to ensure that investment programs are made known to all concerned at the time of their inception. Price movements, by themselves, do not generally form an adequate system of signalling. Indeed, Tjalling Koopmans (1957, p. 146) has been rather critical of what he calls "the overextended belief" of certain economists in the efficiency of competitive markets as a means of allocating resources in a world characterized by ubiquitous uncertainty. The main source of this uncertainty, according to Koopmans, is the ignorance which firms have with respect to their competitors' future actions, preferences and states of technological information. In the absence of a complete set of forward markets in which anticipation and intentions could be tested and adjusted, there is no reason to believe that with uncertainty, competitive markets of the kind which American antitrust laws seek to foster can produce efficient outcomes.[3] The information-circulating function which economic theory attributes to competitive markets is quite simply not discharged by any existing arrangements with the detail and forward extension necessary to support efficient outcomes (Koopmans 1957, p. 163).

Today, there is no area in which uncertainty is higher and the need to coordinate greater than in the development, and possibly the commercialization, of new technology. In many industries, the stupendous foreshortening of product life cycles and the tremendous increase in development and commercialization costs have increased the technological, managerial and financial resource requirements for marketplace success. Moreover, the sources of innovation have become geographically and organizationally more dispersed. Relatedly, imitation and idea borrowing is becoming increasingly easy and common. Most scientific know-how and new product concepts are available to all firms willing and able to invest in the relevant information collection activities. Low cost travel and telecommunications means that the natural protection of distance and language has all but evaporated. While intellectual property law is migrating in a direction which favours innovators, the instruments of the law (patents, copyrights, trademarks, etc.) are inherently weak and cannot protect ideas, only certain of their manifestations. Appropriating the benefits from investment in new technology is thus inherently difficult. Accordingly, the incentives to coordinate via collaboration have markedly escalated. In the global environment of the 1980s, collaboration (horizontal and vertical) is a necessity in many industries.

Not surprisingly, some analysts are coming to realize that collaborative research activities among firms which may be competitors in product markets is likely to improve economic welfare. There are several forms in which such cooperation may take place. At one extreme, firms may simply combine their total activities, including R&D, through acquisition or merger. At the other extreme, one firm could perform under contract all of the R&D needed by both. Intermediate solutions include collaborative behaviour, where firms could simply pool their research activities, in whole or in part, or R&D joint ventures, where a separate entity could be established in which joint R&D activities could be conducted (Pisano, Russo and Teece 1988, pp. 4-16).

Both research joint ventures and research collaborations can assist firms to overcome appropriability (technology leakage) problems because research costs can be shared, and also because the set of firms receiving the benefits is likely to include a greater portion of firms which have incurred R&D costs.[4] The effect of greater appropriability is, of course, to stimulate greater investment in new technology. It is well understood that competitive markets tend to underinvest in new technology because those firms which support R&D have limited capacity to extract "fees" from the imitators (free riders).

In addition, collaborative research reduces, if not eliminates, what William Norris, then CEO of Control Data Corporation, refers to as "shameful and needless duplication of effort" (Davis 1985, p. 42). Independent research activities often proceed down identical or near-identical technological paths. This is wasteful and can be avoided if research plans are coordinated.

The manifold benefits from collaboration activity have been recognized abroad and, more recently, in the U.S. as well.[5] One assessment of the U.S. is that "up until now, however, we have taken it for granted as an article of faith that no cooperation should be permitted, that it is best that we keep companies apart from one another" (Ouchi 1984, p. 103). Japanese competitors have engaged in deep cooperation for decades and have received *de facto* exemption from Japanese antitrust laws to do so. Japanese cooperative activity is not only in the form of R&D joint ventures, but also R&D collaboration. For instance, by the end of 1971, the entire Japanese computer industry (six firms) was paired in order to compete with IBM and its system 370 (Ouchi 1984, p. 105). While the research was done in existing cooperative labs, there was intense interaction and information sharing. Another celebrated example of Japanese collaboration was the VLSI (Very Large Scale Integrated Circuit) Research Association which as an R&D joint venture formed in 1975 with the capital contributed by NEC, Toshiba, Hitachi, Mitsubishi and Fujitsu.[6] At the successful conclusion of the project in 1979, the laboratory was dissolved and the scientists went back to their sponsoring companies.

Since the *National Cooperative Research Act* of 1984, which limits but does not eliminate antitrust risks, some interest has been shown in R&D joint ventures in the U.S. Well known R&D joint ventures include: the Microelectronics and Computer Technology Corp. (MCC) in Austin, Texas; the Semiconductor Research Corporation (SRC) in Research Triangle Park, North Carolina; and Bell Communication Research (Bellcore). These joint ventures are restricted to R&D up to the prototype "stage." For instance, MCC's objective is to engage in advanced long-term research and development in computer architecture, semiconductor packaging and interconnect, software technology, VLSI and CAD. Its numbers include AMD, Boeing, Control Data, Harris, Motorola, Sperry and others. (IBM is conspicuously absent as are Japanese and European-based firms.)

The only form of cooperative research which receives special antitrust treatment (but not exemption) in the U.S. is the R&D joint venture.[7] Other forms of collaborative R&D activity, such as the pooling of R&D projects and the sharing of development data, are subject to deep antitrust exposure. Cooperating using existing facilities is thus perceived to be exposed to serious antitrust risk, particularly if participating firms have significant market shares. Beneficial collaboration in R&D is thus likely to be circumscribed in the U.S. if participating firms are world class competitors.

In order to go beyond laboratory activity and commercialize new technologies, a more challenging and typically more investment-intensive set of tasks must be successfully conducted. The commercialization of technologies is perhaps even more challenging than their initial development. The requirements for cooperation here are also strong.

In idealized treatments of the innovation process, it is common to represent the various steps as being largely sequential but with significant overlaps. In the textbook treatment, one does basic/applied research, then prototyping or pilot plant design, production planning and manufacturing set-up, manufacturing start-up, and marketing start-up. The impression is often left that one step mechanically leads to the next. Feedback loops from manufacturing to research, from sales and marketing to manufacturing, and from sales and marketing to research are often omitted, particularly in treatments of the innovation process by policy analysts. (Managers generally know better.)

The innovation process is, however, decidedly non-linear. The reason is that with incomplete information at the outset, there are shortcomings and failure which demand rapid, accurate feedback with follow-up and redesign. Radical, or revolutionary, innovation prospers best when provided with multiple sources of informational input. Ordinary, evolutionary innovation requires iterative fitting and trimming of the many necessary criteria and desiderata. In either case, feedbacks and trials are essential. An implication of this is that it is difficult to organizationally separate R&D from commercialization. Hence, antitrust statutes which view collaboration with respect to R&D sympathetically, but collaboration with respect to commercialization antagonistically, are inherently in conflict.

Moreover, the successful commercialization of technology often involves collaboration among firms that have different pieces of the puzzle. The relevant manufacturing capacities need not be resident within the firm responsible for the other activities in the innovation process. In order to capture value from the innovation, it may therefore be necessary for a number of firms to collaborate, with different firms being responsible for different activities (Teece 1986). In some cases, these firms may be horizontal competitors and antitrust may block desirable collaboration.

Strictures on collaboration after the prototype stage and pursuant to earlier involvement in an R&D joint venture also create technology transfer burdens even if the prototype is fully optimized. The reason is that key personnel from the R&D joint ventures will drift back to their particular companies where they will be inaccessible to competitors for post-prototype consultation. One can therefore predict that the various R&D joint ventures which have recently taken root in America, such as MCC, will face a considerable challenge in transferring technology back to the sponsoring companies, and successfully commercializing it. The fact that communication among the sponsoring companies is cut off, or at least attenuated by antitrust constraints, once commercialization commences must limit the productivity of R&D. In short, public policy which cautiously permits R&D joint ventures but maintains hostility or ambiguity towards other forms of R&D cooperation and extreme hostility towards collaboration with respect to commercialization activities when the firms involved are significant market players is unlikely to satisfactorily promote long-run economic welfare.

It is thus apparent that while a pragmatic case for adopting a new vision of competition, and of public policy towards competition and cooperation, is required in several Western nations, the intellectual-theoretical case has yet to be fully articulated. This reflects inherent shortcomings in the body of orthodox economic theory which many analysts bring to bear on economic problems. These deficiencies are particularly embarrassing when matters of innovation and adjustment are at issue. Unfortunately, it is these conditions which are at the essence of today's global economy.

4.0 CONCLUSIONS

The corporation and the nature of competition have changed. Traditional conceptualizations of each have always been inadequate, but those inadequacies are particularly hazardous as a guide to policy in today's global environment. The corporation today is an animal quite different from the textbook caricature. Moreover, the population of corporations is rather different from what existed barely two decades ago. Giant enterprises are becoming islands in a sea of smaller, entrepreneurial technology-based enterprises, located especially in California and the northeastern seaboard. Some of these corporations are "hollow" in the sense that they contract out for manufacturing and other key services. Others take on more traditional levels of vertical integration. Larger companies often source technology from them or with them. These smaller companies often have non-traditional control structures with flat hierarchies and significant equity ownership by employees. Economic theory, and perhaps management theory as well, has a way to go if it is to incorporate key features of these new institutions into mainstream theory.

Likewise, American economists and policy analysts must reconceptualize competition in order to reconcile theoretical tensions between cooperation and competition. While much antitrust law has been revised in recent years to produce relaxed standards with respect to many vertical issues, cooperation among competitors is still regarded with suspicion in North America. Elsewhere, nations recognize that competitiveness in the global marketplace may require close collaboration with respect to matters ranging from R&D to standardization.[8] The Japanese in particular have a different view of competition, and see collaboration as ultimately pro-competitive in many circumstances. Economic theory, and perhaps managerial theory, needs to be unshackled from orthodox paradigms so that an appropriate competitive policy can be fashioned for today's global economy.

NOTES

1. It is true that many specialized firms adopted diversification strategies and then divested many of their former acquisitions (e.g., ITT).

2. By assumption they could not be because, if they were, no manager would seek to execute one. At least, this is the reasoning advanced by many orthodox financial economists. See the paper by Eckbo, Chapter 7 in this volume.

3. Koopmans (1957, p. 147) goes on to point out that, because of this deficiency, economic theorists are not able to speak with anything approaching scientific authority on matters relating to individual versus collective enterprise.

4. If the R&D industry is specific and all firms in the industry participate in funding, the appropriability problem will be substantially solved, particularly if a coordinated marketing program is also put in place.

5. According to William Norris, U.S. corporations were not willing to give collaborative research a try until "these companies had the hell scared out of them by the Japanese" (Davis 1985, p. 42).

6. A Japanese government laboratory was also involved.

7. In Canada, R&D joint ventures are exempt from the merger provisions of the *Competition Act* enacted in June 1986.

8. Canada's new *Competition Act* makes provision for specialization agreements to be registered with the Competition Tribunal and hence exempt from the conspiracy and exclusive dealing sections. Agreements with respect to defining product standards, the sizes and shapes of containers in which an article is packaged or the adoption of the metric system of weights and measures are exempt from the conspiracy provisions of the *Competition Act*.

REFERENCES

Aoki, M., (1984) *The Economic Analysis of the Japanese Firm* (Amsterdam: North Holland).

Chandler, A.D., (1977) *The Visible Hand: The Managerial Revaluation in American Business* (Cambridge, MA: Harvard University Press).

Coase, R., (1937) "The Nature of the Firm," *Econometrica*, Vol. 4, pp. 386-405.

Davis, D., (1985) "R&D Consortia," *High Technology*, October.

Gerlach, M., (1987) "Business Alliances and the Strategy of the Japanese Firm," *California Management Review*, Vol. 30(1) (Fall).

Hounshell, D., (1984) *From the American System to Mass Production, 1800-1932* (Baltimore: Johns Hopkins University Press).

Knight, F.H., (1965) *Risk Uncertainty and Profit* (New York: Harper & Row).

Koopmans, T., (1957) *Three Essays on the State of Economic Science* (New York: McGraw-Hill).

Lazonick, W., (1983) "Technological Change and the Control of Work," in H. Gospel and C. Littler (eds.), *Managerial Strategies and Industrial Relations* (London: Heinemann).

_____, (1987) "The Social Determinants of Technological Change: Innovation and Adaptation in Three Industrial Revolutions," (unpublished manuscript, Barnard College – Columbia University, August).

Ouchi, W., (1984) *M-Form Society* (New York: Avon Books).

Pisano, G., M. Russo, and D. Teece, (1988) "Joint Ventures and Collaborative Arrangements in the Telecommunications Equipment Industry," in D.C. Mowery (ed.), *International Collaborative Ventures in U.S. Manufacturing* (Washington, DC: American Enterprise Institute, forthcoming).

Pollard, S., (1968) *The Genesis of Modern Management* (Harmondsworth: Penguin Books).

Richardson, G.B., (1960) *Information and Investment* (Oxford: Oxford University Press).

Samuels, R.J., (1987) "Research Collaboration in Japan," (MIT-Japan Science and Technology Program, Working Paper No. 87-02, April).

Shepherd, W.G., (1979) *The Economics of Industrial Organization* (Englewood Cliffs, NJ: Prentice-Hall).

Smith, M.R., (1982) *Harpers Ferry Armory and the New Technology* (Ithaca, NY: Cornell University Press).

Teece, D.J., (1982) "Towards Economic Theory of the Multiproduct Firm," *Journal of Economic Behavior and Organization*, Vol. 3, March, 39-64.

_____, (1986) "Profiting from Technological Innovation: Implications for Integration, Collaboration, Licensing and Public Policy," *Research Policy*, Vol. 15(6), December, pp. 285-305.

Williamson, O.E., (1975) *Markets and Hierarchies* (New York: Free Press).

_____, (1985) *Economic Institutions of Capitalism* (New York: Free Press).

Takeovers: Determinants and Effects

Chapter 5

Mergers, Competition Policy, and the International Environment*

James A. Brander
Faculty of Commerce and Business Administration
University of British Columbia

1.0 INTRODUCTION

In Canada, as in many countries, merger activity takes up considerable newspaper space. Mergers are to the *Financial Post* what UFOs are to the *National Enquirer*. As I write, a significant public controversy is developing over the proposed takeover of Dome Petroleum by Amoco Canada for over $5 billion.[1] More generally, there is considerable concern in Canadian policy circles over the appropriate role of mergers in economic activity, and over the appropriate role of merger policy. The principal objective of this paper is to examine the implications of international considerations for the role of mergers and for merger policy.

Mergers figure prominently in the public consciousness; they also figure prominently in legislation. Canadian competition law has had explicit provisions concerning mergers since 1910. Despite the attention paid to mergers in the law of competition policy, however, the practice of merger activity seems to have been little affected by policy. Since 1910 only eight merger cases have gone to court (Reschenthaler and Stanbury 1977a). In one case a guilty plea was entered. All the other cases were contested and ended in acquittal.

It is possible that the mere existence of merger law has prevented anti-competitive mergers from being attempted. A more plausible inference is

* I wish to thank Bill Stanbury for many helpful suggestions, and Barbara Spencer for her comments on early drafts of the paper. I also thank the Centre for International Business Studies at UBC for research support.

that Canadian competition law has been weak and permissive to the point of having almost no restraining power over the merger process. Some analysts, of course, would argue that this is a good thing, and that the merger process is one of the forces that makes market economies perform well.

The status of merger law has changed substantially as a result of the *Competition Act* of 1986, which removed merger law from the Criminal Code and placed it in a "civil reviewable" category.[2]   A companion piece of legislation, the *Competition Tribunal Act*, created a Tribunal, consisting of judges and "lay" persons, to adjudicate civil reviewable matters, especially mergers.   In addition, the *Competition Act* creates a pre-notification requirement — parties to large mergers are to provide notification and certain information to the Director of Investigation and Research (Bureau of Competition Policy) prior to the actual merger date.[3]

The net effect of the two *Acts* will be to allow more effective, or at least more, policy intervention in the merger process. The basic mandate of the Tribunal is to dissolve or modify a merger if it finds that the merger substantially lessens competition. (See Bill C-91, *Competition Act*, Section 64). This allows more scope for policy action than pre-1986 anti-combines legislation, which required that "public detriment" also be demonstrated.[4]   In addition, the Tribunal itself, rather than being limited to a finding of guilt or innocence, as the courts were, has considerable latitude in modifying mergers.

In setting out the factors to be considered by the Tribunal, the *Competition Act* (Section 65) cites two factors (out of eight) related to international trade. Specifically, the Tribunal is to consider "the extent to which foreign products or foreign competitors provide or are likely to provide effective competition" and to consider "tariff and non-tariff barriers to international trade . . . and any effect of the proposed merger on such barriers."

In addition, in a separate section of the *Act* (Section 68), the Tribunal is instructed to allow mergers to take place if "gains in efficiency . . . will offset the effects of lessening of competition." Furthermore, the Tribunal is also instructed to consider whether the efficiency gains will result in "a significant increase in the real value of exports; or a significant substitution of domestic products for imported products."

While the *Act* does not specify in what way the Tribunal is to take into account increases in exports or substitution for imports, the implication seems to be that such effects are to be favourably regarded. In short, the Tribunal is to be particularly lenient toward a merger that is believed to promote "international competitiveness." The special treatment of mergers related to international trade is consistent with a frequently articulated view in parts of the business community that Canadian firms need to be larger in order to compete in world markets. J. Trevor Eyton (1986), CEO of Brascan Limited, makes the following argument:

> Where then are our world class companies who are going to compete toe to toe with the largest U.S. and other foreign competitors? . . . Because corporate size and economies of scale are linked, this leads to the conclusion that the small[ness] of

Canada's corporations constitutes a very real constraint on our ability to compete in the global village featuring increasing international trade.... Is size important to Canada's economic well being? Well, I think it is.... Note that virtually all of Canada's foreign trade is accounted for by larger Canadian corporations.

The basic theme of Eyton's argument is that mergers will help Canadian firms become large enough to compete effectively in world markets. Policy, therefore, so the argument goes, should not restrict, and perhaps should encourage, mergers between firms that are, or hope to be, involved in international trade. My reading of the business press, however, puts Eyton in a minority camp. Bank of Montreal chairman William Mulholland has argued: "People are finding it cheaper making money with money than to make better goods or new products ... The wave of takeovers without productive investment is wrong, just wrong."[5]

Professor W.T. Stanbury has been quoted in *Maclean's* as saying: "If we are not careful, we are going to end up with a handful of corporate monsters that totally dominate the economy, wielding an enormous amount of power."[6] Diane Francis (1986) has written a Canadian best-seller on precisely this theme. The concerns of Mulholland, Stanbury, and Francis do not specifically address the special role of international trade in mergers, but they do directly contest the benign view of mergers held by Eyton.

As I see it, the logical core of the debate over mergers subdivides into the following three questions:

1. What is the central economic role of mergers? In other words, why do mergers occur and what are their economic consequences?

2. Given the economic role of mergers (whatever it is), what is an appropriate merger policy?

3. To what extent does explicit consideration of international business activity affect the answers to questions 1 and 2?

I do not propose here to answer all of these questions, or any of them for that matter. I do hope to provide some new insights, especially concerning question 3. Both questions 1 and 2 are the subject of a very large academic literature. Question 3, on the other hand, has, to my knowledge, not been very thoroughly addressed in the academic literature.

Section 2 of the paper selectively reviews parts of the literature on the economic role of mergers and merger policy. Section 3 presents some background material on the large and expanding role of international trade, investment and financial transactions in Canada's economy, and Section 4 analyzes the relevance of international considerations for merger activity and merger policy. Section 5 contains concluding remarks.

2.0   THE ECONOMIC ROLE OF MERGERS

2.1   Some Definitions

A merger is the amalgamation of two firms, or parts of two firms, into a single firm. Most mergers are "takeovers"; one firm (the "bidder" or "acquiring firm") buys and absorbs another firm, or part of another firm (the "target"). The difference between a merger and a simple (non-merger) purchase of physical assets is that a merger involves the purchase of a business unit as a going concern.

It is normal to distinguish between three types of mergers — horizontal mergers, vertical mergers, and conglomerate mergers. Horizontal mergers are mergers between two business units that produce essentially the same product, for example, the merger of Amoco and Dome Petroleum referred to earlier. Both firms are in the oil exploration business (among other things). A vertical merger is a merger between two firms that would otherwise be in a potential buyer-supplier relationship; a merger between firms carrying out adjacent steps in a production process. If Dome Petroleum had been taken over by Trans Canada Pipelines, the merger would have been a vertical one. A conglomerate merger is a merger between firms carrying on different lines of business; like, for example, if Dome had been bought by Alcan Aluminum. Many mergers have both vertical and horizontal elements, so the distinction between the three types is not always clear in practice. This distinction is, however, conceptually useful.

The merger process is often referred to as the "market for corporate control," reflecting the idea that the important aspect of mergers is that they transfer control of business units from one set of owners and managers to another.[7] This buying and selling of business units is a market like any other. One can then apply the standard economic analysis of markets to this "market" for corporate control. For example, if this market satisfies the conditions of perfect competition, then control over business units should wind up in the hands of those who can most effectively use them. If, on the other hand, market imperfections, such as asymmetric information, are important in this market, then we might expect it to perform poorly from the public interest point of view.

2.2   Horizontal Mergers: Theory and Evidence

The debate over merger policy is most acute with respect to horizontal mergers. The standard analysis of horizontal mergers (see for example Williamson 1968) focuses on the tradeoff between the reduction in competition caused by a merger and the increase in efficiency due to the exploitation of the advantages of size or "economies of scale."

Consider an extreme case. Suppose there are two firms in an industry, and that production in the industry is characterized by very strong economies of scale (like production of wide-body jet aircraft), so that both firms have downward sloping average cost curves over all reasonable ranges of production. If the firms merge, the new firm could, if it chose, produce the same output as the two firms had previously, and at lower average cost. There is an obvious efficiency gain arising from realization of economies of scale.

Unfortunately, the new firm would not choose to produce the old level of output. If the new monopoly firm wishes to maximize profits, it will restrict output, raise price, and cause an increase in the standard allocational inefficiency associated with monopoly power. Depending on the nature of competition in the original duopoly situation, the monopoly outcome resulting from the proposed merger might be welfare-improving or welfare-reducing, using the standard surplus measures of economic policy analysis.

An example of this type is examined in Brander (1981), assuming that the duopoly is of the Cournot type, and assuming linear demand. In that example, the duopoly solution is more socially efficient than the monopoly, even though there are unexploited economies of scale to be had. In other words, the proposed merger would be welfare-reducing from the social point of view. It is worth emphasizing that the firms themselves would do well. If stock markets behave rationally, both target firm and bidder firm should be able to get an excess return. That excess return is based, however, on a transfer from consumers, not on a net improvement in efficiency.

Suppose, on the other hand, that despite substantial economies of scale, there were many firms in the industry, as if producers of wide-body jet aircraft were as prolific as corner groceries. At this extreme it seems obvious that a few mergers would be in the social (and private) interest. Where should the line be drawn? In some countries there has been an effort to use concentration ratios as a guide. The four-firm concentration shows the fraction of sales accounted for by the largest four firms. One simple rule would be that if this ratio were to go above a certain level, then a merger should not be allowed.

Unfortunately, the use of concentration ratios is not well grounded in economic analysis. Whether a horizontal merger is welfare-reducing or welfare-improving depends crucially on the nature of demand in the industry, on the structure of costs, and perhaps most importantly, on the mode of competitive rivalry between firms in the industry. Interestingly, Canada's new *Competition Act* explicitly states (Section 64[2]) that concentration data should not be the sole basis for finding that a merger substantially lessens competition.

A lot of empirical work has been done on mergers. In Chapter 7 of this volume, Espen Eckbo reviews a large number of papers that use financial stock market data to evaluate mergers. Most of this work, unfortunately, does not directly address the social costs and benefits of mergers. These papers ask whether mergers generated net gains to the firms involved, as measured by changes in the stock market prices of the shares of bidder and target firms around the merger announcement date. The general conclusion of this work is that there are private gains to mergers, and that most of the gains go to shareholders of target firms; there is a significant increase in share prices of target firms during the merger process, and a smaller increase in share prices of bidder firms.

The problem with trying to use these results for an evaluation of merger policy is that even if there are gains to firms involved in the mergers, it does not follow that the public interest is necessarily being served. As mentioned above, the gain to the firms might arise either from efficiency gains, or from an increase in monopoly power, or from some combination of the two. If the gains come from an increase in monopoly power, then social welfare is probably being reduced, not increased.

One of the few stock market papers that addresses the market power hypothesis directly is Eckbo (1985). In this paper Eckbo evaluated the effects of horizontal mergers on the stock market performance of rival firms in the industry. If reductions in the number of firms cause a significant increase in monopoly power, then product prices in the industry should rise, and all firms in the industry should earn higher profits. These higher profits, if rationally anticipated by investors, should lead to a rise in stock prices of the rival firms at the merger date. If we can assume that rival firms should experience no change in their efficiency levels, then the stock market return to these rivals represents a "pure" measure of the change in (anticipated) monopoly power.

Eckbo concludes that his analysis, based on a very large sample of U.S. mergers, shows no evidence in favour of the market power hypothesis. My own reading of Eckbo's results is slightly different: that there is weak but significant evidence in favour of some market power effects.

The other major line of empirical work that bears on the effects of horizontal mergers has been generated by economists working in the area of industrial organization. This line of work tests the relationship between concentration and profitability, using cross-section accounting data. In effect, the analyst looks across a sample of industries and asks whether industries with high levels of concentration have higher than normal profits. If so, and if these above normal profits are attributed to monopoly power, and if mergers increase concentration (which they would do unless offset by induced new entry or by very strange behaviour in the industry), then there is some evidence that mergers create monopoly power. Three studies of this type using Canadian data are Bloch (1981); McFetridge (1973); and Jones, Laudadio, and Percy (1973). Weiss (1974) surveys 54 such studies, most of which examine U.S. data. The overall conclusion of this work is that there is a modest but significant link between concentration and profitability.

Finally, one other empirical study of horizontal mergers should be mentioned. In a recent piece of work, Ravenscraft and Scherer (1987) analyze the actual *ex post* performance of mergers and acquisitions using U.S. accounting data.[8] They examine the balance sheets and income statements of the business units involved at the merger date and again several years later. (The length of time between these accounting "snapshots" of the business units varied from merger to merger.) This is the most direct attempt to evaluate the private performance of mergers, although there are natural problems with the kind of data used. Ravenscraft and Scherer found small negative private returns to horizontal mergers. The study does not try to estimate social losses or gains.

2.3   Vertical and Conglomerate Mergers

Although there is a substantial literature on vertical mergers or "vertical integration," the basic economics of vertical mergers is much less clear than the theory of horizontal mergers. This lack of clarity arises from lack of general agreement among analysts over what the essential aspects of vertical mergers are, and from ambiguity in the results coming from most models of vertical integration. In short, there is no "received theory" of vertical mergers. Williamson (1971) is a standard reference in the area, and Kaserman (1978) is a valuable survey of the literature on vertical integration.

The natural reaction to a proposed vertical merger is that it may reduce competition. Surprisingly, however, there is a well-known line of argument that runs in exactly the opposite direction. Suppose that firm A is a monopoly supplier of some important input to firm B, which is in turn a monopolist in consumer markets. If the two firms are separate, then firm A charges a monopoly markup on the input sold to firm B, raising firm B's costs. Firm B then charges a monopoly markup in the consumer market. If firm A and firm B were to merge, then the distortion associated with charging a monopoly price for the transaction between firm A and firm B disappears, and overall allocational efficiency may rise. In effect, vertical mergers reduce the number of steps at which monopoly power is used, and may, therefore, reduce the total social cost of monopoly power.

The case just described is the case of bilateral monopoly. Moving to other market structures greatly complicates the analysis. My reading of competition law and competition policy discussions is that vertical mergers are of greatest concern in oligopoly situations. Suppose there is one firm in an "upstream" industry, and that there are several firms in a "downstream" industry. The downstream industry buys essential goods or services from the upstream industry. The fear seems to be that if one downstream firm merges with the upstream firm, the merged firm will discriminate against the rival downstream firms. If it refused to deal with the downstream rivals altogether, then it could, in the absence of entry, establish a monopoly in the downstream industry.

In more complex situations, such as "bilateral oligopoly" — oligopoly in both upstream and downstream industries, economic theory is ambiguous concerning the effects of vertical mergers on performance (judged by standard economic welfare criteria). This leaves the question to empirical work. I am aware of very little empirical work that directly addresses the social performance of vertical mergers. There is work that assesses the private performance of vertical mergers, using both stock market returns and accounting data. As already indicated, the stock market evidence reviewed by Eckbo in Chapter 7 of this volume generally suggests positive private returns to mergers. This summary statement includes both horizontal and non-horizontal mergers. Eckbo (1986) finds that in Canadian merger data, the private performance of horizontal mergers is better, but not significantly better (in the statistical sense) than the private performance of non-horizontal mergers. Ravenscraft and Scherer (1987) find that vertical mergers had negative private returns, and performed more poorly, as measured by accounting profits, than horizontal mergers.

As for conglomerate mergers, economic theory has relatively little to say. Presumably, the basic rationale for such mergers is that there is some advantage to carrying out two separate activities in the same firm. (Such advantages are referred to as "economies of scope.") For example, it is often suggested that the marketing network in place to market one line of products can be effectively used to market another line of products acquired by the firm through a merger. In any case, conglomerate mergers have no obvious effect on the competitiveness of particular markets, because, by definition, conglomerate mergers are mergers involving firms producing in different markets.

Some critics, such as Francis (1986), have argued that conglomerate mergers lead to undesirable concentrations of political power.[9] This concern focuses on "aggregate concentration" – the fraction of total economic power (usually measured by sales or by total assets) accounted for by some small subset of large firms, such as the largest 10 firms or largest 50 firms.[10] I know of no research that would suggest what the "danger point" for such concentration ratios would be.

2.4   Merger Waves

Any theory of mergers should be able to explain the main facts of merger activity. Probably the most striking fact about mergers is that they seem to occur in waves. Table 1 shows the number of mergers in Canada from 1960 through 1986, and reports the number of "large mergers" from 1978 through 1986.

The general character of the merger data is seen more easily in graphical form. Figure 1 shows total merger activity and shows the breakdown of total mergers into domestic and foreign. Foreign takeovers have increased sharply in relative importance in the 1980s.

The data from the *Annual Report of the Director of Investigations and Research, Competition Act,* is based on counting mergers as they are announced in newspapers, and is published with a warning that it may be less than completely accurate. The data on large mergers collected by W.T. Stanbury is also based on newspaper sources. The number of mergers is probably a less important number (for most purposes) than is the total (constant dollar) value of mergers, which is not readily available. Also, as economic growth occurs and new firms are created, one would expect the number of mergers to rise correspondingly. It is hard to determine how to "normalize" or deflate the data, but in Figure 2, I show the ratio of mergers to real GDP.

Even these relatively crude data show one important aspect of merger activity. Mergers seem to occur in waves. In Canada, one wave peaked in 1969 and a second wave seems to be peaking in 1986 or 1987. The 1961 year could also possibly be regarded as a peak. U.S. merger data shows a similar pattern.[11] Shughart and Tollison (1984) construct a diagram of U.S. merger activity for the period 1895 to 1980 which shows very striking peaks in 1901, 1929, 1946, 1956, and 1968. In addition, like Canada, the U.S. seems to be experiencing a merger peak currently.

The term "wave" in this description is used rather loosely. What analysts mean by a "wave" in this context is simply that the merger series rises and falls with an amplitude that is large compared to the average level of merger activity. The wave pattern is not sufficiently regular to be

Table 1
Mergers in Canada, 1960-1987

Year	Foreign	Domestic	Total	Large	Year	Foreign	Domestic	Total	Large
1960	93	110	203		1974	78	218	296	n/a
1961	86	152	238		1975	109	155	264	3
1962	79	106	185		1976	124	189	313	3
1963	41	88	129		1977	192	203	395	1
1964	80	124	204	data	1978	271	178	449	9
1965	78	157	235		1979	307	204	511	9
1966	80	123	203	not	1980	234	100	414	13
1967	85	143	228		1981	200	291	491	23
1968	163	239	402	avail-	1982	371	205	576	2
1969	168	336	504		1983	395	233	628	3
1970	162	265	427	able	1984	410	231	641	4
1971	143	245	388		1985	466	246	712	16
1972	127	302	429		1986	641	297	938	42
1973	100	252	352		1987p	622	460	1082	47

Definitions: Foreign means the acquiring company is foreign owned. Domestic means the acquiring company is Canadian owned. Large means "over $100 million (nominal) in transaction value."

Sources: Annual Report, Director of Investigations and Research, *Competition Act*; W.T. Stanbury's list of "large mergers" in Canada — see Appendix 1 of this volume.

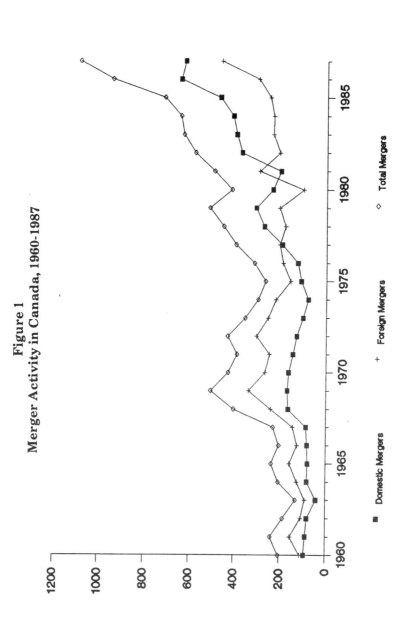

Figure 1
Merger Activity in Canada, 1960-1987

■ Domestic Mergers   + Foreign Mergers   ◇ Total Mergers

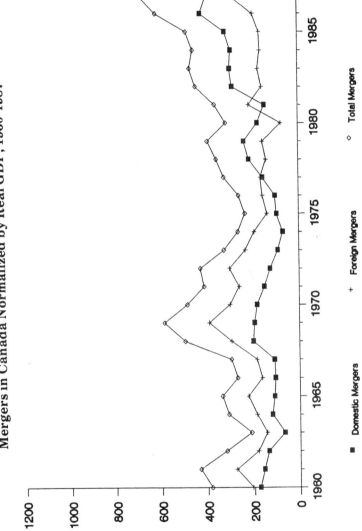

Figure 2
Mergers in Canada Normalized by Real GDP, 1960-1987

■ Domestic Mergers   + Foreign Mergers   ◇ Total Mergers

described as a "cycle." Somewhat surprisingly, however, Shughart and Tollison (1984) conclude that the U.S. merger series is not statistically different from a random walk. A random walk would arise if the number of mergers in a particular year was equal to the number in the previous year plus a random error term with expected value zero. My view is that the interpretation offered by Shughart and Tollison is flawed, and that the term "wave" describes the data well.

2.5 Implications for Merger Policy

The basic theory and empirical work on mergers described above have several implications for merger policy. First, theory and evidence do suggest that merger activity is a legitimate policy concern. Some mergers can be expected to increase monopoly power to an extent that is damaging to the public interest. More policy concern should be addressed to horizontal than vertical mergers, which in turn are of greater concern than conglomerate mergers. (Close to half of Canada's mergers are horizontal at the two digit Standard Industrial Classification (SIC) level.[12]) However, particularly with vertical mergers, and even with horizontal mergers, it is difficult to formulate general procedural rules that would allow determination of which mergers are in the public interest and which are not. Any general rule, such as a concentration ratio rule, would dissolve some desirable mergers and let through some undesirable mergers. It might still be in the public interest to have such a rule. As with traffic lights, sometimes a red light stops cars when there is no reason to stop them (i.e., when there are no cars coming the other way), but red lights are still a valuable policy tool.

3.0 THE INTERNATIONAL ENVIRONMENT

The principal objective of this paper is to consider the implications of the international environment for merger activity and policy. Section 2 carried out the necessary first step of reviewing the basic theory and evidence concerning mergers. No specific consideration of the international environment was undertaken. In Canada, however, the international environment is important for almost any area of potential policy concern, because Canada's economy is very heavily integrated with the world economy. Furthermore, the role of international activity has been growing.

As Table 2 shows, about one-third of Canada's GDP is exported. Even those firms that are not in the business of exporting or importing are affected by the international environment. Many are in competition with imported products, many depend on imports for essential inputs to their own production, many raise money in foreign financial markets, and virtually all are affected by the conditions of international financial markets.

Table 3 makes two striking points – the international or foreign component of Canadian chartered bank assets is very high; and it has grown sharply since 1970. (We might also note in passing that the real size of chartered banks has also grown very substantially since 1970.) This table is evidence of the financial integration of Canada with the rest of the world.

Table 2
Canadian Exports, 1960-1985

Year	Exports	GDP	Exports/GDP
	(in billions of 1981 dollars)		
1960	23	110	17%
1965	33	157	19%
1970	55	265	25%
1975	70	283	22%
1980	93	343	27%
1985	125	246	32%

Source: *Economic Review*, (Ottawa: Department of Finance, 1986).

Table 3
Chartered Bank Assets
(billions of 1981 dollars)

Year	Domestic	Foreign	Total	Foreign Share
1970	82.7	33.7	116.4	29%
1975	127.4	51.5	178.9	29%
1980	189.7	121.7	311.4	39%
1985	197.6	165.0	362.6	45%
1986	204.9	162.9	367.8	44%

Source: Calculated from Bank of Canada, *Financial Review* (Ottawa, various issues).

Table 1 illustrates the importance of foreign firms in the merger process *per se.*

Various other pieces of data could be used to verify the "openness" of the Canadian economy — foreign investment in Canada is very substantial and Canadians are heavy investors in other countries; foreign currency transactions are an important part of Canadian financial transactions; Canadian dollar instruments are held as assets by foreign banks and individuals; and the cyclical movements of Canada's economy are closely correlated with events in the rest of the world.

One very important fact about Canada's integration with the world economy is that it consists mostly of integration with the U.S. economy. For example, about 75 per cent of Canada's trade is with the U.S. A similar proportion applies to most other indicators of international integration. Pragmatically, from Canada's point of view, international really means "Canada-U.S." Canada, of course, is also the most important trading partner of the U.S., but the fact that Canada is only about 10 per cent of the size of the U.S. means that the relative impact of Canada on the U.S. is small.

For some months, Canada and the U.S. have been involved in "free trade" negotiations. Trade barriers between the two countries have fallen dramatically over the past 20 years already, as a result of multilateral tariff reductions under the General Agreement on Tariffs and Trade (GATT), and as a result of the Canada-U.S. Automotive Agreement (Autopact). Even so, a further reduction in trade barriers would increase integration between the two economies even more.

To summarize this section, the business environment confronting Canadian firms is, to a very large extent, determined outside of Canada. In fact, it is hard to know what a "Canadian" firm really is. Many firms that have their head offices in Canada are more that 50 per cent foreign-owned, as was true of the great bastion of Canadian nationalism, Dome Petroleum. Conversely, Canadian investors, especially institutional investors such as pension funds, have very substantial equity holdings in foreign firms. By far the most important part of the international environment for Canada is the U.S. economy.

4.0   MERGER ACTIVITY AND POLICY: INTERNATIONAL CONSIDERATIONS

4.1   International Integration and Merger Activity

The creation of an international market for corporate control tends to increase merger activity. Consider the case of two very small countries, each of which is "protected" by various government restrictions on foreign ownership and outflows of financial capital. If the two countries remove capital controls between themselves, merger activity should rise.

The basic point is that as the population of firms in a particular market grows, the chance of two firms finding a mutual coincidence of wants grows. Thus the increasing integration of the world economy would be expected to increase the proportionate amount of merger activity. The usual gains from trade should follow from this process. This does not refer to gains from trade in final products, but gains from trade in shares of corporations; in the market for corporate control.

The other observation is that the times series pattern of merger activity in one country should be similar to the time series pattern in those countries with which it is closely integrated. Thus, for example, one would expect Canada's merger activity to have a similar wave pattern to merger activity in the U.S., which it does. We do not, however, have a good explanation for why U.S. merger activity seems to follow a wave pattern.

4.2 International Competitiveness and Merger Policy
In this section I examine the case made by Eyton (1986) and others, that mergers are required so that Canadian firms can compete in world markets. The importance of this argument rests first on the importance of economies of scale. As mentioned earlier, economies of scale are advantages that arise from increasing the scale or amount of production. If all production processes were characterized by constant returns to scale, so that average cost was the same whether output was very large or very small, then there could be little in the way of efficiency reasons for mergers.

If, on the other hand, economies of scale and scope are important in most industries, then large firm size would be important in achieving high levels of efficiency, and in promoting the public interest. The first empirical question, therefore, is "how important are economies of scale?" Measuring economies of scale is, unfortunately, rather difficult. The degree of economies of scales varies substantially from industry to industry and, as technology changes, over time within any industry.

There have been several attempts to put together estimates of economies of scale for Canadian industries. See, in particular, Gorecki (1976), Caves *et al.* (1980), Harris with D. Cox, and Daly and McCharles (1986). None of these researchers would place great confidence in the estimates of economies of scale that they have gathered. However, the general picture these various estimates paint is probably fairly reliable. It is that there are substantial unexploited economies of scale in many Canadian industries, particularly manufacturing industries.

In a country that is isolated from foreign competition, it might be worth foregoing realization of economies of scale so as to avoid concentrations of monopoly power. For example, before 1965, Canada's automobile industry was protected from foreign (including U.S.) competition by significant tariffs. Nevertheless, the major auto manufacturers all operated in Canada, and produced a full line of models, even though this meant that all models were produced at inefficiently low scales of production. Much lower average costs could have been achieved by having a single firm produce one or two models only. The disadvantage would have been that the single firm would have had too much monopoly power, and consumer variety would have been restricted. Therefore mergers in this situation would not have been a good idea.

However, as trade barriers fall, domestic monopoly power is very sharply constrained by foreign competition. Even if there is only one producer of some product in Canada, that producer will not have much market power if there are five or six foreign producers that have open access to the Canadian market. Increasing foreign competition allows increased exploitation of economies of scale, more competition, and greater product variety all at the same time. From the businessperson's point of view, the situation resulting from trade liberalization looks much as Eyton (1986) suggests. The business firm perceives pressure to rationalize production, possibly by merger, possibly by increasing specialization within the firm. Merger activity would, therefore, be promoted by trade liberalization, and this is not a force that should be resisted, for it is from this process that gains from trade arise.

The discussion so far relates to horizontal mergers. We can expect horizontal mergers as a reaction to an increasingly competitive environment caused by trade liberalization. Furthermore, there is also a role for conglomerate mergers. Any major trade liberalization will produce winners and losers. In Canada, a Canada-U.S. free trade agreement will likely cause a decline in the textile and clothing industries, for example. One way of dealing with industrial decline is to have declining firms merge with expanding firms in related industries that can make use of the human and physical resources in these declining firms. In short, merger activity is a natural and relatively painless way of organizing the economic restructuring that is required by changing external circumstances.

4.3   Merger Policy and "Rent-Shifting"
The conclusion to be drawn from the preceding discussion of international competitiveness is that the same principles apply to mergers of firms involved in international trade that apply to firms in purely local markets. Both groups of firms should be competitive. The difference is that international markets provide a lot of competition from foreign firms, and this should be taken into account in assessing the anticompetitive effects of mergers.

In this section, however, a different principle is introduced, although it follows from the discussion of mergers and market power in Section 2 above. The idea is simply that monopoly power is not such a bad thing, from a domestic point of view, if domestic firms can earn monopoly rents from foreign markets. Therefore, the optimal domestic merger policy is different for industries that are export oriented than for domestically oriented industries.

As discussed in Brander and Spencer (1981, 1984) policy can be used to shift economic rents between countries. Suppose that the objective of domestic merger policy is to maximize domestic welfare. Consider first an industry that produces and sells strictly in the home market. The appropriate policy is to have the economy operate as closely as possible to Adam Smith's competitive ideal, which means blocking or dissolving anticompetitive mergers. Increases in market power resulting from mergers would increase the profits of domestic firms, but at the expense of domestic consumers, and there would be an additional loss due to allocational inefficiency. Anticompetitive mergers would therefore be undesirable.

If, however, an industry were producing strictly for export markets, the situation would be quite different. In this case, domestic welfare would be maximized by having the industry organize as a monopoly cartel. As a cartel the industry would extract the maximum profits it could. In this case, however, there are no losses to domestic consumers, for the simple reason that there are no domestic consumers. Total returns to domestic nationals consist of profits to domestic shareholders of the firm, taxes to the government, and rents to the workers of the industry. This benefit is maximized by having the industry earn monopoly profits from the world market. Foreign consumers lose, of course, but that is not the concern of the domestic government. In short, merger policy has a rent-shifting aspect to it. Economic benefits can be transferred from foreign consumers to domestic nationals.

In the case of an industry that both exports and sells domestically, there is a tradeoff. The more important domestic consumption is as a share of total sales, the more competitive the industry should be. The practical policy implication of this reasoning is that mergers should be encouraged in industries that are export oriented, and restricted in industries that produce for domestic consumption, if the objective is to maximize domestic welfare.

Politicians do not use such reasoning directly in public debate, but this effect seems consistent with much of what we observe. The OPEC oil cartel was an obvious example. The large net exporters of oil such as Saudi Arabia and Iraq did not want competitive firms extracting and selling petroleum. Their solution was to take over the management of the petroleum industries in their countries, and try to run the industry like a cartel. They made enormous gains by doing so.

This rent-shifting effect of mergers is a "beggar-thy-neighbour" policy. It is rare, however, that such policies have political repercussions in consumer nations. The main reason is that in order to earn monopoly profits, the domestic cartel has to cut back the total quantity sold in the foreign market. The cartel raises prices and earns higher profits, but quantity sold falls. This is bad for foreign consumers, but it is good for foreign producers who compete with exports from the cartel. It seems that foreign producers are much more effectively represented in national political processes than consumers are.

In fact, it is frequently the case that governments encourage cartel behaviour by foreign firms (with or without mergers). One well known example is the Japanese automotive voluntary export restraint (VER) of 1981-1985. In 1981, the U.S. government negotiated an agreement with the Japanese government and with Japanese auto manufacturers to reduce exports of automobiles from Japan to the U.S. (see Feenstra 1985). In effect, this converted the industry into a cartel. The net effect was to increase the average price of new American cars by something in excess of $1000 per car.[13]

As a result of the VER, the U.S. auto manufacturers made very substantial profits, and the policy is generally regarded as having been a "success." Both U.S. and Japanese firms did well, but the price was paid by U.S. consumers in the form of higher prices (on all new cars, not just

Japanese imports) that averaged at least $1,000 per car. In 1986, Lee Iacocca, CEO of Chrysler, received $20.5 million in income from Chrysler.[14] In addition he wrote a best-selling autobiography (the royalties on which he gave to charity). He is widely regarded as a folk hero. While Iacocca very likely is a good manager, and has probably made many improvements at Chrysler; by far the single most important factor improving the fortunes of Chrysler was the VER.

The point of this case is that the VER forced the Japanese producers to restrict sales to certain quotas. In order to restrict sales, prices were allowed to rise toward monopoly levels. In effect, U.S. policy, under pressure from heavy lobbying by Iacocca and others, induced the Japanese auto industry to extract rent from the U.S. economy through monopoly pricing. The net cost to U.S. consumers, was, of course, far higher than the gain to the U.S. auto companies, which was substantial in itself. At $1000 extra per car, it requires sales of only 20,500 cars to cover Iococca's income in 1986.

Canada also imposed VERs on Japanese auto manufacturers in 1983.[15] This policy is even less rational for Canada than for the U.S., because a large share of the profits going to the "Canadian" auto companies flows to U.S. shareholders.

Similar reasoning applies to the recent controversy concerning sales of softwood lumber from Canada to the U.S. The American producers argued that Canadians were selling too much softwood lumber at subsidized prices in the U.S. market. After prolonged wrangling involving many parties, the net effect was that Canada was induced to impose a 15 per cent export tax on softwood lumber shipped to the U.S. Prices of softwood lumber in the U.S. have risen and Canadian sales have fallen. However, for the first time in many years, Canadian citizens are actually receiving general revenue from the forest resource of the country. In addition, the rate at which the forest resource is being "mined," while still too high,[16] is depleting the forest stock less rapidly than was the case before the export tax. U.S. consumers, of course, are paying higher prices for softwood lumber.

My view is that the Canadian public interest is being very well served by the export tax, despite the fact that the Canadian government was, for public consumption at least, dragged kicking and screaming into the "agreement." The U.S. public interest, on the other hand, is being damaged by the agreement, despite the fact that it was for U.S. political reasons that the tax was imposed. The effect of the policy has been to shift economic rents arising from the forest industry from the U.S. to Canada.

Analysis of these cases, and many less publicized cases, suggests that the "rent-shifting" effects of various policies, including merger policies, can be important. Another point illustrated by these cases is that many policy areas seem to be completely controlled by producer interests, at the expense of the national public interest.

5.0   CONCLUDING REMARKS

Canadian merger policy prior to the *Competition Act* of 1986 had very little impact. I believe that antimerger policy has been underutilized in Canada, and that the economy would have performed better if Canadian authorities had undertaken more policy actions to increase the competitiveness of the economy. Part of the reason for the ineffectiveness of merger policy in Canada has been an unworkable set of competition laws that were written remarkably badly.[17] One suspects that people intent on reducing the power of the competition policy have had a major hand in writing such laws over the years. The *Competition Act* of 1986, however, is a great improvement over its predecessors, and is, in my view, a very good piece of legislation.

The reform in competition law has come at a time when Canada is engaged in trade liberalization negotiations with the U.S. If the negotiations are successful, the need for active antimerger policy will be much reduced, because the competitiveness of the Canadian economy will rise to the more competitive level of the U.S. economy. The *Competition Act* of 1986 has tried to deal explicitly with concerns arising from international economic activity.

We still do not understand the reasons for mergers very well. Analysts have not been able to agree on the relative importance of efficiency improvements as opposed to monopoly power entrenchment in the recent history of mergers. Moreover, we have no good explanation for the striking wave-like time series behaviour of mergers (recall Figure 1). We do know that the informational requirements for assessing any particular merger are very high, and include considerable amounts of confidential material which is not available to academic researchers for careful scrutiny.[18]

In this paper, I have addressed the economic effects of mergers. However, much of the concern expressed over mergers, for example, in Francis (1986), is a concern over the political consequences of merger activity. Francis criticizes what she sees as a tendency for power and influence to become concentrated in the hands of family dynasties through the merger process. International considerations do not bear on this phenomenon, for competition from foreign imports creates very little corresponding domestic political power. Political power is more closely correlated with ownership of production capacity in Canada than with sales. Furthermore, Canadian nationalists are very upset by the prospect of foreign firms or individuals exercising political influence in Canada.

Merger policy, however, is a very bad tool for trying to prevent concentration of power. If family dynasties are a problem, they should be dealt with through inheritance laws (which are badly in need of revision). If individual levels of wealth and influence are too highly concentrated, tax laws should be amended to remove the many tax loopholes that allow the wealthy to pay very modest taxes. In addition, there are incentives for merger activity created by tax laws. These distortionary tax laws should be changed, but that is the subject of another paper.[19]

The principal objective of this paper has been to shed some light on the role of international considerations for merger activity and merger policy. I believe that the international environment does have important implications for mergers. Canada's increasing openness to the international economy expands the size of the market for corporate control, and increases its proportionate importance and its efficiency. Furthermore, the international environment increases competition in Canadian product markets and creates pressure on Canadian firms to rationalize. In addition, if domestic firms exercise their monopoly power in foreign markets, then Canada gains as a result, and these gains may offset losses due to monopoly power within in Canada. All of these factors increase the appropriate level of permissiveness for merger policy.

There is, of course, still an appropriate role for merger policy. Some mergers restrict competition unreasonably and should be dissolved or modified. Of particular concern are areas where international competition is not very important. Reflections on the behaviour of Canada Post, Air Canada, and agricultural supply management schemes, however, suggest to me that the greatest abuses of monopoly power in Canada are in areas where monopoly power has been created by government.

NOTES

1. See, for example, "Dome's Last Deal," *Maclean's*, May 4, 1987, pp. 34-42. After increasing its bid by over $400 million, Dome's bankers agreed to the takeover in November 1987.

2. See Stanbury (1986) for a description and critical review of the *Competition Act* and the *Competition Tribunal Act* of 1986 (Bill C-91). See also Goldman, Chapter 21 in this volume.

3. The pre-notification sections of the *Competition Act* came into effect on July 15, 1987.

4. The leading case was *K.C. Irving*, see Reschenthaler and Stanbury (1977a).

5. As quoted in Peter C. Newman, "Business Watch," *Maclean's*, December 15, 1986, p. 36.

6. *Maclean's*, August 26, 1985, p. 26. More generally, see Ghert (1985).

7. More generally, see the paper by Eckbo, Chapter 7 in this volume.

8. Scherer summarizes some of their results in Chapter 8 of this volume.

9. See also the paper by Stanbury, Chapter 17 in this volume.

10. See the papers by Khemani and Marfels, Chapters 1 and 3 in this volume.

11. See also the data in Marfels, Chapter 3 in this volume.

12. Eckbo (1986) reports 389 horizontal mergers and 484 non-horizontal mergers for the 1964-1983 period, using the 2-digit SIC. This was the entire population of mergers for which Eckbo (1986) was able to obtain SIC information for both acquiring and target firms.

13. From 1980 to 1982 new car prices rose by $2,600. A study by Wharton Econometric Forecasting Associates (1983) attributes $1000 of this

price rise to the VER. Presumably, post 1982 increases were also substantial.

14. *Business Week*, May 4, 1987, p. 51.

15. *Globe and Mail*, "Talks begin on quotas with Japan" May 15, 1984, p. B2.

16. There is considerable dispute over the appropriate rate at which to harvest timber. Useful discussions of this issue can be found in the Economic Council of Canada (1984), Wilkinson (1985) and MacKay (1985).

17. My colleague Bill Stanbury emphasizes that criminal law was simply the wrong tool for the job.

18. Indeed, one of the problems with the scrutiny of mergers by the Bureau of Competition Policy is that where the Director decides *not* to challenge a proposed merger before the Competition Tribunal, the public (and academics) are able to obtain very little information with which to "second guess" the Director.

19. See the paper by Blenkarn, Chapter 23 in this volume.

REFERENCES

Bloch, Harry (1981) "Concentration and Profitability in Canadian Manufacturing: An Indirect Test of the Effect of Aggregation," *Canadian Journal of Economics*, Vol. 14, February, pp. 130-135.

Brander, James A. (1981) "Intra-industry Trade in Identical Commodities" *Journal of International Economics*, Vol. 11, February, pp. 1-14.

Brander, James A. and Barbara J. Spencer (1981) "Tariffs and the Extraction of Foreign Monopoly Rents Under Potential Entry," *Canadian Journal of Economics*, Vol. 14, August, pp. 371-389.

_____ (1984) "Trade Warfare: Tariffs and Cartels," *Journal of International Economics*, Vol.16, May, pp. 227-242.

Caves, R., M.E. Porter, M. Spence, and J.T. Scott (1980) *Competition in the Open Economy: A Model Applied to Canada* (Cambridge, Mass.: Harvard University Press).

Consumer and Corporate Affairs Canada (various years) *Annual Report, Director of Investigation and Research, Competition Act* (formerly Combines Investigation Act) (Ottawa: Ministry of Supply and Services).

Daly, Donald J. and D.C. McCharles (1986) *Canadian Manufactured Exports* (Montreal: Institute for Research on Public Policy).

Eckbo, B. Espen (1985) "Mergers and the Market Concentration Doctrine: Evidence from the Capital Market" *Journal of Business*, Vol. 58, pp.325-349.

_____ (1986) "Mergers and the Market for Corporate Control: the Canadian Evidence," *Canadian Journal of Economics*, Vol. 19 (May), pp. 236-260.

Economic Council of Canada (1984) *Western Transition*, (Ottawa: Ministry of Supply and Services).

Eyton, J. Trevor (1986) "Corporate Concentration – its Impact on Canada's Economy" address to the *International Trust Executive Forum on the Management of Change*, Ontario Club, September 29, 1986.

Feenstra, Robert C. (1985) "Automobile Prices and Protection: the U.S.-Japan Trade Restraint," *Journal of Policy Modelling*, January.

Francis, Diane (1986) *Controlling Interest: Who Owns Canada?* (Toronto: Macmillan).

Ghert, Bernard (1985) *Brief on the Green Paper: The Regulation of Canadian Financial Institutions* (Toronto: Cadillac Fairview Corporation).

Globerman, S. (1977) *Mergers and Acquisitions in Canada*, Study No. 34 for the Royal Commission on Corporate Concentration (Ottawa: Ministry of Supply and Services).

Gorecki, P.K. (1976) *Economies of Scale and Efficient Plant Size in Canadian Manufacturing Industries* (Ottawa: Ministry of Supply and Services).

Harris, Richard G. (with David Cox) (1984) *Trade, Industrial Policy and Canadian Manufacturing* (Toronto: Ontario Economic Council).

Jones, J.C.H., Leonard Laudidio, and Michael Percy (1973) "Market Structure and Profitability in Canadian Manufacturing Industry: some Cross-Section Results," *Canadian Journal of Economics*, Vol. 6, August, pp. 356-368.

Kaserman, D.L. (1978) "Theories of Vertical Integration: Implications for Antitrust Policy" *Antitrust Bulletin*, Vol. 23, pp. 483-510.

MacKay, Donald (1985) "You Can't See the Forest," *Canadian Business*, Vol. 58, February, pp. 54-58.

McFetridge, Donald G. (1973) "Market Structure and Price-Cost Margins," *Canadian Journal of Economics*, Vol. 6, August, pp. 344-355.

Newman, Peter C. (1986) "A Banker Lashes Out at Takeovers," *Maclean's*, December 15, p.36.

Ravenscraft, David J. and F.M. Scherer (1987) *Mergers, Sell-Offs, and Economic Efficiency* (Brookings: Washington, D.C.).

Reschenthaler, G.B. and W.T. Stanbury (1977a) "Benign Monopoly: Canadian Merger Policy and the K.C. Irving Case," *Canadian Business Law Journal*, Vol. 2(2), pp. 135-168.

_____ (1977b) "A Clarification of Canadian Merger Policy," *Antitrust Bulletin*, Vol. 22, pp. 673-85.

Shughart, William F. II and Robert D. Tollison (1984) "The Random Character of Merger Activity," *Rand Journal of Economics*, Vol. 15 (Winter), pp. 500-509.

Stanbury, W.T. (1986) "The New Competition Act and Competition Tribunal Act: "Not with a Bang, but a Whimper," *Canadian Business Law Journal*, Vol. 12(1), pp. 2-42.

Weiss, Leonard W. (1974) "The Concentration-Profits Relationship and Antitrust" in Harvey J. Goldschmid, H. Michael Mann, and J. Fred Weston, eds. *Industrial Concentration: The New Learning* (Boston: Little, Brown).

Westfield, Fred M. (1981) "Vertical Integration: Does Product Price Rise or Fall?," *American Economic Review*, Vol. 71, June, pp. 334-346.

Wharton Econometric Forecasting Associates (1983) *Impact of Local Content Legislation on U.S. and World Economies*, July.

Wilkinson, Bruce W. (1985) "Canada's Resource Industries: A Survey," in John Whalley, ed. *Canada's Resource Industries and Water Export Policy*, Vol. 14, Research Studies, Royal Commission on the Economic Union and Development Prospect for Canada (Toronto: University of Toronto Press).

Williamson, Oliver E. (1968) "Economics as an Antitrust Defence: The Welfare Tradeoffs," *American Economic Review* Vol. 58, March, pp. 18-36.

_____ (1971) "The Vertical Integration of Production: Market Failure Considerations," *American Economic Review*, Vol. 61, May, pp. 112-123.

Chapter 6

Merger Boom – 1986

R.F. Mason
Merger and Acquisition Specialist
Woods Gordon
Management Consultants
Toronto

1.0 INTRODUCTION

I propose to give a practitioner's view of the so-called merger boom which Canada has recently been experiencing. Indeed, 1986 was a busy year for Canadian corporations and their financial advisors. The $100 million plus club had 25 members transacting at an aggregate value of approximately $10 billion.[1] This group included $2 billion-plus events: the Gulf Canada acquisition of Hiram Walker Resources and the Imasco acquisition of Genstar.[2] For comparative purposes you should note that 1985 saw 19 mega deals with an aggregate value of $9.8 billion, but 1984 had only four deals totalling $700 million.[3] In the United States there were 454 mergers worth at least $100 million in 1986, including 39 transactions in excess of $1 billion each.[4]

Undeniably a merger boom exists today in the U.S. and Canada, with new announcements appearing weekly.[5] In 1987 W.T. Stanbury's data indicate there were 47 takeovers in Canada in which the value of the transaction exceeded $100 million. Their average value was $556 million.[6] Interestingly, though, the U.S. data indicate that we appear to be experiencing a surge in the dollar value of mergers, not a dramatic increase in the number of combining entities. To illustrate; approximately 3,200 merger announcements with a value in excess of $1 million were made in the U.S. during 1986.[7] In 1969, however, 6,100 announcements were made and in 1970 some 5,200 transactions were reported. These years, of course, reflected the final excesses of the conglomerate era, that period when small- to medium-sized companies found a way to manufacture earnings per share increases by rather indiscriminate acquisition of other unrelated small- to medium-sized companies. While this transaction count data may be revealing, the most startling difference between 1969 and 1986 is the dollar value of the transactions which occurred in the past year. In 1969, there were 2,300 transactions which reported prices paid with a total value of $23.7 billion. In 1986, there were 1,400 transactions which disclosed prices with a total value of $147.6 billion. Here we have the phenomenon of roughly half the number of transactions producing nearly seven times the value. Even allowing for inflation, something fundamentally different seems to be going on.

What has been occurring, of course, is a trend toward very much larger companies being involved in merger transactions. As I noted above, the $100 million-plus club in Canada had 25 members in 1986[8] and 454 members in the United States.

2.0 CAUSES OF MERGERS

In my view the following four factors largely account for the current level of merger activity in Canada and elsewhere in much of the western world:

1. The prospect of economic gain,

2. The availability of "product,"

3. Government policy,

4. Sufficient financial capital.

I believe these factors to be pervasive in explaining what we have seen in 1986, and are seeing in the first quarter of 1987. I propose to examine each in greater detail.

2.1 Prospect of Economic Gain

In our capitalistic society, businessmen are usually motivated to transact by the prospect of economic gain. Recent years have seen a general return to more stable economic conditions, at least for some industries, although businessmen in the oil and gas industry would hotly debate that conditions are more stable, not to mention better.

Notwithstanding the difficulties in the oil patch, economic conditions have improved, as is evident to many businessmen. We have seen these improved economic conditions in the form of reduced rates of inflation and interest on borrowings, and increased corporate profits. For most industries, though, this healthier economic climate has not brought with it much in the way of real growth. Without real growth, or with only modest real growth prospects, businessmen have to temper their aspirations in terms of further improvement in corporate profits, once the last of the more readily obtainable efficiency gains are squeezed out of the system.

In the Canadian food industry I have labelled this problem "the tonnage gap." This is the difference between physical units which would have to be produced to meet business plan expectations and those which are likely to be produced based on market share and market growth of, say, 2 per cent per annum. As this problem is analyzed, companies decide to invest resources in two main areas: new product development, and acquisition programs.

The first alternative is by nature something less than a quick fix, and fraught with uncertainty. Despite these difficulties, new product development is pursued, and must be pursued, by those committed to the industry. It is the second alternative, though, which has the greatest short run appeal, because if the right acquisition candidate can be found growth can be manufactured through the combination of two businesses. That is, the acquirer is able to show real growth in its business through the act of acquiring another business.

There is a catch in this apparently simple process which is related to the price which may have to be paid to get the deal. For example, during 1986 a reasonably well-known private company in the food industry, Primo Foods, came on the market. This company was attractive because of its size, its well-known pasta brands, and its general position in the store-door distribution channel. The prospect was hotly pursued by a number of multinational food companies, and it sold quickly at a price estimated to have exceeded 20 times its most recent year's earnings.

The United States multinational which acquired Primo achieved the instant growth in volume which an acquisition affords, but what about the accompanying gain in profitability? At a purchase price of 20 times earnings, not much falls to the bottom line after financing costs, even in today's environment of cheaper money. There is no simple answer to this particular dilemma, but we are in the era of strategic planning and the strategic business plan usually lets the purchaser convince himself, maybe quite rightly, that the profit performance of his new subsidiary will grow significantly over a three- to five-year period. This optimism is usually justified by the strategic rationale of the business plan and the much greater resources of the multinational. Whether the benefits of multinational ownership will be realized is for the future to tell, but the prospect of economic gain is evident.

Up to this point I have talked about only one fairly obvious form of economic gain—first create volume, then profit will follow, but there are others which also propel businessmen to transact. I would like to examine one other situation which might, for want of a better term, be labelled "the strategic move."

The Bombardier acquisition of Canadair is a recent example of a sizeable "strategic move," some might say a strategic gamble.[9] Bombardier is a transportation company which is best known for its mass market introduction of snowmobiles in 1959. Today its interests range broadly into mass transit vehicles and a variety of other motorized vehicles and equipment. In December 1986 it entered the airframe business when the previously announced Canadair transaction finally closed after being sanctioned in Parliament. But why did Bombardier enter the very difficult field of executive jets sweetened with some defence contract offset work? The difficulty with this business is that it is not only highly competitive but also extremely variable in terms of volume. To make matters worse, the Canadair domestic market is not nearly large enough to support a manufacturer of this highly exotic product. Despite these difficulties, Bombardier appears to have concluded that since it was able to acquire the Challenger airframe technology at no front end cost ($1.5 billion of development costs having previously been written off by the government), and with this technology having a 20 plus year life, it made for a viable strategic investment.

Both of these examples illustrate how companies might be induced to transact for large sums and sometimes at high prices for the prospect of economic gain. In a higher real growth economy, it is possible that neither of the above transactions would have taken place as the purchasers could well have been preoccupied with internal growth opportunities demanding both capital and executive time.

2.2 Availability of Product
It is trite to say but nevertheless axiomatic that the willing buyer cannot buy unless the willing seller will sell. Recent years have definitely seen an upsurge in the quantity of available acquisition product. At this point I should digress slightly to define two different types of sellers:

1. Those placed on the market, often labelled divestitures,

2. Those dragged into the market, sometimes called takeover targets.

I suppose there could be a third category of transaction, namely, those that just seem to happen without much malice of forethought on either side. However, the less consciously made deal is fading in this strategic marketing age.

On the divestiture front, over 1,200 of the reported 3,000 United States transactions of 1985 were defined as being divestitures.[10] I do not have comparable divestiture data for Canada, nor have I tallied the exact number of hostile takeovers in either country. But on the takeover battlefield the evidence of exotic measures and countermeasures with such colourful names as the "front end loaded bust up bid" and the "poison pill" speak loudly enough regarding the frequency and significance of the hostile tactic. Even the relatively staid capital markets of Canada have seen the likes of Union Enterprises,[11] Hiram Walker,[12] R.L. Crain,[13] and most recently, Canadian Tire.[14]

What are the factors which bring acquisition product to market? The most fundamental and pervasive factor has been labelled economic restructuring. I am not an economist and I do not profess to understand why, in a relatively short timeframe, so many basic economic relationships have been challenged and upset. However, it seems that the 1980s ushered in an economic environment characterized by disinflation, increased global competition and rapid technological advances which contemporaneously created new markets and weakened others. Many corporate managers spent long hours in corporate strategy sessions debating how their businesses could best be repositioned in the face of new realities. Those that didn't probably woke up to find that their companies, undervalued by the stock market, had been taken over, or sold by a dissatisfied parent. Suffice it to say that strategic thinking and economic restructuring seem to go hand in hand. Frequently a by-product of these deliberations and events is a decision to sell. Sometimes the decision to sell was preordained at the very moment of acquisition, such as in the Kohlberg, Kravis & Roberts leveraged buyout of Beatrice Foods, or in our own most recent example of Imasco buying Genstar with the immediately ensuing second stage divestitures of the non-financial service businesses.[15]

In another contemporary example the Laurentian Group bought Eaton Financial Services during July 1986 in a share exchange transaction valued at $101 million. Eaton Financial Services (EFS) came to market after Eaton's had concluded that the marketing of consumer oriented financial services through its retail chain could be greatly enhanced under the auspices of a major financial institution. The Laurentian Group, dedicated to building a diversified financial services business, recognized the opportunity to gain access to a new distribution channel as well as forming an alliance with a major consumer marketing organization. Eaton's converted its 100 per cent interest in EFS for a significant minority holding in a diversified, multinational financial services institution.

In addition to product brought to market by restructuring or strategic asset redeployment, a secondary but not unimportant source is the family business. Obviously, succession of ownership of family businesses is not a new phenomenon. However, it now appears that many of these businesses are too large for ready transfer between generations, or the current generation for various reasons is not particularly interested in carrying on. In any event, many of these businesses now come to market in the form of an organized divestiture. Primo Foods, to which I referred above, is a good example.

The last factor I would like to touch on is that of market momentum. Put simply, the more divestitures that are done in a visible and successful manner, the more that will be done. It does not take long for a market success to get around the business community and create an impetus to transact for those who might be considering divestiture but were reluctant to expose their situation to the market. Frequently financial advisors encounter new potential divestiture situations when out in the market talking to purchasers about the particular acquisition product they may currently have on offer.

2.3 Government Policy

The issue of government policy could be an endless subject and I propose to touch on it in the broadest possible manner. One view of government policy is that businessmen will do almost anything that is economically sensible unless prevented from so doing by law or regulation and may often be encouraged to do what is not very sensible by sufficient government incentive. Many of Canada's more marginal natural resource investments attest to the efficacy of public monies at work. However, let me focus on the types of policy which seem to relate most directly to merger activity; which are:

1. Economic nationalism,

2. Competition policy legislation,

3. Fiscal regulations.

In Canada, economic nationalism, when on the ascendancy, has manifested itself in direct government ownership of corporate assets, a classic example being Petro-Canada; and in the systematic exclusion of non-Canadian investors from the marketplace through the Foreign Investment Review Agency (FIRA). In the last few years a wholesale reversal of the policies supporting economic nationalism has taken place, and headlines in the financial press now scream "Canada for Sale" — in both the public and the private sectors.[16] Interestingly, from the merger perspective, both nationalization of business and privatization of government assets add to the volume of deals in the market. I have already referred to Canadair; more recently, but at long last, Teleglobe has been acquired by a private sector purchaser, Memotec.[17] On the other hand, FIRA clearly did prevent merger consummation, or in some cases incubation, where no domestic buyer was evident. Conversely, Investment Canada is accommodating to the foreign investor, maybe too accommodating for the liking of some observers.

Market oriented competition policy in Canada is just emerging and so far it has been used to frustrate the proposed sale of Palm Dairies to a consortium of western dairy cooperatives.[18] This attempt by Unicorp to regurgitate a piece of Burns Foods picked up during the Union Enterprises takeover has for the moment been stopped by the Competition Tribunal.[19] The braking force which it might apply to merger trends is not yet clear as there is still insufficient experience in the administration of the new statute. Undoubtedly this new law will become a factor in Canadian mergers, particularly where dominant market shares might result.

In the United States, by way of contrast, the easing of antitrust rules has stimulated merger activity, particularly in larger deals. The Reagan Administration's free market approach has stressed the irrelevancy of size and importance of efficiency, paving the way for large-scale vertical and horizontal mergers between suppliers and customers, and between competitors respectively.

No discussion of government policy as it affects mergers can ignore fiscal or tax policy as it is known in the corporate world. Tax laws generally affect three things in any given transaction:

1. The percentage of the proceeds retained by the vendor,

2. The ultimate cost of the acquisition financing to the purchaser,

3. The return on investment generated by the acquired business for the new owner.

The rules which affect these three factors are complex and subject to amendment with each federal budget. Most businessmen would argue that they are presently too restrictive but I doubt that they are a major disincentive to transact in Canada.

2.4 Sufficient Financial Capital

The Western world appears to have experienced a great accumulation of financial capital in recent years in the banking system and in other financial pools such as insurance companies and pension funds.

An increasing share of these funds have been directed toward various forms of acquisition financing. The trend is most evident in the United States where a number of financing specialists have established leveraged buyout pools funded by insurance companies and pension funds which, together with bank support, are capable of acquiring corporations valued in the billions of dollars.[20] Earlier I mentioned the Beatrice Foods transaction sponsored by Kohlberg, Kravis & Roberts, which had a price tag of US $6.2 billion. While the tolerance of heavy debt financed deals by these institutions may be surprising or even shocking to some observers, to me they appear to have been undertaken in response to the same economic conditions which created the "tonnage gap" for the food companies. Like the food companies, the institutions have looked to the acquisition market for economic gain. Lack of real growth in conventional lending or investing has propelled these institutions into the promising acquisition market with its higher margins and greater risks for the players.

So, we have economic factors both creating a demand for acquisitions, and creating a supply of available product as well as a flow of funds to make the transactions possible. The whole acquisition financing market in the U.S. has become even more attractive to the institutional participants as it is now possible to liquidate some or all of their initial positions into a secondary market. We have not reached the secondary market stage in Canada yet, but the lesser liquidity of our market has not impaired the flow of funds in support of mergers.

3.0 IMPLICATIONS OF MERGERS

It is most unnerving to try to synthesize the future out of events past and present. It appears that the size barrier in corporate mergers has been breached, which I suspect must create some insecurity within the ranks of management. Almost no entity is too large to be taken over or divested for lack of performance or creation of value for the shareholders.[21] The positive effect of this insecurity may be leaner and more astute corporate management. The negative effect may be shorter range planning to create value today at tomorrow's expense.

Financial institutions are in the merger business to stay; as providers of funds, advisors, and deal initiators. However manifested, this constitutes a move toward investment banking which will demand a rethinking of culture and structure within these organizations. Much dislocation, and many mistakes, will occur.

The debate on foreign ownership of the Canadian economy will once again be raised. Hopefully, FIRA will not re-emerge as we cannot expect to maintain our standard of living in a global economy if we approach business with a parochial mind set.

The Competition Tribunal will be busy trying to adjudicate the conflict between the need for large national entities capable of functioning in global markets and the interests of Canadian consumers.[22]

We will continue to see excesses in the markets such as of foolishly high prices, attempts to abuse minority shareholders, and ponderous restructurings of dubious merit.[23]

It should be interesting.

NOTES

1. In Appendix 1 of this volume, data are provided on mergers in Canada involving a change of control in which the transaction value exceeded $100 million. This series indicates there were 42 such mergers in 1986 with an average value of $389 million.

2. See Appendix 1 of this volume.

3. According to Professor Stanbury's data (Table 1, Appendix 1), there were 16 large mergers with a total value of $8.2 billion in 1985 and four in 1984.

4. See also the paper by Marfels (Table 9), Chapter 3 in this volume.

5. See, for example, "Let's Make a Deal," *Time*, December 23, 1985, pp. 44-55; "Deal Mania," *Business Week*, November 24, 1986, pp. 74-93; "The Top 200 Deals: Merger Mania's New Accent," *Business Week*, April 17, 1987, pp. 273-292. See also "The Gathering Takeover Frenzy," *Maclean's*, August 26, 1985, pp. 26-28; "The New Takeover Frenzy," *Maclean's*, April 7, 1986, pp. 26-28; "Takeover?" *Globe and Mail*, January 3, 1987, pp. D1, D8.

6. See Appendix 1 of this volume.

7. W.T. Grimm & Co., *Mergerstat Review 1986*, p. 2. See also *Business Week*, April 17, 1987.

8. See Note 1 for a much higher estimate.

9. "Bombardier steps into the billion-dollar class, Everyone wins in Canadair sale," *Financial Times*, August 25, 1986, p. 6; "Ottawa selling Canadair to Bombardier," *Globe and Mail*, August 19, 1986, pp. B1-B2; "Bombardier flying into some rough weather," *Financial Post*, August 30, 1986, p. 3.

10. See, for example, "Splitting Up: The Other Side of Merger Mania," *Business Week*, July 1, 1985, pp. 50-55; "For Better or For Worse: The Biggest Restructuring in History Winds Down. What Did It Mean?" *Business Week*, January 12, 1987, pp. 38-40.

11. See Elaine Dewar, "Takeover," *Canadian Business*, November 1985 and December 1985 (2 parts).

12. See Peter Fosher, "Let's Make a Deal," *Saturday Night*, September 1986, pp. 15-22.

13. "Crain family split heartens acquisitors," *Globe and Mail*, September 11, 1986, p. B3; "Crain takeover bid back in judge's lap," *Globe and Mail*, February 13, 1987, p. B7.

14. See, "The Epic Struggle," *Maclean's*, January 26, 1987, pp. 26-33.

15. See, for example, "Crawford's Imasco," *Financial Post*, February 27, 1987, pp. 1-2. The article notes that Imasco paid $2.6 billion for Genstar in mid-1986, and realized $2,568 million from its divestitures. In other words, it obtained the prized Canada Trustco for almost nothing! Yet in 1985 Genstar Corp. paid $1,250 million for Canada Trustco. See also "Imasco sells U.S. real estate business it acquired through Genstar acquisition," *Globe and Mail*, June 9, 1987, p. B6. This article indicates that with its 13th spinoff Imasco will have generated over $2.8 billion from Genstar's assets.

16. See Warren Grover, "The Investment Canada Act," *Canadian Business Law Journal*, Vol. 10(4), 1985, pp. 475-482.

17. See, for example, "Small firm tops big rivals' bids for Teleglobe," *Globe and Mail*, February 12, 1987, pp. A1-A2; "Win puts underdog Memotec in big league," *Globe and Mail*, February 12, 1987, pp. B1-B2; "Memotec's Tangled Roots," *Maclean's*, March 23, 1987, pp. 42-45.

18. "Unicorp Fuels a Fight," *Maclean's*, January 5, 1987, pp. 14-15.

19. "Palm Dairy sale halted by bureau," *Globe and Mail*, January 16, 1987, p. B3.

20. See, for example, "Power on Wall street: Drexel Burnham is Reshaping Investment Banking—And U.S. Industry," *Business Week*, July 7, 1986, pp. 56-63.

21. See, for example, "Takeover Tugs-of-War," *Time*, October 20, 1986, pp. 72-73; Gary Hector, "Is Any Company Safe From Takeover?" *Fortune*, April 2, 1984, pp. 18-23; "Let's Make a Deal," *Time*, December 23, 1985, pp. 44-55; "The Battle for Corporate Control," *Business Week*, May 18, 1987, pp. 102-109. More generally, see the paper by Espen Eckbo, Chapter 7 in this volume.

22. See the discussion in Goldman, Chapter 21 in this volume.

23. See, for example, "Bigger Yes, But Better?" *Time*, August 12, 1985, pp. 32-33; "New? Improved? The Brand Name Mergers," *Business Week*, October 21, 1985, p. 108-116; Anne B. Fisher, "The Decade's Worst Mergers," *Fortune*, April 30, 1984, pp. 262-270.

Chapter 7

The Market for Corporate Control: Policy Issues and Capital Market Evidence*

B. Espen Eckbo
Faculty of Commerce & Business Administration
University of British Columbia

The directors of such [joint-stock] companies, however, being managers rather of other people's money than of their own, it cannot be well expected, that they should watch over it with the same anxious vigilance with which the partners in a private copartnery frequently watch over their own. Like the stewards of a rich man, they are apt to consider attention to small matters as not for their master's honor, and very easily give themselves a dispensation from having it. Negligence and profusion, therefore, must always prevail, more or less, in the management of the affairs of such a company (Adam Smith, [1776] 1937, p. 700).

1.0 INTRODUCTION
1.1 The Issues
Over the past decade, few economic phenomena have attracted as much empirical research — and public attention — as the various forms of transactions in what Manne (1965) dubbed "the market for corporate control." Corporate events such as mergers, tender offers, proxy fights, spinoffs, defensive takeover tactics, etc., are fascinating not the least due to the vast amount of money involved. Transactions in this market in 1985 were at a record level of $180 billion in the U.S., with 3,000 deals of which 36

* Financial support from the Ministry of Finance and Corporate Relations of the Province of British Columbia is gratefully acknowledged.

exceeded one billion dollars.[1] Because there are clear "winners" and "losers" in many of these transactions, it is not surprising that the changes associated with corporate control transactions have stirred considerable political controversy. Corporate managers who face the possibility of being fired after a "hostile" tender offer understandably complain, both directly through the media and indirectly through their political representatives, that takeovers are damaging to the morale and productivity of their organizations and that they force an excessive preoccupation with short-term profits. While this argument is clearly self-serving[2] – and appears inconsistent with empirical evidence[3] – the resulting pressure on regulators and legislatures to enact restrictions that would curb takeover activity has been sufficiently strong to produce a myriad of state and federal regulations of transactions in the corporate control market. In early 1986, even the U.S. Federal Reserve Board joined the regulatory bandwagon by issuing a new and controversial interpretation of margin rules that restricts the use of debt in takeovers.[4]

Opponents to federal and state intervention in the market for corporate control argue that such intervention fundamentally curbs the flow of corporate resources toward more productive uses and helps to insulate inefficient management from the disciplinary forces of the market place. Inherent in the separation of ownership and control observed in publicly held corporations is a fundamental conflict of interest between the owners (the shareholders) and their agents (managers) who themselves own little – if any – of the corporation's shares. Since the vast majority of shareholders diversify their holdings across firms in order to reduce their exposure to firm-specific risk[5], large corporations end up with shareholder clienteles consisting, in large part, of investors who individually hold only a small fraction of the total number of shares outstanding. In this situation, the costs of monitoring incumbent managers will exceed the benefits for each (small) investor, and the majority of the firm's shareholders will remain passive owners of the corporation. Implicitly, these shareholders must rely on market forces, such as competition among managers, to align the interests of managers and owners. In the vernacular of Jensen and Ruback (1983. p. 6):

> The managerial competition model . . . views competing management teams as the primary activist entities, with stockholders (including institutions) playing a relatively passive, but fundamentally important judicial role. Arbitrageurs and takeover specialists facilitate these [corporate control] transactions by acting as intermediaries to value offers by competing management teams, including incumbent managers. Therefore, stockholders in this system have relatively little use for detailed knowledge about the firm or the plans of competing management teams beyond that normally used for the market's price setting function. Stockholders have no loyalty to incumbent managers; they simply choose the highest dollar value offer from those

presented to them in a well-functioning market for corporate control, including sale at the market price to anonymous arbitrageurs and takeover specialists. In this perspective, competition among managerial teams for the rights to manage resources limits divergence from shareholder wealth maximization by managers and provides the mechanism through which economies of scale or other synergies from combining or reorganizing control and management of corporate resources are realized.

Under this view, curbing takeover activity fundamentally threatens the basic structure which supports the survival of large publicly held corporations as an efficient organizational form. While there may indeed be instances where regulation of the possible actions taken by *incumbent management* (as opposed to the market) can be optimal,[6] regulators must carefully avoid external effects on the corporate control market which threatens to "throw the baby out with the bath water."[7]

From the above, it is clear that a policy of regulating corporate control transactions involves a certain risk in terms of reducing the overall efficiency of the corporate sector. The central issue, however, is an empirical one. To what extent can one argue that the intended benefits of regulation in fact are likely to outweigh the social costs? The purpose of this review is to provide a perspective on this difficult issue by bringing together the results of recent capital market based research. While most of the traditional evidence on corporate acquisitions that was generated prior to 1984 is well summarized elsewhere,[8] this review emphasises new results, including recent evidence based on acquisitions in Canada, the United Kingdom, and France, as well as studies that directly analyze the wealth impact of various federal and state regulations of the market for corporate control.

1.2 Outline of the Paper

Section 2 reviews the literature which is primarily concerned with documenting the gains/losses to bidder and target firms. To what extent does this evidence indicate the nature of the sources of gains from takeovers? What are the implications for a general analysis of the effect of regulating corporate control transactions? This section provides an international comparison of the performance of bidders and targets in mergers and acquisitions.

Section 3 analyses some of the implications of recent methods used by incumbent target management in order to fend off a bidder. Are certain defensive strategies likely to be more harmful than beneficial to target shareholders? Is it reasonable to assume that market forces fail to eliminate defensive strategies which are not in the shareholders' interest?

Section 4 discusses actual effects of implementing rules requiring bidder and target firms to publicly disclose their private information which (presumably) motivates the takeover attempt. Do we need government regulation to ensure that shareholders have sufficient time and information to make "informed decisions" in takeovers? What are the likely social costs of such regulation? Should one automatically require certain types of takeover bids to be made via a public offer rather than allowing the acquisition to take place in a private transaction? The discussion in this section draws on evidence from takeovers in the U.S. and in France.

Section 5 discusses the traditional — and still controversial — issue of monopoly and antitrust, with reference to the law enforcement history in the U.S. Do mergers between producers in the same industry, which by definition increase industry concentration, harm consumers by increasing the market power of the merged firm? Are the regulatory agencies able to discriminate between truly anticompetitive and truly efficient mergers through their criteria for selecting which mergers to prosecute? To what extent will an aggressive antitrust policy accidentally deter socially desirable, efficient mergers?

Section 6 looks at the recent Canadian experiment with a policy of restricting foreign participation in the domestic market for corporate control. To what extent did the Canadian government succeed in its objective of using the corporate control market to increase the national benefits from investments by foreign individuals and corporations?

Each section has a four-part structure: The first part contains descriptive and institutional characteristics; the second part provides a theoretical perspective on central hypotheses; the third part reviews the empirical evidence; and the fourth part discusses policy issues and implications of the evidence. Section 7 presents a brief summary of some of these policy implications.

1.3   On the Comparative Advantage of Stock Price Evidence

Before turning to the evidence itself, note that the fundamental issues discussed in this paper are all addressed by means of testable hypotheses which yield predictions concerning the reaction of *stock prices* to public announcements of firm-specific news. The approach of studying stock price reactions to major corporate events has several important comparative advantages. Suppose a merger has the effect of changing the price the firm can obtain for its output as well as the prices it must pay for the factors used in the production of this output. Accurately assessing the impact of the merger on firm profitability using *factor and output prices* (instead of stock prices) would be possible only if one could correctly specify the firm's demand and cost functions. Since such specifications would be arbitrary, empirical inferences would be unreliable. Arbitrary assumptions would also have to be made concerning the *time delay* between the stockholder approval of the merger and the merger's actual impact on product and factor prices. Moreover, the analysis would necessitate an arbitrary definition of what constitutes a *normal* product price change, i.e., the product price change that would have occurred if the merger had not taken place.

In contrast, there is ample evidence that an unbiased assessment of the effects of public information releases about firm profitability is quickly incorporated into stock prices.[9] Thus, the firm's stock price will change immediately upon the public announcement of the merger, and this stock price change measures directly the present value of the net change in the firm's future profit stream (long-term as well as short-term) expected to take place due to the merger. Under weak assumptions, such as stationarity of the distribution of stock returns over the year prior to the merger announcement, this merger-induced stock price change can be used to draw reliable inferences concerning underlying hypotheses explaining the microeconomic effects of merger activity. Stock prices are readily available from the University of Chicago Center for Research in Security Prices covering daily records of all firms on the New York and the American Stock Exchanges since 1962, and the University of Laval covering monthly records of firms listed on the Toronto Stock Exchange since 1963. Hence this approach allows for the use of large samples of mergers, which tends to eliminate the noise present in individual firm data. Attesting to the robustness of the empirical methodology, the conclusions drawn by different authors who focus largely on overlapping merger samples, but who use different methods for estimating merger-induced wealth effects, are virtually indistinguishable.[10]

Note also the fundamental difference between an analysis based on data measuring *ex ante* expectations vs. *ex post* realizations. As always, managerial decisions are made *ex ante*, i.e., without the benefit of *ex post* hindsight. Thus, the question of whether mergers represent "good business judgment" cannot be properly evaluated if the researcher uses hindsight. To illustrate, a finding that a certain number of completed mergers fail to live up to manager's *ex ante* expectations of making a profit represents a manifestation of the trivial fact that a merger, like almost any other investment, is indeed a *risky* venture.[11] Risk in itself has never constituted an argument against undertaking an investment project. The issue is whether mergers, *given* the perceived riskiness, are valuable investment projects. It is precisely this issue which the market addresses when it responds to the announcement that the firm is going to merge. In this sense, the stock price reaction to the merger announcement is an *ex ante* measure of the profitability of the merger investment.

The exclusive focus in this review on studies based on capital market data by no means implies that other data sources are uninteresting. As discussed below, there are situations where stock price data is insufficient to discriminate between the underlying hypotheses. Furthermore, there are also non-trivial problems associated with estimating the *total* acquisition-induced abnormal stock return. Ideally, one would prefer to complement the stock price evidence with a variety of other firm-specific characteristics, such as organizational structure, capital structure (in terms of market values), details of the production/investment strategy, and ownership structure. Data of this type is extremely costly to produce and has therefore not been analyzed for large samples. Furthermore, as pointed out above, the absence of general theories describing the equilibrium values of these firm characteristics — and how they should change in response to takeovers — makes it particularly difficult to draw consistent and meaningful inferences from this type of data.

Attempts to analyze complementary (non-stock-price) data are perhaps particularly useful when it appears that a managerial action systematically causes a share price *decrease*.[1,2] A share price decrease is consistent with the class of hypotheses which holds that non-trivial monitoring costs allow entrenched managers to undertake actions which benefits themselves at the expense of shareholders (referred to as "the managerial entrenchment hypothesis"). The problem is that unless one can reasonably identify the nature of the managerial benefits from the action studied, one cannot draw any strong conclusions in favor of the entrenchment hypothesis based on the share price decrease alone. The stock price decline could be an error due to the market's lack of inside information possessed by managers, or, even if the managerial decision itself is value-maximizing, *the price decline could result from an exogenous reduction in profitability that the managerial action reveals to the market*.[13] Here, accounting, ownership, and institutional data may provide a clue to understanding the hypothesized managerial benefits underlying the managerial entrenchment argument. More generally, such data can help provide additional insights into the difficult issue of what constitutes the sources of the observed wealth effects of takeovers. Thus, although not reviewed here, complementary research based on information other than security price data is clearly important in order to fully understand the economics behind the market for corporate control.[14]

2.0   WEALTH EFFECTS OF TAKEOVER BIDS

2.1   Methods for Acquiring Corporate Control

Takeovers can occur through merger, tender offer, or proxy contest, and sometimes elements of all three are involved. In mergers or tender offers the bidding firm offers to buy the common stock of the target at a price in excess of the target's previous market value. Mergers are negotiated directly with target managers and approved by the target's board of directors before going to a vote of target shareholders for approval. Since the target's management has veto power in a merger (they can refuse target shareholders the opportunity to vote on the merger), a merger is sometimes dubbed a "friendly" takeover in the sense that target management do not necessarily lose their jobs after the merger.

Tender offers, on the other hand, are offers to buy shares made directly to target shareholders who decide individually whether to tender their shares to the bidding firm. The tender offer is outstanding for a fixed period of time, usually three to four weeks. Offers can be "any-or-all," where the bidder agrees to purchase any shares that are tendered; "all-or-nothing," where the bidder accepts no shares unless a prespecified minimum number of shares is tendered; and "two-tiered," e.g., consisting of a tender offer for a sufficient amount of shares to get voting-control of the board as well as a follow up merger offer (usually at a somewhat lower price per share). Since tender offers can occur without target management's approval, this takeover method is particularly useful when the bidder firm's objective is to replace the target management. Thus, some tender offers are dubbed "hostile" takeover bids. Note, however, that tender offers can also be "negotiated," in the sense that the target management may have agreed to support the offer and actually assisted in structuring, say, a two-part deal. Third, a proxy contest occurs when an insurgent group, often led by a dissatisfied former manager or large stockholder, attempts to gain controlling seats on the board of directors. A proxy contest typically begins in the months prior to the firm's annual meeting where shareholders elect the board of directors. Prior to the meeting, both incumbent management and the dissident group seek votes from the shareholders in a manner similar to a political campaign. They forward proxy solicitation materials to stockholders, who in turn sign and return the proxy form of the preferred group, authorizing the agents nominated in the form to vote the shares. The group obtaining a majority of the votes will generally elect a majority of the board:

> The proxy contest can be regarded as a device to instigate a change in corporate management when the board has failed to respond to pressure for such a change. Rather than replace only the top managers, a successful proxy contest achieves a wholesale change by replacing the board as well. Furthermore, it is quite conceivable that the initiative for the contest be generated not just by shareholders, but also by alternative managers or directors, from inside or outside the firm, who are unable to convince the board to dismiss the incumbent officers. As such, proxy contests represent another form by which the managerial labor market . . . operates to discipline corporate managers. In the range of possible disciplinary actions, the proxy contest lies somewhere between a board dismissal of management and an outside takeover by another corporation (Dodd and Warner 1983, p. 405).

2.2   Theoretical Issues

2.2.1   Six Hypotheses Explaining the Motives behind Takeovers:

In order to succeed, the bidder must offer a price per target share which exceeds the target share price just prior to the offer. In fact, the offer premium (i.e., the difference between the offer price and the pre-offer target share price) typically exceeds 20 per cent. Where does the resources needed to pay for this premium come from? Several possibilities have been suggested:

Hypothesis #1: Takeovers generate economic synergies.
This class of theories includes the cost-savings realized as the production and investment policies of the bidder and target firms are integrated, including economies of scale and scope, enhanced organizational efficiencies, increased market power, and various tax benefits.[15] Under this scenario, the acquisition is in principle no different from buying, say, a computer for your secretary: the cost of the purchase (i.e., the purchase price in excess of the second-hand value of the asset) is more than offset by the resulting cost-reduction, broadly defined, elsewhere in the organization. The synergy hypothesis predicts that the takeover increases the market value of both the bidder and the target firm.

Hypothesis #2:   Takeovers replace inefficient target management.
While relocating managerial resources is conceptually equivalent to other resource allocations which generate synergy gains, the issue of replacing inefficient management is typically analyzed separately. As emphasized in the introduction, the market for corporate control places a unique constraint on managerial behaviour. In general, as discussed by Fama (1980), a competitive and efficient labour market will adjust the managerial wage rate to the point where it reflects management's marginal productivity in the best alternative employment opportunity. Thus, the managerial labour market provides a certain safeguard against managerial exploitation of shareholders: assuming the manager has not yet reached retirement, the salary will adjust ex-post to compensate shareholders for wealth losses incurred due to unexpected managerial shirking.[16] However, whether this salary adjustment is sufficient to *completely* eliminate shareholders' concern with managerial shirking is an empirical issue. There may be situations where the value of perks consumed at the expense of shareholders, or the wealth loss incurred due to poor managerial decisions, by far exceeds the current value of the manager's stream of future salary payments. In this case, it is necessary to *replace* the management, not only adjust their salaries. While the responsibility for firing inefficient management rests with the firm's board of directors, the board, which is frequently influenced by the top level management itself, sometimes fails to exercise this power. In this case, the last resort is a takeover, either through a proxy fight or through a tender offer. In addition to predicting that the takeover is beneficial to the shareholders of both the bidder and the target firm, one might expect, under this hypothesis, to find that a target with inefficient management has experienced a period with relatively poor economic performance prior to the takeover.

Hypothesis #3:   The market undervalues the common stock of the target.
The bidder firm may have acquired information which indicates that the target shares are currently undervalued by the market. In order to benefit from this information, the bidder attempts to acquire as many target shares as possible without revealing the information until after the close of the transaction. Of course, if target shareholders understands the motivation behind the bid, they will prefer to keep their shares in order to capture the full benefit of the bidder's information themselves.[17] Thus, this scenario presumes that the bid itself does not perfectly reveal the intention of the bidder. Empirically, this hypothesis predicts that the target share price after a successful tender offer exceeds the offer price.

Hypothesis #4:   Takeovers exploit ex post minority target shareholders.
The minimum number of voting rights needed to replace the board of directors generally differs across firms, with a range from two-thirds of the votes to as high as 90 per cent in some corporate charters. Invariably, it is possible to acquire control of the board without holding 100 per cent of the voting rights. This fact has lead to the following conjecture: a bidder acquiring control of the target will be able to use this control to exploit the

minority target shareholders. To illustrate, suppose (1) it takes 67 per cent of the votes to control the board, and (2) 67 per cent of the target shares can be purchased at the market price prevailing prior to the offer is made (i.e., at a zero offer premium). The bidder purchases 67 per cent and proceeds to "raid" the target minority shareholders by transferring target resources to the bidder at prices below marginal cost.[18]   If the transfer itself does not consume resources, then there is a 33 cent net gain to the bidder on every dollar transferred.   Note that assumption (2) above is crucial for this argument.   Competition among bidders to raid the target will tend to drive the price for the controlling (67 per cent) interest to 100 per cent of the value of the target shares, at which point there is no incentive left for bidders to acquire targets for the purpose of exploiting the minority target share-holders.   The degree of competition depends on whether the technology for transferring resources is available to more than one bidder. For example, if all it takes is a majority vote to merge the target assets with the bidder firm at a sufficiently low price, then one would $-a$ $priori$ $-$expect competition among raiders to be sufficiently strong to eliminate any substantial concern over the possibility of corporate raiding. However, the issue can only be solved empirically, and the unique prediction of this hypothesis is that the target share price after the bidder acquires majority control should be lower than the target share price prior to the tender offer.

Hypothesis #5: Successful bidder firms overestimate the true value of the target shares.

Roll raises the possibility that merger bids arise simply because some managers overestimate the true value of the merger:

> Consider what might happen if there are no potential synergies or other sources of takeover gains but when, nevertheless, some bidding firms believe that such gains exist. The [bidder's] valuation [of the takeover] ... can then be considered a random variable whose mean is the target firm's current market price. When the random variable exceeds the mean, an offer is made; otherwise there is no offer... The takeover premium in such a case is simply a random error, a mistake made by the bidding firm. Most important, the observed error is always in the same direction. Corresponding [negative] errors in the opposite direction are made in the valuation process, but they do not enter our empirical samples because they are not made public [since no offer is being made]. (Roll 1986, p. 199.)

Thus, Roll considers the possibility that mergers are purely the result of irrational bidder behaviour, driven by "hubris" with respect to their own ability to accurately estimate the true value of the takeover gains. Coupled with the proposition that *there are zero true gains from takeovers*, Roll's hubris hypothesis implies that the average gains to bidder firms in observed takeover bids is negative.   This follows because the population average is presumed to be zero, and because bids below the target firm's market price (which would give bidders a positive gain) are not observed and therefore not included in the *sample* averages. Note that the hubris hypothesis does not rely on the assumption that managers *consciously* act against the best interest of their shareholders. It is sufficient that managers act, *de facto*, against shareholder interests by issuing bids founded on mistaken estimates of target firm value.[19]

Hypothesis #6:   Takeovers are initiated by size-maximizing entrenched management.
While the preceding five hypotheses are all consistent with the assumption that managers attempt to act in their shareholders' interest, the "size-maximization hypothesis"[20] explicitly postulates that managers are sufficiently insulated from the "revenge" of the labour and capital markets to pursue goals which benefit themselves at the expense of shareholders. Thus, this hypothesis predicts that, at the margin, merger attempts are negative net present value projects for acquiring firms. This does not preclude the possibility that successfully completed mergers sometimes increases acquiring-firm shareholder wealth. However, "if all acquirors behave as size-maximizers, merger prices will be bid up to the point where merger attempts, on average, have a negative impact on acquiring-firm shareholder wealth" (Malatesta 1983, p.157).

2.2.2 Measuring the Economic Value of Takeover Attempts: The commonly used empirical methodology for measuring the price effect of a merger/acquisition announcement was pioneered by Fama, Fisher, Jensen and Roll (1969) in the context of stock splits. The procedure starts with the assumption that stock returns follow a multivariate normal distribution, which implies that the return on security j is characterized by the following "market model":[21]

$$\tilde{r}_{jt} = a_j + \beta_j \tilde{r}_{mt} + \tilde{\varepsilon}_{jt}, \tag{1}$$

where $\tilde{r}_{jt}$ is the continuously compounded rate of return on security j over period t, $\tilde{r}_{mt}$ is the continuously compounded rate of return on the value-weighted portfolio of all stocks traded in the market over period t, and ε_{jt} is a normally, identically distributed, serially uncorrelated zero mean disturbance term.

Model (1) incorporates the fact that most securities tend to move up or down with the market. Thus, the realized returns are adjusted for market-wide movements to isolate the component of the returns due to news events related to the merger/acquisition. The parameter β_j measures the sensitivity of the j'th firm's return to market movements. The term $\beta_j \tilde{r}_{jt}$ is the portion of the return to security j that is due to market-wide factors. The parameter a_j measures that part of the average return on the stock which is not due to market movements. Lastly, the term ε_{jt} measures that part of the return to the firm which is not due to movements in the market or the security's average return.

The Ordinary Least Squares estimate of equation (1) provides an unbiased forecast of the normal or expected return to security j. Unexpected news events will cause the *realized* return to differ from this *ex ante* expected return, the difference referred to as the security's *abnormal* return (AR_j) over the period. It is this abnormal or unexpected return which is the subject of event studies: AR_j will reflect the firm-specific valuation consequences of news that firm j is involved in a takeover. The "news date" is generally taken to be the date of the first public announcement of the merger/ acquisition event in a major paper such as the (U.S.) *Wall Street Journal* or the (Canadian) *Globe and Mail.*

A typical procedure for estimating the abnormal return is the following: In order to account for the possibility that the merger event itself changes the regression constant α_j and/or the systematic risk β_j two sets of coefficients are estimated, one based on data before the merger event and one based on data after the event. Let τ denote a time period measured relative to the news date. That is, τ equals 0 on the news date, $+1$ one period after the news date, -1 one period before the news date, etc. The abnormal return over event period τ is then computed as

$$AR_{j\tau} \equiv \begin{cases} \tilde{r}_{j\tau} - (\hat{\alpha}_j^b + \hat{\beta}_j^b \tilde{r}_{m\tau}) & \text{for } \tau \le 0 \\ \tilde{r}_{j\tau} - (\hat{\alpha}_j^a + \hat{\beta}_j^a \tilde{r}_{m\tau}) & \text{for } 1 \le \tau \end{cases} \qquad (2)$$

where superscript "hat" denotes OLS-estimate, and superscript b (a) denotes that the coefficient has been estimated using pre-event (post-event) data only. Thus, the procedure employs a pre-event benchmark to estimate abnormal returns up through period 0, and a post-event benchmark to estimate performance after period 0. Time periods used to compute abnormal returns are systematically excluded from the estimation period.

The abnormal return $AR_{j\tau}$ will reflect the valuation impact of all news announcements in period τ, not just the merger/acquisition announcement. In order to randomize the impact of news announcements unrelated to the takeover itself, the researcher collects a sample of merger/acquisition announcements using different firms in different calendar time periods. The abnormal return over event period τ averaged across J such independent merger/acquisition announcements, AAR_τ, where

$$AAR_\tau \equiv \frac{1}{J} \sum_{j=1}^{J} AR_{j\tau}, \qquad (3)$$

is then an unbiased estimate of the average valuation effect of merger/acquisition announcements. If there is uncertainty as to which period is the true news date, it is also useful to construct the abnormal return cumulated over an extended period of time around event period 0:

$$\text{CAAR} \equiv \sum_{\tau=\tau_1}^{\tau_2} \text{AAR}_\tau , \qquad\qquad (4)$$

where τ_1 and τ_2 are the beginning and ending periods in the cumulation, relative to period 0.[22]

Simulations performed by Brown and Warner (1980, 1985) and Malatesta (1986) indicate that the procedure described above has the following characteristics: (i) it is well specified whether one uses monthly or daily time intervals to measure security returns, (ii) it performs at least as well as a Generalized Least Squares procedure designed to take into account any contemporaneous correlation in the residuals of the market model,[23] and (iii) it performs as well as or better than procedures based on more restrictive equilibrium models (such as the CAPM).

The robustness of the econometric technique notwithstanding, the standard methodology does not entirely resolve the following two problems associated with measuring the *total* gains to bidder firms: First, while target firms are acquired only once, acquiring firms frequently merge with several firms over time. Abnormal stock returns measure only the *unanticipated* component of the gains from a takeover, and it is possible that a significant part of the gains to acquiring firms is anticipated prior to the press announcement of the merger and therefore already reflected in the bidder firm's share price.

Second, a measurement problem of a somewhat different nature arises when the bidder firm is large (in terms of total equity) relative to the target. In this case, even if the dollar gains from the merger are split evenly between the bidder and target shareholders, the dollar gains translate into a relatively small *percentage* gain for the bidder. Furthermore, the *precision* of the estimated gain is lower for the larger bidder because the normal variation in equity value is also large relative to a given dollar gain. The analogous problem arises if one were to estimate the change in General Motors' stock price from an important firm-specific event using only a time-series of returns to the value-weighted NYSE index. One possible remedy is to constrain the sample to mergers and acquisitions where the bidder and target firms are of approximately equal size. The problem with this approach is that it typically leads to unacceptably small sample sizes.[24] A second approach is to measure merger gains directly in terms of abnormal *dollar* gains instead of abnormal returns. This can be done by multiplying each return observations in equation (1) by the beginning-of-period firm value. The problem with this approach is that if the disturbances $\bar{\varepsilon}_{jt}$ in model (1) are homoscedastic, as is usually assumed, then the dollar-value weighted disturbances will be heteroscedastic: Disturbance variance will be positively related to the beginning-of-period firm value. Thus, caution must be exercised when making statistical inferences based on abnormal dollar gains as well.

2.3   Empirical Evidence
2.3.1 Successful Mergers and Tender Offers: Table 1 summarizes the abnormal returns to bidder and target firms in successful mergers and acquisitions as reported in the most frequently cited studies in this area. From the evidence in Dodd and Ruback (1977), Bradley (1980) and Eckbo and Langohr (1988), successful bidder and target firms in *tender offers* in the U.S. and target firms in France earn on average significantly positive abnormal returns over the period immediately surrounding the offer announcement date.[25] For *target* firms in the U.S., the abnormal return ranges from 20.6 per cent to 32.2 per cent, with an average across six studies (see footnote a of the table) of 29.1 per cent, all numbers highly significant. For France, Eckbo and Langohr (1988) document 22.0 per cent abnormal return to target firms in tender offers, and 15.3 per cent to targets in privately negotiated controlling-block trades.[26] There is also evidence of significantly positive gains to bidder firms in tender offers: In the U.S., the bidder gains range from 2.8 per cent to 4.4 per cent, with a six-study average of 3.8 per cent. The t-values of these abnormal returns indicate statistical significance on the 5 per cent level or higher. In France, bidders in public tender offers earn 2.7 per cent abnormal returns with a t-value of 6.0, while bidders in privately negotiated controlling-block trades earn 4.2 per cent, with a t-value of 3.0, i.e., both numbers statistically insignificant. There is, to my knowledge, no comparable large-sample evidence on public tender offers in the United Kingdom or in Canada.

Furthermore, there is strong evidence that *targets* in successful *mergers* earn large and significant abnormal returns over the month preceding and including the first public announcement of the merger. In the U.S., the gains range from 13.3 per cent [Asquith (1983)] to 23 per cent [Dodd (1980)]. In the U.K, Franks and Harris (1986) document 23.3 per cent abnormal returns to targets, while Eckbo (1986a) show that targets in Canada earn a somewhat lower 4 per cent average abnormal return in the announcement month.[27] Furthermore, bidder firms appear to make zero or positive abnormal return in the period immediately leading up to and including the announcement date. In the U.S., the abnormal returns range from an insignificant 0.2 per cent [Asquith (1983)] to a significant 3.5 per cent [Asquith, Bruner and Mullins (1983)]. The weighted average across the five studies in the table is 1.3 per cent. In the U.K., Franks and Harris (1986) report a statistically significant announcement month abnormal return of 1 per cent, while Canadian bidder firms on average earn a significant 0.8 per cent over the same month [Eckbo (1986a)].

Of the merger studies in the Table 1, only Dodd (1980) reports significantly negative abnormal returns to bidder firms in mergers over the day of the offer announcement itself. Using larger samples, both Asquith (1983) and Eckbo (1983) report essentially zero bidder firm performance over the announcement day.[28] The *post-merger* performance of bidder firms in successful mergers is, however, subject to more controversy. As shown in Table 2, while bidder firms in successful tender offers earn on average zero abnormal returns in the 12-month period following the offer, there is some mixed evidence that bidders in successful mergers earn significantly

Table 1
Per cent abnormal returns associated with successful tender offers, privately negotiated controlling-block trades and mergers, measured relative to the first public announcement of the offer

(Sample size and t-statistic in parenthesis)

Study	Sample period	Event period	Bidder firms	Target firms
I. Tender offers in the United States				
Dodd and Ruback (1977)	1958-78	Offer announcement month	2.8 (124, 2.2)	20.6 (133, 25.8)
Bradley (1980)	1962-77	Forty days surrounding offer announcement day	4.4 (88, 2.7)	32.2 (161, 26.7)
Weighted average across 6 studies[a]	1956-81		3.8 (478, n.a.)	29.1 (653, n.a.)
II. Tender offers in France				
Eckbo and Langohr (1988)	1966-82	Offer announcement week	-0.3 (53, 0.2)	16.5 (90, 37.6)
III. Privately negotiated controlling-block trades in France				
Eckbo and Langohr (1988)	1972-82	Offer announcement week	0.2 (45, 0.4)	9.5 (93, 22.3)

Table 1 (cont'd)

Study	Sample period	Event period	Bidder firms	Target firms
IV. Merger bids in the United States				
Dodd (1980)[b]	1970-77	20 days before through the first public announcement day	0.8 (60, 0.7)	21.8 (71, 11.9)
Asquith (1983)[c]	1962-76	19 days before through the first public announcement day	0.2 (196, 0.3)	13.3 (211, 15.7)
Eckbo (1983)[d]	1963-78	20 days before through 10 days after first public announcement	1.6 (102, 1.5)	14.1 (57, 7.0)
Asquith, Bruner and Mullins (1983)	1963-79	20 days before through the announcement day	3.5 (170, 5.3)	20.5 (35, 9.5)
Malatesta (1983)	1969-74	Public announcement month	0.9 (256, 1.5)	16.8 (83, 17.6)
Weighted average across the above 5 studies	1962-79		1.3 (784, n.a.)	15.9 (457, n.a.)

Table 1 (cont'd)

Study	Sample period	Event period	Bidder firms	Target firms
V. Acquisitions in the United Kingdom				
Franks and Harris (1986)	1955-85	Public announcement month	1.0 (1058, 2.3)	23.3(1814, 60.6)
VI. Acquistions in Canada				
Eckbo (1986a)	1964-83	Public announcement month	0.8 (1138, 3.0)	3.6 (413, 6.9)

a. Dodd and Ruback (1977), Bradley (1980), Kummer and Hoffmeister (1978), Jarrell and Bradley (1980), Bradley, Desai and Kim (1982, 1983), Ruback (1983).

b. Abnormal return over the day before and the day of the offer announcement is -1.1 (60, -3.0) for bidder firms and 13.4 (71, 23.8) for target firms.

c. Abnormal return over the day before and the day of the offer announcement is 0.2 (196, 0.8) for bidder firms and 6.2 (211, 23.1) for target firms.

d. Abnormal returns over the day before and the day of the offer announcement are 0.1 (102, -0.1) for bidder firms and 6.2 (57, 10.0) for target firms.

negative abnormal return over the same post-offer interval. While Mandelker (1974) and Malatesta (1983), as well as Eckbo (1986a) on Canadian data, report insignificant abnormal bidder firm performance over the year following the merger announcement, Langetieg (1978) and Asquith (1983) report significantly negative post-merger abnormal returns. Interestingly, as is apparent from the table, the studies that report negative post-merger bidder firm abnormal performance generally use a *pre-merger benchmark* to estimate post-merger abnormal returns, while the studies reporting zero post-merger performance generally use a *post-merger benchmark*. The effect of the choice of benchmark is particularly striking in the study by Loderer and Mauer (1986), who compute abnormal returns using both types of benchmarks. Thus, the "evidence" of post-merger negative bidder firm performance is most likely induced by a measurement problem. Bidder firms tend to perform abnormally well *prior* to undertaking mergers, and this abnormal performance tends to overstate the constant term a_j in the market model [eq. (1), section 2.2.2]. When the market model is subsequently used as a benchmark to compute abnormal return in the post-merger period, it will overstate the normal or expected return, causing the abnormal returns to appear negative. When the parameters of the market model is estimated using post-event data, this problem disappears, and there is then no evidence of negative post-merger abnormal stock returns to bidder firms. Thus, although additional research on this problem is needed, the reader is cautioned against interpreting the results in Table 2 as evidence of negative post-merger bidder performance.

Finally, while bidder firms may not lose from mergers, the evidence certainly is consistent with the proposition that competition among bidders grants most of the merger gains to target shareholders. However, from the discussion toward the end of section 2.2.2, this is not the only interpretation of the evidence. Measurement problems induced by relative size and early anticipation of merger gains will generally attenuate the measured returns to bidders. Consistent with this view, Schipper and Thompson (1983) find that firms earn significantly positive abnormal returns when they initially announce the intention to embark on an entire acquisition *program*. This positive abnormal performance is expected if the acquisitions themselves are viewed by the market as value-increasing investments. Moreover, Eckbo (1986a) documents that, in Canada, merger gains appear to be more equally shared between bidder and target firms. In his sample of mergers, the average equity size of the bidder is approximately equal to the average equity size of the target. Additionally, as shown by Eckbo (1988), U.S. bidder firms acquiring Canadian targets appear to show the same pattern as U.S. bidders in general, and the average equity value of these foreign bidders is about eight times the average equity size of the Canadian target. This evidence is consistent with the presence of an attenuation bias in the measured abnormal returns to bidder firms, and it seriously raises the possibility that the announcement-induced abnormal returns to bidders generally reported by U.S. studies substantially understate the true abnormal gains.

Table 2
Summary of per cent post-outcome abnormal returns for bidder firms in successful tender offers and mergers.

(Sample size and t-statistic in parentheses)

Study	Sample period	Event period	Bidder firms
I. Tender offers in the United States			
Dodd and Ruback (1977)	1958-78	Month after through 12 months after the offer announcement	-1.3a (124, -0.41)
II. Mergers in the United States			
Mandelker (1974)	1941-62	Month after through 12 months after the merger completion date	0.6a (241, 0.3)
Langetieg (1978)	1929-69	Month after through 12 months after the merger completion date	-6.6a (149, -3.0)
Asquith (1983)	1962-76	Day after through 240 days after the outcome announcement	-7.2a (196, 4.1)
Malatesta (1983)	1969-74	Month after through 12 months after approval of merger	-2.9b (121, -1.1)
Loderer and Mauer (1986)c	1963-80	13 months after through 24 months after first announcement of merger bid	-5.2a (146, -3.1) 1.1b (105, 0.3)

Table 2 (cont'd)

Study	Sample period	Event period	Bidder firms
III. Mergers in Canada			
Eckbo (1986a)	1964-83	Month after through 12 months after merger announcement	1.0[b] (1138, 1.9)

a. Abnormal returns are computed using an estimate of expected returns based on data prior to the first merger announcement (pre-merger "benchmark").

b. Abnormal returns are computed using an estimate of expected returns based on data starting at least 13 months (in Loderer and Mauer (1986) starting 25 months) after the merger announcement (post-merger "benchmark").

c. Loderer and Mauer (1986) also document a significant increase in the average bidder firms' dividends over the two years following the merger announcement. They fail to observe a dividend increase in a sample of unsuccessful mergers.

2.3.2 Unsuccessful Mergers and Tender Offers: At the time of the merger proposal, there is uncertainty as to whether stockholders of the bidder and target firms will eventually approve the proposal. As a result, the market reaction to the merger proposal announcement reflects the expected gains from the merger weighted by the probability of stockholder approval. Thus, if the expected gains are typically positive, the merger/takeover announcement will cause an increase in the share price also of those offers which *ex post* turn out to be unsuccessful (rejected by shareholders). This prediction is confirmed by Asquith (1983). He found that over the two months prior to and including the first press announcement of a merger proposal the cumulative average abnormal return (CAAR) rises to approximately 16 per cent for targets in successful offers and to approximately 11 per cent in unsuccessful offers. Similarly, Bradley (1980) documents that the CAAR of successful targets in tender offers is approximately 40 per cent by the time of the offer, with a similar result for unsuccessful targets.[29]

As the uncertainty concerning the stockholder reaction to the bid is resolved, the share prices of the bidder and target firms are further adjusted. Asquith (1983) finds that, in unsuccessful merger bids, the market reverses the initial positive excess returns for both target and bidding firms. Stock prices of targets in unsuccessful *tender offers*, however, frequently remain substantially above their pre-offer level even after the failure of the offer. Intrigued by this, Bradley, Desai and Kim (1983) present an extensive examination of the post-failure price behaviour of a sample of 112 targets of unsuccessful tender offers. They segment the offers into two main categories: 86 targets that received *subsequent* takeover offers and 26 targets that did not receive such offers. They distinguish between hypotheses which hold that the expected gains from a takeover are *bidder specific* and those which presume the gains are *target specific*. Examples of bidder specific takeovers are those listed under the synergy hypothesis discussed in section 2.2.1, above, and the idea is that the takeover gains can only be realized if the production/investment policies of the target and (some) bidder firm are actually combined. The source of target-specific gains can be information, revealed to the market as a result of the offer, that some of the target's own resources are undervalued in their *current* use,[30] or information which causes the target management to adopt a higher-valued operating policy on their own.[31]

The main findings of Bradley, Desai and Kim (1983) are summarized in Table 3. From panel II of the table, the 26 targets that did not receive any subsequent successful offers within five years of the initial (unsuccessful) bid earned a 29 per cent abnormal return over the two months preceding and including the initial offer and a -28 per cent abnormal return over the two years following the initial offer. Thus, the initial gains are completely reversed when the market realizes that no subsequent successful offer will occur. This contrasts with the sample of 86 targets that subsequently are taken over within three months to five years after the initial offer: For these targets there is no evidence that the gains from the initial offer is subsequently reversed. In sum, the evidence indicates that the initial gains

Table 3
Summary of per cent abnormal returns to bidder and target firms in initially unsuccessful tender offers in the study of Bradley, Desai and Kim (1983) on U.S. data, 1963-1980

(Sample size and t-statistic in parentheses)

Target subsequently taken over?	Event period	Abnormal return
I. Initial bidder firms		
No, no change in the control of the target over the 180 days following the initial, unsuccessful offer	20 days before through 180 days after the initial offer day	1.2 (27, 0.2)
Yes, a rival bidder acquired control over the target during the 180 days following the initial, unsuccessful offer	20 days before through 180 days after the initial offer day	-8.2 (67, 2.1)
Yes, a rival bidder acquired control over the target during the 180 days following the initial, unsuccessful offer	10 days before through 10 days after the announcement of the successful takeover	-2.8 (67, -2.4)
II. Target firms		
No, not within five years of the initially unsuccessful offer	Month before through month of initial offer	29.4 (26, 10.7)

Table 3 cont'd

Target subsequently taken over?	Event period	Abnormal return
No, not within five years of the initially unsuccessful offer	Month after through 24 months after the initial unsuccessful offer	-27.5 (26, 2.9)
Yes, a rival bidder acquired the target within 3 months following the initial unsuccessful offer	Month before through month of initial offer	48.2 (65, 29.4)
Yes, a rival bidder acquired the target within 3 months following the initial unsuccessful offer	Month after through 24 months after initial offer	-0.5 (65, n.a.)
Yes, a rival bidder acquired the target after 3 months but within 5 years following the initial, unsuccessful offer	Month before through month of initial offer	23.0 (21, 10.3)
Yes, a rival bidder acquired the target after 3 months but within 5 years following the initial, unsuccessful offer	Month after through 24 months after initial offer	31.77 (21, n.a.)

to unsuccessful targets are *conditional* on the event that the target will actually be taken over, either by the initial bidder or by a subsequent rival bidder. Obviously, this is inconsistent with the hypothesis that the target gains are purely target-specific.

Bradley, Desai and Kim (1983) also present some interesting evidence concerning the post-offer performance of the unsuccessful *bidder* firm. In panel I of Table 3, the abnormal performance of these bidder firms is, on average, zero over the six months following the unsuccessful bid *as long as no other bidder takes over the target*. If, however, the target receives a successful bid (by someone other than the initial bidder) over this period, the initial bidder realizes, on average, a statistically significant abnormal return of -8 per cent. The abnormal return is -3 per cent over the month centered on the announcement of the successful rival bid. Bradley, Desai and Kim interpret this as evidence that the successful takeover by a rival bidder is expected to put the initial bidder at a competitive disadvantage in product markets. The evidence is also consistent with the simpler hypothesis which holds that (1) the takeover would have been a value-increasing investment for the bidder firm, and (2) the probability that the initial, unsuccessful bidder will return with a subsequent successful offer is driven to zero when a rival bidder acquires the target firm. Thus, at a minimum, this evidence further supports the hypothesis that takeover bids benefit shareholders of (successful) bidder firms.

2.3.3 Minority Buyouts and Going Private Transactions: In a minority buyout, the majority shareholder purchases the remainder of the outstanding target shares. Since the bidder (the majority shareholder) already has control of the firm, the buyout involves no obvious synergies that potentially characterize the acquisition of control. In light of this, it is interesting to note that target shareholders in minority buyouts appear to earn abnormal returns of a magnitude similar to the abnormal return in control-oriented tender offers. As summarized in Table 4, Dodd and Ruback (1977) document announcement-month average abnormal returns of 17 per cent to targets in a sample 19 successful minority buyouts in the U.S. Furthermore, Eckbo and Langohr (1988) document abnormal returns of 29 per cent over the offer announcement week in a sample of 29 successful minority buyouts in France. The abnormal return to the bidder firms in these buyouts appears to be zero or positive.

Eckbo and Langohr (1988) also show that the bidder on average pays a premium for the remaining target shares which is comparable to the premium paid in control-oriented tender offers. Where does the bidder find the resources to pay for this premium? Perhaps, as suggested by Dodd and Ruback (1977), the premium is analogous to an "out-of-court" settlement, i.e., a payment to avoid even larger expected litigation costs in the event that minority shareholders elect to legally challenge the firm's operating strategy. It is also possible that the majority shareholder is attempting to acquire the remaining shares prior to adopting a value-increasing change in the firm' production/investment policy, and is forced to share part of the gains from this change with the minority holders.[32]

Table 4
Per cent abnormal returns to successful bidder and target firms in various corporate control transactions

(Sample size and t-statistic in parentheses)

Study	Sample period	Sample description	Event period	Bidder firms	Target firms
I. Minority buyouts and going private transactions					
Dodd and Ruback (1977)	1958-78	"Clean-up" tender offers	Month of offer announcement	2.7 (19, 1.9)	17.4 (19, 6.7)
Eckbo and Langohr (1988)	1970-82	Cash minority buyouts	Offer announcement week	-0.8 (15, -0.5)	28.7 (29, 36.7)
DeAngelo, DeAngelo and Rice (1984)	1973-80	Going private transactions	Day before and day of public announce- ment of proposals to go private	n.a.	22.3 (72, 41.6)
Lehn and Poulsen (1986)	1980-84	Going private transactions	Day before and day of public announce- ment of proposals to go private	n.a.	13.9 (92, 41.1)

Table 4 (cont'd)

Study	Sample period	Sample description	Event period	Bidder firms	Target firms
II. Cash vs. securities as payment in acquisitions					
Wansley, Lane and Yang (1983)	1970-78	Mergers paid with cash	40 days prior to and through the offer announcement day	n.a.	33.5 (102, n.a.)
"	"	Security exchange mergers	40 days prior to and through the offer announcement day	n.a.	17.5 (87, n.a.)
Eger (1983)	1958-80	Security exchange mergers	Day before and day of merger announcement	-0.6 (37, -0.3)	5.5 (36, 16.0)
Eckbo and Langohr (1988)	1970-82	Cash tender offers	Offer announcement week	0.6 (12, 1.3)	28.1 (34, 41.8)
"	"	Stock exchange tender offers	Offer announcement week	-0.9 (26, -0.9)	5.4 (31, 6.6)
Huang and Walkling (1987)	1977-82	Cash mergers and tender offers	Day before and day of announcement of acquisition	n.a.	29.3 (101, n.a.)

Table 4 (cont'd)

Study	Sample period	Sample description	Event period	Bidder firms	Target firms
"	"	Security exchange mergers and tender offers	Day before and day of announcement of acquisition	n.a.	14.4 (32, n.a.)
III. When the bidder is the Government					
Eckel and Vermaelen (1986)	1973-82	Purchases of stock in *regulated* firms by Canadian Provincial or Federal Government	Four weeks prior to through week of offer announcement	n.a.	11.9 (7, 2.4)
"	"	Purchase of stock in *unregulated* firms by Canadian Provincial or Federal Government	Four weeks prior to through week of offer announcement	n.a.	-5.9 (7, -1.4)
Boardman, Freedman and Eckel (1986)	1981	Case study of the Domtar takeover by two Quebec Crown Corporations	Day following the day of the public announcement of the takeover	n.a.	-14.1 (1, -9.6)

After a minority buyout, the target firm usually, but not always, is delisted from the stock exchange. In a "going private" transaction, however, such delisting directly motivates the stock purchase. In a "going private" transaction, the entire equity interest in a public corporation is purchased by a small group of investors that includes members of the incumbent management team, and the firm is subsequently delisted from the exchange. These transactions differ from minority buyouts also in that (1) the bidder group typically do not hold a majority interest prior to the transaction, and (2) *the incumbent management* is the driving force behind the initiative. In some management buyouts the management ends up holding 100 per cent of the equity, while in others a small outside equity interest is allowed. Management buyouts frequently involve substantial short- as well as long-term borrowing by the private company and are therefore commonly dubbed "leveraged buyouts."[33] As shown in panel I of Table 4, the empirical evidence indicates that the announcement of proposals to go private is associated with substantial increases in stock prices. Over the two days preceding and including the announcement day, the average abnormal return is 22 per cent in the sample of 72 buyouts studied by DeAngelo, DeAngelo and Rice (1984), and 14 per cent in the sample of 92 buyout proposals studied by Lehn and Poulsen (1986).

How can management afford to pay a substantial premium for the shares purchased in order to go private? Several potential sources of gains have been suggested: (1) avoidance of registration, listing, and other stockholder servicing costs incurred by public companies,[34] (2) improved managerial incentives to maximize the value of the firm, (3) the replacement of a dispersed, largely passive body of shareholders with a small group of new (outside) investors who play a more active role in monitoring and managing the firm, (4) benefits from the additional leverage capacity caused by increased profitability and (frequently) a closer relationship with institutional lenders, (5) income tax benefits at the corporate level (through additional depreciation made possible by an "asset writeup"), and (6) redistribution of wealth from bondholders and preferred stockholders. While Lehn and Poulsen (1986) present some preliminary evidence which contradicts Hypothesis (6), there is so far little evidence to discriminate between Hypotheses (1) through (5).

2.3.4 The Payment Method: In perfect markets with symmetrically informed agents and no taxes, the medium of exchange used to purchase the target shares does not affect the level or distribution of the gains between the bidder and target firms. However, there is both theoretical and empirical support for the proposition that offer premia and offer-induced abnormal returns ought to be — and are in fact — a function of whether the bidder pays the target with cash, securities or a combination of the two. The most familiar argument points to the fact that, in a merger, payment to the target in the form of securities in the combined firm avoids, under certain conditions, the realization of a potential capital gains tax liability implied by an all cash offer.[35] Thus, in a cash offer, the bidder must raise the offer premium in order to compensate target shareholders for the relative tax penalty associated with this particular payment method.

A more subtle argument holds that information asymmetries between the bidder and target firms can lead to an optimal mix of cash and securities. Fishman (1986), Hansen (1987) and Eckbo, Giammarino and Heinkel (1987) all discuss how private information about (1) the true value of the securities to be exchanged, and (2) the contribution of each firm to the synergy gains from the takeover, affects the bidder firm's choice of payment method. Intuitively, cash is a costly medium since the bidder alone bears the cost of overpaying for the target. This contrasts with a securities offer where the target shareholders effectively share in the post-offer decrease in the market value of the bidder firm which occurs whenever the market realizes that the bidder paid too much for the target shares. The resulting trade-off between the two exchange media leads to predictions concerning the characteristics of bidder firms that chose one medium over the other.

As summarized in panel II of Table 4, there is evidence that *target firms in cash offers outperform targets in security exchange offers* in terms of offer-induced abnormal returns. For example, Eckbo and Langohr (1988) document average target firm abnormal returns of 28 per cent over the offer announcement week in cash offers, as opposed to only 5 per cent average abnormal returns to targets in stock exchange tender offers. Similarly, Huang and Walkling (1987) find two-day announcement induced abnormal returns of 29 per cent to targets in cash mergers and tender offers vs. only 14 per cent to targets in security exchange offers.

The difference in the abnormal returns to targets in cash and securities offers seems too large to be explained by a tax argument alone. Eckbo and Langohr (1988) provide further information on this issue by decomposing the total tender offer premium, $(P_0 - P)$, into two components $P_0 - P = (P_0 - P_e) + (P_e - P)$ where P_0 is the offer price, P is the pre-offer target share price and P_e is the post-offer target share price conditional on the offer being successful. The first component, $(P_0 - P_e)$ can be viewed as an *information-adjusted* control premium, and represents a form of compensation received exclusively by those target shareholders that decide to tender their shares. Since a tax liability is realized only if the shares are tendered, this information-adjusted premium must reflect any relative tax disadvantage to cash as a medium of exchange. However, Eckbo and Langohr (1988) do not find that this component of the total premium differ across cash and exchange offers. In contrast, they find that the second component, $(P_e - P)$, is substantially larger in cash than in security exchange offers.[36] This component, which can be viewed as an *information effect*, reflects the impact of new target-specific information revealed by the tender offer. Apparently, the information effect is larger in cash offers than in security exchange offers, which is consistent with the notion that the choice of payment method itself conveys information to the market concerning the true value of the target shares.

2.3.5 When the Bidder is the Government: While the evidence reviewed above strongly indicates that mergers and acquisitions are value-increasing investments for the target firms, the picture appears to be dramatically different when the bidder is a firm controlled by the *government*: As summarized in panel III of Table 4, Eckel and Vermaelen (1986), in a sample of seven *unregulated* firms purchased by the Canadian federal or provincial governments, document abnormal returns to target firms of -5.9 per cent (t-value of -1.4) over the month ending with the offer announcement. In contrast, in a sample of seven *regulated* firms, the corresponding target firm performance is a statistically significant 12 per cent. The authors hypothesize that the dismal performance of the unregulated targets is driven by an increase in agency costs when a private firm is transformed into a mixed — or fully government owned — enterprise. Furthermore, the authors argue, the superior performance of the regulated over the unregulated targets is expected if internal regulation through direct ownership by the government is less costly than external regulation. Moreover, direct government ownership in a regulated firm may give shareholders a greater access to low-visibility subsidies.

In a related case-study, Boardman, Freedman and Eckel (1986) document a statistically significant 14 per cent abnormal decline in the stock price of Domtar Inc. on the day after the announcement by the Quebec government that it would acquire the pulp and paper giant. The stock price dropped another 6 per cent (in excess of the market) on the second trading day after the takeover announcement. According to the authors, "investors' negative reaction to the acquisition was generated by fear that control by the Parti Quebecois government would lead to increased intervention in Domtar's activities, the pursuit of non-profit objectives and decreased Profitability" (Boardman *et al.* 1986, p. 278). They conclude that "a loss of between 8 and 19 per cent, equivalent to $50 million to $117 million, can be attributed exclusively to government control and the anticipated pursuit of non-profit objectives" (p. 284).

2.4   Policy Issues

Mergers and acquisitions allow firms to quickly enter or leave an industry. Instead of wasting resources duplicating the production technologies already existing in an industry, the new entrant can focus on reallocating existing resources to a higher-valued use. The existence of a corporate control market effectively puts a ceiling on the degree of inefficiency that can develop within an industry. Furthermore, since the cost of a takeover, such as fees to lawyers and consultants, normally do not increase in proportion to the size of the firm being taken over, this entry mechanism works equally well in industries with relatively large production units as in industries characterized by small firms. Thus, firm size *per se* does not deter entry through the corporate control market.[37]

From the shareholders' point of view, are there generally too many takeovers? The answer would have been "yes" if there was evidence that takeovers on *average* reduced the *combined* market values of the bidder and target firms. The evidence reviewed above, however, indicates that the opposite is true: target shareholders realize significant gains while bidder shareholders do not on average lose from these investments. This evidence is not particularly surprising. If takeovers were typically harmful to shareholders, they could simply change the corporate charter in order to deny managers the right to undertake these investments. Furthermore, the argument that bidder firms exploit target minority shareholders through "corporate raiding" is thoroughly rejected by the evidence. In the vast majority of the cases, non-tendering as well as tendering target shareholders capture significant gains from the takeover in the form of an increased price for their shares.

Is merger activity excessive from the society's point of view? In other words, are there social costs of takeovers which are not entirely borne by the private participants in the takeover market? The prime issue here is to what extent horizontal mergers generate market power which can be used to exploit consumers and/or influence the political process. This issue is examined extensively in Section 5. The evidence reviewed there rejects the proposition that the gains from horizontal takeovers come from the creation of monopoly power. What about distortions created by government regulations? Certainly, government tax/subsidy policies can affect takeover activity in a way which is socially suboptimal. Furthermore, given the evidence, it is questionable whether takeovers of unregulated, private-sector owned targets by the *government* are in the society's interest.

3.0 MANAGERIAL RESISTANCE TO TAKEOVER BIDS
3.1 Frequently Used Defensive Tactics
There are generally two different classes of takeover defenses; those requiring shareholder approval, and those which can be implemented purely at the discretion of management. Corporate charter amendments designed to increase the cost of takeovers belong in the former category, while strategies like asset restructuring – including the sale of "crown jewels," targeted share repurchases and issuance of "poison pill" securities – fall in the latter. The following is a quick summary of some of the most commonly used defensive tactics under each category.

3.1.1 Defenses Which Require Prior Shareholder Approval: This class of defenses consists of amendments to corporate charters that condition and restrict the transfer of managerial control, frequently dubbed "shark repellents." While anti-takeover amendments were observed as early as the 1960s, the frequency and form of such amendments have changed considerably in the 1980s,[38] in part due to the flurry of new takeover techniques emerging in the corporate control market over the last decade. Jarrell and Poulsen (1986) identify another reason for the increased frequency of amendments in the 1980s: State anti-takeover laws have become largely invalidated since 1982,[39] and antitrust regulators have lowered the barriers to mergers between large firms and between competitors since 1980. Anti-takeover amendments are substitutes for the protection against hostile takeovers once afforded by state anti-takeover and Federal antitrust laws.

Supermajority amendments: Supermajority amendments require approval by holders of at least two-thirds (and sometimes by as much as 95 per cent) of the voting power of the outstanding common stock to approve a merger, tender offer, consolidation, or sale of major assets of the firm. In some cases the supermajority provision is triggered when the stockholding of the merger partner reaches a certain minimum (usually 5 or 10 per cent), and in most cases the supermajority requirement is waived if a majority of the target's board of directors approve the merger. Recently, supermajority provisions have also included the requirement that a (super-)majority of the *minority* shareholders approve the merger. These amendments are almost always accompanied by "lock-in" provisions that require the same supermajority voting approval to change the amendments. The amendments delay or block a bidder from implementing an operating or merger strategy even when the bidder controls the target's board of directors.

Fair-Price amendments: The typical fair-price provision waives the above supermajority provisions if the bidder agrees to pay a "fair price" for all shares purchased. A "fair price" is usually defined as the highest price paid by the bidder for any of the shares it has acquired in the target firm during a specified period of time. The basic purpose of this provision is to prevent a bidder that has gained control of the target from "squeezing out" minority shareholders by purchasing the remaining shares at a price below the price paid for the majority shareholding. Thus, the bidder can normally avoid the supermajority provisions if it makes a uniform, fair price offer rather than a two-tier, non-uniform takeover bid.

Classified boards: This type of amendments divide, or classify, the board of directors into equal-sized groups (usually three), whose members each serve a three-year term of office. Importantly, the terms of office of the three classes are staggered so that only one-third of the directors are elected each year. Thus, it will take at least two years for the bidder to gain control of the board even if the bidder owns a supermajority of the outstanding voting shares. The amendments also typically prevent the bidder from diluting the effect of the classification by inhibiting the bidder from expanding the number of directors.

Other anti-takeover provisions: Examples of other observed anti-takeover provisions are those eliminating "stockholder rights to (i) call special meetings without board approval, (ii) to take action by written consent rather than at a meeting, (iii) to nominate candidates for the board without pre-meeting written notification, and (iv) to remove board members without establishing cause" (DeAngelo and Rice 1983, p. 331). Linn and McConnell (1983, p. 367, n. 8) also refer to "amendments eliminating cumulative voting, amendments creating a class of unissued preferred stock with voting rights to be specified by the board of directors at the time of issuance, amendments requiring that 'social impact' be considered before a merger may be consummated, ... and amendments granting specific rights of appraisal to minority shareholders in a merger."

3.1.2 Defenses Which Do Not Require Prior Shareholder Approval: A multitude of strategies have been used by management of target firms to delay, stall, redirect, counter, or totally eliminate a bid for control of the firm. These include the following which are part of the everyday language in financial newspapers and magazines: "white knight" (a "friendly" merger partner sought out by the target in response to a "hostile" takeover bid); "Pacman defense" (the target firm counters a hostile bid by issuing a tender offer for the bidder firm's shares); sale of "crown jewels" (assets which are thought to be the main attraction of the bidder); "greenmail" (the target repurchases the shareholding of the bidder at a premium above the market price, usually in return for a "standstill" agreement, i.e., a commitment by the bidder not to increase its holding in the target); and "poison pills" (securities entitling the target firm's shareholders to unusual rights and privileges if the firm becomes the subject of a takeover bid and which makes it more costly and difficult for the bidder to acquire control). Other defenses include the acquisition (by the target firm) of a business which raises antitrust issues concerning the bidder's attempt to acquire the target, and lawsuits filed by the target firm alleging various conflicts of interest, insider trading, and/or discrimination between shareholder groups on the part of the bidder.   Further details on some of these defenses are given in Section 3.3, along with the discussion of the empirical evidence.

3.2   Theoretical Issues

3.2.1 The Communal Resource Problem: When a takeover generates gains that are specific to both the target and the bidder firm, the two are effectively locked in a bilateral monopoly bargaining situation. The outcome of this process, (the division of the gains between the two parties) depends on each party's ability to resist the temptation to close the deal at a suboptimal point in the bargaining process. Target shareholders maximize their share of the synergy gains whenever they bargain as one cooperative unit. In reality, however, as pointed out by DeAngelo and Rice (1983), the bidder can exploit the fact that "control" of the target firm is a communal resource: The right to transfer control to the bidder is shared by any subgroup of the target shareholders who collectively own a controlling interest in the target. Since the bidder pays a premium only for the number of shares necessary to gain control, non-colluding target shareholders will tend to compete for the control premium. As a result, they will fail to appropriate the maximum possible premium.

This problem of suboptimal tendering behaviour is best illustrated in the case where the bidder uses a "two-tier" offer to acquire the target.[40] Suppose (1) the target firm has a current market value of $10 per share, (2) the bidder is willing to purchase any, or all, of the target shares for $15 per shares, and (3) target shareholders assign a high probability to the event that another bidder will offer $18 per share in an any-or-all offer in the near future. The optimal strategy for target shareholders as a group is obviously to hold out and wait for the higher-valued offer at $18 per share. However, the first bidder can in fact induce non-colluding target shareholders to accept the lower-valued offer at $15 per share. He specifies a two-tier offer in which he will purchase, say, 50 per cent of the target shares at $20 per share and, after expiration of this first offer, $10 per share for the remaining shares.

The average price in this two-tier offer is $15, the same as in the any-or-all offer. Faced with this two-tier offer, each target shareholder will reason as follows: (i) if other shareholders tender, then I should tender to avoid receiving only $10 for my shares; (ii) if other shareholders do not tender, then I should tender to receive the first-tier price of $20 per share for all my shares. Thus, it is rational to tender despite the strong expectation of a higher-valued any-or-all offer at $18 per share down the road.[41]

The communal resource problem would be solved if the target shareholders had a perfect agent that would centralize their individual tendering decisions. Suppose the target management is such an agent. Then the observed managerial resistance to takeover bids are tantamount to an auctioneer's attempt to keep the auction open until he or she believes the highest-valued bid has materialized. Naturally, the alternative hypothesis is that entrenched target management attempts to protect their jobs by fending off profitable bids at the expense of their shareholders. As summarized below, in order to discriminate between these two opposing hypotheses, empirical research have focused on the market reaction to the announcement of various takeover defenses.

3.2.2 The Role of Greenmail: Alternative Hypotheses[42]: In a targeted share repurchase the firm buys back a block of its common stock from a single shareholder, excluding all other shareholders from participating in the transaction. In several cases the targeted blockholder has already disclosed his or her intention to ultimately acquire control over the firm and signed a "standstill" agreement, thereby abandoning further attempts to acquire control, in return for selling the block to the firm at a premium above the stock's market price.[43] While targeted repurchases may occur for reasons not related to corporate control, the term "greenmail" refers in particular to repurchases where the blockholder is perceived as a potential bidder for control.

Under the managerial entrenchment hypothesis, the greenmail payment is evidence of managerial expropriation of (non-participating) shareholders' wealth for the purpose of maintaining control. Thus, paying greenmail should cause the firm's stock price to decline. Importantly, under this hypothesis, the negative price reaction would not have occurred if managers had chosen not to pay greenmail.

Alternatively, under the shareholder interest hypothesis it is suggested that paying greenmail benefits non-tendering shareholders as well. Broadly speaking, the argument is that a targeted share repurchase in return for a standstill agreement can increase in the type of investment activity which ultimately leads to higher-valued takeover opportunities. Importantly, while this hypothesis maintains that the current value of these opportunities is positive, it does not necessarily follow that greenmail will be met with a share price increase. Indeed, Schleifer and Vishny (1986) prove the existence of a rational expectations equilibrium in which the firms paying greenmail are precisely those for which the market overestimated the value of the firm's takeover opportunities prior to the share repurchase. In their model, while informed managers realize that paying greenmail will cause the stock price to fall today, they rationally decide to undertake the share repurchase because it will prevent an even larger price drop in the future.[44]

A somewhat different version of the shareholder interest hypothesis is suggested by the motive for targeted share repurchases usually given by managers. The following statement is typical in that the *large blockholder* is the source of the greenmail problem:

> In some cases, the purchaser [of a large block of shares] may not be truly interested in taking over the company but uses the threat of a proxy fight and/or a bid to take over the company as a means of either forcing the company to repurchase its equity position at a substantial premium over market price or obtaining for itself a special benefit which will not be available to all of the company's shareholders. The board believes these tactics are generally not in the best interest of all of the shareholders. . . . (Management to shareholders of Atlantic Richfield Co., March 18, 1985).

Under what circumstances would value-maximizing managers feel compelled to repurchase the equity position of an investor which they think "may not be truly interested in taking over the company"? One possibility is that incumbent managers, with their inside information about the firm, know when (outside) shareholders generally overestimate the value of the post-acquisition production/investment policy proposed by the raider.[45] However, given the inherent conflict of interest (the managers may be perceived as defending their jobs), it may be difficult to credibly communicate this information to shareholders. Contrary to the Schleifer and Vishny type of argument, management cannot in this situation expect to rely on current or future competition among raiders to solve the problem, and paying greenmail may be the value-maximizing solution.[46] The greenmail payment will cause the stock price to fall, reflecting the cost of the repurchase premium and, if the management's information is revealed, the downward adjustment as the market realizes it overestimated the value of the firm's current takeover opportunity.[47]

3.3 Empirical Evidence

3.3.1 Anti-takeover Charter Amendments: Panel I of Table 5 lists the major results of studies estimating the market reaction to anti-takeover charter amendments. DeAngelo and Rice (1983) examine 100 NYSE-listed firms adopting supermajority provisions, staggered board, fair price and lock-up provisions over the 1974-79 period. Anti-takeover charter amendments are typically not announced in the *Wall Street Journal* and the authors use the two-day period starting with the day the proxy statement was mailed out to shareholders as the relevant event period. The abnormal return over this two-day interval is -0.2 per cent with a t-statistic of -0.4. They fail to find a statistically significant market reaction over the 10 days before through 10 days after the proxy mailing date as well. The authors

Table 5

Summary of per cent abnormal stock returns associated with various defensive corporate actions which directly or indirectly affect the likelihood the firm will become the subject of a takeover bid.

(Sample size and t-statistic in parentheses)

Study	Sample period	Type of defensive strategy	Event period	Per cent Abnormal return
I. Adoption of charter amendments				
DeAngelo and Rice (1983)	1974-79	Adopt supermajority, staggered board, fair price and lockup provisions	Day of and day after the proxy mailing date	-0.2 (100, -0.4)
"	"	"	10 days before through 11 days after proxy mailing date	-0.9 (100, -0.7)
Linn and McConnell (1983)	1960-80	Adopt classified board, limitations of the right of shareholder to act by written consent, supermajority, fair price, and lockup provisions	Proxy mailing date	0.02 (378, -0.01)
"	"	"	Day after mailing date	0.1 (378, 1.3)

Table 5 (cont'd)

Study	Sample period	Type of defensive strategy	Event period	Per cent Abnormal return
"	"	"	Proxy mailing date through stockholder meeting date	1.4 (307, 3.4)
Jarrell and Poulsen (1986)	1979-85	Supermajority, classified board, fair price provisions	20 days before through 10 days after proxy mailing date	-1.3 (551, -2.3)
Eckbo (1987)	1984-85	Adopt anti-greenmail charter amendment	Proxy mailing day and day after	-0.4 (32, -1.1)
"	"	"	4-day period including proxy mailing day and day after, and stockholder meeting day and day after	-1.2 (32, -1.9)

Table 5 (cont'd)

Study	Sample period	Type of defensive strategy	Event period	Per cent Abnormal return
II. Targeted share repurchases and adoption of poison pill securities				
Bradley and Wakeman (1983)	1974-80	Targeted share repurchase without subsequent merger termination	One day before public announcement through one day after	-1.4 (40, -2.0)
"	"	Targeted share repurchase with subsequent termination of merger bid	One day before public announcement through one day after	-5.5 (21, -7.1)
Dann and DeAngelo (1983)	1977-80	Standstill agreement not accompanied by targeted share repurchase	Day before through day of public announcement	-4.0 (19, -4.5)
"	"	Targeted share repurchase not accompanied by standstill agreement	Day before through day of public announcement	-1.2 (34, -2.2)
Mikkelson and Ruback (1986)	1978-83	Targeted share repurchase not accompanied by standstill agreement or prior control contest	Day before through day of public announcement	-1.0 (50, -1.4) [8.6]a

Table 5 (cont'd)

Study	Sample period	Type of defensive strategy	Event period	Per cent Abnormal return
"	"	Targeted repurchase accompanied by prior control contest but no standstill agreement	Day before through day of public announcement	-2.6 (18, -2.2) [12.7]a
"	"	Targeted share repurchase accompanied by standstill agreement but no prior control contest	Day before through day of public announcement	-7.1 (20, -11.6) [0.7]a
Malatesta and Walkling (1988)	1982-86	Adoption of poison pill securities by firms that were not subjected to takeover bids during the 2 prior months	Day before through day of public announcement	-0.8 (61, -3.1)
"	"	Adoption of poison pill securities by firms that were subjected to takeover bids during 2 prior months	Day before through day of public announcement	-1.8 (12, -2.6)
Ryngaert (1988)	1983-86	Adoption of poison pill securities by firms that were not subject to takeover speculation	Day before through day of public announcement	-0.4 (142, -1.5)

Table 5 (cont'd)

Study	Sample period	Type of defensive strategy	Event period	Per cent Abnormal return
"	"	Adoption of poison pill securities by firms that were subject to takeover speculation	Day before through day of public announcement	-1.7 (37, -3.6)

a   This number is the per cent abnormal return over (i) the date the targeted investor initially purchased his/her shares in the firm through two days before the investor's subsequent 13D filing with the Securities and Exchange Commission, (since 1970, 13D filings are required by investors accumulating 5 per cent or more of any class of the company's voting equity securities) plus (ii) the day before and the day of the 13D filing announcement, plus (iii) the day before and day of any "significant" control-related announcements between the 13D filing and the targeted share repurchase. Thus, this abnormal return is a measure of the total acquisition-related abnormal return leading up to the targeted share repurchase. For the total sample of 111 repurchasing firms, this return is 7.4 per cent with a t-value of 7.9.

interpret their evidence as weakly supporting the managerial entrenchment hypothesis.

Linn and McConnell (1983) examine a sample of 378 NYSE-listed firms adopting classified boards, limitations on the rights of shareholders to act by written consent, and supermajority, fair price, and lockup provisions over the period 1960-1980. They fail to find any significant market reaction around the proxy mailing date. However, for a subsample of 307 cases, they report statistically significant average abnormal returns of 1.4 per cent cumulated over the period from the proxy mailing date through the subsequent shareholder meeting date (t-value of 3.4). They take this as weak evidence in favor of the stockholder interest hypothesis.

Jarrell and Poulsen (1986), who use a sample of 551 firms proposing supermajority provisions, classified board and fair price provisions between 1979 and 1985, document statistically significant average abnormal returns of -1.3 per cent over the 30-day period starting 20 days prior to the proxy mailing date (t-value of -2.3). Separating the amendments by type, they find that fair price amendments have virtually no effect of stock prices, while the supermajority and classified board provisions have more substantial and negative effect on stock prices. Interestingly, they also find that the most harmful amendments are proposed by firms that have relatively high insider and low institutional stockholdings. They argue that large insider holdings can help management win majority shareholder approval of an amendment that reduces stock value, while sophisticated, well-informed institutional shareholders are more likely to oppose such amendments.

3.3.2 Greenmail and Poison Pills: Panel II of Table 5 summarizes the results of studies examining targeted repurchases with or without standstill agreements. The evidence indicates that the market reaction to targeted share repurchases which are not accompanied by standstill agreements, or which do not in any obvious way interrupt a control contest, is only marginally negative. For example, Bradley and Wakeman (1983) find average two-day announcement period abnormal returns of -1.4 per cent (t-value of -2.0) in a sample of 40 repurchases that were not associated with a subsequent merger termination. Dann and DeAngelo (1983), based on 34 repurchases not accompanied by standstill agreements, find the corresponding announcement-period abnormal return to be -1.2 per cent (t-value of -2.2). Finally, Mikkelson and Ruback (1986), in their sample of 50 repurchases 'not accompanied by standstill agreements or prior control contests' find an average two-day announcement period abnormal return of -1.0 per cent (t-value of -1.4).

The market reaction is significantly negative when the targeted repurchase is accompanied by a standstill agreement: In this case, Mikkelson and Ruback (1983) report an average abnormal return of -7.1 per cent in a sample of 20 cases, with a t-value of -11.6. Similarly, when the repurchase terminates a merger bid, Bradley and Wakeman (1983) document abnormal returns of -5.5 per cent, t-value of -7.1, in a sample of 21 cases. The standstill agreement in of itself appears to cause a negative market reaction: Dann and DeAngelo (1983), in a sample of 19 standstills that were not accompanied by targeted repurchases, document two-day announcement-induced average abnormal returns of -4.0 per cent (t-value of -4.5).

Mikkelson and Ruback (1986) also find that the abnormal return cumulated over the period from the initial Schedule 13D filing by the large blockholder[48] through the date of the targeted repurchase is positive and significant. Since Mikkelson and Ruback (1985) document significantly positive average announcement-induced abnormal returns to both "buyers" and "sellers" in a large number of Schedule 13D filings, it appears reasonable to assume that the market starts to anticipate a possible future takeover bid by the raider as early as the time of the initial 13D filing. Thus, the evidence in Mikkelson and Ruback (1986) suggests that targeted repurchases do not on average drive market expectations of future takeover bids to zero.

Eckbo (1987) examines the greenmail controversy from a somewhat different angle by reporting abnormal stock returns and firm characteristics of a sample of 32 firms adopting antigreenmail charter amendments.[49] The typical antigreenmail charter amendment restricts the firm from repurchasing some or all of the common (voting) stock of an "interested" shareholder, usually defined as a shareholder who owns 5 per cent or more of the outstanding common stock and who acquired this ownership position within the past 2.3 years. Virtually all firms retain the option to pay greenmail as long as (1) two-thirds or more of the "disinterested" shareholders approve of the action, or (2) if the shares are purchased at a "fair" price, usually defined as an average of the stock's trading prices over the 90 days immediately preceding the share repurchase.

Why would managers *precommit* not to pay greenmail when they can simply decide not to pay? Eckbo (1987) argues that, under the managerial entrenchment hypothesis, incumbent management precommits not to pay greenmail in order to reduce investors' incentives to collect acquisition-oriented information about the firm. Thus, since this hypothesis maintains that the unrestricted option to greenmail is valuable to stockholders (it enhances takeover activity), the removal of this option is predicted to reduce shareholder wealth. In contrast, the shareholder interest hypothesis, which also maintains that the unrestricted option to greenmail is valuable to shareholders, predicts that a precommitment not to pay greenmail will occur when the associated deterrent effect on takeover activity is minimal. This could be, for example, when the firm has positively identified a valuable bidder. Thus, this hypothesis predicts a positive market reaction to the precommitment. As shown in panel I of Table 5, Eckbo (1987) documents zero or negative abnormal return over the two-day event period starting with the proxy mailing day. As discussed above, a non-positive market reaction to antigreenmail charter amendments is consistent with the proposition that the *unrestricted* option to pay greenmail is *valuable* to shareholders.

Another managerial tool for thwarting unwanted takeover bids is the "poison pill" security which started to surface in 1982. While there are several different forms of poison pills, these securities generally give their owners certain rights in response to certain triggering events which include a hostile takeover bid or the acquisition by an outside party of a sufficiently large block of the company's stock. The triggering events entitles the poison pill security holders to purchase common stock in the newly merged company at a substantial discount or, in some cases, to swap their shares for other, higher-valued debt securities. Some poison pill plans also imply that the acquiring firm loses substantial voting power, after the takeover, relative to other securityholders of the target firm. Clearly, the major purpose of the poison pill is to make the target prohibitively expensive to acquire through a hostile takeover. The evidence summarized in the last part of Table 5 is therefore hardly surprising. The announcement that the firm intends to issue poison pills to their shareholders is on average met with a significantly negative market reaction. Malatesta and Walkling (1988), in a sample of 61 firms adopting poison pills, document a two-day announcement period average abnormal return of -0.8 per cent, with a t-value of -3.1. Ryngaert (1988) also find a negative market reaction, with abnormal returns of -1.7 per cent (t-value of -3.6) in the sample of 37 firms that were not subject to 'takeover speculation' prior to the adoption of the poison pill.

3.4   Policy Issues

Since shareholders have the power to reject management-sponsored charter amendment proposals which they believe will reduce stockholder wealth, the question of regulation is limited to those managerial actions that do not require prior shareholder approval. In the U.S., the favorable treatment accorded large block stockholders in targeted share repurchases is in fact legally valid under extant corporate laws:

> The courts have consistently allowed differential payments to large block stockholders as long as firms demonstrate a valid business purpose for the transaction. Moreover, the courts have given broad interpretation to factors which represent a valid business purpose for the transaction. According to Nathan and Sobel (1980, fn. 2), court-accepted purposes include (1) a '... difference in business philosophies between the corporation's management and the selling shareholders' or (2) '... eliminating what appeared to be a threat to the future of the business and preserving an established management's business policy (DeAngelo and Rice 1983, p. 276).

While it is theoretically possible, as pointed out earlier, that greenmail payments benefit the firms shareholders, the current evidence presents a dilemma in terms of discriminating between the managerial entrenchment and stockholder interest hypotheses. Clearly, the practice of greenmail seen in the U.S. violates the fundamental principle of equal treatment of all shareholders, a principle which has strong protection in Canadian, French and British corporate law. The argument for banning the use of poison pill securities is even stronger, since I am not aware of even a consistent theoretical argument that would picture these securities as protecting the firm's shareholders. Implementation of the principle of equal treatment of all shareholders eliminates poison pill securities as well.

4.0   THE EFFECTS OF DISCLOSURE REGULATIONS
4.1   Disclosure Regulations in the U.S. and in France[50]

Disclosure rules governing cash tender offers in the U.S. were introduced in 1968 through the Williams Amendment to the U.S. Securities and Exchange Act. Under the Williams Act, the bidder is required to disclose any plans to liquidate the target firm, sell its assets, merge it or make any changes in its basic corporate structure. A general antifraud provision prohibits material misstatements, omissions or other receptive acts in connections with the offer. Furthermore, while there were no restrictions on the *duration* of a tender offer prior to 1968, the *Williams Act* requires that all bids for 5 per cent or more of a firm's common stock must be public offers to remain open for a minimum of 10 days.[51]

Mandatory disclosure of information in public tender offers were introduced in France as well. As of 1970, bidder and target firms in France must disclose "all important facts" for target shareholders to make "informed decisions," including the bidder's prior ownership in the target, the rationale behind and financing of the offer, shareholdings of members of the target's board of directors, and the target board's evaluation of the offer. Furthermore, as of 1973, bidders are required to disclose a detailed justification for the offer price or exchange ratio, as well as the ownership structure, research policy, business policy orientation, production/ investment strategy, and a forecast of end-of-year sales for every firm represented by a security given to the target firm in a security exchange deal. The target firm must disclose similar information about itself. Finally, as of 1978, bidders in France must also disclose the identity of any shareholders who own more than 5 per cent of its common stock, and a detailed description of the business activities of its subsidiaries. The target board must disclose the vote structure concerning the tender offer, and target board members who are also shareholders must disclose their *intended* response to the offer.[52]

4.2   Theoretical Issues

To what extent are tender offers likely to be vulnerable to mandatory information disclosure? Suppose that (1) part of the takeover gains can be generated by firms other than the initial bidder, (2) the initial bidder and the market are asymmetrically informed as to the source of the takeover gains, and (3) disclosure rules force the initial bid to reveal some of the bidder's private information to the market. Under this set of assumptions, one would predict an increase in the cost to the bidder firm of buying the target shares as public disclosure induces competition which bids up the target share price. Thus, one should observe an increase in the average offer premium paid in tender offers, and a concomitant reduction in the frequency of tender offers, following the introduction of disclosure rules.

The value to potential rival bidders of any offer-related information revealed by the initial bidder firm obviously depends on the length of time the initial offer will be outstanding. For example, when the response time given rival bidders is short, such as in the "Saturday night raids" or "midnight mergers" observed in the U.S. prior to 1968, any information disclosed by the bidder is of limited value to potential rivals. In this situation, disclosure regulations are also unlikely to substantially increase competition for the target shares. On the other hand, an increase in the minimum tender offer period, such as the one introduced by the amendment to the *Williams Act* in 1970, gives rival bidders time to thoroughly analyze the disclosed information and establish their own valuation of the target. As discussed below, evidence on this issue has been developed based on both U.S. and French takeover bids. The French case is particularly interesting in this regard, since the introduction of disclosure rules in this country *did not alter the required minimum tender offer period*: A minimum tender offer period of four weeks were established in 1966, while the disclosure rules were first introduced in 1970. Thus, while observed changes in tender offer premiums associated with the introduction of the U.S. *Williams Act* is the product of disclosure rules and the increased mandatory (10-day) offer period, the corresponding changes in offer premiums paid in French tender offers are due to the disclosure rules alone.

4.3 Empirical Evidence

4.3.1 Tender Offers in the U.S.: As summarized in Table 6, Jarrell and Bradley (1980) report that the average cash tender offer premium (relative to the target firm's pre-offer share price) increased from 32 per cent to nearly 53 per cent following the passage of the *Williams Act* in 1968. They attribute the higher average offer premium to the Act's disclosure requirements and mandatory minimum tender offer period, which effectively provide potential rival bidders with both time and information to formulate competing bids. Using a data base which includes the Jarrell and Bradley (1980) sample, Eckbo (1986c) shows that the average premium increase following the introduction of the *Williams Act* depends on the nature and outcome of the tender offer auction: (i) the average premium in tender offer contests where the first bid won the auction increased from 33 to 56 per cent, (ii) in tender offers where multiple bids were observed, but where the initial bidder eventually won the auction, the average premium increased from 26 to 102 per cent, (iii) in multiple-bid contests where the initial bidder eventually lost to a rival bidder, the increase in the average premium of the successful bid was from 46 to 96 per cent, while the initial bid (by the first bidder who eventually lost to the rival) increased from 33 to 57 per cent. Thus, the largest premium increases occurred in tender offer contests where more than one bid is made.

Nathan and O'Keefe (1986) find that the premium increase after the introduction of the *Williams Act* is not restricted to cash tender offers: Cash mergers experienced an increase in the average premium from 30 to 67 per cent, while security exchange mergers saw an increase in the average premium from 30 to 54 per cent.[53] Interestingly, Nathan and O'Keefe (1986)

Table 6
Per cent offer premium over the pre-offer target share price in successful acquisition bids before and after the implementation of disclosure rules

(sample size and median value in parentheses)

Study	Sample period	Sample description	Per cent offer premium without disclosure rules	Per cent offer premium with disclosure rules
I. Acquisitions in the United States (Williams Act effective July 1968)				
Jarrell and Bradley (1980)	1962-77	Cash tender offers	32.4 (47, n.a.)	52.8 (94, n.a.)
Eckbo (1986c)	1963-80	Single-bid tender offer contests	33.1 (63, 31.8)	56.4 (138, 48.2)
"	"	Successful bid in multiple-bid tender offer contests; initial bidder eventually successful	26.2 (5, 26.2)	104.4 (24, 86.7)
"	"	Successful bid in multiple-bid tender offer contests; initial bidder unsuccessful (rival eventually successful)	46.3 (7, 43.3)	95.7 (36, 95.7)

Table 6 (Cont'd)

Study	Sample period	Sample description	Per cent offer premium without disclosure rules	Per cent offer premium with disclosure rules
"	"	Unsuccessful bid by initial bidder, multiple-bid tender offer contest (rival bidder eventually successful)	32.7 (7, 31.2)	56.7 (36, 57.4)
Nathan and O'Keefe (1986)	1963-78	Cash tender offers	45.0 (31, 38.8)	70.1 (66, 61.8)
"	"	Cash mergers	29.7 (19, 31.6)	66.6 (46, 59.0)
"	"	Security exchange mergers	29.8 (135, 27.6)	53.6 (174, 43.9)
II. Acquisitions in France (disclosure rules as of January, 1970)				
Eckbo and Langohr (1988)	1966-82	Cash tender offers	33.8 (13, 31.9)	73.3 (34, 59.0)
"	"	Privately negotiated controlling-block trades after February 1973 (exempted from disclosure rules)	n.a.	27.4 (93, 18.3)

show that the increase in the average offer premium in their samples does not appear to take place until after 1972. They raise the issue of whether the premium increase is in fact due to the *Williams Act* (which was amended in 1970), or to some other, yet to be identified, economic phenomenon. While this possibility cannot be ruled out, it should be noted that a time delay in the increase in the average offer premium is not necessarily inconsistent with the proposition that the increase is caused by the *Williams Act*: Disclosure rules affect only "information-sensitive" takeover bids, i.e., bids where the acquiring firm does not rely on ownership of unique resources to generate gains, and it is not impossible that the *Williams Act* in fact caused some bidder firms to put such takeover bids "on hold" for a period of a couple of years in anticipation of the information problem caused by the new disclosure rules.

Other studies also support the view that the *Williams Act* has been costly to bidder firms: Smiley (1975) reports that compliance with the disclosure regulations in some cases has raised the direct transaction costs of a tender offer by as much as 25 per cent. Asquith, Bruner and Mullins (1983) find that gains to bidder firms in mergers are on average lower after 1968. Furthermore, Schipper and Thompson (1983) present some evidence indicating that a sample of frequent acquirors earned significantly negative abnormal returns over the months surrounding announcements of the introduction of the *Williams Act*.

4.3.2 Tender Offers in France: As summarized in Table 6, using a sample of successful cash tender offers where the bidder acquires voting-control of the target firm, Eckbo and Langohr (1988) find that the average offer premium relative to the pre-offer target share price increased from 34 per cent to 73 per cent immediately after the introduction of disclosure regulations in France in January 1970. Since, as pointed out above, the minimum tender offer period remained at one month, this indicates that disclosure requirements alone can cause an increase in average offer premiums of the magnitude documented by Jarrell and Bradley (1980) on U.S. data. Eckbo and Langohr (1988) also document that the compensation required to induce target shareholders to tender their shares has on average remained relatively unchanged over the entire sample period: the average offer premium relative to the post-offer target share price (i.e., the information-adjusted premium) is 15 per cent before and 24 per cent after 1970.[54]

The proposition that the disclosure rules have affected offer premiums in France is further supported by a comparison of two substitute procedures for acquiring voting-control of a publicly listed French firm. Following rules introduced in 1973, the acquisition of control of a French company must take place either through the regular public tender offer procedure or through a so-called negotiated controlling-block trade procedure. The latter applies to all *privately* negotiated trades of a controlling block of shares and requires that, on the day the block trade is executed, the block price, the size of the block and the identity of the buyer and seller be publicly announced. As explained earlier, the buyer must then be prepared to accept *all* additional shares tendered at the block price within the subsequent 15 trading days. Thus, the procedure essentially converts a privately negotiated controlling-block trade into a subsequent public tender offer for 100 per cent of the target firm's shares. As a mitigating factor, however, the procedure *exempts* the parties in the block trade from the disclosure requirements covering the regular tender offer procedure.

Consistent with the results of the pre- and post-1970 analysis of tender offers, Eckbo and Langohr (1988) find that offer premiums are significantly larger in public, control-oriented tender offers than in privately negotiated controlling-block trades. As shown in Table 6, in the latter sample, the average premium relative to the pre-offer target share price is 27 per cent. Interestingly, weighted by the number of observations in each offer category, the average offer premium across *all* control-oriented cash offers in France in the post-1970 period is 34 per cent, which is identical to the average premium for control-oriented cash tender offers prior to 1970. Since the Eckbo-Langohr data base contains almost the entire population of control-oriented (public or private) offers in France after 1972, this is what one would expect if the 1970 disclosure regulations caused marginally profitable control-oriented offers to take place through the privately negotiated block-trade procedure rather than through the public tender offer procedure.

4.4   Policy Issues

The purported intent of disclosure rules is to protect target shareholders by providing them with more information about the acquirer and by giving them more time to decide whether or not to tender. The idea is that disclosure provisions coupled with greater time for deliberation allow target shareholders to make relatively better decisions. While this is a reasonable conjecture, the major flaw is the assumption that the costs of these regulations consist mainly of administrative costs of preparing the required disclosure documents. In fact, an important consequence of forcing greater disclosure and delaying takeover bids is to dilute the acquirers property rights to the knowledge of how to accomplish valuable corporate combinations. This dilution of property rights is expected – and appears – to be reflected in higher tender offer premiums. The social welfare implications are obvious:

> In response to receiving a smaller share of the social gains [from takeovers], potential acquirers produce less knowledge about how to accomplish valuable combinations. Therefore, some otherwise profitable takeovers are deterred, and all takeovers occurring after [disclosure] regulation produce relatively smaller social gains (Jarrell and Bradley 1980, p. 404).

Essentially, disclosure rules and forced delay of execution increases the degree of competition for the target firm at the time of the takeover. As Grossman and Hart (1980) have argued, perfect competition among bidders at the time of the offer is inconsistent with (i) costs of searching for targets and (ii) rational expectations of those searching for acquisitions. Given (i) and (ii), a well-functioning market for corporate control will exist only if the initial bidding firm can reasonably expect to have an advantage over other bidders. It is precisely this advantage which is being reduced by means of regulations like those in France and in the U.S.

Finally, the idea that target shareholders need protection in takeovers follows from the "corporate raiding" theory which, in Section 2, was shown to be thoroughly rejected by evidence. *Ex post* minority target shareholders have systematically realized large capital gains in takeovers both *before* and after the introduction of disclosure laws. Corporate raiding is a myth upon which no far-reaching and costly public policy ought to be built.

5.0 ANTITRUST POLICY TOWARD HORIZONTAL MERGERS
5.1 U.S. Antimerger Policy

With the *Celler-Kefauver Act* of 1950, Section 7 of the *Clayton Act* of 1914 replaced Section 2 of the *Sherman Act* of 1890 as the principal federal antitrust law regulating corporate mergers and acquisitions. Under Section 7, a *potential* threat to competition constitutes a (civil) offense, and it is not necessary to prove a horizontal relationship between the bidder and target firms. Furthermore, anticipated economic efficiencies are not a defense against the illegality of a merger that may "substantially lessen competition."[55] Prior to the *Celler-Kefauver Act*, Section 7 applied to the transfer of corporate stock only and was applied exclusively to horizontal mergers.

Since 1950, the U.S. Department of Justice (DOJ) and Federal Trade Commission (FTC) have filed more than 500 antitrust complaints against firms involved in mergers, on the grounds that these mergers would violate Section 7 of the *Clayton Act*. Approximately 85 per cent of the complaints were filed against horizontal combinations, and most resulted in divestiture or cancellation of the merger. Stigler (1966) perceives another consequence of these prosecutions; he attributes the decline in the relative frequency of horizontal mergers in the United States to the deterrent effect of vigorous Section 7 enforcement.

In September 1978, the *Hart-Scott-Rodino Antitrust Improvements Act* (*HSR Act*) took effect, significantly increasing the legal powers of the law enforcement agencies to obtain private information needed for judging a merger's anticompetitive impact *before* filing a complaint.[56] The *HSR Act* addressed two perceived handicaps borne by the agencies charged with enforcing Section 7 of the *Clayton Act*. First, under the 1962 *Antitrust Civil Process Act* the DOJ could not require third parties, such as competitors and trade associations to provide information about corporate acquisitions until after a Section 7 complaint had been filed. This frequently caused the DOJ to drop an investigation altogether for lack of information or to file a "skeleton" complaint based on scanty data. The *HSR Act* established the right of the DOJ to issue Civil Investigative Demands to the merging firms and to other parties not directly involved in the merger prior to filing a complaint.

Second, until the *HSR Act*, the government could not require postponement of proposed acquisitions pending investigation. The agencies regard prevention of mergers as the most efficient way to cure anticompetitive problems. The agencies can always request a court to enjoin a proposed acquisition, but they must provide the court with evidence that the acquisition is likely to be anticompetitive. Such evidence is difficult to accumulate on a few days' notice. The *HSR Act* required firms planning "large" mergers[57] to notify the FTC and the DOJ before completing the transaction. Such a merger cannot be completed until 30 days after the notification has taken place, and a request for further information by the agencies trigger a further time delay. According to the FTC, the notification requirements and delay have largely eliminated the "midnight merger." They assure that "virtually all significant mergers or acquisitions occurring in the United States will be reviewed by the antitrust agencies prior to the consummation of the transaction."[58] The information provided by the parties "usually is sufficient for the enforcement agencies to make a prompt determination of the existence of any antitrust problems raised by the transaction."[59]

The empirical tests discussed below examine both to what extent the DOJ and the FTC has succeeded in selecting truly anticompetitive mergers for prosecution, and whether there is any evidence that the *HSR Act* has indeed, as claimed by the FTC, increased the precision with which defendants are chosen.

5.2 Theoretical Issues

5.2.1 The Market Concentration Doctrine:
The U.S. government selects Section 7 cases against horizontal mergers largely on the basis of market share and industry concentration.[60] The agencies' reliance on structural standards for selection of merger cases is rooted in the market concentration doctrine, one of the oldest and most controversial propositions in industrial economics. This doctrine, which is an implication of oligopoly models in the tradition of Cournot ([1838] 1927) and Nash (1950), holds that the level of industry concentration is a reliable index of the industry's market power. The empirical implication is that a relatively high level of industry concentration, which in the presence of entry barriers is believed to facilitate intra-industry collusion or dominant-firm pricing, should be associated with relatively large industry-wide monopoly rents.[61]

Following Bain (1951), numerous studies have attempted to test this proposition by estimating the cross-sectional correlation between accounting measures of industry profits and the level of industry concentration.[62] However, although this correlation is indeed typically found to be positive, the same studies have generally failed to discriminate between the market concentration doctrine and alternative propositions, including the hypothesis that the positive correlation is simply driven by inter-industry differences in risk or average costs of production.[63]

As noted by Eckbo (1985), a horizontal merger produces a measurable change in the industry's level of concentration, as well as a change in the risk-adjusted present value of industry rents that is *directly associated* with the concentration change. Under the market concentration doctrine, this change in industry rents should, *ceteris paribus*, be positively correlated with the change in concentration. This value-based test in the *changes* of the two variables allows more specific inferences than can be drawn from the traditional correlation between the *levels* of (accounting) profits and concentration. A summary of the test results reported in Eckbo (1985) are given below.

5.2.2 Collusion vs. Productive Efficiency: Two general hypotheses explaining the sources of economic gains from horizontal mergers are the "market power" and "productive efficiency" hypotheses. The predictions of these two competing hypotheses for the abnormal returns to the merging firms and their close competitors are summarized in Table 7. The abnormal returns are in response to major events which either increase or decrease the probability that the merger will be fully consummated. Probability-increasing events are the merger proposal announcement and the announcement of a pro-defendant decision in a complaint under Section 7 of the *Clayton Act*. Probability-decreasing events are the announcement of a Section 7 complaint filed against the merger or a pro-government Section 7 decision by the courts. Since the market power and productive efficiency hypotheses have identical predictions for the abnormal returns to the *merging* firms, the abnormal returns to the industry rival firms are used to distinguish between the two hypotheses.

According to the market power hypothesis, a horizontal merger will encourage industry-wide collusion or dominant firm pricing which causes an increase in (quality-adjusted) product prices and/or a reduction in factor prices. The resulting price "umbrella" benefits all firms in the industry. Therefore, when a collusive merger is proposed, the market will impound the expected increase in future monopoly rents in the stock prices of the combining firms and their product market rivals. Conversely, the announcement of a subsequent antitrust complaint against the proposed anticompetitive merger reduces the probability of merger consummation, leading to abnormal losses (i.e., reduced monopoly rents) for all industry members' shareholders. Further losses to the rival firms will occur when a pro-government decision in a Section 7 suit is announced and the market realizes that there is zero probability the merger will be consummated. Similarly, a victory for the defendant will again increase the probability of merger consummation and produce positive abnormal stock returns to the rival firms.

In contrast, the productive efficiency hypothesis suggests that mergers take place because the merger partners can lower production and/or distribution costs by combining their productive resources. The fact that the merged firm under this hypothesis becomes a tougher competitor-placing the rivals at a competitive disadvantage, tends to reduce the market value of the rivals when the merger proposal is announced. The prediction of the efficiency hypothesis is, however, somewhat more complex. The merger announcement can also signal opportunities for productivity increases available to non-merging rivals, or the existence of undervalued industry-

Table 7
Abnormal returns to the merging firms and their rivals as predicted
under the market power and economic efficiency hypotheses

Theory predicting the source of the merger gains	Abnormal returns to merging firms	Abnormal returns to rival firms

A. Probability-increasing events: merger proposal or prodefendant decision

Market power:
Collusion — Positive (monopoly rents) — Positive (monopoly rents)

Economic efficiency:
Productivity increases — Positive (cost savings) — Negative (competitive disadvantage)

Information — Positive (undervalued resources) — Zero or positive (undervalued resources and or possible productivity increases)

B. Probability-decreasing events: Antitrust complaint or progovernment decision

Market power:
Collusion — Negative (loss of monopoly rents) — Negative (loss of monopoly rents)

Economic efficiency
Productivity increases — Negative (loss of cost savings) — Positive (avoiding competitive disadvantage)

Information — Zero — Zero

Under the assumption of managerial value maximization, the sum of the gains to the *merging* firms will be positive, regardless of the sources of the gains.

Examples of positive information effects on rival firms are the case where the merger announcement reveals possibilities for efficiency gains also available to nonmerging firms and the case where the merger signals an increase in demand for resources generally owned throughout the industry of the merging firms.

specific resources owned also by the rival firms. Thus, depending on the relative magnitude of the negative competitive disadvantage effect and the positive information signalling effect, the *net* effect on the rival firms of the announcement of an efficient merger can be positive, zero or negative. What gives predictive content to the efficiency hypothesis is the fact that the announcement of a subsequent antitrust complaint (or a pro-government Section 7 decision) reverses the competitive disadvantage effect without removing any valuable information disseminated through the earlier merger proposal announcement. Thus, the efficiency hypothesis predicts zero or a positive rival firm abnormal performance in response to the antitrust complaint. Eckbo (1983) and Eckbo and Wier (1985) report tests of these predictions, and their major findings are reviewed below.

5.3   Empirical Evidence

5.3.1   Intra-Industry Wealth Effects of Horizontal Mergers: Eckbo (1983) examines intra-industry wealth effects of 191 horizontal mergers in the U.S. between 1963 and 1978, 65 of which were challenged by either the Department of Justice or the Federal Trade Commission with violating Section 7 of the *Clayton Act*. A sample of 68 vertical mergers, of which 11 were challenged, is also examined. For each merger, a set of horizontal competitors of the merging firms that were listed on the NYSE or the American Stock Exchange (ASE) at the time of the merger proposal announcement is identified.[64] As called for by hypotheses in Table 7, the paper reports estimates of the abnormal stock returns to the merging firms and their horizontal rivals (i) relative to the merger proposal announcement and (ii) relative to the subsequent announcement that the DOJ or the FTC has filed a Section 7 complaint against the horizontal merger.

The paper reports that the observed sequence of abnormal returns across the proposal and antitrust complaint announcements do not follow the pattern predicted by the collusion hypothesis. Rivals of the 65 horizontal challenged mergers earn small but significantly positive abnormal return around the merger proposal announcement, followed by zero or positive abnormal returns in response to the antitrust complaint announcement. According to Table 7, this pattern of abnormal return to rival firms is inconsistent with the collusion hypothesis but consistent with a combination of the economic efficiency and information arguments.

The paper also reports that the average intra-industry wealth effect of unchallenged horizontal mergers is indistinguishable from the average intra-industry wealth effect of unchallenged vertical mergers. Since vertical mergers are unlikely to have collusive effects, this supports to some extent the view that also the horizontal unchallenged mergers in the sample were not expected to be anticompetitive. Interestingly, there is no evidence that proposed horizontal mergers are expected to *reduce* the value of the competitors of the merging firms:

> Thus, if mergers typically take place to realize efficiency gains, we cannot conclude that the "synergy" effect is expected to produce a significant expansion of the merging firm's share of

the market along with an increase in industry rate of output. If scale economies are involved, then these seem on average to be insufficient to make the rivals worse off. Furthermore, the same evidence contradicts the argument that the merging firms were expected to initiate a (monopolistic) "predatory" price war after consummation of the merger (Eckbo 1983, pp. 271-272).

Clearly, the focus on the horizontal rivals of the merging firms allows a relatively rich set of inferences with respect to the nature of the sources of merger gains.

How can the government's apparent failure to prosecute truly anticompetitive mergers be explained? One proposition is that case selection criteria based on *ad hoc* measures and levels of market shares and industry concentration are unlikely to be of much use. Empirical tests of this proposition is reported in section 5.3.2, below. A second proposition is that legal constraints in effect during the Eckbo (1983) sample period essentially prevented the agencies from obtaining the information needed for accurately judging a merger's competitive impact before filing a complaint. As described above, the implementation of the *Hart-Scott-Rodino Antitrust Improvements Act* in September 1978 significantly relaxed those constraints. A major purpose of this Act was to increase the precision with which defendants are chosen by providing the agencies with more information about potential Section 7 violations and more time to analyze the information before they take legal action.

Eckbo and Wier (1985) examine the proposition that the *HSR Act* has improved the performance of the enforcement agencies by testing the collusion hypothesis on a sample of horizontal mergers challenged after September 1978. Their results are summarized in Table 8. As the Table shows, the results for this sample is indistinguishable from the results for the 65 challenged mergers in Eckbo (1983) which took place before 1978: Over the 31 days (-20 through 10) surrounding the merger proposal announcement, the rival firm normal performance is on average 2.4 per cent in both sub-periods (t-values of 2.6 and 1.9, respectively). Furthermore, there is no evidence of a subsequent negative rival firm performance in response to the antitrust complaint announcement, which contradicts the collusion hypothesis.[65] Thus, the evidence does not support the proposition that the Antitrust Improvements Act has in fact improved the agencies ability to select truly anticompetitive mergers for prosecution.

5.3.2 Merger-Induced Changes in Market Shares and Concentration: Suppose the agencies do in fact succeed in challenging some truly anticompetitive mergers while also making "mistakes" by blocking some efficient ones. In this case, the above tests which are based on sample averages may fail to uncover the evidence of anticompetitive mergers. In part to control for this possibility, Eckbo (1985) performs cross-sectional regressions of the following form:

$$AR_j = a_0 + a_1CR_j + a_2dCR_j + e_j , \tag{5}$$

Table 8
Summary of per cent abnormal returns to bidder, target and rival firms in 82 horizontal mergers challenged under Section 7 of the U.S. Clayton Act, relative to the merger proposal and antitrust complaint announcements as reported in Eckbo and Wier (1985).

(Sample size and t-statistic in parentheses)

Type of firm	Sample period	Event Period	
		Twenty days before through 10 days after public announcement	Day before through day after public announcement
I. Merger proposal announcement			
Target firms	1963-81	25.7 (38, 10.7)	10.5 (38, 15.0)
Bidder firms	1963-81	3.0 (68, 1.8)	0.8 (68, 2.3)
Rival firms	1963-Aug 78[a]	2.4 (65, 2.6)	0.2 (65, 0.4)
Rival firms	Sept 78-81	2.4 (17, 1.9)	0.3 (17, -0.4)
II. Antitrust (Section 7) complaint announcement			
Target firms	1963-81	-6.5 (22, -2.4)	-7.6 (22, -7.9)
Bidder firms	1963-81	-1.8 (55, -1.5)	-1.4 (55, -3.0)
Rival firms	1963-Aug 78[a]	0.8 (56, 0.5)	0.1 (56, 0.7)
Rival firms	Sept 78-81	-0.5 (10, -0.1)	0.6 (10, 1.5)

a   The Hart-Scott-Rodino Antitrust Improvements Act took effect in September 1978. The 65 cases in the sample prior to 1978 were compiled by Eckbo (1983).

where CR_j is a measure of the pre-merger level of concentration in the industry where the horizontal merger is taking place, dCR_j is the change in concentration caused by the merger, and AR_j is the abnormal return to an equal-weighted portfolio of the rivals of the merging firms around the merger proposal announcement. Under the market concentration doctrine, and assuming there are some anticompetitive mergers in the samples of challenged mergers compiled by Eckbo (1983) and Eckbo and Wier (1985), one should find that $a_2 > 0$. This is because the AR_j of rivals of an anticompetitive merger represents increased monopoly rents, and the market concentration doctrine holds that the increase in monopoly rents will be larger the larger the increase in concentration caused by the merger. Furthermore, under the stronger proposition embedded in antimerger policy, which holds that a merger is more likely to have anticompetitive effects the larger the pre-merger *level* of concentration, one should also find evidence of $a_1 > 0$.

While the form of equation (5) is similar in spirit to the regression models typically estimated in the "structure-conduct-performance" literature, there are some notable qualitative differences: For example, while the dependent variable AR_j in equation (5) measures directly the *market value* of the *increase* in industry profits expected to follow from the *increase* in industry concentration, the tradition has been to regress an *accounting measure* of the *level* of industry profits on the *level* of concentration. The traditional approach has been criticized on the grounds that accounting profits are a poor proxy for economic profits, and that any cross-sectional variation in the level of industry profits can simply reflect differences in risk. This criticism does not apply here, since AR_j is measured using market values and represent a *risk-adjusted* change in the level of industry rents. Equally important is the fact that since equation (5) is specified in the form of changes in the central variables, AR_j can be meaningfully interpreted without specifying a structural model relating the level of industry profits to concentration.

The most important results reported in Eckbo (1985) emerge from regressions of equation (5) using the sample of 80 horizontal mergers which were challenged compiled by Eckbo (1983) and Eckbo and Wier (1985). The four-firm concentration ratio (CR_4) of the major four-digit SIC industry of the target firm is used to represent CR_j while the change in the industry's Herfindahl index (dH) measures dCR_j.[66] While data on CR_4 is generally available, the market shares of the bidder and target firms, which yield dH, were collected from case-related court records and publications. In the sample of challenged mergers, the average level of CR_4 is 58 per cent (ranging from 6 to 94 per cent), while the average value of dH is 3.3 per cent (ranging from 0.02 to 24.2 per cent).

Table 9 summarizes the main regression results based on three alternative measures of abnormal returns to the rival firms and two event periods surrounding the merger proposal announcement. The event periods are the 31-day interval -20 through 20 and the 7-day interval -3 through 3. The first dependent variable, AR_j, is the measure of rival firm abnormal

Table 9

OLS estimates of the coefficients in cross-sectional regressions of merger-induced abnormal returns to portfolios of industry rivals on the level and change in industry concentration. Sample of 64 horizontal challenged mergers, 1963-81, reported in Eckbo (1985).

(t-values in parentheses)

Dependent variable[1]	Event period (days)[2]	Independent variables[3]				
		Constant	CR_4	dH	R^2	F
AR	-20 through 10	3.715 (1.13)	-0.004 (-0.67)	-0.420 (-1.70)	0.045	1.43
	-3 through 3	4.279 (2.92)	-0.060 (-2.58)	-0.075 (-0.66)	0.115	3.97
AR'	-20 through 10	1.927 (0.25)	0.088 (0.73)	-0.849 (-1.45)	0.037	1.17
	-3 through 3	7.584 (2.32)	-0.119 (-2.31)	-2.07 (-0.82)	0.102	3.45
dP	-20 through 10	-0.218 (-0.18)	0.020 (1.04)	-0.087 (-0.62)	0.025	0.70
	-3 through 3	0.163 (0.26)	0.01 (0.14)	-0.038 (-0.55)	0.006	0.16

1. As defined in the text, AR is the abnormal return to an equally-weighted portfolio of the industry rivals of the bidder and target firms relative to the merger proposal announcement, AR' is $AR/(1-\pi)$ where π is a maximum likelihood estimate of the probability the proposed merger will be successfully challenged by antitrust authorities, and dP is $AR'X/S(1-\tau)$ where X is current (pre-merger) net earnings, S is current sales, and τ is the corporate tax rate. Under a constant-growth valuation framework, dP can be interpreted as the permanent change in the industry's product price consistent with abnormal returns of AR' to the average industry rival.

2. Day zero is the day of the merger proposal announcement in the *Wall Street Journal*.

3. CR_4 is the four-firm concentration ratio, dH is the change in the industry's Herfindahl index.

return defined above and in section 2.2.2. The second dependent variable is defined as

$$AR'_j \equiv \frac{AR_j}{1 - \pi} , \tag{6}$$

where π is a maximum likelihood estimate of the probability, given the information available at the time of the merger proposal announcement, that the proposed merger will be successfully challenged by the government.[67] At the time of the merger proposal, while the most anticompetitive mergers may have the largest industry wealth effects, the *measured* abnormal return to the rival firms will be small if the merger has a relatively small chance of surviving government scrutiny. The above probability adjustment is "undoing" this antitrust "overhang," giving the cross-sectional regression a somewhat better chance of revealing evidence (if any) consistent with the market concentration doctrine.

The third form of the dependent variable is given by

$$dP \equiv \frac{X_0}{S_0 (1 - \tau)} AR'_j , \tag{7}$$

where X_0 is the current (pre-merger) net earnings available to stockholders, S_0 is the current level of sales, and τ is the (constant) corporate tax rate. As shown by Eckbo (1985, pp. 329-330), under a constant-growth firm valuation model, dP represents a hypothetical expected change in the industry's product price consistent with merger-induced abnormal returns of AR'_j to the representative rival of the merging firms. Thus, the regressions with dP as dependent variable ask the question of whether there is any evidence that the expected merger-induced product price change is correlated with the change in industry concentration. Of course, dP is only *hypothetically* a measure of an underlying product price change: If the mergers are efficient, then AR'_j represents the value of future cost savings, and dP must be interpreted as the percentage expected decrease in the merging firms' average cost of production. Thus, as with the other two dependent variables, evidence of $a_2 > 0$ does not discriminate between the market power and productive efficiency arguments. The important point, however, is that evidence of $a_2 < 0$ is inconsistent with the former argument while being consistent with the latter.

The regressions in Table 9 are all based on the sample of challenged mergers, which, if anything introduces a bias in favor of the market concentration doctrine (all the mergers were accused by the government of "monopolizing" product markets). Despite this potential bias, the table shows no evidence whatsoever supporting the concentration doctrine. The coefficient multiplying the change in the Herfindahl index is uniformly negative across all the regressions. For example, increasing dH by 1 per cent implies a reduction of 0.42 per cent in the abnormal returns (AR_j) to the average portfolio of rival firms. This coefficient is statistically significant on a 10 per cent level, with a t-value of -1.70. For both AR'_j and dP, the coefficient multiplying dH is negative, although the t-values are too low to conclude that they are statistically different from zero. As reported by Eckbo (1985, Table 6), similar results emerge when one uses the abnormal returns to the *merging* firms as dependent variable. Since the results do not support the market concentration doctrine, it is also inappropriate to continue to refer to dP as a product price change estimator. One consistent interpretation is that AR'_j, and therefore dP, is driven by merger-induced cost-savings.

5.4   Policy Issues

The accumulated evidence on U.S. antitrust enforcement rejects the hypothesis that the typical challenged horizontal merger would have been anticompetitive if allowed to go through. There are at least two plausible arguments for why the regulatory process may in fact result in efficient mergers being blocked. First, although preventing efficient mergers harms consumers, the *rivals* of the merging firms clearly benefit as they avoid having to face competition from an increasingly efficient merged firm. The rivals can indeed form a politically strong interest group in situations where they perceive a significant threat to their existing industry equilibrium. Perhaps a case in point is Chrysler's vocal opposition to the joint venture between GM and Toyota. At the time the venture was announced, Chrysler demanded that the Federal Trade Commission stop the venture for reasons that it would "harm competition." An alternative interpretation of Chrysler's opposition is that the firm suspected that the venture would make GM a tougher competitor, placing Chrysler at a competitive disadvantage. If the joint venture were expected to promote intra-industry collusion, Chrysler would benefit (through the higher product price) and it is doubtful that Chrysler Corporation would have complained. It is tempting, in this context, to cite Posner's (1969) more general assertion that the FTC is indeed significantly impaired in its task of promoting the public interest. He claims that FTC investigations are initiated "at the behest of corporations, trade associations, and trade unions whose motivation is at best to shift the costs of their private litigation to the taxpayer and at worst to harass competitors" (Posner 1969, p.88). Posner's antitrust "pork barrel" model is certainly not contradicted by the anecdotal nor by the more scientific evidence discussed above.

A second, and I believe quite relevant, reason for the failure of antitrust policy is plain ignorance. The anticompetitive significance of a horizontal merger can only be assessed *indirectly*, it does not represent a directly observable characteristic. Thus, policy makers are forced to rely on largely untested theories, among which the market concentration doctrine has been a favorite, in order to justify their decisions. As noted by Nobel Laureate George Stigler (1982), the economics profession has supplied "precious little" in the way of *tested* knowledge to support the market share and concentration criteria which (still) form the basis for U.S. antimerger policy. In fact, with the above recent evidence, it is becoming ever more clear that the market power hypothesis rests on an extremely weak empirical foundation. As long as those responsible for antimerger policy continue to insist on rigid structural standards for evaluating the competitive effects of mergers, it is reasonable, given the evidence, that special interest groups, including those representing relatively inefficient producers and/or a rigid work force, will continue to take advantage of the regulatory process.

The empirical evidence implies that past antimerger policy has been costly in terms of foregone opportunities to reallocate corporate resources to a higher-valued use. Furthermore, there is an additional – and somewhat more subtle – costs implied by prenotification rules such as those in the *Hart-Scott-Rodino Antitrust Improvements Act:*

> If a merger proposal conveys to the market some of the valuable inside information held by the bidder firm, the delay in the execution of the merger transaction required by the pre-merger notification rules can reduce the bidder's expected return from the investment. The evidence indicates that rival firms benefit from the news of a merger proposal, and a delay in execution gives these rival firms additional time to exploit the news, perhaps by competing for the target firm. This potential public-good problem lowers the *ex ante* expected returns to the firm initiating the merger negotiations, whether the merger will have anticompetitive effects or not (Eckbo and Wier 1985, pp. 139-140).

Thus, prenotification rules entails the same public-good problem as the one associated with disclosure rules in general (see Section 4). Indeed, shifting antitrust enforcement from an *ex post* analysis of anticompetitive effects to an *ex ante* assessment of the likelihood of reduced competition means that the regulatory agencies not only forego the benefit of the larger and more complete data set available *ex post*, they also impose the costs caused by mandatory disclosure rules and the associated delay in the execution of takeovers.

Of course, evidence that antitrust policy is costly does not necessarily rule out the possibility that the same policy is socially optimal. It is possible that the threat of a challenge also deters a sufficient number of collusive mergers from even reaching the state of a merger proposal. The benefit of the previous studies is then to refocus the debate on the perhaps most important remaining issue. What is the likely social value of the deterrent effect? Empirical evidence on this difficult issue is virtually non-existent. Until there is substantial evidence that a significant number of socially inefficient, anticompetitive mergers are likely to take place in an unregulated economy, I believe the only logical conclusion to be drawn from the existing evidence is to have a largely permissive merger policy constrained to *ex post* examination of anticompetitive effects.[68]

6.0 FIRA AND FOREIGN ACQUISITIONS IN CANADA

6.1 The Foreign Investment Review Agency[69]

The period 1974-1984 saw a unique experiment in Canadian industrial policy. During these years, the Foreign Investment Review Agency (FIRA) effectively regulated the acquisition of control of Canadian business enterprises by foreign individuals, corporations, governments, or groups containing foreign members. Under Section 2(2) of the 1973 Foreign Investment Review (FIR) Act, such acquisitions must provide "significant benefits" to Canada in order to be approved.[70] The FIR Act was in part motivated by the Gray Report (1972) which lists several potentially "undesirable impacts" of foreign direct investments in Canada, allegedly restricting Canadian sovereignty over its industrial policy.[71] Between 1974 and December 1984, when the new Mulroney government introduced legislation renaming FIRA "Investment Canada" and which substantially curtailed the agency's authority, FIRA reviewed approximately 2,100 foreign acquisition attempts, of which 9 per cent were disallowed.[72]

6.2 Theoretical Issues

The history of FIRA's enforcement activity represents another interesting laboratory for studying the effects of direct government intervention in the market for corporate control. In Eckbo (1986b), I interpret the "significant benefit" requirement of the FIR Act synonymously with a transfer of economic rents from foreign bidders to Canadian interests. In this framework, examining the relative "success" or "failure" of FIRA's enforcement activity is equivalent to examining the joint proposition that (1) prior to FIRA's intervention, foreign acquirers did in fact earn positive economic rents from acquiring Canadian targets, and (2) some or all of these rents have been transferred to Canadian interests through FIRA's (implicit or explicit) bilateral negotiations with the acquiring firms.

Since the stock price reaction to acquisition attempts captures the present value of the rents from acquisition activity, this joint hypothesis can be tested directly by examining the acquisition-induced abnormal stock price performance of firms involved in foreign takeovers before and after 1974. The main prediction is that the abnormal return to foreign acquirers has become significantly lower as a result of FIRA's enforcement policy. Irrespective of the nature of the "significant benefit," it must be paid for through the rents otherwise earned by the foreign bidders. Thus, this prediction is valid whether one argues that the benefit is in the form of a local employment subsidy (e.g., by maintaining production in plants that would otherwise have been closed down), in the form of "political flexibility" over domestic industrial policy, or simply in the form of an "entry fee" into the Canadian market for corporate control.[73]

With approximately 9 per cent of all applicants rejected,[74] and given the costs to foreign investors of going through a FIRA application process, entry into the Canadian takeover market by foreign bidders is effectively restricted, an interesting question is whether this entry restriction benefits rivals domestic bidders. Reduced foreign competition for Canadian target firms leads to an increase in the gains to domestic bidders and a decrease in the gains to domestic targets, a proposition that can be addressed empirically by the event study methodology. It is also possible to test the hypothesis that domestic target firms, through FIRA, have received a rent transfer from their foreign merger partners by comparing gains to targets of foreign bidders in the periods before and during FIRA's enforcement activity.

6.3 Empirical Evidence

Eckbo (1986b) tests some of the above predictions using a sample of approximately 450 foreign acquisitions where the bidder firms are U.S. corporations listed on the New York Stock Exchange (NYSE). The results for this sample are also contrasted with the performance of domestic bidder firms listed on the Toronto Stock Exchange (TSE), using a subsample of the more than 1,900 domestic mergers analyzed in Eckbo (1986a). All the acquisitions were successfully completed, i.e., no disallowed cases are included in the sample. The focus on successful cases follows from the fact that FIRA's policy is one of approving foreign acquisitions subject to constraints rather than one of rejecting acquisitions *per se*. The basic issue is whether these constraints have materially affected the rents earned by successful foreign bidders.

The main empirical results, which are summarized in Table 10, fail to reject the hypothesis that foreign bidders seeking Canadian targets on average earn zero economic rents from the acquisition activity, whether one focuses on the 10-year period 1964 through 1973 or the subsequent ten-year period, 1974 through 1983. The 281 successful foreign bidder firms from the period 1964-1973 earned on average a statistically insignificant -0.8 per cent abnormal return over the month the merger was first announced in the financial press. Furthermore, the 190 successful bidder firms from the 1974-1983 period earned a statistically insignificant -0.7 per cent over the same announcement month. If foreign bidders typically earn zero rents even in the absence of FIRA, it is not surprising to find that they also typically earn zero abnormal returns in the 1974-1983 period.[75]

As listed in Table 10, Eckbo (1986a) reports that a sample of 1,138 domestic bidder firms on average earned 0.8 per cent announcement month abnormal returns, with a t-value of 3.0. Thus, domestic bidder firms appear to outperform foreign bidders acquiring Canadian targets. The results in Table 10 further shows that the average performance of domestic bidder firms over the 1964-1973 period is indistinguishable from the performance in the 1974-1983 period. This evidence does not support the proposition that FIRA has benefitted domestic bidders by reducing competition from foreign firms. Furthermore, there is no systematic evidence that domestic target firms earn larger gains as a result of FIRA's activity. In sum, there is no evidence that FIRA has materially altered the distribution of gains between bidder and target firms in successfully completed acquisitions.

6.4 Policy Issues

As discussed above, there is no evidence that the enforcement of the FIR Act affected the level or distribution of merger gains between parties directly involved in successfully completed foreign or domestic acquisitions. Since

Table 10
Summary of per cent average abnormal returns to bidder and target firms in domestic and foreign acquisitions in Canada, as reported in Eckbo (1986b) for the month of the first public announcement of the acquisition. All foreign bidders are listed on the New York Stock Exchange, while the listed Canadian bidders and targets are listed on the Toronto Stock Exchange

(Sample size and t-statistic in parentheses)

Type of Firm	Per cent Abnormal Return

I. Sample period 1964-73, before FIRA

Domestic bidder firms	0.7 (669, 2.10)
Foreign bidder firms	-0.8 (281, -1.6)
Canadian targetsa	6.2 (151, 6.5)

II. Sample period 1974-83, with FIRA

Domestic bidder firms	0.8 (513, 2.1)
Foreign bidder firms	-0.7 (190, -1.6)
Canadian targetsa	2.4 (262, 4.0)

a Over the entire sample period, 1964-83, Canadian targets of domestic bidders earned on average 3.9 (336, 6.9) per cent abnormal return while Canadian targets of foreign bidders earned 2.5 (77, 2.2) per cent abnormal return over the month of the first public announcement of the acquisition.

foreign bidder firms earned minimal (if any) gains from Canadian acquisitions also prior to 1974, it is unlikely that any other (third) party can have received a significant rent transfer through FIRA. Rather, the evidence indicates that competition facing foreign bidders drives most – if not all – of the gains from acquisitions to the target shareholders, with or without intervention by FIRA.

At a minimum, this evidence makes it difficult to justify the costs to Canadian taxpayers of FIRA's regulatory policy, such as the direct costs of FIRA's operations and potential indirect costs as foreign firms are deterred from investing in Canada, by referring to a potential benefit in the form of a rent transfer from foreign bidders. Note also the interesting fact that, given the evidence from the 1964-1973 period, it would have been possible to draw this conclusion already in 1973, before FIRA was established.

7.0 CONCLUSIONS

This paper presents an extensive discussion of various financial theories and capital market evidence concerning the economic effects of regulations of the market for corporate control. A central message emerging from the large number of academic studies reviewed is that the market for corporate control plays a vital role in promoting an efficient allocation of corporate resources. The recurring theme is that government regulations which make it more difficult to transact in the corporate control market are likely to result in a socially suboptimal allocation of corporate resources without any clearly offsetting benefits. While there are many important details in the above discussion, government agencies responsible for generating a public policy response to the corporate takeovers should, in particular, be aware of the following.

Concentration of share ownership facilitates the takeover process. Acquisition of a widely held firm is made difficult by the fact that small shareholders, who find it too costly to coordinate their selling decisions, will under certain circumstances decide to keep their shares even when the acquisition would have benefitted both bidder and target shareholders (recall the discussion of the "free rider" problem in Section 3). Large shareholders have a greater incentive to make sure opportunities for profitable share transfers are fully exploited, thereby providing a significant service to minority shareholders as well. Placing a maximum limit on individual shareholdings promote managerial inefficiencies. Large shareholders also have a greater incentive to actively monitor the performance of incumbent managers. The issue of self-dealing, which is sometimes cited as a reason for imposing limits on individual shareholdings, ought to be addressed, if necessary, by more effective – and most likely less costly – forms of regulations, such as rules requiring equal treatment of all shareholders (which is a basic principle of Canadian corporate law).

Placing a limit on the number of different corporate entities that can be operated under a given ownership umbrella is likely to entail a social cost in terms of foregone efficiency gains. As discussed in Section 5, even in industries where there have been strong *a priori* reasons to fear monopolization effects of horizontal mergers, the enforcement record of the antitrust authorities over the last three decades show that such *a prio,* arguments are for the most part empirically unfounded. On the other hand, the evidence is consistent with the proposition that corporate combinations enhances efficiency.

Mandatory information disclosure, prenotification rules, and delayed execution of takeover bids significantly raise the cost of a takeover. The usual argument for such rules is that (1) target shareholders need time and information to make rational decisions, and (2) government agencies need time to form an opinion concerning the potential anticompetitive effects of horizontal mergers before the mergers are consummated. As discussed in Sections 2 and 4, the evidence strongly indicates that target shareholders benefit greatly from takeovers whether or not disclosure rules are in place, and that the underlying "corporate raiding" theory of takeovers is false. The evidence also shows that the introduction of disclosure rules have led to a significant increase in the cost to bidder firms of purchasing the target shares, which means that a number of otherwise profitable (and socially desirable) takeovers are being deterred.

The idea of judging the anticompetitive effects of horizontal mergers before the mergers have actually occurred shifts the emphasis of antitrust policy from an *ex post* analysis of actual merger effects to an *ex ante* analysis based on theoretical arguments which have an extremely weak empirical foundation in the economics literature. The evidence based on U.S. antitrust enforcement activity after the introduction of prenotification rules rejects the argument that prenotification rules have improved the enforcement agencies' ability to select truly anticompetitive (as opposed to efficient) mergers for prosecution. At the same time, prenotification rules, just as disclosure rules in general, entail a social cost in terms of reducing the *ex ante* expected return from merger activity, thus deterring a number of efficient mergers.

Restrictions on foreign ownership participation in Canadian firms is, if anything, likely to reduce the level of competition in domestic markets and restrict access to international markets and projects by domestic firms. The Canadian economy can only benefit from the additional pool of investment capital made available from foreign investors. Furthermore, any foreign expertise supplied through foreign direct ownership participation in domestic ventures further enhances the competitiveness of domestic firms. Fears that unrestricted foreign ownership in Canadian firms will drive domestically-owned firms out of business have no basis in empirical evidence and should not constitute the basis for a public ownership policy.

Attempts by the government to extract benefits from foreign investors as a condition for granting the right to invest in Canadian firms are likely to be unsuccessful. As shown in Section 6, the evidence indicates that FIRA did not succeed, over the period 1974-1983, in affecting the distribution of gains between the various players in the market for corporate control (including the domestic target, the foreign bidder, and rival domestic bidders). Importantly, while FIRA's activity clearly deterred some foreign investments in Canada, there is no evidence that the cost of this deterrent (including the cost of running the agency itself) has been offset by a benefit in terms of extracting economic rents from foreign bidders. It appears that competition among bidder firms, with or without intervention by FIRA, effectively transfers most of the economic rents from foreign bidders to their respective Canadian targets.

NOTES

1.   See W.T. Grimm, *Mergerstat Review* (1985). For more recent data see *Mergerstat Review 1986* and *Business Week*, April 17, 1987.

2.   "It is questionable how much more long-term planning America's shareholders can stand. What many managements seem to be demanding is more time to keep making the same mistakes" (Pickens 1986).

3.   The office of the Chief Economist of the U.S. Securities and Exchange Commission (SEC), in a study entitled "Institutional ownership, tender offers, and long-term investments," SEC (1985a), reports that firms with high research and development expenditures are not more vulnerable to takeovers. Furthermore, aggregate spending on research and development reached a record level in 1984, which was also a year of record acquisition activity (see, e.g., *Business Week*, July 8, 1985, p. 86 ff).

4.   The Federal Reserve Board apparently disapproves of the use of high risk, high yield ("junk") bonds to finance takeovers. Junk bonds are rated below the investment grade by the bond rating agencies and carry interest rates that are 3 to 5 percentage points higher than the yields on government bonds of comparable maturity. The bonds provide a claim on the proceeds of the merger venture, using the assets and cash flow of the target plus the equity contributed by the acquirer as collateral, which is a common method of financing in other areas (e.g., a mortgage in a home purchase). See Jensen (1986) for an illuminating discussion of the myths and realities associated with the use of junk bonds in corporate takeovers.

5.   For an introduction to portfolio theory, see, e.g., Elton and Gruber (1987).

6.   For example, the principle of equal treatment of all shareholders may need court protection in order to prevent corporate self-tenders which discriminate against certain groups of shareholders. This principle is entrenched in Canadian and French corporate law. Allegations of abusive defensive practices have led to proposed legislation in the U.S. which, if adopted, would limit the target managers' ability to adjust their firm's assets and ownership structure in response to a takeover

bid (Tender Offer Act, H.R. 5693, 98th Congress, 2d Session, May 22, 1984).

7. "[T]ake-overs, like bankruptcy, represent one of Nature's methods of eliminating deadwood in the struggle for survival. A more open and efficiently responsive corporate society can result," Samuelson (1970), p. 505.

8. See Jensen and Ruback (1983), Halpern (1983), Roll (1986), Jensen (1986).

9. See, e.g., Fama (1976) and Schwert (1981) for a review.

10. A common misconception is that the empirical evidence based on stock returns necessitates the strong assumptions underlying the Capital Asset Pricing Model (CAPM) pioneered by Sharpe (1964), Lintner (1965) and Mossin (1966). What is needed is an unbiased estimate of the individual security's expected return. Under the assumption of stationarity the historical mean return is an appropriate measure of the expected return. Indeed, the main results emphasized below are typically invariant to whether one uses this simple historical mean or a more sophisticated approach (e.g., the CAPM) to estimate expected returns.

11. When the managerial action proves to reduce the stock price *ex post*, "it is difficult, given uncertainty, to distinguish between managerial incompetence, managerial opportunism, and mere bad luck" (Jensen and Ruback 1983, p. 612).

12. Common stock issues, convertible debt calls and targeted share repurchases are examples of managerial actions which appear to systematically convey negative information about the firm. See Smith (1986) for a review.

13. The latter are revelations of the type "the house is on fire but the management is doing something about it."

14. See, e.g., Ravenscraft and Scherer (1986) for accounting-based evidence on the profitability of mergers. It is summarized in Chapter 8 of this volume. Furthermore, for a lively discussion on the relative merits of accounting-based profits studies, see Benston (1985), as well as the subsequent comment and reply by Scherer *et al.* (1987) and Benston (1987), respectively.

15. From the point of view of the synergy hypothesis, economic efficiencies and market power are equivalent sources of takeover

gains. A discussion which contrasts the two basic sources of gains is given in Section 5, below.

16.   The *ex ante* managerial contract accounts for the expected level of managerial shirking.

17.   See Grossman and Hart (1980) for a theoretical analysis of this situation.

18.   Such a transfer of resources could take place, e.g., by forcing the target to purchase inputs from the bidder at prices exceeding marginal costs or to sell the target's output to the bidder at a price below marginal cost. Alternatively, the bidder may vote a full merger with the target at a price below the true value of the target shares.

19.   Roll's hypothesis raises the question of why shareholders, if all takeovers were indeed prompted by hubris, do not stop the practice by forbidding managers ever to make any bid. The fact that such prohibitions are not observed is explainable under the hubris hypothesis only if the deadweight costs of takeovers are negligible, leaving well-diversified shareholders indifferent to takeover activity. As a result, even under the extreme hubris hypothesis there is no obvious role for a policy of government intervention in the merger process. A further discussion of this point is given in section 2.4, below.

20.   Other frequently used terms for the same hypothesis are "growth maximization" and "empire building."

21.   See Fama (1976) for a description of the market model.

22.   The following is a common procedure for inferring the statistical significance of the average abnormal return: Standardize AAR_τ by dividing each individual $AR_{j\tau}$ by an unbiased estimate of its standard deviation. Such an estimate is given by

$$\hat{\sigma}(AR_{j\tau}) = \hat{\sigma}(\varepsilon_j)[R_{m\tau}(R'_m R_m)^{-1} R'_{m\tau} + 1]^{1/2},$$

where $R_{m\tau}$ is the vector of observations on the independent variables in period, R_m is the matrix of observations on the independent variables used in the estimation period, and $\hat{\sigma}(\varepsilon_j)$ is the OLS estimate of the standard error of the regression disturbances over the estimation period. See, e.g., Theil (1972, pp.122-123). If the mergers/acquisitions in the sample represent independent events, (i.e., assuming the mergers take place in strictly non-overlapping calendar periods), then this average standardized abnormal return ($ASAR_\tau$) is distributed approximately normal with variance l/J. Consequently, $Z(AAR_\tau) \equiv ASAR_\tau \sqrt{J}$ is approximately a standard normal variate under the null hypothesis of $AAR_\tau = 0$. Furthermore, assuming serial independence in the $Z(AAR_\tau)$s, it follows that

$$Z(CAAR) \equiv 1/\sqrt{L} \sum_{\tau=\tau_1}^{\tau_2} Z(AAR_\tau)$$

is also approximately unit normal under the hypothesis that $CAAR = 0$. For an elegant, and more complete, exposition of hypothesis testing in the event-study framework, see Thompson (1985).

23. This conclusion presumes the events being studied do not overlap in calendar time.

24. An exception is mergers in Canada. See Eckbo (1986a, 1988).

25. The studies by Jarrell and Bradley (1980), Bradley, Desai and Kim (1983) and Ruback (1983) use, in large part, the data bases underlying Dodd and Ruback (1977) and Bradley (1980), and report results consistent with the two earlier studies. Note that, in several cases, the major focus of a particular study goes beyond simply documenting the gains to the bidder and target firms. Several of these other aspects are discussed in subsequent sections of this paper.

26. In France, since 1973, a privately negotiated controlling- block trade must be followed by a public offer to purchase *all* additional shares tendered to the bidder at the controlling-block trade price. This public offer, which effectively converts a privately negotiated controlling-block trade into a public tender offer for 100 per cent of the target shares, must be outstanding for a minimum of 15 days. See Eckbo and Langohr (1988).

27. Eckbo (1986a) also reports that targets in Canada earn on average 10 per cent abnormal return over the four months leading up to, and including, the announcement month.

28. Eckbo (1986a) and Franks and Harris (1986) use monthly data and do not, therefore, report announcement-day abnormal returns.

29. In unsuccessful tender offers the market price per share of the target firm drifts to a level above the offer price during the offer period, causing target shareholders to keep their shares rather than tender.

30. In the vernacular of Bradley, Desai and Kim (1983), the offer reveals to the world that the target firm is "sitting on a gold mine."

31. Bradley, Desai and Kim (1983) refers to this as the "kick in the pants" hypothesis.

32. Note that there may be sufficient communication between the majority and minority shareholders to avoid the free-rider problem discussed by Grossman and Hart (1980). That is, even if the minority shareholders anticipate the value-increasing change in the firm's operations, the bidder may, through bilateral negotiations, succeed in acquiring the minority shares at a price favorable to both parties.

33. See Lehn and Poulsen (1986, pp 3-5) for a description of the typical financing of leveraged buyouts.

34. DeAngelo, DeAngelo and Rice (1984) claim that the capitalized value of these costs can be in the range of $1 million, which is a substantial number given that the median equity value of the firms in their sample is $6 million.

35. In the U.S., a necessary condition for tax-free status is that at least 50 per cent of the value of the transaction is paid in the form of securities. In Canada, the corresponding requirement is 100 per cent.

36. For successful cash offers, the average magnitude of this premium component is 47 per cent, while it is on average -1 per cent in exchange offers.

37. It is a popular myth that the billions of dollars spent purchasing target firms are somehow wasted because the money is paid to target shareholders rather than invested elsewhere. The notion that the money leaves the financial system as soon as it is paid to target shareholders is, of course, false: The purchase price in a takeover represents a *transfer* of claims on resources and not the *consumption* of these resources. Direct transaction costs of takeovers, which represent resources actually consumed in the takeover process, are generally in the order of 0.1 per cent to 0.2 per cent of the dollar value of the deal.

38. For example, of the Standard & Poor's 500 corporations, 13 had passed anti-takeover amendments prior to 1983, while an additional 99 passed amendments over the two-year period 1983-84.

39. "In June 1982, the Supreme Court struck down the Illinois business Takeover Act on the grounds that it pre-empted Federal law and was overly burdensome to interstate commerce [*Edgar* v. *Mite*, 102 S. Ct. 2629 (1982)]. This decision effectively invalidated most antitakeover statutes passed since 1970," (Jarrell and Poulsen 1986, n. 7).

40. The following example is taken from SEC (1985b, pp. 12-13).

41. This situation is logically equivalent to the so-called "prisoner's dilemma." Place two suspected perpetrators of a crime in separate rooms and present each with the following proposition. If you confess and your partner does not, he receives the harshest punishment and you go free. If he confesses and you do not, then you receive the harshest punishment and he goes free. If both confess, then both receive moderate punishment. The rational prisoner will confess to avoid the harshest punishment, even though no confession results in both going free.

42. The following exposition is based on the discussion in Eckbo (1987).

43. "A standstill agreement is a voluntary contract between an issuing corporation and a substantial stockholder which limits the stockholder's ownership of voting shares to some maximum (less than controlling) percentage for a stipulated number of years. In a typical standstill, NVF Company and affiliates and City Investing recently agreed that the former's ownership position in City Investing be limited to a maximum of 21 per cent for the next five years. The agreement stipulates that NVF will not solicit proxies or otherwise participate in a control contest against the incumbent management of City Investing. Also, should NVF decide to sell its large block, City Investing has the right of first refusal to repurchase the shares. The ownership limitation agreement is not binding if a third party makes a tender offer for more than 21 per cent of City Investing or if City Investing proposes a merger with a third party. Standstill agreements sometimes include a stronger transferability restriction which specifies that the issuing firm's approval must be obtained before the large block holding can be sold" (Dann and DeAngelo 1983, p. 276).

44. Since the firm must fully compensate the raider for the takeover gains foregone by signing a standstill agreement, this argument presumes that future potential acquirers can generate substantially larger total takeover gains than can the initial raider. In this sense, greenmail can buy even more valuable future takeover opportunities. In the Schleifer and Vishny (1986) model, the greenmail payment has the additional effect of informing the market that the current takeover opportunity is less valuable than anticipated, causing a net negative adjustment in the firm's stock price.

45. As discussed by Bradley (1980) and Grossman and Hart (1980), the expected value of this post-acquisition policy is a crucial determinant of the success of a tender offer for a less than 100 per cent controlling interest in the firm.

46. With symmetric information, competition among raiders would raise the acquisition price of the target to the point where shareholders would at least get the full value of the firm under the current management. If, however, everyone but the management over-estimate the post-offer target share price under the raider's control, competition is effectively deterred.

47. An argument based on the prisoner's dilemma phenomenon discussed in section 3.2.1 above, and which does not necessitate the type of information asymmetry described in the above paragraph, will yield the same prediction. Note also that while fair price provisions in the corporate charter can effectively protect target shareholders from expropriation through a two- tiered tender offer, no such protection is offered for the case where the market simply overestimated the post-offer value of the target firm under the raider's control.

48. With the 1970 Amendment to the 1968 Williams Act, U.S. investors are required to file Schedule 13D, disclosing to the Securities and Exchange Commission the accumulation of more than 5 per cent of any class of a company's voting equity securities (between 1968 and 1970, the threshold investment position was 10 per cent). An amended Schedule 13D must be filed in response to subsequent major changes in the investment position.

49. These amendments started to surface in 1984, and by the end of 1986 approximately 50 firms had precommitted not to pay greenmail.

50. The discussion throughout Section 4 follows the discussion in Eckbo and Langohr (1988).

51. For further details, see Jarrell and Bradley (1980).

52. For references and a further description of the corporate control market in France, see Eckbo and Langohr (1988).

53. Nathan and O'Keefe (1986) do not provide information on the number of bidders involved in the mergers, nor do they examine the premium in unsuccessful merger bids.

54. The concept of an information-adjusted offer premium was explained earlier in section 2.3.4.

55. *United States* v. *Procter and Gamble* (386 U.S. 568 at 580 (1967)).

56. Eckbo and Wier (1985) analyze the impact of the *Hart-Scott-Rodino Act*.

57.   See Eckbo and Wier (1985, p.122 at 123) for the definition of "large" in this context.

58.   Sixth FTC Annual Report to Congress concerning HSR ACT (1983, p. 11). During the period September 1978 through December 1982 the DOJ and the FTC observed 4,274 reported transactions and received 7,761 notifications (more than one filing may be received for a single transaction where there are multiple parties and where the transaction is completed through several steps).

59.   *Ibid.* at p. 11.

60.   The Justice Department's Merger Guidelines of 1968 state market shares that were likely to trigger an antitrust complaint. The critical aggregate market shares varied according to the four-firm market concentration ratios. For example, a merger between two firms each having 4 per cent of the sales in a market with a four-firm concentration ratio of 75 per cent or more was likely to be challenged. The Department's 1982 Merger Guidelines use the Herfindahl Index of concentration and are somewhat less restrictive than the old guidelines, but their focus is also on market structure. For a perspective on the 1982 Guidelines, see Tollison (1983). Note that the government does not strictly adhere to its own guidelines: Rogowsky (1982) finds that 20 per cent of the mergers challenged under the 1968 guidelines actually fell below the guidelines, and one-third of these were found in violation of Section 7 of the *Clayton Act.*

61.   A closely related but somewhat less general prediction is that high level of concentration should be associated with relatively high, supracompetitive *product prices.* Although evidence of supra-competitive pricing is sufficient to conclude that market power is present, it is clearly not necessary: Monopoly rents can also be generated by means of collusion on non-price variables, by monopsonizing inputs, or by sophisticated price discrimination schemes that need not be evident through the observed product price.

62.   For a survey of the literature on the "structure-conduct- performance" paradigm, see, e.g., Scherer (1980) and Weiss (1974).

63.   Brozen (1970), Demsetz (1973), Peltzman (1977), and Carter (1978) present evidence supporting the theory that industry concentration is predominantly a result of the expansion of relatively cost-efficient producers. The issue of cross-industry variation in risk is not explicitly addressed in this literature.

64.   The rivals are defined based on overlapping 5-digit Standard Industrial Classification (SIC) codes. For the challenged mergers, the relevant product market is the one identified in court records as being

the market 'threatened' by the 'anticompetitive' merger. For unchallenged mergers, the relevant product market is the target's major product line, as defined in the Standard & Poor's *Registry of Corporations*. As shown by Eckbo and Wier (1985), the empirical results based on the 5-digit SIC rivals are robust. They duplicate the tests using rivals identified by the DOJ or the FTC as being relevant competitors, and they draw precisely the same inferences.

65.   Notice, in Table 8, that the non-negative rival firm performance in response to the complaint announcement contrasts with the significantly negative abnormal returns to both the bidder and target firms around this event. Thus, one cannot argue that the insigificant abnormal returns to rivals is simply driven by prior anticipation of the complaint. If this were true, no reaction would have been detected in the prices of the bidder and target firms shares either.

66. $CR_4 \equiv \sum\limits_{i=1}^{4} s_i$, and $H \equiv \sum\limits_{i=1}^{n} s_i^2$, where s_i is the market share of firm i, (in CR_4 the sum is over the four firms with the largest market shares), and n is the total number of firms in the industry. The change in the Herfindahl index caused by the merger between firms i and j in the same industry is therefore given by $dH = 2s_i s_j$.

67.   Eckbo (1985) estimates π using binary logit regression with the number of firms in the industry, CR_4 and the market values of the bidder and target firms as explanatory variables, and using the total sample of challenged as well as unchallenged horizontal mergers. As expected, π turns out to be significantly positively related to CR_4 and significantly negatively related to the number of firms in the industry. For the challenged mergers π ranges from 0.06 to 0.81 with a mean and standard deviation of 0.45 and 0.21, respectively. For the unchallenged mergers π ranges from 0.01 to 0.78, with a mean and standard deviation of 0.20 and 0.14.

68.   This point is also made by Tollison (1983), written while he was Director of the Bureau of Economics of the Federal Trade Commission. As to the prospects for future evidence on the deterrent effect of merger policy, I am currently in the process of repeating the above test strategy on horizontal mergers in Canada, which until recently faced no effective antitrust restriction. If there is such a thing as an anticompetitive mergers, it is more likely to take place in Canada than in the U.S. Thus, a comparison between the U.S. and Canadian merger experience may uncover some evidence on the deterrent effect of U.S. antitrust policy *per se*. A characterization of Canadian competition policy and how it compares with U.S. antitrust legislation is found in Stanbury and Reschenthaler (1981).

69. The discussion throughout Section 6 follows the exposition in Eckbo (1986b).

70. In the 1973 FIR Act, Canadian participation is a key consideration in industries dominated by foreign ownership. Avoiding bankruptcy is also considered a "significant benefit" in this context. "Small acquisitions" (i.e., targets with less than $250,000 in assets, less than $3 million in revenues, and less than 100 employees) do not have to meet the "significant benefit" test, only a "no detriment" test.

71. For a vivid account of the events which led to the FIR Act, and the international (in particular, U.S.) reaction to the resulting unilateral trade restrictions, see Clarkson (1982).

72. See FIRA annual reports, 1975 to 1983.

73. The delay and extra paper work caused by FIRA represent an obvious cost to foreign bidders and, by itself, constitute an entry fee. The important issue of whether the benefits hypothetically extracted by FIRA in fact exceed these and other costs of operating the bureaucracy has not been addressed in the literature, and is not addressed by the prediction stated in the text.

74. Since rejected applications tend to be among the largest proposed acquisitions, the rejection rate is greater in terms of market value.

75. Marginally profitable foreign bidders will drop out of the Canadian takeover market in response to the costs imposed by FIRA. Since, in fact, not all foreign bidders were deterred by FIRA, and assuming FIRA indeed does impose costs on foreign bidders, it cannot literally be true that these bidders all would have earned zero rents in the absence of FIRA. What the evidence does show, however, is that these rents were not statistically distinguishable from zero.

REFERENCES

Asquith, P. (1983) "Merger bids, uncertainty, and stockholder returns," *Journal of Financial Economics*, Vol. 11, pp. 51-83.

Asquith, P., R.F. Bruner and D.W. Mullins, Jr. (1983) "The gains to bidding firms from merger," *Journal of Financial Economics*, Vol. 11, pp. 121-139.

Bain, J.S (1951) "Relation of profit rate to industry concentration: American manufacturing, 1936-1940," *Quarterly Journal of Economics*, Vol. 65, pp. 293-324.

Benston, G.J. (1985) "The validity of profits-structure studies with particular reference to the FTC's line of business data," *American Economic Review*, Vol. 75, 37-67.

Benston, J.S. (1987) "The validity of studies with line of business data: Reply," *American Economic Review*, Vol. 77, pp. 218-223.

Boardman, A., R. Freedman and C. Eckel (1986) "The price of government ownership," *Journal of Public Economics*, Vol. 31, pp. 269-285.

Bradley, M. (1980) "Interfirm tender offers and the market for Corporate control," *Journal of Business*, Vol. 53, pp. 345-376.

Bradley, M., A. Desai and E.H. Kim (1983) "The rational behind interfirm tender offers: Information or synergy?", *Journal of Financial Economics*, Vol. 11, pp. 183-206.

Bradley, M. and L.M. Wakeman (1983) "The wealth effects of targeted share repurchases," *Journal of Financial Economics*, Vol. 11, pp. 301-328.

Brown, S. and J. Warner (1980) "Measuring security price performance," *Journal of Financial Economics*, Vol. 8, pp. 205-257.

Brown, S. and J. Warner (1985) "Using daily stock returns: The case of event studies," *Journal of Financial Economics*, Vol. 14, pp. 3-31.

Brozen, Y. (1970) "The antitrust task force deconcentration recommendation," *Journal of Law and Economics*, Vol. 13, pp. 279-292.

Carter. J.R. (1978) "Collusion, efficiency, and antitrust," *Journal of Law and Economics*, Vol. 21, pp. 435-444.

Carney, W. J. (1985) "Two-Tier tender offers and shark repellents," *Midland Corporate Finance Journal*, Vol. 3, pp. 48-56.

Clarkson, S. (1982) *Canada and the Reagan Challenge* (Toronto: James Lorimer & Co.).

Cournot, A.A., [1838] (1927) *Researches into the mathematical principles of the theory of wealth*, (New York: Macmillan).

Dann, L. Y. and H. DeAngelo (1983) "Standstill agreements, privately negotiated stock repurchases, and the market for corporate control," *Journal of Financial Economics*, Vol. 11, pp. 275-330.

DeAngelo, H., L. DeAngelo and E. Rice (1984) "Going private: Minority freezeouts and stockholder wealth," *Journal of Law and Economics*, Vol. 27, pp. 367-401.

DeAngelo, H. and E. Rice (1983) "Antitakeover charter amendments and stockholder wealth," *Journal of Financial Economics*, Vol. 11, pp. 329-360.

Demsetz, H. (1973) "Industry structure, market rivalry, and public policy," *Journal of Law and Economics*, Vol. 16, pp. 1-9.

Dodd, P. (1980) "Merger proposals, management discretion and stockholder wealth," *Journal of Financial Economics*, Vol. 8, pp. 105-138.

Dodd, P. and R. Ruback (1977) "Tender offers and stockholder returns: An empirical analysis," *Journal of Financial Economics*, Vol. 5, pp. 351-374.

Dodd, P. and J.B. Warner (1983) "On corporate governance: A study of proxy contests," *Journal of Financial Economics*, Vol. 11, pp. 401-438.

Eckbo, B.E. (1983) "Horizontal mergers, collusion, and stockholder wealth," *Journal of Financial Economics*, Vol. 11, pp. 241-273.

Eckbo, B.E. (1985) "Mergers and the market concentration doctrine: Evidence from the capital market," *Journal of Business*, Vol. 58, pp. 325-349.

Eckbo, B.E. (1986a) "Mergers and the market for corporate control: The Canadian evidence," *Canadian Journal of Economics*, Vol. 19, pp. 236-260.

Eckbo, B.E. (1986b) "FIRA and the profitability of foreign acquisitions in Canada" (Unpublished paper, University of British Columbia).

Eckbo. B.E. (1986c) "Synergy, information and intra-industry wealth effects of tender offer contests" (Unpublished paper, University of British Columbia).

Eckbo, B.E. (1987) "Antigreenmail charter amendments and the targeted share repurchase controversy" (Unpublished paper, University of British Columbia).

Eckbo, B.E. (1988) "Gains to bidder firms: Methodological issues and U.S.-Canadian evidence," *Journal of Financial Economics*, forthcoming.

Eckbo, B.E., R. Giammarino and R. Heinkel (1987) "Information asymmetries and the medium of exchange in mergers: Theory and evidence" (Unpublished paper, University of British Columbia).

Eckbo, B.E. and H. Langohr (1988) "Information disclosure, means of payment, and takeover premia: Public and private tender offers in France," *Journal of Financial Economics*, forthcoming.

Eckbo, B.E. and P. Wier (1985) "Antimerger policy under the Hart-Scott-Rodino Act: A reexamination of the market power hypothesis," *Journal of Law and Economics*, Vol. 28, pp. 119-149.

Eckel, C.C. and T. Vermaelen (1986) "Internal regulation: The effects of government ownership on the value of the firm," *Journal of Law and Economics*, Vol. 29, pp. 381-403.

Eger, C.E. (1983) "An empirical test of the redistribution effect in pure exchange mergers," *Journal of Financial and Quantitative Analysis*, Vol. 18, pp. 547-572.

Elton, J.E. and M.J. Gruber (1987) *Modern Portfolio Theory and Investment Analysis*, 3rd ed. (New York: John Wiley & Sons).

Fama, E.F. (1976) *Foundations of Finance*, Basic Books.

Fama, E.F. (1980) "Agency problems and the theory of the firm," *Journal of Political Economy*, Vol. 88, pp. 288-307.

Fama, E.F., L. Fisher, M.C. Jensen and R. Roll (1969) "The adjustment of stock prices to new information," *International Economic Review*, Vol. 10, pp. 1-21.

Fishman, M. (1986) "Preemptive bidding and the role of the medium of exchange in acquisitions" (Unpublished paper, Northwestern University).

Franks, J.R. and R.S. Harris (1986) "Shareholder wealth effects of corporate takeovers: The UK experience 1955-85" (Unpublished paper, London Business School).

Gray, H. (1972) *Foreign Direct Investment in Canada* (Ottawa: Queen's Printer).

Grossman, S. and O. Hart (1980) "Takeover bids, the free-rider problem, and the theory of the corporation," *Bell Journal of Economics*, Vol. 11 (Spring), pp. 42-64.

Halpern, P. (1983) "Corporate acquisitions: A theory of special cases? A review of event studies applied to acquisitions," *Journal of Finance*, Vol. 38, pp. 297-317.

Hansen, R.G. (1987) "A theory for the choice of exchange medium in the market for corporate control," *Journal of Business*, Vol. 60, pp. 75-95.

Huang, Y.S and R.A. Walkling (1987) "Target abnormal returns associated with acquisition announcements: Payment method, acquisition form, and managerial resistance", *Journal of Financial Economics*, Vol. 19, pp. 329-349.

Jarrell. G.A. (1985) "The wealth effects of litigation by targets: Do interests diverge in a merge?", *Journal of Law and Economics*, Vol. 28, pp. 151-177.

Jarrell, G.A. and M. Bradley (1980) "The economic effects of federal and state regulations of cash tender offers," *Journal of Law and Economics*, Vol. 23, pp. 371-407.

Jarrell, G. A. and A. B. Poulsen (1986) "Shark repellents and stock prices: The effects of antitakeover amendments since 1980" (Unpublished paper, U.S. Securities and Exchange Commission).

Jensen, M.C. (1986) "The takeover controversy: Analysis and evidence," *Midland Corporate Finance Journal*, Vol. 4, pp. 6-32.

Jensen, M.C. and R. Ruback (1983) "The market for corporate control: The scientific evidence," *Journal of Financial Economics*, Vol. 11, pp. 5-50.

Kummer, D. and R. Hoffmeister (1978) "Valuation consequences of cash tender offers," *Journal of Finance*, Vol. 33, pp. 505-516.

Langetieg, T. (1978) "An application of a three-factor performance index to measure stockholders gains from merger," *Journal of Financial Economics*, Vol. 6, pp. 365-384.

Lehn, K. and A. Poulsen (1986) "Leveraged buyouts: Wealth created or wealth redistributed?" (Unpublished paper, Washington University).

Linn, S. and J. McConnell (1983) "An empirical investigation of the impact of 'antitakeover' amendments on common stock prices," *Journal of Financial Economics*, Vol. 11, pp. 361-400.

Lintner, J. (1965) "The valuation of risk assets and the selection of risky investments in stock portfolios and capital budgets," *Review of Economics and Statistics*, Vol. 47, pp. 13-37.

Loderer, C.F. and D.C. Mauer (1986) "Acquiring firms in corporate mergers: The postmerger performance" (Unpublished paper, Purdue University).

Malatesta, P.H. (1983) "The wealth effect of merger activity and the objective functions of the merging firms," *Journal of Financial Economics*, Vol. 11, pp. 155-181.

Malatesta, P.H. (1986) "Measuring abnormal performance: The event parameter approach using joint generalized least squares," *Journal of Financial and Quantitative Analysis*, Vol. 21, pp. 27-38.

Malatesta, P.H. and R. Thompson (1985) "Partially anticipated events: A model of stock price reactions with an application to corporate acquisitions," *Journal of Financial Economics*, Vol. 14, pp. 237-250.

Malatesta, P.H. and R.A. Walkling (1988) "Poison pill securities: Stockholder wealth, profitability, and ownership structure," *Journal of Financial Economics*, Vol. 20, in press.

Mandelker, G. (1974) "Risk and return: The case of merging firms," *Journal of Financial Economics*, Vol. 1, pp. 303-335.

Manne, H.G. (1965) "Mergers and the market for corporate control," *Journal of Political Economy*, Vol. 73, pp. 110-120.

Mikkelson W. H. and R. S. Ruback (1985) "An empirical analysis of the interfirm equity investment process," *Journal of Financial Economics*, Vol. 14, pp. 523-553.

Mikkelson W. H. and R. S. Ruback (1986) "Targeted share repurchases and common stock returns" (Unpublished paper, University of Oregon).

Mossin, J. (1966) "Equilibrium in a capital asset market," *Econometrica*, Vol. 41, pp. 867-887.

Nathan, K.S. and T.B. O'Keefe (1986) "The rise in takeover premiums: An exploratory study" (Unpublished paper, Oakland University).

Nathan, C.M. and M. Sobel (1980) "Corporate stock repurchases in the context of unsolicited takeover bids," *Business Lawyer*, July, pp. 297-314.

Nash, J.F. (1950) "Equilibrium points in N.person games," *Proceedings of the National Academy of Sciences of the U.S.A.*, Vol. 36, pp. 48-49.

Peltzman, S. (1977) "The gains and losses from industrial concentration," *Journal of Law and Economics*, Vol. 20, pp. 229-263.

Pickens, T. Boone Jr. (1986) "Professions of a short-termer," *Harvard Business Review*, Vol. 64, pp. 75-79.

Posner R. (1969) "The Federal Trade Commission," *University of Chicago Law Review*, Vol. 37, pp. 47-89.

Ravenscraft, D.J. and F.M. Scherer (1986) "The profitability of mergers" (Unpublished paper, Federal Trade Commission).

Rogowski, R.A. (1982) "The Justice Department's merger guidelines: A study in the application of the rule" (Unpublished paper, Federal Trade Commission).

Roll, R (1986) "The hubris hypothesis of corporate takeovers," *Journal of Business*, Vol. 59, pp. 197-216.

Ruback, R.S. (1983) "Assessing competition in the market for corporate acquisitions," *Journal of Financial Economics*, Vol. 11, pp. 141-153.

Ryngaert, M. (1988) "The effect of poison pill securities on shareholder wealth," *Journal of Financial Economics*, Vol. 20, in press.

Samuelson, P. (1970) *Economics*, 7th ed. (New York: McGraw-Hill).

Scherer. F.M. (1970) *Industrial Market Structure and Economic Performance,* (Chicago: Rand McNally).

Scherer, F.M.. W.F. Long, S. Martin, D.C. Mueller, G. Pascoe. D.J. Ravenscraft, J.T. Scott, and L.W. Weiss (1987) "The validity of studies with line of business data: Comment," *American Economic Review,* Vol. 77, pp. 205-217.

Schipper, K. and R. Thompson (1983) "Evidence on the capitalized value of merger activity for acquiring firms," *Journal of Financial Economics,* Vol. 11, pp. 85-119.

Schleifer, A. and R. W. Vishny (1986) "Greenmail, white knights, and shareholders' interest," *Rand Journal of Economics,* Vol. 17 (Autumn), pp. 293-309.

Schwert, G.W. (1981) "Using financial data to measure the effects of regulation," *Journal of Law and Economics,* Vol. 24, pp. 121-158.

Securities and Exchange Commission (1985a) "Institutional ownership, tender offers, and long-term investments" Unpublished paper, Securities and Exchange Commission).

Securities and Exchange Commission (1985b) "The economics of any-or-all, partial, and two-tier tender offers" (Unpublished paper, Securities and Exchange Commission).

Sharpe. W.F. (1964) "Capital asset prices: A theory of market equilibrium under conditions of risk," *Journal of Finance,* Vol. 19, pp. 424-442.

Smiley, R. (1975) "The effect of the Williams amendment and other factors on transactions costs in tender offers," *Industrial Organization Review,* Vol. 3, pp. 138-145.

Smith, C. W. (1986) "Investment banking and the capital acquisition process," *Journal of Financial Economics,* Vol. 15, pp. 3-29.

Stanbury. W.T. and G.B. Reschenthaler (1981) "Reforming Canadian competition policy: Once more unto the breach," *Canadian Business Law Journal,* Vol. 5, pp. 381-437.

Stigler, G.J.. (1982) "The economist and the problem of monopoly," *American Economic Review,* Vol. 72, pp. 1-11.

Theil, H. (1971) *Principles of Econometrics* (New York: John Wiley).

Thompson, R. (1985) "Conditioning the returns-generating process on firm-specific events: A discussion of event study methods," *Journal of Financial and Quantitative Analysis*, Vol. 20, pp. 151-168.

Tollison, R.D. (1983) "Antitrust in the Reagan Administration: A report from the belly of the beast," *International Journal of Industrial Organization*, Vol. 1, pp. 211-221.

Wansley, J., W. Lane and H. Yang (1983) "Abnormal returns to acquiring firms by type of acquisition and method of payment," *Financial Management*, Vol. 12 (Autumn), pp. 16-22.

Weiss, L.W. (1974) "The concentration-profits relationship and antitrust," in *Industrial Concentration: The New Learning* ed. H.J. Goldschmid, H.M. Mann, and J.F. Weston, (Boston: Little, Brown).

Chapter 8

The Effects of Mergers in the United States

F.M. Scherer
Department of Economics
Swarthmore College

1.0 INTRODUCTION

Professor Eckbo (Chapter 7 of this volume) and I present two sides of a methodological dispute, indeed, a good old-fashioned *Methodenstreit*, that rages among economists these days. Professor Eckbo describes in detail the stock-market event-studies and the use of the efficient markets hypothesis to analyze mergers. My focus is on the analysis of inside company financial information to find out how mergers fare.

In particular, I discuss the success of mergers in the United States over recent history, with the warning that the U.S. perspective may be different from that of Canada. Enterprises are larger in the United States, both absolutely and relative to minimum optimal scales, and the markets in the United States tend to be less concentrated than those in Canada.

One might expect greater opportunities for efficiency gains from Canadian mergers, all other things being equal. What one finds in the United States is not a terribly attractive record. My analysis, carried out with David Ravenscraft of the Federal Trade Commission, is based on line of business data for some 3,500 lines covering roughly 6,000 mergers occurring between 1950 and 1976.[1] The focal point is the merger wave that peaked in 1968. This was preponderantly a conglomerate merger wave, that is to say, it involved companies pursuing more or less unrelated businesses.

The event-studies that Professor Eckbo describes show a rather rosy picture for these typically conglomerate mergers. They reveal that, if anything, conglomerate acquisitions were received by the stock market somewhat more favourably than horizontal and vertical acquisitions.

However, from a longer-term perspective, the record is one of widespread failure.

2.0 SUMMARY OF MAJOR FINDINGS

I now review some of the major findings that come from our study. First, we find that approximately one-third of the 1960s and early 1970s mergers were subsequently undone through sell-off. Of the sold-off acquisitions, conglomerate acquisitions were the most likely to be divested.

We find too that in the year before divestiture commenced, the operating income of the to-be-divested units was on average negative, minus 1 per cent on average. This is a clear sign of failure. Hence about one-third of the acquisitions were failures by virtue of having been sold off with a negative average profitability.

Let's turn now to the other side of the picture. First, pre-merger, the acquired companies, whether subsequently divested or not, had superior profit records on average. They were not poorly managed companies; their operating income averaged about 20 per cent of assets. That can be compared to an average operating income/assets ratio of 11 per cent for all manufacturing corporations. And again, this superiority of pre-merger profit performance existed both for the acquired companies that were not subsequently sold off, and for those that were relatively successful and were retained. For a matched sample of pre- versus post-merger returns, with a lapse of eight to nine years on average between the pre-merger period and the period of observation on post-merger returns, profits fell at an average rate of one-half to one percentage point per year. Over the period profits fell on average from about 22 per cent down to about 10 or 12 per cent. This decline in profitability occurred for both conglomerate and horizontal acquisitions. One possible explanation of the post-merger profit decline is that the profits before merger were unsustainably high. However, from a control group analysis, we find that the post-merger decline in profitability was more rapid than would have been expected if simple Galtonian regression to the mean had occurred.

2.1 Reasons for Poor Performance

Through a series of case studies and also through other statistical analyses, we attempted to ascertain the reasons for this declining profit experience. Basically, we found two main reasons. First of all, acquisition put the acquired unit, which had previously been a relatively simply structured firm, into a much more complex conglomerate organizational structure. As a result of the complex information flows in this more complex organization structure, because the top management of the conglomerate did not understand deeply the business of its typical acquired unit, there were severe losses of control. Once things got out of control, the conglomerate's top management did not know how to straighten out the situation. The other problem was one of a breakdown in managerial incentives. That is, managers who had previously operated in a fairly simple incentive framework were suddenly confronted with quite complexly structured incentives. They responded in a variety of ways that turned out to be counterproductive. The end result was declining profitability and on average, rather poor performance.

To be sure, these are statistical averages. Some of the mergers in our sample were quite successful. One exception, indeed the main statistical exception to the declining profitability result we observed, appeared in what we called "mergers of equals." "Mergers of equals" were cases where two companies of roughly equal size, differing from each other in pre-merger size by not more than a factor of two, came together. Those mergers of equals may have achieved slight efficiency improvements on average. The statistical evidence is ambiguous. Our explanation, and it is more of a leap than some of our other explanations, is that when you engage in a merger of equals – and I might note this seems to be more typical in Canada – the managements on both sides realize that they have a lot at stake in making the merger work. They work very hard to eliminate the problems that we observed in our more asymmetric acquisition cases.

Dennis Mueller (1986) of the University of Maryland has done independent research on a large sample of mergers for the nearly same time period. His results parallel ours and in some respects extend ours. He found that the average merged unit not only suffered from a decline in profitability, but also suffered a decline in market share. This was especially true for conglomerate acquisitions, although it held in weaker form also for horizontal acquisitions.

2.2 Tender-Offer Takeovers

Our sample of some 6,000 mergers is composed mainly of voluntary mergers, where the buyer and seller voluntarily agreed to come together. The sample also includes, however, 95 acquisitions precipitated by tender offer – a merger form more common in the 1980s than it was during the 1960s and early 1970s. Examining the pre-merger profits of tender-offer targets, we found that they were only slightly less profitable on average than their peers, on average 3 to 7 per cent less profitable. The difference was barely significant statistically. So although they were slight underperformers, we don't get strong support for the hypothesis that tender-offer targets are real sluggards who are not, on average, performing well. Nine years after takeover, on average, the tender-offer lines were much less profitable than peers in the same industry with similar market shares. Further analysis revealed that much of this decline in profitability for the tender-offer target lines came from write-ups in the asset base. That is, when the tender-offer was made, a substantial price premium over the pre-takeover book value of assets was typically paid. The tender-offer acquisitions were typically covered by what is called in the United States "purchase accounting." Therefore, assets (the denominator of our profitability ratio) were written up. Depreciation write-offs also increased, so the numerator was reduced while the asset base was written up. And that was the main reason why the decline in profitability occurred.

When we analyzed cash flow, which is stripped of depreciation charges, and related it to sales, which are not written up as a consequence of the takeover, we found that the baseline profitability of the tender offer targets was neither improved nor significantly degraded on average. So, in essence, the acquirers paid rather substantial prices to take over units that they ran no better than they had been run pre-takeover.

3.0 SUMMARY
To sum up, the historical evidence reveals that, even though they were regarded favourably by the stock-market at the time, mergers in the United States in the 1960s and early 1970s were, on average, either clear failures or only limping successes. It is possible, to some extent, to reconcile the stock-market evidence with the kind of internal financial performance evidence we've gathered. When one looks at the acquiring companies' share values two to three years after takeover, what most studies have shown is that there is a decline, seldom statistically significant, in the value of the shares of the acquirer relative to overall market trends. So it appears that it took the stock market a while to figure out that the mergers weren't going to work well. One confirmatory bit of evidence comes from the recent Ivan Boesky affair.[2] When Mr. Boesky got advance information about a hostile takeover, not only did he buy the shares of the target firm before the offer was announced, he sold short the shares of the acquiring firm.

The evidence that Ravenscraft and I have compiled is strictly historical. It is difficult to know whether it will hold for the most recent wave of U.S. mergers; which have tended to be larger, more horizontal, and more hostile than the sample we investigated. It is also possible that managers have become smarter about making mergers and making them work. We are going to have to wait on that eight or 10 years to find out. I would also hesitate to extrapolate our findings to the situation in Canada. Still, these findings should at least serve as warning that the merger route is not a certain road to greater efficiency and financial success.

NOTES

1.   See Ravenscraft and Scherer (1987).

2.   See, for example, "True Greed," *Newsweek*, December 1, 1986, pp. 48-63. "Who'll Be the Next To Fall?" *Business Week*, December 1, 1986, pp. 28-35.

REFERENCES

Mueller, Dennis C. (1986) "Mergers and Managerial Performance," (Washington, D.C.: Federal Trade Commission, Working Paper No. 137).

Ravenscraft, David and F.M. Scherer (1987) *Mergers, Sell-Offs and Economic Efficiency* (Washington, D.C.: The Brookings Institution).

Chapter 9

Post-Acquisition Performance of
Partially Acquired Canadian Firms

Vijay M. Jog and Allan L. Riding
School of Business
Carleton University

1.0 INTRODUCTION

The question of whether changes in corporate control enhance shareholders' economic benefits continues to fascinate economists. A major reason behind this continued fascination is the lack of convincing evidence on this issue. Although substantial empirical research has been devoted to the analysis of economic benefits from these changes, there are significant variations in the conclusions drawn by financial economists from the results of this research. The main purpose of this study is to add to existing research evidence by identifying whether, in the long-term, changes in corporate control result in changes in valuation and performance. This study, however, differs from so-called "event studies" as well as from most other related work, in that it analyzes target firms involved in "partial" acquisitions.

The literature in the area of "the market for corporate control" can be classified into three broad categories.[1] The first category encompasses studies which document and analyze the immediate (stock) market value impact of the takeover announcement – "event" studies. An excellent summary of some of these (essentially U.S. studies) can be found in Jensen and Ruback (1983).[2] The second category of studies analyzes the postmerger performance of merged conglomerate firms, and are exemplified by the work of Weston and Mansinghka (1971).[3] The third category of studies includes those which analyze the characteristics of acquired firms and the motives behind their acquisition (e.g., Harris *et al.* 1982). A common theme underlying all these studies is the determination of the economic benefits arising from changes in corporate control.

The purpose of this study is to explore the economic benefits arising from a change in corporate control in a different manner. It will proceed by explicitly analyzing publicly traded firms which experienced a change in corporate control, but which still maintained their publicly held status and continued to be listed on their respective stock exchanges subsequent to having been partially acquired. More specifically, the study analyzes both the stock market *and* the financial performance of publicly traded firms which were only "partially" acquired by an identifiable individual, group, or other firm. The analysis is conducted by comparing the performance of these firms during the pre-acquisition period with that of the post-acquisition period, necessary adjustments being made for overall market conditions.

The study differs from existing studies in three ways. First, it is concerned with the long-term value and performance implications attributable to changes in corporate control. The period of analysis employed here encompasses 10 years surrounding the year in which such a change take place. Thus, it differs significantly from the studies in category one, the "event" studies, which concentrate on the immediate impact on stock-market prices. While these "event" studies analyze the immediate impact on prices arising from the markets *perceptions* about the future benefits, this work analyzes actual benefits, if any. As will be shown later, this long-term focus allows abstraction from the implicit valuation uncertainty about the takeover as reflected in share prices immediately following the announcement.

Second, the study concentrates only on partial acquisitions, and, thus is different from the studies in category two, which analyze the fully merged firm during the post-acquisition period.[4] Choi and Philipatos (1983) have identified particular problems (see Section 2 of this paper) with comparisons of the pre-acquisition and post-acquisition performance of acquiring firms. This study, which is to deal with only partially acquired firms, is less subject to such problems.

Third, by concentrating only on "partial" acquisitions, this work allows a more direct test of the hypothesis that changes in corporate control imply long-term changes in valuation and performance, and, therefore, enhance economic benefits.[5]

The rest of the paper is organized as follows. Section 2 provides a summary of relevant research and elaborates on the motivation of this study. Section 3 summarizes the data used in the study. In Section 4 the methodologies are presented and the results of their application described. Section 5 discusses the conclusions, limitations, and implications for further research.

2.0   PREVIOUS RESEARCH AND MOTIVATION OF THE STUDY

As noted in the previous section, the empirical research on issues relating to the market for corporate control can be grouped into three categories. The first category consists of those studies which document and analyze the impact on stock-market values of takeover announcements on bidders and targets. The main purposes of these studies are: to identify the nature and the amount of gains from takeovers (as evidenced by the stock prices of the firms in the takeover contest); and to identify the source of these gains. Jensen and Ruback (1983) and Halpern (1983) provide excellent summaries of at least 40 papers based on U.S. data. Studies by Calvet and Lefoll (1985a, 1985b), and later by Eckbo (1986) provide Canadian evidence. Almost all of these studies can be classified as "event" studies and essentially use estimates of the abnormal stock price changes around the offer announcement date as a measure of the economic effects of the takeover.[6] These estimates are studied for the aggregate sample as well as for various sub-samples (e.g., successful versus unsuccessful, merger versus tender offer, cash offer versus stock offer, regulatory-opposed versus -unopposed, etc.). The underlying hypothesis behind these studies is that if the bidder firms, on average, exhibit positive (negative) abnormal returns, then stock market participants can be presumed to have concluded that the takeover was a wealth-maximizing (minimizing) transaction.[7]

In their summary paper, Jensen and Ruback (1983, p. 47) interpret the evidence based on U.S. studies as follows: "that corporate takeovers generate positive gains, that target shareholders benefit, and that bidding shareholders do not lose."

Roll (1986, p. 213) on the other hand, re-interprets these and other recent studies and concludes that:

> the final impression one is obliged to draw from the currently available results is that they provide no really convincing evidence against even the extreme (hubris) hypothesis that all markets are operating perfectly efficiently, and that individual bidders occasionally make mistakes. Bidders may indicate by their actions a belief in the existence of takeover gains, but systematic studies have provided little to show that such beliefs are well founded.

The Canadian evidence leads Calvet and Lefoll (1985a, p. 198) to conclude that, on average, the bidder firms' performance does not deteriorate either at the announcement date or thereafter (up to 12 months post-announcement). Moreover, they find that target firms experience high abnormal returns at the time of the event, but that the returns of those targets which remain listed on the stock market deteriorate substantially thereafter (again up to 12 months post-announcement (Calvet & Lefoll 1985a, p.199). Recently, Eckbo (1986, p. 258), using an expanded sample, concludes that for both the target and bidder firms listed on the TSE earn, on average, large and significant gains from takeover activity result. His aggregate results, however, do not show any significant deterioration in the targets' performance subsequent to the announcement of the merger (Table 5, p.249). The evidence presented in these two Canadian studies seems as contradictory as the evidence based on U.S. data.[8]

In summary, it seems that researchers have not, in general, concentrated on directly analyzing the long-term performance of firms involved in takeover activity. Rather, they seem to have focused exclusively on the immediate impact of the merger on share prices. (Recent U.S. studies use daily data and concentrate on approximately 120 days surrounding the event; the studies using monthly data provide conflicting evidence and end their analysis a maximum of 12 months after the announcement period.) These periods may not be long enough to evaluate actual economic benefits arising from changes in corporate control.[9] The assumption underlying these analyses is that the share price reaction reflects accurate capitalization of perceived future benefits, perceptions which may differ from actualization (see Black 1966).

The second set of studies concentrate on detecting potential operating or financial synergies of takeovers by analyzing the post-merger performance of *only* the combined firm.[10] The general methodology is to compare the performance of the combined firm with what could be inferred about the future performance of the individual firms in the absence of a takeover. These studies use both accounting and stock-market data for detecting superior performance and again show conflicting results. Hogarty (1970), the Federal Trade Commission (1972), Mueller (1977, 1979), and Melicher and Rush (1973) find little or no improvement in efficiency and performance of the combined firm during the post-merger period. On the other hand, Mason and Goudzwaard (1976), Choi and Philipatos (1984), Weston and Mansinghka (1971), and Loderer and Mauer (1986), show improvements in performance.

Regardless of the conflicting evidence, there is an additional problem with the interpretation of the results of these studies. The results are based on the performance of the combined firm, the performance of which may change independently of changes in the performance of the acquired firm. Thus, even if one finds a difference in post-merger performance, it is difficult to argue that this difference is entirely attributable to the particular takeover itself. An explicit (or direct) test of the changes in the post-merger performance of *individual* firms is, of course, not attempted because most of the takeovers analyzed in these studies resulted in a 100 per cent acquisition of the target.[11]

The third category of empirical research is related to the determination of the motives behind mergers or takeovers. The studies in this category include Smith and Schreiner (1969), Harris, *et al.* (1982), Haugen and Langtieg (1975), Gueard (1982), and Choi and Philipatos (1983), among others.[12] The main emphasis in these studies is to identify particular motives (such as diversification, operational and financial synergy, debt capacity, financial conditions of the targets, etc.) behind takeovers. As Choi and Philipatos (1983) point out: "recent empirical research...has not recognized explicitly the confounding effects of sample heterogeneity, and how this may distort our understanding of the post-merger market performance of the combined firms." Moreover, (as in the first two categories) the studies in this category concentrate on the analysis of the merged firm, as no data exists for the totally acquired target.

The literature reviewed above essentially deals with one of two topics: the immediate market value impact around the announcement date; or the post-merger performance of the combined firm. Studies of the latter, in general, suffer from the following problems: an inability to correctly identify benchmark firms; sample heterogeneity; an inability to separate the post-merger performance of the combined firm from that which would have obtained in the absence of the takeover; and difficulties in identifying whether the acquirer actually improved the target's performance. From a consideration of this literature, it is still not clear whether a change in corporate control actually brings long-term economic benefits.

It should also be noted that theoretical developments in the area of corporate control do not unambiguously predict the effect of changes in corporate control on a firm's profit potential. Following the seminal work of Berle and Means (1932), various studies argue that diffuse ownership structures may adversely affect corporate performance (see, for example, Fama and Jensen 1983). The basis of this argument is that the interests of the agents (managers) need not, and, in general, do not naturally coincide perfectly with those of the principals (the shareholders). This implies that the corporate resources are not used entirely in the maximization of share-holders' wealth. According to this reasoning, it is reasonable to expect that an increase in ownership by an identifiable group, such as might occur in a "partial acquisition," may reduce the so-called agency costs, and may lead to an improvement in managerial performance.[13]

A contrasting view is offered by Demsetz (1983) who claims that the ownership concentration and profit rate should essentially be unrelated. In a more recent paper, Demsetz and Lehn (1986, p. 1158) try to empirically test what they term as the "profit potential," which they define as the wealth gain achievable through more effective monitoring of managerial perform-ance by a firm's owners. Based on their empirical results, they conclude that "doubt is cast on the Berle-Means thesis, as no significant relationship is found between ownership concentration and accounting profit rates (for this set of firms)" (Demsetz & Lehn 1986, p.1155).

Thus, neither theoretical nor empirical developments in the literature on "the market for corporate control" provide unambiguous evidence on the long-term economic benefits from changes in corporate control. Accordingly, the motivation behind this paper is to seek further empirical evidence of economic benefits from changes in corporate control. This analysis is to be based on measurements of financial and stock market performance of Canadian firms which underwent "partial" acquisition by an identifiable individual, group, or other firm during the 1972-1981 period. In all cases, these firms continued to trade publicly on the Toronto Stock Exchange subsequent to the partial acquisition. By confining the study to partial acquisitions, an explicit test for economic benefits and corporate control is intended.

At the outset, however, one caveat is worth noting. It is not claimed here that a partial acquisition automatically implies changes in top manage-ment and/or changes in corporate strategy. It may or it may not. What is assumed here is the ability of the new, significant shareholder to induce, directly or indirectly, an enhanced sense of value maximization to the firm's management by effectively realigning the management's interests with those of the shareholders. At this time, data on the percentage ownership sought by new owners or the amount of direct control exercised over the management is unavailable.[14]

3.0 DATA

The primary data base of this study consists of 2,466 merger and acquisition bids in Canada that were made during the period 1964 through 1983.[15] For each transaction, the data base identified, among other things, the identity of the bidder and the target; the month of the announcement; the newspaper in which the announcement was reported; the ticker symbols if listed on the North American Stock Exchanges; and the type of the transaction (whether it is total or partial).

The criteria for sample selection for this study were as follows:

i) the transaction should not be classified as a "total acquisition"

ii) the target firm must be listed on the Toronto Stock Exchange

iii) the transaction was announced during the period 1970-1981. This was necessary to allow the analysis of pre-merger (five years prior) through the post-merger period (at least four years post-merger).

The distribution of the sample firms in each of the twelve years is shown in Table 1.

Table 1
Derivation of Firms in the Sample

Year of Announcement	Targets on Data Base	Listed on TSE	Study Sample
1970	138	12	3
1971	156	25	6
1972	180	27	6
1973	173	30	14
1974	125	27	7
1975	114	32	10
1976	138	38	9
1977	179	54	15
1978	53	9	1
1979	129	31	0
1980	107	23	2
1981	113	27	3
Totals	1605	335	75

A total of 335 target firms were listed on the TSE during the entire 1970-81 period in the merger data base, only of which 145 were available on the Laval University data base.[16] Of these, 70 firms were further eliminated as they were not available contiguously for at least 60 months prior to the acquisition and 48 months post-acquisition. Therefore, the final sample consisted of 75 firms, which can be classified as "partial" acquisitions. The changes in corporate control for these 75 firms were verified by checking the corresponding newspaper articles and various issues of the Survey of Industrials, and Survey of Mines and Energy Resources published by the Financial Post.

4.0　METHODOLOGY AND RESULTS
4.1　Stock Market Performance
A variety of market-based performance measures were employed to evaluate the market performance of the 75 firms used in this study. Total returns, defined as the "wealth relatives" were calculated according to:

$$WR_t = (P_t - P_{t-1} + D_t)/P_{t-1} \qquad (1)$$

where P_t and D_t are the price and dividend paid on the security in the period t. The "price relative" return, which captures the capital gain component of the yield on a security is computed simply as the difference between the wealth relative and the dividend yield, where the latter is defined as D_t/P_{t-1}. Two risk measures are employed in this work. The first, which estimates total risk on a security, is the standard deviation of the time series of wealth relatives. The second measure, which expresses the average volatility of the security's total return relative to a market index (here, the TSE 300), is the well-known beta measure.

Each of these measures was estimated, using monthly data, for each of the 75 securities for the pre- and post-acquisition periods. The pre-acquisition period extended from 60 months prior to the acquisition to six months prior. The post-merger period extended from six months subsequent to the takeover to 60 months (or to the end of the available data series, as appropriate). The 12 months surrounding the change in corporate control was not included in order to abstract from the informational effects noted by Eckbo and others. In addition, both the pre- and post-merger periods were split in to sub-periods corresponding with the months from -60 to -30 ("-" indicates pre-merger), -29 to -6, +6 through +29, and +30 through +60.

Findings: Return Measures: Total returns (as measured by wealth relatives), averaged across the 75 firms, increased from 0.865 per cent per month for the pre-merger period to 1.782 per cent per month for the post-merger period. While this difference seems large, it is not statistically significant due to the high variance across wealth relatives. In addition, the frequencies of statistically-significant increases in wealth relatives among the 75 firms are not significantly different from the frequencies which would be expected spuriously. Again, this result may be attributable to the relatively large return variances. However, the wealth relatives of 58.7 per cent of the 75 firms in the sample (i.e. 44 firms) increased from the pre-merger levels to the post-merger period.[17]

Similar findings obtained for the price relatives, or capital gain related component of total returns. On average, price relatives increased from 0.678 per cent per month to 1.475 per cent per month. Again, although the average difference is not statistically significant, a total of 46 of the 75 firms recorded increases in price relatives over the pre-merger to post-merger period.

These findings were consistent across the sub-periods. Figure 1 demonstrates the components of total returns for the four sub-periods investigated in this research. While the magnitude of the increases seem large, and a large number of firms did show improvement in performance, it should be noted that the average difference is not statistically significant.

The change in dividend yield, evident from Figure 1, was found to be statistically significant at the 1 per cent level. Dividend yields increased, on average, from 0.187 per cent (monthly average) pre-acquisition to 0.307 per cent subsequently. Moreover, dividend yield increases were recorded by 49 of the firms, permitting rejection (at the 1 per cent level) of the null hypothesis that dividend yield increases are as likely as decreases.

In general, prices on the stock-markets during the sample period tended to have been increasing during the 1970-1981 period under consideration here. In order to determine whether increases in total returns might be attributable to market factors, net-of-market returns were estimated as the difference between the wealth relative for a given security in a particular month and the return of the TSE 300 index for that month. Note that this approach assumes that the sample firms have the same systematic risk (beta = 1) as that of the market index. The next section, which addresses this assumption, finds that the average beta estimate across the sample conforms to this assumption. Net-of-market returns were found to have increased from an average (across the 75 firms) of 0.306 per cent per month for the pre-partial acquisition period to 0.649 per cent monthly subsequent to the acquisition. These are shown in Figure 2 for the various sub-periods. Although the average increases were large, there was large cross sectional variation in these increases, and these differences were found not to be statistically significant. Moreover, only 39 of the 75 firms recorded increases in returns when expressed on a net-of-market basis, thus the null hypothesis that net-of-market returns were as likely to increase as decrease, could not be rejected.

The findings of this study as they relate to measures of return can be summarized as follows. First, significant increases in dividend yields were identified, and the frequency of increased dividend yields was higher than would be expected by chance. Second, while large increases in total returns and price relatives were noted, these increases could be attributed to market factors as opposed to possible acquisition-related factors. Finally, it can be said that although the increases in net-of-market returns are not statistically significant, they are nonetheless positive. Thus it seems that if nothing else, target firms in partial acquisitions seem to at least maintain their performance levels.

Figure 1
Components of Total Return:
Sub-periods Prior to and Subsequent to Acquisition

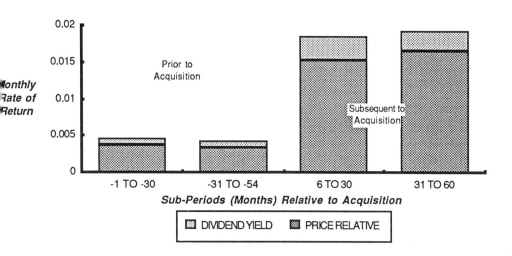

Figure 2
Average Net-of-Market Returns: Acquisition Sub-periods

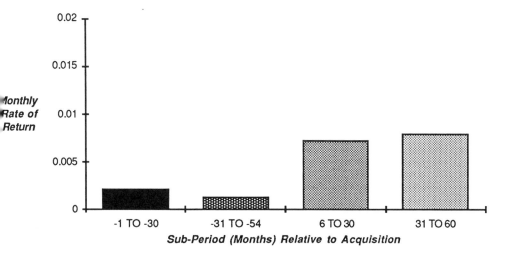

An analysis of two risk measures was also conducted in a manner similar to that for return measures. No differences in total risk, as measured by the standard deviations of returns could be discerned between the pre- and post-partial acquisition periods. Standard deviations of both price relatives and of wealth relatives were invariant across the time-frames of the 75 partial acquisitions studied here. Approximately as many firms recorded increases in standard deviations of wealth relatives (34 firms) as recorded decreases (41 firms).

This cannot be said, however, about the estimates of beta, the coefficient of systematic risk. The average of the ordinary least squares (OLS) beta estimates of the 75-firm sample before acquisitions was found to be 1.06. Subsequent to the mergers, the cross sectional average beta estimate was 0.92. In addition, a statistically significant proportion of these firms (50 of the 75) recorded decreases in individual firm beta estimates. While these decreases may be attributable to decreased risk, it is also possible that they are simply a result of thin trading in the stock. It seems likely even that trading of the shares of the 75 firms might have been less active subsequent to the partial acquisition than before. Therefore, the analysis was repeated using standard methods which attempt to correct for thin trading.

The effects of thin trading on risk measurement are well-known (Fowler, Rorke, and Jog 1979), typically resulting in beta estimates which are biased downward. The problem is essentially that of an errors-in-variables problem in linear models. To test whether the thin trading problem is biasing the results, a procedure proposed by Scholes and Williams (1980) was used.

Application of the Scholes-Williams estimation techniques to these data confirmed the results obtained from use of OLS estimators. The cross sectional average of the Scholes-Williams beta estimates of the 75-firm sample, prior to the merger, was found to be 1.37. Subsequent to the mergers, the average Scholes-Williams beta estimate decreased to 0.95, again, a statistically significant change.

Moreover, 52 of the 75 firms recorded decreases in beta estimates subsequent to the merger according to the Scholes-Williams estimates. This proportion is significantly different, at the 1 per cent level, from that which would be expected given a null hypothesis that increases and decreases are equally likely.

Findings: Return to Risk Measures: The previous sections analyzed the return and risk measures independently. The purpose of this section is to integrate these measures by analyzing the tradeoffs between return and risk. The classical performance measures recognized by the literature of contemporary finance are typically single measure ratios of return to risk. Two such measures, return-to-standard deviation and return-to-systematic risk, are employed in this study.

It has been noted that little change was found in the measure of total risk. It is not surprising, therefore, that the ratios of wealth relatives to standard deviation lead to the same conclusions as consideration of wealth relatives alone: that larger increases are observed in the values of this measure in post-partial acquisition period than pre-acquisition period. In contrast to the standard deviations reported above, large and frequent increases in the return-to-risk measures were found. On average, this performance measure increased from 0.99 per cent prior to the merger, to 1.98 per cent subsequent to the change in control. Moreover, 50 of the 75 firms recorded increases in this ratio. Similar findings were recorded using the Scholes-Williams estimates of systematic risk.

It is clear that shareholders may benefit in the event of a partial acquisition in either or both of two ways. Benefits are received, *ceteris paribus*, either by increased returns, or by decreased risk, or both. In this context, it is useful to examine Table 2, which shows that contingency breakdown for two measures of return (wealth relatives and net-of-market returns) by two measures of risk (beta and variance).[18]

On the basis of Table 2, it is possible to classify the 75 partial acquisitions into three groups. The first group, for which risk estimates decrease *and* returns increase, are clearly of benefit to shareholders, and might be termed "winners." The second group, where decreasing returns are accompanied by increasing risk, are clearly not of benefit to shareholders, and might be termed "losers." Finally, in those instances in which risk and return both shift in the same direction, it is not possible to determine unambiguously whether shareholders benefit or lose.

When beta, or systematic risk, is used as the measure of risk, it is clear that winners outnumber losers. The null hypothesis that winning and losing are equally likely is rejected at a 1 per cent level of significance, for both measures of return.

Table 2
Contingency Results; Risk and Return

Risk Measure	Direction of Shift	Wealth Relatives		Net-of-Market Wealth Relatives	
		Increase	Decrease	Increase	Decrease
BETA	Increase	13	10	10	13
	Decrease	31	31	29	23
VARIANCE	Increase	22	12	19	15
	Decrease	22	19	20	21

When total risk, as estimated by variance (or standard deviation), is used as the risk measure, the conclusion is not clear. While the frequency of winners nominally exceeds that of losers, the null hypothesis of equal likelihood cannot be rejected, even at high levels of significance.

Conclusions about whether, in general, shareholders gain or lose, depend upon assumptions about shareholders' portfolios. If it is believed that shareholders hold diversified portfolios --an assumption commonly invoked in financial theory – then beta is the most appropriate measure of risk. If so, the results shown in this study indicate that shareholders of the partially-acquired firms, in general, seem to have benefited.

4.2 Changes in Financial Performance

To complement the results of the stock-market based performance measures, this section attempts to identify changes – if any – in the financial accounting performance of these partially acquired firms surrounding the year of acquisition. The results in this section are based on the annual balance sheet and income statements of those firms for which data was available on the machine readable data base maintained by the *Financial Post*.[19] Of the 75 companies analyzed in the previous section, the necessary information was available for 42 firms for the contiguous seven year period surrounding the event.[20]

According to the standard textbook literature, many indicators are deemed appropriate for the analysis of financial performance; here, four such measures were employed.[21] The selected measures highlight the performance of the firm, related to efficiency and financial leverage.[22] These four measures were:

i)   *sales-to-asset ratio*, indicating the efficiency achieved in employing assets to produce a given level of output;

ii)   earnings before interest and tax-to-sales ratio (*net operating margin*), measuring the firm's overall operating performance, and which is independent of its capital structure;

iii) *return on equity*, indicating the effectiveness with which management is serving shareholders;

iv)   total *debt-to-assets* ratio, indicating a firm's reliance on leverage.

Each of these four ratios was calculated for each of the seven years surrounding the year of partial acquisition. The results from these calculations are shown in Tables 3 and 4. Table 3 shows the average value for each of the four ratios across firms in each of the three-year pre- and post-acquisition periods.

The results from Table 3 indicate that there is a general improvement in the performance of the sample firms, as evidenced from the yearly cross sectional averages of the three efficiency measures. There is only a slight improvement in turnover, but both the net operating margins and the return on (book) equity show a larger improvement. At the same time, the sample firms seem to have increased their reliance on external debt during the post-acquisition period. This increased reliance on debt suggests that the beta measure of market risk ought to have increased; however, as noted in the previous section, such is not the case. This implies that these increases in leverage ratios may be as a result of excess debt capacity. The statistical significance of these improvements is difficult to ascertain for two reasons. First, the sample size is small and there is a chance that the averages may be unduly affected by outliers. Second, and more importantly, the distributional properties of these rations are unknown. To partially alleviate these problems, Table 4 sorts the sample firms according to the percentage changes in each of the four measures between the post- and the pre-acquisition periods.

The results show that except for the ROE measure, the firms are evenly distributed. That is, that as many of the firms show improvements in the three measures as show no improvements. However, 27 of the 41 firms in the sample show an improvement in the ROE measure, a possible indication of

Table 3
Cross Sectional Averages of Four Financial Measures for Seven Years Surrounding the Acquisition Year

	Sales/ Assets	EBIT/ Sales	R.O.E.	Total Debt to Assets
#Firms	41*	41*	41**	42
Years				
-3	1.26	.091	.010	.185
-2	1.32	.101	.125	.184
-1	1.32	.085	.154	.179
0	1.26	.091	.138	.181
1	1.38	.107	.129	.202
2	1.35	.129	.158	.198
3	1.37	.132	.149	.200

*   Data on sales for Agra Industries for year + 3 was unavailable.

**   One firm, Strathcona Resources, was removed from the sample as it had a significantly negative ROE (-300%). Its inclusion would have resulted in meaningless overall averages.

Table 4
Distribution of Sample Firms According to the
Percentage Change Between Post- and Pre-acquisition Periods

	Sales/ Assets	EBIT/ Sales	R.O.F.	Total Debt to Assets
#Firms	41	41	41	42
%Change*				
less than 50%	2	4	8	5
-25% to -50%	3	2	2	4
0% to -25%	14	12	4	11
0% to +25%	14	**0	9	11
+25% to +50%	3	2	1	1
more than 50%	5	11	17	10
Total	41	41	41	42

*   Defined as a cross sectional average of the percentage change in the average three-year post-acquisition period from that of the pre-acquisition period. Except for the debt-to-total assets ratio, a positive value can signify an improvement in performance.

**   Includes two firms whose average EBIT/Sales ratios changed from negative to positive.

improved effectiveness with which management is serving its shareholders. It is quite possible that a large percentage of the improvement may be attributable to greater reliance on external debt in the post-acquisition period. However, analysis of the interest coverage ratios for the 29 firms for which the ratio was meaningful suggests no significant deterioration in the post-acquisition period.

5.0   SUMMARY, CONCLUSIONS, AND DISCUSSION
The empirical findings presented in this study lead to three conclusions. First, it is evident that the stock-market performance of the share of firms which had been partially acquired is at least as good as that of those same

firms prior to the acquisition. Indeed, results from the return-to-systematic-risk measures indicate that the stock-market performance of such firms may have improved subsequent to the partial acquisition. Second, accounting measures of performance provide consistent results to the effect that return on equity measures appear to increase following partial acquisition, and that there is an increased reliance on debt sample firms in the post-partial acquisition period. No statistically significant differences are found in asset turnover and net operating margin. Third, any improvement in stock market performances must be viewed in the context of a possible increase in firm's leverage.

Two caveats are worth noting before policy conclusions can be drawn. First, it is clear that the study results are based on a sample of only 75 firms. Although this sample size is the maximum possible, and that "survivorship" bias has been accounted for (see Footnote 6), questions of generalizability can still be raised. One way to increase the sample size would be to concentrate on accounting-based performance measures for partially acquired private firms. However, the ready availability of such data is questionable.[23] Second, some partitioning of the sample firms may be attempted in accordance with the percentage ownerships sought by the new owners in these partial acquisitions. This may provide some correlation between direct and indirect control by concentrated ownership and firm performance.

In spite of these difficulties, the evidence presented in this study is sufficient to demonstrate that there is, in general, improvement in the performance of partially acquired firms subsequent to the acquisition. Minority shareholders do, on average, seem to benefit. Certainly, the results clearly indicate that the performance of these firms, at least, does not deteriorate in the post-partial acquisition period. However, whether this improvement is due to the ability of the new owners to influence and change the firm's management remains to be determined.

NOTES

1. This categorization excludes studies in the general area of corporate concentration and macroeconomic issues. The emphasis is mainly on that segment of the literature that concentrates on identifying empirically the benefits of corporate takeovers.

2. A more recent survey was done by Espen Eckbo, Chapter 7 in this volume.

3. A more recent study by Ravenscraft and Scherer is summarized by Scherer in Chapter 8 of this volume.

4. This is the case for almost all of the U.S. studies (e.g., Guerard, 1982; Shrieves and Pashley, 1984) which analyzed the performance of the 'acquirer' firms. The analysis of the 'acquired' (target) firm was not conducted, simply because the target was 'totally' acquired, and, thus, ceased to exist as an independent entity after acquisition.

5. The term "changes in corporate control" is only loosely defined here. No assumptions are made about the *actual* degree of control exercised by these new "partial" owners.

6. The methodological basis for these studies, and the exact details can be found in Fama *et al.* (1969), and Brown and Warner (1980).

7. The analysis of abnormal returns of just the target firms is not as interesting, because, by the very fact that they receive high premiums from the bidder firm.

8. It should be noted that both studies investigate the performance of the target firms up to 12 months in the post-announcement period. It is not clear whether this period is sufficient to allow the bidder to initiate changes, if any, in the target firm's management; especially when there may be a time lag between announcement of the offer and the assumption of actual control (or influence) by the bidder. For example, the FTC (1972) study stated that only for a quarter of cases, the top three managers of the acquired firm had left within three years after the acquisition (pp. 42-46).

9. In one recent U.S. study using monthly data, Langtieg (1978, p. 377) shows that the bidding firms show a significant price decline continuing in the combined firm after the merger outcome.

10. As most of the U.S. studies are based on "total" takeovers, none could evaluate the actual performance of the target under the new ownership following the acquisition.

11. The FTC study (1972) attempted to analyze the performance of firms acquired by nine sample conglomerates. The study found the profit rates of the acquired firms did not tend to improve following the mergers. To the best of our knowledge, this is the most exhaustive study of the post-merger performance of the acquired firms.

12. We abstract ourselves from the substantive economic empirical literature concerned with explaining the motive behind the *aggregate* changes in the merger activity.

13. It is assumed that the new owners will not issue side payments to themselves at the expense of other minority shareholders. Thus, any gains from an increase in managerial efficiency or a decrease in agency costs will reflect in improved performance.

14. We also assume that the benefits, if any, would be reflected in the financial and stock market measures. Thus, side payments and increased (and unobserved) prerequisite consumptions are implicitly assumed as being negligible. As all of the sample firms are publicly traded firms, with stringent disclosure rules, such an assumption is thought to be a realistic one.

15. We thank Dr. Shyam Khemani of the Bureau of Competition Policy, Department of Consumer and Corporate Affairs, for providing us with

this machine readable data base. This data base is based on the acquisitions reported in the *Merger Register*, which is compiled by the Bureau of Competition Policy.

16. It provides the monthly stock returns for all firms listed on the Toronto Stock Exchange from 1963.

17. These results do not appear to be attributable to a "survivorship" bias in the sample selection. In order to evaluate the potential impact of any survivorship bias, the performance of a separate sample of 24 firms listed on the Laval file, but which did not meet the full data requirements for inclusion in this study (108 months of continuous listing) was investigated. For these 24 firms, post-merger return performance was found to be higher than return performance prior to the merger. Of course, for this sample, the time frame was shorter (and variable) than that used in the rest of this study.

18. Scholes-Williams (1980) beta estimates are employed here. Note that while the average of the Scholes-Williams beta estimates was not materially different from the average obtained by means of OLS, for certain individual firms, the differences between the two beta estimates was material.

19. This data base consists of annual balance sheets and income statements of approximately 500 large companies in Canada. Currently the data is available for years 1959 through 1985, with varying coverage for individual companies.

20. A restriction on the data being available for 11 years surrounding the event would have resulted in a sample of 29 firms only. A choice of seven years was deemed to be a reasonable tradeoff between data availability and sample size.

21. One standard finance textbook lists a minimum of 16 (interdependent) measures for assessing firm's performance.

22. Two other measures were also calculated: earnings before interest and tax-to-interest ratio (interest coverage), indicating firm's ability to service its borrowing; and dividend payout ratio, indicating firms' willingness to provide cash flows to its shareholders. However, in 13 of the 42 cases, these were not meaningful because the firms either had no interest payments, or the EBIT values were negative for one of the six years. Due to the reduction of sample, it was decided not to report the results of these two ratios.

23. It is possible that this type of study can be attempted by using the database of Statistics Canada collected under the *Corporations and Labour Unions Returns Act* (Catalogue No. 61-210). All conditions of confidentiality would, of course, have to be met.

REFERENCES

Brown, S.J. and J.B. Warner (1980) "Measuring Security Price Perform-ance," *Journal of Financial Economics*, Vol. 8, pp. 205-258.

Berle, A.A. and G.C. Means (1932) *The Modern Corporation and Private Property* (New York: MacMillan).

Black, F. (1986) "Noise," *Journal of Finance*, Vol. 46, pp. 529-543.

Calvet, A.L. and J. Lefoll (1985a) "The Market for Corporation Acquisition in Canada - Part I," *Proceedings of the Administrative Sciences Association of Canada* (Montreal), Vol. 6, pp. 192-205.

_____ (1985b) "The Market for Corporate Acquisition in Canada - Part II," *Proceedings of the Administrative Sciences Association of Canada* (Montreal), Vol. 6, pp. 206-212.

Choi, D. and G.C. Philipatos (1983) "An Examination of Merger Synergism," *Journal of Financial Research*, Vol. 6, pp. 239-256.

_____ (1984) "Post-Merger Performance Among Homogeneous Firm Samples," *The Financial Review*, Vol. 19, pp. 173-194.

Demsetz, H. (1983) "The Structure of Corporate Ownership: Causes and Consequences," *Journal of Political Economy*, Vol. 93, pp. 1155-1177.

_____ (1983) "The Structure of Ownership and the Theory of the Firm," *Journal of Law and Economics*, Vol. 26, pp. 239-256.

Eckbo, E.B. (1986) "Mergers and the Market for Corporate Control: the Canadian Evidence," *Canadian Journal of Economics*, Vol. 19, pp. 236-260.

Fama, E.F. and M.C. Jensen (1983) "Agency Problems and Residual Claims," *Journal of Law and Economics*, Vol. 26, pp. 327-349.

Fama, E.F., L. Fisher, M.C. Jensen and R. Roll (1969) "The Adjustment of Stock Prices to New Information," *International Economic Review*, Vol. 10, pp. 1-21.

Federal Trade Commission (1972) *Conglomerate Merger Performance: An Empirical Analysis of Nine Corporations*, (Washington, D.C.: U.S. Government Printing Office).

Fowler, D., C. Rorke, V. Jog (1979) "Heteroscedasticity, R2 and Thin Trading on the Toronto Stock Exchange," *Journal of Finance*, Vol. 34, pp. 201-1210.

Guerard, J.B. Jr. (1982) "The Role of Employment and Capital Expenditures in the Merger and Acquisition Process," in M. Keenan and L. White, (eds.) *Mergers and Acquisitions* (Lexington, MA.: Lexington Books), pp. 243-265.

Halpern, P. (1983) "Corporate Acquisition: A Theory of Special Case? - A Review of Event Studies Applied to Acquisitions," *Journal of Finance,* Vol. 38, pp. 297-317.

Harris, R.S., J.F. Stewart, and W.T. Carleton (1982) "Financial Characters of Acquired Firms," in M. Keenan and L. White (eds.) *Mergers and Acquisitions* (Lexington, MA: Lexington Books), pp. 1003-1013.

Haugen, R.A. & T.C. Langtieg (1975), "An Empirical Test for Synergism in Merger," *Journal of Finance,* Vol. 30, pp. 1003-1013.

Hogarty, T.F. (1970) "Profits from Merger: The Evidence of Fifty Years," *St. John's Law Review,* Vol. 44 (Spring), pp. 379-391.

Jensen, M.C. and R.S. Ruback (1983) "The Market for Corporate Control," *Journal of Financial Economics,* Vol. 14, pp. 5-50.

Langtieg, T.C. (1978) "An Application of a Three-Factor Performance Index to Measure Stockholder Gains from Merger," *Journal of Financial Economics,* Vol. 6, pp. 365-383.

Loderer, C.F. and D.C. Mauer (1986) "Acquiring Firms in Corporate Mergers: The Post-Merger Performance," (Working Paper, Purdue University).

Mason, R.H. and M.B. Goudzwaard (1976) "Performance of Conglomerate Firms: Recent Risk and Return Experience," *Journal of Finance,* Vol. 31, pp. 381-388.

Melicher, R.M. and D.F. Rush (1974) "Evidence on the Acquisition Related Performance of Conglomerate Firms," *Journal of Finance,* Vol. 29, pp. 141-149.

Mueller, D.C. (1977) "The Effects of Conglomerate Mergers: A Survey of Empirical Evidence," *Journal of Banking and Finance,* Vol. 1, pp. 315-342.

_____ (1979) "Do We Want a New, Tough Antimerger Law?" *The Antitrust Bulletin,* Vol. 24(4), pp. 807-836.

Roll, R. (1986) "The Hubris Hypothesis of Corporate Takeovers," *Journal of Business,* Vol.59(2), pp. 197-216.

Scholes, M. and Williams, J. (1980) "Estimating Beta from Nonsychronous Data," *Journal of Financial Economics*, Vol. 8, pp. 309-328.

Shrieves, R.E. and M.M. Pashley (1984) "Evidence on the Association Between Mergers and Capital Structure," *Financial Management*, Vol. 13, pp. 39-48.

Weston, J.F. and S.K. Mansinghka (1971) "Tests of Efficiency Performance of Conglomerate Firms," *Journal of Finance*, Vol. 26, pp. 919-936.

Chapter 10

Corporate Concentration and Power

Walter Adams
Distinguished University Professor
Department of Economics
Michigan State University

1.0 INTRODUCTION

My objective is to discuss recent antitrust developments in the United States in the context of the debate over international competitiveness. To achieve it I propose to discuss the findings in a recent book, which I co-authored with Professor James W. Brock.[1]

In the book, we analyze the quintessential myth of America's corporate culture, namely that giant corporate size is the handmaiden of operating efficiency, technological progress, and international competitiveness. We examine the contentions of the neo-conservative Darwinians and the neo-liberal advocates of "industrial policy," and the hostility of both camps toward traditional U.S. antitrust, and we find the contentions of both groups to be unsupported by empirical evidence. Indeed, we find that antitrust – far from being a policy albatross – actually *promotes* efficiency, productivity and innovativeness at home, and competitiveness abroad.

2.0　THE PERFORMANCE OF BIG FIRMS

By most objective standards, America's corporate giants have not performed very well over the last 15 years. They have lost markets to the Japanese and the newly industrializing countries. They have lagged in innovation. The quality of their products has often been inferior and unreliable. And, taken together, America's 500 largest industrial corporations have failed to generate a single new job since 1970.

Bigness has not delivered the goods, and this fact is no longer a secret. Influential business publications have repeatedly called attention to the malaise of the "bigness complex." In recent cover stories, for example, *Business Week* has argued that "small is beautiful"; in response to the question "do mergers really work?" its answer was "not very often — which raises questions about merger mania"; and in noting the trend toward "splitting up," it has reported that some large corporations are now "divesting assets, spinning off divisions, even liquidating themselves."[2] *Forbes* has provided case studies to document what would seem an obvious fact; that "soap and pastrami don't mix."[3] The *Economist* (London) has featured articles entitled "Big Won't Work" and "Big Goes Bust."[4]

3.0 MERGER BOOM

Paradoxically, America is in the midst of an unprecedented wave of mega-mergers and acquisitions — fuelled by the astronomical promoter fees of Wall Street's M&A shops, the sale of junk bonds, and the benign neglect of Washington's antitrust authorities. If the trend continues, we may soon be approaching the day when (in the words of *Fortune*) "the United States economy might end up completely dominated by conglomerates happily trading with each other in a new kind of cartel system."[5]

The merger boom amounts to a process of mass "corpocide." Since 1980, as Table 1 shows, there has been a dramatic increase not only in the number but also in the size of mergers and acquisitions. The extent of this corpocide process in a single major industry, petroleum, is illustrated by Table 2.

Table 1
Value of Corporate Acquisitions in the U.S., 1980-1986

Year	Number of Acquisitions	Total Reported Value (in billions)	Number of large Takeovers ($1 billion or more)
1980	1,565	$ 33.06	3
1981	2,326	66.96	8
1982	2,295	60.39	9
1983	2,345	52.25	7
1984	3,064	125.23	19
1985	3,165	139.13	26
1986	4,022	190.00	34

Source: Information published in Mergers & Acquisitions. Information on value compiled only for those transactions for which a purchase price is available.

Table 2
Selected Acquisitions and Mergers Involving Major Oil Companies, 1955-1986
(Assets in Millions of Dollars)

Year	Acquiring Company	Assets	Acquired Company	Assets
1955	Sunray Oil	300.0	Mid Continent Pet.	186.3
1956	Gulf Oil	2,160.0	Warren Pet.	163.9
1960	Standard (N.J.)	9,894.7	Monterey Oil	102.2
1961	Standard (Cal.)	2,782.3	Standard (Ky.)	141.9
1963	Gulf Oil	4,243.6	Spencer Chem.	123.3
1963	Cities Service	1,505.8	Tennessee Corp.	100.0
1965	Union Oil	916.5	Pure Oil	766.1
1966	Conoco	1,679.5	Consolidation Coal	466.1
1966	Atlantic Ref.	960.4	Richfield Oil	499.6
1967	Kerr McGee	383.3	Amer. Potash	117.7
1967	Tenneco	3,756.8	Kern County Land	435.3
1967	Signal Oil	678.1	Mack Trucks	303.0
1967	Diamond Alkali	275.6	Shamrock Oil	173.7
1968	Occidental Pet.	779.1	Hooker Chem.	366.5
1968	Occidental Pet.	779.1	Island Creek Coal	115.2
1968	Tenneco	1,911.4	Newport News Ship.	139.3
1968	Sun Oil	1,598.5	Sunray DX Oil	749.0
1969	Atlantic-Richfield	2,450.9	Sinclair Oil	1,851.3
1970	Standard (Ohio)	772.7	British Pet.	657.3
1974	Burmah Oil	2,590.9	Signal Oil	340.1
1976	Marathon Oil	2,005.4	Pan Ocean Oil	139.5
1976	Mobil	18,767.5	Montgomery Ward	1,500.0*
1977	Atlantic Richfield	8,853.3	Anaconda	2,050.9
1977	Gulf Oil	13,449.0	Kewanee Ind.	389.0
1977	Union Oil	4,226.8	Molycorp Inc.	163.6
1977	Tenneco	7,177.1	Monroe Auto Equip.	190.3
1979	Standard (Ind.)	14,109.3	Cyprus Mines	733.9
1979	Exxon	41,530.8	Reliance Elect.	613.3

Table 2 (continued)

Year	Acquiring Company	Assets	Acquired Company	Assets
1979	Shell Oil	16,127.0	Belridge Oil	3,660.0*
1979	Getty Oil	6,031.9	ESPN	
1979	Mobil Oil	27,505.8	General Crude Oil	792.0*
1980	Mobil Oil	32,705.0	Vickers Energy/ Transocean	715.0*
1980	Getty Oil	8,266.7	Reserve Oil & Gas	628.0*
1980	Getty Oil	8,266.7	ERC Corp.	536.0*
1981	Occidental Pet.	8,074.5	Iowa Beef Proc.	795.0*
1981	Standard (Ohio)	15,743.3	Kennecott	1,800.0*
1981	Gulf Oil	20,429.0	Kemmerer Coal	325.0*
1981	DuPont	23,829.0	Conoco	7,600.0*
1981	Tenneco	16,808.0	Houston Oil & Min.	400.0*
1981	U.S. Steel	13,316.0	Marathon	6,500.0*
1982	Occidental Pet.	15,772.5	Cities Service	4,000.0*
1984	Texaco	27,000.0	Getty Oil	10,100.0*
1984	Socal	23,500.0	Gulf	13,200.0*
1984	Mobil	36,000.0	Superior	5,700.0*
1986	U.S. Steel/ Marathon	18,989.0	Texas Oil & Gas	2,930.0*
1986	Occidental Pet.	12,273.1	Midcon	3,000.0*

* Reported purchase price

Source: Subcommittee on Fossil and Synthetic Fuels, House Committee on Energy and Commerce, Oil Industry Mergers: Hearings on H.R. 5153, H.R. 5175, and H.R. 5452, 98th Congress, 2d. session, 1984.

Nota bene that these statistics do not include the myriad of quasi-consolidations, or "joint ventures" which have been countenanced; notably between the American auto oligopoly and its foreign rivals: GM/Toyota; GM/Daewoo; GM/Isuzu; GM/Suzuki; GM/Lotus; Ford/Mazda; Ford/Mazda/Kia; Chrysler/Mitsubishi; Chrysler/Mitsubishi/Hyundai; Chrysler/Samsung; and Chrysler/Maserati.[6] The anticompetitive impact of such joint ventures on the U.S. automobile market requires little adumbration or explication.

The trend is not without its apologists. Bigness, they say, promotes efficiency and technological progress. If a merger did not promise to achieve these objectives, why would a profit-maximizing firm ever want to consummate it? The fact that it does proves that the merger is beneficial – not only to the firms involved but, in the long run, to consumers as well. Hence, there is no need to examine the facts or to amass voluminous evidence. It *must* be so; otherwise it would not happen; it would not be done.

Mergers, the apologists claim, have other virtues. Every time a merger takes place, a superior management replaces an inferior management. The market for corporate takeovers protects stockholders against the poor performance of incumbent managers who, in the absence of takeover threats, could continue to suboptimize the investment of their owners. How do we know this? Logic indicates that it must be so. There is no need to investigate further.

Unfortunately, the Reagan Administration has accepted the unsubstantiated claims of the merger apologists. It has refused to enforce the *Clayton Act* to stem the rising tide of mega-mergers. It has promulgated Merger Guidelines in 1982 and 1984 which effectively emasculate Section 7.[7] Finally, it has proposed the *Merger Modernization Act* which would, if enacted, insure the euthanasia of our traditional anti merger policy.

4.0 MERGER POLICY
The Reagan Administration's merger policy, I submit, is fatally flawed because it is based on empirically unproved assumptions and driven by ideological quackery.

4.1 New Learning
The Reagan Administration uncritically accepts the "new learning" that mega-mergers are the touchstone for enhanced production efficiency, technological innovation, and world-class competitiveness. Yet, objective empirical research casts considerable doubt on this currently fashionable belief. In one exhaustive study of the statistical evidence regarding conglomerate mergers, Dennis C. Mueller (1980) reports "a surprisingly consistent picture. Whatever the stated or unstated goals of managers are, the [conglomerate] mergers they have consummated have on average... *not* resulted in increased economic efficiency." Mueller (1986) reports similar findings in an updated econometric study expanded to include all varieties of mergers – horizontal and vertical, as well as conglomerate. Other careful researchers reach similar conclusions. Moreover, the high post-merger divorce rate – up to 40 per cent of the 1970s acquisitions, according to W.T. Grimm and Co. – is further evidence that the efficiency-through-merger hypothesis is a dubious basis for formulating public policy.

Nor do mega-mergers seem conducive to technological innovation. According to one analyst, the "vast majority of acquisitions of high-technology companies by large corporations [including acquisitions by Exxon, Burroughs, 3M and Westinghouse] have ended in disaster."[8] An important reason, the *Wall Street Journal* reports, is that the "giants' many layers of bureaucracy often paralyze the freewheeling entrepreneurial style typical in the high-tech world."[9] Conversely, managers of divested operations released from control by corporate giants are "freed from endless hours of explaining proposals to corporate headquarters and waiting months, often years, for approvals on new projects. . . ." This creative backwardness of bigness has recently been noted by both top corporate executives and high government officials. Martin S. Davis, president of Gulf & Western, confided to *Business Week*: "Bigness is not a sign of strength. In fact, just the opposite is true."[10] Similarly, Richard G. Darman (1986), Deputy Secretary of the Treasury, points to "corpocracy" (i.e., "large-scale corporate America's tendency to be like the government bureaucracy that corporate executives love to malign: bloated, risk-averse, inefficient, and unimaginative") as a problem of increasing national concern.

Incidentally, such evidence is not new. For example, Livermore's (1935) analysis of the turn-of-the-century merger movement in the United States revealed that nearly one-half of the consolidations between 1888 and 1905 subsequently failed; if "success" attributable primarily to patents or monopoly power are excluded, the failure rate exceeds 50 per cent.

Nor is such evidence confined to the United States. With respect to the United Kingdom, for example, one authoritative study found that

> Taking a broad sweep of the results, the picture is one in which it is difficult to sustain the view that merger is in fact a necessary or sufficient condition for efficiency gain. In many cases efficiency has not improved; in some cases it has declined, in other cases it has improved but no faster than one would have expected in the absence of merger . . . More generally we have various pieces of evidence from our investigations that merger has led to no apparent improvement in international competitiveness or export performance... (Cowling *et al.* 1980, pp. 370, 371.)

4.2 Exemption from Antitrust

The Reagan Administration believes that exempting U.S. industries that have been adversely affected by imports from the antitrust laws, and permitting them to freely merge, will cure the malaise of such industries as steel and autos, and bolster their ability to compete against imports. This assertion is flawed, not only because (as has just been argued) mega-mergers seldom contribute to improved economic performance. Beyond this, it ignores the fact that the import "problem" suffered by many major American industries is typically the result of oligopolistic giantism and noncompetitive industry structures *at home* – industry structures that have bred cost inefficiency, poor productivity, lethargic innovation, and most generally, the bureaucratic dry-rot of unchallenged oligopoly power. Indeed, if mammoth size and especially merger-induced giantism were truly conducive to world-class competitiveness, the American steel and automobile oligopolies should be the efficiency and innovation marvels of the world. Clearly, they are not.

General Motors is the world's largest auto company. Its dollar sales are roughly equivalent to the *combined* sales of nine Japanese auto makers. The sales of GM and Ford equal the *combined* sales of 12 leading foreign auto companies - the three largest in Japan, Germany, France and Great Britain respectively. Even without AMC, Chrysler is bigger than all but two of the Japanese producers. Can it really be argued that the U.S.A.'s big three are too small to be efficient, or that massive mergers and joint ventures are imperative to make them competitive in world markets? Certainly, if bigness were truly the guarantor of efficiency, GM would not find it necessary to enter into joint ventures with foreign companies (e.g., Toyota, Daewoo, *et al.*) in order to learn how to produce cars economically.

As for steel, it is clear that firm size (as distinct from plant size) is not the problem of our major integrated producers. They dwarf not only many of their foreign competitors, but also the domestic minimills that have captured increasing shares of the U.S. market. It is equally clear that merger-induced giantism, consummated over three quarters of a century, has not infused the steel oligopoly with an *elan vital.* Merging two major steel companies saddled with antiquated, inefficient facilities – LTV and Youngstown in the mid-1970s, and LTV and Republic in the mid-1980s – does not solve the efficiency problem. As LTV's recent collapse into bankruptcy confirms, combining two losers does not make a winner. Mating ugly ducklings does not produce a swan. If the objective is to become competitive in world markets – to compete successfully against Japan – what is needed is new, modern, state-of-the-art plants that are cost-effective. Mergers are not the means to that end.

Indeed, it is highly significant that in the one instance when antitrust action blocked a major merger – *United States v. Bethlehem Steel*[11] – the performance effects were singularly positive. Bethlehem proceeded to do what it had persistently pleaded was unfeasible: it constructed a giant, state-of-the-art facility at Burns Harbor, Indiana – "the only integrated green-field blast furnace oxygen converter rolling mill complex built during the 1960s and 1970s to provide a U.S. counterpart to the modern steel-making capacity growing by leaps and bounds abroad" (Scherer 1980, p. 546). One can only wonder what the state of the steel industry might be today if the antitrust agencies had blocked the spate of mergers and acquisitions that produced Big Steel, beginning with the U.S. Steel Corporation in 1901.

4.3 Foreign Competition

The Reagan Administration posits that foreign competition renders domestic industry structure irrelevant, and obviates the anticompetitive consequences of mergers in import-sensitive industries. But this postulate, too, is erroneous. It ignores the well-documented reality that giant international rivals recognize that their mutual self-interest lies in cooperation and collusion, *not* hard competition; and further, that concentration of domestic industries enhances the fruits, means, and incentives for forging global market control. As Sir Alfred Mond, organizer of ICI, the giant British chemical combine, pointed out long ago, "You cannot discuss big problems of industry with other countries until your own industries are organized first." Viewed in this light, domestic consolidation may *not* portend more vigorous international rivalry (as the Administration presumes). Instead, it may well mark an important first step toward transnational oligopolization, a concomitant diminution of competition, and a return to the global market controls – cartels, joint ventures, transnational mergers, and mutually agreed upon spheres of influence – of the inter-war years.

4.4 Impact on Prices

The Administration proceeds on the assumption that the only anti-social problem posed by mergers is a capacity on the part of the merged firms to affect price in some "relevant" market. Apart from such influence, Administration policy-makers seem to believe, mergers and acquisitions are unobjectionable, regardless of how large the combining firms may be. In reality, however, this is a profoundly naive conception of the politico-economic consequences of bigness and power. The "bigness complex" in autos illustrates the point; when Chrysler (then the nation's tenth largest industrial concern) confronted bankruptcy in 1978-79 as the result of poor performance, it did not passively submit to the rules of the competitive market game. Instead, the firm – joined by the United Auto Workers, as well as by suppliers, subcontractors, governors and mayors, senators and representatives, Republicans and Democrats – mobilized the power of giantism to manipulate the state and obtain a federal bail out.

In 1981, when the entire domestic oligopoly confronted the competition of Japanese imports (after having ignored the market for decades), the bigness complex in autos 'companies and the Union' engineered a bailout from global competition of the whole industry through governmentally negotiated "voluntary" Japanese export restraints. In 1985, GM and Ford seized upon the power of their size, and obtained a relaxation of government fuel economy standards, by threatening economic sabotage on a grand scale – plant closings, shutdowns, layoffs and unemployment – should their demands be denied. Alas, Brobdingnagian size permits privileged firms and industries to demand – and, more often than not, to obtain – tax favors, dispensations, governmentally-subsidized loans, governmentally subsidized services, and tax holidays from states and communities across the country. In a representative democracy, the power of giantism is not limited solely to the ability to influence price in an isolated "relevant" market; it encompasses the far more ominous capacity to manipulate the state to anti-social ends. Not the least threatening of these is government protection from foreign competition and federal bailouts – an outcome which the Administration purportedly seeks to avoid, but which merger-induced giantism renders more feasible and more difficult to resist.

4.5 Benign Mergers

The Administration policy makers assume that, at worst, mergers are merely benign. After all, they seem to reason, if a merger fails to produce better economic performance, the combination will be undone, the acquired operations divested, and society will be none the worse for it. However, this ignores the key economic principle of "opportunity cost" and its most important corollary – that there is no such thing as a free lunch, (a proverbial truth that this Administration should be expected to embrace).

Thus, two decades of managerial energies devoted to sterile paper entrepreneurialism and the quick-growth-through-merger game are, at the same time, two decades during which management attention has been diverted from the critical task of investing in *new* plants, *new* products, and state-of-the-art manufacturing techniques. Billions of dollars spent on shuffling ownership shares are, at the same time, billions of dollars *not* spent on productivity-enhancing plant, equipment, and research and development. The millions of dollars absorbed in legal fees and investment banking commissions are, at the same time, millions of dollars *not* plowed directly into the nation's industrial base. The opportunity costs of merger mania are real. And they bode ill for the reindustrialization of America.

5.0 POLICY ACTIONS

What, then, should be done? What kind of merger policy would be best calculated to promote the national interest? I submit that one way of allaying concerns over the alleged conflict between the social goal of preserving a decentralized power structure and the social goal of promoting efficiency and consumer welfare, would be to prohibit mega-mergers (e.g., acquisitions by the Fortune 500) *unless* their proponents can demonstrate affirmatively that the proposed consolidation would (1) increase operating efficiency, (2) promote innovation efficiency, (3) enhance international competitiveness; *and* that these objectives cannot be achieved in a manner that is less likely to lessen competition or to foster further concentration of power. Difficult though it might be to adjudicate these issues in an administrative tribunal, it would at least spare us from the drumfire repetition of unsubstantiated claims in support of a laissez faire policy toward giant mergers and the alleged beneficence of corporate giantism in promoting efficiency and consumer welfare.

NOTES

1. See Adams and Brock (1986a).

2. See "Deal Mania," *Business Week*, November 24, 1986, pp. 74-93; "Splitting Up: The Other Side of Merger Mania," *Business Week*, July 1, 1985, pp. 50-55; "For Better or For Worse: The Biggest Restructuring in History Winds Down. What Did It Mean?," *Business Week*, January 12, 1987, pp. 38-40; "The Top 200 Deals, Merger Mania's New Accent," *Business Week*, April 17, 1987, pp. 273-292; "New? Improved? The Brand Name Mergers," *Business Week*, October 21, 1985, pp. 108-116. See also "Let's Make a Deal," *Time*, December 23, 1985, pp. 44-55.

3. See *Forbes*, December 2, 1985.

4. See *The Economist*, December 25, 1976 and April 17, 1982.

5. See *Fortune*, June 1985.

6. See Adams and Brock (1986b, pp. 1532-1537).

7. See U.S. Department of Justice, *Merger Guidelines*, June 14, 1982, and *Merger Guidelines*, June 14, 1984. For a contrasting view, see *Antitrust Enforcement: Horizontal Merger Guidelines of the National Association of (State) Attorneys General*, March 10, 1987.

8. See Cohen, "Failed Marriages," *Wall Street Journal*, September 10, 1984.

9. *Ibid.*

10. See *Business Week*, July 1, 1985.

11. See 168 F. Supp. 576 (S.D.N.Y. 1958).

REFERENCES

Adams, Walter and James W. Brock (1986a) *The Bigness Complex,* (New York: Pantheon Books).

Adams, Walter and James W. Brock (1986b) "The 'New Learning' and the Euthanasia of Antitrust," *California Law Review,* Vol. 74, pp. 1515-1566.

Cowling, Keith, P. Stoneman, J. Cubbin, J. Cable, G. Hall, S. Domberger and P. Dutton (1980) *Mergers and Economic Performance,* (New York: Cambridge University Press).

Darman, Richard G. (1986) "Looking Inward, Looking Outward: Beyond Tax Populism," (Address to the Japan Society, New York, November 7, mimeo).

Mueller, Dennis C. ed. (1980) *The Determinants and Effects of Mergers: An International Comparison* (Cambridge, Mass.: Delgeschlager, Gunn & Hain).

_____ (1986) "Mergers and Managerial Performance," (Washington, D.C.: Federal Trade Commission Working Paper No. 137).

Livermore, Shaw (1935) "The Success of Industrial Mergers," *Quarterly Journal of Economics,* Vol. 50, pp. 68-88.

Scherer, F.M. (1980) *Industrial Market Structure and Economic Performance* (2nd ed.) (Chicago: Rand McNally).

Chapter 11

Strategic Goals and Operational Problems: The Implementation Gap in Mergers and Acquisitions

*Gordon A. Walter**
Faculty of Commerce & Business Administration
University of British Columbia

1.0 INTRODUCTION

There is a considerable gap between strategic goals in mergers and acquisitions and their actual consequences. This gap seems to be due to consistent errors in strategy implementation. A simple way to think about this gap is in terms of operational problems that arise for particular types of mergers and acquisitions. Countless articles in the business press testify to the disruptive nature of mergers and to the post merger dynamics of corporate power. Serious scholarly effort to specify problems and remedies has only recently made noticeable progress in this area.[1] From this and other research, critical factors in mergers and acquisitions are beginning to emerge. The purpose of this paper is to explore the implementation realities associated with one set of strategic contingencies and to describe the gap between strategic objectives and operational outcomes in mergers.

This paper is in two parts. The first part describes managerial objectives for mergers and acquisitions in Canada. Four types of mergers serve as pivotal categories for this description. These are vertical, horizontal, concentric,[2] and conglomerate. Each type is related to objectives that have been judged by mergers and acquisitions intermediaries to be important to acquiring managers (Walter 1986). The second part of the

* The empirical research reported in this paper was made possible through a grant by the Department of Consumer and Corporate Affairs, Government of Canada. The author gratefully acknowledges the help of Jay Barney in the data analysis and interpretation presented in sections 2.2 and 2.3.

paper relates these managerial objectives to post-acquisition organizational problems as identified in the academic and professional literature.

2.0 MANAGERIAL OBJECTIVES IN MERGERS AND ACQUISITIONS

Substantial literatures in economics, finance, business strategy, and organization theory exist concerning the objectives of merger and acquisition minded managers. One approach is to list numerous possible goals for key actors such as acquiring company managers or selling company owners (e.g., Steiner 1975). Another approach is to concentrate on one particular goal to explain managerial action in both acquiring and target firms (Amihud & Lev 1981). Unfortunately, both the goal lists and the single goal approaches fail to explain many important aspects of mergers and acquisitions such as goal priorities in different merger situations. The research reported in this paper used a broad list of 20 goals to empirically derive focused clusters of goals for managers of acquiring firms who were engaged in different types of acquisitions (Kitching 1967; Chatterjee 1986). The list of 20 goals that was used for this research taps a variety of perspectives and themes in the acquisitions literature. A few of these are noted before the details of the study are described.

The fields of organization theory and strategy explain merger goals in ways that are often highly compatible. For example, resource dependence and transaction cost theorists argue that mergers and acquisitions are responses to uncertainty in obtaining key organizational resources (Pfeffer & Salancik 1978; Williamson 1975, 1979; Galbraith & Stiles 1984).

Similarly, diversification strategy also tends to make uncertainty management[3] and the imperative for growth[4] a high priority. On the other hand, unrelated diversification strategy is predicated on an approach to uncertainty management that is quite different from the approach implied in the resource dependency model.

The financial economics field has generated a wide variety and large number of competing explanations for mergers and acquisitions. For example, mergers and acquisitions have been seen as the capital markets' way of replacing poor management (Manne 1965; Jensen & Ruback 1983), as a mechanism for firms to obtain financial leverage (Lewellen 1971; Levy & Sarnat 1970), and as a way managers can enhance their personal power and income (Jensen & Meckling 1976; Mueller 1969) while simultaneously reducing their own career risks (Amihud & Lev 1981). More recently, an "agency theory" imperative to utilize free cash flow has been advanced as a key goal (Jensen 1986). Roll (1985) suggested that mergers and acquisitions are a manifestation of managerial hubris, a false belief that they can manage an acquired firm better then that firm's current management.[5]

One important controversy about horizontal mergers is between the goal of exploiting market power and the goal of creating economic efficiencies. The market power view emphasizes advantages of significant market share and oligopolistic pricing opportunities (Mason 1939; Bain 1956; Ellert 1975; 1976). Others have argued that managers engage in mergers and acquisitions to obtain synergies (Lev & Mandelker 1972; Halpern 1973; Mandelker 1974), or to improved operating efficiency (Eckbo 1983; 1985). Eckbo (1983) offers convincing results, from stock price data, for the dominance of efficiency over market power in horizontal mergers in the U.S. and more mixed results for Canadian horizontal mergers (Eckbo 1986). The debate on this issue is far from resolved.

The approach developed in this paper combines the comprehensiveness of the lists approach with the striving for focus of the single goal approach. It also is comprehensive in the sense that concerns from economics, finance, organization theory, and business strategy are all represented. Rather than attempting to specify what managerial motives should or should not be according to a single exogenous theoretical framework, and rather than speculating on managerial actions in a single situation, a taxonomy of objectives for mergers and acquisitions is developed inductively from the responses of merger professionals to a questionnaire.

2.1 Approach

The multitude of possible goals in mergers and acquisitions were accumulated from the range of sources noted above and regrouped into 20 specific goals within the areas of efficiency, marketing, entrepreneurial actions (e.g., growth), and finance. See Table 1. These goals served as key question items in an empirical study of managerial motives in mergers and acquisitions (Walter 1982; Walter 1986). The study collected data from 32 individuals intimately involved in developing and managing mergers and acquisitions in Canada. These people were all *professional merger intermediaries* who have conducted or scrutinized the analyses associated with numerous mergers and acquisitions and who have a substantial network of associates involved in mergers and acquisitions (Boucher 1980). These are "insiders" to many major merger activities including deal-making itself. They include professional accountants who are merger specialists, banking merger specialists, venture capitalists, financial advisory specialists and analysts, executives of financial underwriting firms, and corporate lawyers. All had offices in New York, Toronto, or Vancouver. Approximately half the sample were partners, vice-presidents, executive-vice presidents, presidents, chairman of the board, or held similar very senior positions in their institutions. Continuous solicitation of names of important merger and acquisition intermediaries and the fact that the major important merchant banks and other institutions were heavily represented in the sample gave confidence that a rich and representative sampling of key members of the merger and acquisition community had been obtained. Moreover, this circle of intermediaries quickly closed on itself, as is often the case in "snowball" samples of this sort (Barnett 1974). Data was collected through structured, confidential interviews held at the office of each of the participants, and were approximately two hours in duration.

Each participant was asked to rank managers' five most important goals for each of seven categories of mergers. For each ranking task, participants were given a randomized set of 20 3" x 5" cards. On each card was placed one of the 20 merger and acquisition goals listed in Table 1.

Table 1
Strategic Goal Items for Mergers and Acquisitions

Productivity

1) Utilize the acquired company's personnel, skills or technology in other operations of the acquiring company.

2) Utilize the acquiring company's expertise in marketing, production or other area within the acquired company.

3) Expand capacity at less cost than assembling new facilities, equipment, and/or physical assets.

4) Create economies of scale by relevant capacity expansion.

5) Improve efficiencies and reduce risk in the supply of specific goods and/or services to the acquiring company.

Distribution/Marketing

6) Attain improved competitiveness inherent in holding a sizable market share or important market position.

7) Improve economies of scale by utilizing the acquired company's distributional capacities to absorb expanded output.

8) Penetrate new markets by utilizing the acquired company's marketing capacities.

9) Reduce risks and costs of diversifying products and services delivered to customers within an industry.

10) Broaden the customer base for existing goods and services of the acquiring company.

Table 1 (cont'd)

Entrepreneurial

11) Reduce risks and costs of entering a new industry.

12) Accelerate growth or reduce risks and costs in a particular industry in which the acquiring company has a strength such as executive wisdom.

13) Utilize interlocking and mutually stimulating (synergistic qualities of the acquired company vis-à-vis the acquiring company.

14) Promote visibility with investors, bankers or governments, with an eye to subtle benefits later.

15) Fulfill the personal ambitions, vision or some particular goal of the acquiring company's chief executive.

Financial

16) Utilize financial strengths of the acquired and/or acquiring company such as foreign tax credits, tax loss, or borrowing capacity.

17) Divest poor performing elements of the otherwise undervalued acquired company, in portfolio management style.

18) Gain valuable or potentially valuable assets with the cash flow or other financial strengths of the acquiring firm.

19) Gain complementary financial features such as those that balance earnings cyclicality.

20) Pursue opportunities to sell stock at a profit by such acts as pressing management of the acquired firm for improved earnings.

Source: Walter (1986)

Participants then sorted the cards, selecting and ranking the five most important goals for a given merger and acquisition category. The first ranking task was for mergers and acquisitions in general, and served to help familiarize participants with the ranking task. The next four ranking tasks were for types of mergers and acquisitions defined by Kitching (1967) and others (e.g., Reid 1968; Rumelt 1974; Williamson 1975; Pitts 1977; Montgomery & Wilson 1986): vertical, horizontal, concentric, and conglomerate. Definitions and examples of each of these types of mergers and acquisitions were presented to each participant, and reviewed just before ranking for a particular type of merger and acquisition began. After ranking the five most important goals for each of these *types* of mergers and acquisitions, participants were directed to rank the five most important goals for "big" and "small" mergers and acquisitions (Porter & Lawler 1964; Kitching 1967; Lubatkin 1983; Cable 1983). As before, both definitions and examples were provided to help participants understand what these categories of acquisitions included.

2.2   Analysis: Building A Taxonomy of Merger and Acquisition Objectives

Cluster analyses were performed on the collected data to develop a taxonomy of merger and acquisition objectives (Hartigan 1975). Several different types of analyses were performed. In one, data from all five ranking tasks were included. In another, all ranks were recoded in a binary form (1 = a motive was ranked among the top five most important by a respondent, 0 = otherwise), and data from all five ranking tasks was included. Both these analyses were repeated including only the four types of mergers and acquisitions cited in Kitching (1967) (i.e., vertical, horizontal, concentric, and conglomerate).

Results of these different analyses were almost identical. Indeed, only one goal switched clusters as a result of changing analyses (goal number 17 in Table 1). This is an unusually high level of consistency across different clustering analyses (Hartigan 1975; Barney 1982) and suggests quite robust results (Boorman & White 1976). In order to conserve space, only results for the analysis that makes the fewest statistical demands on the data are reported. This analysis included only the four types of mergers and acquisitions cited earlier (i.e., vertical, horizontal, concentric, and conglomerate), and treated the data as binary (White, *et al.* 1976; Breiger, *et al.* 1975; Arabie, *et al.* 1978). All four of these data matrices were considered simultaneously in developing the taxonomy of objectives. The clustering algorithm used in this analysis was CONCOR (Breiger *et al.*, 1975).

CONCOR is a hierarchical clustering algorithm that successively splits data into smaller clusters resulting in a tree pattern (Hartigan 1975). CONCOR results for these ranking data are presented in Table 2.

The five clusters derived from the analysis are also labeled in Table 3. The goals grouped together in *cluster I* suggest that *mergers and acquisitions are a way that managers obtain and exploit economies of scale and scope.* This objective is similar to the synergy and efficiency oriented work of Eckbo (1983), Lev & Mandelker (1972), Halpern (1973), & Mandelker (1974).

Table 2
Clustering Results

Data was binary (1 = motivation ranked in top five of importance for a given type of merger/acquisition). All four types of mergers/acquisitions (vertical, horizontal, concentric, and conglomerate) considered simultaneously. Algorithm was CONCOR (Breiger, Boorman, & Arabie 1975). ALPHA cutoff was .95.

Cluster Number	Goal Numbers	Description of Cluster (objectives)
I	2, 4, 1	Mergers are a way managers obtain and exploit economies of scale and scope (Synergy I: efficiency in utilization)
II	12, 13, 5	Mergers are a way managers deal with critical and ongoing interdependencies with others in a firm's environment (Synergy II: creative connection)
III	6, 9, 8, 7, 10, 3	Mergers are a way managers expand current product lines and markets (Market expansion)
IV	18, 11, 15	Mergers are a way managers *enter* new business (Diversify assets & hedge on diversification risk)
V	14, 16, 19, 17, 20	Mergers are a way managers maximize and utilize financial capability (Assets not considered)

The goals grouped together in *cluster II* suggest that *mergers and acquisitions are a way that managers deal with critical and ongoing interdependencies with firms in their environment.* This cluster or objective, is similar to the central concerns about the sources of stimulation for mergers cited by resource dependence (Pfeffer & Salancik 1978; Thompson 1967; Galbraith & Stiles 1984) and transaction cost theorists (Williamson 1975).

The goals which group together in *cluster III* suggest that *mergers and acquisitions are a way that managers expand their current product lines and markets.* This growth orientation is (surprisingly) not overtly emphasized in the merger literature (e.g., Cable 1983), although the growth goal is pivotal to many strategies and is related to both the market power arguments of

Bain (1956) and Mason (1939), and the synergy arguments of Lev and Mandelker (1972), Halpern (1973), and others. *Cluster IV* goals (gain valuable or potentially valuable assets with the cash flow or other financial strengths of the acquiring firm; reduce risks and costs of entering a new industry; fulfill the personal ambitions, vision, or some particular goal of the acquiring company's chief executive) suggest that *mergers and acquisitions are a way that managers enter new businesses.* For goal 13, the cash flow obtained through an acquisition is used to gain valuable or potentially valuable assets. Presumably, these assets could be in an acquiring firm's current business, or in another business. However, goal 13, in combination with goals 16 and 18 strongly suggests that these firms are motivated to look beyond their current markets and products in their merger and acquisition activities. Again, much of the current work on merger and acquisition goals does not directly emphasize this class of objectives. The results of Cable (1983), for example, are consistent with this objective but are interpreted by Cable as evidence of "search" behaviour rather than serious entry behaviour. Research on mergers and acquisitions directed at diversification (Pitts 1977) and financial leverage (Lewellen 1971) are also related to this "new business" objective.

Finally, *cluster V* included the following goals: promote visibility with investors, bankers, or governments, with an eye to subtle benefits later; utilize financial strengths of the acquired and/or acquiring firm such as foreign tax credits or borrowing capacity; gain complementary financial features such as those that balance earnings cyclicality; divest poor performancing elements of the otherwise undervalued acquired company, in portfolio management style; and pursue opportunities to sell stock at a profit by such acts as pressing management of the acquired firm for improved earnings. It suggests that *mergers and acquisitions are a way that managers maximize and utilize a firm's financial capabilities.* That is, each of these goals focuses directly on sources of capital or on the exploitation of capital assets to gain economic advantage. This objective is very consistent with the arguments presented by Lewellen (1971) concerning the advantages of leverage that are mobilized in mergers and acquisitions. It is also consistent with the synergy literature, if synergies are limited to *financial synergies* (Copeland & Weston 1979). It is important to emphasize that in a statistically simple "goodness of fit" analysis this financial objective was very salient.

2.3 Objectives for Specific Types of Acquisitions
The analysis to this point suggests that some useful different objectives, which include a variety of specific goals, are identifiable. The comprehensive, yet economical, pattern of results is quite distinct from what is typical of either the "lists" or the single goal views of mergers and acquisitions that pervade previous work.

To characterize these goal patterns, the cluster solution (shown in Table 2) was applied to each of the data matrices for vertical, horizontal, concentric, and conglomerate types of mergers. This was done by rearranging the rows of each of these data matrices to match the goal partition obtained from the cluster analysis. Then, the average ranking of entries within each cluster for each type of merger or acquisition was computed. To maintain consistency, the binary versions of each of these data matrices were analyzed in this manner. The average ranking of all participants in each cluster for each type of merger acquisition thus represents the percentage of respondents that felt that the goals in a given cluster of objectives were among the five most important for a given type of merger or acquisition. The resulting averages are presented in Table 3.

The overall mean of these averages was 0.26, with a standard deviation of 0.19. Following methods outlined in White, Boorman, & Breiger (1976), a designation of "H" (for high) was given to any cell average that is one standard deviation or greater above the overall mean. A designation of "L" (for low) was given to any cell average one standard deviation or more below the overall mean. Averages within one standard deviation below or above the mean were designated by an "M" (for medium). The patterns which emerge from this analysis are quite striking (see Table 3).

Table 3
Percentage of Times Objectives of Specific Clusters
are Cited as Important for Different Types
of Mergers and Acquisitions *

Cluster Number (Objective)	I	II	III	IV	V
Merger Type					
Vertical	.135 M	.583 H	.266 M	.302 M	.069 L
Horizontal	.271 M	.302 M	.255 M	.406 M	.106 M
Concentric	.208 M	.260 M	.474 H	.177 M	.044 L
Conglomerate	.031 L	.031 L	.036 L	.656 H	.525 H

* Legend:

H - High
M - Medium
L - Low

For *vertical* mergers and acquisitions, objective (cluster) II (*mergers are a way managers deal with critical and ongoing interdependencies*) is very high, while objective V (mergers are a way managers maximize and utilize financial capability) is very low. The other objectives are seen as playing some role in vertical mergers, but not a dominant role. These results are consistent with the transaction cost and resource dependence views of mergers and acquisitions (Pfeffer & Salancik 1976; Williamson 1975). Both these models focus on the problems of managing ongoing business transactions by means of mergers and acquisitions; issues at the core of goals in cluster II. These results also suggest that purely financial objectives are rarely pivotal in vertical mergers and acquisitions.

For *horizontal* mergers, no clusters of goals emerge as dominant, and none emerge as unimportant. This suggests that a broad variety of different goals all operate for horizontal mergers. No single theoretical perspective dominates in this context. There are important immediate implications of this finding. For example, it seems unlikely that the debate between market power (Ellert 1975, 1976) and efficiency (Eckbo 1983) models of horizontal mergers will be resolved in the near future.

For *concentric* mergers and acquisitions, objective III (*mergers are a way firms expand current markets*) is seen as very important, while objective V (mergers are a way firms maximize and utilize financial capabilities) is seen as unimportant. This is consistent with Rumelt's (1974) observations concerning the reasons for related diversification strategies, and builds on research concerning the synergistic benefits of mergers and acquisitions (Copeland & Weston 1979). Such strategies are seen as a way of expanding current businesses in related product markets, without resorting to a full conglomerate form of organization or strategy (Salter & Weinhold 1979). The low ranking of the financial cluster (objective V) in this type of merger activity is consistent with this business, as opposed to a more purely financial orientation (Lewellen 1971).

Finally, *conglomerate* mergers are seen in Table 3 as being motivated very strongly by objective IV (*entering new businesses*) and by objective V (*utilize financial capabilities*). When new business goals are combined with financial goals, the resulting mergers and acquisitions tend to be of the conglomerate type. Just as striking are the very low averages for the other objectives, suggesting that economies of scale and scope (cluster I), managing ongoing interdependencies (cluster II), and expanding current markets (cluster III) are *not* important objectives in conglomerate mergers. These findings are consistent with research on conglomerate mergers by Rumelt (1974), Williamson (1975, 1985), Lewellen (1971), etc.

3.0 OPERATIONAL PROBLEMS IN MERGERS AND ACQUISITIONS

Problems of integrating acquisitions are many and varied (Walter 1982, 1985; Searby 1969; Yunker 1983; Huguet 1985; Kitching 1967; Goldberg 1983). The main challenge is not to find or identify dysfunctional reactions, but to economically categorize, report, and analyze those that have been widely observed. Problems are considered under three headings in this paper. These headings are losses in the target, incentives in the total situation, and organizational failures. Each heading will be used below for a discussion of each type of merger and acquisition. Generalizations are made from years of observing business press and other case reports plus discussions of events with acquirers, since little formal research into these problems has yet been reported. The emphasis is on *how* specific problems arise in each type of acquisition situation, managerial reactions, and how objectives are often not realized.

3.1 Losses in the Target

The majority of mergers and acquisitions begin in an atmosphere of hope and optimism.[6] Acquiring managers see a variety of great gains within their objectives and even beyond (e.g., Howell 1970; Salter & Winehold 1978). Possible losses are de-emphasized and even excluded from thought and communication (Janis 1972). It is assumed that target managers will "get on board" and make the deal a success (e.g., Howell 1970; Yunker 1983). The idea that many target managers have a lot to lose in the situation gets buried. Even the idea that managers in both organizations may be at cross purposes is largely ignored (Pritchett 1985). Losses depend on many factors, including the type of mergers and acquisitions involved. The four merger types provide the structure for this discussion of the losses in the target associated with mergers and acquisitions.

Vertical: Vertical acquirers want to reduce their vulnerabilities in the environment. Thus suppliers and distributors of critical factors are prime targets. For those targets, one important loss is that of self-direction and entrepreneurship (Sales & Mirvis 1984; Walter 1985). Closely related is the effect of becoming a small element in a large bureaucratic organization. This leads to both a shift in decision making authority and to a loss of a sense of importance. For example, Kitching (1967) reports that when the target's size is less than 2 per cent of the acquirer, poor performance is very likely to occur because the insignificant, small subsidiary gets "lost" in the shuffle. Marks & Mirvis (1985) vividly describe the sense of loss of power managers of small firms experience when brought under control of the new parent company.

Managers in the target firm often react to the controls by *resistance*. This can take a strong form of "circling the wagons," or it can be more subtle and passive (Hirsch 1985). A political dynamic is stimulated which further reduces the entrepreneurial nature of the target, making it less satisfying to the most entrepreneurial managers. Managers who react to the imposition of external control are more likely to quit during the post-acquisition integration period. While such terminations impose few immediate costs on the acquirer, they do intensify the sense of loss among remaining target company managers and this feeds into the negative reaction dynamic. Acquirers typically want to purchase "good" vertical targets. Thus, on average managerial talent *is* lost. Moreover, vertical acquirers have limited ability to assess performance in such diversified acquisitions.

Horizontal: Horizontal objectives vary. When efficiency is the goal, the loss in the target can be quite substantial. Here the likelihood is high that one's unit will be integrated into the acquirer and that jobs will be lost. Theoretically, horizontal consolidations should eliminate the less competent of each firm and expand success opportunities for the best (Buono, *et al.* 1985a; 1985b). In reality, most of the cuts are generally borne by the target organization. For example, one administrative structure is better than a blend of two and so the *target's administrative* structure is almost assuredly seen as redundant. Horizontal mergers in the service sector have often eliminated virtually the entire staff of the target organization and retained only the client list (e.g., Critchley 1985).

When growth and "synergy" are sought in horizontal mergers, threat of job loss is diminished but not eliminated. For example, when market share is expanded, many units (such as sales forces) face overlapping jurisdictions. In the confusion that surrounds "undermanaged" integrations with these characteristics, political infighting between the various units can become vastly more competitive (and even vicious) than between the company and "real" competitors (Huguet 1985). Client alienation, poor image and a host of other dysfunctions inevitably accompany such intense intra-corporate conflict (Pritchett 1985).

Concentric: Concentric mergers emphasize the objective of expanding current product lines and markets. They do so by building around specific talents within the acquiring firm. Acquirers are in a position to closely evaluate the competence of managers and staff in targets. Acquirers often make good strategic choices to gain valuable talents not already possessed in the firm (e.g., IBM acquisition of ROLM). When the target has a unique and valued capacity, problems can arise from imposing other systems from the acquirer onto the new subsidiary. Organization theory (Connor 1980) holds as axiomatic the notion that related systems need to be congruent with key internal technologies and tasks. This principle is often violated in concentric mergers because, after buying the desired technology, the acquirer often eliminates the systems that have been developed over years to manage the technology. Then, as a result of *managerial drive for control* (Searby 1969), the parent imposes systems that displace the ones that have evolved in the subsidiary (Souder & Chakrabarti 1984). Subsidiary staff are not just disrupted by such actions. Now they must deal with systems that, in important ways, are incongruous with the task they are addressing. They lose an effective administrative context within which to perform.

When the technologies of the acquirer and target firms are the same, the incongruency factor may be much less, but other losses can occur. Concentric mergers seem particularly vulnerable to a kind of technical arrogance on the part of the acquirer (Souder & Chakrabarti 1984; Magnet 1984; Altendorf 1986). Thus the acquirer staff tend to impose their technological priorities on the target. They do this without balanced consideration or analysis about the viability of the target's approach. They ignore "equifinality" in organizations (i.e., the notion that several approaches can yield comparably good results). The importance of these and related shifts in the target organization are often discounted or ignored by acquirers. These changes dull career accomplishments and reduce the subsidiary manager's capacity to contribute and to succeed in the new order.

Conglomerate: Conglomerate acquisitions are, for the most part, the most benign of all the types considered in this paper. Often the short term threat to managers is low, since only desirable candidates are acquired by most conglomerates. ("Turnaround" is considered a sub-specialty, outside "normal" merger procedures and not considered viable by conglomerates). The imposition of tightened financial control, however, means the loss of self-direction by executives who previously had substantial capital discretion and had been able to "manage the board" reasonably well (Sales & Mirvis 1984; Mirvis 1985).

Financial control is legitimized in a number of ways. In recent years debt has been increasingly used to perform this function (Jensen 1986). Increased competition for desireable target companies and enhanced defensive strategies and tactics of target company managers have resulted in higher purchase premia. No one talks about acquiring "undervalued assets" in 1988. Thus the normal financial controls of acquirers become intensified by the pressure to service enormous debt loads. Some argue that such debt creates *needed pressure* on otherwise complacent managers (Jensen 1986) and this point will be returned to at the end of this paper. However, it is clear that certain flexibility, internal investment options, perks, working arrangements, and so forth, are also lost within the subsidiary (McKinsey & Co. 1987). Substantial losses are experienced by staff in newly acquired firms. No direct estimate of these losses, nor of their consequences have been made on a systematic basis.

3.2 Incentives in the Total Situation

The second source of problems associated with takeovers involves the incentives mobilized in the new structure. As with the previous section, the discussion starts with vertical acquisitions. Both positive and negative incentives are considered such as financial gain versus the "fear" component.

Vertical: The entrepreneurial incentives that are pervasive in small independent companies are superfluous in vertically integrated subsidiaries. The parental need is for steady, cost-effective, supply or distribution. Thus, vertical mergers not only generate increasing bureaucratization and formalization, but also adjust the incentive system to guarantee predictability rather than profitability. Individuals, who prior to the takeover could look forward to substantial bonuses and "perks," find these curtailed so that personnel systems across all subsidiaries are consistent. For example, in bank takeovers of investment dealers such adjustments even include trading-in the BMWs and Porsches for Buicks. The subsidiary's staff must not upstage headquarters executives, who are driving Cadillacs. Reducing incentives that signal identity often reduces performance and leads to the loss of key staff (Halloran 1985).

Often there is substantial ambiguity about incentive arrangements in the new regime. Jemison and Sitkin (1986) demonstrate and emphasize the dysfunctional nature of post-merger ambiguity. Ambiguity is, among many things, the absence of incentive. The possibility that post-merger ambiguity may be intentional and that it may serve an important purpose is ignored by Jemison and Sitkin. For example, one useful purpose is to *avoid confronting* all of the incongruities in incentives between the parent and the subsidiary organization. That is, acquirers can slowly allow the incentives that matter to be revealed to participants in the subsidiary. The advantage of the ambiguous approach is that one gets an "honest" baseline measure of subsidiary staff activities (Hunt, *et al.* 1987). A second advantage of ambiguity is that turnover of the disenchanted is spread over time and the power of subsidiary staff to leave "en masse" is thwarted.

The disadvantage of ambiguity is motivational. Disillusionment and demoralization occur as new incentive priorities slowly become clear to subsidiary personnel. Key accounts and proprietary information are often lost as managers leave the organization and take their legacy with them. Note that the issue is not redundancy or competence, but priorities. Some of the most talented staff are lost because no provision is made to mobilize and use their contributions. The theme that dominates the incentives question in vertical mergers is that acquirer *managers* are so driven to establish *control* in the subsidiary that they often sacrifice the most basic incentives to perform in, or even to stay in the organization.

Horizontal: Redundancy factors are key sources of incentives in horizontal mergers and acquisitions. On the threat side, redundancy is assumed by top management to create intense pressure to perform in the fashion they desire. Ambiguity seems to be assured to heighten this "incentive." Unfortunately top management both under-estimates and over-estimates specific aspects of the rationality of subsidiary's staff. At one level subsidiary staff are less rational than top management typically assumes. They experience the increased pressure in such threatening ways that they are motivated to react against the threat rather than respond to its incentive aspect. In short, they move to protect themselves rather than to perform.

These self-interest moves can take the form of the vicious internal competition, referred to in the previous section (Huguet 1985). Reactive moves can also take the form of "consuming" whatever benefits exist in the job, (e.g., travel perks, client loyalty, etc.). This often is highly costly to acquirers. The recent wave of securities dealer consolidations, serves as an example. Here a major goal is expansion of client lists (market expansion). However, it is also true that many of the best brokers leave the target firm, because of perceived limitations and risks in the new entity. Because of these losses, acquirers in essence get *less* than they purchase. With a little attention to the particulars of the target firm's staff, acquirers could retain substantially more of the value of their acquisition. The absence of managing the transition in such a fundamental way could be taken as *circumstantial evidence* that the acquirer's priority in the acquisition is not efficiency and growth, but the elimination of an institutional competitor (market power over efficiency). On the other hand, such mismanagement could be taken as evidence of a level of incompetence heretofore not attributed to acquirers. This issue is treated again in the conclusions.

Concentric: In concentric mergers the desirability of retaining human capital is even more pervasive and important than for horizontal mergers and acquisitions. Here, however the bureaucratic pressures for internal consistency are buttressed by the self-interest of the acquirer's technical staff. These individuals are in a powerful position to *define competence* and to set incentives to be consistent with that definition. They clearly wish such an arrangement to be consistent with their competencies. So where differences in style between the acquirer and their new subsidiary are substantial, acquirers impose their priorities. Sometimes this imposition is shockingly swift and pre-emptive, but it also may be slow and implicit. When slow it is less brutal, but not necessarily more kind since it simultaneously engenders the problem of ambiguity.

Unique organizational dynamics are created when the change is intense and accompanied by dramatic acts to "announce" the change. An acquisition in the food processing industry serves as an example of the dramatic approach. The acquirer had a "high-tech/high cost" approach while the target had a low tech/low cost approach. Historical evidence indicates that profitability in each of the two approaches was reasonably comparable (equifinality). None the less, the week following the takeover technical staff of the acquirer "studied" the new subsidiary and loudly announced (in front of subsidiary staff) that the operation was a disaster. They made abundantly clear future criteria for criticism and rewards. Employees who were masters of cost savings saw little incentive to try or even to stay. Performance deteriorated rapidly and a very costly technical renovation soon became necessary. Subsequently, the acquisition purchase team was blamed for "paying" too much for the "poorly run" target.

Even when change is slow, dysfunction can occur. Souder & Chakrabarti (1984) report that parent corporations in concentric mergers seem to be nearly unable to resist the temptation to move in and "help" the new subsidiary. This occurs through the provision of advice about (and rewards for) "proper" action. Demoralization can spread through a subsidiary like the rising tide on mudflats, as subsidiary core technical skills are ignored and other priorities imposed (Yunker 1983; Arnold 1984). First, the technical skills rewarded may well be possessed by individuals of relatively low skill in other important areas. Thus the discount to the old skills is experienced acutely. Second, rewards are status. Granting rewards to otherwise low status people also constitutes a redefinition of the status system. Age-old internal contracts are broken (both overt and relational, Williamson 1979, 1985). The corporate culture is disrupted. Subsidiary staff are in a fundamental, and nearly legal, sense "violated" by these new actions. Contracts are broken in the horizontal mergers also, but in concentric mergers it is not so much the threat that proves dysfunctional. In concentric mergers it is the insult that seems to be most central. In the final analysis these actions undermine employee commitment.

Conglomerate: The previous section described the conglomerate's emphasis on financial control. Clear incentives generally accompany this assertion of control. The incentive problem here arises as an extreme form of the problems just described for concentric mergers. The key concentric element in conglomerates is financial expertise and power. Growth of conglomerates is through the assertion of these financial competitive advantages. By contrast, subsidiary managers have a rich internal system and culture in which a variety of contributions that indirectly build the bottom line are also valued. For example, targets often value core technical skills higher than they do financial skills. They value production and marketing more than financial controls. Since conglomerate management cannot fully appreciate these detailed contributions in their highly diverse empire, they must rely on financial performance and presentation over "direct" indicators. Thus rewards for critical contributions can be eliminated and performance can erode.

The issue of values requires more elaboration. Values are to managers as culture is to organizations. As the values of the parent are made clear in the subsidiary via incentives, the culture of the subsidiary changes. Some people go. Some people rise in importance, others go down in status (Walter 1985). The old governing coalition changes or even disintegrates. A new one arises. Skilled individuals, who do not wish to exchange their expertise for one that is more oriented to financial calculations and reporting, move on to other opportunities. Again, some of the human capital that was "purchased" is simply and, it seems unintentionally, discarded.

3.3   Organizational Failures
There are an almost infinite number of specific organizational problems which arise when two companies are combined. Sometimes they arise from oppressive control aspects of what essentially is "over-organization". Sometimes they arise from a variety of "under-organization" gaps, overlaps, and errors. Jemison and Sitkin (1986) emphasize the ambiguity of the post merger organization and de-emphasize the over-organization aspects in their analysis. The following analysis will show the unique proclivity for different types of mergers (simultaneously) to generate *both under-organization* and *over-organization*. However, in most managerial situations the failures tend to be primarily of either one or the other variety (Huse & Cummings 1985; Wilensky 1967). As with the other problem categories, each type of merger and acquisition is treated separately.

Vertical: Vertical acquisitions tend to have less trouble with confusion and under-organization than other types of mergers and acquisitions. However control is often a major source of trouble. Efforts to mitigate this problem source can create substantial ambiguity. First, consider some over-organizational dynamics. Remember that the key *managerial* goal in vertical takeovers emphasizes ways of dealing with critical ongoing interdependencies with others in the firm's environment. The implications for control are simple yet profound. Consider for a moment that the act of acquisition is not one of expansion *per se* nor one of using financial power. In competitive strategy terms, vertical acquisitions are largely *defensive* rather than offensive (according to this study's interviewees). This means that the central sensitivities and concerns of acquiring managers are also largely defensive in nature. Cost control, distributional reliability, and so forth take priority over creative, market oriented activities. The imposition of bureaucratic controls and the tightening of financial, production and other planning tasks often occurs. If the new subsidiary is substantially smaller than the parent, it is likely to be much less formalized. Thus increased formalization is experienced in the subsidiary as unnecessary "overburden." Few things are more demoralizing than superfluous supervision (Beer 1981). Reactions in the subsidiary range from reduced commitment to active rebellion. Key executives leave when they see that the controls will eliminate creative moves that can enhance their careers. For most of those who remain, the situation signals that their careers are dramatically limited. In these cases active rebellion gives way to plodding conformity. Motivation levels are low.

Some acquirers attempt to avoid these dysfunctions by "going slow" in implementing tight controls (Hunt, *et al.* 1987). They give lip service to an entrepreneurial mandate. Paradoxically, managers in the subsidiary do not experience the absence of control as freedom, but instead as ambiguity. They ask "What do they want of me? What are their priorities? How should I act? Should I repair or replace this equipment?" They know a new game has started. They know that "score" is being kept. They do not know how to get a good score. The firm drifts. It is under-organized.

Horizontal: Organization and management should be relatively simple when firms in the same business combine. Competencies can be assessed, redundancies can be rationally identified, and so forth. Since horizontal acquirers seek a variety of alternative goals, (e.g., growth, market power, and efficiency). It would seem a straightforward exercise to use the existing hierarchies to seek specific desired outcomes. The fact that these issues are theoretically very manageable tends to mask three critical factors: (1) differences in corporate culture and style, (2) the dynamics of self-interest, and (3) upward communication pathologies of a unitary chain of command. These can make the "rationalization" process proceed in very irrational ways.

The culture of an organization includes the shared values, attitudes and beliefs of its members. The concept of equifinality used above is profoundly applicable to culture. The condition of equifinality, again, means that there is a vast range of possible ways that an organization can get to the same performance level or to the same set of outcomes. Similarly, many alternative cultures would work quite well for a given organization. Corporations and societies need *a* culture, not necessarily a particular culture (Wilson 1975). Corporate culture is built-up over time and is the result of key people, key events, myths, personnel hiring history, and a host of other factors (Frost, *et al.* (eds.) 1985). Two merging organizations often have major culture incompatibilities (Buono, *et al.* 1985a,b). Both organizations could work well separately, but neither work well within the cultural pattern of the other. It is for this reason that many horizontal mergers generate *negative* synergy.

Closely related to the grand issue of culture are the smaller but equally important issues of style and procedure. Negative synergy is experienced daily in the merging organizations. This is experienced as value conflicts and climate differences and also as more pragmatic irritations. Approvals, personnel transfer sequences, rewards, and even business forms are different. The all important area of customer relations suffers, since each side of the merger has a unique marketing emphasis and approach. For example, one store's marketing emphasis features wide aisles while another has rapid turnover of displays and freshness as key. One bank tries to display an image of solidity and stability while another sells friendliness. Employees are put in "double-binds" daily in their most fundamental work activities. Psychologists tell us that double-binds not only are a source of discomfort, they drive people crazy. It is not hard to appreciate that these incongruencies can confuse identity and diminish performance (Halloran 1985).

The dynamics of self-interest are a related source of problems of this type in horizontal mergers. Self-interest is harnessed through incentive systems, the standard hierarchy and specific controls in normal, on-going organizations. Most internal competition is channeled into constructive performance striving. Unfortunately, managers come to rely on and have faith in competition as the key source of "motivation" for staff. Seeing competition as their friend, managers sometimes fail to perceive the destructive dynamics of intergroup competition. For example, Huguet (1985) documents a case of the horizontal combination of four sales forces which were allowed to continue to operate in territories which existed prior to merger and which overlapped. With their internal performance evaluations on the line, the competition was much more fierce *among* the groups than between them and their "true" outside corporate competitors. Dysfunction included lies about and deprecation of other sales units within the firm to common customers! Clearly, the system was under-organized. Most top managers do not seem to know how to organize for proper motivation *outside the normal assumptions* of ongoing and unified organizational structure.

Concentric: The dominant organizational problems in concentric mergers closely parallel the over-organization type problems in horizontal mergers and acquisitions. This may be somewhat surprising, since presumably it is harder to manage subsidiaries that have merely similar technologies than ones that are in virtually identical businesses. For this reason one might expect problems of under-organization to predominate over problems of over-organization in concentric mergers and acquisitions. However, this is not the case. The discussion below shows the reasons for the critical importance of over-organization problems in concentric mergers and acquisitions. This discussion begins with a reminder of the key objective of the concentric type of acquisition.

The dominant managerial objective in concentric mergers and acquisitions is expansion of current product lines and markets. This is quite different from vertical acquisitions, where defensive objectives appear to dominate. Concentric acquirers are on the offensive. They move out into the competitive environment in their effort to expand by emphasizing areas of competence and competitive advantage. With this growth objective key, the concentric merger can be understood to be less a use of technology per se and more a type of related diversification, one that sticks to core and linked technologies (Rumelt 1974). It is the mobilization of competencies in service of the growth objective that is important (McKelvey, 1982). Bureaucratic control is a necessary part of this and it is here that the problems of over-organization are generated.

Jemison & Sitkin (1986) use the term "management systems misapplication" to identify circumstances where imposing the parent's routines and policies has these kinds of effects. Souder & Chakrabarti (1984) used a similar idea in their empirical study of concentric merger failures and successes. They report that failing acquisitions are typified by meddlesome and over-controlling parent relations. Technological specialists went in and "helped" subsidiary staff too much. Systems misapplications also include situations in which technical priorities of the parent are imposed on subsidiaries. This is often done in spite of the fact that these priorities do not reflect the optimal arrangement for them. A vivid example of such misapplication is provided by Magnet (1984). Schlumberger acquired Fairchild Camera and Instrument and "arrogantly imposed its do-it-by-the-numbers manner on the once agile semiconductor manufacturer. Fairchild's top engineers left in droves," revenues declined (Magnet 1984; p. 22).

The picture that emerges from scholarly and business observers is grim. There seems to be an inability of monolithic control structures *to restrain their managers' proclivities* toward imposing their "will" on subordinates in dysfunctional ways. Bureaucratic controls are misused. The reasons for this organizational failure are simple. First, most organizations are designed to "overdetermine" outcomes. A basic principle is "recurrence of past mistakes is prevented by institutionalizing controls and routines." A complex web of structures grows that specifies what is desired and disdained. Organizations cannot create desired outcomes as readily as they can suppress that which is not desired. Managers' careers in a single organization pivot around these institutional realities. To succeed they must actively pursue and avoid specified outcomes. In a concentric merger, many parent structures are tied to the technology. Parent representatives in subsidiaries know that perceptions in headquarters matter. Thus, even if acquirers see existing structures in the subsidiary as legitimate and relevant, acquirer managers have a strong incentive to change things so that they are consistent with the parent. Given the incentive/motive situation, selective perceptions of participants is easily biased toward seeing problems in the subsidiary and not seeing effectiveness in the subsidiary. Such biasing also yields conclusions that parent approaches are the solutions to perceived problems. These dynamics make it difficult for headquarters to appreciate or even discover the damage done to subsidiary processes and procedures. The irony of concentric mergers is that the power of technology to misapply parent systems in subsidiaries is not counterbalanced by equally good ability to monitor and limit such potential *control excesses*. The monolithic character of bureaucracy creates a "self-sealing" quality that undermines such self-limitation. The board of directors almost never finds out what went wrong and why.

Conglomerate: Conglomerates can be thought of as a special form of concentric acquisition in which the central technology is finance rather than marketing or production. Conglomerates can also be seen as engendering a more diversified form of growth than is pursued in other concentric acquisitions. This concept of conglomerate is not speculative. It comes directly from the opinions of participants who provided the data reported in the first half of this chapter. They saw acquirer managers' objectives to be *utilizing financial capabilities* of the firms and *entering new businesses*. Given this reality and the financial control emphasis in conglomerate management, one would expect problems of an under-organization variety to predominate in conglomerate acquisitions. However, in reality, problems of both under-organization and over-organization coexist in the conglomerate type acquisitions.

Problems of under-organization are pervasive because diversification acquisitions are outside the acquirer manager's decision making expertise (Rumelt 1974; Biggadike 1979; Buhner 1987). Headquarters has a position between that of a true line control relation with subsidiaries and that of a creditor or stock holder. The poor performance of highly diversified conglomerates in the late 1970s and early 1980s made it fashionable to criticize growth by diversification "strategies" (e.g., *Business Week*, 1985). Unfortunately, what such criticism ignores is that if one has grown as much as is practical in a given business environment (e.g, General Electric, Brascan), diversification may be the best (and only) alternative managers have for using the firm's financial power (Grant & Thomas 1987). One must not compare ITT with a focused smaller firm such as Proctor and Gamble, since the excess capital power "problem" and the business environment for ITT are not the same as for Proctor and Gamble. Proctor and Gamble has different unique stategic problems and opportunities.

Today, successful conglomerates tend to be of the "rifle" rather than "shotgun" variety (Dundas & Richardson 1982; Rumelt 1982; Kuswett 1985; Prahalad & Bettis 1986). They concentrate on three or four industries that are complementary (e.g., primary products, consumer products, and financial services at Brascan). In this way adequate executive expertise can be accumulated at headquarters in each business area and specific (horizontal and concentric) decisions can be delegated to the major operating "groups." But even such successful conglomerates have problems.

Under-organization problems arise in conglomerates from the inherent limitations when finance is the primary "technology." Reporting, performance definition, and other systems are imposed by headquarters. Too often this is done without adequate tailoring to the uniquenesses of the subsidiary. One result is that upward reporting is rather anemic. When financial performance figures decline, little information is available to headquarters that can guide efforts to change the situation (e.g., Loomis 1979). Delegation of various decision making responsibilities to "group" managers can mitigate this and other important limitations in diversification (Stengrevics 1986). Unfortunately, these structures build extra layers of hierarchy and introduce greater time lags for financial decision making (say, capital investment) and more time for political subterfuge. Overhead is increased rather than decreased. These factors would be labeled "dis-economies of scale" by an economist, rather than sources of under-organization. However, the term under-organization seems to be more descriptively rich even if less judgmentally prescriptive.

Absolute size is not the problem here. The problem comes when a firm's size relative to its business environment restricts growth and (full capital utilization). Proctor and Gamble has been in the greatly expanding market of home products. Drucker (1985) argues that good managers will always find a way to expand markets in this way. However, many other firms chose to diversify when market limitations became apparent. G.E., American Can and many other firms have done "industry swaps" to escape limited environments (Hofer & Chrisman 1985) while ITT chose a more wide reaching approach to diversification.

Over-organization problems also can diminish subsidiary performance. Financial reporting can be burdensome as well as irrelevant (Sales & Mirvis 1984). Further, pressure to reduce all performance to financial figures can create overly formalized and largely irrelevant decision making. The CBC program "Venture" vividly documented how this brand of over-organization destroyed the potential of the high-tech firm AES. Long financial decision making cycles of its owner, the Canada Development Corporation rendered impossible rapid product design and production decisions. Subsidiary priorities can become biased toward making the numbers look good, rather than striving to improve operations in ways that have less clear links to explicit performance indicators. Admittedly, such a change may not always be destructive. Unfortunately once priorities change so also do many systems within the subsidiary. Subsidiary management may not have adequate capabilities for financial tasks in such a way that important performance capacities are preserved. Even if they do, such massive shifts in style and procedure are highly disruptive. At the very least, these reorganizations contribute to the under-organized situation in subsidiaries. Given that there are so many ways a highly diversified corporation's subsidiaries can run into problems, it should not be surprising that many diversification attempts in the past few decades have gone *so* badly.

When things do go wrong in the under-organized situation, parents have little choice but to assign specialists to the "problem child." The parent managers put in charge are literally seen to be "riding herd" on the subsidiary. The portfolio management proclivity to not only fire individuals, but also to sell "weak" companies makes such arrangements very coercive. Reactionary over-organization replaces under-organization. Many subsidiary staff react poorly to the threats and punishments that attend this over-organization. The commitment of subsidiary mangers declines, good people leave, others withdraw or rebel. Firms experiencing such a sequence can be bought and sold two or three times before the downward spiral reaches its nadir.

4.0 CLOSING OBSERVATIONS AND CONCLUSIONS

This paper has documented the goals of acquiring company managers and has shown how these goals can lead managers into self-defeating organizational dynamics. The general tendency of acquirers to experience nearly zero stock price gain compared to target shareholder gains of 17 per cent (Jensen & Ruback 1983) may reflect the stock market's pessimism about these limits. Eckbo (1983, 1985) found positive stock holder gains for *horizontal* acquirers. This is hardly surprising since high redundancy gains are relatively easy to realize in horizontal consolidations, even when there also is massive waste of the variety discussed in this paper. It is hoped that the descriptions in this paper have a sobering effect on enthusiastic acquirers.

Managing the combining of companies is fundamentally different than managing a single, on-going organization. Differences arise from inter-unit linkages and the way managers react to the inter-organizational tensions and linking activities. Thus, a gap arises between the objectives of acquirers and outcomes. Why then do mergers occur? What implications are there for the debate about what is wrong with North American management (e.g., Hayes & Abernathy 1980)? What are the implications for the use and abuse of power?

4.1 Why Mergers Occur

This paper has concentrated on the difficulty of pursuing managerial objectives via mergers and acquisitions. Despite enormous problems there remain several imperatives driving mergers and acquisitions. What are the alternatives to this form of strategic behaviour? What else are firms to do to cope with vertical vulnerabilities, growth limitations/opportunity, consolidation potential, pressure to mobilize financial power? The fact that many mergers and acquisitions are badly managed does not diminish from their strategic importance. In fact, given that acquirers pay large premia to target shareholders, one must accept that capital market efficiency is sponsored by mergers and acquisitions in the short term. This good does not lessen the necessity for striving for effective post merger management. The manager's challenge is twofold. First is to improve management of the transition and second is to properly assess the costs of the implementation period rather than assuming that a merger in itself solves the firm's strategic problems.

4.2 Implications for the Crisis in North American Management

Hayes & Abernathy (1980) essentially argue that executive entrancement with finance and ambitious strategic maneuvers has meant that the candy store is being left unattended. That is, the common tasks of management are ignored in the executive scramble for opportunity. Such careerists attend too closely to observables and not closely enough to important, value creating, unobservables. Mismanagement of the post-merger situation could be seen as support for the Hayes and Abernathy critique. Unfortunately, the opposite could also be true.

On the other side of the argument is Boone Pickens (1985; 1986; 1987). Pickens claims the chief problem in business is that 80-90 per cent of North American managers are *incompetent*. Worse, they are incompetent and entrenched. Since boards of directors cannot bring such managers under control, acquirers take on that function (and receive raider rewards for doing so). Acquirers "shake-up" entrenched and self-serving management groups. Pickens implicitly asserts that the dysfunctions discussed in this paper are a byproduct of renovations and housecleaning that are overdue. The short term problems of mergers and acquisitions are trivial compared to the long term discipline that is being reintroduced into the larger system. Unfortunately, the litany of difficulties in integrating subsidiaries explored in this paper does not suggest that raiders are a solution to the competitive problem due to their own limitations.

The literature is filled with arguments against the Pickens position. All of these are appealing, but few are convincing. One that is convincing and that has the most credible business source asserts that in attempts to wrest control from managers, raider corporations "*damage*" target organizations (Rohatyn 1986). That is while gaining capital advantages and replacing some managers constitute important goods for mergers, there are also bads which can be substantial and which often are greater than the good. Evidence of damage is pervasive in this paper. In mergers and acquisitions one sees strategic gain and management waste, not management gain following strategically neutral moves. There is little real hope that a Pickens will do a better job managing targets than his objects of scorn. In fact, his way is the way of the financier, the anathema of Hayes and Abernathy! Mesa's raid on Gulf and subsequent "flip" netted capital gains that were critical to the survival of Mesa. Mesa was on the brink of bankruptcy while Gulf was safe and secure due to a more conservative management approach. Which firm was really the best managed? If the takeover attempt *proves* Picken's superiority, we are reduced to a simple "financial" *might makes right* test of goodness. This paper must support the view of Hayes and Abernathy that, in recent years, a strict financial/coercive approach to mergers and acquisitions has been a major part of the problem, not an untarnished sterling solution.

The current problems of the economy are being strategically addressed by mergers and acquisitions but the problems may be more fundamental than we realize. The ageing industries, increasing economies of scale and scope, and other issues which recur in merger and acquisition situations may be real yet superficial. It seems that something even more fundamental is wrong. Perhaps this level of the "problem" is best appreciated in broad historical terms. Important sectors of the North American economy are at the end of the greatest period of rising affluence in history. Less rich and more spartan nations have not yet enjoyed this affluence and are anxious to do so. Their populations are *motivated* to perform in ways the North

American population can barely remember. In other words, at least in relative terms, North American culture is complacent about critical things that make an economy vital. Stronger historical and ethical critics argue that the west is not merely complacent, but actually decadent and corrupt (e.g., Parkinson 1963; McIntyre 1981). The culture is not only polycentric, it is so much so as to be "lost," exhausted, or dissipated. This possibility may be less absurd than one first imagines. The incredible success of *Pursuit of Excellence* (Peters & Waterman 1982) and other "strong culture" management techniques is evidence that organizations now create what one would normally assume a society's culture would provide.

4.3 Implications for the Use and Abuse of Power
There is plenty of evidence that both pecuniary and real economies are gained by mergers and acquisitions.[7] For example, horizontal mergers can yield significant operations consolidations and conglomerates can use capital in ways that, it is fair to claim, add real value. On the other hand, horizontal mergers also squeeze out competition at times and the value of most mergers pivot on tax considerations. Most analyses of mergers and acquisitions ignore the problems and externalities treated in sections of this paper.

New questions arise in light of this paper. How can it be that managers who have been delivering an impressive string of profits for decades are suddenly "exposed" as incompetent by a crusading Boone Pickens? If raiders are reformers, why do they pick targets that are generally in the *top half* of competitors in a given industry? When massive numbers of managers in target companies are dismissed or demoted, what are the "shake-out" effects on taxes, middle class values, and so forth? While answers to such questions cannot be known completely, it is striking that so little curiosity exists about these matters.

When many subsidiary mangers are dismissed, are they replaced by lower paid managers? If so, are mergers merely a *convenient* structural *device* for breaking managerial *contracts* that can now be fulfilled by a new generation? Over-active business schools are graduating ever increasing numbers. If a new set of career rules is being imposed as a result of enhanced supply of managerial personnel, should not those who are dismissed be given severance pay and outplacement counselling? Remember most managers cannot demand a golden parachute. They can only hope for a silver handkerchief. Is avoiding proper severance payment an important component in the "efficiencies" created by mergers? Much of the dysfunction documented above testifies to the defensive character of subsidiary managers actions in today's organizations. Hirsch (1987) argues that this generation of managers is sufficiently traumatized by events to be likely to embrace a whole new managerial ethic. This ethic may prove to be cynical and corrosive. Will this ethic on balance be better or worse than that which is now being replaced? Are we assuming that the exercise of power proves its value? Is it in the interest of society to simply back the top dog, even if he is inefficient? Are takeovers the overdue solution to our problems or the ultimate managerial expression of abuse of power? At the very least it is clear that there is a substantial gap between strategic rationality that drives mergers and acquisitions and the pervasive irrationality observed in their implementation. This paper shows that mergers and acquisitions may be as much a part of the problem as they are a solution to today's economic difficulties.

NOTES

1. See Goldberg (1983), Souder & Chakrabarti (1984), Jemison & Sitkin (1986), Blake & Mouton (1985).

2. Concentric refers to mergers between firms with highly similar production or distributional technologies. (FTC product extension/ conglomerate mergers. Thompson (1967), Perow (1970), Reid (1968), Galbraith & Stiles (1984).

3. See Rumelt (1974); Hofer & Schendel (1978); Salter & Weinhold (1979).

4. See Hofer & Schendel (1978); Allen, Oliver & Schwallie (1981); Hofer & Crisman (1984).

5. For a comprehensive discussion of financial economics, see the paper by Eckbo, Chapter 7 in this volume.

6. Hostile takeovers are on the decline for a variety of reasons. First, boards of directors have better armed executives to defend against takeovers in order to maximize selling price. Thus the raiders incentives and opportunities have been curtailed. Second, the "market for reputation" is such that hostile acquirers pay higher acquisition premia than friendly acquirers. Third, hostile attacks often require hostile follow-through and thus serve as an enormous incentive for target managers to find other suitors and solutions. For example, "scorched earth" policies by targets can *destroy* the value purchased by hostile acquirers and thus make the approach self defeating and futile.

7. See the paper by Eckbo, Chapter 7 in this volume.

REFERENCES

Allen, M.G., R.A. Oliver, and E.H. Schwallie (1981) "The key to successful acquisitions," *Journal of Business Strategy*, Vol. 2, pp. 14-24.

Altendorf, D. M. (1986) "When cultures clash: A case study of the Texaco takeover of Getty Oil and the impact of acculturation on the acquired firm," (Los Angeles: University of Southern California, unpublished doctoral dissertation).

Amihud, Y. and B. Lev (1981) "Risk reduction as a managerial motive for conglomerate mergers," *Bell Journal of Economics*, Vol. 12, pp. 605-617.

Arabie, P., S.A. Boorman, and P. Leavitt (1978) "Blockmodels: How and why," *Journal of Mathematical Psychology*, Vol. 17, pp. 21-63.

Arnold, J.D. (1984) "Special challenges in merging manufacturers," *Mergers and Acquisitions*, Vol. 19(3), 49-55.

Bain, J.S. (1956) *Barriers to New Competition* (Cambridge, Mass.: Harvard University Press).

Barnett, V. (1974) *Elements of Sampling Theory* (London, England: English Universities Press).

Barney, J.B. (1982) *The structure of informal social relations in organizations: A comparative approach* (Unpublished Dissertation, School of Organization and Management and Department of Sociology, Yale University)

Beer, M. (1981) *Organizational Change and Development* (Bel Air, CA: Goodyear).

Biggadike, R. (1979) "The risky business of diversification," *Harvard Business Review*, May-June, pp. 103-111.

Blake, R.R., and J.S. Mouton (1985) "How to achieve integration on the human side of the merger," *Organizational Dynamics*, Vol. 13(3), pp. 41-56.

Boorman, S.A. and H. White (1976) "Social structure from multiple networks. II: Role structures," *American Journal of Sociology*, Vol. 81, pp. 1284-1346.

Boston Consulting Group (1971) *Growth and financial strategies* (Boston: The Boston Consulting Group).

Boucher, W.I. (1980) *The Process of Conglomerate Mergers* (Washington, D.C.: Federal Trade Commission).

Breiger, R., S.A. Boorman, and P. Arabie (1975) "An algorithm for clustering relational data, with applications to social network analysis and comparison with multidimensional scaling," *Journal of Mathematical Psychology*, Vol. 12, pp. 328-383.

Buhner, R. (1987) "International diversification of West German corporations," *Strategic Management Journal*, Vol. 8, pp. 25-27.

Buono, A.F., J.L. Bowditch, and J.W. Lewis III (1985a) "When cultures collide: The anatomy of a merger," *Human Relations*, Vol. 38(5), pp. 477-500.

_____ (1985b) "The human side of organizational transformation: A longitudinal study of a bank merger" (San Diego, CA: Paper presented at the 45th Annual Meetings of the Academy of Management).

Business Week (1980b) "ITT: Groping for a new strategy," Dec.15, pp. 66-80.

Business Week (1985) "Do mergers really work? Not very often which raises questions about merger mania," June 3, pp. 88-100.

Cable, J. (1983) "A search theory of diversifying merger," in W.H. Goldberg (ed.) *Mergers: Motives, Modes, and Methods* (New York: Nichols), pp. 17-34.

Chatterjee, S. (1986) "Types of synergy and economic value: The impact of acquisitions on merging and rival firms," *Strategic Management Journal*, Vol. 7, pp. 119-139.

Connor, P.E. (1980) *Organizations: Theory and Design* (Palo Alto, CA: Science Research Associates).

Copeland, T. and J.G. Weston (1979) *Financial Theory and Corporate Policy* (Reading, Mass.: Addison-Wesley).

Critchley, B. (1985) "The merger that became a takeover," *Financial Post*, Feb. 8, pp. 1.

Drucker, P.F. (1985) *Innovation and Entrepreneurship: Practice and Principles* (New York: Harper & Row).

Dundas, K.M.M. and P.R. Richardson (1982) "Implementing the unrelated product strategy," *Strategic Management Journal*, Vol. 3, pp. 287-301.

Eckbo, B. E. (1983) "Horizontal mergers, collusion, and stockholder wealth," *Journal of Financial Economics*, Vol. 11, pp. 241-274.

_____ (1985) "Mergers and the market concentration doctrine: Evidence from the capital market," *Journal of Business*, Vol. 58(3) pp. 325-349.

_____ (1986) "Mergers and the market for corporate control: The Canadian evidence," *Canadian Journal of Economics*, Vol. 19, pp. 236-260.

Ellert, J.C. (1975) *Antitrust Enforcement and the Behavior of Stock Prices*, (Chicago: Unpublished doctoral dissertation, Department of Economics, University of Chicago).

_____ (1976) "Merger, antitrust law enforcement, and stockholder returns," *Journal of Finance*, May, pp. 715-732.

Frost, P.J., L.F. Moore, M.R. Lewis, C. Lundberg, and J. Martin (eds.) (1985) *Organizational Culture* (Palo Alto, CA: Sage Press).

Galbraith, C.S. and C.H. Stiles (1984) "Merger strategies as a response to bilateral market power," *Academy of Management Journal*, Vol. 27, pp. 511-524.

Goldberg, W.H. (1983) *Mergers: Motives, Modes, Methods* (New York: Nichols).

Grant, R.M. and H. Thomas (1987) "Diversification and profitabilitiy: Empirical findings and management implications," (Hollywood, CA: Paper presented at the 28th Annual Meeting of the Western Academy of Management).

Halloran, K.D. (1985) "The impact of M & A programs on company identity," *Mergers and Acquisitions*, Vol. 20(1), pp. 60-66.

Halpern, P.J. (1973) "Empirical estimates of the amount and distribution of gains to companies in mergers," *Journal of Business*, Vol. 46, pp. 554-575.

Hartigan, J.A. (1975) *Clustering Algorithms* (New York: Wiley).

Hayes, R.H. and W.J. Abernathy (1980) "Managing our way to economic decline," *Harvard Business Review*, Vol. 58(6), pp. 67-77.

Hirsch, P. M. (1985) *Implications of two conflicting perspectives for mergers and acquisitions* (San Diego, CA: Paper presented at the 45th Annual Meeting of the Academy of Management).

_____ (1987 in press) *Pack Your Own Parachute* (Reading, Ill.: Addison Wesley).

Hofer, C.W. and D. Schendel (1978) *Strategy Formulation: Analytical Concepts* (New York: West).

Hofer, C.W. and J.J. Chrisman (1984) "First diversification and the strategic management process: A new perspective," (Boston, Mass.: Paper delivered at the 44th Annual National Meeting of the Academy of Management, August 12-15).

Howell, R.A. (1970) "Plan to integrate your acquisitions," *Harvard Business Review*, Vol. 49, pp. 66-76.

Huguet, J.H. (1985) "Blending sales forces after the acquisition," *Mergers and Acquisitions*, Vol. 19(4), pp. 52-57.

Hunt, J.W., S. Lees, J.J. Grumbar, and P.D. Vivian (1987) *Acquisitions - The Human Factor* (London: London Business School/Egon Zehnder International).

Huse, E. and T.C. Cummings (1985) *Organizational Development and Change* (New Haven, Conn: West).

Janis, I.L. (1972) *Victims of Groupthink* (New York: Houghton Mifflin).

Jemison, D.B. and S.B. Sitkin (1986) "Corporate acquisitions: A process perspective," *Academy of Management Review*, Vol 11 (1), pp. 145-163.

Jensen, M.C. and W.H. Meckling (1976) "Theory of the firm: Managerial behavior, agency costs, and ownership structure," *Journal of Financial Economics*, Vol. 3, pp. 305-360.

Jensen, M. C. (1986) "Agency costs of free cash flow, corporate finance, and takeovers," *American Economic Review*, Vol. 76(2), pp. 323-329.

Jensen, M.C. and R.S. Ruback (1983) "The market for corporate control: The scientific evidence," *Journal of Financial Economics*, Vol.11, pp. 5-50.

Kitching, J. (1967) "Why do mergers miscarry?," *Harvard Business Review*, Vol. 46, pp. 84-101.

Kuswitt, J.B. (1985) "An exploratory study of strategic acquisition factors relating to performance," *Strategic Management Journal*, Vol. 6, pp. 151-169.

Lev, B. and G. Mandelker (1972) "The microeconomic consequences of corporate mergers," *Journal of Business*, Vol. 45, pp. 85-104.

Levy, H. and M. Sarnat (1970) "Diversification, portfolio analysis, and the uneasy case for conglomerate mergers," *Journal of Finance*, Vol. 25, pp. 795-802.

Lewellen, W.G. (1971) "A pure financial rationale for the conglomerate merger," *Journal of Finance*, Vol. 26, pp. 521-545.

Loomis, C. J. (1979) "How ITT got lost in a big bad forest," *Fortune*, Dec. 17, 42-55.

Lubatkin, M. (1983) "Mergers and the performance of the acquiring firm," *Academy of Management Journal*, Vol. 8, pp. 218-225.

MacIntyre, A. (1981) *After Virtue: A Study of Moral Theory* (Notre Dame, Ind: University of Notre Dame Press).

McKelvey, B. (1982) *Organizational Sytematics: Taxonomy, Evolution, Classification*, (Los Angeles: University of California Press).

McKinsey and Co. (1987) "The effects of purchase price on post-merger performance," (unpublished generalizations from current practice).

Magnet, M. (1984) "Acquiring without smothering," *Fortune*, Vol. 110(10), pp. 22-30.

Mandelker, G. (1974) "Risk and return: The case of merging firms," *Journal of Financial Economics*, Vol. 3, pp. 303-335.

Manne, H.G. (1965) "Mergers and the market for corporate control," *Journal of Political Economy*, Vol. 73, pp. 110-120.

Marks, M.L. and P.H. Mirvis (1985) "Merger syndrome: Stress and uncertainty," *Mergers and Acquisitions*, Vol. 20(2), pp. 50-55.

Mason, E.S. (1939) "Price and production policies of large scale Enterprises," *American Economic Review*, Vol. 29, pp. 61-74.

Mirvis, P.H. (1985) "Negotiations after the sale: The roots and ramifications of conflict in an acquisition," *Journal of Occupational Behavior*, Vol. 6, pp. 65-84.

Montgomery, C.A. and V.A. Wilson (1986) "Mergers that last: A predictable pattern?" *Strategic Management Journal*, Vol. 7, pp. 91-96.

Mueller, D.C. (1969) "A theory of conglomerate mergers," *Quarterly Journal of Economics*, Vol. 83, pp. 643-659.

Parkinson, C. N. (1963) *East and West* (Boston: Houghton Mifflin).

Perrow (1970) *Organizational Analysis: A Sociological View* (Belmont, CA: Wadsworth).

Peters, T.J. and R.H. Waterman, Jr. (1982) *In Search of Excellence: Lessons from America's Best-Run Companies* (New York: Harper & Row).

Pfeffer, J. and G.R. Salancik (1978) *The External Control of Organizations: A Resource Dependence Perspective* (New York: Harper).

Pickens, B. (1985) "Management interest vs. shareholder rights," *Beta Gamma Sigma - Interview*, December, pp. 1-6.

_____ (1986) "Professions of a short termer," *Harvard Business Review*, Vol. 64(3), pp. 75-83.

_____ (1987) "Boone speaks," *Fortune*, Vol. 15(4), pp. 42-56.

Pitts, R.A. (1977) "Strategies and structures for diversification," *Academy of Management Journal*, Vol. 20, pp. 197-208.

Porter, L. and E.E. Lawler III (1964) "The effects of tall versus flat organization structures on managerial job satisfaction," *Personnel Psychology*, Vol. 17, pp. 135-148.

Prahalad, C.K. and R. A. Bettis (1986) "The dominant logic: A new linkage between diversity and performance," *Strategic Management Journal*, Vol. 7, pp. 485-501.

Pritchett, P. (1985) *After the Merger: Managing the Shock Waves* (Dallas, Tex: Dow Jones-Irwin).

Reid, S.R. (1968) *Mergers, Managers, and the Economy* (New York: McGraw-Hill).

Rohatyn, F.G. (1986) "Needed: Restraints on the takeover mania," *Challenge*, May-June, pp. 30-34.

Roll, R. (1985) "The Hubris Hypothesis," (Los Angeles: Unpublished, Graduate School of Management, UCLA).

Rumelt, R.P. (1974) *Structure, Strategy, and Economic Performance* (Cambridge, Mass: Harvard University Press).

_____ (1982) "Diversification strategy and profitability," *Strategic Management Journal*, Vol. 3, pp. 359-369.

Sales, A.L. and P.H. Mirvis (1984) "When cultures collide: Issues in acquisition," in J.R. Kimberly, and R.E. Quinn, (eds.) *Managing Organization Transitions* (Homewood, IL: Irwin), pp. 107-133.

Salter, M.S. and W.A. Weinhold (1978) "Diversification via acquisition: Creating value," *Harvard Business Reviews*, Vol. 56, pp. 166-176.

_____ (1979) *Diversification Through Acquisition: Strategies for Creating Economic Value* (New York: Free Press).

Sandberg, C.M., W.G. Lewellen, and K.L. Stanley (1987) "Financial strategy: Planning and managing the corporate leverage position," *Strategic Management Journal*, Vol. 8, pp. 15-24.

Searby, F.W. (1969) "Control postmerger change," *Harvard Business Review*, Vol. 45, pp. 4-12, 154, 155.

Souder, W.E. and A.K. Chakrabarti (1984) "Acquisitions: Do they really work?," *Interfaces*, Vol. 14(4), pp. 41-52.

Steiner, P.O. (1975) *Mergers: Motives, Effects, Policies* (Ann Arbor, Michigan: University of Michigan).

Stengrevics, J.M. (1986) "Managing the group executive's job," in M. Jelinek, J.A. Literer, and R.E. Miles (eds.), *Organizations by Design (Second Ed.)* (Plano, Tex: Business Publications Inc.).

Thompson, J. (1967) *Organizations in Action* (New York, McGraw-Hill).

Walter, G.A. (1982) "The morning after," *Cornell Executive*, Vol. 83, pp. 15-19.

_____ (1985) "Culture collisions in mergers and acquisitions," in P.F. Frost, L.F. Moore, M.R. Lewis, C. Lundberg, and J. Martin, (eds.) *Organizational Culture* (Palo Alto, Calif: Sage Press), pp. 301-314.

_____ (1986) "Management objectives for mergers and acquisitions in Canada," (Report to The Department of Consumer and Corporate Affairs, Government of Canada).

White, H., S.A. Boorman, and R. Breiger (1976) "Social structure from multiple networks: I. Blockmodels of roles and positions," *American Journal of Sociology*, Vol. 81, pp. 73-80.

Williamson, O.E. (1975) *Markets and Hierarchies: Analysis and Antitrust Implications* (New York, Free Press).

_____ (1979) "Transaction cost economics: The governance of contractual relations," *Journal of Law and Economics*, Vol. 22, pp. 233-261.

_____ (1985) *The Economic Institutions of Capitalism* (New York: Free Press).

Wilensky, H.L. (1967) *Organizational Intelligence: Knowledge and Policy in Government and Industry* (New York: Basic Books).

Wilson, E.O. (1975) *Sociobiology: The New Synthesis* (Cambridge, Mass.: Belknap Press of Harvard University Press).

Yunker, J. A. (1983) *Integrating Acquisitions: Making Corporate Marriages Work* (New York: Praeger).

Chapter 12

Notes on Corporate Concentration and Canada's Income Tax

Michael C. Wolfson*
Social and Economic Studies Division
Statistics Canada

"The law in its majestic equality forbids the rich as well as the poor alike to sleep under bridges, to beg in the streets, and to steal bread."
Anatole France via Gordon Bale (1981)

1.0 INTRODUCTION
The *Report of the Royal Commission on Corporate Concentration* (1978) accepted the conclusion of the background study by Stikeman, Elliot, Tamaki, Mercier and Robb (1976, p. 39): "In summary, the (Income Tax) Act does not appear to contain any fundamental bias which is either in favour of or detrimental to corporate concentration." On the other hand, recent newspaper columns by Parizeau (1987) and Blenkarn (1987) have called for major changes to the corporate income tax system precisely in order to remove what they see as a bias toward corporate concentration.

In this chapter the question of tax system bias is examined in two main stages. First, several corporate income tax provisions that are relevant to takeovers and mergers are examined. These provisions tend to attract attention because takeovers are themselves much more likely to arouse journalistic attention and public interest. This part of the analysis is necessarily anecdotal and impressionistic because of the paucity of data, and the technical complexities of both the provisions themselves and the way transactions are typically structured to use these provisions.

* The author accepts full responsibility for any errors or omissions, and for all views expressed herein. The analysis should not be taken as necessarily representing the views of the Government. It is part of a larger analysis of the distributional impact on firms of Canada's corporate income tax/transfer system.

While corporate takeovers may generate headlines, one firm growing more quickly than another rarely occasions much public interest. Yet if larger firms tend systematically to have relatively higher after-tax profits, whether to plough back into existing operations or to grow via corporate acquisitions, then this would also appear to constitute a source of bias toward concentration. On this question of the impact of the tax system on after-tax profitability, there is a considerable amount of data. This chapter provides a more detailed empirical assessment, based on a sample of corporate income tax returns. These data are well suited to determining the effective rates of tax actually paid by firms, although they are not able to shed any light on the taxation aspects of corporate takeovers and other forms of reorganizations. The main empirical part of the analysis examines the relationship between firm size, effective tax rates, and the utilization of various corporate income tax provisions.

The basic conclusions of the analysis are in two parts. First, it is argued that the effects of the tax provisions relating specifically to mergers and takeovers on corporate concentration may be overstated, particularly in light of the greater journalistic attention they have recently received. Second, however, the empirical analysis of effective tax rates seems to indicate a more fundamental and pervasive bias toward concentration. Put simply, larger firms systematically tend to pay less tax.

2.0 PRELIMINARIES

In any assessment of the extent of bias in the income tax system with respect to corporate concentration, it is desirable to be precise about the concepts being used. Unfortunately, this is difficult. For example, we refer to corporate concentration, but in fact in common parlance the objects of interest are not legal corporations but groups of corporations linked by common ownership and control, often referred to as enterprises. (The generic word "firm" where it is not likely to be ambiguous.)

Concentration often is measured by the amount of a given market accounted for by the k largest firms. But this begs the questions of how to measure the size of a market and the sizes of the firms in that market (typical measures are the shares of total sales or assets accounted for by the four or eight largest firms), how to define a firm, and how to define a market. In this analysis, the focus will be on whether or not there are biases in the corporate income tax system that allow large firms to grow relatively more quickly, so there is no need for a precise definition of market. The analysis might in fact be considered to be applicable mainly to the question of aggregate concentration. Also, the quantitative analysis uses corporate data, so there is little scope for exploring alternative definitions of the firms.

Another conceptual issue concerns the precise meaning of an assertion that the tax system is biased toward corporate concentration. The notion of bias only makes sense when the current tax system is compared to some other hypothetical tax system. One approach could be to compare the current corporate income tax system with an hypothetical tax system that is identical in all respects to the current tax system except that the provision in question is absent. An alternative is to compare the current tax system to a well-defined benchmark tax structure which is neutral with respect to concentration.

The former approach is easier to understand, but is unsatisfying because of its naivete: it is either unlikely that the corporate income tax would ever be amended in such a simplistic way, or such simple amendment would fail to recognize some of the more basic concepts built into the corporate income tax system. The latter approach is more probing and rigorous. Yet there is ongoing dispute even about what it is that the corporate income tax taxes (see Stiglitz 1976; Boadway, Bruce and Mintz 1981), so that the construction of a "neutral" tax system is a difficult task. In the first part of the analysis, both of these approaches will be considered, while in the second empirical part of the analysis the principal focus will be on comparisons with a neutral "benchmark" corporate income tax structure.

3.0 MERGERS AND TAKEOVERS AND TAX LAWS

The tax provision that tends to receive the most attention as constituting a bias toward external growth, i.e., growth by acquisition of another firm, is the interest deduction on funds borrowed to buy shares. For example Bale (1981) and Blenkarn (1987) both single out this provision. Two other provisions that have been noted in the popular press are the tax-free flow of intercorporate dividends, and the continuation of tax losses through a takeover if certain conditions are met. A fourth provision that tends to receive relatively little popular attention is the system of capital gains rollovers allowed in takeover situations, provided they are appropriately structured. In this section, these provisions are examined to assess the extent to which they can be said to be biased toward concentration.

In the case of interest deductibility, the main concern is that the costs of borrowing the funds required to make a "paper" as opposed a real physical investment are a deductible expense for tax purposes, while the resultant flow of income from this purchase of shares takes the form of non-taxable intercorporate dividends. This, however, is a simplistic view. When one company wants to buy the assets of another, there are several strategies and hence a variety of tax planning trade-offs. The purchaser can buy the physical assets of the target company, or its shares. In the case of a share purchase, there can be either a cash purchase or an exchange of shares.

If the purchaser uses cash, which in turn has been raised by borrowing, they benefit by the possibility of paying those interest costs with 50 cent dollars. This is because interest is, for tax purposes, a deductible expense against a combined federal and provincial corporate income tax rate of about 50 per cent. (This will be somewhat lower if the proposed corporate income tax reform proposals are implemented.) However, the vendor will typically realize a capital gain in a cash sale, and in order to protect the after-tax value of the proceeds of the sale of the company, will probably ask a higher price. Furthermore, if the purchaser is in a non-taxable position already, or has a relatively small amount of taxable income, little if any of the interest expense would prove to be useful as a deduction for tax purposes. Thus, most or all of the interest could have an after-tax cost of 100 cents on the dollar.

More importantly, even if a firm is in a position to use interest expenses as a tax deduction, the firm does not need to engage in a takeover to increase its debt-equity ratio; it can borrow to buy more assets or to buy back some of its own shares. It is also not clear why we should be any more offended at a firm borrowing money to buy a stream of tax-free intercorporate dividends than at a firm borrowing money to buy physical assets eligible for accelerated write-offs. At least in principle, the intercorporate dividends reflect corporate income that has already borne tax. In contrast, the asset purchase directly involves a mismatch in the timing of the expense incurred to earn income and the resulting income.

Turning the question around, one can ask what the impact would be if the interest deductibility provision were restricted in the case of share purchases. As noted when the restriction was removed in the 1972 tax reform, it would place domestic firms at a comparative disadvantage relative to U.S. firms in financing a takeover, since interest is deductible in these situations under the U.S. tax code. It would also have a stronger adverse impact on nonfriendly takeovers. The reason is that in friendly takeovers, the deal could be structured as a sale of assets rather than as a sale of shares, in which case interest on money borrowed would be deductible. Also, nonfriendly takeovers more often involve a cash bid. More generally, removal of interest deductibility would have a somewhat haphazard impact, depending not only on whether or not the takeover was friendly, but also on whether the parties to the transaction would have found it beneficial to borrow to finance the transaction.

(I shall not comment at length on any moves to tax intercorporate dividends as a means to curtail the incentives for corporate takeovers. If this were done generally, it would clearly constitute double taxation, and would be akin to hitting the proverbial fly with a sledgehammer. Note that the new taxes on intercorporate dividends proposed by the Minister of Finance on June 18, 1987 are selective and have limited application — see the Postscript to this chapter.)

One alternative is for the purchaser and vendor to arrange the sale via an exchange of shares. Typically, such share for share exchanges are structured to avoid triggering any realization of capital gains. In this latter case, the vendor can ask a lower price (in terms of the purchaser's shares) because he will not have to pay any tax on the capital gains — they are deferred until the time he chooses to sell the shares he has received from the purchaser.[1]

Thus, it is not at all clear that the preferred route for a corporate takeover is to borrow money for a cash transaction. Unfortunately, there exist virtually no data that would allow a careful analysis of the relative quantitative importance of interest deductibility and capital gains rollovers in Canada. Instead, I shall appeal to some anecdotal evidence.

In the federal budget of May 6, 1974, section 85.1 allowing share-for-share exchanges was introduced, along with the enrichment of a number of other capital gains rollovers for corporate reorganizations. The only mention of these proposals was given in the technical part of the document on supplementary information. In the summary table on the revenue impacts of the budget's proposals, no mention was made of these enhanced rollovers. In the budget of March 31, 1977, these rollover provisions were again enriched and again the only mention was in the detailed technical language of the Ways and Means motions of the Supplementary Budget Papers. There was no mention of these changes in the Budget Speech, and they were not mentioned in any of the tables showing the revenue impact of all the budget's proposals.

Any reader would thus appear justified in concluding that the introduction and enhancement of capital gains rollover provisions related to corporate reorganizations were of a minor technical nature and had no revenue consequences. As a result, if the Minister of Finance were to propose subsequently to tighten these provisions, this should occasion no comment. However, when just such tightening was proposed in the November 11, 1981 budget, there was a very large outcry. The first Saturday after the budget, Bill Richards president of Dome Petroleum flew to Ottawa to say essentially that the proposed restriction on the capital gains rollovers (as well as restrictions on the use of term preferred shares) would prevent Dome from proceeding with the takeover of Hudson Bay Oil and Gas. Comments at the time suggested that the tax implications would be in nine figures. The tightening of the capital gains rollovers was one of the very first budget proposals upon which Mr. MacEachen retreated, as indicated in a press release dated November 18, 1981.

While it is not clear what reaction would greet a budgetary proposal to remove interest deductibility on funds borrowed to buy shares in a takeover situation, it would clearly have to be fairly substantial to equal the outcry caused by the prospective tightening of the capital gains rollovers. This in turn suggests that the role of interest deductibility in facilitating corporate mergers and takeovers may be over-stated relative to other provisions.[2]

Another set of provisions governs the ability to carry tax losses through a merger or takeover. For example, in the popular commentary on the recently proposed takeover of Dome Petroleum by Amoco Canada. It has been noted that there are $2.5 billion in "tax loss credits to lure a buyer."[3] Tax losses arise both when a firm has actual economic losses, and when a firm is profitable. Particularly in the latter case, the tax losses typically reflect the use of various accelerated write-offs and incentive provisions. These tax losses can be carried forward by a corporation and used up to seven years later to offset subsequent years' taxable income. In principle, a firm could become a takeover target if it has substantial tax losses that it is unlikely to be able to use itself. There is a restriction in the tax system that allows the losses to be used after a takeover only against income earned in the same line of business. Nevertheless, a firm in the same industry that is taxable could well find it attractive to merge with another with a bank of otherwise unusable tax losses solely for this reason.

The anecdotal evidence suggests that these provisions in the income tax system may provide an inducement to corporate takeovers and mergers. By this, we mean that the removal of any one of the provisions for interest deductibility for share purchases, the tax-free flow of intercorporate dividends, capital gains rollovers in corporate reorganizations, and the carryforward of tax losses through a change in control would probably discourage at least some takeovers.

However, there are several reasons for caution in concluding that this in turn represents a fundamental tax system bias toward corporate concentration. The first point is that the inducements should more properly be measured relative to some benchmark tax structure that is neutral with respect to takeovers and mergers. What might such a tax structure look like? To give one example of the conceptual issues this question biases, consider capital gains. Since gains are taxed on a realization basis, if a realization were triggered on the change in control of a company (which is one of the key tests in many other jurisdictions tax codes), this would result in the well known lock-in effect of the taxation of realized capital gains – the owners would be less likely to sell as compared to a situation in which there were no taxation of capital gains. This lock-in has been ameliorated by providing generous rollover provisions, but this is tantamount to the abolition of taxation of capital gains if ways can always be found to defer realization indefinitely. Alternatively, as proposed by the (Carter) Royal Commission on Taxation (1966), capital gains on company shares could be essentially taxed as they accrue via full integration of the corporate and personal income taxes. Something like this which is close to full accrual taxation of capital gains would remove the lock-in effect. Compared to these polar opposite benchmarks – either full taxation of capital gains on an accrual basis or the complete exclusion of capital gains from taxable income – the existing rollover provisions would not appear biased toward takeovers.

Similarly, the full deductibility of interest costs to buy a stream of tax-free intercorporate dividends clearly represents a bias in comparison to the abolition of this specific provision. But interest deductibility as currently allowed raises broader questions. How biased would it appear when compared to a tax system in which interest deductibility was more generally limited not only as it now is to investments made for business purposes, but was also limited to the amounts of taxable income which those business activities actually generated year by year. In this case, the bias would not appear so great. For example, the tax deductibility of interest costs incurred to buy a physical asset eligible for accelerated depreciation is equivalent to an immediate tax deduction in respect to a deferred stream of taxable income. The deductibility of interest to buy a stream of non-taxable intercorporate dividends does not appear to be as great a tax preference in this light.

Finally, the takeover motive related to tax losses would be substantially reduced if there were provisions to allow the sale of tax losses by themselves. This example of an alternative benchmark illustrates the fundamental issue of the treatment of losses in the tax system, which is discussed more fully below.

These points suggest that the tax system bias toward mergers and takeovers depends critically on what benchmark tax system is taken as a point of reference. If we take as the benchmark tax system one with full accrual-based taxation of capital gains, a full matching of interest expense deductions with the taxable income streams they are used to purchase, and fully symmetric treatment of losses for tax purposes, then none of the three groups of measures just discussed — capital gains rollovers on corporate reorganizations, interest deductibility on financing of purchases of shares, and tax loss flow throughs on change of control — would represent a very strong tax system bias toward mergers and takeovers.

Notwithstanding this argument, a second broad reason for caution in interpreting the anecdotal evidence above as a bias toward concentration is that small as well as large firms may engage in takeovers and mergers. A bias toward concentration would only arise if any tax system bias toward mergers and takeovers was relatively stronger among already large firms. One might speculate that larger firms have a greater capacity to borrow and hence to benefit from interest deductibility, that larger firms are more likely to be able to tender their own shares in a takeover bid using a share for share exchange since the vendor will likely view those shares as more secure or liquid, and that larger firms are more likely to be able to benefit from an ability to utilize tax losses in an acquired company if those tax loss accounts are allowed to continue through a change in control. However, except for the last point which is discussed later, we are not aware of any strong evidence to support these speculations.

4.0 THE TAX SYSTEM AND PROFITABILITY

The ability of a firm to grow depends critically on its profitability. This is true whether the firm grows externally by purchasing other companies, or grows internally by purchasing productive assets; it is also true whether the firm finances its investments out of retained earnings, share issues, or new borrowing.

In the rest of the chapter the focus is on the question of whether the income tax acts in any systematic way to bias after-tax profitability in relation to firm size. To the extent that it does, it results in a potentially more pervasive and fundamental bias toward concentration than the provisions just discussed relating to mergers and takeovers. The key indicator of any such tax system bias is effective corporate income tax rates as a function of firm size. In turn, any differences between effective and statutory tax rates are largely attributable to tax expenditures — tax provisions whose purpose is similar to direct spending programs rather than the simple raising of revenue.

4.1. Variation in Effective Tax Rates (ETR's) by Firm Size

The basic accounting framework and definitions of benchmark tax and income are developed in the Annex. In this section, the resulting effective tax rates (ETR's) are shown for firms within the corporate universe arrayed by size. The basic results are shown in Table 1 for 1983. The most striking observation is the "inverted U" pattern of ETRs by asset size. The overall average ETR of net federal income taxes less transfers received (top row) was 11.5 per cent; but this average covered average ETRs ranging from 9.7

Table 1
Various Effective Tax Rates and Information Items by Net Asset Size, 1983

Variable	Net Asset** Size Range ($ millions)								All Sizes
	0-.5	.5-1	1-2	2-5	5-10	10-25	25-100	>100	
Effective Tax Rates									
Federal Income Tax less Transfers	9.7	11.1	11.9	16.5	15.3	17.1	15.4	9.6	11.5
Provincial Income Taxes	3.2	3.8	4.5	5.9	6.6	6.8	6.4	5.5	5.3
Sub-Total	12.9	14.9	16.4	22.4	21.9	23.9	21.8	15.1	16.8
Federal and Provincial Resource Taxes	0.4	--	0.4	--	2.8	2.9	4.1	24.8	13.2
Indirect Taxes*	9.5	11.6	15.6	13.4	9.9	8.2	4.6	4.6	7.1
Total	22.7	26.5	32.4	35.8	34.6	35.0	30.5	44.5	37.1
Counts									
Sample Size (000s)	12.4	1.7	1.6	1.2	1.3	1.3	1.6	0.8	21.9
Estimated Number of Firms (000s)	378.5	43.3	23.4	12.8	4.0	2.6	1.6	0.8	466.8

Table 1 (cont'd)

Variable	Net Asset** Size Range ($ millions)								All Sizes
	0-.5	.5-1	1-2	2-5	5-10	10-25	25-100	>100	
Percentage Distributions									
Firms	81.1	9.3	5.0	2.7	0.9	0.6	0.3	0.2	100.0
Benchmark Income	11.6	5.6	4.8	6.0	4.0	5.6	11.4	49.7	100.0
Assets	7.5	3.1	3.2	4.8	3.0	4.6	9.3	61.5	100.0
Fixed Asset to Labour Cost Ratio (Capital Intensity, %)	80	141	143	132	146	195	199	323	210
Proportions of Firms with Positive									
Book Profit After-Tax	61	72	70	74	67	71	72	79	63
Benchmark Income	65	75	74	72	70	74	72	76	67
Income Tax Paid	44	58	58	56	48	49	45	42	46

*   Note that transfers and indirect taxes are both seriously understated.

**   Net Assets are total assets less investments in affiliates.

per cent in the smallest asset size group up to 17.1 per cent in the $10 to 25 million asset size group and then back down to 9.6 per cent in the top $100+ million asset size group. This latter group of very large firms accounted for 0.2 per cent of all firms, but 49.7 per cent of all positive benchmark income and 64.5 per cent of all assets.[4]

This pattern of ETRs suggests that above a certain size threshold (in the range of $10 to $25 million in total assets), the corporate income tax system is systematically (albeit anonymously – recall Anatole France) biased toward concentration. For some complex of reasons, the largest firms face declining ETRs, and hence higher after-tax profitability than they would under a neutral benchmark tax structure.

It should be noted that total assets as used in virtually all publications based on these data are subject to some double counting due to intercorporate holdings. However, in this analysis, an approximation to total assets net of intercorporate holdings has been used.

The "inverted U" pattern carries through provincial income taxes, and for total taxes with the exception of the top (over $100 million in assets) size group. In this latter case, resource taxes impose high effective tax rates (24.8 per cent in the $100 million plus range), though as we shall see shortly this is an artifact of a very small number of large resource firms.

The bottom of Table 1 shows that fairly similar proportions of firms within each size range are profitable from both the shareholder (book profit after tax) and the benchmark/economic perspectives. The largest firms are most often profitable from shareholder's perspective. However, there is a sharp difference in the proportions which are taxable. In fact, the largest firms are the least likely to pay any income tax. A point to which we shall return later is that capital intensity increases quite strongly in relation to size.

Figures 1 and 2 extend the results in Table 1 by showing the dispersion of ETRs within each of the asset size ranges, where Figure 1 shows ETRs for federal income taxes net of transfers (i.e. corresponding to the first row in Table 1) and Figure 2 shows ETRs for total net taxes from the shareholder's perspective excluding only provisions for deferred tax (i.e. the "Total" row in Table 1). Generally, these micro level results corroborate the overall results. ETRs follow an "inverted U" pattern. Figure 2 in particular shows that even when resource taxes are included, at least up to the 90th percentile of firms there is still a generally "inverted U" shaped pattern of ETRs. Thus, the very high effective tax rate in Table 1 applies to only a very small fraction of the largest firms.

As a further elaboration of the "inverted U" pattern of ETRs overall, Table 2 presents ETRs by net asset size range and broad industry group. Generally, the same pattern holds within each industry group with the exception of energy, wholesale trade and services, where the largest size group of firms pays relatively higher taxes. In the other seven industry groups, the firms in the top size range pay relatively less tax than firms in the next smaller size range. However, the patterns by firm size within each broad industry group tend to be more jagged than the pattern for all industries combined.

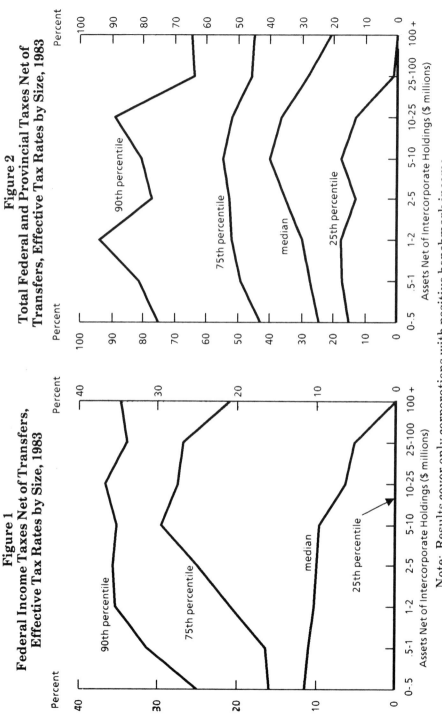

Figure 1
Federal Income Taxes Net of Transfers,
Effective Tax Rates by Size, 1983

90th percentile

75th percentile

median

25th percentile

Percent

40

30

20

10

0

Percent

40

30

20

10

0

Assets Net of Intercorporate Holdings ($ millions)

0-.5   .5-1   1-2   2-5   5-10   10-25   25-100   100 +

Figure 2
Total Federal and Provincial Taxes Net of
Transfers, Effective Tax Rates by Size, 1983

90th percentile

75th percentile

median

25th percentile

Percent

100

90

80

70

60

50

40

30

20

10

0

Percent

100

90

80

70

60

50

40

30

20

10

0

Assets Net of Intercorporate Holdings ($ millions)

0-.5   .5-1   1-2   2-5   5-10   10-25   25-100   100 +

Note: Results cover only corporations with positive benchmark income.

Table 2
Federal Corporate Taxes less Transfers, Effective Tax Rates (#), 1983

Broad Industry Category	Net Asset Size Range ($ millions)								All Firms
	0-.5	.5-1	1-2	2-5	5-18	10-25	25-100	>100	
Agriculture, Forestry and Fishing	-8.4	-1.9	4.0	6.1	6.1	12.1	6.6	--	-1.7
Mining	9.6	10.2	13.2	12.7	14.1	14.2	16.0	6.5	9.0
Energy	4.5	2.2	-13.2	26.4	10.4	7.9	6.4	8.8	8.7
Manufacturing	5.1	2.5	4.3	15.7	19.4	19.5	18.1	10.8	13.2
Construction	9.8	13.9	14.0	11.6	27.9	14.4	23.1	20.3	14.1
Transportation	8.7	11.0	13.2	8.1	19.9	21.0	15.0	7.2	9.0
Wholesale	11.6	13.0	12.1	20.2	16.2	21.4	22.1	27.7	17.8
Retail	11.3	10.1	12.1	14.1	15.7	18.7	21.6	13.4	13.3
Finance	14.3	17.9	17.7	16.3	12.3	10.6	7.6	6.7	11.4
Services	8.2	10.9	12.8	21.3	7.8	23.9	20.5	27.1	15.1
All Industries	9.7	11.1	11.9	16.5	15.3	17.1	15.4	9.6	11.5

5.0 MAJOR TAX PROVISIONS AFFECTING CORPORATE CONCENTRATION

I turn now to consider a number of specific provisions of the income tax system. The basic question is whether any particular tax provisions can be identified that account for the overall patterns of ETRs. Table 3 shows the impact of the major provisions on effective tax rates. The figures show the hypothetical change in effective tax rate that would result if the particular provision were removed. In the case of exploration and development expenses and depletion claims, and depreciation claims, the alternative assumption is that only book amounts would be claimable. Equivalently, Table 3 expresses the values of the tax provisions as a percentage of benchmark income.[5]

5.1. Losses for Tax Purposes

One might expect that larger firms with multiple product lines, different geographical markets or more diversified customers would be more likely to have profitable segments of the business against which to offset losses in other segments. In turn, this would imply both that tax losses for large firms are less likely to arise and also that if they do, they are more likely to be carried back or utilized in the following tax year.

Table 3 indicates that there was some variation in the current year tax loss experience by size of firms, but no clear patterns.

5.2. Tax Incentives and Capital Intensity

The tax system contains a number of provisions that provide incentives for capital investments. These include the investment tax credit, the Scientific Research Tax Credit (SRTC), the two-year write-off of manufacturing and processing machinery and equipment, other accelerated depreciation cases, and the overall generosity of the capital cost allowance system. As is evident from Table 3, both tax depreciation in excess of book depreciation and the investment and scientific research tax credits are biased towards larger firms.

This pattern can be explained by the fact that larger firms are on average relatively more capital intensive than small firms (recall Table 1). This might be anticipated both because of the nature of the industries in which they operate and because of the type of production processes adopted. In other words, general incentives directed toward capital investment will lower the effective tax rates of larger firms on average more than for smaller sized firms, and thus tend to contribute to corporate concentration.

5.3. Resource Sector

In terms of effective tax rates the resource sector provisions – fast write-offs of exploration and development expenses and the additional earned depletion deduction – are clearly biased toward larger firms.

5.4. Inventory Valuation Adjustment

The 3 per cent inventory deduction tended to be relatively most important for medium-sized firms. This provision has been abolished. It provided partial relief for the impact of inflation in creating purely nominal gains from holding inventory.

5.5. Small Business
The small business deduction (a misnomer since it is actually a tax credit) is by far the most important tax provision related either directly or indirectly to firm size. Its impact on effective tax rates is so great that if it were eliminated, effective tax rates would decline almost monotonically when moving up the asset size ranges.

5.6. Manufacturing and Processing
The manufacturing and processing deductions (again actually a tax credit) is somewhat more beneficial to medium to large as opposed to small and very large sized corporations.

Figure 3 provides a graphic summary of these data on the relative impact by size of firm of some of the tax provisions shown in Table 3. The bottom and darkest portion of the bars in the graph shows the actual average ETRs within each size range. Here, the pattern in the inverted "U" that has already been noted; medium-size firms on average pay more federal corporate income tax than either smaller- or larger-size firms. Next, the dark plus the shaded portions of the bars show what the average ETRs would have been in the absence of the special low tax rate for small businesses. In this hypothetical situation, ETRs would decline systematically with increasing size. Thus, the special low tax rate for small businesses does generally lower ETRs for smaller firms.

Finally, the unshaded top segment of each bar shows the value of a number of other major tax expenditures expressed in terms of their impact on ETRs. These tax expenditures are mainly incentives for investment. Figure 3 shows that these tax measures tend primarily to benefit the largest corporations. In their absence, and without the special low small business tax rate, this accounting for the values of various major tax expenditure provisions suggests that average ETRs would be roughly flat across size ranges.

6.0 SUMMARY AND CONCLUSIONS
This chapter set out to assess the role of the corporate income tax system in relation to corporate concentration. The analysis started with a brief impressionistic review of the main provisions relating to mergers and takeovers. One provision that has received considerable attention recently is the deductibility of interest expenses on funds borrowed to buy shares in a takeover situation. I have argued, however, that the importance of this provision may well be overstated relative to the provisions allowing capital gains rollovers and flow throughs of losses in corporate reorganizations where there is a change in control.

All three of these groups of provisions can be seen as providing a bias in the corporate income tax system toward mergers and takeovers as compared to a tax system where these provisions were simply absent. However, this is

Table 3
Values of Selected Federal Corporate Income in Terms of Effective Tax Rates*

Tax Provision	Net Asset Size Range ($ millions)									All Firms
	0-.5	.5-1	1-2	2-5	5-10	10-25	25-100	>100	
Tax Losses									
Current Year	7.5	7.6	7.2	9.4	8.8	9.4	9.8	6.1	7.3
Current Year Carried Back	2.1	1.8	1.8	1.5	2.3	1.5	1.1	0.6	1.1
Prior Year Applied	3.0	2.4	2.7	4.9	3.7	3.5	4.5	3.1	3.4
Accelerated Depreciation	-1.6	-1.9	-2.6	-1.9	-1.8	-0.4	1.5	4.0	1.5
Investment Tax Credits	0.5	0.8	1.2	1.1	1.3	1.5	1.7	2.2	1.6
SRTC	--	--	--	--	0.1	0.6	0.6	1.8	1.0
Resource Exploration and Development	--	--	--	0.6	0.6	0.5	0.2	3.3	1.8
Inventory Valuation Adjustment	1.0	1.4	2.1	2.4	2.1	2.1	2.0	1.3	1.5
Small Business Dedn.	14.2	13.0	9.1	3.6	0.6	0.2	--	--	3.3
Manufacturing and Processing Dedn.	0.6	0.9	0.8	1.1	1.3	1.5	1.5	0.8	0.9

* the value of the tax provision as a percentage of benchmark income.

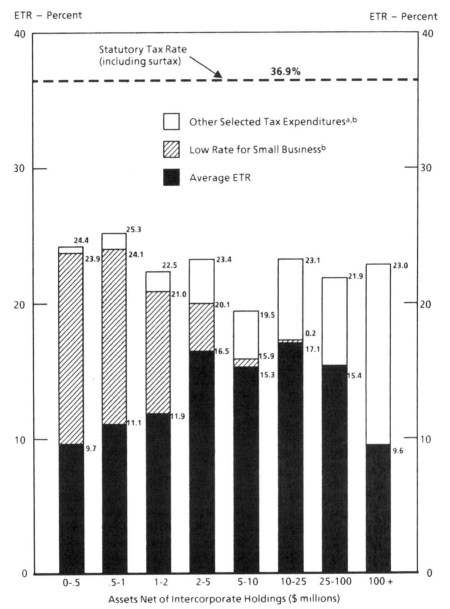

Figure 3
Average Federal Effective Corporate Income Tax Rates (ETRs) by
Net Asset Size and the Impact of Selected Tax Expenditures, 1983

Notes: a. accelerated depreciation, investment tax credit, SRTC, resource
exploration
and development, inventory valuation adjustment, and low rate for
manufacturing and processing.
b. expressed in terms of percentage point reductions in ETRS.

not a conceptually satisfactory alternative. Compared to more conceptually pure but probably academic alternative tax structures, these provisions would not appear to provide very strong incentives to mergers and takeovers.

The main part of the analysis addressed the relationship of the income tax system to variations in profitability by firm size. This is a more fundamental issue because firms' ability to grow, whether externally by mergers and takeovers, or internally by ploughing back after-tax profits, is clearly dependent on their profitability. This in turn depends on firms' effective tax rates. The basic result of the analysis is that, leaving aside the special low tax rate for small businesses, there is a general pattern of effective tax rates that decline with corporate size. Thus, it could be argued that the corporate income tax system is generally structured so that larger firms are able to grow relatively faster than medium- and small-sized firms as compared to a benchmark tax system that is neutral. With these dynamic properties, the tax system can be said to be biased toward corporate concentration, a conclusion contrary to that reached by the Royal Commission on Corporate Concentration (1978).

More specifically, the main group of provisions that account for this bias relates to capital intensity. Large firms tend to be more capital intensive, and a significant proportion of the tax provisions that lower effective tax rates are tax expenditures providing incentives for investment, both in capital equipment and structures (accelerated depreciation and the investment tax credit) and in resource exploration and development.

7.0 POSTSCRIPT – THE TAX REFORM WHITE PAPER

On June 18, 1987, the Minister of Finance tabled a White Paper on tax reform. Several proposals for reform of the corporate income tax are germane to the analysis here:

- lowering the statutory corporate tax rate;

- cutting back on accelerated depreciation, write-offs in the resource sector, and investment tax credits;

- increasing the proportion of capital gains income to be included in income for tax purposes;

- introduction of special additional taxes on dividends on term preferred shares; and

- introduction of a general anti-avoidance rule.

The new taxes on intercorporate dividends arising from term preferred shares, which came into effect on June 18, 1987, are apparently intended to curtail the effective movement of tax losses between corporations. To the extent that this objective is met, there could be more pressure on takeovers as a means of utilizing banks of tax losses whose carryforward would otherwise run into the seven year limit. The increased relative taxation of capital gains could place similar increased pressure on the use of the capital gains rollover provisions. On the other hand, the proposed general anti-avoidance rule, with its particular reference to step transactions (a sequence of transactions each of which is legal where the ultimate effect is that no tax liability is incurred), could well inhibit takeover transactions where a significant aspect is tax loss flow-throughs or capital gains rollovers.

The reduced incentives for investment (accelerated depreciation, resource sector provisions, and investment tax credits) would probably tend to mitigate the results above showing lower ETRs among the largest firms. The impact of the general lowering of the statutory tax rate is not clear. The value of the small business deduction would be increased both absolutely and relatively (from 11 per cent against 36 per cent to 12 per cent against 28 per cent).

The analysis presented in the White Paper shows corporations paying effective tax at a rate of 18.7 per cent (Table 4.9) compared to our figure of 11.5 per cent in 1983. However, the White Paper does not specify which year(s) the data are from, while it does indicate that the concept of benchmark income excludes capital gains income, income used to pay provincial resource royalties, and foreign source income eligible for foreign tax credits.

The White Paper concludes that small firms face lower effective tax rates than large firms (Table 4.10). This result is not inconsistent with our analysis because the White Paper definition of large firms generally corresponds to the top four or five size ranges in our analysis.

NOTES

1. In fact, typical transactions are often much more complex than this and involve "funny" kinds of shares like retractable preferred shares which are much more like GIC's.

2. It might also be noted that Auerbach and Reishus (1986), in a study of U.S. mergers during the period 1968 to 1983, did not find "that significant changes in leverage are associated with mergers and acquisitions, even when the acquired companies are large relative to those making the acquisition."

3. See, for example, *Globe and Mail*, April 14, 1987.

4. It may be noted that similar but less detailed conclusions regarding declining ETRs in relation to firm size were presented in Kierans (1972).

5. Wolfson (1987) provides more detailed data as well as a complete description of the methodology.

REFERENCES

Auerbach, A.J. and D. Reishus (1986), "Taxes and the Merger Decision", mimeo.

Bale, G. (1981), "The Corporate Interest Deductions," *Canadian Taxation,* Vol. 3, No. 4.

Blenkarn, D. (1987), "Tax Reform Can Discourage the Takeover Game", *Toronto* Star, April 7, 1987, p. A19.

Boadway, R., N. Bruce and J. Mintz (1981), "Budget 1981: Implications for the Corporate Income Tax", mimeo.

Economic Council of Canada (1987), *Road Map for Tax Reform: the Taxation of Savings and Investment,* (Ottawa: Minister of Supply and Services).

Kierans, E.W. (1972), "Contribution of the Tax System to Canada's Unemployment and Ownership Problems" in *Canadian Perspectives in Economics,* (Toronto: Collier-Macmillan Canada Ltd.).

Minister of Finance (1987), "Tax Reform 1987, Income Tax Reform", Ottawa.

_____ (1985), "An Account of Selective Tax Measures", Ottawa.

_____ (1981), "Press Release," November 18, 1981, Ottawa.

_____ (1979, 1980), "Tax Expenditure Account", Ottawa.

_____ (1977), Supplementary Budget Papers, Ottawa.

_____ (1976), Supplementary Budget Paper D, Ottawa.

_____ (1974), Supplementary Budget Papers, Ottawa.

Mintz, J.M. and D. Purvis (1985), "Report of the Policy Forum on Reform of the Corporate Income Tax System," John Deutsch Institute for the Study of Economic Policy.

Parizeau, J. (1986), "Fiscal System Encouraging Conglomerates," *Ottawa Citizen,* April 14, 1986, p. B1.

Royal Commission on Corporate Concentration (1978) *Report* (Ottawa: Minister of Supply and Services).

Royal Commission on Taxation (1966) *Report* (Ottawa: Information Canada), 6 Vols.

Statistics Canada (various years), *Corporate Taxation Statistics*, Catalogue Number 61-207, Ottawa.

Statistics Canada (various years), *Corporate Financial Statistics*, Catalogue Number 61-208, Ottawa.

Stiglitz, J.E. (1976), "The Corporate Tax," *Journal of Public Economics*, Vol. 5, pp. 303-310.

Stikeman, Elliot, Tamaki, Mercier and Robb (1976), *Corporate Concentration and the Canadian Tax System*, Royal Commission on Corporate Concentration, Study No. 28, (Ottawa: Minister of Supply and Services).

Waddell, C. and B. Little (1987), "Dome's Huge Tax Loss Credits Lure to Buyer," *The Globe and Mail*, April 14, 1987, p. B1.

Wolfson, M.C. (1987), "Canada's Corporate Tax/Transfer Systems," Analytical Studies Branch Working Paper (Ottawa: Statistics Canada).

The Financial Sector

Chapter 13

Current Issues Facing Canadian
Financial Institutions

André Ryba
Director, Financial Institutions Group
Economic Council of Canada

1.0 DEVELOPMENTS IN THE FINANCIAL SECTOR

The emergence of large conglomerates and financial holding groups is one of the recent developments marking the Canadian financial scene. By actively diversifying into related – and not so related – areas, Canada's chartered banks have become some of the largest financial conglomerates in the country. So have some trust and insurance companies.

Furthermore, since the late 1970s, other financial holding groups have emerged, bringing together trust and insurance companies, merchant banks, and in some cases securities firms and investment counsellors. Trilon, Power Financial, E.L. Financial, Laurentian; to name but a few, have joined the ranks of the Mouvement Desjardins.[1] In 1984, the nine major financial holding groups accounted for 10.3 per cent of total assets of financial institutions up from 6.5 per cent in 1979.[2] Also in 1984, these financial holding groups accounted for over 20 per cent of mortgages on the books of financial institutions (13.2 per cent in 1979) and for 12.4 per cent of all deposits (7 per cent in 1979).

The diversification that led to the growth of conglomerates and financial holding companies also blurred the distinction between the four traditional pillars of the financial system: the banks, the trusts, the life insurance companies, and the securities firms. The original pillar system, as it emerged from the Great Depression and World War II, was based on two fundamental premises: separate institutions for regulatory purposes, and separate ownership of various categories of institutions. Banks, trusts, life insurance companies and securities firms fell under distinct regulatory authorities. Banks could not own trust companies, life insurance companies could not own banks, banks, trust and life insurance companies could not own securities firms. While today many analysts refer to the dismantling of the pillar system, only the ownership structure of the old pillar system is disappearing; separate groups of institutions continue to fall under distinct regulatory authorities.

Another important development is the movement within the financial sector towards closely held ownership. The purchase of Canada Trust by Genstar marked the disappearance of the last widely held large trust company in this country.[3]

A fourth development is the greater mixing of commercial and financial enterprises. A tobacco company now owns Canada's largest trust company;[4] some of the large financial holding groups are part of wider conglomerates bringing together financial and non-financial enterprises. Through Brascan, Trilon is associated with a brewer and a mining company.[5]

These developments are not unique to Canada. They are worldwide. The blurring of the distinction between institutions was quite prevalent south of the border, with securities firms entering the banking business and banks pushing to share into the securities business. The mixing of financial and non-financial activities has also gained ground in the United States. In 1981, Sears purchased Dean Witter and Coldwell Banker and launched the Sears Financial Centers in many of its stores. General Motors plays an important role in the current securitization process.

It should be noted that in some countries, West Germany and Japan for instance, the commingling of financial and non-financial activities and the cross-ownership between commercial and financial firms is not a new phenomenon. For years German banks have had an important stake in German industry. And banks in Japan have been part of large industrial conglomerates; the Mitsui and Mitsubishi groups are examples.

Other developments have marked the Canadian financial scene: financial innovation, new technology, and the internationalization and globalization of financial markets. But these may be somewhat less important to the main theme of this conference than the other issues. Diversification, the growth of conglomerates and the emergence of financial holding companies, the movement towards closely held ownership and the increased commingling of financial and non-financial firms raise important concerns with respect to concentration.

As noted in Dr. Khemani's paper,[6] there are many different measures and even concepts of concentration. Concentration of power reflects the ability of firms to influence political and economic decisions because of their sheer size. Concentration of assets refers to the proportion of assets controlled by a few firms, and may be a proxy measure for concentration of power. Concentration of ownership reflects the proportion of a firm's equity controlled by a single, or a few, shareholders. Market concentration refers to the share of the market controlled by a single or a few firms. Depending on the purpose of the analysis, one concept or the other is relevant.

2.0 CRITICAL CHARACTERISTICS OF THE FINANCIAL SYSTEM

Any analysis of the financial system should first recognize the specific role it plays in the economy. The financial system is quite different from any other sector of activity. It contributes to the maintenance of a payment system, without which no transaction can take place in our monetary economy. It performs the intermediation of funds and risks and thus channels the necessary financing to all sectors of activity. As many have pointed out, it is a backstop of liquidity: it is the oil without which the engine will not run. It also provides for the safekeeping of funds that individuals and businesses put aside for future use, and it offers valuable information on financial conditions and other aspects of the economy. By performing these key roles, the financial system contributes to economic growth and social development.

The specificity of the financial system has been recognized by authorities all around the world. It is on the basis of this specificity that the Minister of State for Finance has built his proposals for a reform of financial regulation (see Hockin 1986). This specificity has also been recognized by Gerald Corrigan (1987), the President of the Federal Reserve Bank of New York. However, this specificity has generally been attached to banks and deposit-taking institutions. As Corrigan (1987) says: "there are public interest considerations associated with the operations of the banking system that call for a higher degree of official supervision and regulation than is needed in other kinds of business enterprise." I would suggest that the specificity that has traditionally been attached to the payment system should be extended to all financial institutions. First, the intermediation of funds and risks is as important to our economies as the maintenance of the payment system. Second, the nature of the means of payment is also changing over time. For instance, as the securitization process moves along at a fast clip – at least in the United States, if not internationally – the contribution of commercial banks to the financing of economic activity is declining and merchant banks and securities firms are playing a much greater role. And – who knows – units in securities pools may be tomorrow's means of payment, replacing bank deposits.

3.0 REQUIREMENTS FOR THE FINANCIAL SYSTEM

For the financial system to perform its role effectively, markets must be competitive, financial institutions must be solvent and benefit from the confidence of the public, and there must be broad access to the services offered by financial institutions and agents.

With competition, a greater variety of financial services are offered at a lower price. Competition leads to more innovation, less conservatism and a better allocation of resources. Without confidence in a solvent financial system, savers would stash their money under the mattress; without confidence investors would require high interest rates to entrust their funds to financial intermediaries or ultimate borrowers; without confidence currency and cheques would not be accepted for the purchase of goods and services or for the liberation of debt. But confidence goes beyond the mere solvency of the major players on the financial scene, it also requires confidence that there will be fair treatment by the various financial institutions. First, the managers of financial institutions must not take excessive risks with the funds entrusted to them, and, in particular, must not pass the risks on to others who are not rewarded for bearing those risks. Second, conflicts of interest, when they arise, must not be abused. Third, where non-arm's length transactions occur, they must be executed at market conditions so that no costs are passed on, either to customers or to minority shareholders. Finally, consideration must be given to the wisdom of mixing financial and non-financial activities within the same organization where such mixing could create the potential for abuse, and for mis-allocation of financial resources.

Access is important because a market functioning well from a private point of view does not necessarily guarantee access to financial services. A situation may arise where potential customers of financial institutions believe that the expected private benefits do not justify the price they have to pay to purchase financial services (a situation where marginal benefits are less than marginal costs). They will not obtain financial services and they will not channel their savings to financial institutions. But from the point of view of the nation as a whole, economic growth and social development require that all funds be reallocated nationwide according to the risk-return combinations. Intermediaries should channel funds to and from all economic agents; thus the importance of the availability of services or accessibility.

Finally, the issue of concentration of power is often raised with respect to financial institutions, although it does not specifically relate to the operation of the financial system.

I will now consider each issue (competition, confidence, access, and concentration of power) in greater detail and investigate how they relate to the theme of this conference.

3.1 Competition

Measuring the degree of competition in any sector of economic activity is always a difficult task. Indeed, competition on any market is reflected in the pricing behaviour of the various participants and in their ability to extract higher than normal profits from transactions in which they engage. But what is an accurate measure of prices and profits? How does one assess competitive behaviour? An easy way out is to use the level of concentration as a proxy in an analysis of competition. It is true that the link between concentration and competition is at times tenuous. A market may be relatively concentrated but still exhibit some form of competitive behaviour. On the other hand, when a market is competitive, the degree of concentration should decline over time. Although one cannot necessarily conclude that a high level of concentration means a low level of competition, a high level of concentration maintained over a long period of time may raise suspicions about the existence of competition.

Here, of course, it is the concept of market concentration that is relevant. It is the ability of a firm to control a specific market that may lead it to indulge in non-competitive behaviour. And it is concentration on domestic markets that should be the focus of the analysis.

Research recently conducted by the Economic Council of Canada (1987), and reported in *A Framework for Financial Regulation*, indicates that while concentration in several financial markets is high, particularly in comparison with other areas of economic activity, it has generally declined between 1979 and 1984, despite recent mergers and acquisitions and the emergence of financial holding groups. In the personal and commercial loan market the four largest firms among banks, credit unions, trust and loan companies and life insurance companies, accounted for over 70 per cent of the business in 1979 but for less than 63 per cent in 1984. The four largest companies controlled almost 54 per cent of the deposit market in 1979 but less than 48 per cent in 1984. The mortgage market is an exception. First, it is much less concentrated than the other two; second, concentration has increased over time. Indeed, the four largest companies controlled 32.6 per cent of the market in 1984, up from 29.9 per cent in 1979. It is probably the market where the growth of financial holding groups has had the largest impact, as these groups usually brought together trust, loan and life insurance companies that are major mortgage lenders.

When trying to link concentration to competition it is important to analyze the extent of turnover over time among the four largest companies. The Council's analysis has shown that the turnover is rather large in the mortgage market but much less in the loan and deposit market. Indeed, in the deposit market the same four banks were the largest institutions in 1979 and 1984; only their ranks changed – albeit only slightly – between the two dates. Similarly, in the loan market there was little turnover among the four largest institutions, although one bank replaced another between 1979 and 1984. In the mortgage market, in contrast, the four largest companies in 1979 were the Desjardins Group, the Royal Bank, the Royal Trust, and Canada Trust; in 1984 they were the Desjardins Group, the Royal Bank, the Canadian Imperial Bank of Commerce, and Trilon Financial Corporation.

Concentration figures tend to underestimate the nature of competition as they do not take into account the competitive pressures coming from markets where substitute instruments are being traded. While Canadian banks dominate the commercial loan market, trust and life insurance companies offer financing instruments that are a close substitute for commercial loans, but are not captured by an analysis of that market. Some commercial mortgage loans are a case in point.

Finally, even though a market may be concentrated, firms would behave in a competitive fashion if there were freedom of entry and exit. Should non-competitive profits arise, freedom of entry would ensure that new players emerge. Competitive behaviour does not require a large number of participants, but rather the potential entry of new participants. Participants behave in a competitive fashion when markets are contestable, to use a term coined by William Baumol.

But barriers to entry and exit do exist. There are quite a large number of legislative barriers in many markets; such as the various incorporation and licensing requirements, capitalization minima, and restrictions preventing specific institutions from operating in some markets. For example, and until legislative changes are implemented, banks cannot engage directly in securities underwriting and dealing; nor can they enter the trust and insurance markets. Trust companies face restrictions with respect to commercial lending and life insurance companies cannot accept deposits.

In fact, rather than striving to provide a level playing-field, the existing regulatory system imposes different costs and constraints on a number of particular activities; the differences depending on the types of institution involved. Quite apart from its lack of fairness, this constitutes a barrier to entry and an impediment to competition.

The existence of a level playing-field requires a regulation-by-function approach. A function – such as banking or insurance – would be the subject of regulation, instead of the institution which performs that function. This would promote a level playing-field, as institutions involved in performing of the same functions would be subject to the same rules relating to that function.

3.2 Confidence

I now turn to confidence, and will first consider solvency, an important factor affecting confidence. The 1980s saw an increasing number of failures of financial institutions. And 1985 was a particularly difficult year as it witnessed the first bank failure since 1923, with the collapse of the Canadian Commercial and the Northland Banks. In the same year, five trust and loan companies went out of business as well as two general insurance companies. Altogether there were 22 failures of financial institutions between 1980 and 1985 (Economic Council of Canada 1986).

Other financial institutions faced serious financial difficulties, and although these did not result in bankruptcies, they often led to mergers with other institutions. In 1981, Quebec's caisses d'entraide economique faced bankruptcy and some of the locals were amalgamated with the Desjardins Group the following year, while others were restructured. At the beginning of 1986 the Mercantile Bank of Canada merged with the National Bank. Also in 1986 the Morguard Bank was purchased by the Security Pacific Bank, a subsidiary of a foreign bank. The Bank of British Columbia and the Continental Bank had to resort to borrowing from the Bank of Canada, and to assistance packages put together by other banks. Later in the year the Continental Bank announced plans to merge with Lloyds Bank of Canada, a subsidiary of Lloyds Bank of London; in November 1986 the purchase of the Bank of British Columbia by the Hong Kong Bank of Canada, a Schedule B bank, was announced. Bank mergers have occurred in the past, but the reorganization that took place in 1986 was the most significant in any single year. Although there have been no failures as such in the securities industries, there were 20 mergers and acquisitions between 1981 and 1985.

In the view of the Economic Council (1987), these failures and financial difficulties are mainly the result of management errors resulting in high loan losses, mismatching of assets and liabilities, and funding problems. But the movement towards conglomeration, and the rise of financial holding groups, raise the issues of the continuing solvency of Canada's financial system. The maintenance of solvency requires, among other things, the identification of activities that can prudently be mixed with certain functions. Can short-term investment be mixed with the provision of pension liabilities? Can short-term commercial lending be safely mixed with the long-term liabilities of life insurance?

Also, the preservation of solvency requires that a separate capital base supports each financial function. A separate capital base should support the banking function; a separate capital base should support the insurance function; a separate capital base should support the securities, trading, and underwriting function. With growing conglomeration; and with the mixing of banking, insurance and securities underwriting functions; this very important principle of a separate capital base, for separate functions is threatened. To preserve a separate capital base and given that solvency relates to an institution as a whole and not to a specific function performed by an institution, the Council (1987) recommended that institutions be limited to the performance of a single major function. Diversification could still take place through cross-ownership of institutions. But to better insulate the individual members of a larger family of financial institutions, the Council recommended that cross-ownership take place through a financial holding group structure — not the structure proposed in the ill-fated federal Green Paper released in April 1985,[7] where financial transactions between members of a holding group were either banned outright or severely limited — but a more flexible structure that would generally permit the movement of funds towards the most profitable opportunities as long, of course, as the members of the group remain solvent.

The fair treatment of customers is the other contributor to confidence. Growing concentration, and particularly the mixing of various functions within a single institution and the commingling of financial and non-financial activities, may lead to abuses of conflict of interest situations and to self-dealing. As noted by the Economic Council (1987), conflict of interest situations could arise when banking and securities dealing are combined within the same institution. A conflict may exist between the institution's deposit business and its stock exchange transactions. The institution might not sufficiently uphold its customers interests in investing in stocks and bonds, since the funds to pay for those investments would most likely come from the customer's deposits in the institution. There could be a conflict of interest between the underwriting and lending business. For example, it might be more advantageous for a financial institution to lend to a firm than to assist it in building up its equity base by underwriting an issue. There is also a potential conflict of interest between a financial institution's stock exchange transactions and its lending business. The institution might withhold information obtained in its credit business from customers in its securities business. Or an institution could use information from its commercial activities to have an advantage over other stock market participants.

The mixture of financial and non-financial firms is also a source of potential abuse. A non-financial entity, through self-deals, may use an associated financial institution to finance its operations at favourable conditions, thereby reducing the institution's profitability. Also the financial institution may be in a position to deny funding to competitors of the parent or affiliated companies. As Gerald Corrigan (1982) noted when he was president of the Federal Reserve Bank of Minneapolis:

> In periods of stress, banks might be called upon to supply credit to borrowers who for one reason or another temporarily do not have access to sources of funds or to make the even more difficult decisions as to which borrowers are experiencing problems of a fundamental or irreparable nature. It is in these particular circumstances that banks must be in a position to make rigourous, impartial and objective credit decisions because it is precisely in such circumstances that the potential for compromise in the impartiality of the credit decision-making process is greatest and the potential for asset quality deterioration is the largest.

Even if no wrong-doing takes place in the relation between financial and non-financial entities, it is the perception by the public at large and by the customers of the financial institution that such potential exists, that may affect confidence in the impartiality of the financial institution itself. Worse still, the financial institution might be placed in a position of severe risk should the non-financial side of the operation suffer losses, and, in the presence of safety nets, the government guaranty is extended to the non-financial affiliate.

The one function/one institution model proposed by the Economic Council (1987) would go a long way towards dealing with some of these abuses. Indeed, it would bring a greater separation between various functions and between financial and non-financial activities. Widespread ownership is another form of control as it reduces the incentive that owners of financial institutions might have to self-deal, and to abuse conflict of interest situations.

3.3   Access to Financial Services

Access to financial services is our third concern; because concentration can reduce access to financial services. Indeed, it has been shown by the Economic Council (1987), that financial institutions with universal powers tend, in the long run, to reduce accessibility to financial services as they compete for the total business of an individual rather than for specific portions of it. In West Germany, for example, banks with universal powers have been a factor in the slower development of equity markets.

3.4   Concentration of Power

Turning finally to the last concern: the concentration of power, one has to look at concentration of assets as a proxy measure. In the Canadian financial sector, there appears to be a large concentration of assets held by a few corporations. Indeed, the four largest institutions accounted for 52 per cent of total assets in 1984; only 17 institutions were needed to account for 80 per cent of total assets (Economic Council 1987), a relatively high degree of concentration. By comparison, in the manufacturing sector, the four largest firms accounted for 11.1 per cent of total assets in 1983. The corresponding figures for four component industries of that sector were as follows: food industry, 15.6 per cent; wood industry, 28.9 per cent; paper and allied product industry, 33.6 per cent; and transportation equipment industry, 75.2 per cent. Against these figures, concentration in the financial sector appears to be somewhat higher than average. However, the level of concentration decreased between 1979 and 1984.

4.0 HOCKIN'S PROPOSALS
The Economic Council's analysis was conducted before the tabling of the federal government's white paper (Hockin 1986). The proposals put forward by the government are a first step in the right direction. They are a first step in a long overdue reform of financial regulation in Canada.[8] But problems still remain.

The federal government's proposals will help to increase competition in the financial system, and more specifically, in the securities industry; when put together with the proposals put forward by the Ontario Minister of Financial Institutions. However, because of the absence of coordination among regulatory authorities – particularly between the provincial and the federal authorities – and because of the absence of a practical regulation-by-function approach, the system will not move as far as it could towards a level playing-field. Solvency and consumer protection, although improved in comparison to the situation that prevailed in the 1980s, still fall short of the ideal. There are indeed dangers in allowing institutions to diversify through direct subsidiaries without going the holding group route. A holding group structure permits the insulation of members from the financial difficulties experienced by other members. It also guarantees that a separate capital base supports each function.

The federal and Ontario governments' proposals, if implemented, may lead to many more mergers, acquisitions and emergence of financial holding groups. But this might intensify competition as new players enter the traditional turf of banks or securities firms – and result in a further decline of market concentration.

NOTES

1. The Mouvement Desjardins, with total combined assets of close to $30 billion, if not more, is not only the largest financial holding group in the country, it is also the oldest. It has been established quietly over the years, drawing little attention, as insurance (life and casualty), trust and investment companies were added to a rich network of cooperative banks.

2. The data in this paper is taken from the Economic Council of Canada (1987). See also Economic Council (1986).

3.   See *Globe and Mail*, April 18, 1986, p. B1.

4.   See, for example, Andrea Gordon, "Imasco gets its way," *Financial Times*, April 7, 1986, pp. 3, 10, 11; Laura Reid, "Battling the takeovers," *Financial Times*, March 31, 1986, pp. 1, 26; Nicholas Hunter, "Imasco proposes Genstar takeover for less than shares trading on TSE," *Globe and Mail*, March 25, 1986, p. B1; David Hatter, "Genstar would fit Imasco's bill," *Financial Post*, March 29, 1986, p. 4; "Genstar says 'yes' to suitor; bill put at $2 billion-plus," Vancouver *Sun*, April 3, 1986, p. H1. Robert Gibbons, "Genstar board endorses Imasco bid," *Globe and Mail*, April 4, 1986, p. B1.

5.   See *Financial Post 500*, Summer 1986, p. 200.

6.   See Chapter 1 in this volume. See also Professor Marfels' paper, Chapter 3 in this volume.

7.   See Minister of State for Finance (1985).

8.   See the extensive discussion by Tom Courchene, Chapter 24 in this volume.

REFERENCES

Corrigan, Gerald (1982) "Are Banks Special? A Summary" in Federal Reserve Bank of Minneapolis, *Annual Report*.

Corrigan, Gerald (1987) "Financial Markets Structure: A Longer View" (New York: Federal Reserve Bank of New York, January).

Economic Council of Canada (1986) *Competition and Solvency: A Framework for Financial Regulation* (Ottawa: Minister of Supply and Services).

Economic Council of Canada (1987) *A Framework for Financial Regulation* (Ottawa: Minister of Supply and Services).

Hockin, Tom (1986) *New Directions for Financial Institutions* (Ottawa: Minister of Finance, December 18).

Minister of State for Finance (1985) *The Regulation of Canadian Financial Institutions: Proposals for Discussion* (Ottawa: Minister of Supply and Services, April).

Chapter 14

The Effects of Concentrated Ownership and Cross-ownership on the Stability and Efficiency of the Financial System

D.G. McFetridge*
Department of Economics
Carleton University

1.0 INTRODUCTION

The debate over the political and economic effects of the large corporations has been both lengthy and inconclusive. The discussion has been enlivened in recent years by the emergence of a new set of issues. A number of not entirely disinterested observers have alleged that closely held deposit taking intermediaries, linked by ownership either to other financial institutions or to corporations active in the real sector, pose a danger to the Canadian financial system. The danger is said to involve both an increased likelihood of insolvency with attendant depositor losses and misuse of privileged information; and abuse of power.

In their defence, the financial conglomerates, as they have come to be called, reply that concentrated and cross-ownership, are motivated by efficiency considerations rather than by opportunities for fraud, misuse of information and abuse of trust.

This paper investigates the respective relationships between concentrated ownership and cross-ownership and abusive self-dealing and conflict of interest. It also examines the efficiency consequences of concentrated and cross-ownership of Canadian financial intermediaries.

*   The research assistance of Sheldon Polowin is gratefully acknowledged.

333

2.0 CONCENTRATED OWNERSHIP

2.1 Definition

The term concentrated ownership has been given a number of different meanings. To some, the problem of concentrated ownership is the size of a corporate entity or linked corporate entities relative to a particular market or to the economy as a whole. These are the problems of market concentration and aggregate concentration respectively.[1]

For purposes of this paper the problem of concentrated ownership is something different. It is the problem created when a corporate entity is closely held, that is, its shares are concentrated in the hands of relatively few individuals.

To distinguish between the two types of concentration, we note that Bell Canada Enterprises and Canadian Pacific Enterprises are large relative to the Canadian economy and relative to certain markets in which they operate. They are also widely held. Their *ownership* is not concentrated.

Edper Investments (the holding company of Edward and Peter Bronfman) is large relative to the Canadian economy, has some subsidiaries which are large relative to the markets in which they operate (e.g., John Labatt) and is closely held. Obviously there are innumerable companies in Canada which are small but closely held and many which are large relative to some markets but are widely held.

2.2 Consequences of Concentrated Ownership

For large segments of the economy the existence of concentrated ownership, that is, of closely held corporations poses no problem. Indeed, the owner-managed firm or sole proprietorship are often viewed in the same terms as the family farm and apple pie.

Concentrated ownership is thought to pose a problem for some types of financial intermediaries. Concentrated ownership is said to facilitate self-dealing by financial intermediaries. This can, in turn, lead to the impairment of an intermediary's capital and, possibly, to failure with an attendant loss of confidence in the nation's financial system.

The task here is to explore the respective links between concentrated ownership and self-dealing, and between self-dealing and insolvency. Self-dealing involves a transaction between a firm and its owner(s), manager(s) or related parties. Self-dealing can be beneficial in that the transacting parties are likely to be well-informed about each other. Self-dealing can also be abusive. Abusive self-dealing occurs when a transaction is detrimental to the interests of some or all of a firm's owners (stockholders) and/or creditors.

Self-dealing can occur in either financial or non-financial businesses. In a non-financial business abusive self-dealing usually involves the exploitation of minority (outside) shareholders by a concentrated majority (inside) interest. This may entail either or both of:

- purchases of assets or services from insiders or their nominees at inflated prices,

- trading in the equity or marketable debt of the firm with the benefit of inside information.

In both cases there is a transfer from outsiders to insiders. Anticipation of this transfer will reduce the demand price for a minority interest if it is offered. This implies that ownership structures comprising a concentrated majority and a dispersed outside minority will not be observed as a equilibrium phenomenon. There is a capital gain to be made from either the elimination (buying out) of the outside minority by the insiders or the dispersion of the inside majority interest. This is generally given as the reason why multinationals are reluctant, unless obliged by the host government, to issue shares in their local affiliates or take on domestic partners.

If a non-financial company is closely held and equity-financed, there is no incentive for abusive self-dealing. The owner would simply be cheating himself. In a widely held non-financial company, individual shareholders have the incentive and the ability to engage in self-dealing. The shareholders have legal recourse if breach of trust or fraud can be proven. If it is merely suspected, shareholders will have difficulty coalescing to replace incumbent management with individuals they deem to be more trustworthy.

Recent research by Demsetz and Lehn (1985) and Demsetz (1986) emphasizes that an ownership structure characterized by an inside majority and an outside minority is a continuing rather than a transitory phenomenon. Drawing on work done by Grossman and Hart (1980), Demsetz hypothesizes that insiders perform a costly monitoring function, that of enforcing efficiency performance on management, for which they receive the benefits of self-dealing as compensation. In this view, dispersion of the majority interest would result in less insider self-dealing but weaker management performance, yielding no net gain. Buy-outs of minority interests would apparently be limited by either the wealth of insiders or their desire to shape at least some of the risk associated with the firm's profit stream.

Closely allied with the problem of self-dealing is what Meckling and Jensen (1976) have called the agency problem of debt. A closely held or a stockholder-welfare maximizing, widely held company will have an incentive to treat the bond and other debt holders as an outside interest and to exploit them. The greater the debt to equity ratio (leverage), the greater the owners' incentive to choose highly risky investments which enrich them in the event of success and impose disproportionate losses on the bondholders in the event of failure. Since this will be anticipated by potential bondholders and other creditors, ownership will be disciplined by some combination of enforceable covenants regarding permissible asset acquisitions and increase in the supply price of debt.

In the case of financial intermediaries there are, again, incentives for both insiders and managers to exploit both outsiders and debt holders (including depositors and the deposit insurer). The difference is that it is more difficult to make and enforce covenants with respect to asset acquisition decisions. The reason is that the essential function of the deposit intermediary is to acquire non-marketable financial assets. The bulk of the assets of a banking intermediary have no readily observable market value. Since the intermediary is the ultimate authority on what its assets are worth, this makes covenants with respect to portfolio behaviour difficult to enforce. It also makes it difficult for depositors or more sophisticated debt holders to relate the supply price of debt capital (including deposits) to the quality of the intermediary assets. In essence, these assets can only be defined to be of poor quality *ex post*.

The implication is that such external quality assurance mechanisms as risk-related deposit insurance premiums, co-insurance and the requirement that subordinated debt be issued may not be effective in reducing the incentive for abusive self-dealing.

Self-dealing by a financial intermediary may involve either the acquisition of assets from principals at inflated prices or making excessively risky loans to principals or related parties.

Self-dealing of the first type could occur among officers and directors in a widely-held intermediary and by insiders in an intermediary characterized by concentrated majority and dispersed minority ownership. The effect on depositors is indirect. The intermediary's capital hence its protection against insolvency is reduced. This type of problem is less likely in the case of closely held intermediaries although it does provide the owner with a way of evading regulatory capital and leverage requirements.

Self-dealing of the second type might be expected under the following circumstances:

-   In the case of dispersed ownership, excessively risky loans may be made to officers or directors. The latter benefit if the investments so financed succeed. If they fail, losses are imposed on the shareholders, and, if the losses are sufficient, on depositors, the providers of deposit insurance and other creditors.

-   In the case of concentrated majority and dispersed minority ownership, risky loans may be made to insiders. The latter benefit if their investments succeed. In the event of failure losses are imposed on insiders, the outside minority interest, depositors, deposit insurance and other creditors. Note, however, that unless losses exceed the intermediary's capital, a significant fraction will be borne by insiders.

-   In the case of a closely held intermediary, risky loans may be made by the owner to himself. If the resulting investment succeeds the owner captures the gains. If it fails the owner bears all the losses up to his equity in the intermediary, at which point depositors, deposit insurance and other creditors begin to share in them.

Has self-dealing been an important cause of insolvency among financial intermediaries? Some evidence from the experience of the United States is summarized in Table 1. It indicates that over the period 1971-1982 poor quality loans were the "major cause" of 36 per cent of the bank failures experienced in the U.S.

A review of the more recent U.S. experience is provided by Hannah, Horne, and Smee (1986). These authors correctly note that some practices such as making excessively risky loans (to principals or others) may be symptoms rather than underlying causes of insolvency. As past losses whittle away at equity, there is greater incentive to make ever riskier loans. Insolvency, the underlying cause of which may have been macroeconomic factors, may be incorrectly attributed to the increasingly risky portfolio held

Table 1
Causes of Commercial Bank Failures 1971-1982
(Cause as a Per cent of Number of Failures)

Causes of Failure	1971-1982 Major	1971-1982 Primary	1980-1982 Major	1980-1982 Primary	1982 Major	1982 Primary
Credit Quality Losses						
Loans	77.4%	61.3%	82.7%	67.3%	76.5%	55.9%
Insider Loan	36.3%	14.5%	26.9%	9.6%	26.5%	14.7%
Poor Funds Management						
Interest rate						
risk	20.2%	4.8%	19.2%	5.8%	17.6%	8.8%
Liquidity	36.3%	2.4%	30.8%	1.9%	17.6%	2.9%
Fraud and Embezzlement						
Internal	13.7%	11.3%	15.4%	11.5%	17.6%	14.7%
External	7.3%	5.6%	5.8%	3.8%	5.9%	2.9%
Number of cases (including assistance cases)	124		52		34	

Note: This table includes 124 commercial banks and 11 mutual savings banks. The commercial banks include four assistance transactions. One bank that failed 11 years after receiving assistance was counted twice. Of the remaining commercial bank cases, only 31 were depositor payoffs, and the rest were closed bank purchase and assumption transactions or open-bank assisted merger transactions. There were no payoffs of mutual savings banks.

Source: *Deposit Insurance in a Changing Environment*, (Washington, D.C.: Federal Deposit Insurance Corporation, 1983). Reprinted from Cooper and Fraser (1984, Table 6-4).

by an intermediary as its leverage ratio increased. Hannah *et al.* (1986) also point out that bank officers may receive indirect compensation in return for making an otherwise undesirable loan and this is often difficult to trace. As a consequence, insolvency may be attributed to poor loan quality when it is, in fact, due to insider malfeasance. Classification problems notwithstanding, actual or probable misconduct by officers, directors, or other insiders was involved in 69 per cent of recent (up to 1984) U.S. bank insolvencies (Hannah *et al.*, 1986, p. 25). This speaks to the concentrated ownership issue only to the extent that these insiders were also large shareholders. The study does not elaborate on this issue.

With respect to the Canadian experience, the Economic Council of Canada (1986) analyzed the failures of financial intermediaries between 1980 and 1985 and found that what it called questionable practices were involved in 10 of 22 cases. All 10 cases involved closely held intermediaries.

2.3 Controlling Self-Dealing

It is evident from the discussion in Section 2.2. that there is no single remedy for abusive self-dealing. What is required is some combination of the following:

- prohibition of certain transactions,

- scrutiny of or size limitations on certain transactions,

- reducing maximum leverage ratios, and

- requiring widely dispersed ownership.

In the case of closely held or concentrated majority intermediaries, potentially damaging self-dealing can be deterred by increasing the minimum capital to borrowing ratio (reducing the maximum leverage ratio) and reducing the maximum size of transactions with insiders relative to capital. More attention will be devoted to the leverage ratio later, but, for the present, it should be noted that reductions in the maximum leverage ratio will reduce the incidence of harmful self-dealing without the necessity of defining that term. For an investment of a given size, insiders face a higher probability that they will bear any losses. Smaller excessively risky inside loans will no longer be beneficial. Big, "bet the firm" loans will continue to be tempting but it is possible that these can be controlled by size limitations. Here the problems of defining an insider and "throwing the baby (good inside loans) out with the bathwater" remain.

For widely held institutions, the benefits of risky loans accrue to the officers and directors receiving them while the costs are borne by shareholders and ultimately depositors, deposit insurers and other creditors. Here an increase in capital borrowing ratios does not reduce the incentive for self-dealing. It merely increases the likelihood that losses will be borne by shareholders rather than depositors and other creditors. In this case, reliance must be placed on the scrutiny and/or prohibition of transactions between an intermediary and its officers or directors.

The essential point is that, from the standpoint of depositor safety, a closely-held or concentrated-majority intermediary may be equivalent to a widely held intermediary with a higher maximum leverage ratio. Indeed, this thinking appears to be reflected in the array of leverage ratios presently imposed on deposit-taking intermediaries. Banks which are widely held are generally allowed higher leverage ratios (between 20:1 and 30:1) than trust companies (12.5:1, higher with permission) (Ontario Task Force on Financial Institutions 1985, p. 31).

The question remains as to the role of widely-dispersed ownership in the control of self-dealing. This has been an important issue in Canada because, while the chartered banks must be widely held, their competitors, the trust companies, need not be, and generally are not, widely held.

Dispersed ownership is widely regarded as the best means of controlling self-dealing. It has been adopted as a central policy goal by the Ontario Task Force on Financial Institutions:

> Because of the threat to solvency posed by self-dealing in closely held institutions and because of the potentially undesirable concentration of power evident in the development of conglomerates, the Task Force believes that, on balance, this objective [solvency] is more likely to be achieved by widely held rather than closely held institutions. Thus we conclude that the bias of public policy should be in favour of having financial institutions widely held. Accordingly, we recommend that:

> ...A basic principle of public policy should be to encourage the development of widely held rather than closely held financial institutions.

> ...In line with a policy to encourage the development of widely held institutions the regulatory authorities should:

> (i) favour when approval is sought for new charters or for changes in ownership and control applications by widely held institutions that intend to confine their activities to the financial business;

> (ii) refrain from approving the creation of closely held institutions unless there is evident need for new entrants to a financial services market and the closely held applicant has clear plans to increase public participation with a view to becoming widely held (Ontario Task Force on Financial Institutions 1985, pp. 59-60).

The Blenkarn Committee also stressed the importance of widely held ownership and of measures that would oblige existing closely held intermediaries to move in that direction:

> The fundamental issue surrounding the ownership of financial institutions is, in effect, an assessment of the costs and benefits of closely held versus widely held ownership structures. One of the costs of permitting closely held cross-ownership of financial

institutions is the greater potential for self-dealing under such a structure. Widely held ownership has traditionally been viewed in Canada as a deterrent for self-dealing transactions between financial institutions and the owners of these institutions. Under widely held ownership, the potential for self-dealing with directors and their other non-financial interests remains but to a much lesser degree than in the case of closely held ownership where controlling shareholders could have undue influence on the financial institutions and abuse their privileged position (Canada 1985, p. 89, mimeo version).

In response to the House and Senate reports, the Minister of State for Finance, Tom Hockin, has recently tabled a set of proposals which addressed the self-dealing problem of self-dealing, first, by prohibiting loans to or purchases of assets from "non-arm's-length persons" (owners of 10 per cent or more of the equity and their families, directors, officers, auditors of the intermediary and of corporate shareholders holding 10 per cent or more) (Hockin 1986, pp. 21-4).[2]

Second, some restrictions on concentrated ownership were proposed. Large chartered banks are to remain widely held. Trust, loan and insurance companies with capital in excess of $750 million are to have at least 35 per cent of their voting shares publicly traded. This requirement can be satisfied if a minority shareholder holding 35 per cent now exists (p.18). Otherwise it implies that the 35 per cent minority must be held in blocks of no greater than 10 per cent of the voting shares. Finally, as of December 18, 1986, no shareholders will be permitted to acquire more than 10 per cent ownership of the above institutions.

Advocates of dispersed ownership argue that prohibitions on inside transactions can never be effective. They are too costly to enforce and becoming more so. In their view, it is necessary to remove the ability to self-deal by ruling out concentrated ownership. As the discussion above has indicated, requiring dispersed ownership eliminates some but by no means all of the ability to self-deal.

The requirement that ownership of financial intermediaries be dispersed may also involve certain economic costs. In this regard, two issues have been identified. The House (Blenkarn) Committee concluded that a requirement that an intermediary be widely held could deter both the entry and initial expansion of new intermediaries:

A widely held ownership structure makes it difficult for new or small financial institutions to raise capital under these conditions [of economic adversity]. Perhaps less restrictive ownership limits in the banking sector could have alleviated the recent difficulties experienced by small regional banks in Canada. Indeed, evidence presented before the Committee favouring closely held ownership cited the benefits of this type of ownership structure in the formation of "de novo" institutions and during the initial growth period for institutions when a widely held ownership structure could otherwise make it difficult for a small and developing institution to raise additional capital for expansion. It was pointed out, for example by Atlantic Trust, that a major shareholder could have a greater interest and ability to provide additional capital for a fledgling institutions especially during periods of adversity (Canada 1985, p. 90, mimeo).

A requirement that no individual hold more than 10 per cent of a firm's capital may raise the cost of capital. It certainly will not reduce it. If it did, given the freedom to choose, all ownership structures would evolve in that direction. Thus, a regulation which rules out some ownership structures must either increase the cost of capital or leave it unchanged. It also constitutes a barrier to entry if existing firms were not obliged to be widely held when they entered the market. More intuitively, it removes from the evolutionary process the classical entrepreneur, the venture capitalist and the turnaround specialist. This leads us to the second possible cost associated with the requirement of widely held ownership. This is the removal of the intermediaries involved from the market for corporate control.

In its simplest form, the market for corporate control hypothesis states that there is an incentive for alternative managerial groups to buy control of poorly performing firms, replace incumbent management and improve operations.[3] The incentive to take this action lies in the capital gain which can be earned by purchasing shares trading at a discount to their potential value (i.e., in the event of good management), installing and providing assurances of continuing good management and reselling the shares or holding the shares and earning economic profits on them.

The relevance here is, of course, that the market for corporate control is just that – a market for control. If control is unattainable, as in the case of Canadian chartered banks, the market does not operate. Is this a serious problem? Would it be a serious problem if the requirement were extended to trust companies?

The market for corporate control is regarded by many as a little more than a theoretical curiosity. There are two reasons for this. First, while the empirical work on the determinants of the probability of a firm being subject to a tender offer, merger proposal or proxy fight, has established that this probability is a decreasing function of the ratio of the market to book value of the firm's equity, the effect is not very large (in terms of the increase in probability), nor is the relationship particularly strong statistically (Scherer 1980, pp. 37-8).

Second, theoretical work by Grossman and Hart (1980) has shown that the operation of the market for corporate control is impeded by some serious free rider problems. In essence, shareholders have no incentive to tender their shares unless the party seeking to acquire control overbids; that is, offers more than the underlying "good management" value of the shares. In this event, the corporate raider gains nothing from the acquisition unless he can somehow dilute the equity (exploit the remaining outsiders) of the target firm.

As it stands, the evidence is that the market for corporate control has not been an important source of discipline on managers of widely held firms. There is, however, another stream of literature which demonstrates that mergers, tender offers, and proxy fights are usually beneficial to the shareholders of the firms involved. The implication is that while it may not have operated on a significant scale, the market for corporate control has operated in the interest of corporate shareholders and perhaps in society's interest also.

This stream of literature which makes use of the effect of mergers and acquisitions on the respective prices of the shares of the firms involved as an indicator of social benefit is summarized in Jensen and Ruback (1983) and by Eckbo in Chapter 7 of this volume. An excellent summary of the United States evidence and its policy implications appears in the Economic Report of the President (1985).

Among the conclusions reached by these studies are, first, that mergers and acquisitions are beneficial to the shareholders of the acquired firms. Second, shareholders of acquiring firms in the United States neither gain nor lose, on average, from acquisitions. This is consistent either with acquiring firms being much larger than acquired firms or with competitive bidding for target firms. Evidence in favour of the latter interpretation has been adduced by Ruback (1983) who finds that losing bidders would have reduced the market value of their respective firms had they paid the price for the target firm which the winning bidder paid.

The ubiquity of target shareholder gains is emphasized in a recent study by Holderness and Sheehan (1985). These authors studied the activities of six of the most "notorious" corporate raiders in the United States. These individuals, it has been alleged in the press, acquired firms largely in order to loot them. There have been calls for curbs on this and other manifestations of "paper entrepreneurship." Holderness and Sheehan find that shareholders of the targets of these six raiders did benefit from the raids. Moreover there is evidence that these benefits were the result of real improvements made by the raider in the target. The evidence is entirely inconsistent with the looting hypothesis.

The clear message of virtually all the recent work on this subject is that on average, transfers of corporate control are beneficial to the shareholders involved. There is, however, reason to believe that while transfers of control are beneficial on average, there may be circumstances when the shareholders of the acquiring firm do lose. One such situation may be when the acquiring firm is management controlled (Lewellen *et al.* 1985).

Mergers and acquisitions can be in the interests of shareholders but not society as a whole. Shareholder benefits derived from better management or the exploitation of synergies or economies of scale are also social gains. Shareholder gains derived from monopoly power, tax avoidance, or additional opportunities for fraud, do not reflect a social gain and indeed, may involve a reduction in aggregate income.

While the evidence on this subject is rather weak, it tends to be incompatible with the market power and tax-saving motives for merger. The implication is that observed shareholder gains are also social gains. Thus, to preclude the operation of the market for corporate control, for example, by requiring that ownership of financial intermediaries be dispersed, is to forego at least some social gains in terms of more efficient operation. Whether the gains which have been or will be foregone are significant, is simply unknown.

The next question is whether a compromise such as the requirement proposed by the Minister of State for Finance (Canada, Department of Finance 1986), that trust, loan, and insurance companies have at least 35 percent of their voting shares widely held has any merit. An initial reaction is that it does not reduce either the incentive or the ability of the controlling (inside) interest to self-deal. Indeed it increases it. Insiders have even greater leverage, being able to impose their losses not only on depositors, deposit insurance, and other creditors but also on the outside minority.

It is precisely the anticipation of this, however, that will drive the demand price for minority shares down so that these shares will sell at discount from their value to the majority. Thus, the cost of insider self-dealing is effectively internalized. Insiders will take whatever steps they can to assure the potential outside minority that it will not be among the victims of insider self-dealing. It will be in the interest of insiders to push this guarantee process up to the point at which the cost of the guarantees provided, in present value terms, is just equal to the increase in the price which outsiders are willing to offer for a minority interest. Of course, protection for the outside minority is also protection for depositors and shareholders. Thus, the requirement that closely held intermediaries sell a minority interest to outsiders effectively forces the majority interest to take additional measures at its own expense to protect depositors and other creditors.

The proposals of the Minister of State for Finance would also have the effect of eliminating the possibility of transfer or acquisition of voting control of a (federally chartered) financial intermediary. The market for corporate control is rendered inoperative as far as financial intermediaries are concerned. This may not pose much of a problem for the intermediaries which are closely held (i.e., stockholder controlled). Whether it entails a significant efficiency loss among intermediaries which are or will be widely held depends on the alternative means available to stockholders to constrain management to operate in their (the stockholders') interest.

The proposals of the House of Commons Finance Committee with respect to ownership limits would allow both more scope for the operation of the market for corporate control, and for a greater variety of potential entrants into financial intermediation (Canada 1985, p. 98). Under the Committee's proposal a single shareholder (linked to the real sector or otherwise) could acquire or maintain voting control of any federally charted financial institution with assets under $30 billion.

3.0 CROSS-OWNERSHIP
3.1 Definition
Two types of cross-ownership are of interest to us here. The first involves participation by one intermediary (or by a number of commonly owned

intermediaries) in a number of different forms of financial intermediation. In a Canadian context this involves common ownership of intermediaries operating under two or more of the "four pillars". The four pillars are the chartered banks, trust and mortgage loan companies, insurance companies, and securities dealers – see Economic Council of Canada (1986).

The second type of cross-ownership involves the common ownership of a financial intermediary and a company involved in the so-called real sector of the economy – manufacturing, trade, services, etc.

3.2 Consequences of Cross-Ownership

Cross-ownership is said to pose several problems for the stability and integrity of the financial system. First, it offers greater opportunities for self-dealing. Thus, a real estate developer owning a bank or trust company might, in the absence of prohibitions from so doing, make excessively risky loans to finance land development. The costs of a sufficiently large default on these loans would be borne by deposit holders, deposit insurers and other creditors.

In the United States it has been argued that participation in non-bank and non-financial businesses which is permitted bank holding companies (BHCs) allows the latter to take on greater risks than would a bank or other purely financial intermediary. According to this argument, BHC management has an incentive to take on these risks if potential losses are covered by deposit insurance and the latter is not priced so as to reflect the probability of bankruptcy (Boyd and Graham 1986).

While this problem is a consequence of inappropriately priced deposit insurance rather than real-financial linkages, it is useful to examine the relationship between the extent of real sector or at least non-bank investment by BHCs and their probability of bankruptcy. This issue has been investigated in detail by Boyd and Graham (1986) who find that, over the period 1971-1983, there is no relationship between the proportion of non-bank assets held by a BHC and its probability of bankruptcy. A positive relationship does exist, however, for the period 1971-1977 which, according to the authors, was characterized by much looser scrutiny and supervision of BHCs and their non-bank activities by the Federal Reserve. The authors conclude that there is a case for active regulatory scrutiny of the non-bank activities of BHCs although there is no case for prohibiting this type of diversification.

Second, cross-ownership may place an intermediary in a conflict of interest situation. One form of conflict of interest is that an intermediary may obtain confidential information in one capacity which would be useful in another. The intermediary is placed in the position of failing to properly serve one client or the other. An example is the potential conflict between the fiduciary responsibilities of trust companies and their commercial lending. A trust company may acquire information as a lender which would be useful in the investment of trust funds it administers. Use of that information may harm one client, failure to use it harms another.

A second example is the combination of brokerage and underwriting functions in a stock broking firm. Information may be available to underwriters which would be of benefit to clients of brokers. Again, use or failure to use this information is damaging to the interest of one of the clients.

Related to the problem of use or misuse of confidential information is the potential incompatibility of incentives. Trust funds may be diverted to companies to which a trust company has lent heavily. Brokers may urge their clients to buy shares which their firm has underwritten.

Notice that these examples are conflicts of interest which could occur without cross-ownership. Another such conflict would be the favouring of one of two competing loan applicants by a chartered bank or trust company.

Conflicts of interest involving inter-pillar operations would include the conflict between the commercial lending business of banks and proposed brokerage and underwriting activities. Other potential conflict of interest situations posed by inter-pillar operations are summarized in Table 2.

When real-financial cross-ownership is considered, additional opportunities for conflict of interest arise. These would include favouring of firms with which an intermediary is linked over other clients, and using confidential information obtained as an intermediary to benefit firms with which it is linked or to damage their competitors.

In addition to conflict of interest, financial and real-financial conglomerates are also thought prone to engaging in the abusive trade practices usually attributed to real sector multimarket firms (tying, reciprocal dealing, mutual forbearance, predation).

All these faults and more are attributed to real-financial conglomerates in the brief submitted to the House (Blenkarn) Committee by Cadillac Fairview Corporation:

> It is conceivable, in the absence of any controls over conglomerate ownership (with the possible exception of the major chartered banks) that, within a decade or so both the financial and the non-financial sectors will be dominated by less than a dozen very large groups which will span both sectors as is the case in Japan. These groups could wield enormous economic power. The concern for public policy is not simply that those with such power will earn excess profits. Rather the concern is that these large groups will have the ability to earn an acceptable level of profits (e.g., sufficient to prevent a takeover) and be able to use their power to achieve objectives other than increasing the shareholders' wealth. This power may be used to alter the behavior of other firms involuntarily, e.g.,
>
> - by advancing the interests of some customers or suppliers and/or penalizing others;
>
> - by undermining the position of rivals in ways inconsistent with maximizing the wealth of one's own shareholders;

Table 2
Conflicts of Interest[1]

	DT	CL	TM	SD	U	IA	PD	I	REB
Deposit Taking[2]		Con	Con			CWE			
Commercial Lending[3]	Con		CWE	CWE	CWE	CWE	CWE		CWE
Trust Mgt.[4]	Con	CWE		CWE	***	CWE	CWE	***	CWE
Securities Dist.[3]		CWE	CWE		***	CWE	***	CWE	CWE
Underwriting		CWE	***	***		***	***		
Invest. Advice	CWE	CWE	CWE	CWE	***		CWE	CWE	CWE
Principal Dealing[6]		CWE	CWE	***	***	CWE		CWE	CWE
Insurance			***	CWE		CWE	CWE		CWE
Real Estate Brokerage		CWE	CWE	CWE		CWE	CWE	CWE	

Con = conflict of interest
CWE = Chinese wall procedures are effective
*** = Chinese wall procedures are effective only in certain circumstances

Table 2 (cont'd)

Notes:

1. This Table is not meant to be an exhaustive list of either the functions performed by financial institutions or the conflicts which may arise when an institution performs multiple functions.

2. Deposit-taking includes basic chequing and savings account functions as well as guaranteed investment certificates and term deposits.

3. Commercial lending includes mortgage lending, financial leasing, factoring and computer services.

4. Trust management includes basic fiduciary activities, as well as acting as trustee for mutual funds and sinking funds, portfolio management, pension fund management and corporate trusteeships.

5. Securities distribution includes recommending trades in securities, soliciting trades, accepting trade orders and risk arbitrage.

6. Principal dealing includes primarily investments and loans by an institution for its own account.

Source: Goodman and Carr (1985, Appendix Table 1).

- by providing excess rewards, pecuniary or otherwise, to the top management coalition that effectively controls the corporation, or

- by using economic power to influence public policy via the political process, i.e., expenditures on lobbying, advocacy, advertising, public relations, campaign contributions and the ability to redirect corporate locational decisions (Cadillac Fairview 1985, 68A: 19, September 23).

The brief argues that in addition to self-dealing and conflicts of interest which result from the combination of intermediating activities, the combination of real and financial activities allows the institution involved

to have an almost immediate impact on other financial or non-financial enterprises by moving funds into or out of another firm; calling a loan; failing to renew a loan — even the economic health of the borrower is unchanged; giving or withdrawing financial guarantees; or acquiring the financial claims of others, e.g., purchasing shares, debentures, loan portfolios, mortgages, rewarding those [the institution] favours and punishing those in disfavour (Cadillac Fairview 1985, 68A: 19, September 23).

In addition to its ability to award or withhold financial favours, the financial intermediary with real linkages is especially well placed to misuse information. The essential feature of deposit-taking intermediaries is that they hold specialized, non-marketable assets and issue fixed value liabilities. The essential function is one of investigating monitoring and certifying. As a consequence:

Financial intermediaries that grant credit to non-financial enterprises are necessarily privy to a great deal of confidential information about their customers. Where the customer concentrates his business with a single seller of a specific financial service he is vulnerable to the discretionary behaviour of that firm. Because of the normally close relationship between borrower and lender, when a lender moves to upset that relationship . . . other firms may interpret the financial institution's move — which is assumed to be made on "inside information" — as containing negative information . . . . Since credit is heavily dependent on reputation the refusal of the financial institution to renew a loan can inflict substantial costs on its former customer (Cadillac Fairview 1985, 68A: 20, September 23).

Granted that an intermediary possesses information that real sector corporations normally do not have, what are its incentives to misuse it? The first problem with the Cadillac Fairview brief is that it is confused regarding the type of ownership structure it finds offensive. A closely held institution is not faced with the threat of takeover and its owners face the full cost of pursuing "power" at the expense of the value of their firm. Why a closely held intermediary would wish to undermine rivals *and* reduce its own net worth is difficult to fathom.

The type of problem identified by Cadillac Fairview is more likely to prevail, if at all, when there is a minority outside interest or in the case of a widely held intermediary (by managers).

The second problem relates to the connection to commercial activities. It is clearly not necessary for a financial intermediary which is determined to abuse its position to have an ownership linkage with the real sector or even with the other "pillars" of the financial system. Executives or insiders in financial intermediaries can capitalize on their knowledge and ability to reward or punish by trading in stock or futures markets or soliciting side payments of various kinds from potential beneficiaries. This is not to deny that ownership linkages can facilitate these abuses. It is simply to state that they are by no means essential.

The third problem concerns the assumptions made with respect to the state of information and competition in the product market. As the Cadillac Fairview brief concedes, an intermediary which becomes known for opportunistic behaviour, let alone capricious, opportunistic behaviour, will see its market share and net worth decline perhaps drastically. Thus, opportunistic behaviour should not be a serious problem over the longer term in a market in which buyers and sellers have alternatives. Even a monopoly intermediary is likely to employ a more systematic and readily anticipated means of extracting surplus.

Let us now examine several examples of tying arrangements by industrial-financial conglomerates. Consider first, the offer by Chrysler Corporation of 3.8 per cent financing on purchases of certain 1987 model cars made by Chrysler. Chrysler will not give you 3.8 per cent financing on a new motor boat or a house or a new Mercedes. Very few would suggest that this type of tie can be banned. Fewer still could suggest that it has occurred because Chrysler is a conglomerate.

An example of the type of tie that might legitimately concern legislators is provided by a recent U.S. case involving Sears Savings Bank, a subsidiary of Sears Roebuck, a large retailer. A real estate developer is sueing Sears for $100 million alleging that, as a condition of its loan to him, Sears Savings Bank

> ... required him to install Sears Kenmore appliances and use other Sears services in a 161-unit condominium project financed by the bank. The developer charges that cheaper and better appliances were available from other sources but that he was forced by the bank to use Sears products anyway.

Sears' response was that the developer

> ... is simply another active and sophisticated litigant who would like to get some money somehow out of Sears. The material allegations of his complaint are not true.

The merits of this suit notwithstanding, the issue is important. What conditions should an intermediary be able to impose on the users of its services? Some appear to argue that it is the tie to another product, rather than forcing arrangement (minimum loan size, compensating balances, collateral requirement, etc.) which is offensive:

> Banks are supposed to be impartial allocators of credit. But Sears is saying, we'll give you credit if you buy our appliances. That doesn't seem impartial to me (Nash 1986, p. B12).

Let us assume for the sake of discussion that Sears engages in this type of tying arrangement and this policy is known to potential borrowers. If the tie is not mutually beneficial, borrowers will go elsewhere. If there are alternative sources of loans, Sears cannot impose a tie that is burdensome to borrowers and expect to retain its share of the loan market.

This raises the possibility that the tie is mutually beneficial. That is, it enables Sears to lend on better terms than the borrower in question could obtain elsewhere. Sears Savings Bank may be able to offer better terms because Kenmore appliances are worth more to it as collateral than those of some other manufacturer. An alternative explanation is that Sears earns economic (excess) profits on appliances which compensate for concessionary financing. This is the same as 3.8 per cent financing of Chrysler products. In either case the tie should not be prohibited. Indeed, borrowers would not wish to challenge it except for opportunistic reasons.

The key concerns here are that the ties be known and understood by customers and that there be alternatives. If these conditions hold, institutions which impose ties which are not beneficial (in terms of a lower price for the package) will decline relative to those which do not impose ties or confine themselves to ties which are beneficial to their customers.

3.3 Remedies for Conflict of Interest

The first remedy for victims of conflict of interest is a suit to recover damages. There have been some recent Canadian examples of successful actions brought against financial intermediaries which have favoured one client over another.

A second remedy is for intermediaries to avoid placing themselves in conflict of interest by effectively preventing the flow of information between functional areas which are potentially in conflict. The set of rules and procedures which compartmentalize information are called "Chinese walls." Goodman and Carr (1985, p. 30) define a Chinese wall as follows:

> A Chinese wall may be defined as a collection of rules, procedures and possibly physical arrangements designed to prevent communication of information from one department to another. The wall may be designed to prevent the flow of all information, only confidential information or only material confidential information, depending on the relevant circumstances.

Chinese walls have been used effectively in several jurisdictions to mitigate a number of potential conflicts of interest. Together with restrictions on certain specific combinations of activities, Chinese walls promise to be effective in a fairly wide range of circumstances. The situations in which Chinese walls are potentially efficacious are summarized in Table 2.

Intermediaries may also make use of separate but commonly owned corporate entities for particular sets of functions as a device for avoiding conflicts of interest. This might be called a "reinforced Chinese wall."

The final remedy is structural. Given freedom to combine financial or financial and real activities, intermediaries may choose to specialize in a combination of functions which avoid the most severe conflicts of interest. This is called specialized ownership.

There are reasons to expect that, in the absence of regulatory restrictions, there would be an evolution of intermediary functions in the direction of minimizing conflict of interest problems. Presumably, potential customers will anticipate to some degree the conflicts of interest to which the intermediaries soliciting their business will be subject. The intermediaries which can provide the most credible undertakings to the effect that their clients will not be the victims of such conflicts, will prevail.

We might also speculate that as the process of experimenting with combinations of Chinese walls, separate corporate entities and specialized ownership evolves, a role for specialized ownership will emerge. A specialist can be more aggressive in seeking out and acting on financial information than can a multimarket intermediary which must always demonstrate that its information was obtained at arm's-length.

Some evidence that intermediaries will have an interest in minimizing their exposure to conflicts of interest which their clients may regard as potentially damaging is provided by the reaction of the trust companies to the announcement (see below) that they will be permitted to own securities dealers. The president of Royal Trustco recently stated:

It is not Royal Trust's intention to go into the brokerage industry . . . . It is difficult to be an asset manager and also be a broker. We are positioning ourselves as advisers and asset managers. In Europe the feeling is growing that it is difficult to serve one's clients if one has feet in both asset-management and the brokerage side (Galt 1987, p. B1).

It is apparently the underwriting and fiduciary functions which, in the view of Royal Trustco, require separate ownership. Royal Trustco, however, will continue to offer a stock transaction service.

It is likely that the combination of intermediary functions which emerges in the future will be less the result of natural selection than of structural regulation. The December 18, 1986 proposals of the Minister of State for Finance regarding the direct extension of the powers of certain types of intermediaries and the reduction of restrictions on intermediary cross-ownership are as follows:

- Trust, loan and insurance companies are to be granted increased powers to engage in commercial and consumer lending.

- Chartered banks and insurance companies are to be granted increased fiduciary powers.

- Chartered banks and federally regulated trust, loan and insurance companies will be permitted to own securities dealers.

- With the exception of retailing insurance, full networking powers will be available to all federally regulated financial institutions.

With regard to real-financial linkages, the government's view is now that "it is desirable to constrain ownership linkages between the financial and commercial sectors of the economy and — where these linkages now exist . . . to encourage a significant minority holding" (Canada 1986, p. 17).

To this end the government has proposed that commercial interests be limited to 10 per cent of trust, loan and insurance companies with capital in excess of $50 million. Commercial interests now in excess of 10 per cent need not necessarily be reduced, but all commercially linked trust, loan, and insurance companies with capital in excess of $50 million will be required to have at least 35 per cent of their voting shares publicly traded (Canada 1986, p. 17).

If the government's proposals are accepted, any federally regulated financial institution would be able to perform any intermediating function except retailing insurance. The four pillars approach to financial regulation will have been laid to rest. Existing real-financial linkages will be reduced somewhat by the requirement that 35 per cent of the voting stock of trust, loan and insurance companies are widely held. The restriction on the acquisition of a voting interest in excess of 10 per cent implies, first, that significant new real-financial combinations cannot be formed and, second, that existing intermediaries with real sector linkages will be prohibited from growth by acquisition.

3.4   The Efficiency Consequences of Restricting Cross-Ownership

Restrictions on cross-ownership have been seen as a means of reducing problems of conflict of interest in financial intermediation. The question now to be addressed is whether restrictions of this nature are likely to have any adverse consequences for economic efficiency. This requires, in turn, the estimation of the magnitudes of any economies to be realized by combining various financial and real activities under common ownership.

When cost savings can be realized by providing two or more services jointly, economies of scope are said to exist. Economies of scope derive from several different sources. The first is the existence of indivisibilities at one or more stages in the production process. In this case, minimum efficient scale at one stage of production is greater than at other stages, hence, idle capacity exists at this stage. In the contest of financial intermediation it is sometimes argued that the computer systems of the chartered banks cannot be used to capacity in their respective banking operations. Economies in the use of computers may be realized by engaging in any or all of the following:

-   joint provision of data processing services,

-   rental of excess capacity to non-bank or non-financial users (networking),

-   provision of financial or non-financial services which make use of idle data processing capacity (cross-ownership), and

-   expansion of banking activity.

Excess capacity can be utilized either internally by cross-ownership or externally by networking. Excess capacity can be utilized by providing new services (economies of scope) or more of the existing mix of services (economies of scale). If there are no economies of scale from this source, it is unlikely that there will be economies of scope. Excess capacity may also be a transitory phenomenon. For example, the introduction of automated teller machines (ATMs) is said to have left deposit intermediaries with idle space in their branch offices. While this idle space could be utilized in the manner suggested above, it may also disappear over time as the size of branches is reduced.

There are some inputs for which there is always idle capacity: public inputs. The most important public input is knowledge. Information and experience accumulated for one purpose can be used for others without diminishing their availability for the first. There are many examples which can be drawn from financial intermediation. Experience accumulated in assessing mortgage applications may be relevant to the assessment of commercial or consumer loan applications. The information provided by loan applicants themselves might be used to evaluate requests for other types of loans. This complementarity could extend to other forms of intermediation with information gathered by, say, life and property insurers being used in the assessment of loan applications and *vice versa*.

The existence of public inputs implies economies of scale as well as scope. Thus, lending experience can be utilized more intensively by engaging in additional lending of one variety or by adding varieties. Public inputs can also be rented or licensed and may be provided by specialists. The existence of public inputs does not necessarily imply that their users must be multimarket firms.

A second source of economies of scope is jointness in production. In this case, an increase in the output of one service reduces the marginal cost of another. At the heart of financial intermediation is the economy of engaging jointly in lending and deposit-taking. As fundamental is the cost (i.e., risk) reduction obtained by adding to the variety of financial assets of which an intermediary's portfolio is comprised. Other examples include economies of joint promotion. It may be less costly, for example, to inform consumers about mortgage and personal loans or term and savings deposits jointly than separately.

The existence of scale and scope economies can be inferred in a variety of ways. Two methods are discussed here. One is the survivor method which assumes that an organizational form occupying an increasing share of the market has efficiency advantages. The second is statistical cost analysis which estimates the relationship between unit costs and the scale and mix of outputs respectively.

Survivor and Trend Evidence: A rough approximation of the survivor method of inferring the efficient combination of financial or financial and real functions, is to examine the evolution of product lines and organizational forms of financial intermediaries both in Canada and elsewhere. As Table 3 indicates, the four pillars have been subject to considerable erosion in Canada even in the presence of regulatory restrictions on cross-ownership.

Table 4 indicates the combinations of financial and real activities now observed in the United States. The combination of fiduciary activities with commercial and consumer lending has always been allowed and normally prevails in the United States. The combination of commercial lending, and the brokerage and underwriting functions has been allowed and generally prevailed in continental Europe and in Britain (Rybczynski 1985).

Although confined by the *Glass-Steagall Act* to the brokerage end of the securities business, U.S. banks have begun to offer discount brokerage services on a significant scale (Cooper and Fraser 1984, p. 202, 211). U.S. Banks have also shown considerable interest in entering both securities underwriting and insurance underwriting and retailing (Mittelstaedt 1987).

The debate over the entry of U.S. banks into the insurance business is instructive. According to the American Banking Association *Banking Journal* (June 1985) some 50 per cent of 750 bank CEOs surveyed by Egan Zehnder International indicated an intention to acquire a non-banking business during the next five years. Some 70 per cent of this group indicated a preference for acquiring a property and casualty insurance business if they were permitted to do so. It was anticipated that these acquisitions would take the form of joint ventures with existing agents or underwriters. It was not expected that these acquisitions would be highly profitable in themselves. Benefits would instead take the form of increased customer convenience which presumably would be reflected in the profitability of the banks' existing operations.

Crum (1986, p. 51) is more explicit about the potential benefits of commercial bank entry into the insurance business:

> For banks seeking increased fee income to cover overhead expenses, insurance offers a large and apparently untapped field that could efficiently utilize their excess lobby space, extensive branch network, frequent customer contacts and credit processing facilities.

Table 3
Financial Services Offered by Various Types of Intermediaries, Canada, 1983

Products & Services

Financial Institutions	Credit Unions	Securi. Dealers	Prov. Insur. Cos	Federal Insur. Cos	Prop. Canada Savings Banks & Trust Co	Prov. Loan Corps	Fed. Loan Cos	Prov. Trust Cos	Fed Trust Cos	Banks
Deposit taking	Y	Y	N	N	Y	Y	Y	Y	Y	Y
Chqing Accts	Y	L	N	N	Y	Y	Y	Y	Y	Y
Comm. Lending	L	N	N	L	L	L	L	L	L	Y
Mort.on Real Prp	Y	Y	Y	Y	Y	Y	Y	Y	Y	Y
Safety Dep Boxes	Y	Y	N	N	Y	Y	Y	Y	Y	Y
Safekping of Prp	Y	Y	N	N	Y	Y	Y	Y	Y	Y
Guartee Inv Cert	N	N	Y/N	Y/N	Y	Y	N	Y	Y	N
RRSPs and RHOSPs	Y	L	N	N	Y	Y	Y	Y	Y	Y
Estate Admin.	N	N	N	N	N	N	N	N	N	N
Secur. Broking	N	Y	Y	Y	N	N	N	N	N	N
Iss. Ins. Pol.	N	N	Y	Y	Y	N	N	Y	Y	N
Mutual Funds	N	Y	N	N	Y	Y	Y	Y	Y	N
Real Est. Bank.	N	N	L	L	Y	Y	Y	Y	Y	N
Trav. Chqs	N	M	Y	Y	Y	N	N	Y	Y	Y
Finan. Leasing	N	M			L	Y	Y	L	Y	Y
Comp. Services	N	Y				L	L			L

Table 3 (cont'd)

Financial Institutions	Credit Unions	Securi. Dealers	Prov. Insur. Cos	Federal Insur. Cos	Prop. Canada Savings Banks & Trust Co	Prov. Loan Corps	Fed. Loan Cos	Prov. Trust Cos	Fed Trust Cos	Banks
Credit Cd Plans	Y	M	N	N	Y	N	N	Y	Y	Y
Porfolio Mgmnt	N	Y	Y	Y	Y	L	L	Y	Y	L
Invstmnt Advice	N	Y	Y	Y	Y	Y	Y	Y	Y	N
Factoring	N	M	N	N	N	N	Y	N	N	Y
Underwriting	N	Y	N	N	N	N	N	N	N	L
Rgstrar&Trav Ag	N	N	N	N	Y	N	N	Y	Y	M
Manging Snking Funds & Act. as Corp. Trustee	N	Y/N	N	N	Y	N	N	Y	Y	Y/N
Invstment Cont.	M	Y	N	N	N	N	N	N	N	M
Admin Advisory & Mgmnt Services	M	Y	N	L	M	M	M	M	M	M
Indexed Sec.	Y	Y	Y	Y	Y	N	N	Y	Y	M
Invstmnt Plan	Y	Y	Y	Y	Y	N	N	Y	Y	Y

Y = yes   N = no   M = maybe   L = Limited

Source: Submission to the Ontario Securities Commission by the firm of Campbell, Godfrey and Newton, September 1983.

Table 4
Comparison of Products and Powers of Selected U.S. Financial and Non-Financial Institutions

	Nat. Bank	State Bank of Calif.	Savings Bank Holdg Co.	Federal Unitary Bank/ Savings Bank & Loan	Thrift Holding Co.	Merrill Lynch	Dreyfus	Prudent. Bach	Sears	Amer Exp
Demand Dep	Y	Y	Y	Y	Y	N	Y	N	Y	N
Savings Dep	Y	Y	Y	Y	Y	N	Y	Y	Y	N
Cert. of Dep	Y	Y	Y	Y	Y	Y	Y	Y	Y	Y
Trans.Acct (Now/ATS,etc)	Y	Y	Y	Y	Y	Y	Y	Y	Y	Y
Federal Ins	Y	Y	Y	Y	Y	Y	Y	Y	Y	N
Comm. Loans	Y	Y	Y	Y	Y	Y	N	Y	Y	Y
Cons. Loans	Y	Y	Y	Y	Y	N	Y	N	Y	N
Resdntl Mrtg.	Y	Y	Y	Y	Y	Y	Y	N	Y	Y
Comm Mrtg.	Y	Y	Y	Y	Y	Y	Y	Y	Y	N
Margin Loans	Y	Y	Y	N	Y	Y	Y	N	Y	Y
Credit Cards	Y	Y	Y	Y	Y	N	Y	Y	Y	Y
Credit Rel. Ins. Agent	Y	Y	Y	Y	Y	Y	N	Y	Y	Y
Genl Ins Agt	N	N	N	Y	Y	Y	N	Y	Y	Y
Ins. Under-writer	N	N	N	N	Y	Y	N	Y	Y	Y
Stock Brokge	N	N	N	Y	Y	Y	N	Y	Y	Y

Table 4 (cont'd)

	Nat. Bank	State Bank of Calif.	Savings Bank Holdg Co.	Federal Unitary Bank/ Savings Bank & Loan	Thrift Holding Co.	Merrill Lynch	Dreyfus	Prudent. Bach	Sears	Amer Exp
Disc Stk Bkge	Y	N	Y	Y	Y	N	N	Y	N	N
Invstmnt Adv	Y	Y	Y	Y	Y	Y	Y	Y	Y	Y
Invstmnt in Corp. Sec.	N	Y	Y	Y	Y	Y	Y	Y	Y	Y
Orgnztn/oprtn of Mutual Fund										
Real Est Bk	N	Y	Y	N	Y	Y	Y	Y	Y	Y
Real Est Dvl.	N	N	N	N	Y	Y	N	N	Y	Y
Real Est Appr for others	N	Y	N	Y	Y	Y	N	Y	Y	Y
Data Prcssing for others	N	Y	Y	Y	Y	Y	N	N	Y	N
Trav Agency	N	Y	Y	Y	Y	N	N	N	Y	N
Leasing Pers.	N	N	N	N	Y	N	N	N	Y	N
Property	Y	Y	Y	Y	Y	Y	N	N	N	N
Retail Sales	N	N	N	N	Y	N	N	N	Y	Y
Manufacturing	N	N	N	N	N	Y	N	N	N	N

Source: Aspinwall (1985)

To gain entry into this market, commercial banks would be obligated to acquire product knowledge, selling and servicing skills, and underwriting expertise. These could be acquired by acquiring, or affiliating with, an existing agent or underwriter.

Commercial bank entry into the insurance business in the United States has been opposed by independent agents groups which expect to lose sales and margins to the new competition. The agents have made skillful use of regulation, legislation and litigation both at the state and federal levels in their efforts to forestall commercial bank entry (Crum 1986, p. 56).

The main arguments against commercial bank entry into the insurance business are that banks would tie the purchase of insurance to the granting of credit and that banks have an unfair advantage in their access to cheap (insured) deposits.

With respect to tying, a coercive tie requires monopoly power, in the credit market which most commercial banks simply do not have. For a commercial bank with some monopoly power, a tying arrangement between loans and insurance is a dubious proposition as a surplus extraction device. It does not provide a meter of the loan customer's consumer's surplus as in the Xerox and Gestetner cases, among others. Indeed, a bank's biggest and probably most valued loan customers would also be the most able to go elsewhere for credit when confronted with a coercive tie. Smaller customers may be more likely to accept a tie but the surplus extracted from them would probably not be sufficient to offset the loss of larger customers.

With respect to the cost of funds argument, banks may or may not have a lower cost of funds. They have lower credit ratings, hence a higher cost of wholesale funds than many industrial corporations. Retail deposits may once have been a "cheap" source of funds. With competition for deposits there is no reason why they should still be "cheap." Obviously the calculation of the cost of deposits as a source of funds should take more than interest rates paid on deposits into account. Whatever the outcome of this calculation, it is relevant for public policy purposes only if retail deposits are a *subsidized* source of funds. Under priced deposit insurance is a subsidy. In the Canadian context, however, the major chartered banks have historically paid deposit insurance premiums which are regarded as excessive in the light of their loan loss experience. In this case deposit insurance does not constitute a subsidy.

The absence of a significant capital cost advantage for commercial banks over insurance companies is supported (although hardly confirmed) by the British experience. British banks have been able to sell insurance for years and have not come to dominate that market (Crum 1986, p. 57).

A final concern is that insurance underwriting exposes depositors and deposit insurance to additional risk. For this reason it has been argued that banks should be confined either to selling or underwriting more stable types of insurance such as life insurance. With reinsurance, underwriting need not be and probably is not any riskier than the current investment activities of chartered banks. The U.S. experience is that among the deposit institutions (non-bank banks, state banks and thrifts) there have been few problems with underwriting losses and few, if any, failures attributable to them.

To summarize, the advantages of combining commercial (Schedule A) banking and insurance selling and underwriting are rather vague. Excess branch capacity arguments appear to conflict with the (U.S.) statistical evidence on scale economies (i.e., their absence). Perhaps excess capacity arguments refer to the post-ATM world of smaller optimal branch sizes while the statistical evidence is less current.

One conclusion reached by all commentators is that the banks would have to acquire underwriting and marketing skills. These are apparently not present in banking organizations. Thus the notion that there are a common set of skills which can be applied to any intermediating activity receives no support from this literature.

While the advantages of combining banking and insurance activities have yet to be demonstrated, so have the disadvantages. The only legitimate objection to this expansion of bank activity is that the latter may be the beneficiaries of subsidized deposit insurance. This is, of course, objectionable in its own right and applies to any expansion of bank activities.

Some would dispute the proposition that the entry of financial intermediaries into new markets necessarily reflects the exploitation of economies of scope. At least some of this movement may reflect internal diversification out of declining markets. For example, Freedman (1985, pp. 11-12) argues that:

> Most of the pressure in Canada for expansion of the powers of financial institutions appears to be coming from the institutions themselves. As far as can be ascertained, with some minor exceptions, there has not been much in the way of complaints by customers as to services or any great demand for financial supermarkets. Furthermore, there is very little empirical evidence of economies of scope from bringing together functions under one roof. Indeed, components of the newly-emerging financial conglomerates do not appear as yet to have made advantageous use of their joint affiliation. Moreover, one can argue that any advantages that might accrue from financial supermarkets can be captured via networking without raising the problems that inhere in the common ownership of a variety of institutions.

Freedman goes on to analyze the motives of trust and insurance companies seeking to expand their powers. With regard to trust companies, Freedman sees two motivating factors. The first is a secular decline in the supply of their principal asset — residential mortgages. The second is a decrease in the term of their liabilities hence the desirability of reducing the average term of their assets. The search for newer and shorter term assets has led trust companies into the commercial and personal loan market.

In this view, the expansion of trust companies into new loan markets stems more from a desire to diversify out of a declining business, than from a desire to exploit scale and scope economies. Continuation of regulatory impediments to this expansion would, presumably, result in the decline of trust companies as a group. It may also reduce competition among deposit taking institutions. This will be discussed later. On the present interpretation of the evidence, it would not result in foregone scale and scope economies by trust companies. Insurance companies have similar motives in Freedman's view:

> With the declining importance of whole life insurance, they have been faced with a fall in their share of financial business. In addition they, too, have faced a significant shortening of the term of liabilities desired by savers and have responded to this development by offering new kinds of annuities that are directly competitive with term deposits. However, they do not appear to have had the same difficulty as trust companies in finding matching assets to cope with the shortening term of their liabilities. The only potential economies that would appear to be pushing them in the direction of expanding their investment powers might be related to their agent delivery network (i.e., the desire to make wider use of their agents) and possibly a less than fully utilized senior management. Since their requests to the federal government for an expansion of powers relate more to the right to purchase trust companies than to expansion of life insurance company powers it would appear that it is the ability of their senior management to extend their expertise into other areas which is dominant in their thinking (Freedman 1985, pp. 14-15).

The findings of Daly *et al.* and Kellner and Mathewson (reported in the section on empirical evidence below) of decreasing returns to scale (in the life insurance industry) cast doubt on the underutilized management argument. Again, the alternative explanation is simply a desire to diversify out of a declining line of business into expanding ones. This is not necessarily inefficient even if the diversifying firms are outperformed by the incumbents in the industries they enter.

There are several examples of the integration of real sector firms into various financial service and intermediary activities, which illustrate both the efficiencies which can be derived by combining the two and the futility of legislating against at least some of these linkages.

A number of real sector (industrial) corporations have been active for years in various forms of sales financing. What is perhaps less well-known is that the bulk of the financing now done by the largest of these formerly "captive" sales finance subsidiaries is on sales of other (unrelated) corporations:

> many of the captive finance companies of these manufacturers who originally financed only the sale of their parents' products have evolved to provide credit, if not to all comers, then to a wide

clientele involved in purchasing goods other than their parents'. For example, by 1981 financing of General Electric Products accounted for less than 5 per cent of GECC's [General Electric Credit Corporation] financing volume, and over 90 per cent of Borg-Warner Acceptance Corporation's income and assets resulted from financing other companies' products. Similarly, Westinghouse Credit extended about 1 per cent of its credit to finance Westinghouse products (Rosenblum and Siegel 1983, p. 2).

The point here is not so much that the financial affiliates of real sector corporations are competing successfully with various financial intermediaries, which they are, but that there does not appear to have been any problem with conflict of interest. That General Electric, Westinghouse and Borg Warner, among others, can finance sales of the products of others to the apparent satisfaction of all concerned implies that borrowers have not been the victims of such conflicts.

This conclusion is supported by the successful expansion of real sector companies into the provision of a virtually full range of financial intermediating services (save deposit taking) in recent years. The in-house banks as they are called perform a range of functions including asset and liability management for the associated corporate group, provision of financial services such as currency trading and swap arrangements for the corporate group and borrowing on the corporate guarantee and relending.

Consider the experience of Peugeot which set up a finance subsidiary in Switzerland in 1981 called PSA International. PSA International's trading activities result from its role in consolidating, managing and hedging the foreign exchange exposures of Peugeot's subsidiaries around the world and taking responsibility for short-, medium-, and long-term financing and currency swaps. "If Peugeot's companies did this individually it would take 360 accountants and they would not be as expert as we [PSA] are" (Crabbe 1986, pp. 24-25).

The experience of BP Finance International is also illustrative:

Last year BP raised an aggregate of $990 million in the Eurobond market with ten public issues denominated in dollars, sterling, yen and New Zealand dollars and one private placement. Often deals involved more than one swap, producing considerable savings. With an AA credit rating, BP is able to raise funds in the capital markets at levels substantially below the Libor rate. Simply by warehousing those funds in a variety of investments for a return of, say, Libor, the oil company is able to make a profit.

The range of activities which comes under the aegis of BP Finance International is impressive: standard treasury operations, including forex trading, which totals around $100 billion annually, the funding of 70 companies associated with BP worldwide, a capital markets group to define new funding products. It also has BP's long-term interest rate swap and trading books, an M&A (mergers and acquisitions) group and a business finance group looking after leasing and property credit (Crabbe 1986, p. 32).

While BP Finance engages in a wide variety of intermediating activities, R.J. Reynolds has focused on cash management:

> Thus Reynolds began to concentrate on banking relationships and investment of surplus funds . . . . Pockets of excess cash were still being held at times by some operating units while others were borrowing short-term from local banks. We had many small, insignificant accounts for various units and could not consolidate activity into our major line banks.

> The company was borrowing up to $130 million overnight and investing $90 to $10 million without being able to put the positions together. The solution was the creation of FINCO in late 1982.

> The Geneva operation comprising only a managing director and two staff with an operating budget of less than one million a year, has since given Reynolds' senior management hands-on control of the company's liquidity and currency exposures. With its own trading rules, direct wires and correspondence banks, FINCO is now Reynolds' bank for its operating units worldwide.

> The mini-bank takes deposits and excess funds of the company's operating units in their functional currencies and on-lends them as needed, to other operating units in their functional currencies.

> Reynolds saves foreign exchange transactions costs and the interest rate spread of netted positions . . . . Say we had a tobacco company in West Germany and a Del Monte unit in France in need of Deutchemarks. The German unit left to its own devices, would invest Deutchemarks while the Del Monte unit would borrow Deutchemarks. FINCO, however, nets out the positions and eliminates the banks altogether.

> After the German unit deposits its excess funds with FINCO, which pays a competitive interest rate, FINCO on-lends the money and charges a competitive rate . . . We just capture the spread that would otherwise go to the banking system. This shows up in FINCO's books as profits but it is really savings 'Other benefits'. Reynolds has been able to close more than 500 tiny operation accounts of its operating units as it consolidates its business with its major-line banks (Crabbe 1986, p. 41).

In-house banking appears to be profitable because corporate treasuries and internal cash management must exist in any case. Various banking functions can be performed internally at marginal cost while banks presumably charge fees or maintain spreads which reflect both incremental and overhead costs. Another interpretation is that the internal performance of various financial functions contributes to the effectiveness of the overall treasury operation. The implication here is that the marginal cost of internal performance of some banking functions may be negative.

The existence of in-house banking implies another source of competition for financial intermediaries. If faced with excessive fees and/or spreads, major corporations can integrate backwards both on their own account and on behalf of others.

In-house banking obviously involves a lot of self-dealing. This does not appear to have bothered the creditors of the in-house banks. The reason is that the in-house banks borrow on the guarantee of their corporate parent. If in-house banks were separate corporate entities (as they often are) and if they borrowed without their parents' guarantee, the situation might be quite different.

In-house banking can give rise to conflicts of interest if it involves lending to outsiders. There do not appear to have been any problems of this nature and this may be because in-house banks tend to hold marketable debt — commercial paper and government and corporate bonds. They are price takers in these markets and have the same information as other holders of these assets. This is not to say that their own industrial operations might not yield information which could be used to advantage in financial markets. The existence of in-house banking not only makes it easier to capitalize on information derived from industrial activities, but also provides an incentive to use industrial operations for the purpose of manipulating financial markets. In a sense this is insider trading on behalf of the shareholders.

Conflict of interest problems would be aggravated if the in-house bank engages in merchant banking functions (such as mergers and acquisitions), as BP Financial does, or engages in commercial lending. In this event the real sector operations of the parent could benefit from information provided to its banking operation by outside clients. Presumably this banking operation would not attract many clients unless it could satisfy them that it would not make use of privileged information on its own account. More generally, financial institutions with real sector linkages would find it in their own interest to assure prospective clients that privileged information will not be misused. There does not appear to be a role for ownership restrictions or regulatory specification of Chinese walls unless clients cannot distinguish one institution from another. This should not be true of either merchant banking or commercial lending. The potential for conflicts of interest in consumer or small business loan markets, in which clients might not be able to distinguish among intermediaries, would appear to be considerably less.

The implications of this discussion are that some types of real-financial linkages are so common they often go unnoticed. The conflict of interest problems which ought to be burdening them have apparently been avoided. They are clearly efficiency enhancing. Prohibition of them would be costly and futile.

Statistical Evidence: The statistical evidence on the existence of economies of scale and scope in financial intermediation is of limited use. U.S. studies summarized by Benston, Henweck and Humphrey (1982) and Gilbert (1984) find that any economies of scale in deposit-taking institutions are exhausted at scales well below that of the smallest Canadian bank as well as most trust companies and many credit unions. One U.S. study (Gilligan, Smirlock and Marshall 1984) was able to confirm that loans and deposits are complementary. Little progress has been made beyond this point.

In a Canadian context, a study of the Canadian life insurance industry (Dale, Rao and Geehan 1985) finds that the scale curve is U-shaped and concludes that the largest firms in the industry (Manufacturers Life, London Life and Sun Life) are experiencing decreasing returns to scale.

There are two statistical studies which allow for both economies of scale and scope in financial intermediation in Canada. Murray and White (1983) estimate cost functions for 61 B.C. credit unions operating during the period 1976-77 and employing computerized posting. They assume credit unions produce three distinct outputs: mortgages, other loans, and other investments. They assume that there are four inputs: capital, labour, demand deposits and term deposits. They find that there are scale economies for credit unions with assets of up to $130 million. Only two credit unions in the province were larger than this.

Murray and White find cost complementarity between mortgage and other lending but no such complementarity between other investments and mortgages and other lending respectively. On the input side, demand and time deposits are found to be complements rather than substitutes. That is, an increase in the price of time deposits *decreases* the intermediary's demand for demand deposits (given the level of output). This would appear to be impossible as these two inputs are essential for the production of output (loans and other investments).

Kellner and Mathewson (1983) estimate a cost function for Canadian life insurers for each of the years 1961, 1966, 1971, 1976. They assume that all input prices are identical for all firms. Thus their cost function has only output terms. Four outputs are included. These are ordinary life insurance contracts, group life, ordinary annuities and group annuities. Output is measured as the number of policies written during the year or the number of individuals in groups served. Cost is defined to include all head office (non-agent) expenses except advertising.

Kellner and Mathewson (1983, p. 41) find that the hypothesis of constant returns to scale cannot be rejected in two years (1961, 1976) and can be rejected in favour of *decreasing* returns (at the average size of firm) in two years (1966, 1971). Testing for local cost complementarity they find that it exists in some cases but is sometimes reversed, indicating local diseconomies of joint production, in other years. Their results are summarized in Table 5.

The absence of any cost complementarities between ordinary and group life again indicates the difficulty of finding statistical evidence of the benefits of combining even the most basic functions of the institutions involved.

In sum, initial attempts to estimate economies of scope in financial intermediation have concluded that they are minimal even within traditional lines of business. Estimation of scale economies in intermediation has been going on for some 25 years and the general conclusion is that these too are minimal. The absence of discernible scale economies also has implications for the existence of economies of scope. The two can be derived from the same source. Thus, the existence of public inputs (know-how, technology, information) and quasi-public inputs (under-utilized physical and human capital) would support the existence of both scale and scope economies. The absence of scale economies implies that a potentially important source of scope economies is also absent.

It is important to realize where these results put the statistical cost literature in relation to policy debate. It is being argued that combinations of such disparate functions as insurance underwriting, portfolio management, securities underwriting, fiduciary trust services, commercial lending, and deposit taking are being driven by economies of scope. Yet research to date has had difficulty establishing the existence of cost complementarities between the basic functions of deposit-taking or insurance intermediaries.

It may be that there are neither scale nor scope economies in intermediation. This leaves the statistical approach at odds with the

Table 5
Local Economies or Diseconomies of Joint Production

	Ordinary Life	Group Life	Individual Annuity	Group Annuity
Ordinary Life	0	none	disecon (61,66) none (71, 76)	econ (61, 66, 71) disecon (76)
Group Life		0	econ (61, 71) none (661, 76)	econ (66, 71) none (61, 76)
Individual Annuity			0	econ (61, 71) none (66) disecon (76)
Group Annuity				0

Source: Kellner and Mathewson (1983, p. 41).

survivor approach. It may also be that the statistical models presently in use are in need of further refinement. Among the refinements needed are:

- a consistent distinction between inputs and outputs; see Hancock, (1985), for a promising approach,

- a consistent definition of the dimensions of output (number of loans, average loan size),

- a distinction between the short- and long-run (particularly with regard to the number of branches),

- the application of the analysis over a wider range of intermediary sizes.

3.5 Prohibition of Cross-Ownership: An Assessment

A review of the evidence suggests that cross-ownership within the financial sector has become increasingly widespread and is now virtually complete in many jurisdictions. Linkages between financial and real activities and the financial and real sectors are also increasing.

There is little in the way of statistical evidence to indicate that this cross-ownership will yield significant economies of scope. Nor have the financial conglomerates themselves provided much evidence regarding the types of economies, if any, that they may be realizing. Indeed, their public statements tend to place more emphasis on the separation of their various activities than on their jointness. Llewellyn (1985) has summed up the British experience as follows:

> There is also the possibility that some customers would prefer to shop in a financial "department store" providing a full range of financial services. But in practice the big financial conglomerates (especially the Clearing Bank groups) have hitherto not in practice offered this, but have conducted their different activities from different premises (frequently through subsidiary companies). Whether this structure confers the advantage of the department store is questionable. In this case the benefit to the consumer must derive from any alleged efficiency advantages to be gained from within the conglomerate. But this is likely to be small if different parts of the group are managed as separate companies. One advantage, however, for a financial conglomerate is that risks are diversified in a holding company conducting a wide range of business . . . . There may also be doubt in some cases whether the different ethos of clearing banking, merchant banking and broking can be mixed. This, in turn, raises the question of the extent to which the different facets of the conglomerates are managed independently and the type of control system within the administrative structure. The dilemma is that if the different areas of the conglomerate are integrated so as to secure the advantage for the consumer of a department store, then questions arise about whether such a diverse but integrated business can be effectively managed. On the other hand, if

different elements of the conglomerate are established as semi-autonomous companies, the question arises as to whether there is any advantage to the consumer of financial services (Llewelyn 1985, p. 24, p. 26).

Some rather vague evidence on the economies which have been realized in the joint provision of financial services is contained in the brief submitted by Traders Group Limited to the House of Commons Finance Committee.[4] Traders Group owns a trust company (Guarantee Trustco), insurance companies (Canadian General Insurance and others), a small loan company (Trans Canada Credit) and a land development company (Guaranty Properties). The brief cites the benefits to the group of transferring the accumulated experience of Traders Finance to the trust company. It also argues that its loan company can raise funds much more cheaply through its trust affiliate than as a consumer finance company. While the nature of the economies involved here is not entirely clear, this financial conglomerate has integrated its operation at least in part.

Additional evidence of the exploitation of firm level economies by a financial conglomerate comes from the brief submitted by the Investors Group, a subsidiary of Power Corporation, to the House Finance Committee.[5] The Investors Group is engaged in investment fund distribution and management. Investors Group "networks" with Great-West Life Assurance and Montreal Trust (also owned by Power Corporation) to provide investment funds, investment certificates, life and health insurance, tax sheltered products, pension funds services, and financial planning services through one organization. However, contact between Investors Group and Montreal Trust and Great West Life respectively is almost entirely at the distribution stage. The investment operations of the trust and life affiliates are autonomous.

There is, in sum, much to commend the view that the observed increase in intermediary cross-ownership reflects diversification out of declining or slowly growing markets rather than the exploitation of economies of scope. If this is the case, the cost of prohibiting cross-ownership is not economies of scope foregone as much as it is the limitation of the opportunities for internal (i.e., intrafirm) reallocation of resources and the elimination of a large number of potential entrants into financial intermediation.

As the proposals of the Minister of State for Finance (Canada, Department of Finance 1986, pp. 16-18) now stand, firms such as General Electric Credit Corporation or General Motors Acceptance Corporation would not be able to incorporate a new (federally chartered) trust, loan or insurance company or acquire one with capital exceeding $50 million. Existing trust companies which are linked to the real sector (such as Royal Trustco and Canada Trustco) will no longer be able to grow by acquisition. Whether the ability of these intermediaries to compete with the chartered banks on a broad scale (which, ironically, they will now be free to do) is significantly impaired as a consequence, is an open question.

While the advantages of cross-ownership are a matter of dispute, the same may be said of the disadvantages. Cross-ownership does increase the potential for conflict of interest. Conflicts of interest have existed, however, within each of the traditional four pillars and there is little to indicate that the additional conflicts to which an extension of powers would give rise are qualitatively different. The devices which have proven effective for remedying existing (within-pillar) conflicts should be equally effective in dealing with new ones.

Suppose this is not the case. Suppose there is no remedy for some conflicts of interest short of ownership specialization. Unlike self-dealing, the degree of specialization of an intermediary is observable at a modest cost. If consumers of a particular set of financial services attach a premium to being invulnerable to conflicts of interest and feel invulnerable only when dealing with a specialized institution, then that is what will emerge. It is not obvious that regulators can short-circuit this process of market experimentation.

With respect to real-financial cross-ownership, there is also widespread integration of real sector corporations into the provision of a broad range of financial services both internally and for others. The resulting efficiencies have been documented. Potential conflicts of interest have been avoided. Conflicts of interest posed by the movement of traditional intermediaries toward the real sector may be greater than the conflicts encountered (and apparently resolved) by real sector firms moving towards intermediation. The reasons why this may be the case are less than obvious. They certainly have not been provided by those advocating continued regulatory separation of the financial and real sectors.

4.0 CONCLUSIONS

Concentrated ownership has been associated with self-dealing and self-dealing has been associated with intermediary insolvency. The marginal contribution of concentrated ownership to the incidence of self-dealing and of self-dealing to insolvency has not been determined. In principle, self-dealing can be controlled by prohibiting certain non-arm's-length transactions, and by reducing maximum leverage ratios. Prohibitions are said to be too costly to enforce. Reductions in maximum leverage ratios are said to leave the institutions involved at a competitive disadvantage.

The dispersion of ownership removes some of the incentive for self-dealing. It also removes the institution involved from the market for corporate control. The magnitude of the efficiency gains foregone as a consequence is not known. With respect to chartered banks in the past, it may not have been very large. This may not be true of the current, less heavily regulated environment.

Cross-ownership has been associated with conflict of interest. This does not affect the solvency of financial intermediaries. It does place them in situations in which they may be forced or at least tempted to favour the interest of one client over another. Given some choice consumers will not patronize institutions which have, or by virtue of their characteristics, are likely to put the interests of others over their own. Where conflict of interest poses a serious problem which can be remedied only by specialized ownership, we would expect that form of institution to prevail. The question is then whether putative regulators can anticipate the result of this evolutionary process.

NOTES

1. See the papers by Khemani and by Marfels, Chapters 1 and 3 in this volume.

2. These are discussed in detail by Tom Courchene, Chapter 24 in this volume.

3. More generally, see the discussion in Eckbo, Chapter 7 in this volume.

4. See *Minutes of Proceedings and Evidence* of the House of Commons Standing Committee on Finance, Trade and Economic Affairs, Issue No. 59, September 11, 1985.

5. *Ibid.*, Issue No. 68, September 23, 1985.

REFERENCES

American Banking Association (1985) "Insurance Products Catch Banker's Eyes," *Banking Journal*, June, pp. 11-12.

Aspinwall, R. (1985) "Shifting Institutional Frontiers in Financial Markets in the United States" (Paper prepared at a Colloquium on Shifting Frontiers in Financial Markets, Cambridge, England, May).

Benston, G.J., G.A. Hanweck and D.B. Humphrey (1982) "Operating Costs in Commercial Banking," Federal Reserve Bank of Atlanta, *Monthly Review*, Vol. 67, November, pp. 7-21.

Benston, G.J., A.N. Berger, G.A. Hanweck and D.B. Humphrey (1983) "Economies of Scale and Scope in Banking" in *Proceedings of a Conference on Bank Structure and Competition* (Chicago: Federal Reserve Bank of Chicago, May), pp. 432-455.

Boyd, J. and S. Graham (1986) "Risk, Regulation and Bank Holding Company Expansion into Nonbanking," *Federal Reserve Bank of Minneapolis Quarterly Review*, Vol. 10, Spring, pp. 2-17.

Cadillac Fairview Corporation (1985) "Brief on the Green Paper: *The Regulation of Canadian Financial Institutions*" (Minutes of the House of Commons Committee on Finance, Trade and Economic Affairs, Vol. 68A, September 23).

Canada, House of Commons, Standing Committee on Finance, Trade and Economic Affairs (1985) *Report on the Regulation of Canadian Financial Institutions: Proposals for Discussion* (Ottawa: Minister of Supply and Services).

Canada, Department of Finance (1986) *New Directions for the Financial Sector* (Ottawa: Department of Finance, December 18).

Cooper, K. and D. Fraser (1984) *Banking Deregulation and the New Competition in Financial Services* (Cambridge: Ballinger).

Crabbe, M. (1986) "Inside the New In-House Banks," *Euromoney*, February, pp. 24-41.

Crum, W. (1986) "Banking in Insurance: A Guide to Chaos," *The Banker's Magazine*, January/February, pp. 51-58.

Daly, M.J., P.S. Rao and R. Geehan (1985) "Productivity, Scale Economies and Technical Progress in the Canadian Life Insurance Industry," *International Journal of Industrial Organization*, Vol. 3, pp. 345-361.

Demsetz, H. (1986) "Corporate Control, Insider Trading, and Rates of Return," *American Economic Review*, Vol. 76, May, pp. 313-316.

Demsetz, H. and Kenneth Lehn (1985) "The Structure of Corporate Ownership: Causes and Consequences," *Journal of Political Economy*, Vol. 93, December, pp. 1155-66.

Eckbo, B.E. (1986) "Mergers and the Market for Corporate Control: The Canadian Evidence," *Canadian Journal of Economics*, Vol. 19, May, pp. 236-260.

Economic Council of Canada (1976) *Efficiency and Regulation, A Study of Deposit Institutions* (Ottawa: Ministry of Supply and Services Canada).

Economic Council of Canada (1986) *Competition and Solvency: A Framework for Financial Regulation* (Ottawa: Ministry of Supply and Services Canada).

Freedman, C. (1985) "Recent Developments in the Structure and Regulation of the Canadian Financial System" (Paper presented to a Colloquium on Shifting Frontiers in Financial Markets, Cambridge, England, May).

Galt, V. (1987) "Royal Trustco to Limit Securities Services," *Globe and Mail Report on Business*, March 6, p. B1.

Gilbert, R.A. (1984) "Bank Market Structure and Competition," *Journal of Money, Credit and Banking*, Vol. 16, November, pp. 617-645.

Gilligan, T., M. Smirlock and W. Marshall (1984) "Scale and Scope Economies in the Multi-Product Banking Firm," *Journal of Monetary Economics*, Vol. 13, pp. 393-405.

Goodman and Carr (1985) "Proposals to the Ontario Task Force on Financial Institutions: Self Dealing and Conflicts of Interest" (Toronto: Goodman and Carr, mimeo).

Grossman, S. and O. Hart (1980) "Takeover Bids, the Free Rider Problem and the Theory of the Corporation," *Bell Journal of Monetary Economics*, Spring, pp. 42-64.

Halderness, C.G. and D.P. Sheehan (1985) "Raiders or Saviours: The Evidence on Six Controversial Investors," *Journal of Financial Economics*, Vol. 14, December, pp. 555-580.

Hancock, D. (1985) "The Financial Firm: Production with Monetary and Non-monetary Goods," *Journal of Political Economy*, Vol. 93, September/October, pp. 859-880.

Jensen, M.C. and W.H. Meckling (1976) "The Market for Corporate Control: The Scientific Evidence," *Journal of Financial Economics*, Vol. 11, pp. 5-50.

Jensen, M.C. and R.S. Ruback (1983) "The Market for Corporate Control: The Scientific Evidence," *Journal of Financial Economics*, Vol. 11, pp. 5-50.

Kane, E.J. (1984) "Technological and Regulatory Forces in the Developing Fusion of Financial Services Competition," *Journal of Finance*, Vol. 39, July, pp. 759-772.

Kellner, S. and F. Mathewson (1983) "Entry, Size Distribution, Scale and Scope Economies in the Life Insurance Industry," *Journal of Business*, Vol. 56, February, pp. 25-44.

Lewellen, W., C. Loderer and A. Rosenfeld (1985) "Merger Decisions and Executive Stock Ownership in Acquiring Firms," *Journal of Accounting and Economics*, Vol. 7, pp. 209-231.

Llewelyn, D.T. (1985) "Evolution of the Financial System" (Paper presented at a Colloquium on Shifting Frontiers in Financial Markets, Cambridge, England, May).

MacDonald, R. (1985) "Bankers and Insurers: Logical Allies," *Banker's Magazine*, January/February, pp. 11-16.

Mittelstaedt, M. (1987) "U.S. banks eager to move into forbidden areas," *Globe and Mail*, February 4, p. B11.

Murray, J.D. and R.W. White (1983) "Economies of Scale and Economies of Scope in Multi-Product Financial Institutions: A Study of British Columbia Credit Unions," *Journal of Finance*, Vol. 38, p. 887.

Nash, N.C. (1986) "U.S. Authorities are at Odds Over Sears Suit," *Globe and Mail*, May 27, p. B12.

Ontario Task Force on Financial Institutions (1985) *Final Report* (Toronto, Ontario Government Printer).

Revell, J.R.S. (1985) "Implications of Information Technology for Financial Institutions" (Paper presented at a Colloquium on Shifting Frontiers in Financial Markets, Cambridge, England, May).

Rosenblum, H. and D. Siegel (1983) "Competition in Financial Services: The Impact of Non-Bank Entry" in *Proceedings of a Conference on Bank*

Structure and Competition (Chicago: Federal Reserve Bank of Chicago).

Rybczynski, T.M. (1985) "Shifting Financial Frontiers: Implications for Financial Institutions" (Paper presented to a Colloquium on Shifting Frontiers in Financial Markets, Cambridge, England, May).

Scherer, F.M. (1980) *Industrial Market Structure and Economic Performance* (New York: Rand McNally).

United States (1985) *Economic Report of the President* (Washington: U.S. Government Printing Office).

Chapter 15

Trends in the Financial Sector

Hal Jackman
Chairman of the Board
National Victoria and Grey Trustco Limited

1.0 CONCENTRATION AMONG FINANCIAL INSTITUTIONS

I want to begin by providing data that puts the concentration among financial institutions in Canada into perspective. Table 1 is taken from the *Financial Post 500* which lists the 500 largest industrial companies and the 100 largest financial institutions. I have broken down the financial institutions into five categories based on their ownership. The first category, Canadian-owned and widely held, includes 12 of the top 100 financial enterprises. These 12 have $413 billion in assets, about 67 per cent of all the assets in the Canadian financial system, and obviously include the six large chartered banks. There are 44 foreign controlled financial institutions, and this category includes all the Schedule "B" banks. Then there are a number of government-owned financial institutions, and a number of cooperatives and credit unions. The last category consists of 18 Canadian-owned, closely held companies. By closely held I mean where there is a significant, identifiable Canadian shareholder interest. These 18 institutions have only 7.8 per cent of the assets in the system. Now to put things in perspective, those 18 institutions out of 100, with 7.8 per cent of the assets in the system, are in total smaller than the smallest of our five major Canadian chartered banks. I believe these data put the issue in perspective.

2.0 POWER OF THE LARGE BANKS

It is apparent, therefore, that the financial intermediary landscape in Canada is very much influenced by the power and size of our large banks. Hence the smaller institutions must generally operate around the fringe of the banks' predominant position and must work very hard to remain competitive. Although the concentration of power in the hands of a few banks, as opposed to the U.S. model of a great number of small regional banks, is now an accepted reality, Canadians have paid a steep price in accepting such a high degree of concentration. Large banks have tended to mean large loans to a few large borrowers, most of whom are represented on the boards of the banks concerned. This fact has undoubtedly contributed to the concentration of corporate power in the non-financial sector in this country.

Similarly, the feeling that regional interests have not been served by the large banks, with their head offices in Montreal and Toronto, has led to the growth of the credit union and cooperative movement which is much stronger in this country than in the United States. Provincial governments, which tend to be more conscious of provincial and regional needs, have encouraged the growth of trust and loan companies where it was perceived that the decision making would be closer to the region involved. This has encouraged the proliferation of trust and loan companies, most of whom are chartered by the provinces (see Economic Council of Canada 1986; 1987).

Therefore, any discussion of the concentration of power in the financial services industry must be related to the question of being able to form viable, competitive entities which will be able to take on the banks on their own turf. I believe that combinations of non-bank financial institutions, which have the effect of increasing competition, should be encouraged.

Table 1
100 Largest Financial Institutions (December 31, 1985)

	No. of Institutions		Amount of Assets ($ billions)	
- Cdn owned and widely held	12	(12%)	413.0	(67.4%)
- Foreign controlled	44	(44%)	62.9	(10.3%)
- Government Owned (Federal and Provincial)	8	(8%)	55.5	(9.1%)
- Co-operatives and Credit Unions	18	(18%)	33.5	(5.5%)
- Canadian Owned (with an identifiable significant shareholder interest)	18	(18%)	48.0	(7.8%)
	100	(100%)	612.9	(100.0%)

Source: *Financial Post 500* (Summer, 1986).

3.0 HOCKIN'S PAPER

Now I want to comment on the recent direction of the federal government as evidenced by the White Paper that was released by Tom Hockin, the Minister of State for Finance (1986a). That paper rejects the four pillar concept and encourages total integration of the financial services sector through allowing cross-ownership, networking, and a relatively full extension of powers within each pillar. Dr. Hockin's paper represents a major departure not only from the Green Paper,[1] but from almost every other report that has been written on this subject.[2]

The banks, which were excluded from the Green Paper, are being given virtually unlimited powers to move into the more profitable aspects of the trust companies and will have the ability to own security dealers outright. In return the trust and insurance companies are being given the power to make commercial and personal loans, in spite of the fact that they did not ask for such all-embracing powers in the first place. Similarly, the three largest trust companies in Canada – the Royal Trust, the Canada Trust, and the National Trust – have all indicated that they do not wish to go into the securities business. They feel that this would be a conflict with their intermediary and other fiduciary operations.

Although everybody here seems to have been given expanded powers, the obvious reality of the situation is that not everybody will be able to expand. As one sector gains advantage, someone must correspondingly lose advantage – a reality which at the moment may have escaped some of the players, if not the government itself. The general view, however, is that the banks are the big winners, because of their size, while non-bank financial institutions will be put at a competitive disadvantage.

The second significant direction in the government's new White Paper is the apparent acquiescence of the federal government in the internationalization and potential disappearance of Canadian-owned investment dealers. This was most surprising as it is contrary to the advice of the Dey[3] and Dupre[4] reports in Ontario, and contrary to the Ontario Government's original position which would have limited outside ownership to 30 per cent.

The reasons given in the White Paper for the integration of investment dealers into our banking system are far from convincing. Dr. Hockin (1986b, p. 1) says: "global forces have challenged existing legislation designed for an earlier and less dynamic era," and "advances in communication technology [that] have facilitated international capital flows abroad and the demand for one-stop financial shopping at home." Although this type of language is reminiscent, perhaps, of the last Trilon prospectus,[5] it hardly represents cogent reasons for the destruction of one of Canada's foremost pillars.

There is, however, a much more compelling yet unstated reason why the banks had to be given such additional powers. In spite of the minister's statement to the contrary, the worldwide financial system, and Canada's banking system in particular, is not as fundamentally sound as the government would like, as the quality of credit risks continues to deteriorate.

3.1. Bank Failures

In the last two and a half years, six Canadian banks have closed their doors.[6] There are only six banks of any size in this country remaining. A 500 per cent batting average is not very good for the Canadian government when it comes to bank regulation. As far as the six remaining banks are concerned, they had actual loan losses of a staggering $3.4 billion in the last fiscal year. Relative to their size, the banks' loss ratio is almost 20 times higher than that of the trust industry. Similarly, non-performing loans ballooned to $9.6 billion, an increase of 29 per cent. Furthermore, the market value of our banks' $23 billion in sovereign loans to developing countries continued to deteriorate, prompting the government to ask for an additional $2 billion in reserves by 1989.

The banks have reacted to their adversity by increasing spreads on domestic business. However, weak balance sheets and increased spreads do not augur well for competition. Many of our banks' largest customers are more creditworthy than the banks themselves and therefore pay lower rates of interest on the commercial paper market than indirectly through a bank. Thus the phenomenal growth of the lucrative commercial paper market, which until recently had been the preserve of the investment dealers.[7] The banks, faced with the loss of their major corporate accounts, really have no other alternative but to seek entry into the more lucrative securities business in order to restore profitability and market share.

3.2. Banks as Securities Dealers?

The suggestion that banks and other commercial lenders should be able to underwrite corporate securities, particularly when the securities dealer will be 100 per cent owned by the commercial bank, will undoubtedly give the government its most serious problem. This is probably the greatest danger inherent in the Government's new White Paper. Although one of the policy objectives was to remove conflicts of interest, there can be no greater potential conflict than that of an investment banker and a commercial banker. It is the conflict between the commercial lender who has the power to securitize his bad loans and push them on to an unsuspecting public that has not been addressed. Recognition of this potential conflict was the rationale behind the *Glass-Steagall Act* passed in 1934 by the U.S. Congress. One can argue that the *Glass-Steagall Act* was an overreaction to the ill-timed and ill-conceived underwritings in the 1920s and that for most of the intervening 50 years such constraints on the financial system were unnecessary. This may have been so in the past. But what of 1987 and beyond? Can we honestly say that the excesses of 1929 are behind us and such constraints are unnecessary?[8]

In recent years we have witnessed a true monetary explosion, a financial system awash with liquidity, which has caused an exponential growth in financial assets and has far outstripped the creation of real productive assets. In the United States the stock of financial assets has quadrupled to over six trillion dollars in the last 10 years, with no corresponding growth in real earning power to support it.

Furthermore, we have seen a steady deterioration in the debt-to-equity ratio of our corporate balance sheets. In Canada, corporate sector indebtedness has risen from $64 billion to $226 billion in the past 10 years. Earnings coverage of interest is now only 2.7 times, down from 7 times in 1976. In Canada, $8.5 billion of common equity has been taken out of the stock market as a result of takeovers since January 1985. Most of this equity has been replaced by debt, and none of this could have been financed in the absence of excessive credit provided by the central bank and the banking system.

One of the reasons suggested by the Minister of State for Finance for the integration of Canada's investment dealers into the banking system is to help provide the additional capital to meet international competition in world markets (Hockin 1986b, p. 2). But while Canada's investment dealers increase their capital, the same can be said for every other country. How will this excess capital be employed? In the era of the "bought deal," the "leveraged buyout," the junk bond flotations, where investment dealers' up-front fees and markups frequently exceed the amount of shareholders' equity in the issuer; one can expect that the dealers themselves will create financing out of air, simply in order to get the fees. This, of course, is what happened in the 1920s with the stock pools, the public utility holding companies and the highly geared investment trusts, almost all of which have long since disappeared. But are they any different from the arbitrage funds, the leveraged buyouts, and some of the takeovers that are taking place today?

One can argue that in a free market economy, it will in due course become self-correcting, as unsound borrowers and banks go to the wall. But in the meantime we seem to be developing a financial system, now unwittingly abetted by the Canadian government, which will facilitate the corporate raiders and may pose a threat not only to long-term investment and productive assets, but to the financial system as a whole. If legislation like the *Glass-Steagall Act* was ever relevant, then surely now should be the time for the government to reinforce such legislation. The Canadian government, however, under pressure from the banks, has chosen to move in the opposite direction.

4.0 POLICIES TO SUSTAIN THE LARGE BANKS

Thus the odyssey of the regulation of our financial institutions is entering a new phase. It started with the 1967 *Bank Act* when the four pillar concept was breached, with the banks being given power to make mortgages and to effectively take over the personal loan companies. Trust and insurance companies were promised compensating additional powers in the 1982 draft amendments of the federal *Trust Companies Act*, but those were withdrawn. We were promised them again in the 1985 Green Paper, but that was also withdrawn. However, the need of the banks to gain even further powers, to restore their profitability and maintain their market share, has led the government to break its promise to non-bank financial institutions not to amend the *Bank Act* until compensatory powers to the other pillars were given. Why, when a clear promise was given, were the powers of the banks once again broadened at the expense of the smaller institutions? The answer clearly must lie in the indisputable fact that the Canadian banks are so large, so all-encompassing; and their health and prosperity so vital to the continued well-being of Canada; that Government policy must be to maintain their prosperity even at the expense of discouraging competition and seeing the disappearance of our smaller institutions. Dr. Hockin said it all in his White Paper when he said that one of his guiding principles was: "to protect the ability of Canadian financial institutions to be world-class participants by assuring that non-residents' access to Canada's domestic market reflects Canadian firms' access to markets abroad." This is simply another way of saying that in order to protect the position of our few large banks, we must be prepared to sacrifice Canadian ownership of our smaller institutions without regard to the possible adverse effects on consumer choice.

Although theoretically trust and other non-bank institutions are being given comparable powers, the government has given clear signals that big is beautiful, as witness the takeover of the last two failed banks, the Bank of British Columbia and the Continental Bank, by large foreign banking concerns, rather than canvassing the Canadian alternatives that were available. This is clearly a damning admission by a Government that it cannot regulate a small Canadian bank as well as a foreign government like Hong Kong can.[9] Thus the government has given out a clear signal that it may not be capable of managing its own system, its own Canadian banking institutions, as well as foreigners can.

5.0 THE FUTURE

I predict that if Dr. Hockin's paper is allowed to stand, the destruction of the four pillars and the consequent removal of protection for the small players in their respective market niches, will lead to increased pressures by the domestically owned non-bank institutions on the federal government. They will request permission to be taken over by the large banks and the foreign conglomerates, for much the same reasons that motivated our investment dealers to acquiesce in their own destruction. If there is to be a virtually unlimited ability of foreign companies to take over investment dealers and the few remaining Schedule "A" banks, it stands to reason that the remnants of the shareholder-owned intermediary system will also want the "benefits" of internationalization that are being given to the banks and the brokers. The small, regionally based trust companies will, in the minds of the federal government, simply become regulatory nuisances and will in all probability be absorbed into the banking system at some future revision of the *Bank Act*.

It is perhaps a shame that Canada does not seem to be able to develop smaller regionally based financial institutions that can be more responsive to local needs, and that at the federal level there is not a more serious attempt to encourage the competition that such institutions might provide. The White Paper of December 18, 1986 is perhaps the simple admission of the reality that the banks have grown so large and powerful that the trend cannot be reversed, and like the partners of the investment firms, the remnants of the two remaining pillars will have little choice but to surrender to the inevitable and to lie back and enjoy it.

NOTES

1. Minister of State for Finance (1985).

2. See, for example, Economic Council of Canada (1987), House of Commons Standing Committee on Finance, Trade and Economic Affairs (1985); Ontario Task Force on Financial Institutions (1985); and the paper by Tom Courchene, Chapter 24 in this volume.

3. Ontario Securities Commission (1985).

4. Ontario Task Force on Financial Institutions (1985).

5. Trilon Financial is controlled by Edward and Peter Bronfman through Brascan Holdings. Trilon owns 55 per cent of Lonvest which owns 100 per cent of Wellington Insurance, 98 per cent of London Life Insurance, 50 per cent of Royal Trustco and 50 per cent of Royal LePage. See *Financial Post 500*, Summer 1986, p. 200.

6. See Economic Council of Canada (1986).

7. See Economic Council of Canada (1987).

8. See, for example, "Jitters! Unsettling Economic Signs Have Americans on Edge," *Business Week*, May 11, 1987, pp. 40-48.

9. The Hong Kong Bank of Canada acquired the Bank of British Columbia for $63.5 million in late 1986. See "A Savior for a Troubled B.C. Bank," *Maclean's*, December 8, 1986, p. 44.

REFERENCES

Economic Council of Canada (1986) *Competition and Solvency: A Framework for Financial Regulation* (Ottawa: Ministry of Supply and Services).

Economic Council of Canada (1987) *A Framework for Financial Regulation* (Ottawa: Ministry of Supply and Services).

Hockin, Tom (1986a) *New Directions for Financial Institutions* (Ottawa: Department of Finance, December 18).

_____ (1986b) "Remarks on the Tabling of the Policy Paper," in *New Directions for Financial Institutions* (Ottawa: Department of Finance, December 18, press release).

House of Commons Standing Committee on Finance, Trade and Economic Affairs (1985) *Canadian Financial Institutions* (Ottawa: Ministry of Supply and Services).

Minister of State for Finance (1985) *The Regulation of Canadian Financial Institutions: Proposals for Discussion* (Ottawa: Ministry of Supply and Services, April).

Ontario Securities Commission (1985) *A Regulatory Framework for Entry and Ownership of the Ontario Securities Industry* (Toronto: Ontario Securities Commission).

Ontario Task Force on Financial Institutions (1985) *Final Report* (Toronto: Ontario Government Printer, December).

Chapter 16

Corporate Concentration and Changes in the Regulation of Financial Institutions

Jacques Parizeau
Professor titulaire
Ecole des hautes etudes commerciales
Montreal

1.0 INTRODUCTION

I begin by making a very simple sort of distinction between two types of concentration. While this distinction sometimes gets blurred, to my mind it is a very fundamental one. On the one hand, we have attained in Canada a very high degree of concentration of assets in a small number of hands.[1] It is in fact remarkable with what can be seen in other countries, and I think that we should underline here the remarkable work done on this subject by Diane Francis (1986). That kind of concentration of assets has brought about a few groups that now find the Canadian "pond," a bit small for them and therefore tend to go to the United States.[2] This explains, to a considerable extent, the fact that direct Canadian investment in the United States now is so much larger than the reverse flow.

On the other hand, there is also a high degree of another kind of concentration in Canada – the concentration of specific economic activities among a small number of firms, and that is very different. The typical example, of course, has to do with the banks and, in comparison to other countries, here again a relatively high degree of concentration has taken place in Canada.

However, when we focus on the concentration of specific economic activities among firms we have to realize that we're still very small fish in relation to others. A recent issue of *Euromoney* provided the first estimate of the market values of the 100 largest banks in the world as of December 31st, 1986.[3] Nine out of the 10 largest banks are Japanese. Except for American Express, the largest U.S. bank is ranked 26th while the largest Canadian bank is ranked 54th. All of the Japanese banks on that list of the hundred have a total market value of $433 billion. The U.S. comes second at $75 billion, the Swiss at $36 billion and Canadian banks are way down the line at $11 billion. It is remarkable that a Japanese banker stated to *Euromoney*: "If only money counted, we'd buy everything."

2.0 LESSONS FROM THE QUEBEC EXPERIENCE

In light of these data, I think we have three questions to ask ourselves: How do we structure the financial industry to allow further concentration of activity? How do we try to induce greater competition? At the same time, how do we avoid concentrating undue power in the hands of a few shareholders? Each of these objectives is essential. In trying to achieve all three objectives, the Quebec experience of the last few years is illuminating – in part because of the problems it has not raised.

The starting point here is the following. The framework of the Quebec financial system was, for all practical purposes, the same as that of Canada for a very long time. The francophone community, as is well known, didn't participate very much in that framework until recently. Then, three changes occurred that transformed the financial system in Quebec. One was the growth of the cooperative movement, the "Mouvement Desjardins." The second was the growth of the National Bank of Canada through a long process of mergers. The third was the creation and growth of the Caisse de Depot.[4] It is a coincidence, but an interesting one, that each of these three enterprises now has assets in the $30 billion range.

For these three enterprises, the development of an indigenous structure was the obvious objective to attain. This could be done within the fairly new context of deregulation and based more specifically on the idea of the financial supermarket. The Province of Quebec made a number of changes in legislation to try to restructure what was going on beyond the three enterprises. The general idea was to get a few large, very diversified financial institutions into competition with each other. This was to be done by starting from a specific core of services, but rapidly overlapping into the activities of the others. This, of course, implied that acquisitions and mergers would be facilitated.

The regulatory reform operation was conducted in steps, and for a long time nobody really paid any attention to what was going on. For instance, in 1981 the principle was accepted that one shareholder could purchase the whole capital stock of a stockbroker.[5] This was years before the 10 per cent rule of the Toronto Stock Exchange was lifted. Secondly, downstream holdings were permitted for mutual life insurance companies under Quebec jurisdiction. Thirdly, Bill 75 was enacted which allowed insurance companies to overlap in the operations of a number of other financial institutions, trust companies for instance. At the same time that such actions were taken, the powers of the Superintendent of Financial Institutions were considerably widened and more extensive discretionary powers were given to him.

The first results of the changes in Quebec are already very noticeable. The Laurentian Group in Quebec, in Canada, and now in the United States, is becoming a very large financial group. Indeed, its rate of development has been exceedingly rapid. The recent merger of two mutual life insurance companies,[6] l'Alliance and l'Industrielle, who now also control a fairly large part of the capital stock of the Trust General du Canada, is also another major institution that is in the offing. Others, smaller than these two, have also evolved.

I note that, for the last two years, the movement on the part of the Quebec government has stopped. There is still a great deal to be done; for instance, to allow trust companies to overlap in other financial activities. Changes should be brought to the charter of the Mouvement Desjardins so as to allow the further diversification of its operations.

However, what the Quebec proposals system *has not* resolved is fundamental. For instance, very little emphasis has been put on what to do with closely held corporations simply because the problem did not arise. Large insurance companies under Quebec charter are mutual companies and therefore you just do not ask yourself whether it is closely held or not or what is going to happen to the shareholders, as the policy holders are the shareholders. The Mouvement Desjardins obviously is a cooperative so the problem does not arise there either. The Caisse de Depot does not raise the problem as it is owned by the Government of Quebec. In other words, the problem of a closely held corporation has not been raised yet in these changes in Quebec's regulation of financial institutions. The role of non-financial interests within financial institutions was not really a major issue except possibly with respect to the purchase of stockbrokers. With respect to non-resident control, the Quebec government did not change the existing rules in any way. Therefore, in spite of the fact that the changes made in Quebec over the last five or six years have not dealt with the major issues cited above, what was done in Quebec acted as a detonator both with respect to Toronto and Ottawa. In a way, a number of the rapid changes that we have seen in the last few years at the federal level and in Ontario are an answer to what Quebec started. It was obvious that that development would be inevitable and it was clearly understood in Quebec when the experiments were launched that sooner or later, but rather sooner than later, Ottawa would have to move in a similar fashion.

From Ottawa we have seen all kinds of proposals – the Green Paper,[7] the House of Commons Finance Committee report,[8] the Senate report,[9] and the recent White Paper.[10] It has not always been easy to separate the main issues that changes in Quebec have not solved, and that have to be solved now; from all kinds of "side shows." Of course, the bankruptcy of the Commercial Bank and the Northland Bank did not help in getting the real fundamental issues out of the hat.[11]

3.0 THE BLENKARN COMMITTEE PROPOSAL

Out of all the proposals that have come out of the various federal reports, I wish to comment on one proposal that seems to be particularly interesting. To my mind it would solve several of the problems we have at the present time. It is the so-called Blenkarn proposal.[12] Mr. Blenkarn chaired the

House of Commons Committee on Finance, Trade and Economic Affairs. Recommendation #50 of the Committee was as follows:

> That domestic ownership limits for all Canadian incorporated financial institutions and holding companies controlling affiliated financial institutions be established on the basis of domestic size as follows:
>
> | *Domestic Asset Size* | | *Ownership Limits* |
> | --- | --- | --- |
> | under $10 billion | - | 100% |
> | $10-$20 billion | - | 75% |
> | $20-$30 billion | - | 50% |
> | $30-$40 billion | - | 25% |
> | over $40 billion | - | 10% |

Past $40 billion in assets the maximum equity interest for any individual would be 10 per cent, exactly the rule applicable to Schedule "A" chartered banks in Canada. Some adjustment could be made with respect to non-financial interests although they are not to my mind necessary to the application of this formula.[13]

The beauty of it is that it can be set in such a way that it applies to residents in the same way as it applies to non-residents. Whether residents or non-residents; a group of shareholders or one corporation, can get involved in just about any kind of financial venture in Canada, and develop it as it sees fit under government regulation. However, these shareholders or that shareholder, knows very well that the more successful the business venture is (i.e., the larger its assets), the more likely that there will come a time where divestment will be necessary and other shareholders will have to be brought in to the picture. By the time the financial conglomerate reaches a certain size ($40 billion in assets), then each individual shareholder or group of shareholders will have to drop to 10 per cent. Therefore, control either by residents or by non-residents will be considerably reduced insofar as one can imagine that these are very large institutions. No single group of interests could have undue influence on the way these very large institutions would function.

Such a formula could be very useful in our present negotiations with the United States. Quite obviously the Americans are pressing us for free trade in services, and therefore in financial services. They are also trying to clarify the issue of national treatment. In this context we would find the Blenkarn formula more useful than the latest recommendations of the White Paper (Hockin 1986). The White Paper of December 18, 1986 suggests that control over foreign interests should not be changed or modified pending the present commercial negotiations. Of course, that cryptic sentence could mean anything. It could even mean the eventual application of the Blenkarn proposal.

4.0 CONCLUSIONS

The Blenkarn proposal and the reforms in Quebec now being widened throughout Canada drive me toward the following conclusions. First, competition in the global village of financial services can undoubtedly be enhanced. However, increased competition needs to be accompanied by a concentration of various financial activities within given firms. In other words, competition will probably be greater on the basis of competition between very large institutions, rather than between a few large institutions and a very large number of small ones. Competition and concentration of activities are not mutually exclusive, on the contrary. Hence, concentration of firms in the Canadian financial system should proceed. Second, we should not be wary of either building or witnessing the arrival in Canada of very large financial institutions. The market will operate better; and competition will be all the more acute; where a large number of very large financial institutions are present.

Thirdly, there are obviously ways to avoid the concentration of economic power in too few hands. In other words, just because we want concentration of activities and of firms to take place, we need not conclude that concentration of economic power in the hands of a small band of shareholders is inevitable.

That is where the Blenkarn proposal is particularly interesting. By all means, we should proceed to try to build large financial institutions that cover a wide range of financial activities. However, concentration of economic power among a few shareholders can largely be avoided. At least it can be reduced relative to the sort of trend that we have been witnessing until now. Yet the Canadian government does not have a great deal of time to deal with these problems. Within a few months we will know if it can reconcile deregulation of financial institutions on the one hand, and a more manageable system of concentration of economic power on the other. Because of the particular interest expressed at Punta del Este, the United States wants to have some kind of agreement with Canada with respect to freedom of access and national treatment in the service industries (particularly financial industries), and the Canadian government will have to answer forthwith. It is obvious that some of these answers have to be on the table by the end of the summer of 1987.

It's an interesting challenge. I think it will be much easier to meet if, in the meantime, we avoid being sidetracked by such an issue as whether provinces or the federal government should be responsible for the securities industry. We should also focus on what we will say to the U.S. in response to their proposals regarding the international deregulation of ownership of, and access to, financial institutions.

NOTES

1. See the data in the papers by Khemani, Marfels and Jackman, Chapters 1, 3, and 15 in this volume.

2. This was one of the reasons given by Robert Campeau for his purchase of Allied Stores for $4.9 billion in the fall of 1986. See Arthur Johnson, "The Best Revenge," *Report on Business Magazine*, March 1987, pp. 22-31. See also "Campeau's cash squeeze," *Maclean's*, March 2, 1987, p. 26.

3. See *Euromoney*, February 1987.

4. See, for example, Olive (1982), Pesando (1984).

5. It was not until 1983 that the Quebec Securities Commission removed the ownership restrictions on provincially-registered securities dealers.

6. See "Life insurers planning merger," *Globe and Mail*, July 3, 1986, p. B4. The new company, Industrial-Alliance Life Insurance Co., will be, based on 1985 statistics, the largest Quebec-based life insurer, 20 per cent larger than any of its competitors with $25 billion in insurance in force with revenues of $604 million in 1985.

7. Minister of State for Finance (1985).

8. House of Commons Standing Committee on Finance, Trade and Economic Affairs (1985).

9. Standing Senate Committee on Banking, Trade and Commerce (1986).

10. Hockin (1986).

11. See Estey (1986).

12. House of Commons Standing Committee on Finance, Trade & Economic Affairs (1985).

13. Note that in its June 18, 1986 report to the House of Commons, the Finance Committee recommended that all "non- financial institutions be prohibited from owning directly, indirectly or beneficially more than 30 per cent of a financial affiliate." The NDP member wanted the limit set at 10 per cent.

REFERENCES

Estey, Hon. Willard Z. (1986) *Report of the Inquiry into the Collapse of the CCB and Northland Bank* (Ottawa: Minister of Supply and Services, August).

Francis, Diane (1986) *Controlling Interest: Who Owns Canada?* (Toronto: Macmillan).

Hockin, Tom (1986) *New Directions for Financial Institutions* (Ottawa: Minister of Finance, December 18).

House of Commons Standing Committee on Finance, Trade and Economic Affairs (1985) *Canadian Financial Institutions* (Ottawa: Minister of Supply and Services, November).

Olive, David (1982) "Caisse Unpopulaire," *Canadian Business*, May, pp. 94-101.

Pesando, James E. (1984) "An Economic Analysis of Government Investment Corporations with Attention to the Caisse de Depot de Placement du Quebec and the Alberta Heritage Fund" (Paper presented to the Economic Council of Canada's Conference on Government Enterprises, Toronto, November, mimeo).

Standing Senate Committee on Banking, Trade and Commerce (1986) *Towards a More Competitive Financial Environment* (Ottawa: Minister of Supply and Services).

Corporate Power and Influence

Chapter 17

Corporate Power and Political Influence

W.T. Stanbury*
UPS Foundation Professor of Regulation & Competition Policy
Faculty of Commerce & Business Administration
University of British Columbia

> Power fascinates us all because it sets in train the most compelling of human emotions, whether the witness to its exercise abhors it, hungers after it, shrinks from its toils, suffers its cruelties, or enjoys its pleasures. The Indians have a word for this sensation: darshan – that glow of warmth and light one gets from the propinquity of the powerful (Newman 1979, p. 462).

1.0 INTRODUCTION
1.1 Purpose and Organization of the Paper
This paper explores the relationship between corporate concentration and political influence in Canada. Canadians have long appreciated that concentration in individual industries/markets is high, largely due to the small size of the economy. However, the recent merger boom (79 takeovers in 1986 and 1987 in which the value of the transaction exceeded $100 million[1]) has prompted a re-examination of the high level of aggregate concentration in Canada[2] and its wider consequences.

   Discussions of the political and economic power of large corporations[3] have also been stimulated by a series of other developments over the past few years: the takeover of major financial by industrial enterprises (e.g., Imasco's takeover of Genstar Inc. in order to obtain Canada Trustco, the nation's largest trust company); the failure of two relatively new chartered banks and more than a dozen smaller financial institutions (Estey 1986; Best and Shortell 1985; Economic Council 1986a); the proposed bailout of Dome Petroleum by the federal government in order to prevent severe difficulties for several of the largest banks (Foster 1985); political incidents which

* I am indebted to Karyn MacCrimmon for efficient research assistance and Paulie McLeod for skillful word processing services and to several colleagues for helpful comments.

resulted in a special parliamentary committee to recommend legislation to register lobbyists (Cooper 1987); several different scandals in which allegations of political influence, bribes, and conflict of interest were made with respect to MPs, cabinet ministers and some firms.[4]

This paper tries to answer a number of important questions that relate to the political rather than the economic consequences of corporate concentration. Has aggregate concentration increased to the point where the largest corporations (or business interests in general) have an "undue" and undesirable amount of influence on the formation of public policy in Canada? Is the political influence of the largest corporations sufficient to undermine the pluralist ideal of a democratic society? Even if the largest corporations do have a great deal of influence in the political process, does that influence constitute a threat to basic democratic values?

After drawing some distinctions between economic and political power, the analytic framework of the paper is presented. Six aspects of the political power of large corporations are explored: the objectives of such power, the concerns regarding large corporations' ability to influence politics and policy making, the sources of corporate political influence, the means by which it is exercised, the various manifestations of the political influence of large corporations, and the constraints on the exercise of political power by large enterprise. Limitations of space preclude a detailed discussion of each of these aspects. The paper focuses more intensively on the concerns about the political power of mega corporations in Section 2, the sources of their political power in Section 3, the manifestations of such political power in Section 4, and the limitations or constraints on the political power of large corporations in Section 5. Some conclusions are offered in Section 6 in respect to Canadian values and the concentration of power.

1.2 Distinguishing Economic and Political Power

Power is a universal attribute of all societies and it is a function of the general need for social order (Porter 1965). While there are many types of power, in general terms, power is the ability of individuals or organizations to intentionally alter the behaviour of others, or to alter some aspect of the physical universe. Power is the capacity to exert successfully one's will upon others so as to change their attitudes, values, beliefs, but most importantly, their behaviour, involuntarily if necessary.[5]

It is important to try to distinguish economic from political power, although the latter is often based on the former.

Economic Power: Economic power is the ability to command scarce economic resources on a large scale relative to others so that the decision maker is able to exercise considerable discretion. If there is absolutely no discretion, even when the scale of resources is large, the manager/owner has little power. He (or she) is, in the extreme, merely a cipher in transmitting coercive market signals to the levers of the firm.

Economic power also consists of having sufficient wealth to be able to *not* have to maximize profits (shareholders' wealth). If a hired manager has a net worth of several million dollars or an owner's worth is tens to hundreds of millions of dollars and this wealth is largely independent of the performance of a firm or even a group of firms under his control, his mind is free to contemplate and to pursue objectives *other* than profits or shareholders' wealth. In fact, real economic power is the ability to *sacrifice* accumulated or anticipated profits in order to achieve some other objective such as status, prestige or other manifestations of ego, such as crushing a rival, shaping public policy in light of one's personal values, or building various types of corporate monuments.[6]

The importance of goals other than profit is reinforced by Canadian society's ambivalence about the relentless pursuit of pecuniary gain.

> Most religions and most philosophies deprecate, to say the least of it, a way of life mainly influenced by considerations of personal money profit. On the other hand, most men today reject ascetic notions and do not doubt the real advantages of wealth. Moreover, it seems obvious to them that one cannot do without the money-motive, and that, apart from certain admitted abuses, it does its job well. In the result the average man averts his attention from the problem, and has no clear idea what he really thinks and feels about the whole confounded matter (J.M. Keynes quoted in Stanbury 1985, p.106).

In the same vein, Joan Robinson, a famous neo-Marxist economist, has argued that "It is precisely the pursuit of profit which destroys the prestige of the business man. While wealth can buy all forms of respect, it never finds them freely given" (quoted in Stanbury 1985, p. 106). One might interpret, therefore, efforts by the leaders of large corporations to extend their influence beyond the domain of profits as designed to raise their status in society.

Political Power: In general terms, political power is simply the exercise of power (e.g., the ability to alter the behaviour of others, involuntarily if necessary) in a *political* context. Political contexts include elections, the exercise of discretion by a government decision maker, and efforts to influence present or future public policy.

The most formal type of political power is the ability to control levers of the state with their capacity to exercise legitimate coercion. The scope of governing instruments is enormous and the constraints on the cabinet of a majority government are relatively few, particularly in the first two years or so after a general election. More generally, political power is the ability to mobilize the resources of the state to advance the values, beliefs, or pecuniary interests of those able to exercise power. C.B. MacPherson (1973, p. 47) put it this way: "political power, being power over others, is used in any unequal society to extract benefit from the ruled for the rulers." One might say that the ultimate goal of an interest group desiring to exercise the greatest scope for its power is to "capture the state". For corporations, political power is the ability to have government advance the interests of a particular firm at the expense of others in the same industry, or at the expense of some definition of a broader "public interest." Fred Harris (1973, p. 25), then a U.S. Senator, described the political power of corporations as "the ability to use public government to obtain private economic goals . . . [it is] the ability of big corporations to have more than their fair share of influence over the decisions of government."

1.3 A Framework of Analysis

Although a substantial number of writers have expressed a variety of concerns about the political power of large corporations (see Section 2 below), there have been very few efforts to provide a general analytic framework within which the problem can be examined in depth.[8] While it is not possible to provide such a framework and develop it in detail in the scope of a single paper, I propose to address six of the most important facets of corporate political power in a democracy. They are outlined in Figure 1. The analysis begins by examining the objectives of the exercise of political power by corporations.

1.4 Objectives of Corporations' Political Power

In a world in which the scope of government activity and influence over the private sector is great,[9] it is not surprising that large business enterprises (and groups of small ones) should seek to influence the political agenda. Governments can confer great benefits on individual firms, on specific industries and on the private sector in general. They can also impose complex and costly burdens as well (taxes, regulation, quotas, etc.). The ways in which a government can act that are beneficial to a particular enterprise are numerous: new or amended legislation or subordinate legis-lation, favourable interpretation of existing policy, and the provision of information to help corporations adapt easily to government policies.

One of the principal objectives of efforts by big business to assert political influence is to create a general climate favourable to its endeavours so that it may grow and prosper. Political power can also be used to obtain specific regulatory, tax, or procurement decisions that are advantageous to a specific firm or to an entire industry. For example, when the domestic automobile industry was unable to meet competition from Japan it sought (in conjunction with the union) help from government in the form of capital subsidies and quotas on imports. As a result, Canadian car buyers were forced to bail out an inefficient industry.

Mega corporations appreciate that effectiveness in the political arena is often based on the role they are able to play in the complex process of making public policy. Therefore they seek to shape the process as a means of influencing the outcomes of particular decisions in the future.

The concerns about large corporations' political power, the sources of such power, the manifestations of large corporations' political power and the limitations on such power are outlined in Figure 1 and addressed in detail later in the paper. However, the *means* by which corporate political power is exercised merit brief comment here.

Figure 1
Corporate Political Power: Objectives, Concerns, Sources, Means, Manifestations and Limitations

1. Objectives of the Exercise of Political Power by Corporations

- to shape the political agenda – which issues are the subject of action by the government

- to create a general climate favourable to big business

- to obtain specific regulatory, tax, subsidy, procurement decisions that are advantageous to the firm or industry

- to shape the *process* by which government policy is made, e.g., who participates, timing, basic assumptions – with a view to exercising more influence in the future

2. Concerns About Corporations' Political Power

- large corporations have excessive influence on public policy based on their economic power

- business leaders are not visible, not representative and not accountable as are politicians

- political power is no longer independent of economic power and able to act as a constraint on its use or abuse

- political activity becomes "monetized" (excessively dependent on economic resources)

- with greater concentration of economic activity private interests and the public interest become less distinguishable to policy makers

- popular (one person, one vote) control over government is reduced; political power becomes more concentrated in the hands of a few

3. Sources/Bases of the Political Power of Large Corporations

- economic power: market power within a specific industry; conglomerate structure; large size where there is a high level of aggregate concentration

- cultural values: deference to authority; trust in concentrations of private or public power

- weakness/absence of countervailing power, e.g., unions, other interest groups

- interconnected elites: business, bureaucracy, politics, cultural/social, media

- ownership/control of the media; influence over the media which in turn shapes the political agenda

- organizational skills

- economic resources that can be utilized in the political arena

- access to government decision makers

- dependency of other groups on the corporation

- public character of large corporations (surrogateship)

- backlog of political success

- high status of business and business managers in society

- poor macro economic performance, hence government's dependence on business to create jobs

Figure 1 (cont'd)

4. Means Through Which Political Power is Exercised

- lobbying: efforts to influence particular policies

- participation in advisory bodies

- strategic use of the legal system

- input to task forces, royal commissions, special inquiries

- media/p.r. campaigns ("louder voices" that help define the policy agenda)

- political contributions

- purchase and strategic use of polling information

- extensive informal contacts with senior bureaucrats and politicians

- formation of political alliances

- funding of policy research organizations whose outputs contribute ideas and data to public policy formation

5. Manifestations of Political Power

(a) Outcomes

- ability to veto policy actions that appear to have wide support

- ability to implement policy actions strongly opposed by other interests

- ability to greatly influence the outcome of elections

(b) Process

- easy access to decision makers; multiple points of access compared to other interests

- institutionalized position(s) in the policy making process

- views receive respectful attention from politicians and bureaucrats

- ability to alter the fundamental assumptions under which policy is being made

- ability to constrain the range of alternatives considered in policy making

6. Limitations on Large Corporations' Political Influence

- competition of other interests in the political arena (countervailing power)

- market for corporate control if managers stray from profit maximization

- competition among political parties, notably pressure from the left which has a different agenda

- conflicting interests within the business community on a host of specific issues

- turnover amongst the largest corporations, this makes coordination more difficult

- need of political parties to balance the need for campaign funds and popular support

- political disadvantages of large corporations; visibility, myth of the little man, insensitive bureaucracies, increased vulnerability to changes in government policy

- government policies designed to curb the political influence of "big business," e.g., funding of opposing voices, constraints on mergers, constraints on lobbying and campaign contributions and/or expenditures

- vast array of coercive powers that may be legitimately used by government

1.5   The Means Through Which Political Power is Exercised[10]

Most people think of lobbying as the principal means by which any group seeks to influence public policy and that term is used to cover a wide range of efforts designed to shape existing or proposed public policies. But large corporations have many other arrows in their political quiver. They frequently obtain preferred access to the policy process through participation in advisory bodies and by invitations to make "inputs" to government task forces, royal commissions and inquiries (see Stanbury and Fulton 1987).

Large corporations can capitalize on their superior economic resources by using them to make strategic use of the legal system (e.g., to mount challenges to the constitutionality of new legislation), and to acquire sophisticated polling information so as to better understand (and anticipate) how politicians are likely to see certain issues. They also have the money to make large contributions to political parties in the expectation that their generosity will not go unrewarded in the fullness of time, although only the naive believe that such contributions can be tied directly to benefits from government, e.g., a lucrative contract, an advantageous regulatory decision, etc.[11]

Corporations may seek to influence policy making by means of media and public relations campaigns. For example, private automobile insurers in Ontario began an advocacy advertising campaign for a limited form of no-fault insurance in March 1987 to try to forestall a government-run no-fault insurance scheme.[12] They were only partly successful as the government promised to regulate auto insurance premiums.

Large corporations, as do other interest groups, find it useful to engage in extensive informal contacts with senior bureaucrats and politicians as another means of exercising the arts of persuasion. They will also form alliances with other groups to advance (or defeat) particular issues. In an effort to compete in the marketplace of ideas, some large corporations have begun to support certain public policy research organizations, e.g., the Fraser Institute — see Section 3.2 below.

2.0   CONCERNS ABOUT THE POLITICAL POWER OF MEGA CORPORATIONS

As shall be documented in this section, a review of the literature reveals a variety of concerns about the power and influence of large corporations on politics and policy making in a democracy. Mega corporations are quite widely perceived as a threat to democracy. However, before we move to these concerns, it may be useful to begin by noting the important characteristics of a democratic form of government:

- Free, periodic elections which are not subject to subversion by bribery, intimidation, or fraud.

- Universal suffrage; prohibitions on the sale or transfer of votes.

- Proportional representation: one person, one vote; constituencies of almost equal size.

- Constitutional controls on the power of government vis-à-vis individuals, e.g., Charter of Rights and Freedoms in the *Constitution Act, 1982.*

- An independent judiciary beyond the reach of the executive and the legislature except in the case of improper/illegal behaviour.

- Active competition by political parties for the electorate's support.

- Diffusion of power among interests competing in the political arena; no interest dominates policy making; no one can "buy" an election or political favours.

- The *assumption* that the collective power of individuals working through political institutions should be able to control any agglomeration of private power, economic or otherwise.

As we review the various concerns set out below it is helpful to ask how and to what extent do large corporations affect each of these assumptions so as to undermine popular democratic government. It may well be that large corporations in an economy with a high level of aggregate concentration may have undue influence over public policy, largely because in the real world a number of factors undermine or limit the achievement of the ideal of popular democracy. These include

- imperfect knowledge and costly information (despite low cost, mass media.)

- high and asymmetric transactions costs,

- imperfect competition in political markets based on the concentration of economic resources, and

- the public good characteristics (notably the "free rider" problem) of many government policies and of representations to obtain such policies.

In other words, these various types of "market failures" in political markets may make it easier for mega corporations to translate their economic power into political power and thereby exercise an undue influence on government policy. For example, in a world of imperfect knowledge and costly information the large corporation may have "too much" influence on policy formation because it can use its economic resources to acquire more and better information than its rivals in the political arena. In addition, in the hope of obtaining beneficial policies, such corporations can provide money to political parties so that the parties can both obtain better information about the electorate's preferences and "sell" their policies or promises to voters.

I now review the issues raised by those concerned about the political power of large corporations.

It is argued by many that big business has "excessive" influence in the formation of public policy and uses its influence to benefit itself often at the expense of other interests in society.[13]   Beck (1985, p. 202), for example, claims that

> it is the largest enterprises . . . whose executives form the powerful network that faces government as the spokesmen for the dominant actors in the economy and who thus set the policy agenda. It is to that voice that government responds in setting national economic policy.

This argument immediately raises several questions. First, what is meant by excessive influence? Is a corporation's political influence excessive if it is merely proportional to its economic resources or its stake in the economy? Second, when a firm exercises its political power to who do we impute the benefits – shareholders, managers, employees, or other stakeholders? Third, are the critics concerned with the *results* of power in terms of policy or merely with the possession of power, i.e., the potential for abuse?[14]

Business leaders who wield great power, it is argued, are not usually identifiable, and they are not accountable, except perhaps to their shareholders.[15] When corporations exercise political power they constitute an "irresponsible government" while elected representatives are ultimately accountable to the people in periodic popular elections.[16] (Yet elections are also influenced by economic and political resources despite the constraints on expenditures during federal campaigns.)

When large corporations operate in the political arena, political power and influence are concentrated in a few hands, not diffused widely.[17] Such positions of power are less fluid than when power is diffused. Competition among interest groups for the attention of decision makers in government more closely resembles a concentrated oligopoly than a perfectly competitive market of the pluralist ideal. Such imperfect political competition means that the more powerful (e.g., large corporations) benefit disproportionately from many government policies.[18]

It has been suggested that economic and political power of large corporations make it incumbent on individuals and smaller (less powerful) interest groups to combine so as to compete more effectively in the political arena.[19] The result is that political markets that were once subject to easy entry and low concentration become substantially more concentrated and the barriers to entry to such markets are increased. Competition among the few, to use William Fellner's phrase, becomes characteristic of political as well as economic markets.

When economic power is concentrated and focused on the political arena, the ability to offset economic power by decisions in the political arena in a democracy is reduced. This violates the widely held belief that politics should act as a counterweight to the concentration of economic power. One of the most common propositions, albeit poorly defended, is that the political process should be used to redistribute income in a more egalitarian fashion from determined market forces.

It is argued that the concentration of economic power creates popular pressures for countervailing political power (Galbraith 1952). This often takes the form of a larger or more intrusive/restrictive government which may be able to curb the excesses of corporate power, but it also may reduce the freedom of individuals. The individual may be caught in the jaws of a vise composed of big business and big government.

It is argued by some that big business has the power in some instances to "suborn the state" to some degree.[20] Marxists speak of the power of big business to reduce the state's "autonomy." But in a democracy how can the state have a large degree of autonomy from the popular political will in periodic elections?

The vast economic resources of large corporations can be converted into political resources such as the following:

- personnel and expertise to operate political organizations,

- public and media relations (to build a "good image"),

- polling (to monitor public opinion),

- lobbying and other forms of representation,

- research (acquisition of political intelligence),

- advocacy advertising, and

- campaign contributions (including leadership campaigns).

This fact changes the *basis* of political power from popular appeal (e.g., grass roots organization building) to a process in which political parties have a symbiotic relationship with large economic interests and political campaigns depend in large part on the economic resources of the parties. In short, political markets become "monetized." It should be appreciated that situation is the product of certain, largely exogenous, forces: imperfect knowledge and costly information, hence political parties require money to "do the Lord's work" and the fact that individuals or small groups have substantially different economic, emotional or ideological stocks of capital whose value can be greatly influenced by public policy. The stage is set, therefore, for an exchange in which large stakeholders provide political parties with cash and other forms of political support in return for promises of policies that are beneficial to them. The concentration of economic resources which can be brought to bear in the political arena results in grossly imperfect competition in politics and policy making. Big business effectively has a louder voice and the resources to out-compete its rivals in the political arena *on average*,[21] if not in every instance.

The scope and depth of government intervention in the economy means that a larger fraction of society's resources are being allocated by means other than market competition (see Courchene 1980). This state of affairs *requires* that corporations, particularly large ones, participate in the political/policy process to protect and advance their interests. If managers did not do so they would be failing in their duty to shareholders — and other groups with a stake in the corporation's well-being.

High aggregate concentration and very extensive government intervention necessarily create a symbiotic relationship between "big business" and government. This means that government needs the cooperation of business to successfully implement economic policy, and that business is both constrained by and benefits from government action (see Beck 1985).

As the economic scope of the largest corporations increases (more employees in more regions, in more industries, accounting for a higher percentage of output and capital investment), its political interests become less distinguishable from the popular or public interest (Galbraith 1973). Actions that are deemed harmful to mega corporations are actions that hurt many people (the firms' various stakeholders) and much economic activity. Galbraith (1973, p. 5) suggests that because such enterprises have "powerful leverage in the community," their "needs are *pro tanto* sound public policy." Moreover, mega corporations become too big to fail – even if they deserve to do so in light of market criteria.[22] The political wash of their failure would swamp too many boats. So political decisions override the judgments of economic markets.

It is evident that thoughtful observers of the role of large corporations in society have raised a number of concerns about such enterprises' impact on politics and policy making. The core of their concern is that for a variety of reasons (size, economic resources, imperfections in political markets) large firms are able to exercise an undue and undesirable amount of influence in the political arena. In most cases, such political power stems from the fact that in western industrial economies "big business" accounts for a large proportion of economic activity at both the industry and economy-wide level.[23] Even where industry and aggregate concentration is far below the high level that exists in Canada, the largest 100 or 200 firms (and the various trade associations to which they belong) are able to command resources that may be utilized in the political arena that are vastly greater than almost all individuals and all but a few interest groups (e.g., unions, professional associations, environmentalists, etc.). I now examine in more detail the sources of large corporations' political power.

3.0   THE SOURCES OF LARGE CORPORATIONS' POLITICAL POWER[24]

Mao argued that political power comes out of the barrel of a gun. Berkeley radicals asserted that such power comes from "the people." This section tries to determine the sources or bases of the political power of large corporations in countries like Canada.

3.1   Organization

A long time student of power, Adolf Berle, Jr. (1969, p. 63), argues that "no group of any kind in and of itself wields power or can use it. Another factor must be present: that of organization." Political scientist Charles Lindblom (1977, p. 26) asserts that organization is the ultimate source of *all* power. Galbraith (1983, p. 6) argues that organization is "the most important source of power in modern societies," more important than property or personality. Organization, he states, "has its foremost relationship with conditioned power. It is taken for granted that when an exercise of power is sought or needed, organization is required." Galbraith (1983, p. 7) continues, "from the organization, then, come the requisite persuasion and the resulting submission to the purposes of the organization." While the state has access to condign power (which "wins submission by inflicting or threatening appropriately adverse consequences"), organized groups "have greater or lesser access to compensatory power through [their] property . . ."

Being large-scale formal organizations, giant corporations have learned to coordinate disparate activities to achieve specific goals under conditions of uncertainty while contending with the actions of rivals. These skills are very valuable when they are applied to achieving political objectives. Most large corporations already have specialized units whose skills are easily adaptable to the political arena, e.g., public relations, government relations, regulatory affairs, government contracting, legal expertise, and advertising.

Almost all of the largest corporations operate in multiple locations nationally and internationally. These units are supported by elaborate communications networks and often by extensive market and political intelligence activities. Large corporations have an enormous variety of human contacts — even if we focus exclusively on major stakeholders: employees, creditors, suppliers, customers, etc.[25] Grefe (1981) emphasizes that these stakeholders can, under certain circumstances, form a considerable force for lobbying government. Large corporations can also form alliances with other enterprises, often through various trade associations.

3.2 Economic Resources

The economic resources of large corporations, as compared with rival interest groups, are enormous. The very largest corporations are able to command resources beyond the scope of some governments (except for the latter's power of taxation). Of critical importance is the ability of the corporation to convert its pecuniary resources into other types of resources that are useful in the political arena. Galbraith (1983, p. 47) notes that "of the three sources of power, property is seemingly the most forthright. Its possession gives access to the most commonplace exercise of power, which is the bending of the will of one person to another by straightforward purchase." He emphasizes that today the direct use of money in public affairs is on the decline. Rather, pecuniary resources are used to effect persuasion or "conditioned power." Galbraith (1983, p. 49) continues, "the modern man of wealth [or corporation] no longer uses his money to purchase votes; he contributes it to the purchase of television commercials and by this means he hopes to win conditioned submission to his political will."

Those with large economic (or emotional) stakes in the system are acutely aware of the ability of government to quickly create or destroy wealth in the name of the public interest. The larger government becomes, the more people that have a big stake in its decisions. In such cases, self-interest requires that one take a more than casual interest in policy making. Large and diversified enterprises are likely to have a larger economic stake in more policy issues and more constituencies than smaller and less diversified firms. In general, more voters will be hurt or helped by government action affecting large conglomerates than other firms. Economic resources of mega corporations provide the means by which to increase a corporation's effectiveness in the political arena. Money is necessary to pay for the following means of influencing political activity.

Political Contributions: Since the 1974 *Election Expenses Act* the Liberal and Conservative parties' dependence on corporate political donations has decreased to about one-half of total revenue. However, large contributions ($10,000 or more) from corporations are still fairly important. At the same time, the expenditures of the parties outside the official campaign period have increased greatly. See Table 1.

If we compare the costs of running political parties in Canada[27] to the profits of some mega corporations in 1984 we find that only 25 per cent of General Motors' profits in 1984 would have been sufficient to finance *all* of the expenditures of the two largest political parties in Canada. If the 10 largest non-financial enterprises had formed an agreement to each spend 1.1 per cent of their net profits on campaign contributions they could have financed the *record* outlays of *both* the Liberals and Tories in 1984. If the top five banks had done the same, each would have had to spend 2.8 per cent of their profits to foot all of the bills of the two leading parties. If Bell Canada Enterprises (#4 on the *F.P. 500* in 1984) had spent 4.8 per cent of its net profits on campaign contributions it could have paid for all of the expenditures of both the Liberals and the Tories in that election year. Recall that outlays in 1984 were three times those in 1983, and the percentage of profits needed to finance the two parties shrink accordingly.

Table 1
Political Contributions and Expenditures, Federal Parties, 1981-1986

	Total Expenditures Outside Campaign Period ($ Millions)		Per cent of Total Party Revenue from Corporations		No. of Corporate Contributions $10,000+		Corporate Contributions $10,000+ as % of Total Revenue	
	Lib	PC	Lib	PC	Lib	PC	Lib	PC
1981	5.1	7.5	53%	37%	na	na	na	na
1982	5.5	8.5	41	28	na	na	na	na
1983	6.3	10.3	49	34	45	43	11.6%	5.3%
1984	12.0	20.8	51	52	113	198	20.4	19.8
1985	7.5	11.1	44	46	54	95	19.8	13.6
1986	10.6	15.6	54	50	102	104	21.5	14.7

Source: Stanbury (1986a, Ch. 10) and tabulations by the author.

The point is that a small fraction of a mega corporation's profits (let alone shareholders' equity) constitutes an enormous fraction of the total amount the federal Liberal and Conservative parties raise and spend, even in off-election years. What is worrying is how easy it would be for a single mega corporation to pay all the bills of both major parties.[28]

Advocacy Advertising, e.g., Gulf Canada spent over $6.2 million on its advocacy advertising program between 1980 and 1982 (see Stanbury 1986a, p. 570 and pp. 570-578). Obviously, large scale campaigns – those most likely to shape public opinion – are only within the reach of large enterprises.

Public Affairs Programs: these can be used to portray the corporation in a favourable light, e.g., Gulf Canada's expenditures on public affairs between 1979 and 1984 totalled $21.6 million (Stanbury 1986a, p. 569). Only the largest corporations (or unions) could afford such expenditures.

Legal Challenges: these can be mounted against government policy initiatives. Legal battles have become so expensive that one is reminded of the Mexican curse to the effect that "may your life be filled with lawyers." The National Citizens' Coalition, for example, spent over $300,000 on the *Lavigne* case up to the trial level. As the case is expected to go to the Supreme Court of Canada the total cost will exceed $500,000 (Stanbury 1986a, p. 195).

Lobbying: Despite the fact that lobbying is expensive, few corporations in Canada spend more than $1 million annually in out-of-pocket costs for lobbying. Their indirect expenditures, notably in terms of the time of senior line executives and on legal advice, can easily double or treble the outlays. The budgets of major trade associations (e.g., the Canadian Chamber of Commerce, Canadian Manufacturers' Association, Canadian Federation of Independent Business), only part of which goes to lobbying directly, fall into the range of $7 million to $15 million annually. Large amounts of money are obviously valuable in efforts to persuade government and public opinion to advance the interests of the corporation. (More generally, see Stanbury 1986a, Ch. 7-9.)

Public Policy Research Organizations: Beck (1985, p. 202) asserts that policy research organizations in Canada such as the Conference Board, C.D. Howe Research Institute, the Niagara Institute and the Fraser Institute, are "for the most part . . . funded by business interests and reflect a consistently conservative point of view."[29] The Fraser Institute, for example, with an annual budget of about $1 million, produces about a dozen books, a number of other opinion pieces and scores of radio, television and newspaper editorials each year. It has developed a reputation as an aggressive "right wing" think tank and its director, Dr. Michael Walker, has a high profile in the media and in some public policy circles. There is no question that the Fraser Institute seeks to shape public policy.[30]

The point is that it costs money to compete in the world of ideas that help to shape public policy in the short run and the long run. When business contributes to a research organization it cannot expect to control what is produced. But, in the case of the Fraser Institute, the ideas put forward are very likely to be consistent with maintaining a favorable political and economic environment for business.

The crucial point to appreciate is that for a few million dollars per year a large firm or a small group of firms could produce several clones of the Fraser Institute, thus quadrupling the output of books, pamphlets, speeches, and media appearances by articulate "right thinking" individuals. In short, it would be relatively cheap to make a serious effort to try to reshape the public policy agenda by injecting new ideas, or by providing more analytical support and higher visibility for existing ones.

Summary: It should be appreciated that for $25 million per year a group of firms could create the dominant actor in each of the following tools of persuasion: lobbying, p.r./media relations, advocacy advertising, political contributions and privately-funded policy research. Given the stakes involved and the resources of giant corporations, this amount seems quite small.

3.3 Access
In most cases it is all but impossible to exercise influence in the political process without access to the key actors at crucial times and places. One of the apparently benign functions of political contributions is to facilitate access (see Stanbury 1986a, pp. 479-481). Harsh critics, however, argue that access is the key to corruption. "To be influenced, the public official must be accessible to the corrupter" (quoted in Stanbury 1986a, p.481). Dalton Camp, writing in 1979, argues that "Toronto money merely maintains access to the parties, keeping open essential lines of communication, corporate hotlines, so to speak, to the right ears at the appropriate times" (quoted in Stanbury 1986a, p. 480). Modern political fund raising is making increasing use of what is called an "access opportunity." For example, for a $1,000 contribution to the Conservatives "500 Club" individuals could attend a "Cabinet Forum," a luncheon and address by Mr. Mulroney followed by a question and answer session. Membership in the 500 Club "also offers private tête-à-tête with Cabinet Ministers, key MPs and party leaders."[31] The net after-tax cost of the $1,000 contribution is only $550 given the generous federal tax credit.[32]

Access, of course, does not guarantee that the corporate official will win the day and get what he wants. On most issues the target politician or senior bureaucrat is the object of "inputs" from other, often opposing, interests. Besides, politicians (and bureaucrats) have their own ideas about what maximizes political support or the public interest.[33]

"Access also results from the size, importance and reputation of corporations" (Epstein 1969, p. 198). The reasons are obvious: those who control such enterprises command resources (jobs, capital investment, raw material inputs) on a gigantic scale.[34] Moreover, the industrial and geographic scope of these giant companies' activities literally spans the nation. No responsible government can afford *not* to grant access to those who control mega corporations. At the level of the individual member of the legislature, "the welfare of an important constituent is automatically of concern to a legislator, notwithstanding the fact that the corporation may have opposed his election" (Epstein 1969, p. 198).

Strong evidence of access is the ability of a *private* organization to have top political decision makers come to the meetings *it* arranges to discuss the items on *its* agenda. Consider the case of the Business Council on National Issues:

> The power of the BCNI was captured in a five-line item on the inside pages of the Toronto Star on June 6, 1984. The item announced that the premiers of Ontario and Alberta had attended a meeting arranged by the BCNI to discuss energy policy. Unremarkable perhaps, but it is hard to think of any other interest group in Canadian society that could secure the attendance of two powerful provincial premiers at a quiet meeting to discuss a national policy issue. Most importantly, such a meeting is not a singular event; similar meetings are typical of the BCNI's method of operation. It is not contended that such meetings, and the work of the BCNI, are somehow sinister. There may be much that is beneficial in regular, informal contacts between leading economic decision makers and senior government officials. The point simply is that the BCNI — what it represents — is a power group like no other in our society and is so recognized by government (Beck 1985, pp. 200-201).

Access to political decision makers is facilitated by a host of means: political contributions, the economic, hence political importance of the corporation/industry, membership on the many advisory committees, task forces, etc. set up by government, social contacts, cultural bodies, kinship, exclusive schools, clubs, etc.), regulatory proceedings, circulation of policy papers/draft bills, etc., appearances before legislative committees, and the fact that members of the business, bureaucratic and political elites move from one to the other over a career of about four decades (see Stanbury and Fulton 1987).

3.4   Patronage by Large Corporations

In this context, patronage refers to the dependency of other social groups upon the activities of the corporation. The number of "stakeholders" in a mega corporation is large: shareholders, customers, creditors, suppliers, employees, and so forth.[35] So long as those who control the corporation have *any* discretion in their decision making they are in a position to favour one group of employees over another, to favour one supplier of raw materials over another, or to favour one group of firms that distributes its products over another. Even where a firm operates in perfectly competitive markets for both inputs and outputs, it still has the power of choice among apparently homogeneous suppliers, wholesalers, etc. In practice, the senior management (or owners) of most large corporations are able to exercise a considerable degree of discretion in dealing with its various stakeholders. Such discretion is an obvious source of power.

Perhaps one of the most obvious situations in which large corporations are able to exercise both economic and political power is the "company town" or fairly isolated region within which a firm employs a substantial fraction of the labour force. While the worst example of local or regional "corporate fiefdoms" have probably passed from the scene, some observers continue to point to the problem.

> ...in company towns...the dominant corporation can control public opinion and political activities – a syndrome which can apply as well to 'company states' like Delaware. While locally dominant corporations can be oppressive, absentee corporations with national interests can be indifferent to community needs ...Sociological, economic, and congressional studies have documented this lack of civic involvement and its erosive effects on community well being (Nader *et al.* 1976, pp. 23,24).

Epstein (1969, p. 204) notes that corporate patronage may take the form of "a satellite or patron-client relationship...with governmental units such as states and municipalities because of the overriding economic importance of the corporation to the area in which it is located." Not surprisingly, in areas of high unemployment local voters put the pressure on all levels of government to provide various types of assistance to create jobs. Indeed, I argue in Section 3.10 that high levels of unemployment give corporations able to create jobs substantial political leverage.

"Patronage as a political resource is most valuable where the alternatives available to the dependent social interest are quite limited. More often [economic] dependence results in a sense of identity with the dominant firm rather than in formal coercion by it" (Epstein 1969, p. 207). This dependency can be used by the corporation to create alliances and to broaden its base of support. Both are likely to increase the large corporation's effectiveness in influencing public policy to its own benefit.

Grefe (1981, pp. 9-10) argues strongly that corporations need to develop a broad *political* base by mobilizing their stakeholders (employees, shareholders, etc.) to develop personal, constituent relationships with lawmakers. He stresses the need for corporations to create allies ("platooning in depth") so as to establish a broader base of support [read votes] for their political positions. As Grefe (1981, p. 46) puts it, "Once an issue has been selected as vital, one reaches out beyond the [corporate] family to mobilize all who are and will be affected by the outcome." Possible allies on an issue of critical importance to a firm or industry include the following:

A. Suppliers of goods: raw materials, manufactured supplies, secondary suppliers

B. Suppliers of services: executives, employees (including the union), banks, insurance companies and agencies, landlords, trucking companies, railroads, lawyers and other professionals on retainer, commerce and trade associations.

C. Natural political support: county officials, town and city officials, political party officials.

D. Friendly competitors

E. Shareholders — in the case of more widely-held firms.

In seeking to influence government policy, Grefe (1981, p. 107) suggests that corporations prepare an "economic profile" to be used as a vehicle to remind decision makers and opinion leaders of the importance of the corporation to the community.

> Information generated from the economic profile can provide the basis of an annual report to every opinion leader of the community. The report should state the contribution of the corporation to the economic vitality of the community; note the cost of adverse public proposals on both the corporation and the community; and open a direct dialogue to offset unsubstantiated attacks by anticorporate polemicists.

3.5 The Public Character of Large Corporations

Finer (1955, p. 285) argues that because private enterprise "affects all members of the community," corporations relate to government as a surrogate or deputy. This is another term for what Galbraith (1973) and others refer to as the public character of the large corporation.

According to Epstein (1969, p. 208), surrogateship assumes a number of forms. First, there is the economic power that stems from concentration in specific markets or industries, particularly when there are significant barriers to entry (due to nature, man or government policy).

Second, because business firms collectively operate a large fraction of the economy, the success or failure of many macro- and micro-economic policies depends on how businessmen (and women) perceive them and react to them. Stanley Beck, now chairman of the Ontario Securities Commission, concludes that

> If economic policy is to be effectively carried out, the collaboration and support of business is essential. In that sense, business is an interest group in our society like no other; government has to heed its voice and attend to its concerns or risk frustration and failure of its policies (Beck 1985, p. 185).

Given the interdependence of business and government on the matter of economic policy, do giant corporations actually exercise the *dominant* influence on policy making? Is the political power of corporate interests vastly greater than their rivals? Power is relative and it is the *disparities* in the power of groups that matter. Moreover, the government and a Government are hardly passive actors. Men and women do not aspire to join the cabinet or become deputy ministers merely to compute the parallelogram of forces exerted by various interest groups in drafting legislation or making administrative decisions. They have egos, ideas, and they enjoy the exercise of power. More importantly, they have, in conjunction with others, access to the very considerable legitimate powers of coercion of the state. Finally, as noted in Section 5, there are important constraints on the influence of large corporations.

Third, business has at least two sources of leverage over government decision makers which are most effective when pursued in a coordinated fashion (no mean feat):

> (i) they can threaten, or deliberately take action that slows down activities government wishes to encourage or speed up processes government is attempting to discourage; (ii) they can threaten a political strike — non-performance of their valuable economic tasks — unless political authorities either take certain actions which they demand or refrain from taking certain actions of which they disapprove (Epstein 1969, p. 209).

Obviously, business' leverage is much greater when the federal government is not able to maintain full employment — see Section 3.10 below. However, one must question whether a "strike" by capital is more than a theoretical concept.

3.6 Corporate Influence Over the Mass Media

The capacity of any interest group to successfully influence the mass media is a political resource of great value. Not only are the media the principal source of the public's information about business (Corrado 1984, p. 84), but more importantly, the mass media greatly shapes the political environment and hence public policy. Siegel (1983, pp. 14-15) suggests that the media's political power derives from five sources:

- the media provide basic political information;

- they are a major link between the public and governments; much of the public discussion of political issues occurs in the media;

- the media have a substantial influence over the political agenda because they must necessarily be selective as to what facts and opinions are reported;

- the print media in particular offer editorial opinions, although in the age of television these may be less important than they were in an earlier era; and

- the mass media influence political actors; indeed, modern election campaigns have boiled down to a battle to get a 30-second clip on the local and national television news programs.

Epstein (1969, p. 212) argues that corporations' influence over the mass media stems from four sources:

the advertising dollar; the ownership of some media outlets by industrial firms; the fact that the media comprise sizable corporate interests with political interests of their own; and the continuous exposure of the public – via the mass media – to efforts by business firms (a) to project a positive image of the importance of corporate enterprise to the American way of life and (b) to create a store of public empathy and support of business which can be valuable in times of political crisis.

In Canada the ownership factor is of particular importance in that within the various media ownership is highly concentrated – including cross-media ownership and in some cases industrial enterprises also control important media outlets (e.g., K.C. Irving; Thomson).

The Report of the Royal Commission on Newspapers (Canada 1981, Ch. 1) provides the following information on this important news medium:

- In most communities in Canada there is only one newspaper. Toronto is a conspicuous exception being served by the *Globe and Mail*, The Toronto *Sun* and the Toronto *Star*.

- Of the 117 daily papers, 88 (75%) belong to chains while 29 are independently owned.

- 88% of average weekly circulation is attributable to papers owned by chains.

- Two chains (Thomson and Southam) which control 54 dailies, account for 59% of total English-language circulation. Power Corp. controls 25% of the French language circulation in Quebec while the Irving family owns all five English-language papers in New Brunswick. Ninety percent of English-language newspapers are owned by three groups, according to Trevor Eyton.

- A number of the leading owners of newspapers (e.g., Thomson, Irving, Sterling) are also major conglomerates with wide-ranging interests in other industries.

- Chain ownership is further complicated by multi-media ownership, e.g., in New Brunswick the Irving family owns the leading television and radio stations in the cities in which it owns all the English-language newspapers.[36]

According to Clement (1983, p. 101), the *Report* of the Royal Commission on Corporate Concentration "found there to be enormous concentration within the media that was detrimental to everyone's interest except, of course, those few who controlled the media." He notes that since the Davey Report in 1970 and the RCCC's report in 1978 concentration in the media has increased substantially. Moreover, shortly after they took office, the Tories reversed the CRTC 1982 order that the Irving family divest their television stations (Francis 1986, p. 18).

Concentration in the ownership of the media can have the following adverse consequences: a reduction in the variety of opinions and sources of news; a reduction in the number of firms available as employers of reporters, producers, etc.; and the ability to engage in cross-subsidization among media outlets to achieve the political objectives of the owners. Tom Kent has described the reporting of the Irvings in their New Brunswick newspapers as follows:

> Irving papers are noteworthy for their obeisance to every industrial interest. They are not known for probing investigations into pollution, occupational health dangers, industrial wastes, or any of the other darker consequences of industrial power" (Francis 1986, p. 17).

Given the extraordinary scope and size of the Irvings' industrial holdings in the province (they employ about 8 per cent of the labour force), this means that the negative externalities produced by their operations receive little coverage in the five Irving papers. Yet the Supreme Court of Canada concluded that Irving did not "control" the editorial policies of the newspapers he owned outright (see Reschenthaler & Stanbury 1977).[37]

There needs to be an inherent tension between government and the media in a democracy, and there is a need to be skeptical of government's efforts to regulate the media. However, the extremely hostile reaction to the Liberals' proposed *Daily Newspaper Act* (July 6, 1983) provides evidence of the political power of the media.

> [Multiculturalism Minister James] Fleming's proposed [Daily] Newspaper Act was designed to distil the findings of a royal commission on newspaper monopoly, and a subsequent court case that demonstrated the wide gaps in existing combines legislation. He talked, at the same time, of trying to ensure the independence of the nation's newsrooms from the influence of the owners, and he proposed government subsidies for a watchdog national press council, and the expansion of news coverage through bureaus at home and abroad. Fleming's proposals summoned the nation's publishers to the ramparts, their voices raised to hitherto unprecedented heights, or depths, of indignation. Nor did the denizens of the newsrooms rally to Fleming's defence, or in support of any of his measures. Freedom of the press was at stake, and Fleming must be burned. When it was over, Fleming was out of the cabinet, and his Newspaper Act was abandoned by the government that had spawned it (Lynch 1985, p. 43).

3.7 A Backlog of Political Success

Epstein (1969, p. 216) argues that "another political asset of significance to some corporations is the backlog of favorable results that they have enjoyed over the years in their relationships with legislative bodies and with administrative agencies and executive departments."[38] Past success in the political arena for any interest group hardly guarantees future success, but it does serve several useful purposes. It provides a generally favourable climate or atmosphere in which to advance new initiatives. It provides corporate leaders with a feeling of confidence, even elan, in their subsequent dealings with government, and other interest groups. Previous success provides the experience upon which to draw in future encounters, although some might argue that failure too provides valuable lessons. When corporate interests have a record of success they may make other interest groups more cautious in their competitive behaviour in seeking to win favour with government. The previous success of corporate interests may have been based, in part, on their ability of corporate interests to win by exhausting the resources of rivals. On the other hand, a string of victories by big business may spur other groups to greater efforts when their positions are eroded by the policy actions generated by big business.

In the long run, the most important consequences of an interest group's past successes may be the following: (i) the creation of *legitimacy* for that group, i.e., when government "ratifies" a group's position it raises its status merely by such recognition; it gives the group and its proposals some measure of validity; and (ii) the integration of the group into the policy making *process* so that in the future it is invited to sit at the table when policy changes are discussed. Moreover, the group gains routine access for its policy initiatives in the future (see Stanbury 1986a; Pross, 1986).

3.8   The Status of Business and Business Managers in Society

"As a result of their position as social and economic notables, corporate managers are frequently opinion makers within their communities" (Epstein 1969, p. 219). High status generally has beneficial consequences when an individual seeks to exercise influence in the political or policy making process. This is particularly true in a society characterized by elite accommodation (see Presthus 1973). "Great deference is paid to the corporation executive, whose job is the symbol of success and who reputedly has mastered the art of managing men and making money" (quoted in Epstein 1969, p. 219). More generally, "many people feel that business leaders are practical and efficient and that therefore the policies they espouse are also practical and efficient..." (Epstein 1969, p. 219). On the other hand, the efforts by some noted businessmen to attain elected office have not been successful, e.g., Peter Pocklington, Stephen Roman, Wallace McCutcheon. Some have succeeded (e.g., Robert Winters, Michael Wilson, C.D. Howe, Ron Huntington), but it was largely despite and not because of their experience in business.

We should not exaggerate the level of status and social prestige of businessmen in Canada. It could be easy to do so at present in light of the various chronicles of the life-styles and corporate deeds of the more visible business executives and the families that own/control large businesses.[39] Although Canadians may be fascinated by the economic and political "games" played by the titans of big business, they may need more time to appreciate some of the less attractive consequences of what has happened over the past few years.[40] History suggests that their long run opinion of business leaders over the long term appears not to be as high as that of their American neighbors.

It should be emphasized that the effectiveness of business leaders in influencing public opinion and government decision makers varies with the issue and the political context in which it arises. The status and influence of businessmen, like the stock market, rises and falls. Presently, there appears to be a greater interest in and public support for business entrepreneurship, competitive markets, individual initiative and a smaller public bureaucracy. But tides go out as well as come in. Businessmen should not let their improved status go to their heads as they will almost inevitably face disappointment within a few years.

Perhaps more important than the social status of businessmen in terms of corporate power is the apparently inherent legitimacy of mega corporations in Canadian society. My argument is based on the following observations. First, there is in North America a cultural predisposition to "worship" the biggest of anything in the vein that the biggest equals best idea. (This is not to say that the "small is beautiful" idea has not gained support since the 1960s.)

Second, there is the widespread belief, endlessly reinforced by leading Canadian businessmen, that firms can only grow into behemoths because they are more efficient, more innovative or have adapted more effectively to changes in the environment. There is vague, but strong feeling of corporate Darwinism. Unlike Darwin, however, the true believers in this idea attach a normative significance to survival and growth. Mega corporations invite an application of Alexander Pope's dictum, "whatever is, is right." Recently Trevor Eyton (1986b), president and CEO of Brascan Limited, a senior executive in a handful of companies in the Edper/Brascan group, and a member of the board of directors of 25 businesses, noted that among the world's largest enterprises, Canada's largest (General Motors of Canada) ranked only 45th. The largest Canadian-owned enterprises ranked about 60th. In his view, "because corporate size and economies of scale are linked, this leads to the conclusion that the smallness of Canada's corporations constitutes a very real constraint on our ability to compete in the global village featuring increasingly international trade" (Eyton, 1986, p. 5).[41] He noted that "virtually all of Canada's foreign trade is accounted for by larger Canadian corporations" (p. 6).

Third, mega corporations appear to benefit from the fallacy of sunk costs, i.e., their existing huge capital investments create a kind of momentum in the world of politics. If such wealth is threatened, it must be protected by government action if need be. (This is not to say that there would not be large disruption costs if a corporate giant was allowed to go broke.) Therefore, politicians are willing to vote tens or hundreds of millions of dollars to bail out a large corporation in order to prevent what they believe will be the destruction of their assets.[42]

3.9 Canadians' Trust in Concentrations of Power
As compared with Americans, Canadians are remarkably trusting of large aggregations of power, whether they are in private or public hands. This constitutes a considerable political resource for mega corporations in Canada. Canadians are less concerned with the rights of the individual than they are with what they feel are the benefits of various types of collective action. On almost every occasion, they have traded increased economic and psychological security for a reduction in personal freedom and individual responsibility. They see big institutions (corporations, governments, unions, etc.) as a desirable means of achieving security, not as threats to their freedom. Canadians usually see concentrations of power in a benign light.

Why have Canadians been so eager to achieve security? Perhaps it is the harshness of the climate and the frequent adversity of nature.[43] Perhaps it is the experience of being a small population in a vast land of greatly varied regions (see Malcolm 1985). Perhaps it is our location adjacent to the economic and political power of the U.S. (see Stanbury 1987). Perhaps it is our colonial heritage, which encourages dependency rather than autonomy. According to Friedenberg (1986, p. 55),

> Peace, order and good government in Canada depend ultimately on the deep acquiescence of the people in the idea that they have no inalienable rights; ultimately, the final decision rests with the cabinet. Instead, they have ombudsmen, negotiators whose responsibility it is to present the citizen's case to the authorities and try to get him a better deal.

Large size in Canada confers legitimacy and authority. The idea is that "they (those who control large private or public institutions) must know what is best for us." The fact is – and it is a crucial one in understanding the growth of corporate power in Canada – that Canadians exhibit a remarkable amount of deference to authority (see Friedenberg 1980). However, as Friedenberg (1980, p. 137) notes,

> In Canada, there has existed and will continue to exist, extreme concentration of economic power. But this fact of itself does not tell us how that concentration affects the quality of life in Canada or the freedom of individual Canadians, and these are much more complex questions.

I return to Canadian values in Section 6.

3.10 Poor Macro Economic Performance
The political influence of big business (or even business in general) is likely to be much greater when governments are unable to achieve full employment and a rising standard of living for a majority of citizens. The sad fact is that the federal government in Canada has been unable to use the levers of macro-economic policy to achieve full employment in recent years. As long as it fails to do so it will be fairly easy prey to business demands, along with

those of provincial and local governments, for economic assistance in order to create jobs. It is not hard to find examples where governments in Canada have been willing to pay directly or indirectly up to several million dollars of taxpayers' money for each new job created or to pay annual subsidies equal to several times the annual income of each worker employed.

These examples are not hard to find because of the generally high level of unemployment (which has averaged over 10 per cent for the past several years) and extremely high levels of unemployment in certain regions (e.g., the Maritimes, parts of Quebec and parts of B.C.). When a major new plant is to be built it is common for several provinces to compete by offering various subsidies, "tax breaks" and other inducements to the corporation involved. One of the worst or best examples recently was the fight over the Hyundai car plant which eventually went to Bromont, Quebec.[44] In this case, not only did Quebec and Ontario compete for the right to greatly subsidize this Korean company, but Quebec and the federal government sought to top each other's bids in terms of economic assistance. A few years earlier the intense competition between Quebec, Ontario and several U.S. states (e.g., Michigan) for a new engine plant to be built by Ford resulted in an agreement to prevent such suicidal bidding wars in the future.

4.0 MANIFESTATIONS OF CORPORATE POLITICAL POWER
4.1 Methodological Considerations
There are formidable methodology difficulties in determining the extent of business interests' influence on public policy. First, how do we identify cause and effect when a firm or group of firms have sought to influence a particular policy? True, in many cases we can identify and perhaps measure their "inputs." With careful research we can often identify the policy "output" associated with particular issues, although it has been suggested that on occasion governments seek to do good by stealth. We may even be able to ascertain the short and longer term *impact* of the policy action on the firm or firms in question. But what is extremely difficult – perhaps impossible – is to penetrate and understand the workings of the "black box" in which all the various forces (including chance) come together to produce the observed policy action.

Second, if the heart of the policy process is opaque, and even if we are able to identify all of the forces (considerations) involved in the policy formulation process – and this is no easy task – then we are very unlikely to be able to disentangle the effects of each "input" into the process. What we really want to know is the size and stability of the coefficients of the independent or explanatory variables in a regression equation designed to predict (explain) policy "outputs."

Because power (or influence) is a relative matter, we want to know the importance of a firm's influence in a set of policy issues relative to all the other factors (inputs) into the black box. Even when a group has more power than others and it is the most important variable, but where there are a large number of other factors influencing the policy output, the percentage of the total variance explained by the group's efforts may be small. In general terms, the process by which public policy is made in Canada is complex, dynamic, subject to conflict and competition, and involves a substantial number of participants (see Stanbury 1986a, Ch. 4). Therefore it should be clear that determining the impact of a particular firm, a trade association, or even big business as a very broad interest group, presents a serious challenge to the analyst.

The task is made more difficult because, *a priori*, there appears to be strong pre-conceptions about the extent of business influence over public policy. There are many people who are sure they "know the answer" and new evidence is very unlikely to be persuasive. At one extreme are those such as many neo-Marxists for whom it is axiomatic that the corporate elite of the capitalist class not only hold the reins of economic power, but they (perhaps together with other elites within the capitalist class) dominate government policy making. For example, William Carroll (1986) argues that the dominant class, in this case "the capitalists in control of the corporations," "play a hegemonic role in shaping the economic and political structures through which it rules."[45]

In the view of Beck (1985), because business interests and government are so interdependent, that government "must, to a significant degree, be acquiescent to the needs and demands of business for to do so is not more than to provide good government." Business interests have a special place in policy making, one that "no other interest group can begin to approach."

There are others who are equally firmly convinced that business exercises very little influence in government policy making. For example, Peter Newman (1979, p. 159), quotes the (former) chairman of Canada Packers as saying, "being a businessman has a negative influence when dealing with government. Business has become impotent." According to a well known Montreal investment counsellor, "politicians must inevitably look at the vote." Because "about 90 per cent of Canadian households earn under $14,000 [this was in the early 1970s], so the vote of the rest doesn't count . . . The 10 per cent of the people with funds to invest are locked out of the democratic process" (quoted in Newman 1979, p. 161). In the same vein, others strongly believe that policy making in Canada is genuinely pluralistic with multiple contending interests that are roughly evenly balanced, or if business does on occasion exercise some influence on policy making that its influence is benign, it is in the public interest. This view is well represented in *Report* of the Royal Commission on Corporate Concentration in 1978.[46]

As a final comment on the methodological problems of determining the relative influence of mega corporations on public policy I note the problem of coincidence of interests (generally, see Forster 1986). How do we distinguish causation from a commonality of interests between government decision makers and business even where we observe a large number of instances in which business "got what it asked for"? Park and Park (1973, p. 54) point out that "the case for the community of interest between the government and big business ultimately rests on an analysis of the actions of government and their effects on big business." Suppose we find that a large fraction of policy actions by government are neutral or beneficial to big business, what do we conclude? Suppose further that we observe that business interests have lobbied strenuously to obtain those policy actions and that other interest groups opposed them vigorously. Can we correctly conclude that business interests generally dominate the process – that they generally get their way?

It would seem reasonable to do so for we have noted that in quite a number of situations where business interests have had to compete with other groups which have opposed them and/or advocated quite different policy actions, business "won" more often than not. There may, however, be another plausible explanation. It may be that business interests tend, on average, to more frequently coincide with the interests of the Government. The point is that a Government *has* interests. It is not a mere cipher. Moreover, it has a variety of governing instruments it can use to achieve its objectives. Unlike business or any other interest group it has the legitimate authority to use coercion (e.g., taxation, regulation, the police power) to implement its policies or to respond to the initiatives of the private sector.[47]

I turn to a discussion of the possible manifestations of the influence of big business on public policy.

4.2   Possible Manifestations of Political Influence

To properly assess the extent of influence (or power) an interest group (or business enterprise) has in the formation of public policy, we need to consider the possible manifestations of political influence – or lack of it. What are the signs that a group has substantial influence? These can be grouped into two categories:

(a)   **Outcome Manifestations**

- The ability to *veto* policy actions that otherwise had wide support.[49]

- The ability to *initiate* and have *implemented* on a regular basis policy actions that are strongly opposed by other major players.[50]

- The ability of a group to alter (or even reverse) a well-established policy when it is seen to work to the disadvantage of that group – despite the fact that the policy is satisfactory to everyone else.[51]

- The ability to shift one's political support to another party (or leader) and thereby move the party from opposition to government (backbencher to leader). In short, I refer to the ability to determine the outcome of elections.[52]

(b)   **Process Manifestations**

- A group has easy access, multiple points of access to the policy making process relative to other interests.[53]

- The group has an institutionalized position (or positions) in the policy making process, i.e., they have a reserved seat at the table across which all the important papers move and the views of the "movers and shakers" are invited.[54]

- Respectful attention: a group's views are always treated seriously, they are weighed carefully if not always followed.

- The group has the ability to create (or change) the fundamental assumptions or "givens" under which a policy is being made, i.e., what are the "facts", what are the priorities, what are the basic values which imbue the process, what are the relevant alternatives to be considered seriously?[55]

- The group benefits from forbearance by politicians and bureaucrats: to limit the alternatives seriously considered in policy formulation in anticipation of the wrath of a particular interest group.[56]

4.3   Other (Macro) Manifestations of Political Power

By concentrating on what are really micro phenomena we have ignored other, broader phenomena. The following macro or *systemic* phenomena provide useful evidence of the political power of big business.

1.   There has been a relatively steady increase in the level of aggregate concentration in Canada, at least between 1965 and 1983. Statistics Canada indicates that the 100 largest non-financial enterprises accounted for 38.6 per cent of the assets of all such firms in 1965 and 52.2 per cent in 1983. No doubt when the data for 1987 are published they will reveal that the top 100's share has increased by several percentage points due largely to the large number of large mergers in 1985 (16), 1986 (43) and 1987 (22 by June 10).[57]

The critical point is this: the federal government has not taken any action to inhibit the growth in aggregate concentration.[58] The reasons for failing to act are hard to discern. Perhaps the government believes that the social benefits of higher aggregate concentration outweigh the current and potential adverse consequences. In other words, they tacitly accept[59] the line of reasoning advanced by prominent Ontario Tory insider Eddie Goodman:

Sure the conglomerates [such as Edper/Brascan/Hees] are far too complex for them [top management] to be in control, but they can occasionally act in concert. But occasionally is not serious. The benefits outweigh the risks. We [Canadians] have to have players on the international market, and our pools of capital are just spits in the ocean. The country needs corporate strength . . . (quoted in Dewar 1985b, p. 61).

Perhaps the various federal governments have failed to act against increasing aggregate concentration because big business has been able to exert sufficient influence to persuade them not to legislate against growing concentration. Perhaps members of the federal cabinet have not felt sufficiently threatened by corporate concentration to see that any legislative or other policy action was necessary.[60]

2.   Although anti-combines legislation was introduced in 1889, one year before the famous *Sherman Act* in the United States, Canada has never had any enforceable provisions in respect to takeovers or mergers(see Reschenthaler and Stanbury 1977). It remains to be seen if the civil merger provisions in the new *Competition Act*, which came into force on June 19, 1986, are effective.[61] As a result, businessmen have been virtually free to alter the structure of any industry as they saw fit in the apparently relentless search for profits. Even today, only those mergers with horizontal and/or vertical elements can be addressed by the new *Competition Act*. Pure conglomerate mergers, no matter how large, are exempt. For example, the new legislation, if it had been in place, could not have touched Imasco's takeover of Genstar.[62]

It should be noted that the concerted lobbying of the business community fought every effort to strengthen Canada's weak antitrust laws between 1969 (when the Economic Council's report on competition policy was published) and 1986.[63] Specifically, between 1977 and December 1985 the federal government introduced four bills (C-42 and C-13 in 1977, C-29 in 1984 and C-91 in 1985) to deal with, *inter alia*, the problem of mergers. The first two were defeated by the vociferous opposition of business firms, trade associations and their legal counsel (Stanbury 1986g). The third, Bill C-29 in 1984, was the product of line-by-line negotiations with the "Gang of Three" (CMA, CCC, BCNI) and, as a result, it was a severely watered-down bill (Stanbury 1985). The fourth bill (C-91) was eventually enacted, but as introduced it was even weaker than C-29 (Stanbury 1986b). It was the product of intensive negotiations between the government (Department of Consumer and Corporate Affairs) and the "Gang of Five" (The Gang of Three plus GPMC and CBA). Somewhat surprisingly, the Consumers Association, academics and CFIB were able to obtain some amendments to improve the bill somewhat.

3.   The Davey Commission (Canada 1970), the Royal Commission on Newspapers (Canada 1981), the Caplan-Sauvageau Report (1986) and other sources indicate that the ownership of newspapers, periodicals, radio stations and television stations is highly concentrated; there is a great deal of multi-media ownership, e.g., the Irving family in New Brunswick, Southam; and a number of the owners of the largest media interests are industrial conglomerates, e.g., the Irving family, the Thomson Organization, etc.

Over the years, the federal government has done little to limit such concentration. When it threatened to do so with the proposed *Daily Newspapers Act* in 1982, it felt the full weight of the newspaper owners and thought better of it as noted above. The Tories revoked the CRTC's order that K.C. Irving sell off some of his media holdings so as to eliminate his ownership of both print and electronic media in several cities in New Brunswick.

4.   Despite the enormous growth of the welfare state (e.g., one-quarter of total Personal Income in Canada takes the form of transfers from governments) and the regulatory state, the long run profitability of private

enterprise has not been reduced in Canada. It has not been reduced over time or in relation to other industrialized countries. Canada remains a generally attractive place for both domestic and foreign capitalists.

Private enterprise remains firmly entrenched and is the dominant form of activity when the economy is viewed as a whole. It is true, however, that it has become common to speak of Canada's "mixed economy" in recognition of the fact that the expenditures of governments now amount to about 48 per cent of GNP whereas they were in the range of 5 per cent to 7 per cent at the time of Confederation (Howard & Stanbury 1984). In addition, there are several hundred federal and provincial Crown corporations. Despite some recent efforts at privatization,[64] and regulatory reform (Stanbury 1987b), government activity in Canada is still very expensive.

Therefore, while the scope of economic activity in the hands of privately-owned enterprises has declined somewhat over the past century, capitalism flourishes. The long run rate of return on capital has not been reduced. Moreover, the growth of government activity has seen the creation of new opportunities for individuals and organizations to advance their pecuniary interests. Rent seeking has grown enormously. People routinely choose to advance their economic interests in political markets rather than the traditional marketplace.

The neo-Marxists emphasize that the growth of the state does not imply that capitalism has been weakened. Indeed, Wallace Clement (1983, p. 125) argues that the state in Canada "is a capitalist state predicated on maintaining [basic] property relations and is thus limited by this basic commitment [to the rights of private property]." Moreover, those who control the largest enterprises "have been effective in using the state apparatus to aggrandize their own power in their respective spheres of concentration..." (Clement 1983, p. 86). According to Clement, the most visible elements of the welfare state "are concessions that sustain the prevailing system and do not interfere with the rights of private property". Many forms of intervention effectively "socialize the costs of maintaining capitalism" because the state provides services that would otherwise be left to the individual or corporation (Clement 1983, p. 123).

The neo-Marxists go through elaborate and interesting contortions seeking to explain the continued existence, indeed, the good health, of capitalism in Western industrialized countries. Marx' prediction of the imminent death of capitalism reminds one of Mark Twain's statement that reports of his demise had been greatly exaggerated. No modern Marxist predicts that capitalism's end is near. This fact should not only provide encouragement to practicing capitalists, but it should also be cited as evidence of the political power of the corporate elite or business class. They could hardly be said to be dominant if their fundamental institutions were imperiled.

5.0   LIMITATIONS ON THE POLITICAL POWER OF MEGA CORPORATIONS

5.1   Identifying the Constraints

What are the factors or forces constraining the political power of large corporations? Epstein (1969, Ch. 8) identifies the following:

- political resources are not equivalent to political power,

- other social interests have political resources (countervailing power),

- opposition of the general public, particularly the emphasis on social pluralism, and

- constraints within the business system such as problems of coordination and internal conflicts over public policy.

This list is obviously incomplete. I have classified the constraints on corporate political power into two categories as follows:

(a)   *Natural*

- The political power of large corporations is constrained by the competition (countervailing power) of other interests: labour, consumers, environmentalists, nationalists. Canada is a pluralist society in the sense that a number of different interests are contending for a place in the sun and competing to influence government policy. This does not mean that reality is close to the pluralist ideal of a very large number of contending interests (reflecting the full diversity of substantive interests in society), or that such interests are "balanced" in that there is some sort of parity of power or influence over the formation of public policy.

- Business managers' behaviour is constrained by the market for corporate control. The capital market can extract its revenge on inefficient managers – including those who have pursued political objectives at the expense of profits for shareholders.[65]

- Competition among political parties, notably from the left ("contagion from the left") represents an important limitation on the political power of corporations – see Chandler (1977).

- The values of populism, the belief in the tenets of popular democracy, and the distrust of "vested interests" by at least some fraction of the electorate all limit the exercise of political power by large corporations.

- Abuses and scandals with their attendant media exposure also act as a constraint. Nothing promotes reform like well publicized excesses.

- Lack of unanimity within the business community or even among the top 50 limits the actual impact of big business' potential political power. There are numerous cleavages on specific government policies by industry, ownership, and region.

- The absolute size of the corporate elite militates against a conspiracy to exercise political power. It is hard to have a conspiracy among a few thousand people – even if one-quarter went to Upper Canada College! (this is not to say that such individuals do not have a loose community interest.)

- Politicians intent upon seeking or retaining power can be amoral. They may not be constrained by any philosophical commitment to individual freedom or small government or other specific issues favoured by large enterprises. They must balance competing interests in order to retain power – see Section 5.2 below.

(b) *Government Policy*

In principle, governments have the power to curb the growth of aggregate concentration in a number of ways:

- Antitrust policy which inhibits very large mergers, including conglomerates.

- Tax policy that prohibits the deduction of interest on money borrowed to finance takeovers.

- Prohibitions or several limitations on the ownership of large financial institutions by industrial interest.

- Limitations on cross-media ownership and the ownership of major radio, television or newspapers by industrial interests.

- "Countervailing policies" such as
   - funding of opposing voices (interest groups),
   - registration of lobbyists,
   - "government in the sunshine" legislation,
   - conflict of interest legislation, and
   - inheritance taxes that reduce personal concentrations of wealth.

- The use of scientific polls by government to assess public opinions in part to counteract pressures from organized interests.

5.2 Maintaining Political Support: The Need for Populism

A Government's primary interest is to retain office.[66] To retain power, the rational strategy is to practice marginal voter politics, the essence of which is to focus policy initiatives on what are believed to be voters in marginal constituencies. But political activity requires financial and other resources. Inevitably, the Government (and opposition parties) must necessarily exchange policy actions (or promises of policies) for political support, including campaign contributions from those individuals or groups that have a large stake in government policy.

At the same time, however, the Government must *balance* the need for specialized support (campaign contributions, information, media coverage, etc.) with the need for large numbers of votes (see Wolfe 1985). To gain a majority of seats, even with a three-party system, a party must appeal to the "masses", not simply the elite. If a government in Canada is seen to attend very closely to the publicly expressed views of the major business or trade associations – the institutionalized interests primarily of "big business" – it is unlikely to be re-elected. While in politics perception is reality, and the art of smoke and mirrors is frequently practiced, trade-offs must be made. Policies must be put in place that benefit hundreds of thousands of lower or middle income voters even at the expense of the economic elite. Brokerage of differing interests is essential. The politician's art lies in retaining the support of both groups more effectively than rival parties. *A priori*, therefore, we should expect that some government policies should favour business interests while others should favour other interests even at the expense of business. We should also expect the balance of advantage to change over time even when the same party is in office and also to change somewhat when a different party forms a government.

Wolfe (1985, p. 144) points out that "the key to the success of the centrist [federal] government that served through most of the postwar period was its ability to balance competing claims of the broad political constituencies from which it drew its electoral support." The Liberals were able to generally please business, or at least not alienate it, while at the same time offering lower and middle class voters transfer programs and satisfying symbols (e.g., national unity, a new flag, etc.) more effectively than the Conservatives or the NDP. To gain and hold office a national party needs both money (from business) and votes (from blue and white collar workers). Finding the right balance is difficult – as it is in any high wire act.[67]

The balancing act is complicated by the fact that both the Liberals and the Tories have to contend with the NDP and its substantial share of the federal popular vote (about 20 per cent). "Contagion from the left" is a real phenomenon (Chandler 1977). Indeed, between elections the leader of the NDP's popularity rises to rival or even exceed the leaders of the other parties. The Tories also have to deal with the Liberal Party's consistent record of adopting – albeit in a modified way – NDP policies so as to maintain a position of being generally left of centre (see Chandler 1977). The welfare state in Canada[68] has broad support, much to the chagrin of at least some business leaders. While the welfare state is not the creation of business interests, this is not to say that each and every brick in its edifice was violently opposed by business. What some business interests have done, however, is to pressure the state (successfully) to create a wide variety of "welfare" programs for business.[69] The list is long: tariff and non-tariff barriers; generous tax expenditures; growing direct cash subsidies in the name of regional development; agricultural products supply management schemes (government-mandated cartels). The list could go on – indeed, the former Department of Industry, Trade and Commerce published a 300-page book listing hundreds of programs designed to assist business with subsidies, grants, etc.

Clement (1983, p. 89) argues that "a great deal of state policy is directed at moderating the glaring inequalities of capitalism" in the interests of harmony and the continued dominance of the capitalists, "but it draws the line at the greatest inequality, that of the private power of property." With respect, Clement is moving toward a tautological argument and he may also fail to appreciate the ability of left-wing/liberal elements in a democratic society to use the power of the state to restrict the rights of private property. Rent control in Ontario – introduced in 1975 provides such an example (see Stanbury & Thain 1986). Stringent controls, which were changed in many important respects, over the past decade, effectively obviated many of the traditional rights associated with the ownership of real property. In most cases, large opportunity losses were imposed on the owners of rental properties in the name of providing affordable housing for low income families and to prevent rent gouging. In summary, the power of the state – at the behest of renters – was used to very severely attenuate the very rights of private property that Professor Clement suggests are beyond the pale in a capitalist-dominated democracy.

5.3 Coercive Powers of Government
Governments in Canada possess extensive and unique powers to influence the behaviour of individuals and organizations. Only governments have the legitimacy in a democracy to exercise coercion in the name of that philosophically troubling concept of "the public interest." They can tax, regulate, spend, create Crown enterprises, invest in privately-owned ones, use suasion, borrow/lend and even print money in the case of the federal government (see Howard and Stanbury 1984). Governments also have the right of eminent domain and so may seize private property (with compensation). The powers given to governments by citizens are breathtaking and they are but modestly circumscribed by the new *Constitution Act, 1982*. In fact, the cabinet of a majority government in Canada is a periodically elected kingship that has a wide range of coercive governing instruments and subject to few *formal* constraints (e.g., popular elections must be held at least every five years). The real constraints are informal, although real in practice. These include:

- The ability of the mass media and opposition parties to expose malfeasance, scandal and questionable behaviour;

- The power of public opinion when it is aroused and channeled by the media and opposition politicians;

- The countervailing actions of other governments, both at home and abroad; and think of the terrible toils of federal-provincial relations;

- The failure of the government to obtain active support of the senior functionaries of the vast public service and related agencies (even uncoordinated resistance to initiatives of the bureaucracy in a democracy, where the scope of government is great will thwart the designs of an aggressive government).

5.4 Turnover Among the Largest Corporations

Even though aggregate concentration has increased in Canada since the mid-1960s, we must consider the fact that there is turnover within the set of dominant firms. As the neo-Marxist William Carroll (1986, p. 75) puts it, "the largest firms do not comprise a fixed and unchanging bloc of capital, insulated from the competitive rigours of the market". Turnover among mega corporations probably has the effect of such enterprises on the political system.

There are several types of turnover among mega corporations. First, there is the use of the same legal entities, in same rank order, run by the same persons, over a specific period. In this situation aggregate concentration could either rise or fall. Second, the level of aggregate concentration (e.g., the fraction of all non-financial assets accounted for by the largest 100 firms) could remain constant over time, but (a) the identities of the top firms could – at the extreme – change completely,[70] (b) even if the identity of each firm is unchanged, the identity of those persons that control it could change over time. This turnover may not matter much if the leaders of all dominant corporations act in a similar manner. If, in other words, they act as a class the fact that their identity changes is irrelevant. Clement (1983), for example, argues that individuals among the corporate elite act as a class.

5.5 The Market for Corporate Control

It is usually argued that the market for corporate control provides an arena in which alternative management teams compete for the right to manage corporate resources.[71] It is argued that takeovers are the "revenge of the capital market" on inefficient and/or ineffective management or controlling interests that do not have a majority of the voting stock. However, as aggregate concentration increases there may well be a reduction in the threat from the market for corporate control for at least two reasons. First, due to the absolute size of these mega corporations, it may be impossible to finance a takeover via a hostile tender offer.[72] Second, ownership linkages from non-financial firms to financial firms (banks, trust companies, insurance, securities dealers, etc.) may restrict the sources of finance to make a tender offer.

In Canada, however, the possibilities of a hostile takeover by means of a public tender are far less than they are in the U.S. Why? Because such a large fraction of publicly traded firms are *not* widely held.

> The situation in Canada [is] revealed by a 1984 Toronto Stock Exchange (TSE) study . . . Some 283 public companies make up the TSE 300 composite index. Legal control (50 percent or more) was present in 137 companies (40 percent); effective control (20 percent to 49.9 percent) was present in 84 companies (30 percent) and 61 companies (21 percent) were widely held. Looked at another way, close to 80 percent of the listed companies are controlled by a single family and/or group. Conversely, the Standard & Poor's 500 index in the United States shows 426 (85.2

percent) of the companies to be widely held. The Financial Post's list of Canada's top 500 companies, ranked by sales, shows only 17 (3.4 percent) to be widely held, that is, with no one owning more than 10 percent. Another 21 are owned by cooperative members or employees. Some 75 of the top 200 companies (37.5 percent) are majority or wholly owned by foreign corporations. In short, the picture in Canada is one of very significant control of the economy by a small number of families and foreign corporations. (Beck 1985, p. 196)

Francis (1986, p. 4) states that only 20 of Canada's 400 largest public corporations are widely-held, i.e., no one individual family or corporation holds more than 15 per cent. In 374 corporations a controlling interest of at least 25 per cent to 30 per cent is held by a family or conglomerate. Of the 100 largest public companies, which account for about one-half of all corporate assets, 25 per cent of the sales and assets are family-controlled, 25 per cent are in the hands of widely-held conglomerates, 25 per cent are foreign-controlled and 25 per cent are public enterprises or co-operatives.

A superb example of a very large enterprise that is closely controlled is ,the Edper/Brascan complex controlled by Edward and Peter Bronfman. They directly or indirectly control a substantial number of firms ranked in the *Financial Post 500* or on related lists of large enterprises:[73]

- F.P. 500: #18, 26, 40, 42, 136, 148, 172, 316, 397

- 100 lgst. fin. inst.: #10, 34

- 100 lgst. subsidiaries: # 33, 59, 64, 65, 86

- 100 cos. of tomorrow: #53, 55, 99

- 15 lgst. real estate sales: #1

- 25 lgst. life insurers: #7

This means that not only is it not possible to acquire *any* of these companies by means of a hostile public tender offer, but is also not possible for control of the entire Edper group of companies to pass to other owners unless the two brothers agree to sell. They are immune from the revenge of the market for corporate control almost regardless of how badly they manage their "empire." If they manage it badly, not only do the brothers dissipate their own fortune, they also reduce the wealth of thousands of public shareholders who collectively have a large stake in Brascan companies. They are, however, constrained by creditors. If the group as a whole cannot generate sufficient income to meet its interest payments assets could be seized and sold off or a corporate reorganization forced upon the brothers. Even if interest obligations are met creditors will not continue to extend credit if they are not confident that the value of the firm's assets will continue to exceed its liabilities. This means that at the operating level profits and cash flow must be (or expected to be) sufficient to maintain the value of the firm's assets.

Amicable takeovers (or mergers) of closely-held corporations are almost certainly likely to increase aggregate concentration. This is the case because a group of "outsiders" who form a coalition to make a public tender offer are likely to be seen as hostile by the selling group. Moreover, as macro-concentration increases, the number of potential buyers is reduced. These are likely to be other large or very large enterprises.

5.6   Political Disadvantages of Large Corporations
Large corporations do have certain disadvantages in the political arena. They are generally more *visible* politically when it comes to asking for and receiving "handouts." (This is reinforced by access to information legis-lation.) However, tax expenditures are easier to hide than cash subsidies.

Thirty small firms equal in size to one large one will have more clout when they are able to coordinate their lobbying efforts.

For a variety of reasons, perhaps philosophical, at least some people fear bigness in terms of its disproportionate political influence; it contradicts the democratic ideal. They are hypersensitive to obvious efforts to exert influence.

Clever opponents can at least temporarily hobble giant corporations by using "David and Goliath" tactics in the media, e.g., Ralph Nader and GM. One thinks also of the inbred hostility to the CPR in western Canada; it has been a favorite whipping boy of politicians for generations.

Large enterprises are large bureaucracies. While they have organizational skill, they may not be able to be highly responsive to changes in their environment. They may well be politically insensitive and hence perceived as inept.

As aggregate concentration increases, governments have a greater opportunity to "coerce" firms because the larger multi-industry enterprise "interfaces" with government at more points. The opportunity for log rolling or making trade-offs among a number of issues is increased. See Stanbury and Fulton (1984) on government's use of suasion.

6.0   CONCLUSIONS: CANADIAN VALUES AND THE CONCENTRATION OF POWER
Peter Newman (1979, p. 464) argues that the idea of a Canadian Establishment, "the notion of the existence of an undemocratic class structure, comes as a profound shock to many Canadians. It negates the populist belief in the wide open spaces, the notion of Canada as a land of freely accessible opportunities." With respect, Newman is quite wrong. Most Canadians — if they think of the issue at all — are quite comfortable with the idea of an establishment or even of a group of interconnected, highly undemocratic elites dominating the key institutions of life in Canada: the economy, politics, the media, etc.[74] If they were uncomfortable, why have they designed or tolerated the domination of elites in so many areas of national life? As Edgar Friedenberg (1980, p. 152) has pointed out,

Canadian society is peculiarly consistent. All its institutions are designed or, at least, have evolved to concentrate control at the top, reduce the effectiveness of influences originating at lower levels, and insulate themselves from external stimuli until they have been cleared by persons in authority.

Newman (1979, p. 463) contends that "it was not until 1965 that the power structure of this country was examined in detail" with the publication of John Porter's *The Vertical Mosaic.* Yet a fair number of academics, social critics (largely on the left) and other only slightly sophisticated observers appreciated that the interrelated elites ran the show. The Family Compact in colonial times has been the model upon which Canada has developed. What formal research and richly detailed anecdotal accounts such as those in Newman's several books have done is to document what was essentially common knowledge.

It is a fact that most Canadians are not instinctively populists or even pluralists, although the rhetoric of pluralism pervades discussions of the relationship between power and public policy (see, for example, Beck 1985). Rather, most Canadians suffer from strong feelings of insecurity. To gain security they have put their trust in large aggregations of power – both private and public. They have steadily supported scores of different governments, each of whom left office with a larger public sector (considered in its entirety) than when it was elected (see Howard & Stanbury 1984). They have tolerated, and implicitly encouraged, the growth of closely-held, private business empires in the hope that they would provide them with economic and psychological security. They have sought – and gained – strong father figures (or is it nurturing mother figures?).

Very few Canadians fear any potential loss of liberty associated with the concentration of power. Canadians have systematically traded off individual responsibility for powerful social and economic institutions they believe provide collective security. They are happy to delegate, almost without recourse, to the few in business, politics, culture and the media who seem to know best what's good for them. Competition both as a social and economic process is little esteemed by Canadians. Competition implies conflict and competitors can behave ruthlessly. Moreover, it is a disorderly process and Canadians place a high value on order and predictability. In general Canadians do not see the growth of aggregate concentration as a threat to either their personal political freedom or to their democratic political system.

Perhaps such Canadians feel they can rein in such large and potentially unruly horses should they go too far. But by what means would they do so? Could they reassert their authority over the federal government and mandate it to act to curb the negative externalities of the mega corporations? It may be, however, that these business enterprises have been able to effectively alter the way the political process works, and in particular the way in which public policy is formulated that a "populist revolt" could not succeed.

NOTES

1. See Appendix 1 of this volume.

2. Statistics Canada indicates that as of 1983 the 100 largest non-financial enterprises accounted for 39.2 per cent of the sales and 52.2 per cent of the assets of all non-financial corporations in Canada. The comparable figures in 1975 were 36 per cent and 46.5 per cent respectively. Obviously these data do not incorporate the effects of the 1985-87 merger boom. More comprehensive discussions of aggregate concentration can be found in Chapters 1 and 3 of this volume.

3. The phrase "large corporations" in this paper refers to those financial and non-financial enterprises which rank in the largest 100 to 200 in each category (i.e., are relatively large in terms of the Canadian economy). Such firms account for a much larger share of aggregate economic activity in Canada than do their American, Japanese, and German counterparts, for example. See Marfels' paper, Chapter 3 in this volume.

4. See, for example, "A political minefield," *Maclean's*, February 2, 1987, pp. 8-16; "Government under siege," *Maclean's*, February 16, 1987, pp. 10-14; "Mulroney's new offensive," *Maclean's*, February 23, 1987, pp. 6-8.

5. Generally, see Berle (1969), Dahl (1957), de Jouvenel (1949), Epstein (1969), Galbraith (1983), Manning (1960), Mason (1950), Pfeffer (1981), Russell (1938), Ulmer (1971), Wrong (1980).

6. Some psychologists argue that there is a hierarchy of need or wants and as lower level needs for food, sex and security are met "higher order" needs associated with ego and self-fulfillment emerge and become much more important. Peter Newman (1979, p. 48) suggests that Paul Desmarais, chairman of Power Corporation, was able to alter the Quebec government's policy concerning independence in 1967 through discussions with the premier. The ability to "make history" must be very rewarding to those with such power.

7. For a discussion of the various concepts of the public interest and its strategic use in lobbying, see Stanbury (1986a, Ch. 4).

8. An obvious exception is the important work of Edwin M. Epstein (1969).

9. See, for example, Howard and Stanbury (1984).

10. For a detailed discussion, see Stanbury (1986a).

11. For example, "According to a CBC report, the controversial fund raising party was held in Montreal in July 1985, with then-public works minister [Roch] La Salle as the guest of honor. Most of the 30 businessmen paid $5,000 apiece—in cash—to attend. In return, they expected to receive federal contracts—but they were apparently

disappointed and later voiced their complaints to La Salle." (*Maclean's*, February 23, 1987, pp. 6-7.) See also Graham Fraser, "La Salle probe called last year, PM says," *Globe and Mail*, February 14, 1987, pp. A1, A5.

12. See William Walker, "No-fault auto insurance 'hottest issue', NDP says," Toronto *Star*, February 28, 1987, pp. A1, A12; Duncan McMonagle, "Public no-fault car insurance 'a very sexy political issue,'" *Globe and Mail*, March 7, 1987, pp. A1, A2; Duncan McMonagle, "Insurers say no-fault plan could cut auto rates 15%," *Globe and Mail*, March 12, 1987, pp. A1, A2; see the full page advocacy ads in the Toronto *Star*, March 13, 1987, p. F7 by the Insurance Bureau of Canada, and Toronto *Star*, March 7, 1987, p. D8 by the Co-operators Insurance Services.

13. For example, in 1921, when he was opposition leader, Mackenzie King denounced "the real though invisible government . . . the little oligarchy of interwoven financial, manufacturing, transportation and distributing interests" (House of Commons, *Debates*, May 19, 1921, p. 3603). More generally, see Campbell (1978), Carroll (1986), Chodos (1973), Clement (1975, 1977, 1983a), Finn (1970), Francis (1986), League for Social Reconstruction (1935), Levitt (1970), Mahon (1977), Marchak (1983), McCollum (1935, 1947), Mintz and Cohen (1977), Park and Park (1973), Starowicz and Murphy (1972), Traves (1979), Slichter (1931, p. 14).

14. Bayless Manning (1960) suggests that what we fear is the power of others to put into place policies to which we object. "The question is not power, it is policy" (quoted in Epstein 1969, p. 190).

15. See, for example, Beck (1985, p. 182).

16. It should be noted that a similar result could flow from large aggregations of private wealth in any form.

17. See, for example, Ghert (1985, 1986), Nader *et al* (1976, pp. 75, 225), Turner (1986).

18. The central problem for most critics is that the concentration of economic resources gives their owners/controllers a degree of influence in the political arena that makes a mockery of the one-person-one-vote maxim of a democracy. Even if political influence is far less than proportional to one's economic resources – as seems to be the case – those with extensive economic resources have greater political influence than those with modest economic resources.

19. See, for example, Galbraith (1952), and T.R. Roosevelt quoted in Lazarus (1973, p. 216).

20. In 1912 Woodrow Wilson argued that "big business interests . . . are so great that there is an open question whether the government of the

United States with the people back of it is strong enough to overcome and rule them" (quoted in Lazarus 1973, p. 220).

21. Business leaders, when faced with the argument that they exercise considerable influence in the policy making process, often point to specific instances where their entreaties failed. They ignore the battles they won and, more importantly, they ignore the "structured inequality" of access that characterizes government policy making in Canada.

22. See Adams and Brock (1986) and the discussion of the proposed bailout of Dome Petroleum in Stanbury (1986g, Ch. 7).

23. See the papers by Khemani and by Marfels, Chapters 1 and 3 in this volume.

24. This section is based loosely on the framework in Epstein (1969, Ch. 8).

25. U.S. Senator Philip Hart has argued that "when a major corporation from a state wants to discuss something with its political representatives, you can be sure it will be heard. When that same company operates in 30 states, it will be heard by 30 times as many representatives" (quoted in Nader et al. 1976, p. 223).

26. Expenditures by parties and candidates during the campaign period are limited by statute – see Stanbury (1986a, Ch. 10). The limit for a party running candidates in all ridings in 1984 was just under $6.4 million.

27. To put Canadian political party expenditures ($57.6 million for the three largest federal parties in 1984, the last election year) into perspective, one should note that in 1983, according to official estimates, the five major parties in Japan spent $523 million, including $184 million by the Communist Party. But this figure underestimates the total spending by the ruling LDP which is conservatively estimated to have spent $323 million in 1983. This is in a country where the official campaign period is 15 days and candidates may not campaign door-to-door because of fears they will bribe voters! Officially, contributions from individuals are limited to $231,000 while a corporation is limited to $1.2 million. In practice (honne), these limits are not enforced and brown bags filled with unreported cash pass frequently from business interests to the leading parties. See Thomas Walkom, "No end of yen: free spending a Japanese political tradition," *Globe and Mail*, June 28, 1986, p. A13.

28. Obviously, such a move would cause enormous controversy as most Canadians believe that their political parties should not rely on contributions from only a few sources. Note that while all contributions over $100 must be publicly reported, there is no limit on the size of individual or corporate contributions at the federal level. Both Ontario and Quebec impose a cap on contributions and Quebec restricts contributions to persons who are registered voters. Recently, federal Conservative MPs from Quebec have advocated that limits be placed on

political contributions and that corporations be prohibited from making contributions. See Graham Fraser, "Quebec PCs send out call for reform," *Globe and Mail*, February 9, 1987, pp. A1, A2; Martin Cohn, "Fund raising curbs urged by Tories in Quebec," Toronto *Star*, February 9, 1987, pp. A1, A12.

29. While he notes the existence of the Institute for Research on Public Policy (stating that an increasing fraction of its budget is coming from corporations) and the now defunct Canadian Institute for Economic Policy, Beck doesn't even refer to the rather independent-minded government-funded research bodies such as the Economic Council of Canada, whose budget exceeds *all* of the other think tanks. Nor does he mention the Ontario Economic Council, some of whose studies stung the politicians and bureaucrats sufficiently to have it put out of business in late 1984. Beck also ignores the frequently-quoted studies of the Canadian Council for Social Development, a major advocate for more social programs, and a champion of the poor and other "disadvantaged" groups.

30. For example, a senior Institute employee and the editor of the recent volume of papers on the *Competition Act* said his objective was to "kill the bill," Bill C-91 introduced in December 1985 (see Stanbury 1986b).

31. Tim Naumetz, "Tory 500 club collars elusive PM," *Globe and Mail*, August 16, 1986, p. A11. For a more extreme version of the paid access opportunity, see William Johnston, "U.S. Senator cancels $10,000 breakfasts," *Globe and Mail*, February 7, 1987, p. A7.

32. This is based on the assumption that the $1,000 is the only contribution the individual makes to a federal party in that year.

33. Dalton Camp, now senior advisor to Brian Mulroney in the PCO, claimed in 1979 that "mature politicians secretly believe board chairmen and company presidents to be political cretins and would as soon take their advice as harken to a herd of mandrills" (quoted in Stanbury 1986a, p. 480).

34. For example, the *Financial Post 500* (Summer 1986) reveals that Canadian Pacific Ltd. had 123,000 employees in 1985 and Bell Canada Enterprises had 108,300. The next eight largest corporate employers had between 48,000 and 72,500 employees. When it comes to capital spending in 1985, five of the 10 largest spenders were Crown corporations (e.g., Ontario and Quebec Hydro). However, Bell Canada Enterprises spent $2.4 billion while Canadian Pacific spent $1.9 billion on capital projects.

35. In May 1985, Jack Cockwell, the chief financial officer of the Edper/Brascan group, testified before the Ontario Energy Board that the total value of the companies in the Edper/Hees/Brascan orbit was "probably . . . about $30 billion." Business journalist Elaine Dewar (1985b, p. 55) noted, "Thirty billion. That's bigger than the GNP of a lot

of countries. A cabinet minister seeing an Edper/Hees/Brascan representative waiting in his lobby would be hard pressed not to fall on his knees before the jobs they represent. There was a respectful moment of silence."

36. In 1976 the Supreme Court of Canada held that the mergers that resulted in K.C. Irving owning all five English language dailies in New Brunswick did not violate the *combines Investigation Act* as the Crown was not able to establish beyond a reasonable doubt that competition had been lessened to the detriment of the public. See Reschenthaler and Stanbury (1977).

37. See Francis (1986, p. 21) for a contrary view.

38. Bell Canada Enterprises and its wholly own subsidiary, Bell Canada, is an outstanding example.

39. See, for example, Newman (1975, 1978, 1981, 1982); Francis (1986); Foster (1986a, 1986b); Goldenberg (1983, 1984); Olive (1986).

40. See, for example, Estey (1986) and Johnson (1986) on the recent bank failures, Best & Shortell (1985) on trust company problems, and Corcoran and Reid (1984) on the trust company scandals in Ontario. See also Cook (1981), Foster (1984), McQueen (1984), Fleming (1986).

41. No analytical justification is provided. The argument is treated as self evident. See also Eyton (1986a), (1986c), and Cohen (1986).

42. Alternatively, they may be willing to provide advantageous changes in regulation to ensure the success of the largest enterprises. This point is made by Tom Courchene in respect to changes in financial regulation that affect the largest chartered banks. See Chapter 24 in this volume.

43. Margaret Atwood (1972, p. 31) argues that the central symbol of Canada is "grim survival."

44. See "Quebec lassoes the Pony," *Maclean's*, November 25, 1985, p. 45. The cost to the federal and provincial governments is estimated to be over $90 million for some 1,200 jobs in the plant.

45. One can find essentially the same conclusion in the writings of other Canadian neo-Marxists, e.g., Mahon (1977), Naylor (1975), Brym (1985), Panitch (1977, 1985), Park and Park (1973), Niosi (1978, 1981), Drache (1983), and Clement (1983, Ch. 4, 9).

46. While the Commission admitted that "representatives of major corporations can and do have greater access to both politicians and public servants than do other individuals," they imply there is some equality of access among all interest groups. They say that "farm and labor groups and . . . many others with special interests" also have greater access than do individuals (Canada 1978, p. 338).

47. For two examples, see Francis (1986, pp. 52, 88-89).

48. In the confines of this paper, one can only sketch some of the evidence. For a much more extensive discussion, see Stanbury (1986g, Ch. 7).

49. For example, it is widely rumoured that prior to meetings between the Prime Minister and Paul Desmarais (Power Corp.) and with Trevor Eyton (Brascan/Edper group) the Minister of State for Finance (Tom Hockin) had proposed to limit the ownership of trust companies by non-financial enterprises to about 30 per cent of their equity as recommended by the Blenkarn Committee in November 1985 and June 1986. The White Paper released in December 1986 effectively "grandfathered" the positions of the companies controlled by these two men. The maximum equity interest for existing owners was set at 65 per cent but will be lower for future owners. See Minister of State, Finance (1986) and the paper by Courchene, Chapter 24 in this volume.

50. For example, see the description of how the big banks were able to persuade the Minister of Finance to request that they limit their loans to finance the takeover of foreign-owned oil companies in Stanbury (1986g, Ch. 7). The consistent political effectiveness of Stephen Roman (Denison Mines) and the Ghermezian family is described by Francis (1986, pp. 85-86, 175). The Reichmanns (Olympia and York) have consistently been successful in obtaining help from the federal government in their big takeovers – see Stanbury (1986g, Ch. 7).

51. For example, in 1981 Eastern Provincial Airways was able to mount a successful appeal (enlisting the aid of all the Maritime premiers) to the federal cabinet to greatly vary the decision of the CTC to award CP Air the right to fly non-stop between Toronto and Halifax. This was despite the fact that CP Air had been encouraged to apply for the route by the Minister of Transport. See Reschenthaler and Stanbury (1982).

52. It has been suggested that K.C. Irving had an extraordinary influence on elections in New Brunswick – see Stanbury (1986g, Ch. 7).

53. This certainly applies to most of the major business and trade associations such as BCNI, CCC, CMA, CFIB, etc. For more detailed examples, see Stanbury (1986g, Ch. 7) in respect to the access enjoyed by the McCain family, Charles Bronfman, Paul Desmarais, Cedric Ritchie (former chairman of the Bank of Nova Scotia), Hal Jackman, and Robert Campeau.

54. This applies to the major business and trade associations, e.g., BCNI.

55. Some firms or business leaders are actually able to alter the course of the policy making process. See Stanbury (1986g, Ch. 7) for two examples: the Irving family and three public or regulatory inquiries; and the role of Conrad Black in the policy investigation of Norcen's attempted takeover of Hanna Mining Co. in 1981. See also Newman (1982) and Austen and McQuaig (1983).

56. For example, because they had to deal with the "Gang of Three" (BCNI, CMA, CCC) on the drafts leading to Bill C-29 (April 1984) and the

"Gang of Five" on drafts leading to Bill C-91 (December 1985), officials in the Bureau of Competition Policy were severely inhibited in the proposals they put forward to amend the *Combines Investigation Act*. See below.

57. These data are based on mergers in which the transaction value exceeded $100 million. The average transaction value was $511 million in 1985, $381 million in 1986 and $577 million in 1987. The data were collected by the author.

58. It is evident that the concentration of economic activity (and of personal wealth) has long been a fact of life in Canada. See Myers (1914), Canada (1937), McCollum (1943), Porter (1956), and Rosenbluth (1960). However, because of methodological difficulties we cannot determine if aggregate concentration was greater or less than it was in the mid-1960s. The empirical evidence indicates that while aggregate concentration has increased markedly since the mid-1960s, industry-level concentration in the manufacturing sector has not increased (see the paper by Khemani, Chapter 1 in this volume). The average level of such concentration, however, is much higher than most industrialized countries including the U.S., the U.K., Japan and West Germany. See the paper by Christian Marfels, Chapter 3 in this volume.

59. It is all but impossible to find an official reasoned argument in support of Canada's high level of aggregate concentration. The most widely quoted semi-official document is the Report of the Royal Commission on Corporate Concentration — see Canada (1978).

60. See the paper by Harvey André, Chapter 20 in this volume.

61. See Stanbury (1986b), (1986c) and the paper by Goldman, Chapter 21 in this volume.

62. See Nicholas Hunter "Imasco proposes Genstar takeover for less than shares trading on TSE," *Globe and Mail*, March 25, 1986, p. B1. David Hatter "Genstar would fit Imascos bill," *Financial Post*, March 29, 1986, p. 4. Imasco subsequently sold over almost all of Genstar's assets (for about $2.8 billion) except Canada Trustco, which incorporated Canada Permanent Trust. See *Globe and Mail*, June 9, 1987, p. B6.

63. See Stanbury (1977, 1981, 1985, 1986b, 1986g).

64. The most notable Crown corporations sold by the federal government to private interests since 1985 were: Teleglobe, de Havilland, Canadair, and Canadian Arsenals. A number of provincial Crown corporations have been sold off, e.g., Quebec sold its 56 per cent interest in Donohue Inc. for $320 million, Ontario sold off the Urban Transportation Development Corporation while Saskatchewan sold off almost one-half of Saskoil. See Stanbury (1987a).

65. This point is developed in detail by Espen Eckbo in Chapter 7 of this volume. For a more popular treatment, see "The Battle for Corporate Control," *Business Week*, May 18, 1987, pp. 102-109.

66. No political party can really do the Lord's work unless they form the Government by commanding a majority of the seats in the legislature (or at least obtain a plurality).

67. Wolfe (1985, p. 146) notes that "the emphasis on redistributive and supply-oriented policies seemed to be accentuated during the early years of the Trudeau government, to the continued dismay of business interests". Eventually, business executives came to loathe Trudeau and they turned toward the Tory alternative. After a relatively brief honeymoon following the general election of September 1984, they came to realize that a prime minister and a cabinet intent on staying in power inherently take a pragmatic view of virtually everything and everyone. Hence, they act in ways they believe maximize political support. Thus only serial attention is paid to the wishes of big business. (More generally, see Stanbury, 1986a, Ch. 4.)

68. For some data on the size of welfare transfers, see Grubel (1984).

69. The reason David Lewis' phrase "corporate welfare bums" had such force in 1972 is that it contained a great deal of truth.

70. See the discussion by Khemani, Chapter 1 in this volume.

71. See the discussion in Eckbo, Chapter 7 in this volume.

72. The takeover of Gulf Oil, the fifth largest oil company in the U.S., by Standard Oil of California, the fourth largest, for $13.2 billion in March 1984 seems to indicate that the money can be found to take over.

73. Based on 1985 revenues reported in the *Financial Post 500* (Summer, 1986).

74. See Porter (1965), Presthus (1973, 1974), Clement (1977), Olsen (1980) and Carroll (1986).

REFERENCES

Adams, Walter and James W. Brock (1986) *The Bigness Complex: Industry, Labor, and Government in the American Economy* (New York: Pantheon).

Ashley, C.A. (1957) "Concentration of Economic Power," *Canadian Journal of Economics and Political Science*, Vol. 23, pp. 105-8.

Atwood, Margaret (1972) *Survival: A Thematic Guide to Canadian Literature* (Toronto: Anansi).

Austen, Ian & Linda McQuaig (1983) "The Law and Conrad Black," *Maclean's*, February 21, pp. 26-36.

Banfield, Edward C. (1961) *Political Influence* (New York: Free Press).

Bannock, Graham (1971) *The Juggernauts* (Indianapolis: Bobbs-Merrill).

Banting, Keith (1986) "The State and Economic Interests: An Introduction" in Banting (ed.) *The State and Economic Interests* (Toronto: University of Toronto Press), pp. 1-34.

Baratz, Morton S. (1956) "Corporate Giants and the Power Structure," *Western Political Quarterly*, Vol. 9 (June), pp. 406-15.

Bauer, Raymond A., Ithiel de Sola Pool and Lewis Antony Dexter (1964) *American Business and Public Policy* (New York: Atherton Press).

Beck, Stanley M. (1985) "Corporate Power and Public Policy" in *Consumer Protection and Environmental Law, and Corporate Power* (Toronto: University of Toronto Press), pp. 181-219.

Berkowitz, Stephen D., Peter Carrington, Yehuda Kotowitz, Leonard Waverman (1979) "The Determination of Enterprise Groupings through Combined Ownership and Directorship Ties," *Social Networks 1*, Vol. 4, pp. 391-413.

Berkowitz, Stephen D., Yehuda Kotowitz, Leonard Waverman, *et al.* (1976) *Enterprise Structure and Corporate Concentration* (Royal Commission on Corporate Concentration Study No. 17) (Ottawa: Minister of Supply and Services)

Berle, A.A. and C.G. Means (1932) *The Modern Corporation and Private Property* (New York: Macmillan).

Berle, A.A. Jr. (1969) *Power* (New York: Harcourt, Brace and World).

Berry, Glyn R. (1974) "The Oil Lobby and the Energy Crisis," *Canadian Public Administration*, Vol. 17(4), pp. 600-635.

Best, Patricia & Ann Shortell (1985) *A Matter of Trust: Power and Privilege in Canada's Trust Companies* (Toronto: Viking Penguin).

Blumberg, P.I. (1975) *The Megacorporation in American Society: The Scope of Corporate Power* (Englewood Cliffs, N.J.: Prentice-Hall).

Booth, Amy (1981) "Corporate Concentration: Empires, Old Sultanates, and New," *Financial Post 500*, June, pp. 8-12, 17, 20).

Brady, Robert A. (1947) *Business as a System of Power* (New York: Columbia University Press).

Bretton, Henry (1980) *The Power of Money* (Albany: State University of New York Press).

Brym, Robert J. (ed.) (1985a) *The Structure of the Canadian Capitalist Class* (Toronto: Garamond Press).

_____ (1985b) "The Canadian Capitalist Class, 1965-1985" in Robert Brym (ed.) *The Structure of Canadian Capitalist Class* (Toronto: Garamond Press), pp. 1-20.

Calvert, John (1984) *Government Limited: The Corporate Takeover of the Public Sector in Canada* (Ottawa: Canadian Centre for Policy Alternatives).

Campbell, Colin (1978) *The Canadian Senate: A Lobby from Within* (Toronto: Macmillan).

Canada (1937) *Report of the Royal Commission on Price Spreads* (Ottawa: King's Printer).

_____ (1978) *Report of the Royal Commission on Corporate Concentration* (Ottawa: Queen's Printer).

_____ (1981) *Report of the Royal Commission on Newspapers* (Ottawa: Minister of Supply and Services).

Canadian Bankers' Association (1985) *Concentration of Power in the Financial Services Industry* (Toronto: CBA, March).

Caneo, Carl J. (1982) "The Network of Directorate Links Among the Largest Canadian Firms," *Canadian Review of Sociology and Anthropology*, Vol. 19, pp. 44-69.

Carroll, William K. (1982) "The Canadian Corporate Elite: Financiers or Finance Capitalists?," *Studies in Political Economy*, Vol. 8, pp. 89-114.

_____ (1984) "The Individual, Class and Corporate Power in Canada," *Canadian Journal of Sociology*, Vol 9(3), pp. .

_____ (1986) *Corporate Power and Canadian Capitalism* (Vancouver: University of B.C. Press).

Chandler, William M. (1977) "Socialism and Policy Impact: Contagion from the Left," *Canadian Journal of Political Science*, Vol. 10(4), December.

Chodos, Robert (1973) *The CPR: A Century of Corporate Welfare* (Toronto: James Lewis and Samuel).

Clark, S.D. (1939) *The Canadian Manufacturers' Association* (Toronto: University of Toronto Press).

Clement, Wallace (1975) *The Canadian Corporate Elite* (Toronto: McClelland and Stewart).

_____ (1977) *Continental Corporate Power* (Toronto: McClelland and Stewart).

_____ (1983a) *Class, Power and Property: Essays on Canadian Society* (Toronto: Methuen).

Cohen, Marshall (1986) "Prosperity means being world class," *Financial Post*, September 13, 1986, p. 8.

Coleman, W.D. and H.J. Jacek (1983) "The Roles and Activities of Business Interest Associations in Canada," *Canadian Journal of Political Science*, Vol. 16, pp. 257-280.

Coleman, William D. (1985) "Analysing the associative action of business: policy advocacy and policy participation," *Canadian Public Administration*, Vol. 25(2), pp. 265-278.

_____ (1986) "Canadian Business and the State" in Keith Banting (ed.) *The State and Economic Interests* (Toronto: University of Toronto Press), pp. 245-290.

Cooper, Albert (1987) "Lobbying and the Registration of Paid Lobbyists," *Minutes of Proceedings and Evidence of the Standing Committee on Elections, Privileges and Procedure*, Issue No. 2, January 27, pp. 1-20.

Cook Peter (1981) *Massey at the Brink* (Toronto: Collins Publishers).

Corrado, Frank M. (1984), *Media for Managers* (Englewood Cliffs, N.J.: Prentice-Hall).

Courchene, T.J. (1980) "Towards a Protected Society: The Politicization of Economic Life," *Canadian Journal of Economics*, Vol. 12(4), pp. 556-77.

Dahl, Robert A. (1957) "The Concept of Power," *Behavioral Science*, Vol. 2 (July) pp. 201-15.

_____ (1973) "Governing the Giant Corporation" in R. Nader and M. Green (eds.) *Corporate Power in America* (New York: Grossman), pp. 10-24.

de Jouvenel, Bertrand (1949) *On Power: Its Nature and the History of Its Growth* (New York: Viking Press).

Dewar, Elaine (1985a) "Takeover" (Part I), *Canadian Business*, November, pp. 26-56, 159-183.

_____ (1985b) "Takeover" (Part II), *Canadian Business*, December, pp. 53-63, 152-154.

Dhingra, Harbans L. (1983) "Patterns of Ownership and Control in Canadian Industry: A Study of Large Non-financial Institutions," *Canadian Journal of Sociology*, Vol. 8, pp. 21-44.

Domhoff, G. William (1967) *Who Rules America?* (Englewood Cliffs, N.J.: Prentice-Hall).

Drew, Elizabeth (1983) *Politics and Money* (New York: MacMillan).

Drucker, Peter (1950) *The New Society: An Anatomy of the Industrial Order* (New York: Harper & Row).

Economic Council of Canada (1986) *Competition and Solvency: A Framework for Financial Regulation* (Ottawa: Minister of Supply and Services).

Epstein, Edwin (1969) *The Corporation in American Politics* (Englewood Cliffs, N.J.: Prentice-Hall).

Estey, Willard Z. (1986) *Report of the Inquiry into the Collapse of the CCB and Northland Bank* (Ottawa: Minister of Supply and Services, August).

Esty, Daniel C. and Richard E. Caves (1983) "Market Structure and Political Influence: New Data on Political Expenditures, Activity, and Success," *Economic Inquiry*, XXI, pp. 24-38.

Eyton, J. Trevor (1986a) "Extract from [an] Address to the Annual General Meeting, Brascan Limited" (Toronto, May 7, 1986, mimeo).

_____ (1986b) "Corporate Concentration: Its Impact on Canada's Economy" (Speech to the International Trust Executive Forum on the Management of Change, Toronto, September 29, transcript).

_____ (1986c) "We're ill-served by attacks on bigness," *Financial Post*, October 11, p. 8.

Finn, David (1970) *The Corporate Oligarch* (New York: Simon & Schuster/Clarion Books).

Fleming, James (1986), *Merchants of Fear* (Toronto: Viking).

Forster, Benjamin (1986), *A Conjunction of Interests: Business, Politics, and Tariffs, 1825-1879* (Toronto: University of Toronto Press).

Foster, Peter (1979) *The Blue-Eyed Sheiks: The Canadian Oil Establishment* (Don Mills, Ontario: Collins).

_____ (1984) *Other People's Money: The Banks, the Government and Dome* (Toronto: Totem Books).

_____ (1986a) "Let's Make a Deal," *Saturday Night*, September, pp. 15-22.

_____ (1986b) *The Master Builders* (Toronto: Key Porter Books).

Fournier, Pierre (1986) "Consensus Building in Canada: Case Studies and Prospects" in Keith Banting (ed.) *The State and Economic Interests* (Toronto: University of Toronto Press), pp. 291-336.

Francis, Diane (1986) *Controlling Interest: Who Owns Canada* (Toronto: Macmillan).

Freeman, Natalie Veiner (1982) "Student of Power [Peter C. Newman]," *City Woman*, Fall, pp. 58-66.

Friedenberg, Edgar (1980) *Deference to Authority: The Case of Canada* (White Plains, N.Y.: M.E. Sharpe).

Galbraith, J.K. (1952) *American Capitalism: The Concept of Countervailing Power* (Boston: Houghton Mifflin).

_____ (1973) "On the Economic Image of Corporate Enterprise" in Ralph Nader and Mark J. Green (eds.) *Corporate Power in America* (New York: Grossman Publishers), pp. 3-9.

_____ (1983) *The Anatomy of Power* (Boston: Houghton Mifflin).

Ghert, Bernard I. (1985) "Brief on the Green Paper: The Regulation of Canadian Financial Institutions" (Toronto: Cadillac Fairview Corporation Limited).

_____ (1986) "Address to the Vancouver Board of Trade and the UBC Alumni Association" (Vancouver, April 10, mimeo).

Gillies, James (1981) *Where Business Fails* (Montreal: The Institute for Research on Public Policy).

_____ (1986) *Facing Reality: Consultation, Consensus and Making Economic Policy in the 21st Century* (Montreal: Institute for Research on Public Policy).

Ginsberg, Eli and George Vojta (1986) *Beyond Human Scale: The Large Corporation At Risk* (New York: Basic Books).

Goldenberg, Susan (1983) *Canadian Pacific: A Portrait of Power* (Toronto: Methuen).

_____ (1984) *The Thomson Empire* (Toronto: Seal Books).

Grefe, E. (1981) *Fighting to Win: Business Political Power* (New York: Harcourt Brace Jovanovich).

Grossack, Irving (1973) "Corporate Power: Myth or Reality," *Business Horizons*, Vol. 16, August, pp. 88-96.

Grubel, Herbert (1984) "The Costs of Canada's Social Insurance Programs" in G. Lermer (ed.) *Probing Leviathan: An Investigation of Government in the Economy* (Vancouver: Fraser Institute), Ch. 3.

Hacker, Andrew (1964) "Politics and the Corporation" in Andrew Hacker (ed.), *The Corporation Takeover* (New York: Harper and Row) pp. 246-69.

Hamilton, W. (1957) *The Politics of Industry* (New York: Alfred A. Knopf).

Harris, Fred R. (1973) "The Politics of Corporate Power" in Ralph Nader and Mark J. Green (eds.) *Corporate Power in America* (New York: Grossman Publishers), pp. 25-41.

Hatter, David (1985) "Charmed Circle Still Firmly in Control," *Financial Post 500*, Summer, pp. 58-61.

Herman, Edward S. (1981) *Corporate Control, Corporate Power* (A Twentieth Century Fund Study) (Cambridge: Cambridge University Press).

Howard, J.L. and W.T. Stanbury (1984) "Measuring Leviathan: The Size, Scope and Growth of Governments in Canada" in George Lermer (ed.) *Probing Leviathan: An Investigation of Government in the Economy* (Vancouver: The Fraser Institute), pp. 87-110, 127-223.

Hunter, Lawson, A.W. (1985) "Notes for an Address to the Conference on the Changing Regulatory Environment for Canadian Financial Institutions" (Toronto: Faculty of Law, University of Toronto, May 23, mimeo). (For an excerpt, see Toronto *Star*, June 24, 1984, p. B10.)

Jacoby, Neil H. (1972) *Corporate Power and Social Responsibility* (New York: Macmillan).

Jardine, Richard and Ann Shortell (1986) "The Top Forty: Our richest people and their record holdings," *Financial Post Moneywise Magazine*, May, pp. 28-41.

Jessup, John Knox (1952) "A Political Role for the Corporation," *Fortune*, Vol. 46 (August) p. 112.

Johnson, Arthur (1986), *Breaking the Banks* (Toronto: Lester, Orpen Dennys).

Johnston, Moira (1986) *Takeover: The New Wall Street Warriors* (New York: Arbor House).

Kariel, Henry S. (1961) *The Decline of American Pluralism* (Stanford, Calif: Stanford University Press).

_____ (1962) "The Corporation and the Public Interest," *Annals of the American Academy of Political and Social Science*, No. 343 (September), pp. 39-47.

Khemani, R.S. (1986) "The Extent and Evolution of Competition in the Canadian Economy" in D.G. McFeridge (ed.) *Canadian Industry in Transition* (Toronto: University of Toronto Press), pp. 135-176.

Lazarus, Simon (1973) "Halfway Up from Liberalism: Regulation and Corporate Power" in Ralph Nader and Mark J. Green (eds.) *Corporate Power in America* (Neive, David (1983b) "Canada's Top Private Companies: Part Two," *Canadian Business*, December, pp. 55-66.

League for Social Reconstruction (1935) *Social Planning for Canada* (Toronto: Thomas Nelson).

Lehmbruch, G. and P.C. Schmitter, eds. (1982) *Patterns of Corporatist Policy Making* (Beverley Hills: Sage Publications).

Levitt, Kari (1970) *Silent Surrender: The Multinational Corporation in Canada* (Toronto: MacMillan).

Lynch, Charles (1985) *Race for the Rose: Election 1984* (Toronto: Methuen).

MacPherson, C.B. (1973) *Democratic Theory: Essays in Retrieval* (London: Clarendon Press).

Mahon, Rianne (1977) "Canadian public policy: the unequal structure of representation" in Leo Panitch (ed.) *The Canadian State: Political Economy and Political Power* (Toronto: University of Toronto Press), pp. 164-198.

Malcolm, Andrew H. (1985) *The Canadians* (New York: Times Books).

Malvern, Paul (1985) *Persuaders: Lobbying, Influence Peddling and Political Corruption in Canada* (Toronto: Methuen).

Manning, Bayless (1960) "Corporate Power and Individual Freedom: Some General Analysis and Particular Reservations," *Northwestern Law Review*, Vol. 55 (March-April), pp. 38-53.

Marchak, Patricia (1979) *In Whose Interests?* (Toronto: McClelland and Stewart).

_____ (1983) *Green Gold* (Vancouver: University of British Columbia Press.

Marcus, Alfred A. (1984) *The Adversary Economy: Business Response to Changing Government Requirements* (Westport, Conn.: Quarum Books), p. 42.

Mason, Alpheus T. (1950) "Business Organized as Power: The New Imperium in Imperio," *American Political Science Review*, Vol. 44 (June), pp. 323-42.

Mason, Edward S. ed. (1966) *The Corporation in Modern Society* (New York: Atheneum) [originally published by Harvard University Press in 1959].

McCollum, Watt Hugh (1935) *Who Owns Canada?* (Regina: CCF Research Bureau).

_____ (1947) *Who Owns Canada?* (Ottawa: Woodsworth House Publishers).

McConnell, Grant, (1966) *Private Power and American Democracy* (New York: Alfred A. Knopf).

McKie, James W., ed. (1974) *Social Responsibility and the Business Predicament* (Washington, D.C.: The Brookings Institution), pp. 79-108.

McQueen, Rod (1984) *The Moneyspinners* (Toronto: Totem Books/Collins Publishers).

Millstein, Ira M. and Salem M. Katsch (1981) *The Limits of Corporate Power* (New York: MacMillan).

Minister of State, Finance (1986) *New Directions for Financial Institutions* (Ottawa: Department of Finance, December 18).

Mintz, Morton & Jerry S. Cohen (1977) *Power Inc.* (New York: Bantam Books).

Myers, G. (1914) *A History of Canadian Wealth* (Chicago, Charles H. Kerr), 2 Vols.

Nader, Ralph, Mark Green and Joel Seligman (1976) *Taming the Giant Corporation* (New York: Norton).

Newman, Peter C. (1975) *The Canadian Establishment* (Toronto: McClelland and Stewart).

_____ (1978) *Bronfman Dynasty: The Rothschilds of the New World* (Toronto: McClelland and Stewart).

_____ (1981) *The Canadian Establishment, Vol. II The Acquisitors* (Toronto: McClelland and Stewart).

_____ (1982) *The Establishment Man: A Portrait of Power* (Toronto: McClelland and Stewart).

Nichols, Mark and Ann Shortell (1986) "The empire strikes back," *Maclean's*, June 9, pp. 32-36.

Niosi, Jorge (1978) *The Economy of Canada: A Study of Ownership and Control* (Montreal: Black Rose Books).

_____ (1981) *Canadian Capitalism: A Study of Power in the Canadian Business Establishment* translated by Robert Chodos (Toronto: James Lorimer).

_____ (1985) *Canadian Multinationals* (Toronto: Garamond Press).

Olive, David (1983a) "Canada's Top Private Companies," *Canadian Business*, November, pp. 33-58.

_____ (1983b) "Canada's Top Private Companies: Part Two," *Canadian Business*, December, pp. 55-66.

_____ (1986) "What's Gone Wrong with the Reichmanns?" *Report on Business Magazine*, December, pp. 35-48.

Olsen, Denis (1980) *The State Elite* (Toronto: McClelland & Stewart).

Ornstein, Michael D. (1984) "Interlocking directorates in Canada: Intercorporate or class alliance?," *Administrative Science Quarterly*, Vol. 29, pp. 210-31.

Panitch, Leo (ed.)(1977) *The Canadian State: Political Economy and Political Power* (Toronto: University of Toronto Press).

_____ (ed.)(1985) "Class and Power in Canada," *Monthly Review*, Vol. 36(11), pp. 1-13.

Pfeffer, Jeffrey (1981) *Power in Organizations* (Marshfield, M.A.: Pitman Publishing).

Porter, John (1956) "Concentration of Economic Power and the Economic Elite in Canada," *Canadian Journal of Economics and Political Science*, Vol. 22, pp. 199-220.

_____ (1965) *The Vertical Mosaic* (Toronto: University of Toronto Press).

Presthus, Robert (1973) *Elite Accommodation in Canadian Politics* (Toronto: Macmillan).

_____ (1974) *Elites in the Policy Process* (London: Cambridge University Press).

Pross, A. Paul (1986) *Group Politics and Public Policy* (Toronto: Oxford University Press).

Reich, Robert (1983), *The Next American Frontier* (New York: Penguin Books).

Reschenthaler, G.B. & W.T. Stanbury (1977), "Benign Monopoly: Canadian Merger Policy and the K.C. Irving Case," *Canadian Business Law Journal*, Vol. 2(2), pp. 135-168.

Rhoades, Stephen A. (1983) *Power, Empire Building, and Mergers* (Lexington, Mass: Lexington Books/D.C. Heath).

Rosenbluth, Gideon (1960) "Concentration and Monopoly in the Canadian Economy" in M. Oliver (ed.) *Social Purpose for Canada* (Toronto: University of Toronto Press).

Rothschild, K.W. ed. (1971) *Power in Economics* (Middlesex, England: Penguin).

Rueber, Grant L. and Frank Roseman (1969) *The Take-Over of Canadian Firms, 1945-61* (Ottawa: Queen's Printer) (Economic Council of Canada Special Study No. 10).

Russell, Bertrand (1938) *Power: A New Social Analysis* (New York: W.W. Norton).

Salamon, L.M. and J.J. Siegfried (1977) "Economic power and political influence: The impact of industry structure on public policy," *American Political Science Review*, Vol. 71, pp. 1026-43.

Schattschneider, E.E. (1960), *The Semi-Sovereign People* (New York: Holt Rinehart & Winston).

Schwindt, R. (1977) *The Existence and Exercise of Corporate Power: A Case Study of MacMillan Bloedel Ltd.* (Ottawa: Supply and Services Canada). (Royal Commission on Corporate Concentration, Study No. 15).

Shleifer, Andrei and Robert W. Vishny (1986) "Large Shareholders and Corporate Control," *Journal of Political Economy*, Vol. 94 (3 part 1), June, pp. 461-488.

Shonfield, Andrew (1965) *Modern Capitalism: The Changing Balance of Public and Private Power* (Fair Lawn, N.J.: Oxford University Press).

Siegel, Arthur (1983), *Politics and the Media in Canada* (Toronto: McGraw-Hill Ryerson).

Slichter, Sumner (1931) *Modern Economic Society* (New York: H. Holt).

Stanbury, W.T. (1977) *Business Interests and the Reform of Canadian Competition Policy, 1971-1975* (Toronto: Carswell/Methuen).

_____ (1985) "The Psychological Environment of Business-Government Relations in Canada," *Business Quarterly*, Vol. 50(2), pp. 105-114.

_____ (1986a) *Business-Government Relations in Canada: Grappling with Leviathan* (Toronto: Methuen).

_____ (1986b) "The New Competition Act and Competition Tribunal Act: Not With a Bang But a Whimper," *Canadian Business Law Journal*, Vol. 12(1), October, pp. 2-42.

_____ (1986c) "The Mother's Milk of Politics: Political Contributions to Federal Parties in Canada, 1974 - 1984," *Canadian Journal of Political Science*, Vol. 19(4), December, pp. 795-821.

_____ (1986d) "Privatization in Canada" (Faculty of Commerce and Business Administration, University of B.C., unpublished paper, mimeo).

_____ (1986e) "Analysis of the Merger Provisions in the New Competition Act" (Vancouver: Continuing Legal Education Society of B.C., September).

_____ (1986f) *The Politics of Canadian Competition Policy, 1976-1986* (Unpublished study, Faculty of Commerce & Business Administration, University of B.C., mimeo).

_____ (1986g) *The Political Consequences of Corporate Concentration and Corporate Power in Canada* (Vancouver: Faculty of Commerce and Business Administration, University of B.C., unpublished manuscript).

_____ (1987a) *Privatization in Canada* (Vancouver: BC Politics and Policy and The Institute for Research on Public Policy).

_____ (1987b) "Direct Regulation and Its Reform: A Canadian Perspective" (paper to be published in *Brigham Young University Law Review* in 1987).

Stanbury, W.T. and Peter Thain (1986) *The Origins of Rent Regulation in Ontario* (Toronto: Ontario Commission of Inquiry into Residential Tenancies).

Stanbury, W.T. and M. Jane Fulton (1984) "Suasion as a Governing Instrument" in Allan M. Maslove (ed.) *How Ottawa Spends, 1984: The New Agenda* (Toronto: Methuen), pp. 282-324.

_____ (1987) "Consultation and Public Participation in Processes in Government Policy Making: A Conceptual Framework" (Vancouver: University of B.C., Faculty of Commerce, unpublished paper).

Stapells, H.G. (1927) *The Recent Consolidation Movement in Canada* (Master's Thesis, University of Toronto).

Starowicz, Mark and Rae Murphy (1972) *Corporate Canada: 14 Probes into the Workings of a Branch Plant Economy* (Toronto: James Lewis & Samuel).

Stokman, Frans N., ed. (1985) *Networks of Corporate Power: a Comparative Analysis of Ten Countries* (Cambridge, Polity Press).

Thorburn, Hugh G. (1964) "Pressure Groups in Canadian Politics: Recent Revisions of the Anti-Combines Legislation," *Canadian Journal of Economics and Political Science*, Vol. 30(2), pp. 157-174.

_____ (1985) *Interest Groups and the Canadian Federal System* (Toronto: University of Toronto Press).

Traves, Tom (1979) *The State and Enterprise: Canadian Manufacturers and the Federal Government, 1917-31* (Toronto: University of Toronto Press).

Turner, Hon. John N. (1986) "Speech to the Confederation Dinner," Sheraton Centre, Toronto, September 17.

Ulmer, Melville J. (1971) "Economic Power and Vested Interests" in K.W. Rothschild (ed.) *Power in Economics* (Harmondsworth, Eng.: Penguin), p. 245.

Useem, Michael (1984) *The Inner Circle* (New York: Oxford University Press).

Vogt, R. (1985) "Corporate Power and the Development of New Competition Policies in Canada," *Journal of Economic Issues*, Vol. 19(2), pp. 551-58.

Weinstein, J. (1968) *The Corporate Ideal in the Liberal State* (Boston: Beacon Press).

Westell, Dan (1984) "Big Chunk of Business in Hands of a Few," *Globe and Mail*, August 25, p. B1.

Westin, Alan F. ed. (1963) *The Uses of Power* (New York: Harcourt, Brace & World).

White, T.H. (1979) "Boards of Directors: Control and Decision-making in Canadian Corporations," *Canadian Review of Sociology and Anthropology*, Vol. 16, pp. 77-95.

Williamson, Oliver (1985) *The Economic Institutions of Capitalism* (New York: The Free Press).

Winter, Ralph K. (1978) *Government and the Corporation* (Washington, D.C.: American Enterprise Institute).

Wolfe, David A. (1985) "The Politics of the Deficit" in G. Bruce Doern (ed.) *The Politics of Economic Policy* (Toronto: University of Toronto Press).

Wrong, Dennis H. (1980) *Power: Its Forms, Bases and Uses* (New York: Harper Colophon Books).

Chapter 18

Mergers and Corporate Concentration: A Labour Perspective

Richard Martin
Vice President
Canadian Labour Congress

1.0 INTRODUCTION

It is not my purpose in this paper to recite the statistics on the level of concentration in key sectors. That is done in the paper by Shayam Khemani.[1] It is enough to note that the Canadian economy has one of the highest levels of concentration of all the Western industrial countries,[2] and that the recent wave of takeovers that has swept Canada,[3] as well as the United States, has only increased that level of concentration.

My purpose is to discuss whether that is a good thing for the workers of Canada. There are some who would say that it is a good thing; others would say that the recent wave of takeovers and mergers, and the level of corporate concentration, is irrelevant as far as the interest of the workers is concerned. Still others, no doubt, would say that the interest of the workers is irrelevant in coming to a conclusion about the value of takeovers and mergers.

I begin by pointing out two things. First, workers are also consumers. What hurts consumers hurts workers, and vice versa. Secondly, workers, as workers and as consumers, have suffered unduly in the past decade from the way the Canadian economy has been run. They have suffered both from unemployment, and from declining purchasing power.

Although we are supposed to be well into a recovery from the recession of the early 1980s, and although we experienced vigorous growth in at least two of the most recent years – 1984 and 1985 – the rate of unemployment and the numbers of unemployed remain unacceptably high.

At the beginning of the recession in the late summer of 1981, our national unemployment rate was below 7 per cent, and the numbers of unemployed were in the area of 800,000. Now, over five years later, our national unemployment rate is still roughly 9.5 per cent, and the unemployed remain in the area of 1.2 million. Moreover, a much larger percentage of the unemployed are long term unemployed than was the case in earlier years, which presents us with serious social problems in addition to the economic problems.

Finally, a large proportion of the jobs that have been created have been part-time jobs, not the kind that provide a decent income or benefits. While a few years ago, about one in 10 jobs in the economy were part-time, now roughly one in six are part-time.

As a result of all these problems, and the depressed state of the economy, the purchasing power of the average weekly wage has been on a long, steady decline for roughly a decade. The purchasing power of the average weekly wage in Canada is now significantly less than it was a decade ago.

The objective of economic policy in Canada, given our extremely high levels of unemployment, should be to provide high levels of employment and income for all Canadians. In the view of most people in the labour movement, the recent wave of takeovers and mergers is likely to make that job more difficult to do, for a number of reasons. The first has to do with the rise of paper entrepreneurship as a substitute for attending to the real problems which the economy faces. The second has to do with the effect of concentration of economic power on the economic and political decision making process in Canada.

2.0   CORPORATE TAKEOVERS AND PAPER ENTREPRENEURSHIP

On the first economic effect of the recent takeover wave, John Kenneth Galbraith said recently that the current round of takeovers in the United States "will eventually be regarded as no less insane than the utility and railroad pyramiding and the investment trust explosion of the 1920's." Galbraith argued that the takeover binge has little or nothing to do with improving the industrial base, which is the only sure, long term way of preserving jobs.

The takeover binge, as well, has little or nothing to do with the welfare of the people who work for the companies affected. In fact, the recent wave of takeovers and mergers represents a use of the energy and initiative of the business community that provides no particular benefit to Canadians, either as consumers or as workers. Paper entrepreneurship, as it has been called, is a substitute for technological and industrial innovation.

A recent newspaper article described some of the new jargon of takeovers:

—   Leveraged buyout, in which a corporate raider uses the assets of the sought after company as collateral to obtain the funds needed for the takeover. Leveraged buyouts usually crate massive amounts of debt, which has to be carried by the new company formed by the buyout, and which requires a steady cash flow to service.

- Junk bonds, which are high risk and high return bonds to finance the takeover, followed, perhaps, by greenmail, where the target company agrees to buy back its own shares – with shareholders' money – for more than the going rate in order to buy off a takeover attempt.

- Or, alternatively, the target company may attempt to provide itself with shark repellant, in order to ward off a takeover. One such form of shark repellant is the creative use of voting and non-voting shares to entrench the management of a company and prevent it from being taken over. One result of this is that a small group of shareholders may wind up with a majority of the voting rights in a company even though they have only a small proportion of the equity.

- Or, alternatively, a white knight will appear, which is a friendly takeover attempt arranged by the management of the target company as an alternative to a takeover by the raider, and as a way of saving their jobs.

- Failing this, the management may resort to a golden parachute, where they arrange to abandon the company, taking with them a good deal of its cash.

- As a last resort they may resort to a scorched earth policy where they dismantle the company and sell off the parts that are attractive to takeover artists.

- Or they may decide to take a poison pill, where they saddle the company with enough debt to make it unattractive to raiders.

If, after all this has gone on, the management of the target company is successful in fending off the raider, it will have done it at the cost of expensive court cases, corporate restructuring designed not to make the company more efficient or productive but less attractive to outsiders, the payment of huge amounts in severance and retirement payments to company executives, and the expenditure of vast amounts of time devoted to simply keeping control of the company in their own hands.

If they are not successful and the takeover is accomplished, the raider may then begin to milk the cash flow of the company in order to pay off the junk bonds,[4] or dismantle the company and sell off its parts in order to do the same thing. Either way, the long term viability of the company, and its ability to provide good, well paying jobs is nowhere on the list of priorities for either side.

Now all of this has a certain fascination – in the same way that "Dallas" and "Dynasty" are fascinating from a certain point of view. Everyone is interested in T. Boone Pickens,[5] and Carl Icahn,[6] and the doings of Ivan Boesky.[7] All of us have followed with some fascination the doings of the Reichmanns and the Belzbergs, and other powerful businessmen in Canada. However, what is remarkably absent from any of this discussion of takeovers and mergers is any sense of how it is beneficial to the economy and to the workers and consumers who make up the majority in that economy.

Most of the jargon cited above, of course, is a recitation of the reality in the United States, where junk bonds, greenmail,[8] poison pills, and hostile takeovers are very much in the news.[9] Is our concern with takeovers and mergers in Canada an overreaction to this American situation, or are there causes to be concerned about the same thing in Canada?

It is true that junk bonds are not part of the Canadian reality. However, what is done in the United States by junk bonds is done in Canada through lines of credit arranged through large banks. Both carry high rates of interest that have to be borne from the cash flow of the companies involved. In addition, Canadian acquirers make use of high yield preferred shares to finance takeovers.

It is true that hostile takeovers have not been as common in Canada as in the United States (although we have had our share recently of hostile takeovers). Part of the reason for this is that the Canadian economy is already concentrated in the hands of a small number of people, and a smaller proportion of Canadian companies are widely held than is the case in the United States. It is also true, however, that takeovers don't have to be hostile to provoke the unproductive paper shuffling and corporate concentration that are the heart of the problem.

Canada has had its share of this kind of unproductive restructuring; designed not to improve efficiency and productivity, but to serve the ends of paper entrepreneurship. The recent Canadian Tire takeover battle has revolved around the creation some years ago of a classic poison pill, whereby the Billes family, who had owned a controlling interest in Canadian Tire, managed to retain control while selling off much of their equity in the company through the stratagem of creating voting and non-voting shares for a handsome gain.[10] In another well known example of a poison pill in operation, union enterprises bought Burns Foods to prevent Unicorp from taking it over.[11] In a similar move, Noranda bought MacMillan Bloedel in order to ward off a takeover by Brascan and the Caisse de Depot.

Similarly, Torstar and Southam exchanged shares a couple of years ago in order to ward off a takeover attempt on Southam.[12] In this case Torstar was acting as a white knight, but the result was the entrenchment of management at both Torstar and Southam, and a dangerous concentration of influence in the newspaper business.

None of the recently publicized phenomena of the takeover wave, then, are absent from the Canadian scene, and it is just as hard in the Canadian context as in the United States context to see how workers, or the economy in general, will benefit from all this activity. In some ways, in fact, the takeover wave is more dangerous in Canada than in the United States, for two reasons: the already high level of concentration in the Canadian economy, and the high level of foreign ownership in the economy.

Takeovers involving United States companies will have effects in Canada, even if the major activity takes place outside the country. A good example occurred recently when Goodyear successfully fought off a takeover attempt.[13] The cost was $88 million in greenmail, a restructuring that involved selling off huge chunks of the company, a program to buy back $2 billion worth of common shares, with borrowed money of course, and — in order to carry the huge load of debt resulting from all this – the shutdown of several tire plants, including one in Toronto that employs over 1,500 people. In this case, because of the branch plant nature of our economy, a takeover involving a United States company resulted in Canadian jobs being lost.

Another takeover attempt that cost jobs was the takeover by British Telecom of Mitel Corporation, which has been the recipient of several million dollars worth of federal government grants and subsidies.[14]

We don't have to restrict ourselves to branch plant situations, however, to encounter takeover situations that are of questionable benefit to Canadians – whether they are workers or consumers.

Will the merger of Pacific Western Airlines (PWA) and Canadian Pacific Air Lines (CPAL) provide benefits to workers and consumers?[15] It is important to understand that the Canadian airline industry – even before this takeover – was characterized by a much higher level of concentration than the United States airline industry, even after a dizzying series of mergers and takeovers in the United States industry over the past couple of years. The PWA-CPAL merger will increase the level of concentration even more.

It is likely, in fact, that the eventual result of this takeover will be a loss of jobs. It is not likely, as industry spokesman have already admitted,[16] to result in lower fares, and if the United States experience with increasing concentration in the airline industry is any guide, it is not likely to result in improved service either.

In fact, the result of the increasing concentration in the United States airline industry, combined with deregulation, has been a loss of service in many parts of the country, and a serious gap between the fare structure that people in the highly populated parts of the country can expect, and that people in smaller towns and cities can expect. In addition, there have been deteriorating safety standards, large layoffs; a loss of job security, wages and benefits for many workers, and a serious deterioration in the labour relations climate in the industry that – in the long run – can only result in poorer service, less efficiency and less job satisfaction for those who work in the industry.[17]

3.0 CONCENTRATION OF ECONOMIC POWER

The already high level of concentration in the Canadian economy means that the recent wave of takeovers has concentrated the ownership of Canadian industry even more into the hands of a smaller number of conglomerates.

Bernard Ghert (1985), the president of Cadillac Fairview, has said in a brief to the parliamentary committee looking at the Green Paper on financial institutions, that the recent rash of takeovers and mergers has created a group of conglomerates that are harmful to the health of the Canadian economy – because of their power to restrict output and raise prices, because they are inefficient and wasteful, and because of their impact on the political system.[18] Ghert goes on to say that:

The concern is that these large groups will be able to use their power to advance the interests of some customers or suppliers and/or penalize others: undermine the position of rivals; provide excess rewards and use economic power to influence public policy via the political process, i.e., expenditures on lobbying, advocacy advertising, public relations, campaign contributions, and the ability to redirect corporate locational decisions (Ghert 1985, p. 13).

If a handful of conglomerates end up dominating our economy, he continued:

> They would wield enormous power in a country the size of Canada. That power would be sufficient to influence significantly the political process itself and ultimately our political freedoms.

Stanley Beck, the chairman of the Ontario Securities Commission, made a similar point when he argued, in a background study for the Macdonald Commission, that big corporations:

> Exercise power that extends far beyond their obvious function as efficient producers of goods and services, in spite of the rise of manifold regulations and the alleged play of countervailing forces, the large corporation yields enormous power that controls, directs and influences large segments of society. . . . A high degree of market concentration and a high degree of concentrated ownership are the hallmarks of the Canadian economy. Together they constitute a centre of power that is rivalled only by government itself (Beck 1985, p. 182).

As he notes, a small number of family groupings controls a large proportion of the largest publicly traded companies in Canada, whose

> Opinions and preferences must necessarily carry great weight in government councils. . . . Increasingly the public is subjected to, and government responds to, a narrow range of ideas (p. 197).

None of this can be good for the Canadian economy, nor for the workers and consumers who make up the majority.

If there were any truth to the suggestion that the takeover wave has resulted in more efficient and more competitive companies, it might be reasonable to say that some of these takeovers have been beneficial. However, there is absolutely no evidence to that effect.[19] In fact, the opposite seems to have happened. The result of the takeover binge in Canada has been a smaller number of even larger conglomerates with increasingly concentrated power and dangerously heavy debt loads.

The heavy debt loads have made these companies reluctant to make the kind of capital investment necessary to rejuvenate the economy, and the concentrated power has given these conglomerates the political clout that makes it possible to manipulate the tax system so that they can make profits without being particularly innovative or particularly risk oriented. The result is good for the people who control the conglomerates, but not especially good for the rest of us.

4.0 POLICY RESPONSES

What can be done about all this? To begin with, we need to be clear that the purpose of competition policy[20] – and economic policy in general – is to protect workers and consumers from the market, not to perfect the workings of the market. In our view, there is no particular reason to expect the market to pass along any benefits to workers and consumers without some government pressure to do so.

In my view, then, the answer to these problems lies in government action, not in expecting the corporate sector, or the market, to solve the problems and to pass the benefits along to the rest of us. We need to begin by making the dangers of the kind of takeover activity we have seen in recent years, and the dangers of the resulting corporate concentration, a political issue that politicians will act upon.[21]

In my view we need a public review of the economic and social effects of conglomerate mergers, so the public and the government are aware of the situation and the issues. This was advocated by Professor W.T. Stanbury (1986) in his testimony on Bill C-91.

This is just as true in the media as elsewhere. The Kent Royal Commission on Newspapers (1981) recommended restrictions on cross-ownership of newspapers and other media, and tax measures to encourage wider ownership of the communications media.

We need better corporate disclosure laws. Information on Canadian companies is often easier to get from the United States Securities and Exchange Commission than from Canadian sources. This is inexcusable.

We need to make sure that tax reform takes into account the effects of the tax system on corporate structure. There is no reason, for instance, why the interest on funds borrowed to buy shares should be tax deductible. As one well-informed commentator noted recently, this encourages more corporate concentration.[22]

We need a continuing strong government presence in key sectors of the economy. Although I am sure not many business people would agree, we in the labour movement see government ownership of key industries as a valuable countervailing force in an economy that tends toward private conglomerates. Air Canada, Petro-Canada and others are important elements in overall economic policy, and they should not be privatized.[23]

Finally, we need a government with the political will to map out, and work on, an industrial strategy. In our view, an industrial strategy would replace the private profit-oriented decisions of businessmen, with the will of the people as expressed by popularly elected governments, as the most important determinant of the direction of our economy. We are, in fact, a long way from that state of affairs. It is important, however, that we work towards it if we are to ensure that the continuing wave of takeovers and mergers that is sweeping Canada and the United States does not result in an even higher level of concentration in economic and political power than now exists.

NOTES

1. See Chapter 1 in this volume.

2. See the paper by Marfels, Chapter 3 in this volume.

3. See, for example, "The gathering takeover frenzy," *Maclean's*, August 26, 1985, pp. 26-28; "The new takeover frenzy," *Maclean's*, April 7, 1986, pp. 26-28; "Takeover!" *Globe and Mail*, January 3, 1987, pp. D1-D8. See also the data in Appendix 1 in this volume.

4. See, for example, "Power on Wall Street: Drexel Burnham is Reshaping Investment Banking - And U.S. Industry," *Business Week*, July 7, 1986, pp. 56-62; "Why Junk-Bond Investors are Losing Sleep," *Business Week*, October 13, 1986, pp. 151, 154.

5. See, for example, "High Time for T. Boone Pickens," *Time*, March 4, 1985, pp. 52-65; "Why Gulf Lost Its Fight for Life," *Business Week*, March 19, 1984, pp. 76-84; "Restructuring Big Oil," *Business Week*, November 14, 1983, pp. 138-150; "Could Boone Pickens Be Stalking U.S. Steel?" *Business Week*, December 3, 1984, pp. 146, 149; "Corporate Fear and Trembling," *Time*, January 14, 1985, p. 45. See Brooks (1987).

6. See, for example, "Carl Icahn: Raider or Manager?" *Business Week*, October 27, 1986, pp. 98-104; "The Man of Steel," *Newsweek*, October 20, 1986, pp. 50-55.

7. See, for example, "True Greed," *Newsweek*, December 1, 1986, pp. 48-64; "Going After the Crooks," *Time*, December 1, 1986, pp. 74-93; "Who'll Be the Next to Fall?" *Business Week*, December 1, 1986, pp. 28-38; "Suddenly the Fish Get Bigger," *Business Week*, March 2, 1987, pp. 28-35.

8. "A Flurry of Greenmail has Stockholders Cursing," *Business Week*, December 8, 1986, pp. 32-36.

9. Generally, see "Let's Make a Deal," *Time*, December 23, 1985, pp. 44-55; "Deal Mania," *Business Week*, November 24, 1986, pp. 74-93; "Splitting Up: The Other Side of Merger Mania," *Business Week*, July 1, 1985, pp. 50-55; "How the New Merger Boom Will Benefit the Economy," *Business Week*, February 6, 1984, pp. 42-54; "Bigger Yes, But Better?" *Time*, August 12, 1985, pp. 32- 33; "Deals, Deals, Deals," *Business Week*, November 17, 1986, pp. 64-67; "The New Food Giants: Merger Mania is Shaking the Once-Cautious Industry," *Business Week*, September 24, 1984, pp. 132- 138; "New? Improved? The Brand-Name Mergers," *Business Week*, October 21, 1985, pp. 108-116; "The

Corporate Shopping Spree Roars On and On," *Business Week*, July 21, 1986, pp. 110-111.

10. See, "The Epic Struggle," *Maclean's*, January 26, 1987, pp. 25-33.

11. See, Elaine Dewar, "Takeover," *Canadian Business*, November 1985, pp. 26-56, 159-183; and December 1985, pp. 53-62, 152-154.

12. See, David Climie, "Did Southam overreact to takeover threat?" *Financial Times*, April 6, 1986, p. 41; "Stalking a media empire," *Maclean's*, July 15, 1985, pp. 24-25.

13. See, "Trying to Beat Sir Jimmy to the Punch," *Business Week*, November 17, 1986, pp. 64-65; "In Akron, Jimmy Goldsmith's Name is Mud," *Business Week*, November 24, 1986, p. 40; "The Two Worlds of Jimmy Goldsmith," *Business Week*, December 1, 1986, pp. 98-102.

14. See, "Mitel buyer to be bound to loan rules," *Globe and Mail*, May 14, 1985; p. B3; "British Telecom breathes new life into Mitel," *Financial Post*, May 18, 1985, pp. 16; "Ottawa approves sale of Mitel to British firm," *Globe and Mail*, February 27, 1986, p. B3.

15. See, "Upstart PWA soars to No. 2 in Canadian skies," *Financial Times*, December 8, 1986, p. 12; "PWA heats up the war," *Maclean's*, December 15, 1986, pp. 32-33. See also Gillen, Stanbury and Tretheway (1988).

16. "Fare rise seen from purchase of CPAL," Vancouver *Sun*, December 3, 1986, p. F5.

17. [Editors' note: There is considerable evidence supporting the view that airline deregulation has been a big success in the U.S. See, for example, the papers in *Logistics and Transportation Review*, Vol. 22(4), December, 1986.]

18. This issue is developed in some detail by Stanbury, Chapter 17 in this volume.

19. [Editors' note: we refer the reader to Espen Eckbo's paper, Chapter 7 in this volume.]

20. See the paper by Goldman, Chapter 21 in this volume.

21. See the paper by the Minister of Consumer and Corporate Affairs, Chapter 20 in this volume.

22. See "New clamor to curb takeover 'tax subsidy'," *Financial Post*, May 31, 1986, pp. 1-2. See also Bale (1981) and the paper by Don Blenkarn, Chapter 23 in this volume.

23. For a review of federal and provincial privatization efforts, see Stanbury (1987).

REFERENCES

Bale, Gordon (1981) "The Interest Deduction to Acquire Shares in Other Corporations: An Unfortunate Welfare Tax Subsidy," *Canadian Taxation*, Vol. 3, pp. 189-202.

Beck, Stanley M. (1985) "Corporate Power and Public Policy" in *Consumer Protection and Environmental Law, and Corporate Power* (Toronto: University of Toronto Press), pp. 181-219.

Brooks, John (1987) *The Takeover Game* (New York: E.P. Dutton).

Ghert, Bernard (1985) *Brief on the Green Paper: The Regulation of Canadian Financial Institutions* (Toronto: Cadillac Fairview Corporation Limited, August).

Gillen, D.W., W.T. Stanbury & M. Tretheway (1988) "Duopoly in Canada's Airline Industry: Consequences and Policy Issues," *Canadian Public Policy*, vol. 14(1), pp. 15-31.

Royal Commission on Newspapers (1981) *Report* (Ottawa: Ministry of Supply and Services).

Stanbury, W.T. (1986) "Testimony on Bill C-91," *Minutes of Proceedings and Evidence of the Legislative Committee on Bill C-91*, Issue No. 3, April 29, 1986, pp. 4-32.

Stanbury, W.T. (1987) *Privatization in Canada* (Vancouver: B.C. Politics and Policy and Institute for Research on Public Policy).

Chapter 19

The Logic of Collective Lobbying: Information Hide and Seek

Robert R. Kerton
Professor of Economics, University of Waterloo
and Chairman, Economic Issues Committee
Consumers' Association of Canada

"The consumers are at least as numerous as any other group in the society, but they have no organization to countervail the power of organized or monopolistic producers." (Olson, 1965, p. 166)

1.0 INTRODUCTION

In *The Logic of Collective Action*, Mancur Olson (1965) points out that where each individual has a small interest in the public good, no individual may invest the time and energy to make sure that the public good is achieved. Each is prepared to be a "free rider" on an effort made by someone else. If *The Logic* is followed to its conclusion no individual would ever work for competition policy. In 1971, when I first gained a view on this as a volunteer for the Consumers' Association of Canada, there were indeed few allies in the trenches.

Olson's thesis assumes that the citizen knows his or her individual interest, but does not have the incentive to act on it because the expected private costs exceed the expected private gain. Unhappily, when the payoff is thought to be small the individual does not even have any real incentive to become informed about the issue. In the language of the literature on "search" (Stigler 1961), it does not pay to invest time and effort seeking out information. Note that this does not depend on the *actual* size of the benefit but on what the individual (rightly or wrongly) thinks the benefit will be. This might often be underestimated, as is frequently the case in consumer markets (Maynes 1985). Competition policy, to the average citizen, is just not right up there on the priority list of things needing study, so its benefits may not be calculated with care.

463

Further, there are economic actors who gain – and handsomely – from *not* having an effective competition policy. It is unreasonable to assume that they will passively sit by and allow the rules of the marketplace to be changed to reduce their monopoly rents. One component of the effort has the attributes of "disinformation." Inputs devoted to this task are wasted (from the overall point of view) very much in the way described by Tullock (1967). Alternatively, this can be viewed as a sub-species of waste now discussed as "dissipation" (of monopoly rent) although this term overlooks the foresight in the "investment" in disinformation. The strategy was highly successful in the 1970s. Relatively few Canadians knew that monopoly profits were rewards for keeping products off the market. Many consumers and business leaders accepted the line that a competition policy would be "interference" with free enterprise. Some smaller business people argued squarely against their own interest, not realizing that they were victims of anti-competitive practices that would be prohibited by the very laws they were opposing. In general, see Stanbury (1977).

To understand the tasks of public interest lobbying it is necessary to recognize that those who might lose their positions of economic power will engage in efforts to maintain their privileges. This sometimes results in an effort to hide information and explains the "hide" in the title. It is useful to distinguish between "technical" and "economic" concealment (Fisher and Kerton 1975). The former exists because science has not yet advanced enough to lift the veil of ignorance. Economic concealment, on the other hand, exists because some agent has an economic interest in keeping us from understanding something. Economic concealment is a special problem when the payoff to search is thought to be small and where the individual does not think it worthwhile to seek information. This is the "seek" problem. Why should anyone spend valuable time becoming informed about an issue in the general public interest?

2.0 HIDING INFORMATION ON THE PUBLIC INTEREST

A theory of lobbying that assumes we start from a benign position of neutral ignorance is in danger of seriously underestimating the difficulty of advocating the public interest. Lobbyists for private interests have been paid for identifying key politicians and media people. They have also presented over-simplified portions of the truth to opinion leaders. It is far more difficult to inform a person whose mind is made up than someone who is prepared to examine all the facts.

Perhaps it is not surprising that the average citizen would be affected by the well-crafted speeches of lobbyists, or by paid messages in the media. What is more remarkable is how often business itself is bamboozled into putting wolves in charge of sheep. One well-studied example concerns the U.S. National Association of Manufacturers, an interest group which has been dominated by a small group of giant corporations (Olson 1965, pp. 146-7). There are other startling examples. In early 1982 when the Consumers' Association of Canada (CAC) went to discuss competition policy with the Canadian Chamber of Commerce – a group which is to represent thousands of retailers and small businesses across Canada – Helen Morningstar and I found ourselves facing three senior executives from some of the country's biggest oligopolies.

In the early 1970s the gasoline retailers came out squarely against proposed changes in legislation concerning monopoly. One wonders who briefed them. In my view, one small but critical turning point in the 19-year campaign for merger laws came when Professor David McQueen (who has also served on CAC's Economic Issues Committee) spoke at a meeting of the gasoline retailers. He explained that they were in fact victims of some anti-competitive practices which would be removed by better laws against abusive monopoly power. It was a turning point because the Petroleum Marketers' Association of Canada eventually developed into a highly effective lobbying group. By 1985 it was able to articulate in public an issue that any car owner could readily understand. The group certainly played a role in the passage of the new *Competition Act* in 1986.[1] That story has a happy ending although this may not always be the case.

Hiding the public interest from the public is easier in Canada than in Europe, for example, because our journalists are expected to be a Jack (or Jill)-of-all-trades. One day the reporter covers computers, the next day family law or softwood lumber exports. My own experience is that writers for the financial press have always shown a clear understanding of monopoly and competition. But most others in print, television, or radio – and these are people who were eager to be fair – had too little training in economics to deal with difficult economic issues.[2] (This is an opinion that many journalists share). I am prepared to accept some blame on account of a professional talent for expository obfuscation. However, in the early years when I tried to explain that a monopolist is rewarded for restricting output and this in turn means that fewer inputs will be hired, I got one of two responses. The first was the thoughtful pause of a journalist politely trying not to snore. The second was an argument that the bigger monopolized unit would hire *more* inputs.

All this changed abruptly on August 27, 1980 when many journalists suddenly developed a keen understanding of economics. At that time newspapers were closed in Winnipeg and Ottawa with unemployment consequences which did much to sharpen the minds of those who had not understood before.[3] Coverage after that was much more helpful in getting the country its first effective law against monopolies. Press releases received more appropriate skepticism. In economic terms, special interest lobbyists opposing change found that the cost of hiding the public interest was sharply higher.

3.0 CONSUMER ORGANIZATIONS

If Olson is right, there may be no consumers' association (as indicated by the quotation at the head of this paper). And for the U.S., he is at least partly right, because Consumer's Union is primarily a product-testing body which operates without local action groups. Specialization has developed in the U.S. with various Nader-initiated groups providing some of the pressure for change (see Berry 1977). Worldwide evidence suggests that the problem of financing the public interest has inhibited but not thwarted the growth of consumer organizations. If we examine only organizations surviving to the 1980s we see that prior to 1950 *only three countries* (U.S.A., Denmark, and Canada) had enduring, national consumer bodies. In the 1950s, organizations were formed in 13 more countries. In the 1960s, 15 countries were added, and in the 1970s, 14 more (Kerton 1981). Nearly every conceivable financing method is evident — from pure volunteerism, to fee-for-service, to government grant. In my view, 100 per cent support from government, as is virtually the case in Sweden or Denmark or Hong Kong, (where it seems to work well) would, in a Canadian context, hopelessly compromise the independence of the Consumers' Association. This is not the view of eminent international consumer leaders who see no insurmountable problem with this public financing of the public interest.

Many national consumers' organizations make use of volunteers. Relatively few can call on an extensive network of locals such as exists in Canada. Among plausible hypotheses proposed to account for the origin of volunteer groups are the following: entrepreneurship, disturbance-response, purposive and historical. A good case is made for using the historical model for explaining the genesis of the CAC, largely because the other hypotheses are inadequate (Morningstar 1977; Forbes 1985, pp. 107-109). The Canadian organization grew from the Wartime Prices and Trade Board and it has been sustained by a continuing sense of public responsibility. Volunteerism is a self-imposed tax paid by those who do not quite agree with the outcomes provided by the niceties of public finance. The payoff is partly explained by Hirschman's (1970) concepts of exit, voice, and loyalty. By making use of consumer information and testing results, consumers either buy the product again or they "exit" (leave a brand). Exit can shift market shares from one brand to another, an important market function, to be sure. But in the sweep of history, it sometimes provides all the rewards that passengers got from shifting around deck chairs on the *Titanic*. "Voice" is action-oriented, directed to a change in the rules of the game.

Truly significant changes come from "voice" rather than from choices among brands. Yet it is a fact of economic life that the resources available to present information on a vital national problem like "ring-around-the-collar" may be a million times as large as the budget we had for monopoly policy. But even a small change in the question from one asking which brand best solves ring-around-the-collar to one asking whether it is the collar or the neck which should be washed, has alarming potential. (Never mind asking if the neck is threatened by a concentration of economic power.) In the end, the decision to use skilled resources on collar sanitation is one based on market structure and economic incentives as signals for resource allocation depend on the framework in which competition takes place. This framework depends on political power which can only be adjusted by those who make the effort to voice the need for change. The volunteer side of CAC is a collective method for expressing "voice."

A simplified view of the Consumers' Association of Canada can identify three distinct centres of activity: (1) a testing organization/magazine (*The*

Canadian Consumer), (2) the Regulated Industries Program, and (3) Association Policy and Affairs, which consists of a network of volunteers. This review has a focus on the third centre and its information cum lobbying experience since 1971. But the Regulated Industries Program (RIP) has also played a critical role, one which has been particularly significant against monopoly power in telecommunications and air transportation. With this program the "free rider" problem is overcome by means of a government grant or an intervention award at a regulatory hearing. Public money has provided an office with at least two lawyers and, importantly, continuing expertise on regulatory matters. The RIP centre has always been under the direction of a board headed by an expert volunteer. In the preparation of competition policy briefs, RIP and the volunteer network (Association Policy and Affairs) have often worked together, as was the case in the successful presentation to the 1986 Legislative Committee on Bill C-91, the new *Competition Act.*

The rewards received by volunteers are sometimes "explained" in strict economic terms but this is probably not a suitable model for persons who received their acculturation in Canada. No doubt Stanbury (1986a, p. 23) is correct in identifying a corporatist strain in Canadians: "These values stress the primacy of group over individual interests and an organic view of society in which the common good transcends individual interests." For expert help, chairpersons of CAC committees often ask for advice from corporate leaders, senior civil servants and others. I think many would be surprised and some would be shocked by (a) the quality of the expertise which is freely made available, and (b) the willingness to set aside private goals to provide advice on what should be done in the public interest. This is done discreetly of course: one would not want to be seen being public spirited. Suggestions received are often re-worked by volunteers of longer standing. It is true that to get volunteer help from experts we lower the effort-cost they have to make. They need not attend meetings—one or two phone calls will suffice. How about the "price" which has to be paid by the more permanent corps of volunteers?

CAC volunteers are often committed to a specific consumer issue: inadequate labelling, meat which is unfit, unsafe baby cribs etc. Yet there is a sense of identity or common purpose which goes well beyond that specific concern. No strict exchange theory can account for the hours of volunteer time given. But the volunteer network does exist and it provides national support for any issue of general concern.

Members of this network have all the characteristics of activists identified by Thorelli and Thorelli (1977) as "information seekers." For competition policy, as for other issues, the existence of these sensitive leaders facilitates the spread of information throughout the network of 10 provincial, two territorial and 30 or more local organizations. CAC has a national magazine (*The Canadian Consumer*), a publication for locals and for active committee workers (*The Watchdog*), regular mailings (including material from its Economic Issues Committee) and enough meetings to intimidate a civil servant. By the end of Maryon Brechin's presidency in 1974 this group of active volunteers was well informed about competition policy. An attempt to use radio talk shows to interest the broader public was not successful at that time. On this issue, as on most matters, the network of volunteers was a valuable asset. There can be no doubt that it did its bit to promote the passage of the 1976 law to bring the service sector under competition policy (see Kaiser 1979). But it was by no means sufficient to overcome powerful lobbyists opposed to effective laws on mergers.

4.0 LEVERS OF POWER

Our experience over the last fifteen years is in accord with the prescient observations of Douglas Hartle (1975, pp. 19-21) about the shift in the focus of political power:

> A Prime Minister or a Premier with a clear majority has enormous power ... This power attracts, like a magnet, individuals who wish to influence the exercise of this power, for this confers prestige on them ... Minority governments are highly dependent upon the performance of particular Ministers — whether by virtue of the votes they can deliver as individuals from their own riding or the votes they can deliver by virtue of the policies adopted with respect to their particular portfolio.

In these circumstances the Consumers' Association of Canada has some power too because, in its effort to help the media inform the public about merger policy, it has the side effect of show-casing the Minister's work in a way he or she could not achieve alone. At a minimum, our coverage in the media shows the Ministry to be working on an important issue deserving public attention.

During times of majority governments, the consulting industries expand — firms can thrive by charging handsome fees for quiet activity to gain or defend some private privilege or some monopoly rent. This economic health is countercyclical for low-budget groups which support the public interest. Yet it is easy to overstate the pessimism if we fail to recognize that Canadian reality — for whatever reason — has given our Prime Ministers a core set of advisors (attracted by the magnet of power) who are self-confident enough not to need *any* independent advice. For example, international comparisons reveal that central agencies like the Prime Minister's Office have typically shown remarkably little interest in obtaining outside views.

> Compared to their British and American counterparts, Canadian officials in central agencies demonstrated the least interest in obtaining the views of outsiders, and fell behind in consultation with business and union leaders, local government officials, religious leaders, leaders of ethnic groups, citizen groups and other professionals (Dobell and Mansbridge 1986, p.13).

There is little reason for the Consumers' Association to resent being excluded, since our experience suggests that even Ministers have had trouble getting a hearing. All of this helps to explain why high profile liaison with government has not been the dominant strategy in CAC advocacy work on monopoly policy. Nor is our experience different from that of other public interest groups. Dobell and Mansbridge (1986) provide results collected from 45 interest groups in Canada on the activities perceived to be effective in influencing government on social policy – see Table 1. At the top of the list is information dissemination and in last spot is formal government liaison and delivery of service. We have results for a set of opinion leaders from the Consumers' Association of Canada on the same question (perceived influence on social policy).

Differences are small but both groups perceive informal government liaison to be more important than formal liaison. CAC respondents may have had trouble interpreting the words "social policy research" but if they held the same notion as those in the IRPP sample, CAC leaders felt research was less influential in affecting government social policy than did those in the interest groups sample of IRPP.

Table 1
Perceived Effectiveness of Activities on Influencing Government Social Policy

	IRPP Group*		CAC Leaders**	
Number in sample	45		22	
Activity	Score	Rank	Score	Rank
Informal government liaison	2.6	3	2.6	1
Delivery of service	2.9	5	2.7	2
Information dissemination	2.3	1	2.9	3
Formal government liaison	2.9	6	3.0	4
Group meetings	2.7	4	3.3	5
Social policy research	2.5	2	3.3	6

*   Average is for 45 Interest Groups as defined in Dobell and Mansbridge (1986, pp. 69, 94).

**   Obtained in survey responses at a seminar organized by the Policy Advisory Council March 20-22, 1987 in Bolton. Respondents are active consumer leaders of CAC local, provincial or national groups.

In sharp contrast, the IRPP results show that *business* groups rate formal (and informal) liaison with government as highly effective, and "information dissemination" as being least effective. As an explanation, the authors suggest "This may indicate that Business finds these channels so effective as to minimize the need to appeal to the general public" (Dobell and Mansbridge 1986, p. 101). A small sample of eight CAC leaders who work on economic issues was surveyed with a similar questionnaire. Their perceptions differ sharply from those of business, probably showing the other side of the same coin. The most effective activities *on competition policy* were perceived to be "briefs and position papers" and "public pressure through media." Two conclusions follow from these differing perceptions. First, for the public interest group, it is not easy to get a real hearing. Second, there is no sense in being cynical about political attentiveness. There are many political advisors who are entirely willing to give the public interest as much attention as they give to private lobbies. But it is necessary for CAC and others to work with the media to make it politically safe for politicians to act in the public interest.

5.0 THE AWAKENING OF ALLIES

With the specific case of monopoly policy we began in a situation where a great deal of misinformation — driven by economic forces — existed. Recall that efforts had been made to hide the importance of a fair framework of rules which would oblige producers to succeed in the market-place with superior products or services. Arguments about economies of scale were abused to further the notion that bigger is better. Platitudes about "government interference" were deployed to hide the fact that powerful economic agents quite liked a *status quo*. Under existing tax and monopoly laws the main route to wealth — especially for those already well en route — was one which encouraged takeovers and the shuffle of paper assets, most of which did nothing for Canada nor for the economy. From such a starting point it is little wonder that our chief task required a public information campaign.

But much more than information was required. Smaller businesses had to learn of their situation and voice their own views. Leadership was provided in the continuing work of the Department of Consumer and Corporate Affairs, the Economic Council of Canada (1969) and by Professor W.T. Stanbury.[4] Public interventions at enquiries by Lawson Hunter, then the Director of Investigation and Research, *Combines Investigation Act*, played a role. But primary importance must be attached to the formation of — and the increasing economic sagacity of — small business organizations. There was as well, a significant increase in the support of labour. By 1984 or so it was no longer so lonely in the trenches. It still was not the least bit obvious that an effective bill could be passed, but the balance of forces was much more promising.

6.0 USE OF CONSUMER RESOURCES TO LOBBY FOR THE PUBLIC INTEREST

The network of "information seekers" provided information to allow CAC volunteers to include a brief discussion of competition policy in their speeches throughout the country. And our publications frequently cover competition. But it is no surprise that the awakening of the general public depends squarely on their being an immediate "felt need" for an explanation. All sellers are not equal as motivators: consumers get more upset over problems with certain products or services than over others. Food is first, in our experience, followed by gasoline retailers and banks. A well-timed explanation at the right moment is worth ten thousand well chosen words at some other time. We made, for example, one major effort to use the *Canadian Consumer* to explain competition policy. Most of the issue of August, 1977 was devoted to articles of high quality by a number of academic experts. It certainly provided an effective resource base for our active workers, and that success must be recognized. But a readership survey would probably have indicated that month's *Canadian Consumer* stands out as one of the least read issues of all time. Most members "did not have time" to read the careful discourses on monopoly. And it was as late as 1983 that CAC added its first full time professional media relations person. This was a resource of absolutely critical importance on a number of fronts. For economic issues it was a crucial method of moving artillery to the front lines. The information battle is no place for amateurs.

In a perverse way, events in the Canadian economy over the span of time have served as persistent reminders of the need for a merger policy. Recent events with the shuffle of paper assets in the financial sector represent the latest motivator to consumers.[5] That example also allows a brief demonstration of one of CAC's successes with public education. Our strategy is a deliberate attempt to lower the effort-cost of understanding economics (decreasing the price the public has to pay for learning). Financial sector reform was to consider the "four pillars:" banks, trust companies, investment brokers, and insurance firms. By changing the image to "four pastures" with each cash cow eager to chomp on the green stuff on the other side of the regulatory fence, we were able to explain why the fences were being broken down. With newspaper interest in four pastures we could educate the public on the gains from competition and on the potential abuse of corporate power through intra-conglomerate deals. And we were first to point out that cross-referrals which could enlarge conglomerate profit were a fundamental threat to unsophisticated consumers who could do better by shopping around. CAC was clearly successful with this strategy of lowering the "price" of learning, but it does have its own problem: It is not easy.

7.0 IS THERE A ROLE FOR LUCK? FOR INTEGRITY?

Sometimes academics are too good at explaining things. Every outcome has a set of explanatory variables with no room left for luck. The first edition of George Stigler's *Theory of Price* had "luck" explain part of economic success.

Later editions are more scientific, luck does not appear. We had 20 years of political roulette since May of 1966 when the Prime Minister announced the intention to ask the Economic Council of Canada for a "... fundamental review" of "... the whole question of combines, mergers, monopolies and restraint of trade ..." (Rea 1976, p. 217) so it may be about time that the public interest had its number come up. To see that luck had at least a minor role consider the special circumstances at work in the hearing process when the new *Competition Act* was passed in 1986.

The Consumers' Association of Canada has been given credit for succeeding in having an impressive list of amendments accepted in Committee and passed into law. Two business lobby groups have signalled their distress at this unexpected turn of events and they have quietly let us know that it will not happen again. We believe that we understood the process and that our presentation dominated the agenda. We are more than eager to take full credit for our part. But a rigorous look at the facts shows a remarkable configuration of circumstances which provided the luck and the drive to achieve a measure of success far beyond what one could reasonably expect. First, the Minister, Michel Coté, understood the distinction between being "pro free enterprise" and "pro existing firms." Second, he had solid expertise in his ministry. Third, the recent 1985 reforms allowed special legislative committees a new and unexplored degree of independence – if they could get away with it.

Many of our previous appearances before legislative committees had all the attributes of a circus, with some members demonstrating that they were under-informed about the economic issue and more interested in political one-liners to each other than in any legislation. Contrast that with our hearing in 1986. The Committee had a strong chairman and government members who were well informed on the issue and willing to show independence. One of the opposition members was David Orlikow, an NDP MP long known for his integrity, and a man who has followed competition policy for years. Another was Andre Ouellet, a former Minister of Consumer and Corporate Affairs with the knowledge that comes from years of experience and a clear view of what was needed.[6] From a public interest point of view this three-party resource base was a remarkably lucky set of circumstances.

Proof that this was luck might be provided by the December 1986 to March 1987 hearings on Bill C-22 (pharmaceutical patents) where the legislative committee was in a circus mode unwilling or unable to marshall any degree of independence in the public interest. The general point though, on the monopoly bill as seen from the perspective of the Consumers Association of Canada, is that we did our part (a) with public opinion and (b) with concise, point form amendments. But success depended as well on the Committee system working at its best. This is a moment to relish but not something that can be counted on routinely.

8.0 CONCLUSIONS

Consumer experience in advocating competition policy in Canada is testimony to the difficulties Olson (1965) describes in organizing a defence of the public interest. But effective lobbying efforts by private interests make the task even more daunting than Olson predicts. If information is successfully hidden, citizens will not even know that they need to search. If one looks back over the long struggle to strengthen Canada's notoriously weak merger provisions, the surprising fact is how long it took for potential winners to see that they could gain from fairer rules. Among the winners are consumers and the country generally. The major purpose of a new policy is to shift the incentive system from one which rewards the shuffling of paper assets to one which tips the balance toward rewarding those who best produce real goods and services. This is no trivial matter as it affects the dynamism of the economy, and the standard of living of all Canadians. That private interests were so successful in delaying legislation is evidence of their skill.

There is nothing to be gained by underestimating the difficulties to be faced in lobbying for collective interests, whether they be difficulties with financing collective action or difficulties in getting participants to seek out accurate information which is important to the public interest. It is certainly unwise to assume that one can start from a benign status of neutral ignorance.

NOTES

1. The contents of the new legislation effective in June 1986 are discussed in Stanbury (1986b) and in the paper by Goldman, Chapter 21, in this volume.

2. See the discussion in Stanbury (1986a, Ch. 11).

3. The simultaneous closings by the Thomson and Southam chains resulted in the Kent Commission (the Royal Commission on Newspapers) which reported in 1981. In the subsequent prosecution for merger, monopoly and conspiracy the two chains were acquired and the Crown did not appeal.

4. Between 1976 and 1987 Stanbury published over 50 articles, book chapters, edited books and books on Canadian competition policy. He has been a consistent advocate of stronger competition legislation. See, for example, Stanbury and Reschenthaler (1981) and Stanbury (1985). The history of efforts to reform the legislation are described in Stanbury (1977), Brecher (1982) and Stanbury (1986b).

5. See the paper by Courchene, Chapter 24, in this volume.

6. Mr. Ouellet had made substantial efforts to introduce new legislation, see Stanbury and Reschenthaler (1981).

REFERENCES

Berry, Jeffrey (1977) *Lobbying for the People* (Princeton: Princeton University Press).

Brecher, Irving (1982) *Canada's Competition Policy Revisited: Some New Thoughts on an Old Story* (Montreal: The Institute for Research on Public Policy).

Dobell, A. R. and S. H. Mansbridge (1986) *The Social Policy Process in Canada* (Montreal: Institute for Research on Public Policy).

Economic Council of Canada (1969) *Interim Report on Competition Policy* (Ottawa: Queen's Printer).

Fischer, D.F. and R.R. Kerton (1975) "Perception of Environmental Diseconomies: Technical vs. Economic Invisibility," *Social Science Information*, Vol. 14(1), pp. 45-54.

Forbes, J.D. (1985) "Organizational and Political Dimensions of Consumer Pressure Groups," *Journal of Consumer Policy*, Vol. 8 (2), pp. 105-131.

Hartle, Douglas G. (1975) "Techniques and Processes of Administration" (Paper delivered to the Annual Meetings of the Canadian Institute of Public Administration, September, mimeo).

Hirschman, A.O. (1970) *Exit, Voice, and Loyalty: Responses to the Decline in Firms, Organizations and States* (Cambridge, Mass.: Harvard University Press).

Kaiser, Gordon (1979) "The Stage I Amendments: An Overview" in Prichard, Stanbury and Wilson (eds.) *Canadian Competition Policy* (Toronto: Butterworths), Ch. 2.

Kerton, R.R. (1981) "The Business of Organized Consumers: National and International," *Canadian Business Review*, Vol. 8(3), pp. 31-33.

Maynes, E.S. (1985) "Towards Market Transparency" (Ithaca, N.Y.: Cornell University, Department of Economics and Housing. Working Paper, June 28).

Ministry of Consumer and Corporate Affairs (1973) *Proposals for a New Competition Policy for Canada: First Stage.* Reprinted in K.J. Rea and J.T. McLeod, *Business and Government in Canada*, Second edition, (Toronto: Methuen, 1976), pp. 205-225.

Morningstar, H.J. (1977) "The Consumers' Association of Canada – The History of an Effective Organization," *Canadian Business Review*, Vol. 4(4), pp. 30-33.

Olson, Mancur (1965) *The Logic of Collective Action* (Cambridge, Mass.: Harvard University Press).

Stanbury, W.T. (1977) *Business Interests and the Reform of Canadian Competition Policy, 1971-1975* (Toronto: Carswell/Methuen).

Stanbury, W.T. (1985) "Half a Loaf: Bill C-29, Proposed Amendments to the Combines Investigation Act," *Canadian Business Law Journal*, Vol. 10(1), pp. 1-34.

Stanbury, W.T. (1986a) *Business-Government Relations in Canada* (Toronto: Methuen).

Stanbury, W.T. (1986b) "The New Competition Act and Competition Tribunal Act: 'Not With a Bang, But a Whimper'," *Canadian Business Law Journal*, Vol. 12(1), pp. 2-42.

Stanbury, W.T. and G.B. Reschenthaler (1981) "Reforming Canadian Competition Policy: Once More Unto the Breach," *Canadian Business Law Journal*, Vol. 5(4), pp. 381-437.

Stigler, G.J. (1961) "The Economics of Information," *Journal of Political Economy*, Vol. 69(3), pp. 213-25.

Thorelli, H.B., and S.V. Thorelli (1977) *Consumer Information Systems and Consumer Policy* (Cambridge: Ballinger Publishing).

Tullock, G. (1967) "The Welfare Costs of Monopoly and Theft," *Western Economic Journal*, June, 1967.

Public Policy Responses

Chapter 20

Corporate Concentration in Canada*

Harvie André, PC, MP
Minister of Consumer and Corporate Affairs Canada
and Minister Responsible for Canada Post

1.0 INTRODUCTION AND BACKGROUND

In this paper I will deal with an emerging issue that is being drawn to the government's attention—aggregate corporate concentration. Over the last few months, we've seen newspaper headlines heralding the dangers of high and increasing concentration. These articles state that the clothes we wear, the milk we drink, the chocolate bars we eat, the gas we pump into our cars, the mortgages we have on our homes, all in one way or another add to the income and profits of a small group of large conglomerates. Some people say that we pay higher prices than necessary for these products or services. Others say the conglomerates are controlled by a few families whose wealth gives them access to the political process. Stories are written about the conglomerate families and the corporate mega mergers they consummate with borrowed money. Editorials have demanded hearings to disallow or review certain takeovers. Others predict Canada will become an economic oligarchy where the corporate elite will preside over the welfare of Canadians. While 1984 is behind us, these articles seem to imply that the Orwellian world has yet to visit us.

There is *one* thing I know for sure, and that is people are becoming more concerned about what's going on out there and what impact it's going to have on them. In a recent Decima poll, of those who said mergers were increasing, more than 70 per cent expressed concern about the trend.

---

* Edited version of a speech to the Gordon Group 1987 Executive Program on Competition and Corporate Concentration at the Sheraton Centre, Toronto, Ontario, March 31, 1987.

But this concern is not new. In 1975 public nervousness prompted the establishment of the Royal Commission on Corporate Concentration. Its report in 1978 documented Canadians' concern over the ability of large corporations to influence public policy.[1] However, the commission concluded there was no real evidence to support those concerns.

Now we're in the 1980s, and concerns over corporate concentration are being raised virtually every day in the national media. Every time another takeover hits the news, it sparks a new round of speculative articles, questions in the House of Commons, political speeches, and even books on corporate concentration in Canada.

The environment we're dealing with now is considerably different from the one in the 1970s. I will discuss that environment because it has contributed significantly to the tone of the current debate.

We have no doubt seen an increase recently in very large takeovers, both within Canada, and in Canadian companies taking over much larger American firms.[2] These processes dominate the headlines for weeks, as the business community and the public follow the story with the same zeal some devote to "Dallas" or other television soap operas. And why not? They are high drama.

When non-financial companies take over financial institutions,[3] concerns are raised over conflict of interest and the protection of life savings. This has been particularly underlined by the failure of two banks and a number of trust companies.[4] Questions have been posed on the integrity of our financial institutions and on the adequacy of our regulatory system – something most people used to take for granted.

"Star Wars" has been replaced by "takeover wars." Target firms hostile to a particular corporate suitor search for "white knights" to rescue them. If what cannot be avoided is inevitable, a "poison pill" is kept in hand. Or other tactics described by equally emotive images such as "scorched earth" and "golden parachutes" are used. As takeover activities have increased, so too has the concentration of wealth in Canada. The press has been preoccupied with comparing the number of billionaire families per capita in Canada and the United States, and even documenting lifestyles of the rich and famous.[5]

There is also a lot of talk these days about "paper entrepreneurship," or investment in ownership and control of existing corporate assets, rather than investments in new business ventures that augment jobs and production. A company which was worth $50 million last year is worth twice maybe three times as much this year because it levered the purchase of a much larger company.

Now, I'm not saying any of this is wrong, illegal, or even otherwise problematic. But, as you know, public perceptions form the political environment in which these kinds of issues will be considered.

Given what's going on, I think I would encourage our children to become intermediaries – lawyers, accountants, brokers and the like. All this shuffling of paper spins off tremendous fees for the professionals involved in putting these deals together.

A billion-dollar company may be changing hands with no net economic gain or loss. But those on both sides of the deal are paying large professional fees to make it happen. Again, there's nothing wrong with that. It does, however, raise questions and speculation about what it all means for the public.

If you look at all of these issues against the political and economic backdrop of the 1980s, there is cause for legitimate public concern. Not so long ago, Canada went through a real economic downturn that cost millions of jobs, increased the federal government's deficit, and almost decimated regional economies. While times have changed and economic indicators are pointing in the right direction, the memory of the early part of this decade lingers. As a result, Canadians are conditioned to be somewhat fearful of any economic or business relationships they may not fully understand. Those fears are raised whenever there are conflict of interest allegations against public officials. It doesn't matter whether those charges are well-founded, whether they focus on public servants or politicians, or whether they're in the municipal, provincial or federal jurisdictions.

Corporate takeover activities and businessmen are often viewed in a similar emotional environment. An emotion-charged debate will sometimes force a government to act in haste to resolve those pressures which exist when the public believes its interests are threatened. It's not the best way to solve a problem, especially when no one is even sure what the problem is.

If action is forced before we even have a rational debate on the issues, the subsequent public discussion will be based upon limited facts, unlimited speculation, and political advantage. So, we must make the debate more deliberate and focused; we must address the real issues rather than succumb to political rhetoric. How do we do this? I cannot offer a ready-made government policy, but I know we must reduce the emotionalism so we can deal with the real issues.

2.0 THE DEBATE ON CORPORATE CONCENTRATION
Conceptually, there are about six different areas around which the debate on corporate concentration should focus. My discussion will be restricted to the following categories:

— competition,

— the governing of corporations,

— financial versus non-financial corporations,

— economic performance,

— the distribution of wealth, and

— government/business relationships.

I must raise more questions than provide answers. But if we can get the questions right, then we have a much better chance of finding the answers. This is important because if we miss the right questions, who knows where we will end up?

The questions I'm going to ask do not come in any policy order or any political framework. They are just questions that are thrown on the table when corporate concentration is discussed.

2.1 Competition

Competition is probably the most volatile emotional issue in the entire debate. High levels of corporate concentration often seem to be equated with a lack of competition.

This issue has several dimensions. All takeovers do not reduce competition. The question at hand is what indicators does one use to determine which takeovers do reduce competition. Corporate concentration in a particular market may increase as the result of an acquisition. But that may make the new competitor more vigorous and efficient. Concentration is an important factor but not the only factor by which one must judge competition. Freedom for new firms to enter, and for small and medium size companies to grow into a particular line of business, range of choice, and price of products and imports are among the host of factors that must also be considered. Besides, competition relates to markets, and the concern that seems to be driving the public debate more often these days is a concern over the absolute size of a corporation.

From my perspective as Minister of Consumer and Corporate Affairs, if we are to advance the public debate we must begin by distinguishing between competition issues specifically, and the problems of increasing corporate concentration. A question that needs to be asked is: What is the relationship between concentration in corporate ownership—one company owning dairy companies, real estate firms, car rental companies, breweries and other organizations—and brand-name market penetration, or price within a specific commodity area? While I don't have the answer, I know it's the question uppermost in people's minds when they address the issue of corporate concentration.

2.2 Corporate Governance

How should corporations be governed in this atmosphere of takeovers? This raises questions of shareholders' rights, information disclosure, the responsibility of corporate directors and so on. The Canadian Tire situation put many of these issues squarely on the table - though I'm not sure that the Canadian public really understood what was going on. The regulators, however, have made it clear that they will not look favourably upon companies who violate the rights of minority shareholders.

Government can move further in these areas with corporate and securities legislation. But that requires extensive understanding and cooperation by two levels of government in two different areas of legislation—and that's only a small part of the issue. The issue of financial institutions is also an essential element in the discussion of corporate concentration.

2.3   Financial vs Non-Financial Enterprises

The relationship between financial institutions and non-financial corporations raises many questions, some of which I alluded to earlier. My colleague, the Minister of State for Finance, has established some directions for the resolution of these issues.

In his paper, *New Directions for the Financial Sector*, the Honourable Tom Hockin articulated four principles that the government should adopt to maintain a sound financial system – a system that would provide Canadians with innovative, competitive and secure services.[7] Integration of the industry, a pragmatic ownership policy, strength in the regulatory system, and an effective, modern supervisory system are the basis for strong financial institutions that will best serve Canadian interests.

2.4   Economic Performance

A fourth topic which must also be addressed is the macro issue of the impact of corporate concentration on economic performance. Do takeovers, large or small, contribute to economic growth? Put the other way, do they diminish economic growth? I suspect the answer is – it depends. The money paid out for an acquisition likely won't add new jobs to the Canadian economy – except maybe for lawyers and other intermediaries. Nor does it necessarily improve the competitive performance of the company that was taken over.

But what about the people who used to own the company and who suddenly have more cash to invest? What do they do with that investment capital? And how do their decisions impact on job opportunities and entre-preneurship? I don't have these answers either. But there must be some economic benefit from that infusion of unattached capital.

Even if those benefits can be demonstrated, we don't know the economic impact on firms that have been the targets of takeovers – the impact in terms of efficiency, effectiveness or risk-taking in the private-sector environment.

More importantly, when very large players in the economy make bad economic decisions, or mistakes, the effects do not just wash through the economy. Rather, because of their size they can have a significant effect on the performance of the Canadian economy. We can probably deal with all those elements through a combination of tax and monetary policies, sectoral policies, and corporations law. The problem is orchestrating all of the legislative powers we have, if we only have a limited understanding of the problems we're trying to resolve.[8]

Do these major corporate takeovers enrich the country or simply create a smaller and smaller corporate elite? And, does this elite have political power – the ability to intervene with politicians and exert influence over policy – that somehow subverts the democratic system?

In this arena, where public confidence in our democratic institutions is being challenged, the questions are clear. The answers, however, are clouded by political rhetoric, by short-term advantage, and by whatever ephemeral issues happen to occupy the headlines of the media.

3.0 POLITICAL ACTION

The government is moving on a number of fronts to counter the emotional response. We are dealing with lobbyists,[9] conflict of interest guidelines, divestiture of Crown corporations that no longer have overriding public policy imperatives, and other related policy issues. We are dealing with changes to the corporate and personal income tax systems.

We are looking at two potentially conflicting issues simultaneously – encouraging investment and entrepreneurship on the one hand, and preserving and enhancing the social safety net on the other – all this while trying to maintain the integrity of the political process.

I suggested earlier that the issue of corporate concentration can be examined conceptually by reducing it to six different issues, all of which have an impact on our economic, social, and political traditions. While the government has moved to resolve many of these issues independently, it will not necessarily ease the public's concern over the generic issue of corporate concentration. That's why more disciplined thought – public, corporate, and government – must take place to ease the public mind, while at the same time ensuring an effective environment for Canadian business nationally and internationally.

I don't want this discussion to be controlled by those scaring the Canadian public for political advantage. I don't want to be forced to develop legislation to respond to issues that are driven by emotion rather than careful reasoning. I don't want to propose solutions to Cabinet before we really understand the problems. Perhaps the public perceptions about the evils of corporate concentration are valid. But what I want is deliberate thought on the issues. Businessmen must understand where public concern is coming from, and help mould the debate from one of 'hysteria' to one of 'deliberation.'

The concepts I've outlined above are just *one* way of looking at these issues. For instance, I haven't talked about Canada's ability to compete in the international marketplace. I haven't talked about the environment of freer trade relationships with the United States, or how the European Economic Community is defining many international trade issues.

The government has already undertaken several initiatives which touch on the issue of corporate concentration. The *Competition Act*, in its first full year of implementation, will go a long way toward ensuring healthy competition in the marketplace.[10] It had been on the public policy agenda for a long time.[11] But we got the job done. Tom Hockin's proposals which have been designed to strengthen our financial system; steps toward privatization, our plans for comprehensive tax reform, and our response to the registration of lobbyists[12] will also address the subject of a fair and open marketplace and political system.

I believe we have a policy and legislative framework in place that allows business to do what it does best – business. I encourage and welcome input from businessmen on our efforts thus far and their thoughts on emerging issues such as corporate concentration. Policy formulation is an ongoing process and businessmen are an integral part of that process.

NOTES

1. See Royal Commission on Corporate Concentration (1978). For a series of critiques, see Gorecki and Stanbury (1979). For a more recent discussion, see Stanbury, Chapter 17 in this volume.

2. See the list of large takeovers in Canada (those with a transaction value of $100 million or more) compiled by Professor W.T. Stanbury in Appendix 1 to this volume.

3. Perhaps the most notable was Imasco's takeover of Genstar Ltd. in 1986. Genstar had recently acquired Canada Trustco, the nation's largest trust company, and in 1985 it acquired Canada Permanent Trust, another large trust company.

4. These are reviewed by the Economic Council (1986).

5. See, for example, the columns of Diane Francis, and her book, *Controlling Interest: Who Owns Canada?* (1986).

6. See, for example, "Canadian Tire takeover focuses spotlight on voting rights," *Globe and Mail*, January 13, 1987, p. B1; "Riding high on coattails," *Financial Times*, January 19, 1987, pp. 1, 38; "The Epic Struggle," *Maclean's*, January 26, 1987, pp. 25-33; "Blowout at the Tire," *Financial Times*, April 27, 1987, p. 3; "Court backs halting of bid for retailer," Toronto *Star*, March 13, 1987, p. E1-2.

7. See Hockin (1986) and the paper by Courchene, Chapter 24 in this volume, for an assessment.

8. I'm reminded of a group of Ontario business people who went to Montreal many years ago to plead the case of expanding passenger rail services before the executive of a major railway company. The Board of Directors took the intervention of these important business interests quite seriously, until the Chairman of the Board looked at his watch and asked the group: "How did you get here in time for this meeting?" The group replied, "We flew, of course," at which point the Chairman of the railway said, "Meeting adjourned, and thank you for coming. I hope you have a pleasant flight home." The moral of that story, of course, is that it's not enough to just state your case; you must demonstrate it as well.

9. See Sawatsky (1987) and Consumer and Corporate Affairs Canada (1985).

10. The government modernized a policy that was long overdue for change. Although there may still be some wrinkles to iron out, we think the legislation contains flexible instruments that recognize the economic realities confronting Canadian business in both the domestic and global marketplace. The new competition policy was developed with a broad consensus among public- and private-sector interests to safeguard competition in Canada. The *Competition Act* passed in June 1986 will

provide a balanced and more stable environment for the private sector to function as effectively as possible. See Goldman, Chapter 23 in this volume.

11. See Stanbury (1986) and the paper by Kerton, Chapter 19, in this volume, and the paper by Goldman, Chapter 21 in this volume.

12. See Cooper (1987).

REFERENCES

Consumer and Corporate Affairs Canada (1985) *Lobbying and the Registration of Lobbyists: A Discussion Paper* (Ottawa: Minister of Supply and Services Canada).

Cooper, Albert, Chairman (1987) "Lobbying and the Registration of Paid Lobbyists," *Minutes of Proceedings and Evidence of the Standing Committee on Elections, Privileges and Procedure*, Issue No. 2, January 20, pp. 2-20.

Economic Council of Canada (1986) *Competition and Solvency: A Framework for Financial Regulation* (Ottawa: Minister of Supply and Services).

Francis, Diane (1986) *Controlling Interest: Who Owns Canada?* (Toronto: Macmillan).

Hockin, Tom (1986) *New Directions for Financial Institutions* (Ottawa: Minister of Finance, December 18).

Royal Commission on Corporate Concentration (1978) *Report* (Ottawa: Minister of Supply and Services).

Sawatsky, John (1987) *The Insiders: Government, Business and the Lobbyists* (Toronto: McClelland & Stewart).

Stanbury, W.T. (1986) "The New Competition Act and Competition Tribunal Act: Not with a Bang but a Whimper," *Canadian Business Law Journal*, Vol. 12(1), pp. 2-42.

Chapter 21

Corporate Concentration and Canada's New Competition Act

Calvin S. Goldman
Director of Investigation and Research, Competition Act, and
Assistant Deputy Minister, Competition Policy
Consumer and Corporate Affairs Canada

1.0 INTRODUCTION

In this paper I discuss the new *Competition Act*, which was enacted by Parliament on June 19, 1986, particularly as it relates to the issue of corporate concentration. At the outset it is important to distinguish between the different dimensions of corporate concentration. In his paper, Shayam Khemani describes the various concepts and inter-relationships between aggregate concentration, industry or market concentration, ownership concentration and conglomeration of financial and non-financial companies.[1]

The type of corporate concentration that is most directly of concern to the *Competition Act* is industry or market concentration. This measure of concentration can influence the nature and extent of competition in a market since it relates to the number and size of competitors in a market.

The *Competition Act* is primarily concerned with competition in markets. In what follows I will describe the major provisions of the Act that impact on the structure and conduct of firms in a given market. However, over time, the enforcement of competition law may also have an indirect effect on aggregate concentration in the economy as a whole and to some extent, on the concentration of ownership. In my view, the vigorous application of competition policy can contribute significantly towards alleviating many of the concerns that often arise from different dimensions of corporate concentration, even though competition policy operates primarily in relation to market concentration. I believe that many of the concerns associated with high levels of corporate concentration can be traced back to the extent to which competition prevails in given markets.

In this paper I will first describe, briefly, the basic objectives of competition policy and relate these objectives to the constraints imposed by the structural characteristics of the Canadian economy. I will then discuss the administrative machinery established for the implementation of competition policy. Following this I will highlight the merger, specialization agreement, abuse of dominant market position, and other provisions of the *Competition Act*. In doing so I will also discuss my initial experience over the past nine months in administering this new legislation. Finally, I will present some concluding remarks on what I perceive to lie ahead for the state of competition in Canada.

2.0 OBJECTIVES OF THE CANADIAN COMPETITION ACT

The purpose clause of the *Competition Act* (S. 1.1) is new and it now states:

> The purpose of this Act is to maintain and encourage competition in Canada in order to promote the efficiency and adaptability of the Canadian economy, in order to expand opportunities for Canadian participation in world markets while at the same time recognizing the role of foreign competition in Canada, in order to ensure that small and medium-sized enterprises have an equitable opportunity to participate in the Canadian economy and in order to provide consumers with competitive prices and product choices.

These objectives will generally be considered in the adjudicative process when cases are brought before the newly established Competition Tribunal, which I describe below, or the courts. There are also a number of underlying principles that thread together the various provisions of the new *Competition Act* which can be summarized as follows. First and foremost, the *Competition Act* is a general law of general application. It is a legislation framework which seeks to maintain and strengthen the role of market forces, thereby encouraging maximum efficiency in the use of our economic resources. Second, the law recognizes the important role international trade plays in exerting competitive pressures in the domestic economy as well as providing export opportunities for Canadian firms. Third, large firm size is not necessarily viewed as being adverse to competition. In some instances, increases in size may be necessary to achieve economic efficiency in order to effectively meet domestic and foreign competition. It is not the size of a firm that is the primary concern under the *Act*, but rather the use and abuse by a firm of its market power. Fourth, where large firm size is necessary for the attainment of efficiency, the efficiency gains should be counter balanced with the impact on competition. This theme flows through the merger, specialization agreement and abuse of dominant position provisions of the new *Act*. Fifth, the *Act* seeks to establish a clear and equitable set of standards — standards which are also effective and enforceable — by which businesses are to conduct themselves in the market place. These standards are aimed at preventing abuses of market power, ensuring firms compete with one another on a fair basis, and providing consumers with product and quality choices at the lowest prices possible.

The approach adopted in the *Competition Act* places it squarely in line with the unique needs of the Canadian economy. There are several characteristics of the Canadian economy, which, when taken together, present a complex configuration in which competition policy must operate. These are the following:

(1)   The small size of domestic markets relative to efficient scale of production which imposes cost disadvantages on firms competing in international markets.

(2)   An open economy in which international trade plays an important role but, which is nonetheless, still characterized by protective measures.

(3)   High levels of market concentration and oligopolistic structure of many industries.

(4)   Geographically segmented markets

These structural characteristics of the Canadian economy dictate that competition policy should have regard to the efficient allocation of resources rather than simply promoting competition for competition's sake. Competition is not an end in itself. It should be viewed as a vehicle to promote economic efficiency and the other objectives referred to in Section 1.1 of the *Act*.

Efficiency considerations may often result in firms of large size and higher levels of concentration. This is not to imply that bigness is necessarily synonymous with efficiency. But in cases where efficiency requires firms to be of relative large size, it is not intended that competition law penalize or act as an impediment to the achievement of that size. The *Act* explicitly recognizes the need to facilitate the process whereby firms can become world class competitors. The new competition law seeks to balance competition-related concerns with efficiency considerations while at the same time facilitating the ability of firms to adapt to changing market circumstances.

The provisions of the *Competition Act* are designed to foster a flexible dynamic and innovative market environment. Such an environment dampens, if not eliminates, tendencies some large firms may otherwise have to exercise market power and engage in anticompetitive practices. High levels of corporate concentration become a major concern when markets are not contestable, that is, when incumbent firms are entrenched in their respective markets and are insulated from the competitive process by regulatory and structural factors. Thus the *Competition Act* is designed to ensure that markets perform their proper function in signalling the flow of economic resources from less to more valuable uses and by rewarding innovative and efficient firms.

3.0 ADMINISTRATION OF COMPETITION POLICY

The *Competition Act* is the principal piece of legislation in the administration of competition policy in Canada. However, like other Western industrial countries, Canada has additional economic policy instruments such as government regulation, tariffs, and tax policy, which influence the structure, conduct, and performance of various sectors of the economy.

Therefore, in the administration of competition policy, a dual set of responsibilities have been assigned to me. First, as the Director of Investigation and Research, my primary responsibility is to enforce the provisions of the *Competition Act*. Second, I am also Assistant Deputy Minister, Competition Policy within the federal Department of Consumer and Corporate Affairs. In this latter role I try to ensure that competition-related concerns are fully considered in the formulation of various aspects of government policy.

The *Act* contains specific provisions which give rise to inquiries by my office and perhaps subsequent proceedings, within the framework of the criminal law in certain instances of offences such as conspiracy and predatory pricing, and within the framework of administrative law in respect of reviewable matters including mergers and abuse of dominant position.

I do not propose to delve into details of the organizational and administrative principles underlying the enforcement of the *Competition Act*. I will, however, briefly mention that inquiries under the *Competition Act* can be initiated in a number of ways. The Director may initiate an inquiry on his own accord if he has reason to believe that an infraction of the *Act* has or is about to be committed. The Director shall also initiate an inquiry, if there exist the necessary grounds, on receipt of a complaint from six persons of not less than 18 years of age, resident in Canada, or on direction from the Minister. The Director, on discontinuing any inquiry, must make a report in writing to the Minister; and in cases of a six-resident complaint, to the applicants; informing them of the reasons for his decision. Provisions exist for the Minister to review any decision and instruct the Director to make further inquiry.

Concurrent with the passage of the *Competition Act*, Parliament also enacted the *Competition Tribunal Act*. This piece of legislation establishes the Competition Tribunal, a unique Canadian institution, which brings together both judicial and lay expertise, to adjudicate cases brought before it by the Director. The membership of the Tribunal include four judicial members and up to eight lay members who may have extensive expertise and background in economics, industry, commerce, or public affairs. The specialized nature of the Tribunal provides the greatest potential for developing expertise in such complex issues as efficiency considerations and the effects of anti-competitive practices.

In an attempt to ensure its impartiality, the Tribunal has been structured purely as an adjudicative body, without any investigative functions. The Tribunal has no role in supervising the investigative powers of the Director, initiating investigations, or providing research or policy advice to the Government. Its jurisdiction extends solely to the civil reviewable matters contained in Part VII of the *Competition Act*. The Tribunal is a court of record, and, with respect to such matters as the examination of witnesses and enforcement of its orders, it possesses the same powers as are vested in superior courts. Appeals arising from decisions of the Tribunal will be heard by the Federal Court of Appeal.

4.0 PROVISIONS OF THE ACT
In this section I focus on some of the specific provisions of the new *Competition Act* and highlight how these provisions address the anti-competitive consequences of market power while maintaining sufficient flexibility to facilitate economic adjustment. In the first section I describe the merger provisions which form an important part of the phenomenon of corporate concentration. Then I go on to discuss in some detail the specialization agreement provisions and the abuse of dominance provisions as these too are relevant to the corporate concentration issue.

4.1 Mergers
The most important and far-reaching reform brought about by the *Competition Act* is the new set of provisions dealing with mergers. The criminal law provisions under the previous legislation, the *Combines Investigation Act*, proved to be totally ineffective and inappropriate to deal with potentially anti-competitive mergers. In the 75 year history of this law, the Crown laid charges in only eight cases, resulting in seven acquittals and one guilty plea. While the great majority of mergers are, on balance, neutral or even beneficial to the economy, there is no doubt that some mergers are clearly anti-competitive. I am confident that the new merger provisions have given us the means to deal effectively with those mergers that are detrimental to competition.

Administrative Law: One of the most important changes in the merger law is that it has moved from a criminal law to a non-criminal, administrative law environment. This change has a number of significant ramifications. First, the standard of proof on the Director has been changed from a criminal burden of proof – the familiar "beyond a reasonable doubt" – to a less onerous non-criminal standard. A non-criminal standard is clearly better suited to the examination of complex economic matters such as mergers, where a wide variety of factors and their effects have to be considered. Second, the reviewing body, the Competition Tribunal, will be composed of judges, and probably, experienced economists and business people who should be more familiar with assessing extensive economic or commercial data. Third, the administrative law provides greater scope and flexibility for introducing evidence, making submissions and granting remedial orders to maintain or restore competition. In the criminal law setting the judge is restricted to the use of fines, incarceration, orders of prohibition, or possibly a dissolution order. Finally, the non-criminal law environment promotes a more positive atmosphere for resolving competition-related problems raised by the merger. Parties to the merger are much more receptive to the voluntary presentation and discussion of their merger proposals, and are often more receptive to altering aspects of the transaction to alleviate our concerns than they were in the past.

The Basic Test: The second major departure from the old merger law is that the basic test the Director must meet has been changed. The Competition Tribunal is now directed to consider the issue of the impact of the merger on competition, instead of the more ambiguous standard of public detriment. As with other non-criminal provisions dealing with tied selling, exclusive dealing, market restriction; in the new abuse of dominant position provision, the Director must demonstrate that the merger "prevents or lessens or is likely to prevent or lessen competition substantially." To assist the Tribunal in its consideration of the arguments and evidence in relation to the substantial lessening of competition, the *Act* sets out a non-exhaustive list of factors that the Tribunal may consider in its deliberations, and in its final decision.

The *Act* makes it clear that the Tribunal cannot find a substantial lessening based solely on the evidence of increased concentration as a result of the merger. This provision ensures that the assessment of mergers is more than a mechanical exercise of adding up market-shares and that the Tribunal will consider the impact of both the quantitative and qualitative aspects in analyzing the impact of the merger. It is an explicit recognition of the fact that it is the substantial lessening of competition, not the size of the merged firms *per se*, that is of primary importance. Size of the firms by itself may tell you nothing about how rival firms compete in a particular market. Although market concentration will remain an important factor in the merger assessment, the Director and the Tribunal will also have to address and consider many other factors such as barriers to entry, the extent of change and innovation, effective competition remaining, removal of a vigorous competitor, and the availability of acceptable substitutes in determining whether the merger prevents or lessens competition substantially in the relevant market. These and other factors are specifically enumerated in Section 64 and Section 65 of the *Act*.

The importance of foreign competition to the Canadian economy is highlighted by placing it at the beginning of the list of factors to be considered, in Section 65. The second factor listed refers to the situation where a firm is failing and about to exit the industry. These two factors reflect the desire of the designers of the *Act* to tailor it to the Canadian environment, where international trade and economic readjustment are prominent features of the economic landscape.

It should be noted that the Tribunal may have regard to other factors which are not listed in Section 65 in order to arrive at its assessment of the competitive impact of the merger. Other factors, such as the countervailing market power of buyers or the history of anti-competitive conduct of the merging parties, may be relevant to determining the competitive effects of the proposed merger. The factors actually taken into account by the Director and the Tribunal, and the weight given to each, will, of course, vary with the circumstances of the case and the relevance of the particular factor to the merger in question. In most cases, no one factor will be decisive and all the factors will have to be weighed together to arrive at a conclusion on the competitive impact of the merger.

Efficiency "Defence": The third major departure from the former merger law is the explicit statutory recognition of efficiencies as an exception to the application of the merger law. The small size of the Canadian market and the diversified nature of production necessitates that efficiency considerations be explicitly accounted for in Canadian merger law. By incorporating an efficiency exception, the *Act* clearly recognizes that the restructuring of an industry can, in certain circumstances, result in net benefits for the economy, even though such a merger may result in higher levels of concentration.

The new merger law provides that the Tribunal shall refuse to prohibit a merger even if the merger would lessen competition substantially; when the parties can satisfy the Tribunal that the merger will bring, or is likely to bring about, gains in efficiency that will be greater than, and will offset, the effects of any prevention or lessening of competition resulting from the merger; and that such efficiency gains would not likely be attained in other ways if the order prohibiting the merger were made. Efficiency gains that may be relevant include economies of scale and scope, plant specialization, and lower transportation costs. In most cases, these savings translate into lower unit-output costs, and would likely qualify as efficiency gains under the efficiency exception. Whether such gains would override a lessening of competition is a question for the Tribunal to decide according to the circumstances and particular facts of each case. It should be noted that costs savings that result from a mere redistribution of income as opposed a real savings in resources are not considered by the *Act* to be efficiency gains. Tax savings associated with a merger, for example, are transfers from the general taxpayers to the merged firm and do not, in my view, qualify as efficiency gains.

I understand that a somewhat similar recognition of efficiencies is currently being taken by the U.S. Department of Justice, and I am told it is one of the more difficult tasks they have experienced in their merger analysis, since sometimes competition-lessening "apples" have to be balanced against efficiency "oranges." Our initial experience over the last nine months reflects a similar challenge in undertaking this rather difficult balancing process, although we have not yet encountered a situation where efficiency gains have resulted in an "even weight" on the scales.

Joint Ventures: In addition to the efficiency exception, the *Act* provides, in Section 67, for a limited exemption for combinations that are joint ventures and which have been formed for the purpose of undertaking a specific project or a program of research and development. A special recognition of the value of joint ventures in the merger law is desirable because of the economic importance of joint ventures, particularly in the Canadian oil and gas industry, which has recently been prominent in research and development programs and in export consortia. The section however, has been carefully drafted to ensure that anti-competitive joint ventures remain subject to the merger law and that parties do not have an incentive to restructure transactions in order to escape the law.

Pre-notification Requirements: While it not my intention to dwell on the procedural aspects of the merger law or on the merger prenotification provisions, I will highlight some important points. In most cases, the better time to challenge a potentially anti-competitive merger is before the proposal is completed. Once the parties have merged their assets and operations, it becomes more difficult to return the parties to their pre-merger positions in the market. Without some form of pre-notification, the Director's ability to make a preliminary assessment of the competitive impact of the merger as well as his ability to take the necessary steps to stop an anti-competitive merger before it is consummated would be seriously constrained. In drafting the prenotification provisions, a balance was struck between the Director's need for advanced knowledge and the desire of the parties to complete their deal with a minimum of bureaucratic delay and intervention. First, the prenotification provisions apply (since July 15, 1987) only to large transactions where the parties' combined assets or revenues exceed $400 million and the value of the acquisition itself exceeds $35 million in assets or revenues. In the case of amalgamations the transaction threshold is $70 million. Secondly, the waiting periods are short, ranging from seven to 21 days. Finally, appropriate exemptions have been included that remove business transactions which would rarely, if ever, raise competition issues. While many mergers will not fall within the prenotification provisions, you should note that the substantive merger law applies to all types of mergers, regardless of their size, and that the Director can challenge a merger up to three years after it is substantially complete, unless an advance ruling certificate has been issued, in which case section 75 of the *Act* governs.

If the Tribunal finds that the merger lessens or is likely to lessen competition substantially, it has a wide range of orders to choose from. In the case of a completed merger, it can order dissolution or disposal of certain assets or shares by the parties to the merger or any other person. In the case of a proposed merger, the Tribunal may order the parties not to proceed with all or part of the merger, and/or may prohibit the doing of certain acts or things if all or part of the merger proceeds. In the case of either a proposed or a completed merger, the Tribunal may also order the parties to take other action the Tribunal deems appropriate if the parties and the Director consent to the order.

As noted above, one of the advantages of having the merger provisions removed from the criminal-law environment is that it encourages businessmen to come forward at an early stage with their proposals to see if it will raise competition problems and, if it will, to see if the deal can be restructured to remove these concerns. The difficulty and expense of "unscrambling the eggs" once the deal is done means that it is in the parties' best interest to come forward voluntarily before the transaction is completed. As a matter of policy, I welcome opportunities to resolve these problems in a cost-effective and expeditious manner. It is my intention to make greater use of negotiated settlements in appropriate cases, particularly in the context of the merger and other administrative law provisions. In cases where a settlement or compliance with the *Act* is otherwise reached, it is likely that one of three vehicles will be employed: an advance ruling certificate, a compliance opinion, or a consent order.

Advance Ruling Certificate: If parties are confident that the merger will raise no competition issues but want greater certainty, they can ask for an advance ruling certificate. Section 74 of the *Act* provides for the issuance of a certificate by the Director where he is satisfied that he would not have sufficient grounds to apply to the Tribunal. The certificate precludes the Director from challenging the merger if it is substantially completed within one year after the certificate is issued and if there is no substantial change in the information upon which the certificate was based. I might add that a number of parties have already applied to my office for an advance ruling certificate. An advance ruling certificate may be issued with or without certain terms or undertakings by the purchaser, depending on the circumstances of the case.

Program of Compliance: Another avenue under which a proposed merger can be reviewed is through the Director's Program of Compliance. In one recent case, for example, the potential purchaser sought our views several months before approaching the vendor in order to ensure that once negotiations for purchase have begun, it would proceed quickly without any unpleasant surprises from the Office of the Director. In these early stages of planning, the Director can give a letter of opinion under the Program of Compliance which states whether or not a proposed transaction, based on the information before him, would cause him to initiate an inquiry under the *Act*. This letter will indicate where the Director's concerns, if any, may lie. If concerns are raised, and the party then satisfies these concerns, compliance with the *Act* can usually be achieved without the need for other proceedings. In some cases, we will give a "no issue" compliance opinion rather than an advance ruling certificate. This will allow the Bureau to monitor a situation which raises no immediate concern, but could, due to the changing state of the market, for example, still raise an issue within the three year period in which the Director could challenge the merger or a portion of it.

Consent Order: A final mechanism for negotiated settlement is the consent order. Under Section 77, the Tribunal may consider granting an order, whose terms have been agreed upon by the parties and the Director, without the necessity of going through a full, contested hearing. Consent orders are likely to be used where it is necessary to ensure enforceability of the terms of the agreement over a comparatively long period of time, or where variation of the terms may prove necessary. It should be noted that the ultimate decision to grant a consent order rests with the Tribunal, while the authority for issuing an advance ruling certificate rests solely with the Director.

Initial Experience: The initial experience we have with the new provision, although brief, is encouraging. From June 1986 to October 1987, there were some 1,300 publicly reported mergers. Of these, 400 were examined at least briefly by the Bureau. Ninety of these required closer scrutiny and were handled as follows:

- in 34 cases the file was closed;

- 21 cases were handled under the Program of Compliance;

- 5 proposed transactions were abandoned;[2]

- 9 resulted in Advance Ruling Certificates under S.74;

- 2 applications were made to the Tribunal; and

- 20 cases were still under review at the end of the period.

In over one-half of the cases that gave rise to extensive examination, the parties have come forward voluntarily, sometimes well in advance of the public announcement of the transaction. As I indicated earlier, this is a practice I hope to foster and encourage. Of the 90 cases examined in detail, one-half exceeded the pre-notification thresholds described above.

The recent merger wave that Canada and most other Western economies are experiencing certainly has raised concerns about rising corporate concentration and market power. For the first time Canada now has an effective merger law that applies to all types of mergers, be they horizontal, vertical, or conglomerate. The merger provisions will be used to prevent those mergers that raise the greatest concern because of their detrimental impact on competition and the competitive process.

4.2 Specialization Agreements

As I noted above, one of the structural characteristics of many Canadian industries is that plants are of suboptimal size and have multiple product lines. When parties are considering merger candidates, they often look for partners that will provide opportunities to rationalize production and increase scale and other economies. I now focus on the specialization agreement provisions of the *Competition Act* which also allows firms to reorganize production and enjoy efficiency gains made possible from longer production runs.

Section 57 of the *Act* defines a specialization agreement as an agreement where each party agrees to discontinue producing an article or service on the condition that each other party agrees to discontinue producing an article or service. Parties may apply, on notice to the Director, to the Tribunal for an order to register the agreement. Registration provides an exemption from the conspiracy and exclusive dealing sections of the *Act*.

However, the Tribunal will register a specialization agreement, only if the parties have demonstrated that the agreement is likely to bring about gains in efficiency that will be greater than, and will offset, the effects of any prevention or lessening of competition that will result. Like the efficiency exception in the merger law, it must also be shown that the gains in efficiency could not be achieved by other means, such as the unilateral specialization of product lines by the firm.

The Tribunal may make the order conditional upon such things as wider licensing of patents, reduction in tariffs, removal of import quotas or partial divestiture of assets, if the Tribunal is satisfied that agreement will produce efficiency gains that offset the lessening of competition, but also that there will be no substantial competition remaining in the market if the agreement is registered. The Tribunal can set out in its order the period of time that the order of registration will be in force. The Director may make an application to the Tribunal to remove the registration if the conditions of registration contained in the section cease to be met.

4.3 Abuse of Dominance

In addition to the merger and specialization agreement provisions, another major reform brought in with the *Competition Act* was the replacement of the criminal offense of monopoly with an administrative provision relating to the abuse of a dominant position.[3] The criminal monopoly provisions, like the criminal merger law, proved to be ineffective. The transition to the administrative-law environment should improve the successful application of the provision, given the lower standard of proof and more specialized expertise of the Competition Tribunal.

As noted above, the new *Act* recognizes the fact that large size may be desirable in order to obtain the economies of scale necessary to compete against foreign producers both in Canada and abroad. High concentration or dominance of a particular market is not, in and of itself, a concern of the *Act*. What becomes objectionable, however, is when the dominant firm uses its market power in an abusive fashion to protect or extend its dominant position, thus damaging the competitive process which ensures that all producers in the market are seeking to meet consumer demands at the lowest possible cost. It is the *conduct* of the dominant firm that becomes the subject of examination under Section 51 of the *Act*.

Under Section 51, the first requirement of a dominant position is obtained when one or more firms substantially or completely control a class or species of business. The term "one or more persons" captures the notion of joint or shared dominance, a concept that has been considered in the Canadian *Large Lamps*[4] case. While it will be up to the Competition Tribunal to give us further guidance on the application of the shared dominance concept, it should be noted that Section 51 is not intended to be a civil conspiracy law.

The usual starting point for determining whether a firm substantially or completely controls a class or species of business will be its share of the relevant market. If high concentration is found to exist, then further examination is required to determine why concentration is high and if it will remain so in the future. Key points to consider in this analysis include the ease of entry, foreign or potential competition, availability of substitutes, and changes in technology. Like mergers, the application of the abuse of dominance provisions will require more than a mechanistic approach based solely on the levels of concentration in the relevant market. The second requirement to be proven under Section 51 is that the dominant firm or firms have engaged in a practice of anti-competitive acts. Section 50 provides a non-exhaustive list of anti-competitive acts. The specified acts include the acquisition of a customer or supplier for the purpose of impeding entry, vertical squeezing of an unintegrated customer, the use fighting brands to discipline a competitor, and the pre-emption of scarce facilities or resources required by a competitor. The list is non-exhaustive so that acts of like character can be held to be anti-competitive by the Tribunal. All of the acts listed require consideration of the *exclusionary purpose, object, or design* of the dominant firm to ensure that the censured conduct is not the product of reasonable competitive behaviour. It should also be noted that the firm must make a *practice* of the anti-competitive act and that an isolated act or temporary expedient is unlikely to constitute a practice.

The third requirement to be proven under Section 51 is that the practice has had, is having, or is likely to have, the effect of preventing or substantially lessening competition in a market. To answer this question, the Director and Tribunal must consider both the dynamic and static effects of the practice in terms of its impact on, among other things, ease of entry, potential competition, product innovation, and pricing. An increase in market concentration in and of itself will not be sufficient to establish a substantial lessening of competition.

In determining whether the practice has had the effect of lessening competition substantially, the *Act* directs the Tribunal in Subsection 51(4) to consider whether the practice is a result of *superior competitive performance*. If competitors leave the market or lose market share because a competitor is simply more efficient than its rivals or is more effective in meeting consumer needs, the lessening of competition is not the result of an abuse of market power, but rather it is a natural consequence of the competitive process. Subsection 51(4), therefore, is included in the *Act* to ensure that efficiency, innovation and similar considerations are given proper weight by the Tribunal in its assessment of the trade practices of a dominant firm or firms.

The Tribunal has a number of remedial orders to chose from in redressing a situation where an abuse of dominance has been found. The most commonly invoked order will probably be an order prohibiting the firm from continuing to engage in the practice of anti-competitive acts. If an order of prohibition is not sufficient to restore competition, the Tribunal may make an order directing such actions, including the divesture of assets or shares, as are reasonable and necessary to overcome the effects of the practice in the market.

In considering the problems raised by rising corporate concentration, it should be kept in mind that most concerns arise when a firm has market power in a particular market and has the ability to abuse that power. It is not market power *per se* that harms the economy, but rather it is the abuse of that market power by those who enjoy it that impairs the free-market system. The abuse of dominance provision has been designed to focus on, and remedy, this type of problem.

4.4   Other Provisions of the Act

Space limitations do not permit me to discuss many other provisions of the new *Competition Act*, but I would like to refer in passing to some of the other important changes in the law. There have been a number of amendments to clarify and strengthen the criminal conspiracy provisions.[5] A new subsection states that the existence of an agreement to lessen competition may be proven from circumstantial evidence with or without direct evidence of communication between the parties. Another subsection makes it clear that the Crown must only prove that the parties intended to enter into the agreement, not that the parties intended to lessen competition unduly when they entered into the agreement. The maximum fine has been increased from $1 million to $10 million. Finally, the export exemption to the conspiracy section as also been clarified and expanded so that it will be easier for firms to use export agreements to compete in global markets.

The new *Act* also expands the application of the law for the first time to Crown corporations and banks. In the *Eldorado Nuclear* case, the Supreme Court of Canada held that agent Crown corporations are not subject to competition law when effecting Crown purposes.[6] The *Act* removes this exemption so that all agent Crown corporations when engaged in commercial activity in competition with private sector firms must play by the same set of rules. In addition, the responsibility for investigating bank mergers and agreements has been transferred to the Director from the Inspector General of Banks. The Minister of Finance, however, has the power to exempt bank mergers or agreements from the application of the *Act* when he certifies they are desirable in the interest of the financial system or financial policy.

In addition to the enforcement provisions, another of the Director's roles that is taking on increasing importance relates to the regulated sector of the economy. The *Act* (S. 97) explicitly authorizes the Director to intervene before federal regulatory boards or commissions to ensure competition policy issues are considered in the formulation of regulatory decisions or policy. The Director, in this capacity, has made numerous representations in both federal and provincial forums on such diverse matters as regulation and deregulation of financial, energy, transportation and broadcasting markets, as well as providing input on the privatization of Crown corporations.

These other provisions, as well as the new law on mergers, specialization agreements, and abuse of dominance which have been described, have been carefully designed to achieve the goals of competition policy, while, at the same time, recognizing and accommodating the need for economic adjustment and change in the Canadian economy. The new provisions are flexible instruments that acknowledge the need for large scale, efficient Canadian producers who can compete effectively in domestic and international markets. The *Act*, however, also responds to the concerns raised by the increase in corporate concentration, by adding provisions, or amending existing provisions, in order to prevent the use or abuse of market power in specific markets for anti-competitive purposes.

5.0 CONCLUSIONS

In Canada, major structural developments are taking place or are about to take place, which bode well for the state of competition and which also serve to lessen the concerns regarding corporate concentration. Major changes in regulatory policy in the transportation, energy and telecommunication sectors have already taken place and the pace of change is likely to continue.

Major pro-competition reforms in the financial sector are currently being discussed. Changes in the *Investment Canada Act* have lowered the restrictions on foreign investment and entry of foreign firms.[7] The average level of Canadian tariffs has been declining, partly as a result of the GATT-Tokyo Round agreements, and as a consequence, there is a healthy injection of import competition in many concentrated industries. The prospect for freer trade with the United States further increases optimism for increased competition in concentrated domestic markets. In addition, new technology has been eroding the cost disadvantages many Canadian companies have traditionally experienced. Public sector holdings are also becoming more exposed to market forces. In the past year, more than $800 million of Crown Corporation assets have been privatized — and winning bidder firms include comparatively small firms such as Memotec's acquisition of Teleglobe.

I refer to these events as evidence of the dynamic change that is occurring in many important sectors of the Canadian economy. Such change has to be kept in sight when discussing the issue of corporate concentration.

NOTES

1. See Chapter 1 in this volume.

2. See, for example, Oliver Bertin, "Palm Dairy sale halted by bureau," *Globe and Mail*, January 16, 1987, p. B3; David Oxtoby, "Dairy truce declared," *Financial Times*, January 12, 1987, pp. 3,14.

3. In general, see the papers by McDonald (1987) and Anderson and Khosla (1987).

4. In *R. v. Canadian General Electric Co. Ltd.* (1976) 29 C.P.R. (2d)1, 15 O.R.(2d)360, Canadian General Electric, Westinghouse Canada and G.T.E. Sylvania Canada Ltd. were charged with operating a shared monopoly to the detriment of the public, and with conspiracy. The accused were convicted of conspiracy and acquitted of the monopoly charge. While the judge in this case acknowledged that the words of the old monopoly section of "one or more persons" could embrace a situation of shared monopoly, he did not elaborate further on what would be required to show a shared monopoly, such as an agreement among the firms, or a long history of conscious parallelism.

5. In general, see Stanbury (1986, pp. 19-27).

6. *R. v. Eldorado Nuclear Ltd., et al.* (1983) 2 S.C.R. 551; 77 C.P.R. (2d) 1.

7. See, for example, Grover (1985).

REFERENCES

Anderson, R.D. & S.D. Khosla (1987) "Reflections on McDonald on Abuse of Dominant Position," *Canadian Competition Policy Record*, Vol. 8(3), pp. 51-60.

Grover, Warren (1985) "The Investment Canada Act," *Canadian Business Law Journal*, Vol. 10(4), pp. 475-582.

McDonald, Bruce C. (1987) "Abuse of Dominant Position," *Canadian Competition Policy Record*, Vol. 8(1), pp. 59-75.

Stanbury, W.T. (1986) "The New Competition Act and Competition Tribunal Act: 'Not with a Bang, but a Whimper'," *Canadian Business Law Journal*, Vol. 12(1), pp. 2-42.

Chapter 22

New Directions for the
Financial Sector*

*Hon. Tom Hockin
Minister of State (Finance)
Government of Canada*

1.0 INTRODUCTION

Canada is fortunate to possess one of the finest financial systems in the world. It is composed of sound world-class institutions. It employs hundreds of thousands of Canadians and serves millions. It is one of Canada's leading export industries. However, the financial industry is in the midst of rapid change. Communications technology has created 24-hour global markets. The importance of international capital flows has dramatically increased. The traditional roles of financial institutions are changing. These global forces have challenged existing legislation designed for an earlier and less dynamic era. That is why, early in its mandate, the government announced its intention to work with the provinces, the public and the financial community to reform financial regulations to seize the opportunities offered by change.

There is widespread appreciation of the key role of the financial sector in economic renewal not just in facilitating investment in Canada, but as an exporter and employer. There is agreement that our financial system is fundamentally sound, and that the basic division of supervisory responsibility for our institutions should remain in place. There is universal acknowledgement of the trend toward integrated financial services, both here and abroad, and broad agreement on the benefits this brings to consumers. There is continuing concern regarding self-dealing and abuses of conflict of interest in both closely and widely held institutions.

---

* Adapted by the editors from the remarks of Mr. Hockin on tabling the policy paper *New Directions for the Financial Sector* in the House of Commons, December 18, 1986.

While there have been diverse views expressed on the best *means* to regulate our financial system, all of us seek the same goal. We all want a sound financial system that provides Canadians with innovative and competitive services, that broadens the range of choice for Canadian savers and investors, and that fosters safe and well supervised financial institutions that can compete effectively around the world.

2.0   A NEW POLICY FRAMEWORK

The essence of our approach is to act in four inter-related areas.

* First, we will allow the integration of financial services through the common ownership of institutions and the extension of powers.

* Second, we will introduce a pragmatic ownership policy that checks the growth of commercial-financial links in the economy while maintaining balanced competition within the financial services sector.

* Third, we will provide a strong framework for prudential regulation.

* And fourth, we will modernize and strengthen our supervisory system.

I will discuss each area in turn.

2.1   Integration of Financial Services

The government believes our laws should reflect today's market reality. Today banks and non-bank financial institutions are not only capable of providing, but are actually providing an ever-more common range of services – services that meet the needs of Canadian savers, borrowers and investors.

To foster such common benefits, the government will end unnecessary institutional barriers within the financial services industry and allow the integration of financial services. Restrictions on common ownership of regulated financial institutions will be removed, allowing common ownership through affiliates or subsidiaries. Separate institutions will be maintained for supervisory purposes. Full networking of services will be allowed between institutions, save for the retailing of insurance.

As well, in-house powers will be broadened for institutions in the various "pillars" of the financial industry. All trust, loan and life insurance companies will be granted full consumer lending powers; the larger ones will be eligible for full commercial lending powers. All federally regulated institutions will be able to offer investment advice and portfolio management services. Banks and insurance companies will be granted ancillary fiduciary powers. From the point of view of Canadian consumers, these policies will allow neighbourhood branches to offer a wide array of innovative and convenient services, with greater potential for one-stop shopping.

The philosophy underpinning financial services integration will be to build – not buy. To protect against harmful concentration, acquisition of financial services companies will require the approval of the Minister of

Finance. As a general rule, large financial institutions will not be allowed to acquire other large institutions.

An exception to this general policy will be made for the securities industry. Given the desire for a viable Canadian presence in this strategic industry, the federal government will permit domestically owned, federally regulated financial institutions to build or buy securities dealer subsidiaries. Necessary legislative amendments to permit such participation in the securities industry will be introduced in the near future.

2.2 Ownership Policy

Current Canadian law requires all large domestic banks to be widely held, and new domestic banks to attain widely held status within 10 years. Trust, loan and stock insurance companies, on the other hand, do not have similar ownership rules. Many of these institutions also have significant commercial links. While this variety of ownership forms is not unique to Canada, the development of significant links between these non-bank financial institutions and companies with commercial interests has been a source of intense debate. Some have emphasized the issue of concentration of power and the potential for self-dealing and conflict of interest. However, there is also widespread recognition that entrepreneurial owners have been a source of dynamism in the industry. They have provided firms with the leadership and financial strength to compete with our large banks.

Both these arguments are valid. As with many issues in this complex age, a balance must be struck. To lessen the potential dangers of commercial-financial links while promoting competition, the government intends to implement the following policy:

(i)   Smaller banks will be permitted to be closely held by domestic investors with no commercial interests. They will be allowed to remain closely held until they attain a capital base of $750 million – a base that will support about $15 billion in assets.

(ii) Banks that exceed this capital threshold of $750 million will subject to the following ownership rules:

- Shareholders with less than 10 per cent of the shares in any class, or any series of any class, will be permitted to acquire additional shares to a ceiling of 10 per cent.

- Shareholders with more than 10 per cent of such shares will not be permitted to acquire additional shares in the same class or series.

- Within five years of reaching the capital threshold, at least 35 per cent of the voting shares must be publicly traded and widely held. The penalty for non-compliance will be a constraint on the bank's ability to grow.

These measures will ensure that major existing banks remain widely held, and that closely held banks of substantial size move towards wide ownership as new equity is issued.

(iii) Ownership policies regarding trust, loan and insurance companies will be complementary, but not identical, reflecting the different histories and circumstances of these institutions. Like many Canadians, the government is concerned with the potential dangers of growing commercial-financial links. Yet we are equally concerned that an over-zealous reaction could limit future competition in the financial sector. We are therefore proposing a policy which arrests the growth of commercial-financial links while maintaining strong sources of innovation and competition in the marketplace.

To achieve these twin objectives, the following regime will be implemented, effective today:

• Approval for the incorporation of new trust, loan and insurance companies will be restricted to applicants with no significant commercial interests.

• Commercial interests will not be permitted to acquire or increase significant ownership positions in non-bank institutions with capital in excess of $50 million.

• Such larger non-bank institutions with commercial links will be required to have at least 35 per cent of their voting shares publicly traded and widely held by December 31, 1991, or within five years of reaching the $50 million capital threshold.

• Trust, loan and insurance companies with no commercial links and with capital in excess of $750 million will also be required to have at least 35 per cent of their voting shares publicly traded and widely held by December 31, 1991 or within five years of reaching the $750 million capital threshold. Once this threshold is exceeded, no shareholder will be able to acquire an ownership position in the institution in excess of 10 per cent and significant shareholders will not be permitted to increase their ownership positions.

These policies will foster wider ownership of large financial institutions in the future while recognizing the existing positions of current investors. By causing current laws protecting minority shareholders to come into play, they will ensure market disclosure, public scrutiny and the presence of strong outside directors.

2.3 Prudent Regulation

Protecting the solvency and integrity of institutions requires more than changes in ownership rules. No single ownership policy can protect against imprudent management or questionable business practices. What is needed is an effective and vigilant system of self-governance, supported by independent and objective directors and an effective supervisory system. That is why we will:

• limit commercial-financial links;

• provide sufficiently broad minority shareholding to ensure market disclosure and public scrutiny;

- introduce cumulative voting rules for the election of directors; and

- create a stronger framework for prudential regulation.

In this strong framework, the government will strictly control self-dealing in all financial institutions. The list of non-arm's-length parties will be expanded and made uniform for banks and non-banks. Most asset transactions between such persons will be banned and service transactions will be strictly controlled. Rules will also be introduced to monitor and control transactions between related financial institutions.

Safeguards against abuses of conflict of interest will be introduced. Procedures and controls to prevent the flow of insider information between fiduciary and other financial activities will be implemented. Disclosure rules will be strengthened.

In accord with the overall approach recommended by Mr. Justice Estey (1986), the basic division of responsibilities for ensuring and monitoring the health of institutions among the supervisory authority, the directors of the institutions and the external auditors will remain in place. A number of proposals, however, will improve directors' supervision of their institutions' operations and strengthen the role of auditors.

All financial institutions will be required to have a minimum of one-third of their directors independent of the institution. These independent directors will be asked to perform additional duties on corporate review committees made up solely of such independent directors.

During the Estey enquiry, considerable time and effort was taken to study current accounting principles. As Mr. Justice Estey (1986) stated, in some cases difficulties were easy to define but solutions were not easy to develop. In line with his recommendations, a number of steps will be taken, in consultation with the accounting profession, to review accounting standards as they apply to financial institutions. As well, measures will be introduced to ensure appropriate communication among auditors, financial institutions they audit, and federal regulators.

These measures to improve the framework for effective regulation will ensure that Canadians can maintain confidence in the integrity of their financial system while enjoying the benefits of dynamic competition.

2.4 Strengthening the Supervisory System

Consistent with the integration of financial services, the Office of the Inspector General of Banks and the Department of Insurance will be consolidated into a new body the Office of the Superintendent of Financial Institutions. The new Office will have full supervisory responsibilities for banks and non-bank financial institutions. The Minister of Finance will have overall responsibility for the new Office. The Superintendent will be clearly responsible for the administration of statutes, the execution of supervisory actions and the assessment of solvency. Measures will also be introduced to clarify and expand the Superintendent's power to deal effectively with unsound business practices and with financially troubled institutions.

The government recognizes that the Superintendent requires a full awareness of market trends and developments. The government will therefore act on Mr. Justice Estey's recommendation to form an advisory committee of technical experts with a broad mandate, including a role in the improvement of early warning systems.

The government believes that the Canada Deposit Insurance Corporation should remain a separate body. This will allow the retention of private sector expertise on the CDIC Board of Directors; and it will preserve CDIC's established relationship with provincial authorities supervising CDIC-insured provincial institutions.

In maintaining the CDIC as a separate agency, the government will equip it with additional powers. Premium levels will also be revised to eliminate the existing deficit in a timely way.

3.0 CONCLUSIONS

The four interrelated sets of changes in regulation and policy will provide a framework for a sound and competitive financial system today and for the future. As the financial services industry enters this new regime, all Canadians will benefit. The ability to provide innovative and competitive financial products mortgages, investments, loans to Canadians in all parts of our country will no longer be artificially limited by outmoded laws. But where necessary, regulation and supervision are being tightened to protect the savings of Canadians.

These proposals will lay a solid foundation for the future. They will help our institutions grow and prosper. And they will ensure that Canadians can continue to have confidence in one of the finest financial systems in the world.

NOTES

1. See John Kohut, "Draft bill broadens powers of trust firms," *Globe and Mail*, December 22, 1987, pp. B1-B2.

2. See Bills C-8 and C-9 given First reading on October 6, 1986.

3. See the report by Wyman (1985).

REFERENCES

Estey, Hon. Willard Z. (1986) *Report of the Inquiry into the Collapse of the CCB and Northland Bank* (Ottawa: Minister of Supply and Services, August).

Hockin, Hon. Tom (1986) *New Directions for the Financial Sector* (Ottawa, Department of Finance, December 18).

Wyman, W.R. Chairman (1985) *Final Report of the Working Committee on the Canada Deposit Insurance Corporation* (Ottawa: Minister of Supply and Services Canada).

Chapter 23

Corporate Power and
Political Influence

Don Blenkarn, MP
Chairman of the House of Commons Standing Committee
on Finance and Economic Affairs

1.0   BASIC PHILOSOPHICAL CONSIDERATIONS

In this age of pragmatism in politics, where decisions are made on what is
popular for today without worrying about tomorrow, it is important that
from time to time we look at the philosophy behind the rules, laws or
regulations involving corporate concentration.   First of all, it is probably
trite to say that a person is only truly free if he has freedom of property, the
right to own, to enjoy ownership, and to use ownership of money, land,
buildings, and machinery; the way he as an individual wants to for his own
private purposes.   Most of us learned something about freedom when we
were able to earn money for the first time and did not need to depend on our
parents for financial help.

It is my view that when a society has free ownership of property and
when that ownership is widely held, then the individuals who make up that
society are usually most prosperous.   That ownership, of course, has to be
separate, distinct, individual ownership.   That separate, distinct, individual
ownership means that there is a marketplace with competing interests to
make sure that the efforts and energies and the savings are allocated in the
most effective and efficient way possible.

Collective ownership is not private ownership.   We all remember the
slogan: "Petro Canada — it's ours."   Many of us said, "Oh yeah? It's their's."
It's the governments.   It's Trudeau's.   It's Mulroney's.   But it sure isn't ours.
There is no difference between collective ownership by the state and the old
form of feudal ownership that existed in times past when the land, tools,
buildings, and livestock were owned by the lord, and the tenant farmer

merely worked under the pleasure and direction of his master. The socialists merely substitute the all powerful state for the lord of the manor. We live in a nation where people came from every part of the world and they came so that they could own their own place, their own tools, their own homes, their own farms and be free from the dictates of their masters. It is from the idea that freedom of property must be individual, that we get into the philosophy of combinations or the control of the industrial and commercial assets in society by relatively few people.

I define ownership as ownership that gives control. Ownership in the sense that you have some equity in an enterprise, as in a preferred share, is really not ownership in the sense that I mean, because it does not permit such shareholders to exercise control.

2.0 OWNERSHIP AND CONTROL OF FINANCIAL ENTERPRISES

It is this philosophy, one that demands widespread ownership, that resulted in Tom Hockin's statement of December 18, 1986 which dealt with financial companies declaring that preference shares are not appropriate in financial companies. The lack of a vote by preference shareholders is the issue in the Canadian Tire case.[1] I am pleased that the Toronto Stock Exchange is contemplating rules against non-voting participating preference issues.

A variation on this position is behind the House of Commons Finance Committee's position concerning ownership of financial companies by non-financial companies or commercially linked companies.[2] The reason for the Committee's view is that the ownership of a financial company carries with it something far different from just the ownership of an individual company. It carries with it the prospect of having your capital levered or geared up 20 times. It is that gearing or leverage that makes a financial company very different from a non-financial company. It creates the need to regulate situations in which, because of a gearing arrangement, an individual has the power of 20 times his own capital by the use of his neighbour's savings held on deposit. That power may be unfair in a competitive market. Therefore, we are concerned about self-dealing in assets that would give the holder of the power all sorts of advantages over competitors in the same business. That power stems from a high degree of leverage.

3.0 CONCENTRATION IN CANADA AND TAKEOVERS

Ownership and control concerns are much more visible in a country like Canada because we are, after all, a relatively small country in terms of population. If there are 10 major companies in the United States in the same business, then if a company the size of any one of the major competitors in the United States is going to operate in Canada, and in Canada alone, it must perforce be a monopoly.[3] The relative size of our market means that our companies must either be relatively small in comparison to companies operating in the United States and other world markets; or there must be very, very few of our companies, compared to companies operating in other larger markets.

It is because of this problem that in Bill C-91, the *Competition Act,* it was made possible for a Competition Tribunal to prevent the acquisition of businesses in a fashion as to substantially lessen competition, but at the same time permit mergers which are based on real efficiency gains.[4] That bill, of course, had nothing to do with what seems to be the current form of acquisition fever that has gripped both Canada and the United States.[5]

This acquisition fever rides on the apparent view that it is easier for a businessman to make money by somehow buying up another businessman's assets and remortgaging them, than actually creating new product, new industry, new goods and wares himself. Senator John Heinz, the Republican Senator from Pennsylvania said recently in the United States Senate that our executives would do better if they tended to the real businesses that they are supposed to be in: "You cannot compete with the Japanese if you're fighting a guerilla war on Wall Street." Not only on Wall Street, but here in Canada we have also had guerilla wars. What interest of Canada was furthered by the massive takeover deal a year ago whereby the Reichman interests obtained control of the Hiram Walker and then sold 51 per cent of the liquor assets to Allied-Lyons PLC of the UK?[6] Did this speculative takeover create anything new?

Takeovers do not really create or lead to new plants or new jobs. In my district we are witnessing the closure of the major Goodyear Tire and Rubber investment in Ontario. Why? Because of a takeover bid. Why? Because the Goodyear executives decided to resist that takeover bid.[7] In doing so they used corporate assets to buy back the company's stock to restrict the amount of stock available but in that effort they pledged the company's assets so extremely that they are now forced to sell off company assets in order to pay the bank. The result is not only no new jobs,[8] but in fact no jobs; fewer shares in the market; less widespread ownership.

4.0 ELIMINATING THE DEDUCTIBILITY OF INTEREST ON DEBT TO FINANCE TAKEOVERS

One of the things the Conservative Government of Brian Mulroney is likely to do in tax reform, is to make the tax laws of the country such that the takeover game is less of a profitable adventure. It is essential that something be done to control the borrowing of money for the purpose of just buying up the assets or shares of a company on the marketplace.[9]

First of all, such borrowing results in the available capital of the country being used to concentrate ownership and control in a few hands. Secondly, no new assets, businesses, structures, plants, or science and technology developments, are created by this borrowing. All that happens is the price of shares, equipment or processes, are bid up. Since the costs of borrowing are deductible for no productive purpose, then surely, in tax reform we must look at a method of controlling such borrowing and surely we must then look at the kind of things they have looked at in the United States to determine whether interest should always be deductible.

Logic would direct that the reason for interest to be deductible from active business activity is that the money is borrowed for active business purposes to create new wealth. If money is borrowed for passive activity like investment then interest ought only to be deductible from passive income coming from investment. Is there any reason why a government should allow a company to use its active business income to borrow money to buy up the shares of another company, deduct the cost of borrowing from its active income, and therefore reduce its taxes so that it can create a larger conglomerate, and reduce the amount of ownership available in the marketplace for the ordinary person?

There are obviously all sorts of situations that one can name where the purchase of a business by new owners is good for the growth of the economy. However, it seems that if that growth is to be financed on a tax deductible basis it ought to be financed out of passive income rather than out of active income. Therefore, if someone has interest receivable, surely they should be able to have interest payable. If they have dividends receivable, then they can have dividends payable. Surely current revenues should not be damaged by an acquisition system that not only reduces government revenues and as a result indirectly raises taxes, but in effect operates to reduce the possibility of widespread ownership of the commercial assets that concentrate control — at the expense of the rest of the taxpayers.

Many takeover efforts have been financed by virtue of the fact that in Canada dividends from one corporation to another corporation are not taxable. There would be nothing wrong with this if taxes had been paid by the original corporation to create tax paid profits from which dividends were paid. However, we have created a tax system that does not necessarily require that taxes be paid in order to pay dividends. A company does not need to show a profit in order to declare a dividend. Furthermore, an accounting or tax genius can often have profitable companies not pay a nickel in corporate income tax. By revaluation of assets, money can be borrowed and made available for the payment of dividends that pass from one corporation to another without corporate taxes. The tax system appears to have the effect of limiting the wide ownership of companies without any benefit whatsoever to the national economy in terms of the payment of taxes.

Our tax laws have been a very major inducement to takeovers. I think one of the major beneficial tax reforms, in addition to those changes which promote fairness in tax rates, could well be a change in tax law that makes the takeover game less attractive.

5.0 CONCLUSIONS

It is my view it is in the interest of our society that we have as much ownership as possible, as widely held as possible, and that people's freedom to own property be encouraged. We need to encourage a great many owners of capital so that there can be an active capital market. You can't have a market for something if there is nothing on the market. What real interest will the average man have in the preservation of a capitalist society if the benefits of the capitalist society accrue only to a very small clique if very few groups own most of the assets of society. It is difficult to get people to defend a capitalist system when they have no realistic opportunity to become owners.

Many of us resent the state telling us that we can't complete a transaction because that transaction may lessen competition. We all should realize that it is in our own long term interest that there be limits on acquisitions, limits on ownership,[10] limits on the use of the tax system, and limits on the use of leverage by financial companies — for the very necessary purpose of making sure that the ownership of society is as diverse as possible.

It would seem to me that the thrust of public policy from our government over the few years, a thrust that is really non-partisan, will likely be to enforce the new competition legislation, to promote wider ownership of financial institutions, and make changes in tax laws to encourage wider ownership generally.

NOTES

1. Generally, see, "The Epic Struggle," *Maclean's*, January 26, 1987, pp. 26-33; "Court backs OSC in blocking Canadian Tire bid," *Globe and Mail*, March 13, 1987, pp. B1-B2.

2. See House of Commons, Standing Committee on Finance, Trade and Economic Affairs (1985, 1986).

3. More generally, see the papers by Khemani, Chapter 1 in this volume, and Marfels, Chapter 3.

4. See the paper by Goldman, Chapter 21 in this volume.

5. See, for example, "Let's Make a Deal," *Time*, December 23, 1985, pp. 44-55; "Deal Mania," *Business Week*, November 24, 1986, pp. 74-93. See also "The Gathering Takeover Frenzy," *Maclean's*, August 26, 1985, pp. 26-28; "The New Takeover Frenzy," *Maclean's*, April 7, 1986, pp. 26-28; "Takeover!" *Globe and Mail*, January 3, 1987, pp. D1, D8. Also see the data in Appendix 1 and the paper by Mason, Chapter 6 in this volume.

6. See the discussion in Peter Foster, "Let's Make a Deal," *Saturday Night*, September 1986, pp. 15-22 and in Foster (1986). The Reichmanns subsequently sold their 49 per cent interest in Hiram Walker for a minority position in Allied-Lyons.

7. See "In Akron, Jimmy Goldsmith's Name is Mud," *Business Week*, November 24, 1986, p. 40; "Trying to Beat Sir Jimmy to the Punch," *Business Week*, November 17, 1986, pp. 64-65; "The Two Worlds of Jimmy Goldsmith," *Business Week*, December 1, 1986, pp. 98-102.

8. I worked in the Goodyear plant once as a summer student; I know the anguish of the men who will lose their jobs. And under present law where interest is deductible the state helps pay for the job loss.

9. See "New clamor to curb takeover 'tax subsidy,'" *Financial Post*, May 31, 1986, pp.1-2. For the origins of the current provisions, see Bale (1981). See also the discussion in Wolfson, Chapter 12 in this volume.

10. This point is also emphasised by Jacques Parizeau, Chapter 16 in this volume.

REFERENCES

Bale, Gordon (1981) "The Interest Deduction to Acquire Shares of Other Corporations: An Unfortunate Corporate Welfare Tax Subsidy," *Canadian Taxation*, Vol. 3, pp. 189-202.

Foster, Peter (1986) *The Master Builders* (Toronto: Key Porter Books).

Hockin, Tom (1986) *New Directions for Financial Institutions* (Ottawa: Minister of Finance, December 18).

House of Commons Standing Committee on Finance, Trade and Economic Affairs (1985) *Canadian Financial Institutions* (Ottawa: Minister of Supply and Services Canada, November).

_____ (1986) "Fifth Report" *Minutes of Proceedings and Evidence of the Standing Committee on Finance and Economic Affairs*, No. 28, June 18, pp. 3-5.

Chapter 24

Re-regulating the Canadian Financial Sector: The Ownership Controversy

Thomas J. Courchene*
Robarts Chair in Canadian Studies
York University

1.0 INTRODUCTION

On December 18, 1986, the Honorable Tom Hockin, Minister of State for Finance, released *New Directions For the Financial Sector* (henceforth referred to as *New Directions* or the Hockin paper) the long-awaited federal blueprint for regulating financial services. The public's reaction thus far to the underlying thrust of the position paper have been very favourable, and appropriately so. *New Directions* responds to the international trend toward the integration across both institutions and markets by proposing an open, flexible and creative regulatory environment that would appear on the surface to enable Canadians and their institutions to participate fully in the global financial revolution. However, as is increasingly evident in the public discussion flowing from the position paper, there is one area that is beginning to cast a pall over the initial exuberance, namely the very restrictive provisions relating to ownership of financial institutions and in particular to the prohibition of any link between commercial and financial interests. It is, of course, true that those who are expressing concern are those who are most affected by the policy (e.g., the commercially-linked narrowly-held institutions). However, it is also true that the concerns they

* My interest in this issue was stimulated by my association with the Senate Committee on Banking, Trade and Commerce. In this context, it is a pleasure to acknowledge the insight and contributions of Gerald Lacoste and Basil Zafirion. Basil also provided comments on an earlier draft of this paper as did Jean-Pierre Bernier of Imperial Life. However responsibility for the views expressed below rests with me. The research for this paper was supported by the Centre for the Analysis of National Economic Policy, Department of Economics, University of Western Ontario.

raise touch upon the very core of, and rationale for, the federal policy, e.g., that *New Directions* may well stifle the very competition it was designed to promote and that in the final analysis the financial sector may become more, not less, concentrated. At the very least, such claims ought to, and will be, subjected to detailed evaluation and analysis.

It is important to recognize that this emerging controversy relates not to the underlying policy principles with respect to ownership but rather to the manner in which *New Directions* chooses to implement these principles. Indeed, the underlying principles in *New Directions* with respect to ownership could hardly be more clearly enunciated:

> The government does not believe that it is appropriate to adopt a broad general ownership policy for uniform application to all financial institutions, particularly in view of the differing ownership circumstances that have developed over time and now exist in the Canadian financial services industry. In a dynamic and competitive financial system, there is room for both widely-held and majority-controlled financial institutions. Each form brings its own strengths, both now exist and have served Canadians well: neither is inherently better than the other (Hockin 1986, p. 15).

By way of policy intent, *New Directions* (p.15) then states: "The government proposes to retain the ownership distinction between banks and non-banks that now exists and reflects the Canadian reality."

These principles clearly applied to the original Green Paper in 1985.[1] They also apply to the existing Quebec legislation and to the proposed Ontario legislation for both trust companies and the securities industry. Ironically enough, however, they would not appear to apply to the provisions of the federal paper itself. Indeed, of the various reports on the financial system over the past few years, *New Directions* is probably the most restrictive when it comes to the issue of tolerating anything other than widely-held ownership.

One of the reasons why the ownership controversy took so long to surface relates to the fact that many of the players confidently assumed that the rather sketchy narrative of *New Directions* (i.e., 40 pages of text which, by one estimate, will convert into close to 1,000 pages of legislation) would, when fleshed out by further elaboration and interpretation, fall back in line with the underlying principles with respect to ownership. While the detailed legislation has not as yet been tabled, there is now little doubt that the federal government's intent is to follow through with its restrictive ownership provisions.

The purpose of this paper is to review and assess the arguments with respect to the ownership of financial institutions. Section 2 of the paper focuses in more detail on the federal and provincial proposals as they relate to the ownership of financial institutions. Section 3 highlights the possibilities for jurisdictional confrontation and outlines the underlying economic issues. Section 4 contains the heart of the analysis. It focuses in detail on the pros and cons of wide and narrow ownership. Much of the material for this section is adopted from the recent hearings on ownership and concentration conducted by the Standing Committee on Finance and Economic Affairs of the Ontario Legislature. Indeed, whenever possible the analysis is conducted in the words of the interested parties. Section 5 is devoted to internal corporate governance and, in particular, to the role of business conduct review committees (BCRCs) as a means for policing abusive self-dealing. Section 6 contains a summary of the analysis followed by two compromise approaches that address the issues raised in the paper. A short conclusion completes the paper.

At the outset, it is important that I reveal my own bias. In my view, *New Directions* has come down far too hard in terms of restricting ownership. More importantly, the implications of this approach are likely to be very far-reaching. Among other things, the paper will argue that on broad economic grounds, the issue is whether the wide-ownership provision will become effectively a barrier to entry and, therefore, inhibit market contestability. On broad pragmatic grounds, the issue is whether wide ownership is the only way to ensure against abusive self-dealing and against the concerns that arise from the co-mingling of the commercial and financial sectors. On jurisdictional grounds, the issue on the domestic front is whether Canada's "big bang" in the financial services area will become a federal-provincial shoot-out. On the international front, the issue is whether domestic capital is being forced off-shore and foreign capital is being given preferential access. My overall conclusion is that, in terms of ownership, *New Directions* in itself is in need of new directions. Specifically, the detailed provisions relating to ownership should conform much more closely to *New Directions* own enunciated principles.

2.0 OWNERSHIP PROVISIONS

2.1 Federal Proposals

New Directions responds to recent global trends toward the internationalization of markets, to the integration of the pillars and to the securitization of loans by allowing ownership integration across the traditional four pillars — banks, trusts, insurance and securities. However, as noted above, it does so in a manner that favours widely-held institutions. Since this is not very evident from a straightforward reading of the federal position paper, the purpose of this section is to elaborate on this theme, focusing first on the regulations pertaining to narrowly-held ownership with commercial linkages.

Commercial Linkages: As of December 18, 1986 (the date *New Directions* was released), approval for the incorporation of new banks, trust companies and insurance companies will no longer be granted for applicants with significant commercial interests. The definition of a "significant commercial interest" has two dimensions. First, the individual or corporation must have more than 10 per cent of the shares of the financial institution, i.e., the owner must qualify as a majority or significant shareholder. Second, a majority shareholder of a financial institution will be defined as "commercially linked" if he/she owns more than 10 per cent of the shares of a commercial company (Weir 1987). This definition of a commercial link will be subject to a *de minimus* test designed to "ensure that significant shareholders of financial institutions whose total commercial interests are small relative to their financial interests do not serve to bring their financial institutions within the purview of the foregoing ownership rules" (Weir 1987, p. 20). Total commercial interests will be measured as the aggregate of book value of all ownership interests involving holdings of 10 per cent or more in commercial corporations. The *de minimus* test will exempt shareholders whose commercial interests are 5 per cent or less of their total interests in regulated financial institutions. More on the implications of this *de minimus* exemption later.

Of more interest are the provisions relating to the *existing* commercially-linked, majority-held financial institutions, e.g., Power Financial, Trilon, Imasco, Canada Trust. *New Directions* dictates that "commercially-linked trust, loan and insurance companies with more than $50 million in capital will be required to have at least 35 per cent of their voting shares publicly traded and widely held by December 31, 1991, or within 5 years of reaching the $50 million capital threshold" (p. 17). Moreover, from December 18, 1986 onward no significant shareholder will be allowed to increase his/her percentage holdings. In effect, this provision "grandfathers" these firms, *but only in their existing range of institutions.* Even if they meet the 35 per cent widely-held requirements, they are still deemed to be commercially linked and hence bound by the previous requirement prohibiting any new incorporations or acquisitions.

Majority-Held Institutions Without Commercial Links: The provisions relating to narrowly-held or majority ownership without commercial linkages are much more lenient. Narrowly held trust, loan, or insurance companies where the owners have no commercial links can remain narrowly held (even wholly owned) provided the amount of capital is less than $750 million. Once this capital threshold is passed, the 35 per cent requirement will become operative, again with a five-year period for compliance. What applies beyond the $750 million capital threshold is not fully evident, but it would appear that the 35 per cent requirement would grandfather the firm in its current range of activities: to embark on any new ventures (incorporations or acquisitions) would require getting down to 10 per cent ownership.

There is an important further provision relating to all narrowly-held institutions, namely that in reducing ownership levels shares cannot be sold to other significant (over 10 per cent) shareholders. This implies that as significant shareholders sell out, ownership must move in the direction of being widely held.

Needless to say, the banks and mutuals (and the credit unions and caisses populaires for that matter) are not affected by any of these provisions since they are either widely held or deemed to be.

Mergers and Acquisitions: The Minister of Finance will retain discretionary power to approve the acquisition of one financial institution by another financial institution. There are two guidelines in aiding the Minister in exercising this discretionary power. First, large financial institutions will not generally be allowed to acquire other large financial institutions. Second, the announced preference for expansion to new areas is to build rather than to buy. More later on the implications of these provisions.

Securities Firms: *New Directions* appears to allow all federally chartered financial institutions to incorporate securities firms or to acquire existing securities firms. Presumably this provision is designed to accommodate the Quebec, Ontario, and other provinces' regulations which do not place any ownership requirements on securities firms.

Corporate Governance and Self-Dealing Bans: Finally, it is important to note that *New Directions* also incorporate provisions relating to self-dealing bans and internal corporate governance. These proposals are closely related to the policy on ownership since they represent alternative ways to monitor non-arms'-length transactions, henceforth referred to as NALTs. Later sections of this paper will highlight these provisions, particularly the role and scope of corporate self-governance.

2.2 Provincial Proposals

Quebec's recent legislation for the insurance and securities sectors contains no ownership provisions. Nor does Bill 116, the proposed legislation for Ontario trust companies, or the recent regulations pertaining to the Ontario securities sector (except for a one-year staged entry for foreign acquisitions of domestic securities firms). Ontario, in particular, has accompanied its trust company legislation with very restrictive self-dealing bans. Neither Ontario nor Quebec requires that financial institutions embark upon internal corporate governance procedures.

With this institutional information as backdrop, it is now appropriate to focus on the likely implications of these differing ownership provisions for the evolution of the Canadian financial services sector. The next section deals first with the potential federal-provincial jurisdictional consequences focuses on some of the economic implications of the federal proposals.

3.0 JURISDICTIONAL AND ECONOMIC ISSUES
3.1 Looming Jurisdictional Battles

It would come as a surprise indeed if the narrowly-held, commercially-linked, federally-regulated financial institutions were not seriously contemplating either (a) incorporating new, or purchasing existing, provincially-regulated financial institutions, or (b) rechartering provincially. It would also come as a surprise if the federal government were not anticipating and "guarding against" such moves. Although I am not a constitutional lawyer, my hunch is that Ottawa may well have the upper hand here, at least in the case of rechartering provincially. But we could well be headed for a Supreme Court challenge.

However, where Ottawa may not have the upper hand is in the following hypothetical scenario. Suppose, for illustrative purposes, that Bell Enterprises decides to purchase or establish an Ontario or Quebec securities firm. Suppose, further, that Bell then decides to purchase or establish provincial trust and/or insurance companies. To this point, there would appear to be no problem, although no doubt there would be substantial concern on the part of the federal authorities. Now suppose, however, that the trust company applies for access to the payments system and for a "money" card.

It is clear that this could be viewed as an end run around the intent of the federal proposals, since a commercially-linked, narrowly-held financial institution is now requesting access to the payments system. (Note that this was perfectly acceptable prior to December 18, 1986, and continues to be acceptable for the grandfathered institutions.) One can hazard a guess that the federal government would attempt to deny Bell access to the payments system. If Ottawa did not take this approach, it would be putting itself in a situation where it would be difficult to deny the other end runs elaborated earlier, namely federally-regulated financial institutions rechartering provincially or acquiring provincially-regulated financial institutions.

The constitutional implications of all of this are far from evident. First of all, to have any case at all, it would seem that the federal government would have to bring in legislation to the effect that access to the payments system is what banking is all about. However, such legislation does not now exist and although the payments system resulted from federal legislation it is more akin to a "national" system than a "federal" system since provincially-regulated institutions also have access. Second, the jurisdictional dispute arises because of what Ottawa has done, not because of what the provinces have done. To take a specific example, consider the situation of the stock insurance companies. Under "New Directions", Ottawa has granted them essentially full banking powers on the asset side of their balance sheets. However, they did not request such powers and are not likely to make full use of them. *New Directions* has also decreed that if they want to take full advantage of the new proposals they must become widely held, again something the insurance companies did not ask for. Throughout all of this, the Ontario and Quebec legislation with respect to insurance companies has not changed in any significant way. In other words, it is the *federal legislation that has precipitated the jurisdictional problems.* Thus it is not at all evident that the courts will come down on the federal side. But what is also evident is that the federal government will likely not accept the situation where the principal implications of "New Directions" is that existing and *de novo* financial institutions will seek refuge in provincial jurisdictions. Again, we are probably headed for the courts on this issue.

3.2 Economic Implications
On first reading, *New Directions* gets high marks for enhancing competition. The proposals do respond to the globalization of markets and to the

integration of pillars. Allowing financial institutions to enter the securities industry recognizes the current trend toward disintermediation (i.e., securitization). Moreover, the granting of additional powers to trust and insurance companies and the enhancing of the banks in-house powers in the securities area will also enhance competition. However, it is also the case that *New Directions* carves out a new power balance across existing institutions: widely-held institutions will find their powers significantly enhanced in absolute terms and relative to narrowly held firms, especially those with commercial linkages. The up side is that several mutual life companies and banks are already taking advantage of these new powers and flexibility. But there is a down side as well. In my view. the Achilles heel of *New Directions* is new entry or, in economic jargon, ensuring that financial markets remain contestable. It is instructive to renew the federal proposals from this perspective.

First of all, *New Directions* prohibits any new commercial institutions from entering the financial sector. Second, the existing commercially-linked majority-held institutions are also locked out of new incorporations unless they commit themselves to becoming widely held. Interestingly enough, these institutions may also be "locked in" to the financial sector since they can only sell their shares in accordance with wide ownership precepts. Given that such institutions may find themselves at a decided competitive disadvantage relative to the banks, mutuals, credit unions and other widely-held institutions (if such exist), it may be difficult to sell these shares except at a capital loss. Note that any resulting capital losses will also impact upon minority shareholders of these institutions. Hence, Ottawa may well have a political as well as an economic problem on its hands.

The *de minimus* rule for defining a commercially-linked shareholder also works against new entry. If I own $10 million of equity in, say, a brewery I cannot incorporate a new, small, federal financial institution. However, if I happen to already wholly own a federal financial institution that has, say, $205 million in capital I will then be viewed as "financial" (i.e., not commercially linked) since my commercial holdings are less than 5 per cent of my financial holdings. Indeed, I am entitled to accumulate $750 million in financial capital before even the 35 per cent rule applies. This seems clearly perverse in terms of catering to new entry concerns.

The federal government will presumably claim that new entry concerns are satisfied by the provision whereby financially-linked majority ownership can accumulate $750 million of capital before triggering the 35 per cent requirement. But who falls in this category? The word from the street is that the *de minimus* rule might imply that the Empire Life group qualifies. This is a questionable example, since Empire Life's holdings tend to be chartered provincially, not federally. My own view is that in terms of domestic financial institutions, this category is close to being an empty set and likely to remain so, although one has to admit the possibility that some existing financial conglomerates may qualify by spinning off their commercial holdings to *de minimus* levels.

The prospect for new entry by widely-held institutions also appears bleak. Most of the score of new widely-held banks that emerged as a result of the 1967 *Bank Act* provisions have either failed or merged, so that this route for ensuring contestability appears weak or non-existent.

This leaves one further avenue – entry by foreign financial institutions. *New Directions* is not entirely clear in terms of its proposals for these institutions. Temporarily, at least, the status quo prevails. Over time, however, it appears clear that institutions such as the Schedule B banks will be brought into the proposals. The recent federally-approved takeovers (Continental by Lloyds and The Bank of British Columbia by the Hong Kong Bank of Canada, a wholly owned subsidiary of the Hong Kong and Shanghai Banking Corporation) point in the direction of treating Schedule B's as *financially-linked* majority-held institutions. In turn, this would imply that they could accumulate $750 million of capital prior to being affected by the federal ownership proposals. This would clearly help out in terms of ensuring entry, but it does so in a manner that is likely to generate considerable political and jurisdictional friction. In the limit, this approach would suggest that Deutsche Bank Canada, whose parent not only has downstream commercial linkages, but has effective control over several of Germany's top 100 commercial corporations (Marfels, chapter 3 of this volume), will be free to maneuver in the domestic financial market in a way that is not open to Power Corporation or Trilon. Moreover, such a preference on the part of the federal government for foreign commercially-linked institutions over domestic commercially-linked institutions would surely compromise any federal constitutional challenge with respect to provincial ownership provisions.

3.3   Recapitulation

This, then, is the descriptive backdrop to the ownership controversy. As these various proposals reach committee stage the debate is sure to intensify. Indeed, the debate is already in full swing. The Canadian Bankers' Association (1987) has argued that *New Directions* ownership rules do not go far enough in the direction of ensuring wide ownership. The conglomerates are also beginning to make their views public (Howlett 1987). In Chapter 16 of this volume Jacques Parizeau attempts to resurrect the Blenkarn Proposal on grounds that *New Directions* is weak in terms of promoting domestic new entrants into the financial sector. And so on.

At this juncture it is instructive to step back a bit and focus on some of the underlying economic dynamics. First of all, the financial services sector is one of the fastest growing industries worldwide. It is at the leading edge of the technological revolution, both in terms of computational and telecommunications developments. Not surprisingly, therefore, capital is being attracted from all parts of the economy to the financial services sector. Some of the attraction is simply portfolio diversification. Some is probably related to exploiting expertise in either or both of telecommunications or computer technology. (There is a rumour that IBM is attempting to buy Merrill Lynch and it cannot be long before Bell Canada Enterprises thinks seriously about a securities subsidiary.) Some is surely motivated by the potential for synergy in terms of offering an integrated range of financial products. And some may be driven by the horizontal integration gains that may arise from co-mingling the real and financial sectors. Underlying all these motives, however, is the quest for the higher returns that are available in the financial sector.

Second, world class financial services firms require enormous amounts of capital. Constraining Canadian financial institutions from raising capital from commercial organizations will put them at a serious disadvantage relative to foreign firms which do not face such constraints.

Third, restrictive Canadian regulatory provisions with respect to ownership of financial institutions will obviously not alter the relative attraction of financial services investment internationally, and perhaps not even in Canada. But they do have the potential for altering the *structure* of the Canadian financial sector. By limiting the ability of commercially-linked capital to flow into the financial sector, the predictable results will be (a) to encourage foreign capital to take up the resulting slack, (b) to enhance the degree of domestic financial concentration among the existing players, and (c) to encourage Canadian capital to go offshore in search of investment in the financial sector. In terms of this latter point, I am sure that institutions like Imasco, Power Financial and Royal Trust are already casting their sights offshore in the event that they are frozen out domestically. Indeed. some of the possibilities are intriguing, even if improbable. For example, might Power Financial not increase both its international and domestic flexibility by relocating its head office to, say, Belgium, and then seeking re-entry into Canada as a Schedule B bank?

To be sure, this is a highly unlikely scenario. However, the fact that such a scenario can be contemplated theoretically surely highlights the core issue in all of this: why is the federal government proposing these ownership restrictions? What are the benefits that will accrue to the financial sector from widely-held ownership? Do these benefits exceed the costs generated by restricting entry? Are there alternative approaches available which are less extreme than Ontario's and Quebec's very permissive proposals on the one hand and Ottawa's very restrictive ones on the other? Or does the federal position simply reflect an overriding public policy concern, regardless of potential economic consequences?

To attempt to get to the heart of this issue is the purpose of the remainder of this paper.

4.0 NARROW VS. WIDE OWNERSHIP: A SURVEY OF THE ISSUES
4.1 The Burden of Proof

There is no question that concerns relating to narrow ownership, and in particular commercially-linked narrow ownership, rose to the fore in the wake of what Jacques Parizeau refers to as the "trust musketeers" (Crown, Greymac, and Seaway). The later failures of the CCB and Northland Bank, both of which were widely held, serve to diffuse the concerns somewhat, at least to the extent that self-dealing problems were now also associated with management and boards of directors. Moreover, the bank failures, more so than the Crown-Seaway-Greymac debacle, directed attention to the inadequacy of the system of supervision. All of these factors, in addition to a rethinking of the powers appropriate for the various financial institutions, were the focus of parliamentary committees in both the House of Commons and the Senate.

It is probably fair to say that one of the critical turning points in terms of both public and legislative awareness of the potential problems associated with narrowly-held ownership of financial institutions was the testimony before the Blenkarn Committee in September, 1985, of Bernard Ghert, then president of Cadillac-Fairview Corporation. The timing and substance of the testimony as well as Ghert's apparent, if not real, impartiality with respect to the issue served to lend substantially greater focus and credibility to the view that widely-held ownership is the only acceptable policy for the financial sector. More recently, this view has been popularized by Diane Francis (1986) in her book, *Controlling Interest: Who Owns Canada?*

As a result the burden of proof in the debate appears to have shifted rather dramatically: the banks can now assert, almost self-righteously, that commercially-linked, narrowly-held ownership of financial institutions is virtually synonymous with abusive self-dealing and it is left to the trusts, stock insurance companies and financial conglomerates to plead that the historical tradition of majority ownership of financial institutions has contributed enough to Canadian society that it be allowed to continue. The extent of this change of attitude is reflected by the fact that the Green Paper contained no limitations on majority-held ownership of financial institutions whereas "New Directions" can, as noted above, be viewed as embodying the principle of 10 per cent ownership.

In order to broach the debate, it seems appropriate to focus first on the views of Bernard Ghert (1985). Basically Ghert fears the consequences of undue concentrations of economic power in huge conglomerates, particularly the exercise of financial power by non-financial companies through financial holding companies. At one level, his concerns relate chiefly to the evils of concentration: "Potential adverse consequences of this concentration are:

(i) ability to misallocate resources by restricting output and raising prices;

(ii) redistribution of income from the firm's customers to its owners;

(iii) firms with excessive power can become inefficient and wasteful;

(iv) a high level of concentration reduces the number and diversity of decision makers in the economy;

(v) large concentrations may be unresponsive to regulatory agencies and have the ability to influence public policy;

(vi) corporate concentration may stimulate greater government intervention as a countervailing power" (1985, p.68A:5).

In principle, these concerns apply to concentrations whether widely or narrowly held. But applying these consequences to commercial and financial intermingling leads Ghert to be very concerned about self-dealing and conflicts of interest "when a financial institution has both a debt and equity interest in a non-financial corporation" (p.68A:6). Noting that the difficulty in experimenting with higher levels of concentration of power is that it may not be a reversible process (since governments may be unwilling or unable to dismantle mega-groups once they are established). Ghert concludes that "Public policy must not facilitate any increase in the concentration of ownership of financial institutions or more importantly in the trend to unification of control of financial and industrial corporations" (Ghert 1985, p.68A:6).

But his main concern would appear to be the implications for macro-level concentration that would arise from the levering of the commercial and financial. One example of this relates to the ability of a commercially-linked, narrowly-held financial institution to discriminate against its owners' real-side competitors:

> The public record has many examples of economic power being used in ways that are not always in our best interests in this country. As an example, I know of an instance where, if witnesses were required to testify under oath, they would tell you of a financial institution which had instructions from senior executives of the parent non-financial company to refuse loans to one of its competitors (Ghert 1985, p.68A:6).

Not surprisingly, the Canadian Bankers Association (henceforth referred to as the CBA) included this quotation in their testimony to buttress wide ownership before the Ontario Standing Committee on Finance and Economic Affairs (CBA 1986).

Ghert's ultimate concern, however, is the accretion of macro-level power to the point where it may take on overtones of political influence:

> Power is the ability to produce intended effects on others; it can also mean the exercise of discretion in decision-making. Another attribute of power is the ability to pursue non-economic objectives. even at the expense of economic considerations. The greater the concentration of power, particularly the exercise of financial power by non-financial companies through financial holding companies, the greater the risk of abuse, either directly or through informal networks and spheres of influence in the business community (Ghert 1985, p.68A:6).

and

> By further concentrating the control of business enterprises, conglomerates [particularly those that unify the control of financial and industrial corporations] may have a greater impact on government policy making. Certainly, a large conglomerate enterprise is likely to "interface" with government in more places than a giant firm whose activities are concentrated in a single industry (Ghert 1985, p.68A:22).

As an overall summary of Ghert's concerns, it is useful to reproduce his response before the Ontario Standing Committee to the question of whether or not concentration or largeness is necessary to compete effectively in the world markets:

> You can have largeness in a sense. Canada needs large financial institutions. Canada needs large steel companies. Canada needs large brewing companies, large merchandisers, large forestry companies, large petroleum companies, mining companies, if those companies are going to have the capital and the management to compete in international markets. But it is when you put those together, large steel companies with large mining companies with large trust companies, into one bag, that I have the concern about the potential for the impact on our economy and our institutions.
>
> ... if you have a big pool of financial assets you can have a major impact on the marketplace. You can have a major impact on getting people to do things that you want them to do (Ghert 1986, p. F.7 and F.26 respectively).

This, then, is a brief overview of Bernard Ghert's views on concentration. While most of his points are not particularly novel, the timing and eloquence of his testimony and evidence surely played a major role in the ownership conversion from the Green Paper to the Hockin paper.

Thus far, however, these concerns have been reproduced without comment or analysis. In many cases, such comment is warranted. For example, Ghert's premise that power is the ability to pursue non-economic objectives, even at the expense of economic considerations, would probably argue against "management-controlled" institutions where the ability exists to ignore the interests of the shareholders. However, the approach I have adopted is to use Ghert's views as backdrop to the more detailed focus on the pros and cons of alternative ownership arrangements. Not surprisingly, many of the issues touched upon derive from the above concerns raised by Ghert.

4.2 Arguments for Wide Ownership

Market Concentration: Setting aside for the time being the so-called macro-level concentration concerns, the issue here is whether or not there are policy implications for wide ownership that derive from concerns relating to the concentration of financial markets. There are several aspects that merit attention.

Dealing first with individual product markets, Table 1 presents aggregate data relating to product market shares by type of financial institutions. The chartered banks (Schedule As and Bs) dominate the consumer and commercial loan markets but have a much smaller influence in the market for mortgage loans. Note that by opening up commercial and consumer loans to the trust and insurance companies, *New Directions* will serve to increase the competition and lessen institutional concentration in

Table 1
Financial Institutions' Market Share - 1984
(expressed as per cent)

	Banks (A&B)	Trust Co.	Life Co.	Credit Unions	Other
Assets	56	8	11	7	18
Deposits	65	18	-	15	2
Commercial Loans	84	2	-	4	10
Consumer Loans	71	5	6	14	4
Mortgage Loans	31	27	16	17	9

Source: Royal Trustco (1986, p. 8).

these markets. However, the traditional measures of concentration (i.e., the percentage accounted for by the four largest companies and the number of companies needed to account for 80 per cent of the market) indicate that concentration is already decreasing in these markets. This is apparent from Table 2. Interestingly enough, the evidence shows that the degree of concentration is increasing in the mortgage market, even though it remains by a considerable margin the least concentrated of the markets in Table 2. Some of the reduced concentration in the consumer and commercial lending markets is presumably due to the advent of the Schedule B banks. One would expect that the impact of *New Directions* would be to decrease the four-company concentration ratio. It is not clear what will happen to the second index (the number of companies needed to account for 80 per cent of total assets). My best guess is that it will rise (i.e., the number of companies will fall), given the ability to integrate ownership across the pillars. More importantly, this likely increase in concentration will be more pronounced if commercially-linked capital is held at bay, since the number of large-scale diversified institutions will be reduced.

A second approach to concentration of the financial sector is to focus on the size of institutions with respect to the overall financial sector. Here one rapidly becomes involved in a battle of the balance sheets. Before the Ontario Standing Committee, Empire Life's Hal Jackman (1986) argued that, according to *Financial Post* data, the amount of assets under control (i.e., excluding assets under management such as Estate, Trust and Agency (ETA) assets)) of closely-held shareholding groupings are relatively small compared to the total assets in the system.[2] Table 3, reproduced from

Table 2
Concentration in Selected Markets Among Major Groups of Financial Institutions,[1] Canada, 1979 and 1984

	Percentage of activities represented by the four largest companies			Number of companies needed to account for 80 per cent of the market[2]		
	Mortgages	Domestic Deposits	Domestic personal & commercial Loans	Mortgages	Domestic Deposits	Domestic personal & commercial Loans
1979	29.9	53.8	70.0	23	9	5
1984	32.6	47.7	62.7	20	12	7

Notes:
1. Full ownership links and holding groups are taken into account.
2. In a study by the Department of Consumer and Corporate Affairs, the degree of concentration is determined by the number of companies that account for 80 per cent of the output or employment of an industry. The degree of concentration is "very high" when the number is four or fewer; "high" with five to eight; "relatively high" with nine to 20 companies; "relatively low" with 21 to 50 companies; and "low" with more than 50 companies.

Source: Economic Council of Canada (1987, Table 3-4).

Jackman's submission, indicates that domestic narrowly-held financial conglomerates account for only 7.8 per cent of the total financial assets of the 100 largest financial institutions in Canada. Indeed, he notes that "according to the figures supplied by the *Financial Post*, all of the closely-held shareholder controlled companies when added together do not equal the assets of any single one of Canada's five largest national banks" (1986, pp. 3-4). Thus implicit, if not explicit, in the Jackman message is that power in the Canadian financial sector is concentrated in the hands of a few large banks. But he goes much further when he stated that "Large banks have tended to mean large loans to a few large borrowers and may have contributed to the concentration of corporate power in the non-financial sector of this country" (p. 4). Moreover, in Jackman's view the perceived feeling that regional interests have not been well served by large banks with their headquarters in Montreal and Toronto has led to the rapid growth of the credit union and cooperative movement, which is much stronger in Canada than in the U.S. where the degree and location of bank concentration is much more diverse.

Table 3
Financial Post Survey
100 Largest Financial Institutions
(December 31, 1985)

	Number of Institutions		Amount of Assets ($ billions)	
Canadian Owned and Widely Held	12	(12%)	413.0	(67.4%)
Foreign Controlled	44	(44%)	62.9	(10.3%)
Government Owned (Fed. & Provincially)	8	(8%)	55.5	(9.1%)
Co-operatives and Credit Unions	18	(18%)	33.5	(5.5%)
Canadian Owned (with an identifiable significant shareholder interest)	18	(19%)	48.0	(7.8%)
	100	(100%)	$612.9	(100.0%)

Source: Jackman (1986, p. 2).

Similar concerns have led to the proliferation of the trust and loan companies, most of which are provincially chartered. One can extend this line of argument to suggest that the emergence of narrowly-held financial trust and insurance companies is in large measure a response to the concentration of existing financial power in the hands of the chartered banks. Jackman (1986, p. 5) concludes:

> Therefore any discussion of concentration of power in the financial services industry must be related to the question of being able to form viable competitive entities which will be able to take on the banks on their own turf without sacrificing the primary requirement of ensuring solvency. Therefore combinations of non-bank financial institutions which have the effect of increasing competition should be encouraged ... fully automated on-line systems, automatic tellers and the requirements of providing full service to customers demand a certain size to be fully competitive with the largest of our institutions.

As an interesting aside, Jackman's contentions appear deserving of further research. In effect, his hypothesis is that the concentration of financial power in the hands of a few national banks has contributed in turn to (a) the concentration in the commercial sector, and (b) to the development of regional trusts, credit unions and eventually large financial conglomerates. Thus, in his view the emergence of conglomerates are a direct result of the powerful position of the banks and, hence, are serving to diffuse concentration.

The CBA view (1986) of all of this is poles apart from Jackman's view. Table 4 presents the CBA approach. While the two tables differ in their coverage (the top 10 in Table 3 vs. all financial institutions in Table 4) and in the manner in which they classify institutions, it is very evident that Table 4 reveals a substantially decreased percentage for chartered banks and a dramatic increase for the combination of trust and life companies. Most of the trust company assets and a substantial portion of the life insurance assets would fall under the Table 3 category of "Canadian owned with an identifiable significant shareholder interest." The principal differences between Tables 3 and 4 are the following: Table 3 focuses on all assets, domestic and foreign, of Canadian financial institutions whereas Table 4 focuses only on the Canadian assets (except for some foreign assets of trust companies which are not segregated out in their balance sheets). Table 3 deletes the ETA (estates, trust and agency) assets and segregated fund assets on grounds that they are not under the "control" of the trust companies. Table 4 includes one-half of these ETA assets as well as one-half of segregated fund assets. Both these modifications are dramatic—chartered bank foreign assets as of June 30, 1985 were $190 billion and ETA funds were in the same range.

The CBA paper then presents a comparison of the six largest banks and the six largest conglomerates, based on the Table 4 methodology. The comparison is reproduced as Table 5. The data indicate that Trilon and

Table 4
Adjusted Canadian Currency Assets of Financial Institutions
(June 30, 1985)

	($ millions)	(% total)
Chartered Banks[1]	$230,195	42.1%
Trust/Mortgage Loan Companies[2]	134,680	24.6
Life Insurance Companies[3]	67,302	12.3
Credit Unions/Caisses Populaires[4]	42,904	7.8
Property/Casualty Insurance Companies[5]	16,545	3.0
Financial Corporations[6]	15,302	2.8
Investment Dealers[7]	12,021	2.2
Quebec Savings Banks[8]	5,940	1.1
Investment Funds[9]	7,377	1.3
Other[10]	15,051	2.8
	$547,317	100.0%

Notes:

1. Total Canadian dollar assets of all Schedule A and B banks including assets of banks' mortgage loan subsidiaries - Bank of Canada Review Table C-3.

2. Includes Canadian dollar intermediary assets as in Appendix II as well as one-half of ETA assets (Statistics Canada 61-006 Table 23) and retirement savings funds (Statistics Canada Table 88) adjusted, where data available, to include Canadian assets only.

3. Includes Canadian dollar assets as in Appendix II as well as one-half of segregated funds (Statistics Canada Table 100).

4. Statistics Canada 61-006 Table 33.

5. Statistics Canada 61-006 Table 114.

6. Statistics Canada 61-006 Table 45.

7. Statistics Canada 61-006 Table 119 (this figure is understated as information was not available on funds under administration by investment dealers).

8. Bank of Canada Review - Chart D-5.

9. Statistics Canada 61-006 Table 73.

10. Includes financial leasing corporations, business financing corporations, real estate investment trusts (REITs), closed-end funds, and accident/sickness branches of life insurance companies in Statistics Canada 61-006 Table 56, 60, 64, 68 and 110 (this figure is understated as it does not include Alberta Treasury Branches, Province of Ontario Savings Offices, etc.).

Source: Canadian Bankers' Association (1986, Appendix VI).

Table 5
Banks and Financial Conglomerates: Corporate Data - 1985

Bank	($ billions)	Conglomerates	($ billions)
RBC	$53.9	Trilon Financial	$40.1
CIBC	48.8	Genstar Financial	35.3
BMO	44.1	Desjardins Group	29.7
TD	32.4	Power Financial	26.1
BNS	25.7	E-L Financial	19.6
NBC	16.1	Traders Group	6.4

Source: Canadian Bankers' Association (1986).

Genstar Financial (now Imasco/Canada Trust) each have financial assets which exceed the domestic operations, as measured by Canadian currency assets of the Toronto Dominion Bank, the Bank of Nova Scotia and the National Bank of Canada. [However, if we made the comparison in terms of total assets of the banks, the bank failures as of December 1985 would be: RBC ($96 billion); Montreal ($82 billion); CIBC ($76 billion); BNS ($61 billion); TD Bank ($50 billion); National Bank ($23 billion).] The thrust of the CBA brief is two-fold – to argue that banks do not have as large a market share as is commonly believed and, relatedly, to emphasize that the conglomerates are much larger than they are typically perceived to be.

In Chapter 1 of this volume R.S. Khemani compares the top five banks with the top five conglomerates. Focusing first on both domestic and foreign assets but excluding ETA funds, the top five banks account for 45.9 per cent of total financial sector assets in 1985. The top five holding companies (one of which, Desjardins, is widely held) account for 11.7 per cent. If ETA assets are included, the percentages are 36.7 per cent and 22.0 per cent respectively.

Finally, Table 6 focuses on the size of institutions in terms of the two concentration ratios. Regardless of whether the comparison is in terms of domestic or foreign assets or including or excluding ETA funds, concentration has decreased slightly over the 1979-1984 period.

Recapitulation: Rather than becoming involved in picking sides in this definitional battle, I prefer to focus on some of the implications as they relate to ownership and concentration.   First of all, markets tend to become concentrated in the Canadian context whenever entry is difficult or the border is closed, or both. Historically, both of these conditions prevailed and they account for the current dominance of the big five banks.   Easing

Table 6
Concentration of Assets Among Major Groups of Financial Institutions[1], Canada, 1979 and 1984

| | Percentage of total assets represented by the four largest companies | | | | Number of companies needed to account for 80 per cent of assets[2] | | | |
| | Total Assets | | Domestic Assets | | Total Assets | | Domestic Assets | |
	W/Out ETA	With ETA	W/Out ETA	With ETA	W/Out ETA	With ETA	W/OutETA	With ETA
1979	53.1	45.0	47.7	39.4	13	14	16	17
1984	50.4	41.0	42.2	35.7	16	15	21	19

Notes:

1. Full ownership links and holding groups are taken into account.
2. See footnote 2 of Table 2.

Source: Economic Council of Canada (1987, Table 3.3).

domestic chartering under the provisions of the 1967 *Bank Act* led to a score of new chartered banks but, as noted above, most have now either failed or merged with the larger banks. Opening the border under the provisions of the 1980 *Bank Act* has proved to be an effective challenge to the major banks, particularly at the wholesale end of their business.

Secondly, the rise of trust companies and credit unions has contributed substantially to enhancing competition at the retail end of financial services. This is clearly evident in terms of hours of service, but it is equally apparent in the increased range of financial products and services.

Thirdly, it is true that the conglomerates have, through mergers and internal growth, made some inroads on the dominant position of the major banks. Some of this has been due to the fact that the banks have been widening spreads between lending and borrowing at the retail end in response to their off-shore and oil-patch losses and the majority held trusts have been able to capitalize on this spread. Some is no doubt due to the fact that the trusts (and credit unions) are not required to hold non-interest-bearing required reserves with the Bank of Canada. However, the greatest impetus to conglomerate growth has been that they have (until *New Directions*) enjoyed far greater powers relating to cross-pillar activity than have the chartered banks.

The fourth point is that *New Directions* will alter rather dramatically the powers available to banks and to conglomerates. Because they are widely held, the banks can now roam acquisitively across the pillars. The conglomerates are stopped dead in their tracks. In my view, even if there were no ownership requirements embodied in *New Directions*, the fact that the power of the banks is unleashed would guarantee that they would more than hold their own in any market showdown with the conglomerates. However, because the conglomerates' ability to maneuver has been reduced under *New Directions*, the spectre of enhanced chartered-bank domination, and enhanced concentration, of the financial sector looms as the almost inevitable result.

It is true that there may be some important counterweights. *New Directions* has also unleashed the patent power of the mutual life companies and some of them are already flexing their new-found financial muscle. The other counterweight to the banks may be found in opening up the border. If the thrust of *New Directions* is to treat schedule B's as financially linked (rather than commercially linked) entities, then they will offer considerable competition to the banks, at least at the wholesale level.

The fifth point also relates to the new federal proposals. "New Directions" embodies a preference for *de novo* institutions rather than acquisitions. This clearly favours the major banks, all of whom have at some point benefitted substantially from mergers. Few of the banks' potential competitors have nationwide coverage. To shut off the merger or takeover route to these firms, whether mutuals or conglomerates, is to entrench the established position of the banks. More generally, the takeover route is an integral part of ensuring new entrants (although as noted earlier *New Directions* shuts this avenue off on two scores — commercial linkages and the preference for building over buying). Moreover, there is an obvious and critically important relationship between new entry and acquisitions, or more generally between primary and secondary markets: if the acquisition or merger route is fettered, this will surely discourage new entrants. Setting aside the ownership concerns, it does not make economic sense to prevent Canada Trust, for example, from entering the Quebec retail market via the merger or takeover route.

In summary, therefore, *New Directions* may well serve to entrench the already dominant position of the chartered banks (Jackman 1987). There may well be sound reasons for inhibiting new entry of commercial enterprises into the financial sector and for curtailing the powers of existing commercially linked conglomerates, but concerns over concentration of financial markets is not one of them. Indeed, curtailing the powers of commercially linked enterprises will serve to enhance financial market concentration.

Concentration of Economic/Political Power: The CBA brief (1986) argues that narrowly-held ownership can lead to a concentration of economic/political power, which it summarizes as follows:

> As fewer people gain control of more of the Canadian economy, their ability to influence and distort the political process grows. In addition, with the growth of large, multi-sector holding companies, the failure of one company in a group can have spin-off effects on other affiliates and the entire Canadian economy. This may weaken the ability of legislators to exercise regulatory control. (CBA 1986).

Again, there are several aspects to this concern.

One relates to the exercise of raw political powers or its obverse, namely that firms become so big or important that regulatory response to them is circumscribed. This situation can, of course, arise under any sort of ownership structure. However, Bernard Ghert's concern, reproduced above – that commercially-linked majority ownership may enhance the exercise of this power since such an institution would have many more opportunities to "interface" with government is probably apropos here. Nonetheless, it is a bit ironic that the CBA should raise this issue. Surely it is axiomatic that the government will not allow one of the big banks to fail. Indeed, the banks have become so influential that rescue attempts typically have to be disguised in order to maintain public confidence in the banking system. In the view of many, this is what the Dome bailout was all about.

Recently, Hal Jackman in Chapter 15 of this volume goes much further by expressing concern that the federal government has essentially tailored *New Directions* as a sophisticated and cleverly disguised bailout of the banks. With some $3.5 billion of loan losses last year and some $9.5 billion of non-performing loans, and with the trend toward investment banking rather than commercial banking. Jackman sympathizes with the predicament of the banks, but he believes that the totality of provisions in *New Directions* are skewed much too far in favour of the banks.

Moreover, in terms of influencing decision-making, I am sure that the financial conglomerates wish that they had just some of the influence of the banks, given the remarkable transition from the *Green Paper* (which was essentially a paper about how the rest of the system, conglomerates included, could get into banking), to Tom Hockin's (1986) paper (which is essentially a paper about whether any other players deserve the new powers that the banks have been granted).

To the extent that the concern here is not so much sheer size as the potential for levering the commercial and financial, one solution may be the resort to selective self-dealing bans. More attention will be addressed to self-dealing bans in the later context of controlling certain types of non-arm's-length transactions. In the present context, the point is simply that given a sufficiently stringent set of self-dealing bans any commercial investment in the financial sector will become akin to a "portfolio" investment than a hands-on investment.

A second aspect embodied in the above quotation relates to the possibility that a failure on the commercial side could spread to the financial side. This, too, is a genuine concern and it is precisely for this reason that the Senate (or Murray) Report (1986), for example, recommended that there be a financial holding company between the commercial and financial institutions. The more recent reports of the Economic Council of Canada (1986, 1987) are especially insistent on the use of financial holding companies as a buffer between the real and financial sectors.

A third possibility is that the underlying issue here is really the concentration of assets in the hands of a few families. In large measure this is the thrust of Diane Francis' (1986) book. The jacket of the book asks, "who are the 32 families who, along with five conglomerates, control one-third of Canada's assets?" To the extent that this is a problem (after allowing for the fact that her statement is way-off base unless one utilizes an extremely narrow definition of just what constitutes "Canada's assets"), it affects all sectors and not only the financial services sector. Hence, the range of solutions should also be generic rather than industry specific. Here, I agree with several of Francis' recommendations, e.g.:

- the application of succession duties or preferably accession duties to mitigate the perpetuation of family wealth across generations; and

- reform of the legislation relating to merger activity so as to ensure that mergers are market-driven rather than tax-driven.

In summary, therefore, there is probably more substance to ownership concerns arising from the economic/political aspect of concentration than there is from the market power aspect. Nonetheless, I find the argument neither compelling nor one that would let the big, widely-held banks off the hook. Moreover, both of these concentration arguments have to be placed in the context of the on-going globalization of financial services. It was not too long ago when several of the Canadian chartered banks made the top 20 list of banks internationally. This is no longer the case. In the most recent *Euromoney* rankings (February 1987), the market value of the Royal Bank is less than 10 per cent of each of the top seven ranked banks and its overall ranking is 55th. In terms of assets, however, it fares much better — 27th. But even here its assets are only 40 per cent of those of top-ranking Citicorp.

Credit Deprivation: The CBA brief (1986) lists "credit deprivation" as a further reason for eliminating the link between the commercial and financial: "a financial firm, giving preferential rates to its industrial affiliate, or refusing credit to competitors of related non-financial companies, distorts the credit allocation process and leads to economic efficiency" (p. i).[3] The CBA elaborates as follows:

> The problem with such a situation lies not only in the fact that the company which was refused credit must spend the time and effort to seek funds elsewhere. An even greater concern is that the information that the company in question was refused credit will become known in the marketplace and could affect the reputation of the borrowing company .... Furthermore, the financial institution which turned down the loan would have information about the competitor which would be of use to its related non-financial company (CBA 1986, p. 5).

In my view the correct response to this concern is contained in the Genstar brief (March 1986). In the quotation that follows Genstar is, of necessity, responding to Bernard Ghert's claims and not to those of the CBA, since the CBA position paper was released only in the fall of 1986. However, given that the CBA comments rather faithfully reproduce Ghert's arguments, the Genstar position applies equally well to the CBA's concern:

> The Cadillac Fairview Corporation, a major real estate developer not affiliated through ownership with any financial conglomerate, expressed a concern in a brief on the Green Paper that the mixture of commercial and financial power could limit the availability of funds to certain borrowers which compete with the affiliates of financial institutions and which have no such affiliation of their own. In a competitive environment, there is no advantage to be gained by the arbitrary refusal of a financial institution to lend to the competitor of an affiliated commercial enterprise. Any such refusal would only be to the financial disadvantage of the lender because the refused borrower would be easily able to obtain financing from a competitive source.
>
> There are enough competitors currently operating in the financial services industry that Cadillac Fairview's concern is unfounded. If its concern ever became a problem, that problem is more appropriately solved by measures to increase competition, such as expanding the commercial lending powers for loan and trust companies, or by specific competition legislation, such as 'refusal to deal' prohibitions, than by indirectly attempting a solution through domestic ownership limitations (Genstar 1986, p. 24).

By enhancing the commercial lending powers of trusts and insurance companies *New Directions* has increased competition in the market for loans, thereby minimizing this aspect of the concern with respect to narrowly-held ownership.

Sometimes this "credit deprivation" argument is phrased in terms of "credit bias." Canadians should have confidence that their financial institutions extend credit in an unbiased manner. It is hard to disagree with this. However, the implicit assumption here is that majority-owned financial institutions will be perceived by the public to give preferential loan treatment to their owners. Not only do I believe that there is not much evidence to support this contention but, more importantly, as a matter of public perception the opposite is surely closer to the truth. Moreover, the public would be far more likely to express a concern that it is the chartered banks that have a lending bias — in favour of their large customers, which would in turn convert this concern into a board-of-directors bias, given the tendency for large customers to find their way onto bank boards. "Tell me which bank had Jack Gallagher [former Chairman of Dome Petroleum] as a director and I'll show you a bank that's overextended in the oil patch" is a familiar refrain.

Since lending to trust company directors is much more restrictive (relative to what is allowed for chartered banks), this concern about lending bias does not generate much in the way of a broadside against majority-held institutions.

Self-Dealing Concerns: We now come to what I believe is the heart of the issue. Concerns relating to self-dealing and conflicts of interest are typically front and centre in any debate over widely-held or narrowly-held ownership. The first part of this section focuses on self-dealing concerns arising from a co-mingling of industrial-financial relationships. The second part is devoted to potential self-dealing arising from boards of directors that are not "independent". Finally, the section concludes with the CBA reaction to the ownership provisions in *New Directions*. The ensuing discussion of self-dealing is not intended to be exhaustive. For example, one of the implications that derives from the analysis is that there are alternative ways, such as corporate governance, to attempt to limit the potential for abusive self-dealing. A description and evaluation of corporate governance appears as a later section of the paper.

Following upon the pattern established earlier, quotations from the interested parties themselves provide most of the analysis.

(a) Commercial Financial Co-mingling: Once again, it appears appropriate to let the CBA set the stage:

> Unlike non-financial companies, financial institutions use public deposits, as well as shareholder investment, in their operations. When one or a small group of investors controls a financial institution, there is an opportunity for owners to channel these deposits for personal use. Because financial institutions are highly leveraged, the cost of failure to participants is significantly

higher than for non-financial institutions. With an average leverage of 20 times deposits to capital in financial institutions, there is much more at risk for depositors than for owners; the high degree of leverage implies that a dishonest owner could bilk depositors of far more than his cost of acquiring the depository. While bad management can occur in any organization, there is little possibility for owners of widely-held financial institutions, such as Canada's banks, to divert funds to themselves.

Common ownership by one or a few individuals of both financial and non-financial institutions produces an added risk. Even with strict laws against self-dealing, the temptation to try to save, for example, a troubled real-estate affiliate by "borrowing" from the financial associate could compel an owner to circumvent regulatory authority (CBA 1986, p. i).

The CBA brief (1986, pp. 2-3) buttresses these arguments by several pieces of evidence. First, it notes that according to a U.S. congressional survey, 61 per cent of FDIC-insured commercial bank failures in the United States from June 1980 to June 1983 can be attributed to insider dealings and major shareholdings misusing their position. Second, the CBA refers to a brief presented to the Blenkarn Committee by the Regional Trust Company in September of 1985 which argued that between December 31, 1982 and mid-1985, 86.9 per cent of the loss provisions of the CDIC related to institutions where material self-dealing is either alleged or demonstrated.[4] (Actually, these two points are somewhat misleading in terms of what they imply about *shareholder* points self-dealing. With respect to the first point, both Jackman (1986) and McFetridge (Chapter 14 in this volume) refer to the same data. McFetridge laments the fact that there is not sufficient detail given with respect to "insider dealings" to be able to distinguish between shareholder dealings on the one hand and management/director dealings on the other. A later quotation from Jackman will indicate that some of these companies were mutuals, where there are no shareholders. In terms of the second point, the CBA is also on questionable grounds in light of the substantial CDIC losses *after* mid-1985 in connection with the failures of the Northland and the CCB (both widely held), particularly since these losses were apparent before the CBA brief was presented.) Finally, the CBA provides an appendix that focuses on the details of 10 international cases of abusive, or suspected abusive, self-dealing. Three of the 10 cases are Canadian (Crown/Greymac/Seaway, Fidelity, and Astra Trust/Remor).

The underlying CBA position is that the only effective way of eliminating the potential for abusive self-dealing is to ensure that all financial institutions are widely-held. Therefore, even in the case of Bill 116 (Ontario's proposals for the trust industry) with its very restrictive self-dealing bans, the CBA recommendation is that the legislation be amended to require a separation of industrial and financial business and to require that financial institutions be widely held.

In *Controlling Interest . . . .* Diane Francis (1986, p. 328) takes the same approach:

> The easiest way to prevent self-dealing is to impose ownership limits on any lending institution taking deposits from the public and insured under the Canada Deposit Insurance Corp. Federal laws now limit bank ownership to 10 per cent, and this limit should also apply to provincially-chartered trust companies. Unfortunately, controlling interest in all trust companies is already held by individuals or conglomerates. Even so, they should be forced to divest over a ten-to-fifteen-year period.

However, Francis (1986, p. 330) adds: "if laws fail to disallow owning both types of assets [commercial and financial], self-dealing rules should be enacted to forbid financial companies from conducting any transactions with their real economy cousins."

Professor Stefan Dupré, Chairman of the Ontario Task Force on Financial Institutions (1985), echoes this concern about the role that ownership provisions can play in minimizing self-dealing. After describing himself as a "regulatory pluralist," by which he means that self-dealing bans, audit committees and business conduct review committees all have an important role to play, Dupré offers the following conclusions before the Ontario Legislative Committee:

> . . . in my respectful view, all the so-called business conduct review committees in the world and all the regulators that can be imagined are not proof against the abuses of self-dealing. In the words of my task force report, assurance that self-dealing will not arise in situations of closely-held ownership requires two acts of faith: the first, in the integrity of controlling owners and the second, in the capacity of regulators to ensure that self-dealing prohibitions are in fact enforced. More than enough incidents have yielded more than enough evidence to tell us that these acts of faith rest on foundations that are anything but robust (Dupré 1986. p. F.31).

This, then, is the case for the likelihood of abusive self-dealing in situations where there is majority ownership and a co-mingling of the real and financial. There is clearly something to these concerns.

For their part, the conglomerates and narrowly-held institutions recognize the problems with abusive self-dealing, but they obviously do not share the above analysis or solutions. Again, the Genstar brief is probably the most effective in terms of presenting an alternative viewpoint and approach:

> Self-dealing is not a danger which only exists in, or because of, closely-held institutions. Every corporation has dominant individuals who exercise effective or significant control over its

activities, whether it is closely or widely held. A closely-held corporation is ultimately subject to effective control by a major shareholder or its representatives, while a widely-held corporation may be effectively controlled by its senior management or some combination of management and directors (Genstar 1986, p. 12).

Not surprisingly, one aspect of the conglomerates counter-attack is to focus on examples of self-dealing involving management and directors of widely-held institutions. Although the following section focuses in more detail on directors, it is instructive to reproduce some of Genstar's (1986) concerns in the present context:

A 1977 study by the Conference Board in Canada found that the directors of banks (the quintessential widely-held financial institution) felt they received their appointments to directorships because:

banks have traditionally reserved the seats on their boards for top executives (or representatives of wealthy families) in the expectation of attracting or keeping them as customers, and in the hope that their names will serve as prestigious advertisements and they themselves as ambassadors for the bank, and thereby attract further business.

In 1978, the Royal Commission on Corporate Concentration found that this disposition to appoint directors for the purpose of attracting business led to a type of self-dealing. It stated, respecting bank boards, that:

These boards are composed largely of the chief executives of major corporations that are customers of the bank (though not necessarily of only that bank), and that will usually borrow from that bank. Another element of the board is usually composed of leading members of legal firms who serve the bank in various parts of Canada. To some degree, therefore, most members of the board have important business relations with the bank in addition to their fiduciary duties as directors. Inevitably this creates the possibility of a conflict of interest, collective as well as individual, where the directors' obligations to the bank may clash with their duties elsewhere.

Not to be outdone by the CBA brief, Genstar (1986, pp. 13-15) also details briefly several examples of self-dealing by widely-held institutions — the takeover of Union Enterprises Ltd., the Standard Investments Limited case, and the CCB.

Hal Jackman of Empire Life takes this argument somewhat further:

> The proposition that concentrated ownership is a primary cause of failure of a financial institution is a most unusual view and only in Canada does this extraordinary thesis gain some currency. In the United States and other western countries, a strong shareholder presence has always been encouraged as an added protection for depositors and as a means to ensure management accountability. In fact in our neighbour to the south 'mutual' savings banks which are owned by their depositors are being encouraged by government to become 'stock' companies for these very reasons.
>
> Although, as many studies in the U.S. have pointed out, 'self-dealing' by directors and management have contributed to an alarmingly large number of failures, no correlation can be shown between those failures caused by improper managers and directors and those with significant shareholder interest. In fact many of the failures attributed to 'self-dealing' involved mutual companies where there were no shareholders at all.
>
> In Canada, the evidence to support the view that shareholders are a primary cause of failure is far from convincing.
>
> The Federal Superintendent of Insurance, Mr. Robert Hammond, in his 1985 testimony before the House of Commons Finance Committee, outlined the causes for failure of 11 federal financial institutions since 1980. Only in the Greymac-Seaway fiasco was self-dealing by owners the cause of the default. A report prepared for the Chairman of the Economic Council of Canada expanded the list to include provincial failures. Of the 21 companies named, only in the Greymac-Seaway group of companies and the Continental Trust could self-dealing by owners be considered the cause of the failure although in a number of other cases, self-dealing by officers and directors, but *not* shareholders, could be considered the proximate cause of default. To this list we must add the two widely held western banks which failed and where director self-dealing was in evidence.
>
> Similarly as Mr. Justice Hughes pointed out in his excellent report on the Atlantic Acceptance and British Mortgage failures in the 1960's, self-dealing by officers and directors, not shareholders, was the cause of the failure of those two companies.
>
> In summary, the whole subject of widely held versus closely held is not capable of sweeping generalizations as it affects solvency. Of course there may be weak owners as we have seen in the Crown Trust-Greymac affair of a few years ago. However there can

equally be self-dealing by directors and management in the absence of control by strong shareholders. It is simply impossible to state what shareholder configuration is appropriate in every case (Jackman 1986, pp. 5-7).

The conglomerates' bottom line on ownership and self-dealing is probably effectively captured by the summary position of Genstar:

> To believe that self-dealing will be eliminated by domestic ownership limitations is illusory. Self-dealing can be controlled more effectively and at a lower cost by alternative means. These alternative means include statutory prohibitions [i.e., self-dealing bans], improved supervisory powers for regulators, enhanced public disclosure, improved internal control mechanisms, increased standards of care owed to a financial institution by its directors, and increased responsibilities for third-party advisors to monitor and report instances of self-dealing (Genstar 1986, p. 11).

To this list of alternative approaches many advocates of the position that there should be no ownership requirements would require that the regulators apply a "reputation" test to any potential owners. However, short of focusing on objective criteria, like the existence of a criminal record, it is not clear how such a test would be, or could be, applied.

(b) Directors and Self-Dealing: The Jackman brief to the Ontario Legislature Committee states:

> The term self-dealing or 'related party transactions' is commonly used to refer to transactions between a deposit taking institution and its shareholders. However it is much broader than that and refers to transactions involving the use of depositors' funds with any person, whether he be a major shareholder, officer or director or employee who has a fiduciary responsibility in respect to those funds. . . .
>
> Unfortunately, at present there are no meaningful self-dealing provisions in the Bank Act. Loans to directors of banks are so commonplace that it is generally conceded that the prime requirement for membership on a bank board is the fact that he or she is affiliated with a substantial customer. [Note that the existing trust legislation does not allow directors to be significant customers of the institution — T.J.C.]
>
> I am not suggesting for one moment that the directors of large banks are in any way dishonest. However a director of any deposit taking institution must take an 'even handed' view in determining his responsibilities to both depositors and borrowers. This may not always be an easy task. For a depositor is interested in the highest possible return consistent with safety. The

borrower, on the other hand, is interested in receiving the greatest amount of money at the lowest possible rate. These views are prima facie in conflict. It is therefore the responsibility of the director to take an even hand in assessing his responsibilities. If you have a banking system where the board of directors are almost entirely made up of management and large borrowers, without any shareholder or depositor accountability, it becomes difficult to ensure that depositor protection may not be sacrificed to imprudent lending. This is what has happened in Canada with director-related loans such as Dome Petroleum and Massey-Ferguson.

This issue goes to the root of governance and control of any financial institution. How can a director effectively judge management if he is beholden to management for a loan? Similarly how can management refuse a loan to a person who is in a position to judge his performance? If self-dealing and conflict of interest rules are appropriate for the trust companies, surely they should also be for the banks.

One further point on the matter of directors' loans. I have outlined the danger that exists when a large financial institution's board of directors is dominated by large corporate borrowers. Not only does the lending institution risk favouring the borrower over the depositor, but the presence of these men may very well have an effect on how credit is allocated among the various parties who compete for loans. [This relates to the issue of "bias" discussed earlier — T.J.C.]

It is difficult for a small businessman in a small town in Ontario to understand why huge amounts of money are lent to conglomerates to help finance takeover bids, when his own line of credit is limited to financing receivables and inventory. Trust companies, loan companies and credit unions do not finance takeover bids. Nor do they make loans to South American governments. The trust and loan industry therefore desires expanded commercial lending powers from the Province of Ontario and from Ottawa so that it can fill the gap in this allocation of credit (Jackman 1986, pp. 9-11).

What the reader is probably intended to conclude from Jackman's comments is that the trust companies, even if they are narrowly held, are by the nature of their business *and* their boards of directors more sensitive to the needs of their depositors and borrowers. But these are my words, not Jackman's.

New Directions responds to these concerns by requiring that at least one-third of the directors of financial institutions meet stringent criteria establishing their independence of the financial institution.[5] Moreover, the audit and corporate governance committees must consist solely of these independent directors. However, in what can only be described as an aberration, *New Directions* requires cumulative voting for directors only for narrowly-held institutions. (With cumulative voting for 25 directors, a shareholding of 4 per cent would be ensured of electing one director. Note that such directors might well qualify as independent directors.) On this issue I support Diane Francis who says that:

> Cumulative voting should be required .... Currently, dissatisfied shareholders are powerless to secure representation on a board unless they put up a complete slate of their own and undertake an expensive proxy fight. Bank boards ... should not include the bank's largest customers (Francis 1986, pp. 325-26).

Despite this concession, the CBA reaction to *New Directions* as it relates to independent directors appears to be extremely negative. The CBA (1987, p. 30) states that the proposals relating to independent directors are a "source of major concern" to the banking industry and that a more detailed evaluation of their concerns will shortly be communicated to the federal government. Now that reference has been made to the CBA reaction to *New Directions*, it is convenient to focus on three other CBA concerns relating to the ownership provisions of the federal position paper.

(c) The CBA and Ownership: In general the CBA welcomes the initiatives in *New Directions* that move the system toward wide ownership. However, the CBA's view is that in at least three areas these initiatives do not go far enough. The first relates to the provision whereby commercial interests will not necessarily be precluded from acquiring or increasing positions in existing trust, loan and insurance companies with capital below $50 million (Hockin 1986, p. 17). Although the CBA recognizes that the intent here was to introduce this exception only for emergency situations (e.g., to save a faltering institution), the CBA (1987, p. 25) recommends that this provision be removed.

The second relates to the grandfathering provisions for narrowly-held, commercially-linked firms. Under the current interpretation, it appears that if a commercial shareholder has 50 per cent of the shares of a financial institution, such a shareholder could maintain this proportion, i.e., take 50 per cent of any new share issue. The CBA preference would be to preclude majority shareholders from acquiring any additional shares until the ownership level falls to 10 per cent. Actually, the CBA goes much further here, repeating its earlier position that the government pursue a policy of active divestiture over a five-year period for any majority shareholdings in financial institutions. According to its estimates, this would require unloading $3.5 billion in shares — less than 6 per cent of TSE equity trading in 1986 and roughly 1 per cent if spread out over five years (CBA 1987, p. 27).

The CBA's third point relates to the provision whereby narrowly-held ownership without financial links will be allowed up to a capital threshold of $750 million (or roughly $15 billion of assets). While the CBA believes that it is appropriate to be more lenient with respect to non-commercially -linked narrow ownership, it also believes that the $750 million capital threshold should be dropped to $250 million. Basically the argument has to do with the interaction between narrow ownership and deposit insurance. With full insurance up to $60,000 there is an incentive for owners of a financial institution to take excessive risk. If the venture fails, the depositors are bailed out by the CDIC. If the gamble pays off, then the majority shareholder pockets the winnings. To minimize such incentives, the CBA recommends (a) lowering the capital threshold from $750 to $250 million, (b) introducing some element of co-insurance in the operations of the CDIC, and (c) establishing separate CDIC "pools."

Note that these latter two recommendations were embodied in the Senate (Murray) report on Deposit Insurance (1985). In order not to unduly exhibit new entry, the Senate's proposal involved full insurance for the first $25,000 and then 20 per cent co-insurance (i.e., 80 per cent CDIC insurance) thereafter up to a total of $75,000. The idea behind the concept of pools (one for the banks, one for the trusts, and one for each of the credit unions and the insurance companies if they wished to be covered by CDIC) was that losses in any of the pools would have to be financed by other institutions in the same pool. In this way, there would be an enhanced incentive for all trust companies, for example, to ensure that the regulatory agencies responsible for the trusts were doing an effective job, because they would be saddled with covering any CDIC losses arising from a trust company failure.

In general, I believe that the CBA is correct when it asserts that the interaction of narrow ownership up to $750 million capital and full CDIC coverage up to $60,000 does provide an incentive for excessive risk-taking, if not self-dealing. The question that arises, however, is whether the fact that the authorities refuse to alter CDIC implies that narrow ownership must be sharply curtailed. Actually, the real incentive for taking advantage of the CDIC arises when the institution is *already* in trouble so that there is little or no equity left. Here excessive risk-taking is costless (unless it involves fraud, etc.) since the value of the equity is already zero. It is precisely for the reason that the Wyman Report (1985), the Blenkarn Report (1985), the Murray Reports (1985, 1986), the Dupré Report (1985), and the Economic Council of Canada (1987) all argued for an "early warning system" that would alert the regulators on a timely basis to any problems besetting the institution. The ECC (1987, Figure 4.2) report suggests a series of components that might be included in such an early warning system. e.g., items relating to capital adequacy, liquidity, asset quality, profitability and management performance. To this list I would add that there be a careful monitoring of the level of and rates paid for brokered deposits which have tended to be a leading indicator of impending financial institution trouble. Unfortunately, *New Directions* does not appear to place much emphasis on the development of an early warning system. However, one hopes that the regulators themselves will find it appropriate to implement such a system.

Nonetheless, some aspects of the CBA concern here will be reflected in the compromise proposals in the concluding section of this paper.

(d)   Recapitulation: The potential for abusive self-dealing is present in virtually all financial institutions and is a valid concern. There is no

question that widely-held ownership can effectively eliminate both the ability of, and incentive for, owners to self-deal. However, there is also no question that with dispersed or widely-held ownership, an incentive is generated for officer- or director-related self-dealing. This is the point of much of Jackman's comments. In Chapter 14 of this volume McFetridge makes a similar point:

> In the case of dispersed ownership, excessively risky loans may be made to officers and directors. The latter benefit if the investments so financed succeed. If they fail, the losses are imposed on the shareholders and, if the losses are sufficient, on depositors, deposit insurance and other creditors.

Hence, it is hard to escape the conclusion that the combination of independent directors, corporate governance procedures, cumulative voting and, in general, the application of trust-company-type restrictions on directors are appropriate for all financial institutions. And in order to control owner-related self-dealing some combination of ownership restrictions and self-dealing bans are probably desirable.

McFetridge (Chapter 14 in this volume) proposes a further method for controlling the potential for damaging self-dealing, namely reducing the maximum leverage ratio:

> The essential point is that, from the standpoint of depositors safety, a closely held or concentrated majority intermediary may be equivalent to a widely-held intermediary with a higher maximum leverage ratio. Indeed, this thinking appears to be reflected in the array of leverage ratios presently imposed on deposit-taking intermediaries. Banks which are widely-held are generally allowed higher leverage ratios (between 20:1 and 30:1) than trust companies (12 1/2:1, higher with permission).

McFetridge adds, however, that for widely-held institutions this would have to be accompanied by some prohibitions on the transactions between the intermediary and officers and directors, since altered gearing ratios do not affect the incentives for management self-dealing.

To conclude this section it seems appropriate to refer yet again to the excellent paper by McFetridge. The issue in question relates to the role that a 35 per cent minority shareholding (widely held) can have on the behaviour of a financial institution. The rationale in the Murray Report (1986) for a 35 per cent widely-held float included the following:

- it is sufficient to prevent a restructuring of the corporation that would be inimical to the minority shareholders since two-thirds of shareholders must agree to any restructuring under the *Canada Business Corporations Act*.

-   it would enhance disclosure and would represent a significant enough float to attract attention from investment analysts.

-   it would enhance in the operations of internal corporate governance, particularly if cumulative voting for directors were required.

-   it would allow Canadians to own equity in their financial institutions.

McFetridge adds a further point with respect to a 35 per cent float:

> The question is whether a compromise such as the proposed requirement that trust, loan and insurance companies have at least 35 per cent of their voting shares widely held has any merit. An initial reaction is that it does not reduce either the incentive or the ability of the controlling (inside) interest to self-deal. Indeed it increases it. Insiders have even greater leverage being able to impose their losses on depositors, deposit insurance, other creditors and on the outside minority.

> In anticipation of this, however, the demand price for minority shares will involve a considerable discount from their value to the majority. Thus, the cost of insider self-dealing is effectively internalized. Insiders will take whatever steps they can to assure the potential outside minority that it will not be among the victims of insider self-dealing. It will be in the interest of insiders to push this guarantee process up to the point at which the cost of the guarantees provided is just equal to the increase in the price which outsiders are willing to offer for a minority interest. Of course, protection for the outside minority is also protection for depositors and shareholders. Thus, the requirement that closely held intermediaries sell a minority interest to outsiders effectively forces the majority interest to take additional measures at its own expense to protect depositors and other creditors (see Chapter 14 of this volume).

Therefore, from my vantage point the bottom line to all of this is the following. If there were no costs to limiting ownership, then the concern over self-dealing might justify the imposition of a 10 per cent ownership provision. But the thrust of this paper is that there are very substantial costs. Hence, alternative approaches must be found to prevent abusive self-dealing. Not only do such alternative approaches exist, they are also likely to be very effective. Nonetheless, it is my view that, for reasons outlined above, some degree of wide ownership is also warranted.

The Federal Reserve (Corrigan) Approach: If one engages in a discussion of *New Directions* with a representative of a chartered bank, the conversation will not get very far along before the "Corrigan Report" comes up. This is the recent position paper *Financial Market Structure: A Longer View* authored by E. Gerald Corrigan, President of the Federal Reserve Bank of New York. It is a wide ranging document on the future of U.S.

Thomas J. Courchene **555**

banking regulation and it presumably has the approval of Federal Reserve Chairman Paul Volker. What appeals to Canadian chartered bankers is the document's approach to the intermingling of commerce and banking. Essentially, *The Longer View* argues in favour of "moving in the direction of a more uniform and integrated approach to the operation of the banking *and* financial system [i.e., integration of the pillars] while still preserving the distinction between "banking and the remainder of the economy" (Corrigan 1987, p. 22).

The core of the argument is two-fold. First, "If there are substantial economic benefits from linking banking and commercial enterprises, then efforts to achieve that separation by regulation would, almost certainly, fail or, if somewhat successful, would remove the very economic incentives for such combinations in the first instance" (Corrigan 1987, p. 25). Implicitly, if not explicitly, this suggests that the commercial side is interested in the financial side *only* because of what it can gain from such things as concentration of assets, market power, self-dealing and the like. Hence, it would appear to rule out or ignore other reasons, such as seeking a higher rate of return on capital, portfolio diversification, arm's-length networking and synergy, and even comparative advantage, defined for example by a computer firm having an ownership stake in a financial institution in order to obtain hands-on knowledge and information relating to emerging computational needs and developments in the financial sector. Nonetheless, the Corrigan approach is probably the correct one if regulators are unable to prevent the abusive self-dealing that can arise from a co-mingling of the commercial and financial.

Corrigan's second point is that it is difficult to see how the financial part of such a commercial-financial entity can have a call on official sources of liquidity and capital unless, at the very least, the authorities have some supervisory influence over the entity as a whole. Corrigan elaborates as follows:

> the affiliates find it difficult to disavow each other or their parents and vice-versa in times of stress. This tendency seems to reflect at least two major considerations. First, when one part of a financial entity has problems, the marketplace generally attributes those problems to the entity as a whole; and, second, when the great intangible - public confidence - is so central to the "going concern" value of the enterprise, overt decisions to "cut and run" simply do not come easily. Strength surely begets strength, but weakness even more surely begets weakness (Corrigan 1987, p. 25).

This is not a new point since it has been raised earlier in the analysis, but it has been stated here with more effect. The earlier comment that part of the answer is to ensure that there is a financial holding company between the commercial and financial side has presumably been found wanting by the New York Fed. More correctly, it has not been addressed.

Corrigan (1987, p. 27) concludes by noting that the entire issue "really comes down to a debate as to what kind of risks do we, as a nation, want to incur as a matter of public policy."

An "official" response was not long in coming. Representative Doug Barnard (Democrat, Georgia), Chairman of the House Subcommittee on Commerce, Consumer and Monetary Affairs challenges Corrigan's views on the separation of banking and commerce. (Predictably, the title of his "op ed' piece in *The Wall Street Journal* is "Wrong-Way Corrigan"!) Barnard (1987) makes several points. The first is probably the most important, namely that while Corrigan's position paper is generally excellent, his view on ownership is the one element that "appears to be derived more from customary Federal Reserve doctrine than from fresh creative thought."

Second, Barnard challenges the blueprint's claim that there is no feasible scheme of legal constraints and/or regulation that can effectively insulate an insured bank or thrift institution from financial abuse if it is owned by a commercial/industrial firm. Without going into detail, Barnard's conclusion here is that "if we want tough regulation of financial holding companies, we can get it, no matter who owns them."

Barnard's next point is more telling. Noting that the integration of the pillars (i.e., the striking down of *The Glass-Steagall Act*) will open up situations where bad loans on the books of banks will provide an incentive to off-load these via an underwriting of securities, Barnard asks if the provisions that will be put in place to control this type of activity are not very similar to those that would also be required to control the commercial/financial linkage. It should be noted that this issue has really not been addressed in the various briefs that serve as the "raw material" for the analysis in this paper. In large measure this is a result of the fact that it was not until December 1986 that both Ontario and Ottawa opened up the securities industry to 100 per cent ownership by Canadian financial institutions. Two comments appear relevant. First, it seems apparent at first blush that the potential conflicts of interest or self-dealing problems of a Molson's owning a securities firm are much more easily kept in check than the problems that would arise with a dominant commercial lending institution owning a securities firm. This point has recently been effectively made by Ontario Securities Commission Chairman Stanley Beck (1987). Second, I think Barnard is basically correct in suggesting (albeit indirectly) that effectively policing this latter conflict of interest is going to be every bit as difficult as policing the commercial-financial overlap. In the Canadian context, it is worthwhile noting that so far several conglomerates have decided not to enter the securities core, whereas all major banks appear to be moving in.

The final substantive argument in the Barnard piece is that it is not possible to draw a clean line between commerce and banking in light of the proliferation of financial instruments in recent years. Keeping the commercial/industrial firms out of the banking club will simply mean that they will offer their quasi-banking services in other ways. It is highly unlikely that the clock will be turned back on the development of "in-house" or corporate banking. There are two main areas where even medium-sized corporations can take on a banking role:

First, they can develop the expertise and systems to replace financial advise previously bought from the banks, and deal with those banks on a more equal footing. Second, asset and liability management can be turned into a profitable activity (Crabbe 1986, p. 28).

Moreover, the big corporations are major players in the world's financial markets. B.P. Financial raised nearly a billion dollars in the Eurobond market in 1985, utilizing a sophisticated range of financial instruments and currencies. General Motors Acceptance Corporation (GMAC) is one of the leaders in the securitization of car loans, although to date it does this through a securities firm. General Electric Credit Corporation eliminated this securities link by recently acquiring Kidder Peabody. These activities are presumably not as well developed in most large Canadian corporations, but it is only a matter of time before they will emerge. One domestic development that merits attention, however, is the networking between Provigo and the National Bank to install "debit cards" in Provigo stores. These are effectively money cards since a customer can debit his account for $100 for a $65 grocery bill and take the $35 in change. Is Petro-Canada next? We are just beginning to see the explosion of such financial activities in the commercial sector. The underlying thrust of the Corrigan Report, and *New Directions* for that matter, to the effect that we can hive off financial activities into a few institutions and generate a complete break between financial and commercial ignores the existing, let along the emerging, reality. In Barnard's (1987) view, it is preferable to encourage the commercial/industrial firms with financial expertise and ambitions to pursue these ambitions as banking-system insiders (and, hence, regulated) rather than as outsiders. Hence he concludes that the qualifications for bank ownership "ought to be set in functional and operational terms (sufficient capital, capable management, etc.) rather than in terms of the prospective owner's 'parentage' ".

Thus, while chartered bankers may take comfort from the views of the Federal Reserve, about the most that can be said on this issue is that the U.S. is also undergoing a rethinking of ownership provisions – except, of course, that it is Congress and not the Fed that will do the legislating! This completes the survey of some of the principal arguments in favour of widely-held ownership of financial institutions. Although the counterarguments from the narrowly-held perspective were generally included in the above analysis, there also exists a set of propositions that are frequently offered to buttress the position that financial institutions should be allowed to be majority held. To these I now turn.

4.2 Arguments for Narrow Ownership
Historically and Competition-Wise, Majority-Held Institutions Have Served Canada Well: *New Directions* itself recognizes this: "each form [of

ownership] brings its own strengths, both now exist and have served Canadians well: Neither is inherently better than the other" (Hockin 1986, p. 15). This is particularly the case in recent years. Not only have the non-bank, deposit-taking institutions, many of which are majority held, been the source of much of the innovation in both service and financial instruments but Canadians have sufficient confidence in them that they have grown more quickly than the banks. Unless one wants to entertain the notion that Canadian consumers are somehow dumb or being misled, it seems to me that this is evidence enough that narrowly-held institutions are meeting the needs and desires of Canadians.

Wide Ownership was Designed to Ensure Canadian Control of Banks, Not to Deter Self-Dealing: Until well into the post-war period, there were no ownership limitations on Canadian financial institutions. Indeed, it is instructive to recall that the introduction of the provision whereby banks were required to be widely held had little or nothing to do with minimizing conflicts of interest or abusive self-dealing. Rather, the rationale was to counter the possibility that foreign banks, particularly U.S. banks, might attempt to gain control of the chartered banks. The combination of the 10 per cent rule and the requirement that in the aggregate foreigners could not hold more than 25 per cent of bank shares (i.e., the so-called 10/25 provision) ensured that the banks would remain in Canadian hands. Indeed, the policy in favour of mutualizing insurance companies arose for the same reasons.

In this light, it is more than a little ironic that the Lloyds Bank takeover of the Continental Bank and the Hong Kong and Shanghai Bank takeover of the Bank of British Columbia (through the Hong Kong Bank of Canada) received Ottawa's blessing. Presumably what prevented Canadian financial institutions (except perhaps for the mutuals) from qualifying as eligible purchasers were the domestic ownership provisions relating to banking. Moreover, the government's acceptance of Lloyds as a purchaser lends credence to the earlier suggestion that the Schedule B's will eventually be viewed as "financially linked" rather than "commercially linked," so that their capital threshold for triggering the 35 per cent publicly traded float is $750 million rather than $50 million. *In other words, while the introduction of the 10 per cent rule was designed to prevent foreign ownership of banks, in the current context of dealing with troubled banks it is serving to preclude domestic ownership!* Personally, I find this unacceptable – not the fact that the Hong Kong and Shanghai Bank should take over the Bank of British Columbia but rather that many Canadian-owned financial institutions were deemed to be ineligible suitors.

Obviously, the fact that the original rationale for wide ownership was not related directly to self-dealing concerns need not diminish the force of such an argument in the current time frame. Nonetheless, it is important to remember why wide ownership was introduced in the first place.

Ownership Provisions World-Wide are Not the Norm: A further point that merits emphasis is that the absence of ownership restrictions on non-bank financial intermediaries is the norm across the industrialized world.

Indeed, in a recent CLHIA questionnaire sent to various foreign jurisdictions, none of the *jurisdictions that have responded thus far have in place ownership limitations of the sort proposed by New Directions.* The preliminary results of this questionnaire appears as Appendix A to this paper.

One can imagine many areas where what the rest of the world is doing may be quite irrelevant. However, the financial services sector is surely not one of these areas if the principal implication is to reduce the inflow of domestic capital to this key sector.

Majority-Owned Firms are Better Directed: Time and again the issue that seemed to consume the members of the Ontario Standing Committee on Finance and Economic Affairs related to the impact of a major shareholder on boards of directors. What does a major shareholder bring to a board? Leadership? Entrepreneurship? Accountability? Sheer power? Beyond some initial observations that tended to emphasize the merits of having majority shareholders on these boards, the representatives of narrowly-held institutions found this to be a delicate question. They had no desire to impune the boards of widely-held institutions, but at the same time they were groping for ways to impress the committee of the merits of majority ownership. The following excerpt from the remarks of Allen Lambert, Chairman of Trilon Financial Corporation, is probably typical:

> In Canada the boards of most big corporations are drawn from across the country with wide geographic representation, and that is as it certainly should be. But that also means that it is a fairly loose association. They are not seeing each other on a regular basis, other than perhaps . . . at board meeting times . . . I have worked with the board of a bank, and it was a very good board and a board of 40-plus at times, but from all parts of Canada, and there was not much leadership amongst the board as such.

> I think a major shareholder brings some leadership to the board. He probably (and the representatives of the major shareholder) would be in the minority, but nevertheless if they sense something is going wrong, they would be the catalyst to start to take some action with the other directors.

> I think it is like a caucus. You have got to have some group that is really going to get things moving, . . . I think we all know of instances of widely held corporations where change was clearly needed but it took a while for the board to really come to grips with it. And that is understandable because no one wants to really be the initiator of something unpleasant, and we tend to often go along with these things; whereas a major shareholder is so much at risk himself that he is less inclined to go along with something that is not right or that is unpleasant. And so he will be the catalyst to bring it to the attention of the whole board and, through the whole board, work for change (Lambert 1986, p. F.11).

In his prepared remarks, however, Lambert effectively proposes an alternative way to compare the performance of financial institutions:

> When evaluating financial institutions, overall performance should, I think, also come into play. Not one Canadian bank ranks among the top 50 banks around the world in terms of return on assets and return on equity, two important performance measurements. Royal Trust, by comparison, achieved in 1985 a return on assets higher than any Canadian bank, and second highest among all North American banks and trust companies, and had the highest return on equity (Lambert 1986, p. F.4).

Brascan's Trevor Eyton takes this point one stage further:

> Royal Trustco shares traded in the market at about three times book value. Five or six of the chartered banks in Canada - we are now talking about the major banks - trade at less than book value. I will ask you a question. Why is it that Royal Trustco shares trade at something like three times the basic price of the share of the chartered banks? I think one of the reasons is our concern for shareholder values, and with it implications for ongoing good financial health for our financial institutions (Eyton 1986, p. F.6).

One can, of course, read too much into these and other similar statements by representatives of majority-owned firms. Nonetheless, it does seem evident that majority-owner representation in boards of directors can have a substantial positive impact on an institution's performance. Certainly, there is nothing here that would lead to the conclusion that the boards of widely-held institutions are preferable and, therefore, nothing in the way of an argument for forcing financial institutions to be widely held. Indeed, just the opposite. I now turn to a closely related issue, the market for corporate control.

The Market for Corporate Control: The Genstar brief states:

> The market for corporate control, or the possibility that a widely-held corporation may be acquired by a major shareholder, exerts a strong disciplinary influence on the management of widely-held corporations. If management becomes inefficient or begins appropriating corporate assets to itself, the corporation will become an enticing target for take-over. The new owner could replace incumbent management and realize a significant increase in returns.

> Domestic ownership limitations on Canadian financial institutions would eliminate the market for corporate control and remove an important check on the activities of the management of widely-held financial institutions (Genstar 1986, p. 29).

This point is supported by Calvin Goldman, Director of Investigation and Research, *Competition Act,* of Consumer and Corporate Affairs Canada:

> While implementation of a *Bank Act* model requiring widely-held or dispersed ownership may be effective in preventing self-dealing abuses arising from non-arm's-length transactions, it does eliminate one very important mechanism for ensuring the efficient operation of financial institutions, namely the market for corporate control. The potential for change in shareholder control of a corporation may act as an effective incentive for efficient managerial behaviour and as a removal mechanism for inefficient management (Goldman 1986, p. 21).

As an important aside, Goldman argues that both traditional approaches to controlling abusive NALTs, namely wide ownership and rigid bans on self-dealing, are too extreme and that "further work is required to explore viable alternatives" (*Ibid.,* p. 22). I concur and shall return to this point in the concluding section.

Back to the central issue. In the historical industrial organization literature relating to the development of the "modern" corporation (i.e., the separation of ownership from management), the market for corporate control represented the principal avenue by which this development was tied to market efficiency. The market for takeovers or more generally the ability to acquire sufficient equity so as to discipline management was viewed as the key to reconciling what in modern jargon is called the "principal-agent" problem. However, mandatory ownership limits eliminate this possibility and, in terms of market efficiency, effectively undermine the rationale for widely-held institutions.

It is important to note, however, that Canadians can still send a message of sorts to their chartered banks by unloading bank shares. But even this avenue is precluded for the mutuals.

The issue can be addressed from a different vantage point: how many heads have rolled as a result of the banks' enormous loan losses and non-performing loans? Canadians can be excused for being somewhat cynical of their banks when they see their neighbour foreclosed and at the same time witness the pomp and circumstance by which one generation of bankers anoints the next. Paraphrasing Trevor Eyton only slightly (1986, p. F.4): "it is clear that 10 per cent ownership limits are fantastic for bankers, it is far from clear that they are good for banks!"

Conflict of Cultures: Commercial vs. Investment Banking: As the Canadian securities industry prepares for the "big bang," the street talk has tended to centre around the question of whether one of the big banks will purchase a major securities firm. Actually, the issue is frequently put the other way around — will a major securities firm be willing to associate itself with a large bank? While there are many variables that enter this equation, the "cultural clash" is one of the most prominent. In the extreme, the commercial banking culture is passive, hierarchical and surely fits well within the traditional "management culture" of Canadian chartered banks. Again in the extreme, investment banking culture is pro-active, entrepreneurial and more consistent with the partnership (non-hierarchical) approach of many of the securities firms. More importantly, the clear trend, world-wide, is away from commercial banking and toward investment banking.

The Naisbitt Group (1986, p. 30) of *Megatrends* fame and among the world's leading trend analysts, confirms this view: "As more companies aggressively work both sides of the balance sheet in combinations of debt and equity, they will come to require fewer services of commercial banks." The Group also states that

> Commercial banks may be hindered by their operating culture. 'Qualities that make you a good commercial banker, such as caution, conservative decision making, and unwillingness to deviate from consensus, would make a failure of an investment banker,' comments James Rawlings II, Managing Director, Drexel Burnham Lambert, Inc. Moreover, corporate clients perceive commercial bankers as a source of funds rather than confidential advice. Most corporate financial officers view commercial banks as too conservative in an age of aggressive financial innovation. Anthony de George, Chief Financial Officer of Grace Geothermal Corporation, states that his company uses commercial banks 'only for checking, money market accounts, and temporary deposits for excess cash. For our long-term financing needs, we turn to investment banks . . . the level of competence [of commercial banks] and the way they are structured makes them less attractive than investment banks' (Naisbitt Group 1986, p. 22).

The point at issue here is not to come down against the chartered banks. Indeed, in recent articles I have argued that the banks must be allowed to enter the securities core (Courchene 1986a, 1986b). Moreover, I am confident that they can make the transition and accommodate any differences in corporate cultures: they have no choice if they want to follow their customers.

Rather, the point is to question why Canada is on the verge of precluding the corporate form that would appear to be most suited to the trend toward investment banking. The issue here is not so much one of whether Power Financial should have the same freedom to maneuver as the banks. It probably has more to do with allowing new entrants to move into the financial sector to market new products or to exploit profitable niches.

Quite frankly I am concerned about the longer-term future of the Canadian financial services industry if the domestic participants are required to be management-driven (widely-held institutions plus the mutuals) leaving the foreigners to be the source of owner-driven institutions.

Market Contestability: Finally, the analysis has come full circle. The rationale for re-assessing the ownership controversy derived from the fact that *New Directions* does not score well in terms of new entry, at least for domestic institutions. One of the arguments in favour of more liberal regulations pertaining to majority ownership is to facilitate new entry and, hence, market contestability.

Surprisingly, the Genstar brief is one of the few that focuses on this critical issue, although in the wake of *New Directions* this will surely change. The brief notes:

> Contestability of financial service markets is determined by barriers to entry (and exit) in the industry. The potential of entry helps to ensure competition, increase efficiency and prevent any competitive abuses that could result from market power. Competition from abroad also serves to enhance the degree of competition in Canadian financial markets . . .
>
> Barriers to entry may be structural or regulatory. . . . The Director convincingly argued that 'the onus should be on regulators to clearly demonstrate the need for maintaining regulations which restrain contestability of markets . . .'
>
> Domestic ownership limitations will reduce contestability further. Achievement of optimal size, either by new entry or by acquisition, will be made more difficult if concentrated shareholdings are not permitted (Genstar 1986, pp. 22-23).

The Blenkarn Committee also recognized the role that majority ownership can play in the new entry process. I shall have more to say about the details of the Blenkarn recommendations on ownership later. For now, the following passage is relevant:

> This risk of self-dealing, however, has to be offset against the benefit of having a strong major shareholder that could provide financial support to a financial institution during its initial formative period and on an ongoing basis especially during periods of economic adversity. A widely-held ownership structure makes it difficult for new or small financial institutions to raise capital under these conditions. Perhaps less restrictive ownership limits in the banking sector could have alleviated the recent difficulties experienced by small regional banks in Canada. Indeed, evidence presented before the Committee favouring closely-held ownership cited the benefits of this type of ownership structure in the formation of 'de novo' institutions and during the initial growth period for institutions when a widely-held ownership structure could otherwise make it difficult for a small and developing institution to raise additional capital for expansion. It was pointed out, for example by Atlantic Trust, that a major shareholder could have a greater interest and ability to provide additional capital for a fledgling institution especially

during periods of adversity (House of Commons Standing Committee on Finance, Trade & Economic Affairs 1985, p. 53).

In his (somewhat surprising) appearance before the Ontario Standing Committee, Blenkarn carries this notion further. In the passage that follows, he is responding to a question about the importance of self-dealing in many of the recent failures. After making the point that bad management was probably more important than self-dealing he notes:

> I think the banks' suggestion that it was totally a matter of self-dealing is an effort to maintain the 10 per cent rule of ownership, which I do not think has served us well in small institutions. In very large institutions it is important that there be widespread ownership, but small institutions need a godfather to look after them.

> That was particularly so, as pointed out to us, with respect to Atlantic Trust in the Maritimes in the course of collapse. The Misener family has a major interest in that trust company and has managed to turn it around. It is now profitable . . . Why? They own pretty well the whole thing. They can afford to put in a chunk of fresh capital to get it straightened around.

> In our view a small institution is well served by a major shareholder who has something to gain by its success and is, therefore, prepared to do more than normal to make it grow. I suspect that the problems we had with the Northland and the CCB would not have been there had those banks had major shareholders. They would not have got into some of the bad deals and they would not have expanded as rapidly as they did. I am not at all convinced that the 10 per cent rule is important for self dealing (House of Commons Standing Committee on finance, Trade and Economic Affairs 1986, p. F.15).

As will be detailed later, the Blenkarn Committee's compromise was to allow wholly-owned financial institutions up to a threshold of $10 billion in assets and thereafter to require graduate dilution according a sliding scale which would generate 10 per cent ownership after $40 billion in assets. From his above comment, however, it would appear that the rationale for the sliding scale has more to do with concentration, writ large, than with concerns about self-dealing.

This completes our analysis of the pros and cons of the ownership controversy. Prior to moving to the concluding section and some compromise proposals, it is important to focus in more detail on internal corporate governance and its potential for controlling abusive self-dealing.

5.0 INTERNAL CORPORATE GOVERNANCE

The Blenkarn Report (1985), The Murray (Senate) Report (1986) and *New Directions* (Hockin 1986) all place considerable emphasis on internal corporate governance as an essential ingredient in monitoring NALTs. Focusing for the present on the Murray Report recommendations (because I am more familiar with them), the proposal for monitoring NALTs consisted of three tiers. The first is a selective ban on certain NALTS which by their very nature can be solvency threatening. The second tier is an internal "Business Conduct Review Committee" (BCRC), composed of independent directors, that will pre-screen all NALTs and allow to proceed only those which by objective criteria are undertaken at market (arm's-length) prices. The third tier is pre-clearance by the regulator for certain types of transactions. e.g., those which exceed a certain size threshold, those for which it is difficult to ascertain the equivalent arm's-length prices, and those which appear to be passable but in tandem with previous NALTs exceed a cumulative threshold level so that regulatory oversight is warranted. Both the Blenkarn and Murray Reports recommend that for *de novo* institutions and for mergers or takeovers, all NALTs must, for a period, be regulator-approved, until the regulators are satisfied that the appropriate internal monitoring procedures have been put in place.

Nonetheless, I think that it is fair to say that our legislators and their advisors at both levels of government, as well as many analysts, do not feel very confident in this mechanism. My own view is precisely the opposite. Effective internal corporate governance is the only way to detect and deflect potentially abusive NALTs on a timely basis, whether the NALTs are owner or management/director related. Regulators become apprized only after the fact. Thus, the question becomes: can the concept of a BCRC be established in a manner that sensitizes the entire upper echelons of the financial institution to the self-dealing issue?

Given my obvious biases on this issue, I was pleased to note that, in some quarters at least, the role assigned to internal corporate governance is being enhanced rather dramatically. In his appearance before the Ontario Standing Committee, Trevor Eyton traces briefly the history of Royal Trustco's business conduct review committee and indicates that it will be introduced into all of Trilon's companies:

> The business conduct review committee looks at all related-party transactions; that is its responsibility. All its members are independent. They have their own legal counsel. They have direct access to the auditors of the company at call. They have the same kind of access to all the senior managers. They have the same kind of access to all the records of the company.
>
> There are mechanisms within the company, including a mechanism in the investment committee, such that all transactions which fall within their purview are automatically referred there. They make their decision. As I say, it is an independent one. They can do it with people present or not.

Ordinarily, no one else is; it is just the members of the committee. Their decision cannot be appealed. That is it; it is gone.

We are going beyond that. Next year in our annual reports we are including a section that is going to feature the business conduct review committee. We are going to picture them so they will be even more aware of their responsibility. We are going to include their charter; that is, what their function is. We are going to include a report on how they have discharged their responsibility and their functions for the year in question, and they are going to sign it off. In that sense, what we are doing is the same process I talked about before. We are forcing them to consider their independence and their responsibility.

More recently, and in answer to some of the queries and concerns of regulators, we have said there was never any reservation about it on our part — that regulators could and should have direct access and perhaps direct reporting between business conduct review committees and the regulators. It seems sensible and doable.

We see no reason that the regulators could not in some way confirm or approve membership on the business conduct review committees. We see no reason that a regulator, at will, on a regular or random basis, could not sit in and listen to the deliberations and the decision-making of those committees. We see no reason that those committees should not, as a matter of course, provide minutes of their meetings to regulators so there is an ongoing information exchange, and we see no reason that those committees could not file those deliberations in some public place so they are open for public scrutiny and inspection.

I can report that the few regulators I have talked to about it have seen it as a positive from two points of view. First, they see the business conduct review committee and the members as a kind of addendum to their own office, one that is operating without public expense and does not cut into their budget. Second, they recognize that there are always limits to what regulators can do. You cannot have enough regulators with enough budget and enough time to cover every conceivable transaction, and the system I was describing of strict and tough self-governance was one that fitted nicely, as long as they were informed and had an opportunity to speak directly to members of the business conduct review committees.

It is working well at Royal Trustco, but it is not perfect yet. We are working on it. It is still a new concept. It was a concept that was specifically blessed by the Senate banking committee in its report. It has been blessed by a number of the regulators I have talked to who have seen it as a way in which they can reconcile an ongoing major shareholder, which is a historic fact today, with the benefits that brings and the balance of independent directors and mechanisms where the independent directors could express themselves and monitor the related-party dealings that might occur within a group (Eyton 1986, pp. F-7-8).

As I noted above, internal corporate governance structured along these lines would seem to offer effective and timely monitoring to ensure that "all third parties and regulators will have a high degree of assurance that any and all self-dealing transactions are in the best interests of the institution, its shareholders, and its customers and are being carried out at prices that would fairly reflect those which occur in arm's length or market transactions" (Senate Committee on Banking, Trade and Commerce 1986, p. 34).

6.0 SUMMARY AND ALTERNATIVES
This final substantive section of the paper will focus in turn on some summary observations and some policy options.

6.1 Summary Observations
- By allowing for ownership integration across the pillars and opening up the Canadian financial services sector to international competition, *New Directions* gets high marks for responding to global financial developments.

- However, the federal position paper accomplishes this in a manner which may result in a rather dramatic reduction in the potential inflow of domestic capital into Canadian financial services. World-wide, capital is being attracted to financial services. The prohibition of new commercial-financial linkages will arrest this trend domestically. As a result, new and existing commercially-linked capital will be enticed to charter provincially or, if this avenue is blocked, to go offshore.

- Under this scenario, markets may remain contestable if the border becomes sufficiently open. In turn, however, this has the potential for generating preferential treatment for foreign over domestic narrowly-held (and commercially-linked) institutions.

- In addition to these concerns relating to domestic entry, *New Directions* is likely to increase rather than decrease concentration in financial markets. The recent decrease in financial market concentration may well be reversed if the conglomerates are prevented from competing head-on with the banks. While the big-should-not-buy-big approach to mergers is probably warranted, the build-not-buy proposal will only serve to entrench the position of the banks by preventing their competitors the ability to develop nationwide networks. Moreover, takeovers provide a valuable avenue for entry. Now that we finally have in place a competition policy with teeth, it seems appropriate to allow its provisions to monitor merger and takeover activity in the financial sector.

- Recent conglomerate growth is a function of a variety of factors. Part of it relates to the fact that the banks have fallen on hard times as a result of their oil-patch losses and Third-World loans. This aspect of conglomerate growth surely enhances competition and benefits all Canadians. Part of the growth may relate to inappropriate incentives encouraging mergers and takeovers. These incentives, which apply to all sectors and not just the financial sector, require legislation to ensure that mergers become market-driven rather than tax-driven. Finally, part of conglomerate growth reflects regulatory barriers: the conglomerates could do what the banks could not, at least until *New Directions* appeared. In my view, even if there were no ownership restrictions in *New Directions*, there would be no threat of a conglomerate "takeover" of the financial services area: the banks and mutuals will more than hold their own. However, with its prohibition against commercially-linked financial institutions, new and existing, *New Directions* may well foster the very concentration among domestic institutions that it purports to combat.

- Concentration of assets in the hands of a few families may be viewed as a problem, but it is not peculiar to the financial sector. Indeed, it is best viewed as a symptom of the fact that markets have not been sufficiently contestable and that mergers have been tax driven. If after adopting appropriate measures on these fronts there is still perceived to be a problem, the appropriate solution is a generic one, like the imposition of accession duties, rather than interfering only with the operations of financial markets.

- Concentration in terms of accumulating "political" power as a result of the co-mingling of commercial and financial interests may also be a factor motivating ownership limits. The suggestion here would be that the Royal Bank would have less political clout in the corridors of power than a commercial-financial conglomerate of the same asset size. As long as there are procedures in place to prevent abusive NALTs and there is a financial holding company between the commercial and the real, I have trouble seeing why this should be the case. This is particularly so if the banks themselves engage in both commercial lending and the underwriting/ distribution of securities. However, I recognize that this aspect of concentration does worry some Canadians and it, rather than any concern about self-dealing, appears to have been the motivating force underlying the Blenkarn formula.

- Concerns relating to potential abuses of self-dealing can also motivate ownership restrictions. However, this is too narrow a view of the self-dealing issue. As one moves towards wide ownership, the ability/incentive for owner-related self-dealing diminishes while the ability/incentive for management- and director-related self dealing increases. Extreme solutions are of course possible – wide ownership and outright bans on all shareholder/management/director self-dealing – but the costs of banning all NALTs in order to be sure to capture those that may be abusive effectively emasculates the synergy potential unleased by *New Directions*. It appears to me that a more even-handed approach working across a range of fronts is both more flexible and more effective. As outlined above, the combination of limited ownership provisions, selective self-dealing bans, internal corporate governance and cumulative voting for independent directors is likely to complement the remainder of the regulatory process in providing for an effective deterrent to abusive NALTs as well as the assurance that those that are allowed to proceed are undertaken at market or arm's-length prices. Moreover, even without enhanced legislative powers, it is surely the case that the regulatory agencies and auditors will, as a result of the recent failures, be far more vigilant in their line of duty.

- *New Directions* appears to be operating under the assumption that one can forge a clean separation between activities that are financial and those that are commercial. In fact, this distinction is becoming increasingly blurred with the rapid growth of in-house or corporate banking and joint ventures like the National-Provigo debit card. Submitting these activities to regulatory overview is more appropriate than ignoring them under the pretext that they are non-financial. It is increasingly difficult to distinguish General Electric Credit Corporation's credit activities, only 5 per cent of which are allocated to the financing of G.E. products (McFetridge, chapter 14 in this volume), from those of a financial institution. Moreover, the real/commercial overlap will likely intensify. Now that deregulation in Ottawa and Ontario has neutralized the lead that Quebec enjoyed in financial deregulation, my hunch is that this province's next move will be to encourage its financial sector to take an active role (along Japanese or perhaps even German lines) in Quebec-based commercial enterprises, with a view to facilitating export penetration.

- In addition to enhancing entry and therefore, contestability and competition. a relaxation of *New Directions* ownership limitations would also provide other benefits. Perhaps "maintaining existing benefits" is the more appropriate phrasing, since by virtually any criteria one cares to apply (service, innovation, rate of return, acceptability by the public) the likes of Empire Life, Royal Trust, Great West Life, Montreal Trust, London Life, etc., are serving Canada well. In this light, it seems incredible that the recent entry of Barclays Bank (Kohut 1987) into the provision of agricultural leasing (via a takeover of Massey Ferguson Finance Corp. of Canada Ltd. to form Barclays Bank Agricultural Finance Corp.) may well be the sort of initiative that *New Directions* would deny to the above-enumerated institutions let alone to potential commercially-linked domestic capital in search of investment opportunities. And if it is O.K. for Barclays, it is presumable also O.K. for commercially-linked Deutsche Bank. What is there about Barclays that makes it preferable to Empire Life? At least we can regulate Empire Life! This would be a questionable policy even for a sector in secular decline. However, to contemplate such an approach for the world's fastest growing, most innovative and probably most high-tech sector, is surely inappropriate. The issue here is not one of preferring large, widely-held banks or mutuals to large narrowly-held conglomerates. Neither is likely to be highly innovative. Rather, it is to allow free entry of new capital to the financial sector to capitalize on profitable market niches, to market new instruments, to exploit new technology and to deploy entrepreneurship consistent with the trend toward the investment banking culture. Under *New Directions*, I fear that we are inviting the foreign financial institutions to play this role. The economic arguments for altering this aspect of *New Directions* appear overwhelming but failing this, "economic nationalism" is a last resort. (I never thought I would ever say this in public!)

-    Thus far, the quotations in this paper have essentially pitted the views of representatives of narrowly-held institutions against those of widely-held institutions. Self-interest probably dictates that the debate will involve in this direction. However, what is really at issue is the future of the Canadian financial services industry. In this context, it is significant that the Laurentian Group (a mutual) has added its voice to those who fear that the ownership provisions of *New Directions* are not in Canada's long-term interest:

> While the Minister recognizes the need to give businesses the means to develop in the new context of international financial markets, some people still persist in ignoring this trend, as they continue to raise the specter of a concentration of power. However, there is no evidence, not a single fact, that points to any real problem . . .

> The new policy is intended to prevent financial institutions from becoming tied to non-financial or commercial business through shareholding. However, as yet, no country has felt it was necessary to introduce legislation along these lines . . .

> When we compare the size of Canadian companies to the large corporations with international operations — the largest Canadian financial institution, the Royal Bank, ranks 54th — we see that the real problem is the competitive capacity of our companies, and not their concentration. It is urgent that something be done now, not tomorrow. To illustrate the scope of the problem, the newspapers last month reported that the powerful Nippon Life had just acquired a 15% interest in the no less powerful American Express-Shearson group, and that the two companies were planning to conquer new markets together. Not only are the big players on the international stage bigger than us, but they're making alliances to boot! In any case, if you look at the problems that we have faced in Canada in the past few years — failures of banks, insurance companies and trust

companies – you can see that these were small firms that were undercapitalized or badly managed!

Some government officials and commentators also seem to be obsessed by the question of conflicts of interest and the dangers inherent in transactions between companies within a single group. However, the self-regulation system developed by many companies over the years has proved it can cope with this. With a few improvements, such as the presence of outside members on the Board of Directors in sufficient number and the creation of committees made up of outsiders with a mandate to examine transactions between cohabiting institutions, this system will surely be worth preserving. Some people still continue to advocate prohibiting any transactions between cohabiting institutions and erecting watertight walls between them. But we know it's not the institutions that practice this kind of deception. So in order to protect against a few individuals who are likely to practice fraud, some people are prepared to paralyze the institutions and our entire system!

Based on what we've seen, we fear that the federal legislation is being drawn up on the principle that all businesses and their executives are inclined to cheat or engage in doubtful practices.... The Asians – especially the Japanese, who are fast becoming our most serious competitors – have understood the dynamic of their companies. It is worth noting that their legislation governing financial services proceeds from the principle that institutions and their executives are generally honest citizens. (Castonguay 1987, pp. 11-15.)

Castonguay does not elaborate as to the reasons why, from the Laurentian Group's standpoint, the ownership provisions in *New Directions* are viewed so negatively. My hunch is that somewhere in their impressive plans for expansion one or more of their domestic and/or international downstream holding companies are going to require capital from outsiders in larger-than-10 per cent tranches. Thus, *New Directions* could seriously interfere with their expansion plans.

- To conclude this summary I want to draw upon an overriding principle of the Murray (Senate) Report (1986, p. 15), which in turn was borrowed from the Green Paper (1985. p. 1) - "in a fast changing financial world, regulatory policy should avoid as much as possible the imposition of a preconceived structure on the financial system." In my view, to pursue ownership restrictions beyond the limits that are required (for example, for adequately controlling self dealing) is to straightjacket the system. Wide ownership may well be appropriate, but the market, rather than the regulators, should decide this.

My view of the above analysis and summary is that it indicates that Tom Hockin's paper is itself in need of new directions in terms of its ownership and entry provisions. Accordingly, the paper concludes with two alternative approaches. The first of these, referred to as the "Modified Blenkarn" approach, rectifies some of the market contestability concerns while at the same time endorses the *New Directions* principle of widely-held ownership for large financial institutions. The second. referred to as the "Modified Murray" approach, is more consistent with the above analysis in the sense that, while it requires that there be some widely-held ownership, it does not go as far as endorsing the notion that there is something sacrosanct about 10 per cent ownership.

The obvious other alternative – no ownership limits at all – seems to be a non-starter in the current environment, whatever its potential merits.

6.2   New Directions on Ownership

Modified Blenkarn: As noted above, Jacques Parizeau in Chapter 16 of this volume argues that the Blenkarn proposal be resurrected as the appropriate way to approach the ownership of Canadian financial institutions. Under Blenkarn, financial institutions could be wholly owned until they reached $10 billion in assets. Between $10 and $20 billion majority shareholders could hold 75 per cent of the shares, between $20 and $30 billion, 50 per cent, between $30 and $40 billion 25 per cent, and the 10 per cent rule would apply beyond the $40 billion assets threshold. These assets limits would exclude both foreign assets, ETA assets, and segregated funds assets. In addition to rectifying the above concerns with respect to new entry (both in terms of *de novo* entry and via acquisitions, which Parizeau would allow), such a proposal would place foreign and domestic financial institutions on a more equal footing.

Since these asset thresholds would presumably be indexed for inflation, one way for *New Directions* to incorporate the Blenkarn-type sliding scale would be to eliminate all reference to "commercially-linked" financial institutions. In other words, the 35 per cent rule could be implemented at the $750 million capital threshold (e.g., roughly $15 billion in assets), with, say, 50 per cent coming in at $25 billion, 75 per cent at $35 billion and 10 per cent at $45 billion. If one wanted to be flexible with these limits, instead of requiring divestiture the institutions could be required to ensure that all new equity issues be widely held if the ownership limits are binding. Moreover, the presumption would be that the issue of mergers and acquisitions would fall under the *Competition Act*, with perhaps an overriding requirement that big should not buy big.

One further advantage of such a proposal is that the Minister of State for Finance would not be involved as much in the day-to-day decision making of financial institutions. Under *New Directions*, the spectre arises of a steady stream of queries to the Minister of State for Finance, e.g., Are we commercially linked? Do our real side investments exceed the *de minimus* level? Is the institution we would like to acquire a big institution, a medium-sized institution or a small one? Can we be exempted from the build vs. buy preference? and so on. Under modified Blenkarn the corporate boardroom will make all these decisions and recognize their implications.

Modified Murray: The Blenkarn alternative, like *New Directions* itself, embodies the 10 per cent principle as the ideal for large financial institutions. My interpretation of the above analysis is that there is precious little in the way of solid argument for the presumption that widely-held institutions are to be preferred. Hence, I would opt for a version of the Murray (Senate) Report.

As it stands, the Murray Report essentially requires all financial institutions operating in more than one pillar (and all commercially-linked financial institutions even if their operations are confined to one pillar) to be 35 per cent widely held. There is no asset threshold level which would trigger this requirement, so that even relatively small financial institutions, if commercially linked or operating in more than one pillar, would be required to have a 35 per cent public float. This recognizes the CBA concern that the $750 million threshold for capital is far too high, particularly given the present workings of deposit insurance. Moreover, it also recognizes the fact that most if not all of the narrowly-held financial institutions that have failed (and where there was evidence of self-dealing) were below this capital limit.

Now there is nothing special about the 35 per cent level, except that, under the CBCA provisions, it is sufficient to block a capital reorganization that might be inimical to minority shareholders. (Indeed, the recent Economic Council (1987) report would not allow a minority shareholding of less than 35 per cent for precisely this reason.) Therefore, it is also possible to implement a sliding scale under Modified Murray, e.g., 35 per cent widely held up to, say, $750 million in capital and 45 per cent or even 50 per cent thereafter.

Included in such a proposal would be the full range of regulatory provisions to prevent abusive self-dealing – independent directors, cumulative voting, internal corporate governance a la Eyton and an early warning system of monitoring. Obviously, nothing would prevent firms from becoming widely held under this scheme and one would expect them to move in this direction if there are gains to be had from wide ownership.

Ontario's proposals (no ownership limits, no corporate governance and very strict self-dealing provisions) would still be offside vis-à-vis Ottawa, but the attraction of chartering provincially would be reduced significantly. First of all, most conglomerates welcome some public shareholding. Second, most holding companies (whether widely held or narrowly held) would probably prefer to institute internal corporate governance procedures rather than be subjected to air-tight self-dealing bans. Thus, while it would be preferable, under the modified Murray approach, for Ontario to adopt similar ownership and self-dealing provisions, failure to do so would not result in the incentive for rechartering or acquiring provincially chartered institutions that currently exist under *New Directions* or would exist under the Blenkarn-type approach.

My overall assessment, therefore, is that some version of the Murray approach to ownership is the ideal compromise. While it represents a rather dramatic departure from the status quo, it trades off the various political and economic concerns about ownership in a manner that at the same time instills greater public confidence in Canada's financial services sector yet allows it sufficient flexibility and ability to respond to the domestic and international challenges of the rapid evolution in global finance.

7.0 CONCLUSION: MAINTAINING PERSPECTIVE

For many Canadians the issue of wide ownership has taken on overtones of an "overriding public policy concern." My plea here is for legislation to recognize the potential costs to Canada and Canadians of such an approach. As OSC Chairman, Stanley Beck, noted before the Ontario Standing Committee.

> A lot of nonsense has been talked about the mix between the real and the financial and the concerns about self-dealing. After all, the great Canadian concern has always been about shortage of capital to develop our Canadian institutions. Now we are saying to elements of the financial industry, 'You cannot have access to pools of Canadian capital because somehow there is a danger in having access to Bell Canada's capital or CPR's capital.' That is an argument I do not buy. But I am probably in a minority these days, because it has become an emotional sort of argument. It needs a good deal of analysis . . .

> But it is no different here from what has happened in the United States, or in the United Kingdom with the Lloyd's scandal. Every country will always have its dramatic financial frauds. But you should not set broad, national economic policy on the basis of a single fraud or on the basis of anecdotal evidence. I worry that this is happening too much in the country today (Beck 1986, pp. F14-15).

The earlier quotation from Claude Castonguay expressed similar concerns. Indeed, even Bernard Ghert shares some of these concerns:

> You have to make your laws and regulations and supervision based on the assumption that you are dealing with honest, well-intentioned people, unless you are prepared to accept a police state where you have a policeman looking over everyone's shoulder all of the time (Ghert 1985, p. 68:12).

A second aspect of maintaining appropriate perspective relate to the fact that the "burden of proof" in the ownership controversy has come to rest on the wrong shoulders. Surely, the dictum of Peter Dey (Stanley Beck's predecessor at the OSC) is appropriate: "the presumption is that any action is permissable unless it can be demonstrated to the contrary to the public interest" (OSC 1983, p. 16). However, those who argue for the 10 per cent rule have never really had to argue the full case. Rather, the presumption has developed that majority ownership ought to be prohibited unless it can be demonstrated to be conclusive to the public interest. This approach serves to "taint" the genuine benefits to Canadians that have been derived from majority-held financial institutions. Widely-held ownership is quickly becoming another of our so-called "sacred trusts," effectively outside the realm of reasoned argumentation. Approaching public policy from such a perspective is questionable at the best of times. It may be disastrous for a sector that is as open internationally and is in as full flight as the financial services sector.

A third and final aspect of maintaining perspective relates to the changing role of the consumer of financial services. Most of the above analysis focused on the dramatic changes in either or both financial instruments and financial institutions. However, an excellent case can be made that the financial services revolution has had its greatest influences at the level of the consumer. He/she now has experienced an increase in information, in access to technology and in the range of available choices of both institutions and instruments that probably exceeds the extra degree of maneuverability associated with the institutions themselves. Thus, the notion that the role for government in the financial services sector is to enact legislation in order to protect consumers from their own actions is increasingly questionable. Phrased differently, there is valuable information content in the observation that trust companies have been growing more quickly than banks and in the fact that shares of narrowly-held institutions trade at a multiple of book value whereas those of some of the major banks trade at less than book. Markets may not be perfect, but to ignore the information content of financial markets where consumers/shareholders have ample access to information and alternatives (moreso than is the case in most other markets) is, in effect, to undermine the value of markets as a signalling device.

Despite all of this, there may well be a case for widely-held ownership. However, my evaluation of the arguments and evidence relating to the ownership issue is that the case for the 10 per cent rule has not been demonstrated. Indeed, the opposite is probably nearer the truth. Faced with a choice of the 10 per cent rule or the Murray approach, I would opt for the latter, *even for the chartered banks*. Fortunately, however, we are not faced with this polar choice.

By way of conclusion, therefore, I reiterate my earlier position that, in terms of ownership, *New Directions* is in need of new directions. Actually, this should not really be a tall order. After all, *New Directions* does embody a set of underlying *principles* with respect to ownership that are indeed admirable. All that is required now is to develop a set of detailed provisions and regulations that will implement these enunciated principles.

NOTES

1. See House of Commons Standing Committee on Finance, Trade and Economic Affairs (1985).

2. Jackman makes a similar argument in Chapter 15 of this volume.

3. As part of its argument, the CBA brief reproduces the Bernard Ghert quotation (which I have also reproduced above) relating to the unnamed, narrowly-held financial institution that refused a loan to one of its commercial competitors.

4. This is a very questionable point for the CBA to be making in light of the substantial CDIC losses after mid-1985 in connection with the Northland Bank and the Canadian Commercial Bank, particularly since these losses were apparent well before the brief was presented.

5. The criteria for independent directors include:

   - that they are not officers, employees or significant (10 per cent) shareholders of the financial institutions or companies related to it;

   - that they do not have significant business links with the institutions or companies related to it, directly or indirectly (which includes being a director and/or officer of a significant borrower);

   - that they do not belong to firms acting as major legal advisers to the institution; and

   - that they are not immediately related by birth or marriage to any person in the above categories.

REFERENCES

Barnard, Douglas (1987) "Wrong-Way Corrigan," *The Wall Street Journal,* February 26, p. 20.

Beck, Stanley (1986) Testimony Before the Legislative Assembly of Ontario. Standing Committee on Finance and Economic Affairs: Corporate Concentration, September 23.

_____ (1987) "A Provincial Regulator's Perspective on Mergers and Financial Power," (Paper presented to the IRPP Conference on Mergers, Corporate Concentration and Corporate Power in Canada, Montreal, March 23-24).

Blenkarn, Don, M.P. (1986) Testimony Before the Legislative Assembly of Ontario, Standing Committee on Finance and Economic Affairs: Corporate Concentration, November 6.

Canadian Bankers' Association (1986) *Corporate Concentration in the Financial Services Sector,* Submission to the Legislative Assembly of Ontario, Standing Committee on Finance and Economic Affairs: Corporate Concentration, October.

_____ (1987) *Response to the Federal Policy Statement: New Directions for the Financial Sector,* (Toronto: CBA, February).

Castonguay, Claude (1987) "The Laurentian Group Corporation in the Era of Deregulation," Remarks to the Montreal District Chamber of Commerce (April 14).

Corrigan, E. Gerald (1987) *Financial Market Structure: The Longer View,* (New York: Federal Reserve Bank of New York).

Courchene, Thomas J. (1986a) *Ontario's Proposals for the Canadian Securities Industry,* Observation No. 29, (Toronto: C.D. Howe Institute).

_____ (1986b) "Some Perspectives on the Future of Banking," *Fraser Forum,* Special Issue (Vancouver: The Fraser Institute).

Crabbe, M. (1986) "Inside the New In-House Banks," *Euromoney,* February, pp. 24-41.

Crownx Inc. (1986) Testimony Before the Legislative Assembly of Ontario, Standing Committee on Finance and Economic Affairs: Corporate Concentration, October.

Department of Finance (1985) *The Regulation of Canadian Financial Institutions* (Ottawa: Ministry of Supply and Services). (This is generally referred to as the Green Paper.)

Director of Investigation and Research, Combines Investigation Act (1985) *Submission of the Director of Investigation and Research, Combines Investigation Act, to the Ontario Government Task Force on Financial Institutions* (July).

Dupré, Stefan (1986) Testimony Before the Legislative Assembly of Ontario, Standing Committee on Finance and Economic Affairs: Corporate Concentration, October 8.

Economic Council of Canada (1986) *Competition and Solvency: A Framework for Financial Regulation* (Ottawa: Minister of Supply and Services Canada).

_____ (1987) *A Framework for Financial Regulation* (Ottawa: Minister of Supply and Services Canada).

Eyton, Trevor (1986) Testimony Before the Legislative Assembly of Ontario, Standing Committee on Finance and Economic Affairs: Corporate Concentration, September 24.

Francis, Diane (1986a) *Controlling Interest: Who Owns Canada?* (Toronto: Macmillan).

_____ (1986b) Testimony Before the Legislative Assembly of Ontario, Standing Committee on Finance and Economic Affairs: Corporate Concentration, October 16.

Genstar (1986) *Domestic Ownership of Canadian Financial Institutions.* (Toronto: Genstar, Inc.).

Ghert, Bernard (1985) *The Regulation of Canadian Financial Institutions,* Submission and testimony before the House of Commons Standing Committee on Finance, Trade and Economic Affairs, Issue No. 68 (September 25).

_____ (1986) Testimony Before the Legislative Assembly of Ontario, Standing Committee on Finance and Economic Affairs: Corporate Concentration, September 30.

Goldman, Calvin (1986) Submission and Testimony Before the Legislative Assembly of Ontario, Standing Committee on Finance and Economic Affairs: Corporate Concentration, October 1.

Hockin, Hon. Tom (1986) *New Directions for the Financial Sector* (Ottawa: Department of Finance, December 18).

House of Commons Standing Committee on Finance, Trade and Economic Affairs (1985) *Canadian Financial Institutions*, (Ottawa: Minister of Supply and Services Canada), known as the Blenkarn Report.

Howlett, Karen (1987) "Crownx head decries 'tragic' deregulation plan." *Globe and Mail*, April 9, p. B6.

Jackman, Henry, N.R. (1986) Remarks and Testimony Before the Legislative Assembly of Ontario, Standing Committee on Finance and Economic Affairs: Corporate Concentration, (September 30).

Kohut, John (1987) "Barclay's Bank sees a niche in farm finance," *Globe and Mail*, March 26, p. B.8.

Lambert, Allen (1986) Testimony Before the Legislative Assembly of Ontario, Standing Committee on Finance and Economic Affairs: Corporate Concentration, October 2.

Naisbitt Group (1986) *The Capital Explosion: A Worldwide Quest for Money*, (New York: KMG Main Hurdman).

Ontario Securities Commission (1983) *Report on the Implications for Canadian Capital Markets of the Provision by Financial Institutions of Access to Discount Brokerage Services* (Toronto: Dataline).

Ontario Task Force on Financial Institutions (1985) *Final Report*, known as the Dupré Report.

Royal Trustco Limited (1986) "Corporate Concentration in the Financial Services Industry," presentation to the Legislative Assembly of Ontario. Standing Committee on Finance and Economic Affairs: Corporate Concentration, September 23.

Senate of Canada (1985) *Deposit Insurance*, 10th Report of the Standing Senate Committee on Banking, Trade and Commerce, (Ottawa: Minister of Supply and Services Canada).

_____ (1986) *Towards a More Competitive Financial Environment*. 16th Report of the Standing Senate Committee on Banking, Trade and Commerce, (Ottawa: Minister of Supply and Services Canada), known as the Murray Report.

Weir, E.K. (1987) "Ownership of Banks and Loan, Trust and Insurance Companies." Background Paper for Insight Conference on the Financial Services Industry in Reform (February).

Wyman, W.R., Chairman (1985) *Final Report of the Working Committee on the Canada Deposit Insurance Corporation (CDIC)*, (Ottawa: Minister of Supply and Services Canada).

APPENDIX A

COMMERCIAL LINKAGES: INTERNATIONAL EVIDENCE

In response to Tom Hockin's (1986) paper, the Canadian Life and Health Insurance Association (CLHIA) asserted that Canada would be virtually alone in restricting the growth of life insurance companies on the basis of any commercial links with non-financial organizations or unregulated financial institutions. To buttress this assertion, the CLHIA undertook a cross-pillar, international poll to see if there were any precedents to the proposals embodied in *New Directions*. The following are extracts of responses received thus far:

Association of British Insurers
"I am writing to confirm that there are no legislative restrictions on the ownership, investment, expansion and/or diversification flexibility of financial institutions in this country when they are linked to commercial (non-financial) enterprises."

American Council of Life Insurance
"You asked whether we are aware of any statutory limitations on the ability of a life insurance company to enter into an upstream or downstream affiliation with a non-depository, commercial enterprise. To the best of our knowledge. no such limitations exist in the United States."

The Life Offices' Association of New Zealand Inc.
"In New Zealand there are no restraints affecting the financial institutions. on grounds that they are linked to commercial (non-financial) enterprises in any way."

Swedish Bankers' Association
". . . concerning restrictions when banks are linked to non financial enterprises I can tell you that there are no such restriction under Swedish law."

Verband de Versicherungsunternehmungen Osterreichs
(Austria)
"There is a lot of regulations for financial institutions but most of them apply regardless of any ownership connection with non-financial enterprises."

Association Internationale des Societes d'assurance Mutuelle
"We can inform you that, as far as insurance companies are concerned, they are not subject to France to the mentioned restrictions."

The Life Insurance Association of Japan

In general, Japanese commercial (non-financial enterprises can establish or acquire financial institutions including a life insurance company."

Swiss Bankers' Association

". . . we hereby inform you that the Swiss banking legislation presently in force does not include any provision limiting acquisitions, investments and development of financial institutions legally or economically linked to commercial institutions outside the financial or banking sector."

While further responses are still being received and processed, the CLHIA has issued an interim bulletin which notes:

Further replies and materials received from various financial services associations in West Germany, Norway, Denmark, Finland, Luxembourg, Belgium, Costa Rica, Sweden, Switzerland and France have reaffirmed the CLHIA statement . . . that "We are not aware of any country in the world where the growth of a financial firm is constrained because of commercial linkage."

Source: Canadian Life and Health Insurance Association, *Quarterly Review.* volume 3, number 2, 1987, pp. 7-8, and CLHIA Circular No. 4471F (March 26, 1987).

Appendix 1

List of Large Mergers and Acquisitions in Canada, 1978 to 1987

W.T. Stanbury
Faculty of Commerce and Business Administration
University of British Columbia

The criteria for inclusion in the list are as follows:

- The value of the transaction exceeded $100 million Canadian at the time it took place, i.e., nominal dollars.

- The acquiring firm obtained legal control (51% or more of the voting shares) or *effective* control.

- The merger must result in an increase in industry level and/or macro concentration in Canada. Therefore the list *excludes*: Canadian firms' acquisition of foreign firms which did not have a Canadian subsidiary, and acquisition of Canadian firms by a foreign firm which did not have a Canadian subsidiary.

- Mergers of two foreign-owned companies, both of which have Canadian subsidiaries, are included.

- Acquisitions of additional voting shares above 51% (legal control) are excluded.

	Acquiring Firm	Acquired Firm	Value of Transaction ($ Millions)
1978			
1.	Hudson's Bay Co.	Simpsons Ltd. (88%)	144
2.	Hudson's Bay Co.	Simpson-Sears (36%) [note, Sears Roebuck also has 36%]	203
3.	Dome Petroleum Ltd.	Siebens Oil and Gas	355
4.	Nu-West Development Corp.	Voyageur Petroleum	198
5.	Petro-Canada Ltd. (Crown Corp.)	Pacific Petroleum Ltd.	1,500
6.	Noranda Mines Ltd.	Mattagami Mines	207
7.	Montreal City and District Savings Bank	Credit Foncier Franco-Canadien	123
8.	VGM Trusto Ltd.	Victoria and Grey Trust and Metropolitan Trust (from 38% and 56% to 99% in both cases)	168 est.
9.	AGTL (now Nova, an Alberta Corporation)	Husky Oil (to 48%, control)	251
1979			
1.	Kaiser Resources Ltd.	Ashland Oil Canada Ltd.	485
2.	Canadian Homestead Oil	Inter-City Gas Ltd.	108

3.	Woodbridge Co. Ltd. (Thomson Interests)	Hudson's Bay Co.	641
4.	Dome Petroleum Ltd.	Trans Canada Pipelines (to 49%)	430
5.	Edper Equities Ltd. (Edward & Peter Bronfman)	Brascan Ltd. (50.1%)	335
6.	Bank Canadian National	Provincial Bank of Canada	100+
7.	Carter Oil and Gas Co. Ltd.	Hamilton Bros. Petrol. Corp. (Cdn properties)	522
8.	Olympia & York Developments Ltd.	English Property Corp. (U.K.) (>74%)	135 (U.S.) 150 (Cdn)
9.	Dome Petroleum Ltd.	Mesa Petroleum Ltd. (Cdn assets)	640

1980

1.	Thomson Newspapers Ltd.	F.P. Publications Ltd.	165
2.	Dome Petroleum Ltd.	Kaiser Resources Ltd. (on shore oil and gas assets)	701
3.	Noranda Mines Ltd.	Maclaren Power and Paper Ltd.	241
4.	Consumers Gas Co.	Hiram Walker Gooderham & Worts Ltd.	1,220
5.	Carma Developers	Allarco Development Co.	168
6.	Atco Ltd.	Canadian Utilities Ltd. (58%)	324
7.	Olympia and York Developments Ltd.	Brinco Ltd. (50.1%)	100
8.	British Columbia Resources Investment Corp.	Kaiser Resources Ltd. (66%)	665

	Acquiring Firm	Acquired Firm	Value of Transaction ($ Millions)
1980 (cont'd)			
9.	Western Forest Industries Ltd. (partnership of Doman Industries, BCFP, and ?)	Rayonier Canada Ltd. (B.C. forest assets)	426
10.	Labrador Mining and Explor. Ltd.	Norcen Energy Resources (to 40%)	367
11.	CanWest Capital and Cavendish Investments	McLeod-Stedman (from Gamble-Skogmo, U.S.)	90 (U.S.) 115 (Cdn)
12.	Extendicare Ltd. (75% Jodrey-Burns Group	Crown Life Insurance Co. (92%)	187
13.	Cominco Ltd. (controlled by CPR)	Bethlehem Copper Corp.	146
1981			
1.	Provigo Inc.	Dominion Stores Ltd. (87 Quebec stores)	108
2.	Petro-Canada Ltd. (Crown Corp.)	Petrofina Inc.	1,460
3.	Olympia and York Dev. Ltd.	Abitibi-Price Inc. (91%)	618
4.	Sulpetro Ltd.	CanDel Oil Ltd.	546
5.	Noranda Mines Ltd.	MacMillan Bloedel Ltd. (49.8%)	627
6.	West Fraser Timber Co. Ltd.	Eurocan Pulp and Paper Co. Ltd.	100
7.	Dome Petroleum Ltd.	Hudson's Bay Oil and Gas Co. Ltd.	1,700 (U.S.) 2,040 (Cdn)

8.	Genstar Corp.	Canada Permanent Mortgage Corp. (53%)	260
9.	Canadian Pacific Enterprises Ltd.	Canadian International Paper Co.	1,100
10.	Canada Development Corp.	Acquitane Co. of Canada (75%)	1,616
11.	Canada Development Corp.	Canadian assets of Texas Gulf Inc.	1,800 (U.S.) 2,160 (Cdn)
12.	Hudson's Bay Oil and Gas Co.	Cyprus-Anvil Mining Corp.	350 est.
13.	Turbo Resources Ltd.	Merland Exploration Ltd. (55%)	132
14.	United Canso Oil & Gas Ltd.	Great Basins Petroleum Co. (Canadian assets)	164
15.	Brascade Resources Inc. (70%) and Brascan, 30% Caisse de Depot)	Noranda Mines (for 39%)	1,600
16.	Drummond Petroleum Ltd.	Union Texas of Canada Ltd.	101
17.	G. Donald Love (60%) and Toronto-Dominion Bank (40%) Love increased his holdings from 10% to 60%]	Oxford Development Group	327
18.	K.C. Irving family	MacMillan Rothesay Ltd. (65%)	145
19.	Husky Oil Ltd.	Uno-Tex Petroleum Corp. (Canadian assets)	371
20.	Fairweather Gas Ltd.	Alamo Petroleum Ltd. and Amax Petroleum of Canada Ltd.	210
21.	Federal Commerce and Navigation Ltd. and Paul E. Martin (50:50 partner)	CSL Group Inc.	195

Acquiring Firm	Acquired Firm	Value of Transaction ($ Millions)
1981 (cont'd)		
22. Cominco Ltd.	Bethlehem Copper (97%)	146
23. Alberta Energy Corp.	B.C. Forest Products Ltd. (25%) [probably not effective control given the 41% in hands of Mead Corp. and Scott Paper]	215
1982		
1. Alberta Energy Corp.	Chieftain Development (56%)	168
2. Fletcher Challenge Ltd. (New Zealand)	Crown Zellerbach Canada Ltd. (84%) from U.S. parent	242 (U.S.) 298 (Cdn)
1983		
1. Trilon Financial Corp. (controlled by Brascan Ltd.)	Royal Trustco Ltd. (42%)	252
2. Bell Canada Enterprises Inc.	Trans Canada Pipe Lines Ltd. (42.3%; increased to 47.2% in 1984)	606
3. Petro-Canada Ltd.	B.P. Refining & Marketing Canada Ltd.	416
1984		
1. Trilon Financial Corp.	Fireman's Fund Co. of Canada	125 est
2. National Trust Co. [amalgamation to create National Victoria & Grey Trust — later National Trust]	Victoria and Grey Trust Co.	100 est

3.	Onex Capital Corp.	American Can Canada Inc.	253
4.	Trizec Corp.	Bramalea Limited (31%)	300 est
	[increased to 43% in 1985 for $150 million and to 65% in 1986]		

1985

1.	Allied Corp., Canadian subsidiaries	Signal Cos. Inc., Canadian subsidiaries	330 (U.S.) 452 (Cdn)
2.	Genstar Corp.	Canada Trustco Mortgage Co.	1,250
3.	Great Atlantic and Pacific Tea Co. (51% owned by Tenglemann Group)	Dominion Stores Ltd. (93 stores in Ontario)	115
4.	Dome Mines Ltd.	Falconbridge Ltd. (30% "controlling interest" from Mobil Corp. (U.S.)	160
5.	Unicorp Ltd.	Union Enterprises Ltd. (48.3%)	195
6.	Cambridge Shopping Centres Ltd.	Real estate assets of Woodward's Ltd.	223
7.	Olympia & York Developments Ltd.	Gulf Canada Ltd. (60.2% from U.S. parent)	2,850
8.	Petro-Canada Ltd.	Ontario and Western Canada retail assets of Gulf Canada (from Olympia & York)	886
9.	Slaight Communications	Standard Broadcasting (85%) [49.1% came from Conrad Black]	129
10.	Southam Inc.	Torstar Corp.	222

[Southam acquired a 25% non-voting interest in Torstar and Torstar acquired a 20% voting interest in Southam; the Southam family owns 20% of Southam Inc.]

	Acquiring Firm	Acquired Firm	Value of Transaction ($ Millions)
1985 cont'd			
11.	Lawson Mardon Group (mgt buyout; 49% owned by Roman Corp.)	Lawson & Jones Ltd. (from U.K. parent)	559
12.	Bell Canada Enterprises Inc.	Daon Development Corp. (69%)	162
13.	Burns family & Jodrey family	Crownx Inc. (Increased holdings from 34.5% to 46%) [Did this change control?]	133
14.	Dome Mines Ltd.	McIntyre Mines Ltd. (53%)	> 100 est
15.	Falconbridge Ltd.	Kidd Creek Mines Ltd. (100% from CDC which got about 35% of Falconbridge shares fully diluted; Dome Mines Ltd. interest fell to 19%)	615
16.	Westcoast Transmission	Texas Pacific Oil Canada Ltd.	130
1986			
1.	Ultramar Canada Inc.	Eastern retail assets of Gulf Canada Ltd. (from Olympia and York)	120
2.	MCA Inc. (U.S.)	Cineplex Odeon Inc. (50%, but only one-third of the votes)	215
3.	Hees International (controlled by Brascan Ltd.)	Norcen Energy Resources (41%) [obtained from Conrad Black]	300

4.	Unigesco Inc.	Provigo Inc. [increased direct holdings from 11% to 17% (to 20% indirectly) for "a dominant influence on Provigo policy and management"]	137
5.	Bramalea Ltd. (controlled by Edward & Peter Bronfman)	Fidinam Properties Inc. (Cdn. firm owned by European investors)	170
6.	Weyerhaeuser Canada Ltd.	Prince Albert Pulp Co. Ltd. (owned by Saskatchewan Govt.)	247
7.	Gulf Canada Corp. (80% owned by Olympia and York Enterprises and O&Y Resources)	Hiram Walker Resources Ltd. (69%)	3,000
8.	Imasco Ltd.	Genstar Corp. (100%)	2,500
9.	Trizec Corp. (controlled by by Edper Equities Ltd.)	Bramalea Ltd. (from 34% undiluted to 65% fully diluted)	580
10.	Laurentian Group Corp.	Eaton Financial Services Ltd.	101
11.	Federal Industries Ltd.	Canadian Corporation Management Co. Ltd.	146
12.	Repap Enterprises	2 pulp mills and saw mill of Westar Timber Ltd. (a subsidiary of BCRIC)	130
13.	Norcen Energy Resources	Superior Propane (from Gulf Canada Ltd.)	120
14.	Montreal Trustco Inc.	Credit Foncier (100% owned by Montreal City and District Savings Bank)	160

Acquiring Firm	Acquired Firm	Value of Transaction ($ Millions)
1986 cont'd		
15. Industrial Life Insurance Co.	Alliance Mutual Life Insurance Co.	> 100 est.
[merged company has $2.2 billion in assets; more than 20% of Quebec market – largest share; to be effective January 1, 1987]		
16. Gordon Investment Corp. and Merrill Lynch Canada Inc.	British Columbia Forest Products Ltd. (41%)	250
[acquired from Mead Corp. and Scott Paper Co., both of U.S. – note in January 1987 this bloc was sold to Fletcher Challenge]		
17. Group Videotron	Tele-Metropole	127
[The CRTC earlier had refused to allow Power Corp. to acquire Tele-Metropole]		
18. Kerr Addison Mines Ltd.	Corp. Falconbridge Copper (50 + %)	119
19. Pepsico Inc.	Seven-Up International (including Canadian operations)	100 est.
20. Interprovincial Pipe Line Ltd.	Home Oil Ltd. (from Hiram Walker Resources)	1,100
[Gulf Canada Corp. owns 40% of IPL and the Reichmanns own 80% of Gulf. Imperial Oil has 21% of IPL; Gulf Canada owns 69% of the voting shares of Hiram Walker and O&Y Enterprises owns 11%]		

21.	SA Cimenteries CBR (Belgium)	Cement and related operations of Genstar Corp. in W. Canada and California	452
	[Includes Genstar Cement Ltd., Genstar Construction Materials Co., Genstar Structures Ltd., Genstar Cement Co. (California)]		
22.	Kohlberg, Kravis, Roberts & Co. (leveraged buyout)	Canada Safeway Ltd. (258 stores)	700 to 1,200 est.
	[KKR paid $4.2 billion U.S. for Safeway Stores Inc. of Oakland, Calif.]		
23.	Steinberg Inc.	Aligro Inc.	136
24.	Power Corp. and Consolidated Bathurst and China International Trust Investment Corp.	BCRIC pulp mill at Castlegar	100 est.
25.	Bombardier Inc.	Canadair Ltd.	205 est.
	[In this very complicated deal, $120 million cash plus royalties on the Challenger jet estimated to be $173 million over 21 years or $20 million in lieu of royalties; the Government said the package was worth $205 to $209 million in cash.]		
26.	Teck Corp; Metallgesellschaft Canada; M.I.M. (Canada) Inc. plus several brokers	Cominco Ltd. (52.5% from Canadian Pacific)	472
	[Teck acquired 30.7%, "a controling interest," for $280 million from CP]		
27.	Gordon Capital and Dominion Securities Pitfield – then resold to institutional investors	Nowsco Well Service Ltd.	100 est.
28.	Allied - Lyons PLC (U.K.)	Hiram Walker Resources liquor business (51%)	1,600
	[1,300 in cash plus take over 300 in debt; the Reichmanns hold the other 49%; in late 1987 the Reichmanns exchanged their 49% for a minority interest in Allied Lyons]		

	Acquiring Firm	Acquired Firm	Value of Transaction ($ Millions)
1986 cont'd			
29.	Société des Ciments Français	Lake Ontario Cement (54% from Denison Mines)	156 *
	[* The value is based on 100% of the shares]		
30.	Lloyds Bank PLC (Cdn subsidiary)	90% of the assets of Continental Bank of Canada (#7 in Canada, assets of $5.9 billion)	200
31.	Central Capital Corp. [controlled by Central Trust]	Continental Bank Leasing Corp.	160
32.	Hollinger Inc. (Conrad Black)	34 papers (26 dailies) including 13 in Canada from Sterling Newspapers; the rest were family owned in the U.S.	130
33.	Macluan Capital Corp. (affiliate)	Seaspan International Ltd. (owned by Imasco)	110
34.	Union Faith Ltd. (Li-Ka-Shing of Hong Kong)	Husky Oil Ltd. (52%)	584 est.
	[Nova Corp's 56.7% will shrink to between 24.5% and 43%.; the rest will be held by CIBC (5%) and the public, but Li will get control as his family (Canadian residents) will have 9% plus his 43%]		
35.	Cadbury Schweppes PLC	Canada Dry & Sunkist operations (from RJR Nabisco Inc.)	230 (U.S.) 300e(Cdn)
36.	Hoechst AG	Celanese Canada (54%)	> 100 est.
	[Hoechst bought Celanese Corp. of N.Y. for $2.84 billion U.S.]		

37.	Pacific Western Airlines Corp.	Canadian Pacific Air Lines (from CP Ltd.)	300
38.	Rothmans of Pall Mall Ltd.	Benson & Hedges (Canada) Inc.	> 100 est.
	[This deal was an amalgamation to be called Rothmans, Benson & Hedges, in which Rothman's Inc. holds 60% and Philip Morris Inc. holds 40%. The combined sales of the two firms in 1985 totalled $959 million and assets totalled $382 million.]		
39.	Canadian Pacific Ltd.	AMCA International Ltd. (from 16.1 to 50.6%)	193
	[purchased from Algoma Steel Corp. Ltd., which is controlled by CP Ltd.]		
40.	Bluesky Oil & Gas Ltd.	Precambrian Shield Resources Ltd. (89%)	> 100 est.
	[Share exchange: 1.15 Bluesky common per share of Precambrian]		
41.	Reynolds Metals Co.	Aluminerie de Becancour Inc. (25% indirect stake)	300
	[25% is also owned by SGF, a Quebec Crown corporation]		
42.	Harnischfeger Corp. (U.S.)	Beloit Canada Ltd.	100 est.

1987

1.	Encor Energy Corp. (formerly Dome Canada)	Aberford Resources Ltd. (95%)	100
2.	North West Co. (Mgt buyout Mutual Trust Co. Investors Group)	Bay Northern Stores (180 stores) owned by Hudson's Bay Co.	180
3.	Onex Capital Corp.	Purolator Courier Ltd (68%) (Canadian operations from parent Purolator Corp.)	238

1987 cont'd

	Acquiring Firm	Acquired Firm	Value of Transaction ($ Millions)
4.	Fletcher Challenge Ltd. (New Zealand)	B.C. Forest Products Ltd. (47%) 42% from Gordon Capital and Merrill Lynch Canada) plus 5% from BCFP treasury)	505
	[Fletcher later increased its interest to over 67% in late 1987 for $220 million]		
5.	Memotec Data Inc.	Teleglobe Canada (from federal government)	608
	[the price includes $102 million a dividend paid to the federal government plus $17 million dividend on December 31/87]		
6.	Unicorp Canada (30%) and Dumez S.A. (70%)	Westburne International Industries Ltd. (94.4%)	249
7.	Ford New Holland Inc. (owned by Ford Motor Co. of Canada)	Versatile Farm Equipment Ltd.	180
8.	Federal Industries Ltd.	Steel products distribution business of Marshall Drummond McCall	110
9.	Quebecor Inc. (51%) and British Printing and Communications (49%)	Donohue Inc. (for 56% from Dofor Inc.)	320
	[Province of Quebec sold off its interest as part of its privatization policy]		
10.	Elders IXL Ltd. (Australia)	Carling O'Keefe Ltd. (50.1% owned by Rothman's)	392*
	[* for 100% as Elders extended the bid to all shareholders]		

No.	Acquirer	Acquisition	$ million
11.	Chrysler Corp. (U.S.)	46% of American Motors Corp. from Renault	> 100 est.
12.	Olympia & York Developments	50% of Scotia Plaza project from Campeau Corp.	300 e
13.	Paperboard Industries Corp. Inc.	Belkin Inc.	235
14.	Large number of private investors [privatization of a joint enterprise]	Fisheries Products International (88.5% purchased from the federal government, 62.6%; Nfld, 26.2%; bank, 11.2%)	177
15.	Group of private investors	Hudson's Bay Wholesale	110
16.	Groupe Metro-Richelieu Inc.	Quebec Super Carnival (retail food business from Burnac Corp.)	135
17.	Amalgamation of Placer Development Ltd. Dome Mines Ltd. [Placer will obtain 45% and Dome will obtain 37% of the new firm]	Dome Mines Ltd., and Campbell Red Lake Mines Ltd.	5,700
18.	Bell Canada Enterprises Inc. [BCE appears to have effective control if it converts its preferred shares.]	Memotec Data Inc. (one-third interest)	196*
19.	JMB Realty Corp. (U.S.) [51% now owned by Cemp Investments Ltd. and 23% by Olympia & York Ltd. Prior to the closing (Oct.31/87) Cadillac sold certain U.S. assets for $600 million to Copley Real Estate Advisors.]	Cadillac Fairview	2,590
20.	Pioneer Concrete Services Ltd. (Australia)	Noranda Pacific Ltd. (28.5%)	107*

[*Pioneer must now offer remaining shareholders the same terms so 100% would cost $375 million.]

1987 cont'd

	Acquiring Firm	Acquired Firm	Value of Transaction ($ Millions)
21.	Hershey Canada Inc.	Nabisco Brands Ltd. – confectionary business (Planters, Lowney, Moirs, Life Savers)	200 est.
22.	British Gas PLC	Bow Valley Industries (33.3%)	837
	[The federal government rejected the original deal, but British Gas got around this in December to get effective control with one-third of the equity.]		
23.	Hillsdown Holdings PLC	Maple Leaf Mills Mills Ltd. (100%) (from CP Ltd.)	361
24.	Bank of Montreal	Nesbitt Thomson Deacon Inc. (75%)	292
25.	Onex Corp.	Citibank Leasing Canada Ltd.	270
26.	Onex Corp.	Beatrice Foods Canada Ltd. (60 + %)	300 est.
27.	Investor group incl. Algonquin Mercentile Corp. (13%) and management (20%)	Balfour Guthrie (Canada) Ltd. (from Dalgety PLC)	155
28.	Central Capital Corp.	Traders Group	466
29.	Williams Holdings PLC	General Paint (based in Vancouver) from Reed International of England	482
30.	Shearson Lehman Bros. (10% to 30%) Pentrust Investments (Bronfman family) 20% plus option on 10%	McLeod Young Weir (June 30)	158

31.	Bank of Nova Scotia	McLeod Young Weir (100%) (Sept.)	419
32.	Sceptre Resources	SOQUIP Alberta (part of a Quebec Crown corp.)	195
33.	T.C.C. Beverages Ltd.	51% of Coca Cola Ltd. (Toronto)	173
34.	Alliance-Industrial Financial Corp.	General Trustco of Canada Inc. (increased to 62.8%)	127
35.	Security Pacific Corp.	Burns Fry Corp. (30%)	100
	[Security can increase to 50% after 3 years, so this appears to give Security effective control]		
36.	Imperial Oil Ltd. (Esso Resources Canada Ltd.)	the assets of Sulpetro Ltd.	680*
	[* plus up to $100 million more based on estimates of reserves]		
37.	Provigo Inc.	Consumers Distributing Co.	120
	[offer for balance of Consumers, conditional on getting 50% of A and 63% of B shares; Provigo owns 45.9% voting and 23.5% equity interest; amount is for 100%]		
38.	Enco Ltd.	Building Products of Canada (Imperial Oil)	125
39.	Amoco Canada Petroleum Co. Ltd.	Dome Petroleum Ltd.	5,500
40.	Royal Bank of Canada	Dominion Securities Ltd. (75%)	385
41.	Can. Imperial Bank of Commerce	Gordon Capital	400
	[creation of a joint venture merchant bank]		
42.	Westcoast Petroleum Ltd.	Canadian Roxy Petroleum Ltd. (69%)	103.5

	Acquiring Firm	Acquired Firm	Value of Transaction ($ Millions)
1987 cont'd			
43.	TransCanada Pipe Lines Ltd.	Encor Energy Corp. (formerly Dome Canada) (97%)	1,100
44.	TrailmobileGroup of Companies	Fruehauf Canada Inc.	105.5
45.	Stelco Inc.	Jannock Ltd.	228
	[joint venture under which Stelco paid $81.3 million for 50% of Jannock's five steel operations and the two assumed liabilities of $65 million. The new venture has $350 million in sales and 1,500 employees.]		
46.	Western Mining Corp. Holdings Ltd. (Australia)	2 mines from Northgate Exploration Ltd.	160
	[sale to close in January 1988]		
47.	Canam Manac Group Inc.	Noverco Inc. (20% from Unigesco)	149
	[The deal gives Canam 23% of Noverco, and it is said to share effective control with the Caisse de Depot.]		

Summary Table

Number of Large Takeovers (over $100 million) in Canada, 1978-1987

Year	Number	Total Value ($ million)	Average Value ($ million)
1978	9	3,149	350
1979	9	3,411	379
1980	13	4,825	371
1981	23	14,231	619
1982	2	466	233
1983	3	1,274	425
1984	4	778	195
1985	16	8,181	511
1986	42	16,230	389
1987	47	26,123	556

Members of the Institute

Board of Directors

The Honourable John B. Aird, O.C.,Q.C. (Honorary Chairman)
Aird & Berlis, Toronto

Roger Charbonneau, O.C., (Chairman)
Président du conseil, Président et Chef de la Direction Interim
NOVERCO, Montréal

Rosalie Abella
Chairman, Ontario Labour Relations Board, Toronto

Dr. Robert Bandeen
President and Chief Executive Officer, Cluny Corporation, Toronto

Nan-Bowles de Gaspé Beaubien
Vice-présidente, ressources humaines, Télémédia Inc., Montréal

Larry I. Bell
Chairman, B.C. Hydro & Power Authority, Vancouver

Marie Bernier
Montreal

Catherine Callbeck
Callbeck Limited, Central Bedeque, PEI

Allan F. (Chip) Collins
Special Advisor, Provincial Treasurer of Alberta, Edmonton

Peter C. Dobell
Director, Parliamentary Centre for Foreign Affairs and Foreign Trade, Ottawa

Dr. Rod Dobell
President, The Institute for Research on Public Policy, Victoria

Peter C. Godsoe
Vice Chairman of the Board, The Bank of Nova Scotia, Toronto

Dianne I. Hall
Ivy-Hall Investment Inc., Vancouver

Dr. Roger A. Blais, O.C.
Directeur, R-D coopératifs, École Polytechnique de Montréal

Jill Bodkin
Director of Financial Services, Clarkson Gordon, Vancouver

George Cooper, Q.C.
McInnes, Cooper and Robertson, Halifax

James S. Cowan, Q.C.
Partner, Stewart, MacKeen & Covert, Halifax

V. Edward Daughney
President, First City Trust Company, Vancouver

Dr. H.E. Duckworth, O.C.
Chancellor, University of Manitoba, Winnipeg

Dr. Stefan Dupré, O.C.
Department of Political Science, University of Toronto

Marc Eliesen
Chairperson and Executive Director, Manitoba Energy Authority, Winnipeg

Emery Fanjoy
Secretary, Council of Maritime Premiers, Halifax

Maureen Farrow
C.D. Howe Institute, Toronto

Dr. James D. Fleck
Faculty of Management Studies, University of Toronto

Dr. Allan K. Gillmore
Executive Director, Association of Universities and Colleges of Canada, Ottawa

Margaret C. Harris
Past President, The National Council of Women of Canada, Saskatoon

Michael Hicks
Principal, Centre for Executive Development, Ottawa

Dr. David Hopper
Washington, D.C.

Richard W. Johnston
President, Spencer Stuart & Associates, Toronto

Dr. Leon Katz, O.C.
Saskatoon

Dr. David Leighton
Director, National Centre for Management Research and Development
University of Western Ontario, London

Terrence Mactaggart
Managing Director, Sound Linked Data Inc., Mississauga

Judith Maxwell
Chairman, Economic Council of Canada, Vanier

Milan Nastich
Canadian General Investments Ltd., Toronto

Professor William A. W. Neilson
Dean, Faculty of Law, University of Victoria

Roderick C. Nolan, P.Eng.
President, Neill & Gunter Limited, Fredericton

Robert J. Olivero
United Nations Secretariat, New York

Gordon F. Osbaldeston, O.C.
Senior Fellow, School of Business Administration, University of Western Ontario, London

Garnet T. Page, O.C.
Calgary
Jean-Guy Paquet
Vice-président exécutif, La Laurentienne, mutuelle d'Assurance, Québec
Professor Marilyn L. Pilkington
Osgoode Hall Law School, Toronto
Eldon D. Thompson
President, Telesat, Vanier
Dr. Israel Unger
Dean of Science, University of New Brunswick, Fredericton
Dr. Norman Wagner
President and Vice-Chancellor, University of Calgary
Ida Wasacase, C.M.
Winnipeg
Dr. R. Sherman Weaver
Director, Alberta Environmental Centre, Vegreville
Dr. Blossom Wigdor
Director, Program in Gerontology, University of Toronto

Government Representatives

Roger Burke, Prince Edward Island
Joseph H. Clarke, Nova Scotia
Hershell Ezrin, Ontario
Allan Filmer, British Columbia
George Ford, Manitoba
Ron Hewitt, Saskatchewan
Barry Mellon, Alberta
Geoffrey Norquay, Canada
Eloise Spitzer, Yukon
H.H. Stanley, Newfoundland
Barry Toole, New Brunswick
Gérard Veilleux, Canada
Louise Vertes, Northwest Territories

Institute Management

Rod Dobell	President
Peter Dobell	Vice-President and Secretary-Treasurer
Yvon Gasse	Director, Small & Medium-Sized Business Program
Barry Lesser	Director, Information Society Studies Program
Jim MacNeill	Director, Environment & Sustainable Development Program
Shirley Seward	Director, Studies in Social Policy
Murray Smith	Director, International Economics Program
Jeffrey Holmes	Director, Communications
Parker Staples	Director, Financial Services
Walter Stewart	Editor, *Policy Options Politiques*

Fellows- and Scholars-in-Residence:

Edgar Gallant	Fellow-in-Residence
Tom Kent	Fellow-in-Residence
Eric Kierans	Fellow-in-Residence
Jean-Luc Pepin	Fellow-in-Residence
Gordon Robertson	Fellow-in-Residence
Alan Maslove	Scholar-in-Residence
James Taylor	Scholar-in-Residence
David Cameron	Scholar-in-Residence
Dennis Protti	Scholar-in-Residence
Eugene M. Nesmith	Executive-in-Residence

Related Publications Available
– September 1988

Order Address

The Institute for Research on Public Policy
P.O. Box 3670 South
Halifax, Nova Scotia
B3J 3K6

James Gillies

Where Business Fails. 1981 $9.95
ISBN 0 920380 53 0

Allan Tupper &
G. Bruce Doern (eds.)

Public Corporations and Public Policy in Canada. 1981.
$16.95
ISBN 0 920380 51 4

Irving Brecher

Canada's Competition Policy Revisited: Some New Thoughts on an Old Story. 1982. $5.00
ISBN 0 920380 57 3

W.T. Stanbury &
Fred Thompson

Regulatory Reform in Canada. 1982. $7.95
ISBN 0 920380 71 9

Robert J. Buchan,
C. Christopher Johnston,
T. Gregory Kane,
Barry Lesser,
Richard J. Schultz &
W.T. Stanbury

Telecommunications Regulation and the Constitution.
1982 $18.95
ISBN 0 920380 69 7

R. Brian Woodrow & Kenneth B. Woodside (eds.)	*The Introduction of Pay-TV in Canada: Issues and* *Implications.* 1983 $14.95 ISBN 0 920380 67 0
Mark Thompson & Gene Swimmer	*Conflict or Compromise: The Future of Public Sector* *Industrial Relations.* 1984 $15.00 ISBN 0 88645 001 2
Samuel Wex	*Instead of FIRA: Autonomy for Canadian Subsidiaries?* 1984 $8.00 ISBN 0 88645 012 8
Paul K. Gorecki & W.T. Stanbury	*The Objectives of Canadian Competition Policy, 1888-1983.* 1984 $15.00 ISBN 0 88645 002 0
W.T. Stanbury (ed.)	*Telecommunications Policy and Regulation: The Impact of* *Competition and Technological Change.* 1986 $22.00 ISBN 0 88645 039 X
Stephen Brooks	*Who's in Charge? The Mixed Ownership Corporation in Canada.* 1987 $20.00 ISBN0 88645 051 9
Louis Raymond	*Validité des systèmes d'information dans les PME: analyse et* *perspectives.* 1987 20,00 $ ISBN 2 7637 7118 1
Jacques Saint-Pierre & Jean-Marc Suret	*Endettement de la PME : état de la situation et rôle de la* *fiscalité.* 1987 $15.00 ISBN 0 88645 042 7
R.S. Khemani, D.M. Shapiro & W.T. Stanbury (eds.)	*Mergers, Corporate Concentration and Power in Canada.* 1988 $29.95 ISBN 0 88645 067 5